D1518564

# SOFTWARE PROJECTS

# PROJECTS

**Pedagogical Aids for Software Education and Research**

**John J. Donavan**
**Stuart E. Madnick**
Massachusetts Institute of Technology
Center for Information Systems Research
Alfred P. Sloan School of Management
Cambridge, Massachusetts

**McGRAW-HILL BOOK COMPANY**
New York  St. Louis  San Francisco  Auckland  Düsseldorf
Johannesburg  Kuala Lumpur  London  Mexico  Montreal
New Delhi  Panama  Paris  São Paulo
Singapore  Sydney  Tokyo  Toronto

SOFTWARE PROJECTS
Pedagogical Aids for Software Education and Research

1 2 3 4 5 6 7 8 9 0   WHWH 7 8 3 2 1 0 9 8 7

The editor was Peter D. Nalle.
The Whitlock Press, Inc., was printer and binder.

**Library of Congress Cataloging in Publication Data**

Donovan, John J
   Software projects.

   1.  Educational technology.  I. Madnick,
Stuart E., joint author.  II.  Title.
LB1028.3.D65       371.3'078      76-57693
ISBN 0-07-017591-8

# ACKNOWLEDGMENTS

Over the years dozens of students, teaching assistants, and colleagues have contributed to the design, implementation, testing, operation, and documentation of the software tools described in this book. It is difficult to individually acknowledge all of these individuals, but special note is extended to Benjamin Ashton, Harris Berman, Glen Brunk, Chad Carpenter, Orville Dodson, Harry Forsdick, Rick Granger, Steven Halfich, Martin Jack, Jerry Johnson, Mike Knaur, Norman Kohn, Susan Kruger, Dennis Linnell, William Michels, Al Moulton, Richard Mulhern, Judy Piggins, David Quimby, Chander Ramchandani, David Schwartz, Suhundra Umarji, Stanley Zaborowski, Charles Ziering, and Steven Zilles.

The SIM 360 simulator was originally developed as part of an M.I.T. Bachelor's Thesis by William Arthur McCray and subsequently extended and refined by many students, most notably Geoffrey Bunza. The Batch Monitor Systems and Modified PL/I(F) compiler were developed and documented as part of an M.I.T. Bachelor's Thesis by Paul G. Gregory. The Sample Operating System is based upon an M.I.T. Master's Thesis by John DeTreville, which was subsequently further extended and debugged by other students, notably Richard Swift and Paul Fredette.

Paul Gregory, with the assistance of Ed DeJong and Stuart Altman, initially pulled together most of the then existing material and worked to improve the quality of many of the programs and their documentation. The efforts of Rich Brudnick, Jim Gabbert, Beth Hoemke, Ellen Nangle, Ed Popko, and Susan St. Onge were instrumental in getting the material into its final form.

The work reported herein has been supported, in part, by the Alfred P. Sloan School of Management, the Department of Electrical Engineering and Computer Science, the Information Processing Services (IPS), the Information Processing Center (IPC), and the Laboratory for Computer Science (formerly Project MAC) at M.I.T. The long continuing support and encouragement of Robert H. Scott of IPC is especially appreciated.

John J. Donovan

Stuart E. Madnick

CONTENTS

```
:_____:
:             :
: CHAPTER  1  :
:_____:
```

## 1.1   INTRODUCTION

   This book describes an environment, specific tools, and a philosophy for teaching software that we have been using for many years at M.I.T. in courses in introductory computer concepts, management science, and computer science, especially those dealing with systems programming and operating systems. Besides using these tools and philosophy at M.I.T., we have also used them in courses that we have given at the University of Pittsburgh, the University of Rhode Island, and several other American and European universities, as well as in industry.

   The computer programs (tools) described here are available through us. Preliminary versions of this material has been made available and successfully used by others at universities such as the University of South Dakota, the University of Notre Dame, Auburn University, New Mexico State University, and Central Connecticut State College, among others.

### 1.1.1   Goals

   On one level, our basic goal is to teach an approach to problem solving with particular focus on the use of a digital computer. On the next level, we wish to teach basic programming techniques, e.g., recursion, structured programming, and modularity. On the next level, we wish to give experience using practical tools for solving problems. Finally, we wish to acquaint the student with existing hardware and machine architecture.

### 1.1.2   Philosophy

   The mastery of software design and development is similar to learning how to ride a bicycle. Although the laws of physics fully describe the process, almost no one learns to ride a bicycle merely by reading a book. A balance is needed between instruction of style, techniques, and algorithms and a variety of actual project activities to develop basic programming skills and experience. The object of these projects is generally not to teach the details of a particular language or computer, but rather to instill an appreciation for the software design and development process.

   To make the projects realistic and to enhance student motivation, we chose real computers and existing languages as vehicles. We chose the IBM 370 as our vehicle for computer architecture since it is the "Latin" of the computer industry (because it is so widely standardized, not because it is dead!). We see no justification for fabricating a "simpler" computer or a formalization; we argue that a 370 or any other contemporary computer is not too complicated for a beginner, whether he is a high school, college, or graduate student. We chose PL/I as our high-level language, as we feel that PL/I, or a language that incorporates similar features, will become the "Latin" of programming languages.

This book will not describe specific courses to fulfill these objectives, as its purpose is to describe a philosophy and a set of tools that can be incorporated into most courses that teach computing. At the end of this chapter we do indicate how we have used these tools in some of our courses.

## 1.1.3   Key Concepts

Let us list several of the important software concepts that an instructor must get across:

1. Machine architecture, concepts of asynchronous processing, multiprocessing.
2. Algorithms, the concept of formalizing a step-by-step procedure.
3. Programming, programming techniques (e.g., recursion, structured programming), differences in run time, load time, and execution time, debugging.
4. Experience with components of operating systems.
5. Analyzing the effectiveness of alternate algorithms.

## 1.1.4   Problem Areas

Let us list the problems that many instructors encounter, especially in large classes, in teaching the above concepts:

1. Motivation of students.
2. Feedback to students about programming errors.
3. Having beginning students write programs without their knowing advanced features, e.g., having them write assembly language programs without knowing I/O programming.
4. Grading student programs.
5. Teaching I/O programming and interrupt programming, which typically require the computer hardware to be operating in privileged mode to execute such programs.
6. Providing experience with a large program without requiring students to write very large systems.
7. Teaching all the above at minimal cost.

Over the last ten years we have developed an approach that helps us to teach the key concepts listed above and, at the same time, have developed tools that eliminate or greatly reduce all the above problems. In the following sections we describe these tools and explain their purposes.

## 1.2   MACHINE ARCHITECTURE:  PROGRAMMING AND DEBUGGING

Our objective here is to familiarize the student with the concepts of computer architecture, machine instructions, interrupts, I/O programming, channels, CPU's, and devices. We feel that the best vehicle for exposing a student to concepts of machine architecture is assembly language programming. We have chosen an existing machine language, as it better motivates the student and provides him with a useful skill for later use.

Several problems immediately confront the instructor:

1.   In the beginning, how does he assign even simple assembly language programs without teaching advanced features of I/O programming or using cumbersome dumps? (Main programs without any input or output are typically not interesting.)
2.   If an IBM 370, or any large system typically found in a computing facility, is used, how does he assign more advanced I/O or interrupt programming tasks? These involve using privileged instructions, which the operating systems usually prevent a user process from executing.
3.   How does he give a student debugging information on each of the student runs?
4.   How does he keep his cost down?

We address ourselves to problems (1) and (2) in Sections 1.2.1 and 1.2.2 and in the later Sections 1.5.1 and 1.5.2 describe mechanisms for coping with problems (3) and (4).


### 1.2.1   Assembly Language Grading Programs

We have developed a set of simple 360/370 assembly language problems. For example, given a bit configuration in a register, count the number of EBCDIC commas represented by those bits and leave the answer in another register. Corresponding to each problem is a grading program whose function is to provide a friendly environment for the student's programs by eliminating the need for the student to write his own I/O and error handlers. The grading program also supplies the student's program with test data and in turn grades the student.

As an interesting note, we have found that grading programs for quite different assignments may be constructed of similar modules. Therefore we have constructed a "meta" grading program with which an instructor can generate his own grading program (using macros) for a large spectrum of student problems.

More specifically, our grading programs are all table-driven to allow the instructor to parameterize them for many different assignments. Each grading program treats the student's program as a subroutine. The grading program passes data to the student program, grades it, and gives appropriate diagnostics.

Examples of some of the types of student assignments for our grading programs are as follows:

-- A palindrome problem: The student is to determine whether or not a string passed to him is the same string if it is reversed, e.g., the string 'RADAR' is a palindrome.
-- Counting the number of special characters in a register.
-- Converting a given number into Roman numerals.
-- Number conversions, for example, converting a fixed binary formatted number into packed decimal.
-- An arithmetic expression evaluator.

A detailed explanation of the assembly language problems can be found in Chapter 2.


## 1.2.2   360 Simulator

A major problem in teaching I/O or interrupt programming is that such programs usually require the use of privileged instructions. Programs containing privileged instructions cannot be run under OS/370 or similar such operating systems. A possible (but unsatisfactory) solution is to run those problems without the operating system. Aside from the typical reluctance of a computing center to let instructors do this, if there were any errors in the program, there would be absolutely no debugging information. For example, if a program running on a bare machine stops, what's wrong? Another solution is to use a virtual machine, e.g., CP/CMS or VM 370. However, these provide limited debugging information and have two additional problems--availability and cost. To solve these problems, we have developed a simulator for an IBM 360 written in PL/I.

The simulator takes an object deck (output of the 360 assembler) as input, loads it into virtual memory starting at location 0, and starts executing the loaded program using the initial program status word stored in location 0 (just as a bare 360 would IPL itself).

The unique aspects of the simulator are that it mimics not only user-level 360 instructions but also privileged instructions and detailed I/O and timing. For example, a student must be careful of any timing conditions that he may encounter on a real 360. As such, the simulator is useful as a research tool for checking out new operating systems for the 360, as well as being a pedagogical aid.

Since the simulator is explained in detail in Chapter 4, we will not explain its features here. Let us give a simple example

for those who know IBM 360 assembly language  so  that  they  can
appreciate the usefulness of SIM 360.

Depicted  in  Figure  1  is  a  simple example of an I/O and
interrupt 360 assembly program.  The program counts to 100  while
simultaneously  doing  single  buffered  I/O (reading and writing
cards).  This program could not be run directly under  OS/360  as
it  contains  privileged  instructions  and  hence  violates  the
protection mechanisms of OS; however, we can  run  it  under  SIM
360, which, in turn, can be run under OS/360.

Figure 2 depicts the output of our simulator for the program
of  Figure  1.  (Note that the TRACE macro in the student program
causes the simulator output  of  Figure  2.)   The  trace  output
indicates  that  two  interrupts resulted from the read Start I/O
(SIO) instruction for the first card (a "channel  end"  interrupt
at  time 465 microseconds followed by a "device end" interrupt at
time 73,499 microseconds.)  Similarly, two interrupts result from
the print SIO for that line, but this time the first interrupt at
time  73,917  microseconds  indicates  both  "channel  end  and
incorrect length" in the channel status word (CSW), since only 80
characters  were  printed  instead  of a full 132-character line.
Many more interesting details can be noted by studying the  trace
output.

A  detailed explanation of the use, operation, and design of
SIM 360 can be found in Chapter 4.

Given the SIM 360 facility, we are able to formulate student
assignments that  provide  experience  and  appreciation  of  the
special  supervisory  computer  mode.   Examples  of  some of the
assignments are as follows:

-- Instruction   simulations.   For   example,   the   370
   instruction  Store Characters under Mask (STCM) causes an
   interrupt on a 360 and must be simulated by an  interrupt
   handler to be written by the student.
-- Multiple terminal message  processing  system.   In  this
   assignment  the  student  is  required  to write the I/O,
   timer,  and  SVC  interrupt  handlers  for  an  "airline
   reservation"-type message handling system.  This includes
   interrupt  processing;  message  buffering,  queuing,  and
   routing; timing and priority message scheduling, etc.

A detailed  description  of  the  above,  along  with  other
interrupt and I/O assignments, can be found in Chapter 5.

```
    EXAMPLE INTERRUPT PROGRAM                                                              PAGE   1

    LOC  OBJECT CODE    ADDR1 ADDR2  STMT    SOURCE STATEMENT                      FO1MAY72   8/10/74
                                       2           PRINT  NOGEN          DON'T PRINT MACROS              00000030
    000000                             3 EXAMPLE   CSECT                                                 00000040
    000000  0000000000000080           4           DC     A(0,BEGIN)                                     00000050
    000080                             5           ORG    EXAMPLE+128    SKIP THE REST OF LOW CORE       00000060
    000080  05F0                       6 BEGIN     BALR   15,0           SET UP BASE REGISTER            00000070
    000082                             7           USING  *,15           TELL ASSEMBLER                  00000080
                                       8           TRACE  INTRPT,I/O,STATUS=(OLD1/O,CSW),REGS=(0)        00000090
                                     1Z #     ON EVERY I/O INTERRUPT, DISPLAY I/O OLD PSW, CSW, REG,0    00000100
    000048                            18 CAW      EQU    X'48'           LOCATION OF CHANNEL ADDRESS WORD 00000110
    000040                            19 CSW      EQU    X'40'           LOCATION OF CHANNEL STATUS WORD  00000120
    000078                            20 IONEWPSW EQU    X'78'           LOCATION OF I/O NEW PSW          00000130
    000038                            21 IOOLDPSW EQU    X'38'           LOCATION OF I/O OLD PSW          00000140
    00008C  D207 0078 F126  00078 001A6  22        MVC    IONEWPSW(8),=A(0,IOHANDLE)                      00000160
    000092  D203 0048 F12E  00048 001B0  23        MVC    CAW(4),=A(READCARD)                             00000170
    000098  8000 F142        001C4   24           SSM    =X'FE'         ENABLE INTERRUPTS               00000180
    00009C  9C00 000C        0000C   25           SIO    X'00C'         START THE CHANNEL READING A CARD 00000190
                                     26           TRACE  DUMP,CORE=(MESSAGE,5)                           00000200
                                     37 #     PRINT OUT A MESSAGE USING THE TRACE FACILITY               00000210
    0000AE  5810 F132        001B4   38           L      1,=F'5000'     COUNT TO 5000                  00000220
    0000B2  1B00                     39           SR     0,0            CLEAR REGISTER 0               00000230
    0000B4  5A00 F136        001B8   40 LOOP      A      0,=F'1'        ADD 1 TO REGISTER 0            00000240
    0000B8  4610 F032        000B4   41           BCT    1,LOOP         DO IT 5000 TIMES               00000250
                                     42           TRACE  DUMP,CORE=(MEND,4)                             00000260
                                     53 #     PRINT ANOTHER MESSAGE, SAYING THE LOOP HAS ENDED          00000270
    0000CA  8200 F0A6        00128   54           LPSW   WAITPSW        GO INTO WAIT STATE             00000280
                                     55 #     THIS IS THE I/O INTERRUPT HANDLER                         00000290
    0000CE  50F0 0054        00054   56 IOHANDLE ST     15,X'54'       SAVE REG. 15                   00000300
    000002  05F0                     57           BALR   15,0           SET UP NEW BASE REGISTER       00000310
    0000D4                           58           USING  *,15                                          00000320
    0000D4  9104 0044        00044   59           TM     CSW4,X'04'     WAS THIS A DEVICE END INTRPT?  00000330
    0000D8  4780 F010        000F0   60           BZ     RETURN         NO: IGNORE THIS INTRPT         00000340
    0000DC  D501 003A F0BC  0003A 001C0  61        CLC    IOOLDPSW+2(2),=X'00C'  IS IT A READER INTRPT?   00000350
    0000E2  4780 F024        000F8   62           BE     READINT        YES                            00000360
    0000E6  D501 003A F0BE  0003A 001C2  63        CLC    IOOLDPSW+2(2),=X'00E'  IS IT A PRINTER INTRPT?  00000370
    0000EC  4780 F032        00106   64           BE     PRINTINT       YES                            00000380
    0000F0  58F0 0054        00054   65 RETURN    L      15,X'54'       RESTORE THE ORIGINAL BASE REG. 00000390
    0000F4  8200 0038        00038   66           LPSW   IOOLDPSW       RETURN BY RESTORING I/O OLD PSW 00000400
                                     67 #     THIS IS THE READER INTERRUPT HANDLER                      00000410
    0000F8  D203 0048 F0B8  00048 001BC  68 READINT  MVC  CAW(4),=A(PRNTCARD)  INITIALIZE THE CHANNEL    00000420
    0000FE  9C00 000E        0000E   69           SIO    X'00E'         START THE PRINTER              00000430
    000102  47FC F01C        000F0   70           B      RETURN         RETURN TO THE POINT OF INTERRUPTION 00000440
                                     71 #     THIS IS THE PRINTER INTERRUPT HANDLER                     00000450
    000106  D203 0048 F0DC  00048 001B0  72 PRINTINT MVC  CAW(4),=A(READCARD)  INITIALIZE THE CHANNEL    00000460
    00010C  9C00 000C        0000C   73           SIO    X'00C'         START READER TO GET NEXT CARD  00000470
    000110  47F0 F01C        000F0   74           B      RETURN         RETURN TO POINT OF INTERRUPTION 00000480
    000114  00000000
    000118  0200013000000050         75 READCARD  CCW   X'02',BUFFER,X'00',80  READ A CARD               00000500
    000120  0900013000000050         76 PRNTCARD  CCW   X'09',BUFFER,X'00',80  PRINT A CARD IMAGE        00000510
    000128  FE02000000000000         77 WAITPSW   DC    FE02000000000000'  I/O WAIT PSW                  00000520
    000130                           78 BUFFER    DS    CL80           BUFFER FOR HOLDING A CARD IMAGE  00000530
    000180  C2C5C7C9D5D40E3C8        79 MESSAGE   DC    CL20'BEGIN THE COUNT LOOP'                       00000540
    000194  C5D5C440D6C64040         80 MEND      DC    CL16'END OF THE LOOP'                            00000550
                                     81           END                                                   00000560
    0001A8  0000000000000000CE       82                 =A(0,IOHANDLE)
    0001B0  00000118                 83                 =A(READCARD)
```

```
    EXAMPLE INTERRUPT PROGRAM                                                              PAGE   2

    LOC  OBJECT CODE    ADDR1 ADDR2  STMT    SOURCE STATEMENT                      FO1MAY72   8/10/74
    0001B4  00001388                 84                 =F'5000'
    0001B8  00000001                 85                 =F'1'
    0001BC  00000120                 86                 =A(PRNTCARD)
    0001C0  000C                     87                 =X'00C'
    0001C2  000E                     88                 =X'00E'
    0001C4  FE                       89                 =X'FE'
```

Figure 1
Example of an Interrupt Program

```
MASSACHUSETTS INSTITUTE OF TECHNOLOGY        SYSTEM / 360 SIMULATOR                                    VERSION 1.3
EXAMPLE TRACE LISTING.   0 CONDITIONS ENABLED.                                                         PAGE  1

LOC  TRACE TYPE          COUNT  TIME                                 OP   INSTRUCTION     ABRI ABRE OPERANDI OPERANDE
---- ----------------    -----  ----------                          ---- ------------    ---- ---- -------- --------


00AE SNAPSHOT              5        11  PSW: FE 0 0 0000  '01'B '00'B 0 0000AE .
          CORE DUMP:
          0180,   384: C2C5C7C9 D540E3C8 C540C3D6 E4D5E340 D3D6D6D7       BEGI N TH E CO UNT  LOOP

0084 I/O INTERRUPT       475       465  PSW: FE 0 0 000C  '10'B '10'B 0 000084
          STATUS:
          OLD I/O: FE 0 0 000C  '10'B '10'B 0 000084          CSW: 0 0 000120  0800 0000   CNT=    0
          REGISTERS:
          R 0: 000000EA,       234-

00CA SNAPSHOT           10013     9,962  PSW: FE 0 0 0000  '01'B '10'B 0 0000CA
          CORE DUMP:
          0194,   404: C5D5C440 D6C64040 E3C8C540 D3D6D6D7        END  OF   THE  LOOP

0000 I/O INTERRUPT     10014    73,499  PSW: FE 0 2 000C  '10'B '00'B 0 000000
          STATUS:
          OLD I/O: FE 0 2 000C  '10'B '00'B 0 000000          CSW: 0 0 000120  0400 0000   CNT=    0
          REGISTERS:
          R 0: 00001388,      5000

0000 I/O INTERRUPT     10025    73,917  PSW: FE 0 2 000E  '10'B '00'B 0 000000
          STATUS:
          OLD I/O: FE 0 2 000E  '10'B '00'B 0 000000          CSW: 0 0 000128  0840 0034   CNT=   52
          REGISTERS:
          R 0: 00001388,      5000

0000 I/O INTERRUPT     10031   172,219  PSW: FE 0 2 000E  '10'B '00'B 0 000000
          STATUS:
          OLD I/O: FE 0 2 000E  '10'B '00'B 0 000000          CSW: 0 0 000128  0400 0000   CNT=    0
          REGISTERS:
          R 0: 00001388,      5000


CPU HAS ENTERED THE WAIT STATE WITH NO INTERRUPTS ENABLED. SIMULATION ENDS.
THE FOLLOWING SIMULATOR-PROVIDED SNAPSHOT SHOULD HELP IN DETERMINING THE CAUSE OF THIS CONDITION.  THE PSW INTERRUPT CODE IS    12
8
0000 SNAPSHOT         10044   172,236  PSW: FE 0 2 0000  '10'B '00'B 0 000000
          STATUS:
          OLD PRG: 00 0 0 0000  '00'B '00'B 0 000000
          REGISTERS:
          R 0: 00001388,      5000 R 1: 00000000,        0 R 2: FFFFFFFF,       -1 R 3: FFFFFFFF,       -1
          R 4: FFFFFFFF,      -1 R 5: FFFFFFFF,       -1 R 6: FFFFFFFF,       -1 R 7: FFFFFFFF,       -1
          R 8: FFFFFFFF,      -1 R 9: FFFFFFFF,       -1 R10: FFFFFFFF,       -1 R11: FFFFFFFF,       -1
          R12: FFFFFFFF,      -1 R13: FFFFFFFF,       -1 R14: FFFFFFFF,       -1 R15: 40000082, 1073741954


ABNORMAL SIMULATOR TERMINATION FOR PROGRAM EXAMPLE




          SIMULATED REAL TIME:    172,236.875

          SIMULATED CPU TIME:      10,022.250


-------------------------------------------------------------------------------------------------------------------
EXAMPLE                          OUTPUT TO PRINTER 00E STARTS AT HEAD OF FORM ON NEXT PAGE
-------------------------------------------------------------------------------------------------------------------


THIS IS THE CARD THAT WAS READ AND THEN PRINTED
```

Figure 2
Simulator Output Followed by the One-Line Virtual Pointer Output
that Resulted from Execution

## 1.3   OPERATING SYSTEM COMPONENTS

Operating systems are certainly as important a topic as machine architecture, for in most cases they provide the interface between the user and the machine. There are three basic approaches to teaching operating systems:

1.  The detailed case studies approach (taking OS 360 or MULTICS, for example). Although a useful part of a student's education, this approach has the disadvantage of not clearly differentiating basic concepts from arbitrary design decisions or trivia. Furthermore, the size of such systems and the quality of the documentation usually make them ill-suited for classroom purposes.
2.  The theoretical approach, which presents those parts of an operating system that have been formalized (for example, paging and thrashing). The disadvantages are that it is not clear how or where this theory is applicable, and that many important components of an operating system are left out, since they have not been formalized.
3.  The development of a framework that encompasses all operating systems and relevant theory. Within this framework each component of any system is functionally identified and studied.

Our philosophy follows primarily the third approach, but our tools are useful in all approaches. Experience can be given in each component of an operating system by having a student write a program to accomplish its task. The instructor faces two problems:

1.  Must the student write an entire operating system to gain experience in one component?
2.  How does the student test his component under real situations (e.g., job streams)?

### 1.3.1   Environment Simulators

To eliminate or reduce the above problems, we have written several environment simulators, including those for a job scheduler, a process scheduler, and a device scheduler. Take, for example, the device scheduler. It allows the instructor or researcher to parameterize the characteristics of a system configuration, e.g., channels and devices, as well as to parameterize a sequence of I/O requests originating from various jobs. The student can then write a scheduler to maximize I/O utilization, minimize queue lengths, etc. The environment simulator simulates both the user program activity (i.e., generation of I/O requests) and the I/O hardware (i.e., timing of completion of I/O activities). The student's device scheduler program must build and maintain the database to keep track of all I/O requests outstanding and their status, to keep track of the status of the I/O hardware (e.g., which channels are free), and to provide the algorithm for determining when to initiate an I/O operation on behalf of an I/O request (a single I/O request may require several I/O operations, such as a "seek" followed by a "read"). The environment simulators also provide the student or researcher with performance information to evaluate the effectiveness of his algorithms.

The environment simulators, although not included in this version of this book, are available from the authors.

## 1.3.2   Sample Operating System

We have also developed a sample operating system that not only can be used as a pedagogical aid in the study of operating systems, but also is an example of structured and hierarchical programming techniques. The operating system consists of approximately 1500 IBM 360 assembly language statements and is similar to an advanced multiprogramming OS for a mini-computer. Students may extend this operating system in several ways, either by replacing existing components (e.g., the process scheduler) or by adding additional facilities (e.g., a file system).

The detailed design and structure of the Sample Operating System is contained in Chapter 7 of Operating Systems (McGraw-Hill, 1974). An explanation of its use and operation can be found in Chapter 6 of this book.

## 1.4    COMPLEX HIGH-LEVEL LANGUAGE PROGRAMS

The largest program that most students ever see has no more than 500 statements and solves only one problem. For such relatively straightforward problems, it is difficult to motivate learning of some of the advanced programming techniques such as hierarchical and structured programming.

We have developed a set of projects that cover a broad spectrum of difficulty and complexity. They have been selected to reinforce a student's understanding of the fundamentals of programming in a high-level language as well as the fundamentals of language processors themselves. PL/I is used extensively in these projects.

### 1.4.1    Intermediate Level PL/I Programming

In order to expose the student to certain useful facilities of PL/I and to give him some experience, a variety of short to intermediate exercises have been developed, including:

-- Cipher problem. Cryptographically encode and decode text messages using a Caesar Cipher.
-- Sorting problem.
-- Desk Directory problem. Maintain a telephone directory, including "inserts," "deletes," and "look ups."

In comparison with these exercises, the next three projects to be described are much larger and utilize many more advanced features of the PL/I language. A complete description of all of these exercises and projects can be found in Chapter 3.

### 1.4.2    Assembler

In this project, the student is required to design and implement a slightly simplified 360 assembler (BAL) using PL/I. This effort reinforces the concepts of machine language and the assembly process, encourages careful program organization (especially if done as a group project), and illustrates the "bootstrapping" and "cross-assembly" programming concepts (i.e., writing an assembler in a high-level language).

### 1.4.3    Lexical Analyzer

We have developed an environment for a student to write a lexical processor for a PL/I-like language in PL/I. Besides illustrating the lexical analysis process, a major element in a compiler, this exercise also emphasizes the use of a variety of complex data structures, especially PL/I structures and based variables.

## 1.4.4   PL/I Subset Interpreter

We  have  also developed an environment that allows a student to write an interpreter for  a  subset  of  PL/I  in  PL/I.   The environment  simulator  provides a few necessary utility routines (e.g., a lexical  processor,  an  input/output  handler,  and  an output formater) and tests the student's interpreter.  This is an extremely  extensive  effort, usually done as a group effort (2-4 students per  group).   Besides  providing  for  a  detailed  and comparative  study  of  compiler  and  interpreter  structure and concepts, this project illustrates many of the problems  involved with a large-scale programming effort.

## 1.5    OPERATIONAL AND ECONOMIC CONSIDERATIONS

As a practical matter, the instructor is usually faced with a limited computer budget, which presents some problems:

1.  If each student's program is run as a separate job, there is a high set-up cost on each job (e.g., 100 students with each student assigned 3 problems and allowed 10 runs per problem equals 3000 jobs!).
2.  If the instructor groups several student runs together in a single batch run, then a single student can "bomb" the run for all students if he makes an error.
3.  If Pl/I is used, compilation time is costly and is usually large, compared to execution time of the student's program.

To reduce the cost of running student programs, we have developed a student monitor system and a faster PL/I(F) compiler.

### 1.5.1  Student Monitor System

The student monitor system runs under OS/360 or OS/370. It allows batching of student compilations and student executions as a single job step, thereby avoiding individual job or step overhead for each student run. At the same time, it provides facilities to recover from most program errors (such as abnormal terminations or infinite loops) and allows continued processing of the student batch. At M.I.T. job set-up cost is over $0.50 per job, which often swamps the cost of compiling and executing most student runs.

A detailed description of the monitor systems available for both assembly language and PL/I use can be found in Chapter 7 (additional information on the PL/I monitor is contained in parts of Sections 3.4 and 3.5).

### 1.5.2  Fast PL/I(F) Compiler

The IBM PL/I(F) compiler has been changed slightly internally so that it makes better use of larger partitions (e.g., 160K) to enable it to compile faster than the original. The compiler accepts the same source code and generates the same output, but does it faster. In most cases that we have studied our modified PL/I compiler operates with less CPU and I/O time.

An explanation of the changes to the standard IBM PL/I(F) compiler and its operation can be found in Appendix A.

## 1.6   SUMMARY

Table I summarizes the contents of this book  and  indicates
the  software  tools explained in each chapter.  In general, each
chapter consists of three parts:

 (1)  A Student's Guide,  which   contains   the   student
      assignments.
 (2)  An Instructor's Guide, which  explains  the  setup  and
      operation necessary for each  assignment, along with
      sample solutions to the student assignments.
 (3)  A Maintenance Guide, which  explains  the   internal
      structure of  the  software  tool  (e.g.,  the SIM 360
      simulator) in  sufficient  detail  to  enable  the
      instructor, or his staff, to modify or enhance it.

We  have found these tools to be an especially valuable part
of the software education process by allowing us to reinforce the
learning  process  with  relevant  practical  experience  on  the
computer within the bounds of reasonable costs.

Table I

| Chapter | Software Tools Described | Our Use |
|---|---|---|
| 2 | Assembly Language Exercises, e.g., Palindrome problem | Introductory programming and systems programming course (Practical 360/370 Assembly Language Programming) |
| 3 | PL/I Exercises and Projects, e.g., lexical analyzer and PL/I-like interpreter | Systems programming and compiler course |
| 4 | System/360 Simulator (SIM 360) | Teaching machine structure, I/O programming, and interrupt processing, especially in operating system and computer architecture courses |
| 5 | Interrupt and I/O Exercises | |
| 6 | Sample Operating System | Used in an operating system course, both as a case study and as a base for students to extend as a project |
| 7 | Batch Monitor System | Used in conjunction with the other tools to decrease operating costs and improve error diagnostics and ease of operation |
| 8 | Distribution Tape Description | Describes the contents and usage of the standard distribution tape that contains the software tools described in this book; this tape is needed to obtain actual machine-processible versions of the tools |
| Appendix A | Modified PL/I(F) Compiler | Used in conjunction with the PL/I exercises, described in Chapter 3, to decrease operating costs |

```
!------------!
!            !
! CHAPTER  2 !
!            !
!_____!
```

## 2.1  INTRODUCTION

This chapter describes a set of tools which expedite testing
a student on her or his ability to write an assembly language
program as a graded exercise. The primary vehicle involved in
the testing and scoring of a student is the grading program or
"grader". This program functions in a supervisory capacity,
establishing an environment with an error handling and reporting
facility superior to what a bare operating system would provide.
In addition the grader functions to minimize the costs of student
error. Limits are enforced for maximum program execution time
and lines of printed output.

The student is given a problem which he or she is to
implement as a subroutine. After the student's subroutine has
been assembled and linked with the grader, the grader establishes
its enviroment and calls the student's program, providing test
data. Upon successful return from the student, the grader checks
his or her answers for correctness. Any errors in answers or
program execution (such as an operation exception) cause the
student's program and registers to be "dumped" and may terminate
the student's test run. This automatic checking of answers frees
the instructor to concentrate on grading programming style and
esthetics.

Realizing that graders for different assignments vary only
slightly, we have designed a system of macros which provide a
framework for writing graders with very little effort. Only
those parts of the grader concerned with the passing of test data
and validating of answers need be written. Standard routines are
provided for handling errors, printing messages, and other common
functions.

As examples of what can be accomplished with these tools, we
include descriptions of six assignments for which we have written
graders and solutions. After reading the assignments, if you
wish to use one you merely refer to section 2.3 for help in
setting up the grader and administering the problem.

Note that any of these graders may be used in conjunction
with the batch monitor to efficiently handle many decks at a
time; see Chapter 7 for details. If you wish to use the batch
monitor the student writeups must be changed in the section
titled "Deck Setup". You must add a "$JOB name" card before the
TITLE card and a "$EOJ" card after the END card.

## 2.2 STUDENT WRITEUPS FOR SAMPLE PROBLEMS

### 2.2.1 Palindrome Problem -- A1

Problem Description:

A palindrome is a word that reads backwards the same as it reads forwords. Examples of palindromes are "MADAM", "RADAR", and "OTTO". Your assignment is to write a 360 assembly language subroutine which determines whether or not a sequence of eight characters (blanks included) is a palindrome.

Communication with the Grader:

Your subroutine will be called by a grading program. This program will pass you test cases and you will return answers. When your subroutine is entered, the general registers will contain the following information:

Registers 0-1, 4-12: The contents of these registers are not significant.

Registers 2-3: This pair of registers contains eight characters. Your program examines these eight characters (leftmost is high order byte of register 2) and determines whether or not they form a palindrome.

Register 13: Address of an 18 fullword area where you may save general registers.

Register 14: The address of the return point in the grading program. You should branch to this address when you have completed processing.

Register 15: Address of the beginning of your program.

When you return to the grading program, the contents of registers 2-12 should be the same as when you were called. Register 1 should contain the fullword binary value '1' if the eight characters sent in registers 2 and 3 were a palindrome. If they do not form a palindrome, register 1 should be set to zero.

Debugging Aids:

Executing the following constant as an instruction in your program will cause the grader to dump your program and registers for debugging purposes and then continue execution:

```
     DEBUG   DC   H'15'            CAUSES DUMP TO OCCUR
```

Use this facility sparingly, however, as you will be  limited  in
the number of lines you may print.


Examples:

| | _Reg. 2_ | _Reg. 3_ |
|---|---|---|
| 1. on entry: | ¦C1 C2 C3 C4¦ | ¦C4 C3 C2 C1¦ |

```
          you return in register 1:  ¦00 00 00 01¦
          (the eight characters did form a palindrome)
```

| | _Reg. 2_ | _Reg. 3_ |
|---|---|---|
| 2. on entry: | ¦C1 C2 C3 C4¦ | ¦C1 C2 C3 C4¦ |

```
          you return in register 1:  ¦00 00 00 00¦
          (the eight characters did not form a palindrome)
```

| | _Reg. 2_ | _Reg. 3_ |
|---|---|---|
| 3. on entry: | ¦C1 C2 C3 C3¦ | ¦C2 C1 40 40¦ |

```
          you return in regster 1:  ¦00 00 00 00¦
          (the eight characters did not form a palindrome)
```

| | _Reg. 2_ | _Reg. 3_ |
|---|---|---|
| 4. on entry: | ¦40 D9 C1 C4¦ | ¦C1 D9 40 40¦ |

```
          you return in register 1:  ¦00 00 00 00¦
          (the eight characters did not form a palindrome)
```

| | Reg. 2 | Reg. 3 |
|---|---|---|
| 5. on entry: | ¦40 40 D5 D6¦ | ¦D6 D5 40 40¦ |

```
          you return in register 1:  ¦00 00 00 01¦
          (the eight characters did form a palindrome)
```

Deck Setup:

Your program must be a CSECT labelled MP1. Use the following deck structure:

```
        TITLE 'Students name - Instructors name'
MP1     CSECT
        USING *,15
        STM  ....
          .
          .   rest of program
          .
        END
```

Run Schedule:

TO BE ANNOUNCED

## 2. ASSEMBLY LANGUAGE PROBLEMS

```
A1W    JOB TO WORK OUT GRADER AND DISPLAY MESSAGES -- A1                                      PAGE   2

  LOC   OBJECT CODE    ADDR1 ADDR2  STMT   SOURCE STATEMENT                                  11 JUN 74

000000                                 2 MP1      CSECT
000000                                 3          USING *,15              ESTABLISH ADDRESSABILITY

                                       5 ***********************************************************************
                                       6 *                                                                     *
                                       7 *       THIS JOB WORKS OUT THE GRADER ERROR HANDLING AND MESSAGE       *
                                       8 *       FACILITIES, PROVIDING A SAMPLE OF GRADER OUTPUT. THE FIRST     *
                                       9 *       ANSWER IS RETURNED CORRECTLY, THE SECOND ANSWER IS RETURNED    *
                                      10 *       INCORRECTLY, AND THE THIRD ANSWER CAUSES A PROGRAM CHECK.      *
                                      11 *       EACH TEST NO-OPS A BRANCH TO CAUSE THE CODE FOR THE NEXT       *
                                      12 *       ONE TO BE EXECUTED.                                            *
                                      13 *                                                                     *
                                      14 ***********************************************************************

000000 47F0 F00C        0000C        15 BRANCH1  B     CASE1          THIS BRANCH WILL BE ZAPPED BY CASE 1
000004 47F0 F016        00016        17 BRANCH2  B     CASE2          THIS WILL BE ZAPPED BY CASE 2
000008 47F0 F020        00020        18 BRANCH3  B     CASE3          THIS BRANCH WILL NOT BE ZAPPED

00000C 9200 F001  00001              20 CASE1    MVI   BRANCH1+1,X'00'  NO-OP BRANCH
000010 4110 0001         00001       21          LA    1,1            TRIAL ONE IS A PALINDROME, SO THIS
                                     22 *                             IS CORRECT ANSWER
000014 07FE                          23          BR    14             RETURN TO GRADER

000016 9200 F005  00005              25 CASE2    MVI   BRANCH2+1,X'00'  NO-OP BRANCH
00001A 4110 0001         00001       26          LA    1,1            TRIAL 2 IS NOT A PALINDROME, SO THIS
                                     27 *                             IS NOT CORRECT
00001E 07FE                          29          BR    14             RETURN TO GRADER

000020 0000                          30 CASE3    DC    H'00'          CAUSE PROGRAM CHECK
                                     31 *                             NO NEED TO RETURN
                                     32          END
```

```
**** ASSEMBLER PROBLEM GRADER HAS BEEN ENTERED FOR STUDENT

PROGRAM ENTRY POINT: 12F790

***YOU WILL BE SENT IN REGISTERS 2-3: A,B,C,D,

***YOU HAVE RETURNED IN REGISTER 1 : 00000004

5 POINTS FOR RETURNING CONTROL
5 POINTS FOR RESTORING REGISTERS 2-12
10 POINTS FOR CORRECT ANSWER

***YOU WILL BE SENT IN REGISTERS 2-3: NONEHERE

***YOU HAVE RETURNED IN REGISTER 1 : 00000004

5 POINTS FOR RETURNING CONTROL
5 POINTS FOR RESTORING REGISTERS 2-12

YOU HAVE RETURNED AN INCORRECT ANSWER OF:   4, CORRECT ANSWER IS:    0

***HERE IS A DUMP OF YOUR PROGRAM:
12F780                                            4700F00C 4700F016 47F0F020 9200F001                  ..0...0..00...0.
12F7A0    41100004 07FE9200 F0054110 000407FE     0000FFFF FFFFFFFF FFFFFFFF FFFFFFFF   .........0.......................
12F7C0    FFFFFFFF FFFFFFFF FFFFFFFF FFFFFFFF      FFFFFFFF FFFFFFFF FFFFFFFF FFFFFFFF   .................................

***YOU WILL BE SENT IN REGISTERS 2-3: -!-!-!-.

***ERROR HAS OCCURRED WITHIN YOUR MACHINE PROBLEM

***TYPE 1 INTERRUPT AT LOCATION 12F7B0 ... PROGRAM DUMP FOLLOWS

PSW AT INTERRUPT WAS: FF B 5 0001  '01'B '11'B F 12F7B2


  REG  0    REG  1    REG  2    REG  3    REG  4    REG  5    REG  6    REG  7
 0000001E  FFFFFFFF  605A605A  605A606B  FFFFFFFF  FFFFFFFF  FFFFFFFF  FFFFFFFF

  REG  8    REG  9    REG 10    REG 11    REG 12    REG 13    REG 14    REG 15
 FFFFFFFF  FFFFFFFF  FFFFFFFF  FFFFFFFF  FFFFFFFF  0012E210  0012D8CA  0012F790


12F780                                            4700F00C 4700F016 47F0F020 9200F001                  ..0...0..00...0.
12F7A0    41100004 07FE9200 F0054110 000407FE     0000FFFF FFFFFFFF FFFFFFFF FFFFFFFF   .........0.......................
12F7C0    FFFFFFFF FFFFFFFF FFFFFFFF FFFFFFFF      FFFFFFFF FFFFFFFF FFFFFFFF FFFFFFFF   .................................

*** TESTING COMPLETE, YOUR TOTAL SCORE IS  30
```

## 2.2.2 Comma Counting Problem -- A2

**Problem Description:**

Your assignment is to write a 360 assembly language subroutine that counts the number of commas contained in a pair of general registers.

**Communication with the Grader:**

Your subroutine will be called by a grading program. This program will pass you test cases and you will return answers. When your subroutine is entered, the general registers will contain the following information:

Registers 0-1, 4-12: The contents of these registers are not significant.

Registers 2-3: This pair of registers contains eight characters. Your program examines these eight characters and counts the number of commas present.

Register 13: Address of an 18 fullword area where you may save general registers.

Register 14: Address of the return point in the grading program. You should branch to this address when you have completed processing.

Register 15: Address of the beginning of your program.

When your program returns to the grading program the contents of registers 2-13 should be the same as when you were called. Register 1 should contain a binary value representing the total number of commas present in registers 2 and 3.

**Debugging Aids:**

Executing the following constant as an instruction in your program will cause the grader to dump your program and registers for debugging purposes and then continue execution:

```
DEBUG   DC  H'15'              CAUSES DUMP TO OCCUR
```

Use this facility sparingly, however, as you will be limited in the number of lines you may print.

Examples:

1. on entry:  registers 2-3:  |C1 6B C2 C3|   |C4 6B 6B C5|

   you return in register 1:  |00 00 00 03|


2. on entry:  registers 2-3:  |05 06 05 C5|   |C8 C5 09 C5|

   you return in register 1:  |00 00 00 00|

Deck Setup:

    Your  program  must  be  a  CSECT  labelled  MP1.  Use  the
following deck structure:

```
        TITLE  'Students name - Instructors name'
MP1     CSECT
        USING *,15
        STM  ....
         .
         .   rest of program
         .
        END
```

Run Schedule:

    TO BE ANNOUNCED

```
A6W    JOB TO WORK OUT GRADER AND DISPLAY MESSAGES -- A6                                      PAGE    2

     LOC  OBJECT CODE    ADDR1 ADDR2  STMT   SOURCE STATEMENT                                 11 JUN 74
   000000                               2 MP1      CSECT
   000000                               3          USING *,15              ESTABLISH ADDRESSABILITY

                                        5 ****************************************************************
                                        6 *                                                              *
                                        7 *       THIS JOB WORKS OUT THE GRADER ERROR HANDLING AND MESSAGE *
                                        8 *       FACILITIES, PROVIDING A SAMPLE OF GRADER OUTPUT. THE FIRST *
                                        9 *       ANSWER IS RETURNED CORRECTLY, THE SECOND ANSWER IS RETURNED *
                                       10 *       INCORRECTLY, AND THE THIRD ANSWER CAUSES A PROGRAM CHECK. *
                                       11 *       EACH TEST NO-OPS A BRANCH TO CAUSE THE CODE FOR THE NEXT *
                                       12 *       ONE TO BE EXECUTED.                                      *
                                       13 *                                                              *
                                       14 ****************************************************************
   000000  47F0 F00C         0000C     16 BRANCH1  B        CASE1          THIS BRANCH WILL BE ZAPPED BY CASE 1
   000004  47F0 F016         00016     17 BRANCH2  B        CASE2          THIS WILL BE ZAPPED BY CASE 2
   000008  47F0 F020         00020     18 BRANCH3  B        CASE3          THIS BRANCH WILL NOT BE ZAPPED

   00000C  9200 F001    00001          20 CASE1    MVI      BRANCH1+1,X'00' NO-OP BRANCH
   000010  5810 F024          00024    21          L        1,REGONE       THIS IS CORRECT ANSWER FOR TRIAL 1
   000014  07FE                        22          BR       14             RETURN TO GRADER

   000016  9200 F005    00005          24 CASE2    MVI      BRANCH2+1,X'00' NO-OP BRANCH
   00001A  5810 F024          00024    25          L        1,REGONE       THIS IS INCORRECT ANSWER FOR TRIAL 2
   00001E  07FE                        26          BR       14             RETURN TO GRADER

   000020  0000                        28 CASE3    DC       H'00'          CAUSE PROGRAM CHECK
                                       29 *                               NO NEED TO RETURN

   000024                              31          DS       0F             FORCE ALIGNMENT
   000024  08                          32 REGONE   DC       AL1(8)         LENGTH OF ANSWER
   000025  000028                      33          DC       AL3(ANSWER)    ADDRESS OF ANSWER
   000028  D4C3D4D3E7E7C9E5            34 ANSWER   DC       C'MCMLXXIV'     ANSWER FOR CASE 1
                                       35          END
```

```
**** ASSEMBLER PROBLEM GRADER HAS BEEN ENTERED FOR STUDENT

PROGRAM ENTRY POINT: 12F790


***YOU WILL BE SENT IN REGISTERS 2-3: ABCDDCBA


***YOU HAVE RETURNED IN REGISTER 1 : 00000001

5 POINTS FOR RETURNING CONTROL
5 POINTS FOR RESTORING REGISTERS 2-12
10 POINTS FOR CORRECT ANSWER


***YOU WILL BE SENT IN REGISTERS 2-3: ABCDABCD


***YOU HAVE RETURNED IN REGISTER 1 : 00000001

5 POINTS FOR RETURNING CONTROL
5 POINTS FOR RESTORING REGISTERS 2-12
YOU HAVE RETURNED AN INCORRECT ANSWER OF:   1, CORRECT ANSWER IS:   0


***HERE IS A DUMP OF YOUR PROGRAM:
12F780                                      4700F00C 4700F016 47F0F020 9200F001            ..0...0..00...0.
12F7A0   41100001 07FE9200 F0054110 000107FE   0000FFFF FFFFFFFF FFFFFFFF FFFFFFFF   .........0.....................
12F7C0   FFFFFFFF FFFFFFFF FFFFFFFF FFFFFFFF   FFFFFFFF FFFFFFFF FFFFFFFF FFFFFFFF   ...............................


***YOU WILL BE SENT IN REGISTERS 2-3: SUPERMAN

***ERROR HAS OCCURRED WITHIN YOUR MACHINE PROBLEM

***TYPE 1 INTERRUPT AT LOCATION 12F7B0 ... PROGRAM DUMP FOLLOWS

PSW AT INTERRUPT WAS: FF B 5 0001  '01'B '11'B F 12F7B2


   REG  0     REG  1     REG  2     REG  3     REG  4     REG  5     REG  6     REG  7
 0000001E   FFFFFFFF   E2E4D7C5   D9D4C1D5   FFFFFFFF   FFFFFFFF   FFFFFFFF   FFFFFFFF

   REG  8     REG  9     REG 10     REG 11     REG 12     REG 13     REG 14     REG 15
 FFFFFFFF   FFFFFFFF   FFFFFFFF   FFFFFFFF   FFFFFFFF   0012B210   0012D8CA   0012F790


12F780                                      4700F00C 4700F016 47F0F020 9200F001            ..0...0..00...0.
12F7A0   41100001 07FE9200 F0054110 000107FE   0000FFFF FFFFFFFF FFFFFFFF FFFFFFFF   .........0.....................
12F7C0   FFFFFFFF FFFFFFFF FFFFFFFF FFFFFFFF   FFFFFFFF FFFFFFFF FFFFFFFF FFFFFFFF   ...............................


*** TESTING COMPLETE, YOUR TOTAL SCORE IS  30
```

## 2.2.3 Arithmetic Operations Problem -- A3

Introduction:

An interpreter is a language processor which accepts a source "deck" and executes each statement as it is read (In contrast, a compiler produces an object "deck" which may subsequently be executed). The advantage of an interpreter lies in the fact that for small one-shot programs much more time may be spent compiling the program than would be spent executing it. Some desk-top calculators are actually interpreters which through a simple algebraic language allow a person to perform procedures which would be very tedious on a normal calculator.

When an interpreter encounters a simple statement like "A = 6 + 1" it must add 6 to 1 and then assign the result, 7, to A. When you implement an interpreter on an IBM 360/370 series machine you find that your input statements are in character (EBCDIC) format, and that there are no arithmetic instructions which operate on character forms. In order to evaluate the expression "6 + 1", you must convert both operands to a suitable arithmetic form and then perform the operation.

Problem Description:

Your assignment is to write a subroutine in 360 Assembly Language (BAL) which will perform arithmetic operations on character form operands. You must perform the arithmetic in fixed point binary and convert the answer to zoned decimal form with leading zeroes removed (see below). Your operands will be character strings containing decimal integer numbers with optionally prefixed sign (e.g. +7, 6, -253, etc). If no sign is present you should assume positive. You must convert your operands to fixed point binary and then perform one of four dyadic operations which will be indicated by a character form operator as follows:

| Operator (EBCDIC) | Result definition |
| --- | --- |
| + | Operand 1 added to operand 2 |
| - | Operand 2 subtracted from operand 1 |
| * | Operand 1 multiplied by operand 2 |
| ** | Operand 1 raised to operand 2'th power |
| / | Operand 1 divided by operand 2 |

Communication with the Grader:

Your subroutine will be called by a grading program. This program will pass you test cases and you will return answers. When your subroutine is entered, the general registers will contain the following information:

26

Register 0:  The absolute storage address of the first  word
    of  a  three  word  control  block  with  the following
    structure:

```
 _____              _____
| REGISTER 0 |  -->  |_Count_1_|_1st_Operand_Address_____|
                     |_Count_2_|_Operation_Address_____|
                     |_Count_3_|_2nd_Operand_Address_____|
                      Byte 0      Bytes 1-3
```

("A --> B" means A contains the  address  of  B,  or  A
"points to" B)

Count  1 is the number of consecutive bytes required to
represent the first operand.

The 1st Operand Address is the absolute address of  the
first byte of the first operand.

Count  2  is  the number of bytes required to represent
the operator.  The operator is one or two EBCDIC  bytes
located at the operation address.

The  third  word in the control block is similar to the
first word.


Note:  The number of bytes in the first and second  operands
    will  be  from one to eight inclusive.  The answer will
    always be small enough to fit into a  general  register
    without overflow.  You need not check for division with
    a  divisor  of  zero or exponentiation with zero as the
    base,  but  the  exponents  may  include  all  integral
    values:  negative, zero, or positive.


Registers 1-12:   Not  significant,  but  must  be  restored
    before you return.

Register 13:  Address of an 18 fullword area you may use  to
    save general registers.


Register 14: Address of the  return  point  in  the  grading
    program.  You  should  branch  to this address when you
    have completed processing.

Register 15: Address of the beginning of your program.


When you return to  the  grader,  the  general  registers  should
    contain:

Register 0: Absolute address of a fullword giving the byte count and absolute address of the first byte of your answer. This answer must be in <u>zoned decimal</u> format:

```
 _____             _____
| REGISTER 0 |  ----->  | Count  | Address of Answer |
 ‾‾‾‾‾‾‾‾‾‾            ‾‾‾‾‾‾‾‾‾‾‾‾‾‾‾‾‾‾‾‾‾‾‾‾‾‾‾‾‾‾‾‾
                          Byte 0     Bytes 1-3
```

The fullword and answer must be located within the limits of your subroutine. The answer must be in the most concise form (no leading zeroes). The student should not alter any of the data sent by the grader.

Registers 1-12: Same as when you received control.


Debugging Aids:

Executing the following constant as an instruction in your program will cause the grader to dump your program and registers for debugging purposes and then continue execution:

DEBUG    DC    H'15'              CAUSES DUMP TO OCCUR

Use this facility sparingly, however, as you will be limited in the number of lines you may print.


Examples:

1.  Problem: (-23) + (+7) . On entry to your program:

```
                                        hexadecimal      EBCDIC
 _____        _____         _____
| REG 0 | -->  | 3 | address |  ---> | 60 | F2 | F3 |    -23
 ‾‾‾‾‾‾‾        | 1 | address |  ---> | 4E |              +
                | 2 | address |  ---> | 4E | F7 |         +7
```

The answer (-16) requires two bytes for representation in zoned decimal. When you return to the grader:

```
 _____        _____         hexadecimal
| REG 0 | -->  | 2 | address |  ---> | F1 | D6 |
 ‾‾‾‾‾‾‾        ‾‾‾‾‾‾‾‾‾‾‾‾‾         ‾‾‾‾‾‾‾‾‾‾‾
```

2.  Problem: (+2) / (3) . On entry to your program:

```
                                                      EBCDIC
 _____        _____         _____
| REG 0 | -->  | 2 | address |  ---> | 4E | F2 |      +2
 ‾‾‾‾‾‾‾        | 1 | address |  ---> | 61 |          /
                | 1 | address |  ---> | F3 |          3
```

28

Note truncation of the answer (+0), which requires one byte.
When you return to the grader:

```
 _____                _____      hexadecimal
| REG 0 |  -->    | 1 | address |  ---->   | C0 |
```

You might find the following instructions useful in the  solution
of this problem:

| | | | | | |
|------|------|------|------|------|------|
| UNPK | MVC  | LM   | TR   | EX   | NI   |
| CVD  | CVB  | PACK | CLI  | SRDA | IC   |

Deck Setup:

Your  program  must  be  a CSECT labelled MP1.  Use the following
deck structure:

```
        TITLE   'Students name - Instructors name'
MP1     CSECT
        USING *,15
        STM   .....
         .
         . (your deck goes here)
         .
         .
        END
```

Run Schedule:

   TO BE ANNOUNCED

```
A3W    JOB TO WORK OUT GRADER AND DISPLAY MESSAGES -- A3                                            PAGE   2

   LOC  OBJECT CODE     ADDR1 ADDR2  STMT   SOURCE STATEMENT                                          11 JUN 74

000000                               2 MP1      CSECT
000000                               3          USING *,15                       ESTABLISH ADDRESSABILITY

                                     5 *************************************************************************
                                     6 *                                                                     *
                                     7 *           THIS JOB WORKS OUT THE GRADER ERROR HANDLING AND MESSAGE   *
                                     8 *           FACILITIES, PROVIDING A SAMPLE OF GRADER OUTPUT. THE FIRST *
                                     9 *           ANSWER IS RETURNED CORRECTLY, THE SECOND ANSWER IS RETURNED*
                                    10 *           INCORRECTLY, AND THE THIRD ANSWER CAUSES A PROGRAM CHECK.  *
                                    11 *           EACH TEST NO-OPS A BRANCH TO CAUSE THE CODE FOR THE NEXT   *
                                    12 *           ONE TO BE EXECUTED.                                        *
                                    13 *                                                                     *
                                    14 *************************************************************************

000000 47F0 F00C           0000C    16 BRANCH1  B     CASE1                      THIS BRANCH WILL BE ZAPPED BY CASE 1
000004 47F0 F016           00016    17 BRANCH2  B     CASE2                      THIS WILL BE ZAPPED BY CASE 2
000008 47F0 F020           00020    18 BRANCH3  B     CASE3                      THIS BRANCH WILL NOT BE ZAPPED

00000C 9200 F001     00001          20 CASE1    MVI   BRANCH1+1,X'00'            NO-OP BRANCH
000010 4100 F024           00024    21          LA    0,IWORD                    THIS IS CORRECT ANSWER FOR TRIAL 1
000014 07FE                         22          BR    14                         RETURN TO GRADER

000016 9200 F005     00005          24 CASE2    MVI   BRANCH2+1,X'00'            NO-OP BRANCH
00001A 4100 F024           00024    25          LA    0,IWORD                    THIS IS INCORRECT ANSWER FOR TRIAL 2
00001E 07FE                         26          BR    14                         RETURN TO GRADER

000020 0000                         28 CASE3    DC    H'00'                      CAUSE PROGRAM CHECK
                                    29 *                                         NO NEED TO RETURN

000024                              31          DS    0F                         FORCE ALIGNMENT
000024 01                           32 IWORD    DC    AL1(1)                     LENGTH OF ANSWER
000025 000028                       33          DC    AL3(ANSWER)                ADDRESS OF ANSWER
000028 C1                           34 ANSWER   DC    X'C1'                      CORRECT ANSWER FOR TRIAL 1
                                    35          END
```

30

```
**** ASSEMBLER PROBLEM GRADER HAS BEEN ENTERED FOR STUDENT

PROGRAM ENTRY POINT: 12FD60

YOU HAVE RECEIVED 10 POINTS FOR SUCCESSFULLY ASSEMBLING YOUR PROGRAM


***WE WILL PASS YOU -> (-1      ) ** (0        ):

 REG   0
0012E764 ----> 12E764: 0212E770 ----> 12E770: 60F1404040404040
                       0212E778 ----> 12E778: 5C5CF04040404040
                       0112E77A ----> 12E77A: F040404040404040


***YOU HAVE RETURNED:

 REG   0
0012FD84 ----> 12FD84: 0112FD88 ----> 12FD88: C1FFFFFFFFFFFFFF

2 POINTS FOR RETURNING CONTROL TO GRADER
3 POINTS FOR RESTORING REGISTERS
2 POINTS FOR SPECIFYING PROPER LENGTH OF RESULT
8 POINTS FOR CORRECT ANSWER


***WE WILL PASS YOU -> (-8      ) * (+8     ):

 REG   0
0012E764 ----> 12E764: 0212E770 ----> 12E770: 60F8404040404040
                       0112E778 ----> 12E778: 5C404FF840404040
                       0212E77A ----> 12E77A: 4EF8404040404040


***YOU HAVE RETURNED:

 REG   0
0012FD84 ----> 12FD84: 0112FD98 ----> 12FD88: C1FFFFFFFFFFFFFF

2 POINTS FOR RETURNING CONTROL TO GRADER
3 POINTS FOR RESTORING REGISTERS
INVALID LENGTH SPECIFIED IN YOUR ANSWER


***HERE IS A DUMP OF YOUR PROGRAM


12FD60   4700F00C 4700F016 47F0F020 9200F001   4100F024 07FE9200 F0054100 F02407FE   ..0...0..00...0...0.....0...0...
12FD80   0000FFFF 0112FD88 C1FFFFFF FFFFFFFF   FFFFFFFF FFFFFFFF FFFFFFFF FFFFFFFF   ........A......................
12FDA0   FFFFFFFF FFFFFFFF FFFFFFFF FFFFFFFF   FFFFFFFF FFFFFFFF FFFFFFFF FFFFFFFF   ...............................


***WE WILL PASS YOU -> (-23     ) + (+7     ):

 REG   0
```

```
0012E764 ----> 12E764: 0312E770 ----> 12F770: 60F2F34040404040
                       0112E778 ----> 12E778: 4E404FF740404040
                       0212E77A ----> 12E77A: 4EF7404040404040
```

***ERROR HAS OCCURRED WITHIN YOUR MACHINE PROBLEM

***TYPE 1 INTERRUPT AT LOCATION 12FD80 ... PROGRAM DUMP FOLLOWS

PSW AT INTERRUPT WAS: FF B 5 0001 '01'B '11'B F 12FD82

```
  REG  0    REG  1    REG  2    REG  3    REG  4    REG  5    REG  6    REG  7
0012E764  FFFFFFFF  FFFFFFFF  FFFFFFFF  FFFFFFFF  FFFFFFFF  FFFFFFFF  FFFFFFFF

  REG  8    REG  9    REG 10    REG 11    REG 12    REG 13    REG 14    REG 15
FFFFFFFF  FFFFFFFF  FFFFFFFF  FFFFFFFF  FFFFFFFF  0012E784  0012D942  0012FD60
```

```
12FD60   4700F00C 4700F016 47F0F0Z0 9200F001   4100F024 07FE9200 F0054100 F02407FE   ..0...0..00...0...0.....0...0...
12FD80   0000FFFF 0112FD88 C1FFFFFF FFFFFFFF   FFFFFFFF FFFFFFFF FFFFFFFF FFFFFFFF   .......A........................
12FDA0   FFFFFFFF FFFFFFFF FFFFFFFF FFFFFFFF   FFFFFFFF FFFFFFFF FFFFFFFF FFFFFFFF   ................................
```

*** TESTING COMPLETE, YOUR TOTAL SCORE IS  30

## 2.2.4 DC-Simulator Problem -- A4

Introduction:

     General purpose computers, including the IBM 360-370 series
allow   for   several   internal   data  formats  such  as  logical,
character, fixed point binary,  fixed  point  decimal,  floating
point  binary,  etc.  This flexibility allows programmers to pick
the format most  suitable  to  the  problems  they  are  solving.
However,   this  variety  of  internal  formats  creates  special
problems for language translators which always  accept  character
format (from cards) as input.

     For   example  when you punch a one ("1") in a card column do
you mean the character "1", a binary 1, or the arithmetic 1.00  ?
Some   translators  make  this decision contextually, while others
like the 360 assembler require a qualifier to indicate  what  you
mean   (eg C'1', B'1', E'1', etc.).  Once the translator decides a
constant's type, it  must  convert  the  constant  from  inputed
character format to the correct internal form.


Problem Description:

     Your   assignment   is  to  write  a  360  assembly  language
subroutine which handles the conversion of constants  from  input
character  form  to  the  correct internal form for the assembler
data types C, X, P, and F.  You will be given a character  string
and asked to convert it to a specific internal format.


Communication with the Grader:

     Your   subroutine   will be called by a grading program.  This
program will pass you test cases and  you  will  return  answers.
When  your  subroutine  is  entered,  the  general registers will
contain the following information:

Register 0: The contents of register zero indicate the  type
        of conversion to be performed, as follows:

        0      Character
        1      Hexadecimal
        2      Packed decimal
        3      Fullword binary

Register 1: The contents of register one indicate the length
        and location of the constant to be converted.  Bits 0-7
        contain  the  byte  count, including any optional sign,
        and bits 8-31 contain  the  absolute  address  of  the
        constant:

```
 _____register__1_____
 I__count_I_____address_____I
 0       7 8                          31
```

Registers 2-12: The contents of registers 2-12 are not significant, but must be saved and restored by your program before returning control to the grader.

Register 13: Address of an 18 fullword area where you may save general registers.

Register 14: Address of the return point in the grading program. You should branch to this address when you have completed processing.

Register 15: Address of the beginning of your program.

When your program returns to the grading program, the contents of registers 2-12 should be the same as when you were called, and register 1 should contain the address of a fullword area in your program. This word should contain the length and address of your answer as follows:

```
 _____           _____
 I_REGISTER_1_I -----> I_Count__I_Address_of_Answer_I
                        Byte 0    Bytes 1-3
```

("A --> B" means that A contains the address of B)

The count should be the length in bytes of the converted constant, and the address should be the absolute address of an area within your program containing the converted constant.


Restrictions and Assumptions:

Character constants will have a maximum byte count of 40.

Data to be converted to hexadecimal will have a maximum byte count of 40, yielding a maximum answer count of 20, and the byte count will be even.

Data to be converted to packed decimal will have at most 15 significant decimal digits not including an optional prefixed plus or minus sign. When you return your answer, it should be as short as possible, that is, with leading zeros removed. You must return the answer with the EBCDIC preferred sign codes C and D.

Data to be converted to fullword binary will also have an optional prefixed plus or minus sign, and a maximum significant digit count of 15. Your answer should be aligned to a fullword boundary.

You must not modify the input strings in any way.

You will not be asked to make conversions on invalid data.


Debugging Aids:

Executing the following constant as an instruction in your program will cause the grader to dump your program and registers for debugging purposes and then continue execution:

DEBUG   DC   H'15'               CAUSES DUMP TO OCCUR

Use this facility sparingly, however, as you will be limited in the number of lines you may print.


Examples:

1. Passed Input:

```
  Reg. 0          Reg. 1           _____
!00000001!      !041_____!--->!C1E1F0F1!
```

Returned Output:

```
  Reg. 1          _____         ____
!_____!--->!021_____!--->!A101!
```


2. Passed Input:

```
  Reg. 0          Reg. 1           ____
!00000003!      !021_____!--->!60F1!
```

Returned Output:

```
  Reg. 1          _____         _____
!_____!--->!041_____!--->!FFFFFFFF!
                                   ▲
                                   !
                              (fullword boundary)
```


3. Passed Input:

```
  Reg. 0          Reg. 1           _____
!00000000!      !041_____!--->!E6C8E86F!
```

35

Returned Output:

```
 Reg. 1                  _____          _____
|_____|--->|041_____|--->|E6C8E86F|
```

4. Passed Input:

```
 Reg. 0            Reg. 1           _____
|000000002|      |051_____|--->|4EF1F2F3F4|
```

Returned Output:

```
 Reg. 1                  _____          _____
|_____|--->|031_____|--->|01234C|
```

Deck Setup:

Your program must be a CSECT labelled MP1. Use the following
deck structure:

```
        TITLE  'Students name - Instructors name'
   MP1  CSECT
        USING *,15
        STM   .....
         •
         •  rest of your cards go here
         •
        END
```

Run Schedule:

        TO BE ANNOUNCED

```
   LOC  OBJECT CODE   ADDR1 ADDR2  STMT   SOURCE STATEMENT                                                       11 JUN 74

 000000                               2 MP1       CSECT
 000000                               3           USING *,15               ESTABLISH ADDRESSABILITY
                                      5 ***************************************************************************
                                      6 *                                                                       *
                                      7 *         THIS JOB WORKS OUT THE GRADER ERROR HANDLING AND MESSAGE       *
                                      8 *         FACILITIES, PROVIDING A SAMPLE OF GRADER OUTPUT. THE FIRST     *
                                      9 *         ANSWER IS RETURNED CORRECTLY, THE SECOND ANSWER IS RETURNED    *
                                     10 *         INCORRECTLY, AND THE THIRD ANSWER CAUSES A PROGRAM CHECK.      *
                                     11 *         EACH TEST NO-OPS A BRANCH TO CAUSE THE CODE FOR THE NEXT       *
                                     12 *         ONE TO BE EXECUTED.                                            *
                                     13 *                                                                       *
                                     14 ***************************************************************************
 000000 47F0 F00C         0000C      15 BRANCH1   B         CASE1          THIS BRANCH WILL BE ZAPPED BY CASE 1
 000004 47F0 F016         00016      17 BRANCH2   B         CASE2          THIS WILL BE ZAPPED BY CASE 2
 000008 47F0 F020         00020      18 BRANCH3   B         CASE3          THIS BRANCH WILL NOT BE ZAPPED

 00000C 9200 F001   00001            20 CASE1     MVI       BRANCH1+1,X'00'  NO-OP BRANCH
 000010 4110 F024         00024      21           LA        1,IWORD        THIS IS CORRECT ANSWER FOR TRIAL 1
 000014 07FE                         22           BR        14             RETURN TO GRADER

 000016 9200 F005   00005            24 CASE2     MVI       BRANCH2+1,X'00'  NO-OP BRANCH
 00001A 4110 F024         00024      25           LA        1,IWORD        THIS IS INCORRECT ANSWER FOR TRIAL 2
 00001E 07FE                         26           BR        14             RETURN TO GRADER

 000020 0000                         28 CASE3     DC        H'00'          CAUSE PROGRAM CHECK
                                     29 *                                 NO NEED TO RETURN

 000024                              31           DS        0F             FORCE ALIGNMENT
 000024 02                           32 IWORD     DC        AL1(2)         LENGTH OF ANSWER
 000025 000028                       33           DC        AL3(ANSWER)    ADDRESS OF ANSWER
 000028 A101                         34 ANSWER    DC        X'A101'        CORRECT ANSWER FOR TRIAL 1
                                     35           END
```

37

```
**** ASSEMBLER PROBLEM GRADER HAS BEEN ENTERED FOR STUDENT

PROGRAM ENTRY POINT: 12FDD0

YOU HAVE RECEIVED 10 POINTS FOR SUCCESSFULLY ASSEMBLING YOUR PROGRAM


***WE WILL PASS YOU A TYPE X CONVERSION ON A101

 REG 1
0412E70C ----> 12E70C: C1F1F0F140404040


***YOU HAVE RETURNED:

 REG 1
0012FDF4 ----> 12FDF4: 0212FDF8 ----> 12FDF8: A101FFFFFFFFFFFF

2 POINTS FOR RETURNING CONTROL TO GRADER
3 POINTS FOR RESTORING REGISTERS
2 POINTS FOR SPECIFYING PROPER LENGTH OF RESULT
8 POINTS FOR CORRECT ANSWER


***WE WILL PASS YOU A TYPE F CONVERSION ON -1

 REG 1
0212E70C ----> 12E70C: 60F1404040404040


***YOU HAVE RETURNED:

 REG 1
0012FDF4 ----> 12FDF4: 0212FDF8 ----> 12FDF8: A101FFFFFFFFFFFF

2 POINTS FOR RETURNING CONTROL TO GRADER
3 POINTS FOR RESTORING REGISTERS

YOU HAVE RETURNED WRONG LENGTH FOR ANSWER, CORRECT LENGTH IS:    4


***HERE IS A DUMP OF YOUR PROGRAM


12FDC0                                     4700F00C 4700F016 47F0F020 9200F001              ..0...0..00...0.
12FDE0    4110F024 07FE9200 F0054110 F02407FE  0000FFFF 0212FDF8 A101FFFF FFFFFFFF  ..0.....0...0.......8........
12FE00    FFFFFFFF FFFFFFFF FFFFFFFF FFFFFFFF  FFFFFFFF FFFFFFFF FFFFFFFF FFFFFFFF  ............................


***WE WILL PASS YOU A TYPE F CONVERSION ON -1

 REG 1
0212E70C ----> 12E70C: 60F1404040404040
```

```
***ERROR HAS OCCURRED WITHIN YOUR MACHINE PROBLEM

***TYPE 1 INTERRUPT AT LOCATION 12FDFC  ... PROGRAM DUMP FOLLOWS

PSW AT INTERRUPT WAS: FF B 5 0001  '01'B '11'B F 12FDF2


  REG  0     REG  1     REG  2'    REG  3     REG  4     REG  5     REG  6     REG  7
 00000002  0212E70C   FFFFFFFF   FFFFFFFF   FFFFFFFF   FFFFFFFF   FFFFFFFF   FFFFFFFF

  REG  8     REG  9     REG 10     REG 11     REG 12     REG 13     REG 14     REG 15
 FFFFFFFF   FFFFFFFF   FFFFFFFF   FFFFFFFF   FFFFFFFF   0C12E734   0012D989   0012FDD0


 12FDC0                                          4700F00C 4700F016 47F0F020 9200F001                  ..0...0..00...0.
 12FDE0   4110F024 07FE9200 F0054110 F02407FE   0000FFFF 0212FDF8 A101FFFF FFFFFFFF    ..0.....0...0..........8........
 12FE00   FFFFFFFF FFFFFFFF FFFFFFFF FFFFFFFF   FFFFFFFF FFFFFFFF FFFFFFFF FFFFFFFF    ................................


*** TESTING COMPLETE, YOUR TOTAL SCORE IS  3C
```

## 2.2.5 Instruction Analyzer Problem -- A5

Introduction:

The IBM 360-370 series of computers has essentially five instruction formats: RR, RX, RS, SI, and SS. When the instruction interpreting hardware of the CPU processes an instruction it must decide the instruction type and length; decode operands into register, address, or immediate type; and perform any address calculations necessary to fetch operands from memory.

Address calculation consists of determining the base register number, obtaining its contents (if the register specified is not zero), adding the assembled displacement value from the instruction, and then if the instruction type allows for indexing and the index register specified is other than zero, the contents of the index register must be added. This resultant value is the absolute core address of an operand.

It should be noted that the interpreting of RR-type instructions involves no address calculation; decoding RX, RS, and SI-type instructions involves one address calculation; while SS-type instructions require two address calculations.


Problem Description:

Your assignment is to write a 360 assembly language subroutine which given the address of an instruction will determine:

1. The length of the instruction in bytes.
2. The number of storage operands contained in the instruction, may be 0, 1, or 2.
3. For any storage operands present, the absolute address of the operand (address calculation).

Your answers will be in the form of a four word (16 byte) long, word-aligned block. For this block:

   word 1 - Length of instruction, in bytes, right justified
       in fixed point binary format.
   word 2 - Number of storage operands.
   word 3 - Absolute address of first storage operand, if
       present, else zero.
   word 4 - Absolute address of second storage operand, if
       present, else zero.

## Communication with the Grader:

Your subroutine will be called by a grading program. This program will pass you test cases, and you will return answers. When control is transferred to your subroutine, the general registers will contain the following information:

**Register 0:**  Not used by the grader, need not be restored.

**Register 1:**  Address of the instruction you are to analyze (on a half word boundary).

**Registers 2-5:**  Only these registers will be used by the given instruction for addressing.

**Registers 6-12:**  Not significant, but must be restored before you return.

**Register 13:**  Address of an 18 fullword area you may use to save general registers.

**Register 14:** Address of the return point in the grading program.  You should branch to this address when you have completed processing.

**Register 15:**  Address of the beginning of your program.

When you complete processing, register 1 should have the address of your answer in the form mentioned above. This address should be in the bounds of your program and the instruction sent to you should not be altered. Registers 2-12 should be restored to the values they contained when your subroutine was entered.

## Notes:

1. If there is only one address field, store it in the 3rd fullword of your answer.
2. Your program should not alter the instruction passed.
3. You must restore registers 2-12 before returning control to the grader.
4. Whenever you see the notational convention "A 4.-> B" the intended meaning is that A contains the address of B or simply that A points to B.

## Debugging Aids:

Executing the following constant as an instruction in your program will cause the grader to dump your program and registers for debugging purposes and then continue execution:

```
DEBUG  DC  H'15'            CAUSES DUMP TO OCCUR
```

Use this facility sparingly, however, as you will be limited in the number of lines you may print.

Examples:

    For the examples below, assume registers two through five contain the following (in hex).

       R(2) = 0000 1000
       R(3) = 0000 00F0
       R(4) = 0000 0008
       R(5) = 0000 2000

Case 1:

| REGISTER 1 | ----->| 1A2B |

Upon Return:

| REGISTER 1 | ----->| 00000002 |
                       | 00000000 |
                       | 00000000 |
                       | 00000000 |

Case 2:

| REGISTER 1 | ----->| FA5B3C4D2E6F |

Upon Return:

| REGISTER 1 | ----->| 00000006 |
                       | 00000002 |
                       | 000000D0 |
                       | 00001E6F |

Hints and Suggestions:

    Before you start coding 150 compare instructions, look at the instructions carefully. Note the ordering of the op-codes:

    bits 0 and 1 of RR instructions are always 00,
    bits 0 and 1 of RX instructions are always 01,
    bits 0 and 1 of RS and SI instructions are always 10,
    bits 0 and 1 of SS instructions are always 11.

Using this information, the problem becomes fairly easy. These instructions should also help:

EX    TM    SLL   SRL


**Deck Setup:**

Your program must be a CSECT labelled MP1.  Use the following
deck structure:

```
          TITLE "your name - your instructors name"
MP1       CSECT
          USING *,15
          STM  .....
            .
            .  (your deck goes here)
            .
            .
          END
```

**Run Schedule:**

    TO BE ANNOUNCED

```
  LOC  OBJECT CODE    ADDR1 ADDR2  STMT   SOURCE STATEMENT                                        11 JUN 74

000000                               2 MP1     CSECT
000000                               3         USING *,15                    ESTABLISH ADDRESSABILITY
                                     5 ****************************************************************
                                     6 *                                                              *
                                     7 *        THIS JOB WORKS OUT THE GRADER ERROR HANDLING AND MESSAGE *
                                     8 *        FACILITIES, PROVIDING A SAMPLE OF GRADER OUTPUT. THE FIRST *
                                     9 *        ANSWER IS RETURNED CORRECTLY, THE SECOND ANSWER IS RETURNED *
                                    10 *        INCORRECTLY, AND THE THIRD ANSWER CAUSES A PROGRAM CHECK. *
                                    11 *        EACH TEST NO-OPS A BRANCH TO CAUSE THE CODE FOR THE NEXT *
                                    12 *        ONE TO BE EXECUTED.                                     *
                                    13 *                                                              *
                                    14 ****************************************************************

000000 47F0 F00C        0000C      16 BRANCH1  B       CASE1       THIS BRANCH WILL BE ZAPPED BY CASE 1
000004 47F0 F016        00016      17 BRANCH2  B       CASE2       THIS WILL BE ZAPPED BY CASE 2
000008 47F0 F020        00020      18 BRANCH3  B       CASE3       THIS BRANCH WILL NOT BE ZAPPED

00000C 9200 F001  00001            20 CASE1    MVI     BRANCH1+1,X'00'   NO-OP BRANCH
000010 4110 F024        00024      21          LA      1,ANSWER    THIS IS CORRECT ANSWER FOR TRIAL 1
000014 07FE                        22          BR      14          RETURN TO GRADER

000016 9200 F005  00005            24 CASE2    MVI     BRANCH2+1,X'00'   NO-OP BRANCH
00001A 4110 F024        00024      25          LA      1,ANSWER    THIS IS INCORRECT ANSWER FOR TRIAL 2
00001E 07FE                        26          BR      14          RETURN TO GRADER

000020 0000                        28 CASE3    DC      H'00'       CAUSE PROGRAM CHECK
                                   29 *                            NO NEED TO RETURN

000022 0000
000024 0000000200000000            31 ANSWER   DC      F'2,0,0,0'  THIS IS CORRECT ANSWER FOR TRIAL 1
                                   32          END
```

44

```
**** ASSEMBLER PROBLEM GRADER HAS BEEN ENTERED FOR STUDENT

PROGRAM ENTRY POINT: 1300F8


***WE WILL PASS YOU:

  REG 1                   INSTRUCTION
0012E602 ----> 12E602: 1A22070007000700


  REG  2     REG  3     REG  4     REG  5     REG  6     REG  7     REG  8     REG  9
00000014   00000028   0000003C   00000064   0014CF50   000000FF   00000000   0014CE90


  REG 10     REG 11     REG 12     REG 13     REG 14     REG 15
00130080   0012D810   4014D04C   0012E60C   0012D998   001300F8


***YOU HAVE RETURNED:

  REG 1                   ANSWER
0013011C ----> 13011C: 00000002
                       00000000
                       00000000
                       00000000


     5 POINTS FOR RETURNING CONTROL TO GRADER
     5 POINTS FOR RESTORING REGISTERS
     2 POINTS FOR CORRECT LENGTH
     2 POINTS FOR CORRECT NUMBER OF ADDRESS FIELDS
     3 POINTS FOR CORRECT OPERAND 1
     3 POINTS FOR CORRECT OPERAND 2


***WE WILL PASS YOU:

  REG 1                   INSTRUCTION
0012E602 ----> 12E602: 5543501407000700


  REG  2     REG  3     REG  4     REG  5     REG  6     REG  7     REG  8     REG  9
00000014   00000028   0000003C   00000064   0014CF50   000000FF   00000000   0014CE90


  REG 10     REG 11     REG 12     REG 13     REG 14     REG 15
00130098   0012D810   4014D04C   0012E60C   0012D998   001300F8


***YOU HAVE RETURNED:

  REG 1                   ANSWER
0013011C ----> 13011C: 00000002
                       00000000
                       00000000
                       00000000


     5 POINTS FOR RETURNING CONTROL TO GRADER
     5 POINTS FOR RESTORING REGISTERS
```

```
INCORRECT LENGTH ... YOUR ANSWER WAS    2 PROPER LENGTH IS    4
INCORRECT NUMBER OF ADDRESS FIELDS ... YOUR ANSWER WAS    0 CORRECT NUMBER IS    1

INCORRECT OP1 ... YOUR OP1 WAS 000000 CORRECT OP1 IS 0000A0
   3 POINTS FOR CORRECT OPERAND 2

***HERE IS A DUMP OF YOUR PROGRAM :


130080                                                  4700F00C 4700F016                        ..0...0.
130100   47F0F020 9200F001 4110F024 07FB9200    F0054110 F02407FB 00000000 00000002    .00...0...0.....0...0...........
130120   00000000 00000000 00000000 FFFFFFFF    FFFFFFFF FFFFFFFF FFFFFFFF FFFFFFFF    .............................
130140   FFFFFFFF FFFFFFFF FFFFFFFF FFFFFFFF    FFFFFFFF FFFFFFFF FFFFFFFF FFFFFFFF    .............................


***WE WILL PASS YOU:

 REG 1              INSTRUCTION
00012E602 ----> 12E602: 98RC503207000700


 REG 2     REG 3     REG 4     REG 5     REG 6     REG 7     REG 8     REG 9
00000014  00000028  0000003C  00000064  0014CF50  000000FF  00000000  0014CE90


 REG 10    REG 11    REG 12    REG 13    REG 14    REG 15
001300B0  0012D810  4014D04C  0012E60C  0012D998  001300F8


***ERROR HAS OCCURRED WITHIN YOUR MACHINE PROBLEM

***TYPE 1 INTERRUPT AT LOCATION 130118 ... PROGRAM DUMP FOLLOWS

PSW AT INTERRUPT WAS: FF B 5 0001  '01'B '11'B F 13011A


 REG 0     REG 1     REG 2     REG 3     REG 4     REG 5     REG 6     REG 7
00000021  0012E602  00000014  00000028  0000003C  00000064  0014CF50  000000FF


 REG 8     REG 9     REG 10    REG 11    REG 12    REG 13    REG 14    REG 15
00000000  0014CE90  001300B0  0012D810  4014D04C  0012E60C  7F12D998  001300F8


130080                                                  4700F00C 4700F016                        ..0...0.
130100   47F0F020 9200F001 4110F024 07FF9200    F0054110 F02407FE 00000000 00000002    .00...0...0.....0...0...........
130120   00000000 00000000 00000000 FFFFFFFF    FFFFFFFF FFFFFFFF FFFFFFFF FFFFFFFF    .............................
130140   FFFFFFFF FFFFFFFF FFFFFFFF FFFFFFFF    FFFFFFFF FFFFFFFF FFFFFFFF FFFFFFFF    .............................


*** TESTING COMPLETE, YOUR TOTAL SCORE IS  33
```

## 2.2.6 Roman Numeral Conversion Problem -- A6

Introduction:

General purpose computers, including the IBM 360-370 series, allow for several internal data formats such as logical, character, fixed or floating point binary, and fixed point decimal. This flexability allows a programmer to select the format most efficient and appropriate to his application. Not all IBM machines have instructions which operate on decimal format data. However, for compatibility those that don't run a software simulator for these instructions as part of the operating system.

Essentially such a simulator converts data from decimal to binary form, performs the indicated operation in binary, and then converts the answer from binary back to decimal form.


Problem Description:

Your assignment is to write a 360 assembly language subroutine which converts integral decimal constants in character form to roman numeral character form.

We will use the standardly accepted definition for roman numerals, with all letters in upper case character (EBCDIC) form. Using our definition, the number 1974 (decimal) would be passed to you as "F1F9F7F4" (hexadecimal) and you would return "MCMLXXIV" (character) or "D4C3D4D3E7C965" (hexadecimal).

When your subroutine is called you will be passed two pieces of information. The starting address and length (in bytes) of the input character string and a pointer to a table generated in the following fashion:

```
TABLE      DS        0H          FORCES HALFWORD ALIGNMENT
           DC        C'M ',H'1000'
           DC        C'CM',H'900'
           DC        C'D ',H'500'
           DC        C'CD',H'400'
           DC        C'C ',H'100'
           DC        C'XC',H'90'
           DC        C'L ',H'50'
           DC        C'XL',H'40'
           DC        C'X ',H'10'
           DC        C'IX',H'9'
           DC        C'V ',H'5'
           DC        C'IV',H'4'
           DC        C'I ',H'1'
```

You are urged to use this table in conjunction with a systematic algorithm to create a compact solution to the problem.

47

Communication with the Grader:

Your subroutine will be called by a grading program. This program will pass you test cases and you will return answers. When control is transferred to your subroutine, the general registers will contain the following information:

Register 0: Will contain a pointer to the address of two fullwords as follows:

```
 _____        _____
|Register 0|--->|_____address_____|---> conversion table
                |count|    address      |---> input argument
                0    7 8                31
```

"A --> B" means that A contains the address of B, or A "points to" B.

The first word contains the address of the roman numeral conversion table described above. The second fullword contains the length and address of the input argument. For simplicity, you may assume that the input data has no leading blanks (see the example below).

Register 1: Not significant.

Registers 2-12: Not significant, but must be restored before you return.

Register 13: Address of 18 fullword area you may use to save the general registers.

Register 14: Address of the return point in the grading program. You should branch to this address when you have completed processing.

Register 15: Address of the beginning of your program.

When you return to the grader, register 1 should contain the address of your answer in bytes 1-3 and the length of your answer (in bytes) in byte 0 (see the example below).


Restrictions and Assumptions:

The maximum length of the character strings you will be passed is eight bytes. The maximum length of your answer (if correct) will be twenty bytes. You must not alter the data you are sent in any way; if you need to change it, make a copy.

Debugging Aids:

    Executing  the  following constant as an instruction in your
program will cause the grader to dump your program and  registers
for debugging purposes and then continue execution:

        DEBUG   DC   H'15'             CAUSES DUMP TO OCCUR

Use  this  facility sparingly, however, as you will be limited in
the number of lines you may print.


Example:

String to be converted to roman numeral format is '+973'

When the student is entered:

```
 _____       _____                    _____
| REG 0 | --> |_____| ----------> | CONVERSION |
             | 4 |      | --           |   TABLE   |
                          |
                          |
                          V_____
                        | E9 | E7 | E3 | (973)
```

When the student returns:

```
 Register 1            _C__ _M__ _L__ _X__ _X__ _I__ _I__ _I__
| 8 |      | ----> | C3 | D4 | D3 | E7 | E7 | C9 | C9 | C9 |
```

Deck Setup:

Your program must be a CSECT labelled MP1.   Use  the  following
deck structure:


```
            TITLE 'students name - instructors name'
    MP1     CSECT
            USING *,15
            STM   ....
              .
              . (your deck goes here)
              .
            END
```


Run Schedule:

    TO BE ANNOUNCED

```
A2W    JOB TO WORK OUT GRADER AND DISPLAY MESSAGES -- A2                                        PAGE   2

   LOC  OBJECT CODE    ADDR1 ADDR2  STMT   SOURCE STATEMENT                                     11 JUN 74

000000                               2 MP1     CSECT
000000                               3         USING *,15                     ESTABLISH ADDRESSABILITY

                                     5 ******************************************************************************
                                     6 *                                                                          *
                                     7 *          THIS JOB WORKS OUT THE GRADER ERROR HANDLING AND MESSAGE         *
                                     8 *          FACILITIES, PROVIDING A SAMPLE OF GRADER OUTPUT. THE FIRST       *
                                     9 *          ANSWER IS RETURNED CORRECTLY, THE SECOND ANSWER IS RETURNED      *
                                    10 *          INCORRECTLY, AND THE THIRD ANSWER CAUSES A PROGRAM CHECK.        *
                                    11 *          EACH TEST NO-OPS A BRANCH TO CAUSE THE CODE FOR THE NEXT         *
                                    12 *          ONE TO BE EXECUTED.                                              *
                                    13 *                                                                          *
                                    14 ******************************************************************************

000000 47F0 F00C         0000C      16 BRANCH1  B     CASE1              THIS BRANCH WILL BE ZAPPED BY CASE 1
000004 47F0 F016         00016      17 BRANCH2  B     CASE2              THIS WILL BE ZAPPED BY CASE 2
000008 47F0 F020         00020      18 BRANCH3  B     CASE3              THIS BRANCH WILL NOT BE ZAPPED

00000C 9200 F001   00001            20 CASE1    MVI   BRANCH1+1,X'00'    NO-OP BRANCH
000010 4110 0004         00004      21          LA    1,4                TRIAL ONE CONTAINS 4 COMMAS, SO THIS
                                    22 *                                 IS CORRECT ANSWER
000014 07FE                         23          BR    14                 RETURN TO GRADER

000016 9200 F005   00005            25 CASE2    MVI   BRANCH2+1,X'00'    NO-OP BRANCH
00001A 4110 0004         00004      26          LA    1,4                THIS IS NOT CORRECT ANSWER FOR
                                    27 *                                 TRIAL 2
00001E 07FE                         28          BR    14                 RETURN TO GRADER

000020 0000                         30 CASE3    DC    H'00'              CAUSE PROGRAM CHECK
                                    31 *                                 NO NEED TO RETURN
                                    32          END
```

```
**** ASSEMBLER PROBLEM GRADER HAS BEEN ENTERED FOR STUDENT

PROGRAM ENTRY POINT: 12FE70

YOU HAVE RECEIVED 10 POINTS FOR SUCCESSFULLY ASSEMBLING YOUR PROGRAM


***YOU WILL BE PASSED: 1974

  REG 0
0012E604 ----> 12E604: 0012E60C ----> 12E60C: CONVERSION TABLE
                       04122E640 ----> 12E640: F1F9F7F440404040
                                      CHARACTER FORM: 1974


***YOU HAVE RETURNED:

  REG 1
0812FE98 ----> 12FE98: D4C3D4D3E7E7C9E5FFFFFFFFFFFFFFFFFFFFFFFFFFFFFFFFFFFF
              CHARACTER FORM: MCMLXXIV

2 POINTS FOR RETURNING CONTROL TO GRADER
3 POINTS FOR RESTORING REGISTERS
2 POINTS FOR SPECIFYING PROPER LENGTH OF RESULT
8 POINTS FOR CORRECT ANSWER


***YOU WILL BE PASSED: 153

  REG 0
0012E604 ----> 12E604: 0012E60C ----> 12E60C: CONVERSION TABLE
                       0312E640 ----> 12E640: F1F5F34040404040
                                      CHARACTER FORM: 153


***YOU HAVE RETURNED:

  REG 1
0812FE98 ----> 12FE98: D4C3D4D3E7E7C9E5FFFFFFFFFFFFFFFFFFFFFFFFFFFFFFFFFFFF
              CHARACTER FORM: MCMLXXIV

2 POINTS FOR RETURNING CONTROL TO GRADER
3 POINTS FOR RESTORING REGISTERS

YOU HAVE RETURNED INCORRECT LENGTH FOR ANSWER, CORRECT LENGTH IS:    5


***HERE IS A DUMP OF YOUR PROGRAM

12FE60                              4700F00C 4700F016 47F0F020 9200F001          ..0...0..00...0.
12FE80   5810F024 07FE9200 F0055810 F02407FE 0000FFFF 0812FE98 D4C3D4D3 E7E7C9E5 ..0.....0...0..........MCMLXXIV
12FEA0   FFFFFFFF FFFFFFFF FFFFFFFF FFFFFFFF FFFFFFFF FFFFFFFF FFFFFFFF FFFFFFFF ................................
```

```
***YOU WILL BE PASSED: 973

 REG 0
0012E604 ----> 12E604: 0012E60C ----> 12E60C: CONVERSION TABLE
                        0312E640 ----> 12E640: F9F7F3404C404040
                               CHARACTER FORM: 973

***ERROR HAS OCCURRED WITHIN YOUR MACHINE PROBLEM

***TYPE 1 INTERRUPT AT LOCATION 12FE90 ... PROGRAM DUMP FOLLOWS

PSW AT INTERRUPT WAS: FF 8 5 0001  '01'B '11'B F 12FE92


 REG  0    REG  1    REG  2    REG  3    REG  4    REG  5    REG  6    REG  7
0012E604  FFFFFFFF  FFFFFFFF  FFFFFFFF  FFFFFFFF  FFFFFFFF  FFFFFFFF  FFFFFFFF

 REG  8    REG  9    REG 10    REG 11    REG 12    REG 13    REG 14    REG 15
FFFFFFFF  FFFFFFFF  FFFFFFFF  FFFFFFFF  FFFFFFFF  0012E650  0012D9F8  0012FE70


12FE60                                  4700F00C 4700F016 47F0F020 9200F001          ..0...0..00...0.
12FE80   5810F024 07FE9200 F0055810 F02407FE  0000FFFF 0812FE93 D4C3D4D3 E7E7C9E5  ..0.....0...0..........MCMLXXIV
12FEA0   FFFFFFFF FFFFFFFF FFFFFFFF FFFFFFFF  FFFFFFFF FFFFFFFF FFFFFFFF FFFFFFFF  ................................

*** TESTING COMPLETE, YOUR TOTAL SCORE IS  30
```

## 2.3  INSTALLING AND RUNNING THE SAMPLE GRADERS

This section describes the procedures necessary to install and run the six sample graders. This discussion also applies to any user defined and created graders provided the conventions discussed later in this chapter are followed.


### 2.3.1  Introduction

The term "grader" as used in this chapter refers to a program which performs three specific functions:

1. Establishes an environment for student programs, with maximal error reporting facilities and enforced execution limits.

2. Provides a student program with test data and checks the student's results.

3. Scores the performance of the student's program in terms of answer correctness and absence of execution time errors (such as program checks, etc).

Realizing that most of each grader's effort is spent in establishing the error reporting environment and enforcing limits, we have created a system of macros and subroutines to make grader writing easier. As a result of this system, each grader presents a uniform external interface to the operating system.


System Requirements:

The graders are written in 360/370 assembler language (BAL), furthermore they make extensive use of IBM Operating System/360 primitives for I/O, error interception, and timing. This ties them down to IBM 360-370 Systems running OS or VS (as opposed to DOS). With approximately a man-week of effort the graders could be converted to run under DOS.

When executing under operating systems without the programmer controlled timer feature, a grader will be unable to detect a student program exceeding allowed execution time, but executing the grader will result in no errors. The graders are fully VS compatible and will function under a system with fetch protection for low core.

The storage required by the graders is much less than that required by the IBM F-level assembler. Thus, the storage requirements for running one of these problems is that of the assembler, 44 K-bytes. This requirement is expanded to 60 K-bytes if the batch monitor is used, see chapter 7.

Overview of the Grader Load Module:

The graders are each stored as a load module, pre-linked
with the grader service subroutines in order to reduce the
overhead involved in linking and running each student. This
pre-linked load module has three unresolved external references:

1. MP1 - The student's subroutine to be tested.

2. DUMMY - A CSECT loaded immediately behind a student so
   the grader can tell when to stop dumping the student's
   program if an error occurs (V(MP1) provides start
   address of dump, V(DUMMY) provides end address).

3. TABLE - Driving table for the grader which contains the
   test cases and answers. This table is kept external to
   allow the instructor to easily change the test cases.

In the event the student does not name his or her CSECT
correctly (MP1), the loader would find MP1 an unresolved external
reference and refuse to execute the grader. This would make it
impossible for the grader to inform the student of his or her
error, so the student could well be confused. To prevent the
occurence of this problem another MP1 CSECT is included directly
behind the DUMMY CSECT.

This extra MP1 CSECT contains a branch to the entry point
"BADNAME" in the grader. This causes an informatory message to
be printed and the student's run terminates gracefully. As long
as the student's CSECT name is correct, the automatic replacement
feature of the linkage loader will prevent the second MP1 CSECT
from being linked.


Overview of OS-Grader-Student Relationship:

Testing a student is essentially a three step process.
First the student's assembly language program must be assembled.
Next the resultant object deck has to be linked to the grader,
along with the dummy CSECT and a driving table.   Finally this
resultant complete load module is executed. The Linkage Loader
combines the second and third steps into one job step so that
only two job steps (in the OS sense) are required to run a
student.

The instructor may pass parameters to the graders which will
set execution limits. For a discussion of these parameters and
how to communicate them to a grader, see the next section.  When
the loader transfers control to a grader it passes a pointer to
any parameters specified.  The grader processes these parameters
to set limits; opens the file SYSPRINT for output; establishes an
error exit and timer exit with the operating system;  and passes
the first test case to the student's subroutine.

When the student finishes processing and returns to the grader, the grader checks her or his answers for validity, assigning a point score. As long as the student does not exceed any execution limits or generate a program check, this testing process continues until all test cases in the test table have been processed. The grader keeps a cumulative total of the student's scores which it puts in register 15 as a return code.

If at any time the student exceeds an instructor established execution limit, testing is terminated and an informatory message is printed. If the student has run out of time the grader abends its _task_ with a completion code of 322 (decimal). This is done to insure that a runaway task is stopped, while at the same time indicating why (via the 322 return code). If the student generates a program check, his or her program along with its registers is "dumped", and testing is terminated. Diagramatically:

Relationship Between OS - Grader - Student

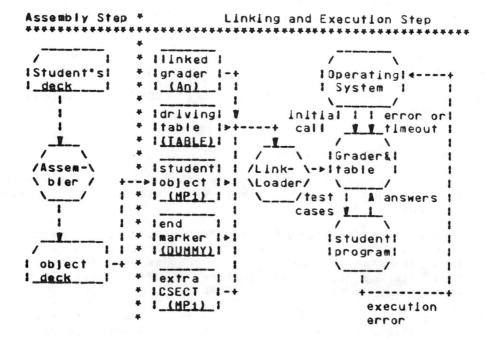

## 2.3.2  INSTALLING THE SAMPLE GRADERS

Introduction:

To use one of the sample graders, or one of your own design-
if you follow convention, you need four modules plus the
student's object deck.  The four modules are:

1. Pre-linked grader load module containing the individual
   grader and all the service subroutines, with entry
   point "GRADER".

2. A driving table which exists as a CSECT labelled
   "TABLE", whose format depends on the particular grader.

3. A CSECT labelled "DUMMY" to be included behind the
   student's CSECT.

4. A CSECT labelled "MP1" which is included behind DUMMY
   in case the student misspells his or her CSECT name.

By convention, the load modules for graders exist as members
of the catalogued PDS "ASSEMMP.LOAD", the sample graders being
members A1-A6.  Furthermore, the corresponding driving tables
exist as members A1-A6 of the catalogued PDS "ASSEMMP.DATA",
which also includes the DUMMY and MP1 CSECT's (combined) as
member DUMMY.


Overview of Grader Generating Process:

In essence, all that is required to run the sample problems
is two partitioned data sets.  These data sets should be  created
in four steps:

1. Create the macro library (PDS) "ASSEMMP.MACLIB",  being
   sure to check the blocksize of "SYS1.MACLIB" to avoid
   later concatenation errors.  The program used to create
   this library is the IBM Utility "IEBUPDTE". (1)  This
   dataset may be deleted after step 3.

2. Using  the  assembler,  create  the  dataset
   "ASSEMMP.OBJECT" which contains the grader service
   subroutines and the parameter processing routine's
   driving table (PTBL) in object form.  This dataset may
   be deleted after the next step.

————————————————————————————————————————————————————————————

(1) A discussion of this program may be  found  in  the  IBM
publication number GC28-6586, OS Utilities.

3. Create the PDS "ASSEMMP.LOAD" which contains the
   pre-linked grader load modules as members A1-A6. First
   the assembler is used to produce grader object decks
   and linkage editor control statements (punched by the
   "PUNCH" assembler psuedo-op), then the linkage editor
   is used to build a library of load modules from the
   assembler output. This dataset should be saved, but if
   you don't wish to create any new graders right away you
   may delete the datasets created by the previous two
   steps.

4. Create the PDS "ASSEMMP.DATA" with driving tables as
   members A1-A6 and The CSECT's DUMMY and MP1 combined as
   member DUMMY, using first the assembler and then the
   IBM Utility program IEBUPDTE. This dataset should also
   be saved.

   The distribution tape contains all the JCL necessary to
accomplish these four steps. Before you sit down to punch up a
lot of JCL you should consult section 8.2 for instructions on how
to retrieve this JCL from the distribution tape.

   It should be noted that these steps are structured in such a
manner as to make use of the Waterloo G-level assembler's
batching capability. If your installation does not have this
assembler or some other batching assembler, these steps are
possible, but much more complex. The distribution tape contains
JCL for both a batching assembler (the preferred way) and the
standard IBM F-level assembler.


Creating the Grader Macro Library:

   The purpose of this step is to create a PDS named
"ASSEMMP.MACLIB" whose members will be the utility macros used in
the generation of service subroutines and graders. The DCB
attributes for this PDS will be: RECFM=FB, LRECL=80, and
BLKSIZE=nnnn, where nnnn is the blocksize of the system macro
library, "SYS1.MACLIB". These blocksizes should match since you
will concatenate these datasets later.

   The macros which will become the members of this PDS exist
as a sequential dataset on the distribution tape, combined with
control statements for IEBUPDTE. After you have determined the
blocksize and decided upon a volume, you run the following job:

```
//MAKEML   EXEC PGM=IEBUPDTE,PARM='NEW'
//SYSPRINT DD   SYSOUT=A
//SYSUT2   DD   DSN=ASSEMMP.MACLIB,DISP=(NEW,CATLG),
//              UNIT=2314,VOL=SER=nnnnnn,SPACE=(TRK,(4,2,1)),
//              DCB=(RECFM=FB,LRECL=80,BLKSIZE=xxxx)
//SYSIN    DD   UNIT=2400,DISP=(OLD,PASS), ... (see note 3)
/*
```

Notes:

1. nnnnnn should be replaced by the volume serial for the
   receiving volume. If this volume is other than a 2314,
   the UNIT and SPACE parameters must be changed
   accordingly.
2. xxxx should be replaced by the BLKSIZE of the system
   macro library "SYS1.MACLIB".
3. This data set exists on the distribution tape, see
   section 8.2.


Creating the Subroutine Object:

   The purpose of this step is to create a sequential dataset
named "ASSEMMP.OBJECT", containing the grader service subroutines
in object form. The distribution tape contains the source for
all these routines plus a CSECT (named PTBL) which acts as a
driving table for the parameter processing routine, run together
into one sequential file. Thus, this step is very simple if you
have the G-level assembler. In this case you run the following
job:

```
//MAKEO     EXEC PGM=ASMBLRG,PARM='NODECK,LOAD,BATCH'
//SYSPRINT DD   SYSOUT=A
//SYSLIB    DD   DSN=ASSEMMP.MACLIB,DISP=SHR
//          DD   DSN=SYS1.MACLIB,DISP=SHR
//SYSUT1    DD   UNIT=SYSDA,SPACE=(CYL,(2,1))
//SYSUT2    DD   UNIT=SYSDA,SPACE=(CYL,(2,1))
//SYSUT3    DD   UNIT=SYSDA,SPACE=(CYL,(2,1))
//SYSGO     DD   DDNAME=SYSLIN
//SYSLIN    DD   DSN=ASSEMMP.OBJECT,DISP=(NEW,CATLG),
//               UNIT=2314,VOL=SER=nnnnnn,SPACE=(TRK,(2,1)),
//               DCB=(RECFM=FB,LRECL=80,BLKSIZE=1600)
//SYSIN     DD   UNIT=2400,DISP=(OLD,PASS)... (see note 2)
/*
```

Notes:

1. nnnnnn should be replaced by the volume serial of the
   receiving volume. If this volume is other than a 2314,
   the UNIT and SPACE parameters must be changed
   accordingly.
2. This dataset exists on the distribution tape, see
   section 8.2.

   If your installation does not have an assembler which
supports batching, this step becomes more complicated. First you
must punch off a copy of the sequential dataset used as input in
the job above. A job to accomplish this is included in the JCL
file on the distribution tape (see section 8.2), which looks
like:

```
//PUNCHSUB EXEC PGM=IEBGENER (1)
//SYSPRINT DD   SYSOUT=A
//SYSIN    DD   DUMMY
//SYSUT2   DD   SYSOUT=B,DCB=(RECFM=F,BLKSIZE=80)
//SYSUT1   DD   UNIT=2400,DISP=(OLD,PASS),...
                            (see note 2, previous)
/*
```

This job will produce a punched deck (about 500 cards) consisting of the source for the grader service subroutines and PTBL, all run together.  You will have to assemble the individual subroutines in separate job steps, concatenating the resultant object decks into one sequential dataset.

About the easiest way to do this involves an in-stream procedure. (2)   The job you run should have the following structure:

---

(1) A discussion of this program may be found in the IBM publication number GC28-6586, OS Utilities.

(2) A discussion of in-stream procedures may be found in Appendix A of the IBM publication number GC28-6704-3, Job Control Language Reference.

```
//AO        PROC
//C         EXEC PGM=IEUASM,PARM='NODECK,LOAD'
//SYSPRINT DD  SYSOUT=A
//SYSLIB    DD  DSN=ASSEMMP.MACLIB,DISP=SHR
//          DD  DSN=SYS1.MACLIB,DISP=SHR
//SYSUT1    DD  UNIT=SYSDA,SPACE=(CYL,(2,1))
//SYSUT2    DD  UNIT=SYSDA,SPACE=(CYL,(2,1))
//SYSUT3    DD  UNIT=SYSDA,SPACE=(CYL,(2,1))
//SYSLIN    DD  DSN=ASSEMMP.OBJECT,DISP=(MOD,PASS)
//          PEND
//ALLOC     EXEC PGM=IEFBR14
//DD1       DD  DSN=ASSEMMP.OBJECT,DISP=(NEW,CATLG),
//              UNIT=2314,VOL=SER=nnnnnn,SPACE=(TRK,(2,1)),
//              DCB=(RECFM=FB,LRECL=80,BLKSIZE=1600)
//          EXEC AO
//C.SYSIN  DD  *
   .  source for subroutine
   .  DCBEXIT
/*
//          EXEC AO
//C.SYSIN  DD  *
   .  source for subroutine
   .  ERROR
/*
   ...  repeated for PARMPROC, RDUMP,
        and SNAP ...

//          EXEC AO
//C.SYSIN  DD  *
   .  source for subroutine
   .  TIMEOUT
/*
//          EXEC AO
//C.SYSIN  DD  *
   .  source for parm table
   .  PTBL
/*
```

Creating the Grader Load Module PDS:

The purpose of this step is to create a PDS containing the
pre-linked load modules for sample graders A1-A6. The
distribution tape contains the source for these graders,
interspersed with "PUNCH" pseudo-op instructions to create
linkage editor control statements. All the graders are
concatenated together in this sequential dataset, suitable as
input to the G-level assembler. The output of this assembly would
consist of a stream of object decks combined with the correct
linkage editor control cards to cause six members to be added to
the PDS defined by the "SYSLMOD" DD statement. If your
installation has a batching assembler, the following JCL will
suffice:

```
//ASSEM    EXEC PGM=ASMBLRG,PARM='NODECK,LOAD,BATCH'
//SYSPRINT DD   SYSOUT=A
//SYSLIB   DD   DSN=ASSEMMP.MACLIB,DISP=SHR
//         DD   DSN=SYS1.MACLIB,DISP=SHR
//SYSUT1   DD   UNIT=SYSDA,SPACE=(CYL,(2,1)),DISP=(NEW,PASS)
//SYSUT2   DD   UNIT=SYSDA,SPACE=(CYL,(2,1))
//SYSUT3   DD   UNIT=SYSDA,SPACE=(CYL,(2,1))
//SYSGO    DD   DDNAME=SYSLIN
//SYSLIN   DD   DSN=&&TEMP,DISP=(MOD,PASS),UNIT=SYSDA,
//              DCB=(RECFM=FB,LRECL=80,BLKSIZE=1600),
//              SPACE=(CYL,(2,1))
//SYSIN    DD   UNIT=2400,DISP=(OLD,PASS),,,,,,
                              (see note 1, below)
/*
//LINK     EXEC PGM=IEWL,PARM='LIST,MAP,XREF,LET'
//SYSPRINT DD   SYSOUT=A
//SYSUT1   DD   DSN=*.ASSEM.SYSUT1,DISP=(OLD,DELETE)
//SYSLIN   DD   DSN=*.ASSEM.SYSGO,DISP=(OLD,DELETE)
//SYSLMOD  DD   DSN=ASSEMMP.LOAD,DISP=(NEW,CATLG),
//              UNIT=2314,VOL=SER=nnnnnn,SPACE=(TRK,(10,2,2))
//OBJECT   DD   DSN=ASSEMMP.OBJECT,DISP=SHR
/*
```

Notes:

1. This sequential dataset exists on the distribution
   tape, please refer to section 8.2 for more information.
2. nnnnnn should be replaced by the volume serial of the
   receiving volume. If this volume is other than a 2314,
   the UNIT and SPACE parameters must be changed
   accordingly.
3. If you do not wish to create any new graders, you
   probably should either move the datasets
   "ASSEMMP.MACLIB" and "ASSEMMP.OBJECT" to offline
   storage or delete them. If you wish to delete them you
   should change the DISP fields of the OBJECT and SYSLIB
   DD statements from "DISP=SHR" to "DISP=(OLD,DELETE)".

If your installation does not have the G-level assembler or
some other batching assembler, again you must do things the hard
way. Before you can proceed, you must punch the grader source
file from the distribution tape. The following job may be run to
accomplish this:

```
//PUNCHGS EXEC PGM=IEBGENER
//SYSPRINT DD   SYSOUT=A
//SYSIN    DD   DUMMY
//SYSUT2   DD   SYSOUT=B,DCB=(RECFM=F,BLKSIZE=80)
//SYSUT1   DD   UNIT=2400,DISP=(OLD,PASS)...
                              (see note 1, previous)
/*
```

The output from this job will be approximately 1,000 cards.
After you have interpreted these cards remove all of the "PUNCH"
pseudo-op statements. Then remove the extra "END" card from the
rear of the deck. Now start looking through the deck from the
front. Every time you find a "END" card, place it and all the
cards before it into a new stack. After you have done this six
times, you should have six stacks of cards, one for each grader.
Then each of these graders must be assembled and linked (two job
steps each), using the following JCL and associated in-stream
procedure:

```
//AG         PROC N=
//C          EXEC PGM=IEUASM,PARM="LOAD,NODECK"
//SYSPRINT DD  SYSOUT=A
//SYSLIB    DD  DSN=ASSEMMP.MACLIB,DISP=SHR
//          DD  DSN=SYS1.MACLIB,DISP=SHR
//SYSUT1    DD  UNIT=SYSDA,SPACE=(CYL,(2,1))
//SYSUT2    DD  UNIT=SYSDA,SPACE=(CYL,(2,1))
//SYSUT3    DD  UNIT=SYSDA,SPACE=(CYL,(2,1))
//SYSLIN    DD  DSN=&&TEMP,DISP=(NEW,PASS),UNIT=SYSDA,
//              DCB=(RECFM=FB,LRECL=80,BLKSIZE=1600),
//              SPACE=(CYL,(2,1))
//L          EXEC PGM=IEWL,PARM="LIST,MAP,XREF,LET"
//SYSPRINT DD  SYSOUT=A
//SYSUT1    DD  UNIT=SYSDA,SPACE=(CYL,(2,1))
//SYSLIN    DD  DSN=&&TEMP,DISP=(OLD,DELETE)
//          DD  DSN=ASSEMMP.OBJECT,DISP=SHR
//SYSLMOD   DD  DSN=ASSEMMP.LOAD(&N),DISP=OLD
//          PEND
//ALLOC     EXEC PGM=IEFBR14
//DD1       DD  DSN=ASSEMMP.LOAD,DISP=(NEW,CATLG),UNIT=2314,
//              VOL=SER=nnnnnn,SPACE=(TRK,(10,2,2))
//          EXEC AG,N="A1"
//C.SYSIN  DD  *
   . source for
   . grader A1
/*
//          EXEC AG,N="A2"
//C.SYSIN  DD  *
   . source for
   . grader A2
/*
   ... continued for A3, A4,
       and A5 ...

//          EXEC AG,N=A6
//C.SYSIN  DD  *
   . source for
   . grader A6
/*
```

**Notes:**

1. Be sure to remove the "PUNCH" pseudo-ops and extra "END" card from the grader source decks.
2. nnnnnn should be replaced with the volume serial for the receiving volume. If this volume is other than a 2314, the UNIT and SPACE parameters must be changed accordingly.

Creating the Grader Driving Table PDS (With DUMMY):

The purpose of this step is to create a PDS named "ASSEMMP.DATA", whose members are the driving tables for the sample graders. These tables are in the form of CSECT's generated by the assembler. Each member contains one CSECT named TABLE, the member names being used to select which table you are using. That is to say that every grader refers to its driving table by "V(TABLE)", but you specify which member (A1-A6) you are dealing with in the JCL when you run a grader. Also included in this PDS is the member "DUMMY" which contains the DUMMY and MP1 CSECT's together.

The distribution tape contains the source for each of the tables run together into one sequential file, with "PUNCH" pseudo-op instructions to produce IEBUPDTE control cards interspersed. This makes generating this PDS very simple if you have the G-level assembler which supports batching. In this case you run the following job:

```
//MAKETB   EXEC PGM=ASMBLRG,PARM='NODECK,LOAD,BATCH'
//SYSPRINT DD   SYSOUT=A
//SYSLIB   DD   DSN=ASSEMMP.MACLIB,DISP=SHR
//         DD   DSN=SYS1.MACLIB,DISP=SHR
//SYSUT1   DD   UNIT=SYSDA,SPACE=(CYL,(2,1))
//SYSUT2   DD   UNIT=SYSDA,SPACE=(CYL,(2,1))
//SYSUT3   DD   UNIT=SYSDA,SPACE=(CYL,(2,1))
//SYSGO    DD   DDNAME=SYSLIN
//SYSLIN   DD   DSN=&&TEMP,DISP=(MOD,PASS),UNIT=SYSDA,
//              DCB=(RECFM=FB,LRECL=80,BLKSIZE=1600),
//              SPACE=(CYL,(2,1))
//SYSIN    DD   UNIT=2400,DISP=(OLD,PASS)... (see note 1)
/*
//STEP2    EXEC PGM=IEBUPDTE,PARM='NEW'
//SYSPRINT DD   SYSOUT=A
//SYSIN    DD   DSN=&&TEMP,DISP=(OLD,DELETE)
//SYSUT2   DD   DSN=ASSEMMP.DATA,DISP=(NEW,CATLG),
//              DCB=(RECFM=FB,LRECL=80,BLKSIZE=1600),
//              UNIT=2314,VOL=SER=nnnnnn,
//              SPACE=(TRK,(2,1,2))
/*
```

**Notes:**

1. This dataset exists on the distribution tape, see section 8.2.
2. nnnnnn should be replaced with the volume serial of the receiving volume. If this volume is other than a 2314, the UNIT and SPACE parameters must be changed accordingly.

If you do not have a batching assemler, you have to follow the by now familiar steps to separate the source for the individual tables and assemble them in separate steps. The first step is to punch the sequential table source file from the distribution tape, using the following job:

```
//PUNCHTB EXEC PGM=IEBGENER
//SYSPRINT DD   SYSOUT=A
//SYSIN    DD   DUMMY
//SYSUT2   DD   SYSOUT=B,DCB=(RECFM=F,BLKSIZE=80)
//SYSUT1   DD   UNIT=2400,DISP=(OLD,PASS) ...
                              (see note 1, previous)
/*
```

The result of this job will be about 100 cards. Once you have interpreted these cards, the first step is to remove all of the "PUNCH" pseudo-op statements and discard them. Next remove the extra "END" card which will now be the last card of your deck. Now you are left with eight distinct CSECT's which must be assembled. If you start from the beginning and separate at each "END" card, you should get eight stacks that start with "TITLE" statements and end with "END" statements. Four of these stacks will contain in-line macro definitions.

A problem arises in that the last two CSECT's (DUMMY and MP1) have to be combined to create the member DUMMY in the new PDS. All other CSECT's are named TABLE and go into members A1-A6 respectively. Because of this difference, please pay close attention to the following example:

```
//AD        PROC N=
//C         EXEC PGM=IEUASM,PARM='LOAD,NODECK'
//SYSPRINT DD   SYSOUT=A
//SYSLIB    DD   DSN=SYS1.MACLIB,DISP=SHR
//SYSUT1    DD   UNIT=SYSDA,SPACE=(CYL,(2,1))
//SYSUT2    DD   UNIT=SYSDA,SPACE=(CYL,(2,1))
//SYSUT3    DD   UNIT=SYSDA,SPACE=(CYL,(2,1))
//SYSLIN    DD   DSN=ASSEMMP.DATA(&N),DISP=OLD
//          PEND
//ALLOC     EXEC PGM=IEFBR14
//DD1       DD   DSN=ASSEMMP.DATA,DISP=(NEW,CATLG),
//               DCB=(RECFM=FB,LRECL=80,BLKSIZE=1600),
//               UNIT=2314,VOL=SER=nnnnnn,
//               SPACE=(TRK,(2,1,2))
```

```
//          EXEC AD,N=A1
//C.SYSIN  DD  *
   . source for
   . table A1
/*
//          EXEC AD,N=A2
//C.SYSIN  DD  *
   . source for
   . table A2
/*
   ... repeated for tables
       A3 - A5 ...

//          EXEC AD,N=A6
//C.SYSIN  DD  *
   . source for
   . table A6
/*
//          EXEC AD
//C.SYSLIN DD  DSN=&&TEMP,DISP=(NEW,PASS),
//             UNIT=SYSDA,SPACE=(CYL,(2,1)),
//             DCB=(RECFM=FB,LRECL=80,BLKSIZE=1600)
//C.SYSIN  DD  *
   . source for DUMMY
   . CSECT
/*
//          EXEC AD
//C.SYSLIN DD  DSN=&&TEMP,DISP=(MOD,PASS)
//C.SYSIN  DD  *
   . source for MP1
   . CSECT
/*
//DUMMY    EXEC PGM=IEBGENER
//SYSPRINT DD  SYSOUT=A
//SYSIN    DD  DUMMY
//SYSUT1   DD  DSN=&&TEMP,DISP=(OLD,DELETE)
//SYSUT2   DD  DSN=ASSEMMP.DATA(DUMMY),DISP=OLD
/*
```

Whichever method you used to create the PDS, you may wish to change the tables, or perhaps add new ones to add variety to your student runs. If you used the G-level assembler, you haven't punched off a copy of the macros used to generate tables A3-A6. In order to create new tables, you should have these macros, so run the previously outlined small job to punch the table source and retrieve the macros. Save the in-line procedure from above, as you will need it to make new tables. The second section after this one contains detailed descriptions of the generating macros and the formats for the tables.

## 2.3.3 Running The Sample Graders

Introduction:

Having performed the requisite forplay you should have two partitioned datasets, "ASSEMMP.LOAD" and "ASSEMMP.DATA" catalogued with all the appropriate members. The next decision you have to make is how to run your students. You are faced with essentially two choices:

1. Using an in-line procedure to reduce the number of individual control cards, allow each student to be assembled and run in two job steps, using the assembler and the linkage loader.

2. Use the special purpose batch monitor to run all the students as one job step, providing extensive logging and control card error recovery.

The first method places the smallest possible core requirement on the system, requiring only 44 K-bytes of storage to run the whole machine problem. This method has several drawbacks, however. The student is required to punch a few JCL cards, which if goofed up could cause an entire run to be lost. Each student is run as a separate step, so the initiator overhead is incurred for each student in addition to any "step charges" imposed by the system. Finally, since each student's output is merged together on the file "SYSPRINT", separating student output becomes a real nuisance for the person running the student jobs.

To overcome these drawbacks we have implemented a simple batch monitor. This monitor greatly reduces the cost of running several students and eases the process of running several students at once. A log of student names along with information cogent to their run is kept and paging separators are supplied at the instructor's option. The only drawback to the monitor is that it increases the storage requirement to about 60 K-bytes. If you think you might be interested in using the batch monitor, please refer to chapter 7 for details on its installation and use.

Regardless of which method you use, you should know the parameters which the graders accept. These parameters (NAME - default - <description>) are as follows:

1. MAXLINES - 500 - Maximum number of lines a student will be allowed to print during execution, not counting assembler output. This parameter must be a non-signed decimal integer.

2. MAXTIME - 100 - Maximum amount of execution time student will be allowed, in hundredths of a second

(i.e. the default of 100 is one second), not counting assembly time. This value must be a non-signed decimal integer.

3. LINESIZE - 55 - Number of lines of output to be placed on each page. This parameter is used by the OUTPUT subroutine to avoid printing on the fold. This parameter should be set appropriately if other than standard forms are used.

4. NAME - ▓▓▓▓▓▓▓▓ - An eight character name to be used to identify the student's grader output. This parameter is used by the batch monitor, if desired, to stop one student from handing in another's output.

5. BADJCL - 0 - This parameter is intended for a batch monitor. If a value other than zero is specified the grader informs the student that he or she has an erroneous job control card. This is used by our batch monitor since it can correct most errors in job control cards.

The method used to pass these parameters depends on which method you are using to run the students. With method one, these parameters are coded in the "PARM" field of the "EXEC" statement executing the grader, while under the batch monitor they are coded as the "GP" subfield of the "PARM" field.

Sample JCL for the two methods follows. Any occurence of the string "An" in the following JCL signifies a grader-particular field. In this case n should be replaced by the number of the sample problem. Thus, the Palindrome Problem would be A1.

JCL Using In-Stream Procedure:

```
//MP1      PROC
//C        EXEC PGM=IEUASM,PARM=(LOAD,NODECK)
//SYSPRINT DD   SYSOUT=A
//SYSUT1   DD   UNIT=SYSDA,SPACE=(CYL,(2,1))
//SYSUT2   DD   UNIT=SYSDA,SPACE=(CYL,(2,1))
//SYSUT3   DD   UNIT=SYSDA,SPACE=(CYL,(2,1))
//SYSGO    DD   DSN=&&TEMP,DISP=(OLD,PASS)
//G        EXEC PGM=IEWLDRGO,COND=(4,LE,C),
//              PARM='NOPRINT,EP=GRADER',
//              TIME=(0,1)
//SYSLOUT  DD   DUMMY,DCB=BLKSIZE=121
//SYSLIN   DD   DSN=ASSEMMP.LOAD(An),DISP=SHR
//         DD   DSN=ASSEMMP.DATA(An),DISP=SHR
//         DD   DSN=&&TEMP,DISP=(OLD,PASS)
//         DD   DSN=ASSEMMP.DATA(DUMMY),DISP=SHR
//SYSPRINT DD   SYSOUT=A
//         PEND
```

```
//ALLOC     EXEC PGM=IEFBR14
//DD1        DD  DSN=&&TEMP,DISP=(NEW,PASS),
//               UNIT=SYSDA,SPACE=(TRK,(2,1)),
//               DCB=(RECFM=FB,LRECL=80,BLKSIZE=1600)
//SMITH     EXEC MP1
//C.SYSIN DD   *
                    •
(SMITH'S DECK GOES HERE)
                    •
/*
//JONES     EXEC MP1
//C.SYSIN DD   *
                    •
(JONES' DECK GOES HERE)
                    •
/*
```

Notes:

1. Every occurence of n should be replaced by  the  grader
number,  i.e.  if you are running the Palindrome Problem
n-->1.

2. Each student is run as a separate invocation of  the
in-stream  procedure  "MP1".  To smooth things along you
should provide pre-punched JCL.   Then  all  a  student
would  have  to  do is punch her or his name in columns
3-10 of your pre-punched EXEC card.


JCL Using Batch Monitor:

```
//ALLOC     EXEC PGM=IEFBR14
//DD1        DD  DSN=&&TEMP,DISP=(NEW,PASS),SPACE=(CYL,
//               (2,1)),DCB=(RECFM=FB,LRECL=80,BLKSIZE=1600),
//               UNIT=SYSDA
//DD2        DD  DSN=&&WORK,DISP=(NEW,PASS),SPACE=(CYL,
//               (2,1)),DCB=(RECFM=FB,LRECL=80,BLKSIZE=1600),
//               UNIT=SYSDA
//DD3        DD  DSN=&&UT1,DISP=(NEW,PASS),SPACE=(CYL,
//               (1,1)),UNIT=SYSDA
//DD4        DD  DSN=&&UT2,DISP=(NEW,PASS),SPACE=(CYL,
//               (1,1)),UNIT=SYSDA
//DD5        DD  DSN=&&UT3,DISP=(NEW,PASS),SPACE=(CYL,
//               (1,1)),UNIT=SYSDA
//RUN       EXEC PGM=MONITOR,
// PARM='LP=(NOPRINT,EP=GRADER),TN=IEUASM,SEP,ZS=(BADJCL=1)'
//STEPLIB   DD  DSN=MONITOR.LOAD,DISP=SHR
//SYSLOG    DD  SYSOUT=A
//*TLIB     DD  DSN=SYS1.MACLIB,DISP=SHR
//SYSWORK   DD  DSN=*.ALLOC.DD2,VOL=REF=*.ALLOC.DD2,
//               DISP=(OLD,PASS)
//SYSPRINT DD   SYSOUT=A
```

```
//SYSUT1    DD   DSN=*.ALLOC.DD3,VOL=REF=*.ALLOC.DD3,
//               DISP=(OLD,PASS)
//SYSUT2    DD   DSN=*.ALLOC.DD4,VOL=REF=*.ALLOC.DD4,
//               DISP=(OLD,PASS)
//SYSUT3    DD   DSN=*.ALLOC.DD5,VOL=REF=*.ALLOC.DD5,
//               DISP=(OLD,PASS)
//SYSGO     DD   DSN=*.ALLOC.DD1,VOL=REF=*.ALLOC.DD1,
//               DISP=(OLD,PASS)
//SYSLOUT   DD   DUMMY,DCB=BLKSIZE=121
//SYSLIN    DD   DSN=ASSEMMP.LOAD(An),DISP=SHR
//          DD   DSN=ASSEMMP.DATA(An),DISP=SHR
//          DD   DSN=*.ALLOC.DD1,VOL=REF=*.ALLOC.DD1,
//               DISP=(OLD,PASS)
//          DD   DSN=ASSEMMP.DATA(DUMMY),DISP=SHR
//MONIN     DD   DATA
$JOB name      student job 1
      •
      •
$EOJ
$JOB name      student job 2
      •
      •
$EOJ

   ... repeated for rest of students ...

/*
```

Notes:

1. The dataset "MONITOR.LOAD" contains the batch monitor
   and its support routines, refer to chapter 7 for more
   details.
2. The file "TLIB" which is currently "commented out", is
   the assembler's macro file. The batch monitor has told
   the assembler to use the file "TLIB" instead of the
   file "SYSLIB".
3. The file "SYSGO" is the output file for the assembler.
   The batch monitor has told the assembler to use this
   file name instead of "SYSLIN".
4. All the student's jobs are run together after the
   "MONIN" DD statement.  The batch monitor is able to
   detect and correct most control card errors, but you
   are still advised to pre-punch $JOB and $EOJ cards.
   The field name should be replaced by the student's
   name.  Eight characters may be used and the rest of the
   card is printed on the logging sheets, but otherwise
   ignored.

### 2.3.4  Modifying the Sample Grader Driving Tables

Introduction:

All of the sample graders use driving tables for their test cases. To allow you the flexibility to change the test cases, the driving tables are kept as CSECT's that are linked to the grader when the student is to be run. You have created a PDS "ASSEMMP.DATA" which contains all of our sample tables as members A1-A6. To insure that you always have a working table, you should not replace these members, but rather you should make a new series such as B1-B6.

If you do not have the G-level assembler then you punched off the source for our sample tables previously. If you do have the G-level assembler, you probably did not in which case you should execute the job shown on page 2-49. This is necessary to obtain the four macros used to generate the driving tables for graders A3-A6.

After you have run this job you must separate the four macros from the source. The macros are labelled TBLA3 - TBLA6. The rest of this section will describe the format of the table for each grader. Once you know how to code entries for the tables you run the following job to create a new table:

```
//AT        PROC
//C         EXEC PGM=IEUASM,PARM="LOAD,NODECK"
//SYSPRINT  DD   SYSOUT=A
//SYSLIB    DD   DSN=SYS1.MACLIB,DISP=SHR
//SYSUT1    DD   UNIT=SYSDA,SPACE=(CYL,(2,1))
//SYSUT2    DD   UNIT=SYSDA,SPACE=(CYL,(2,1))
//SYSUT3    DD   UNIT=SYSDA,SPACE=(CYL,(2,1))
//SYSLIN    DD   DSN=ASSEMMP.DATA(&N),DISP=OLD
//          PEND
//          EXEC AT,N=name
//C.SYSIN   DD   *
  _
 |
 |    macro for table goes here,
 |    if this is for A3-A6
 |_

TABLE      CSECT
    .
    . DC or macro instructions
    . as appropriate
    .
           END
 /*
```

Notes:

1. This in-stream procedure is the same on that  you  used
   to create the tables in the first place if you used the
   F-level  assembler.    There  is  only  one copy of this
   procedure in the JCL file on the distribution tape.
2. name should be replaced with the name you wish your new
   table to have. If this name is the same as  that  of  a
   table  which already exists, then the old table will be
   replaced.
3. Remember that you must go back and change your JCL when
   you run students, so that the DD statement defining the
   driving table, now of the following form:

   //            DD  DSN=ASSEMMP.TABLE(An),DISP=SHR

   contains the correct name for your new table.

   The rest of this section contains  detailed  information  on
the tables for each sample grader.


Table for Palindrome Problem -- A1:

   The  table  for  this problem is very simple, so there is no
generating macro.  Rather, you code directly DC  statements.  You
should  always  make tables with exactly five entries. Each entry
consists of eight characters which will be passed to the student,
followed by a fullword answer (0 if the characters don't  form  a
palindrome, 1 if they do).  An example of a correct table is:

```
TABLE  CSECT
       DC     C'ABCDDCBA',F'1'
       DC     C'ABCDABCD',F'0'
       DC     C'SUPERMAN',F'0'
       DC     C'XXZZZZXX',F'1'
       DC     C'FINISHED',F'0'
       END
```


Table for Comma Counting Problem -- A2:

   The  table  for  this  problem  is very similar to the table
described above. There is no generating macro involved  and  each
table  must  contain exactly five entries. Each entry consists of
eight characters to be passed  to  the  student,  followed  by  a
fullword  constant containing the number of commas in the string.
An example:

```
TABLE CSECT
      DC     C'A,B,C,D,',F'4'
      DC     C'NONEHERE',F'0'
      DC     C'-!-!,-!-',F'1'
      DC     C',,HOPE,,',F'4'
      DC     C'FINISHED',F'0'
```

```
           END
```

Table for Arithmetic Operations Problem -- A3:

The table for this machine problem is fairly complex, so a macro has been provided to aid in creating entries. The name of this macro is TBLA3.

Syntax for TBLA3:

(label)  TBLA3  val3,op,val2,result

> val1 - The first operand for the student to  manipulate
>     (maximum length of 8 characters).

> op - The operation that the student is  to  perform  on
>     the two operands.

> val2 - Second operand for student, similar to val1.

> result - The numeric result of the operation.

Your  table should consist of exactly six entries, delimited by X'FF'. The entries should be generated by the TBLA3  macro  as the following example shows:

```
TABLE      CSECT
TEST1      TBLA3  -1,**,0,1
TEST2      TBLA3  -8,*,+8,-64
TEST3      TBLA3  -23,+,+7,-16
TEST4      TBLA3  +2,/,3,0
TEST5      TBLA3  5,-,-6,11
TEST6      TBLA3  -1,**,-1,-1
           DC     X'FF'      TABLE STOPPING DELIMITER
           END
```

Table for DC-Simulator Problem -- A4:

A  macro  has been provided for the generation of tables for this machine problem.  The name of this macro is TBLA4.

Syntax for TBLA4:

(label)  TBLA4  type,value

> type  -  The  kind  of  conversion  to  be  performed
>     (C=character, X=hexadecimal, P=packed, F=full-word).

> value - String to be converted by student.

Your TABLE should consist of exactly <u>six</u> entries. The last entry should be followed by a delimiter of F'-1', as the following example shows:

```
TABLE      CSECT
TEST1      TBLA4 X,A101
TEST2      TBLA4 F,-1
TEST3      TBLA4 P,-1
TEST4      TBLA4 C,WHY?
TEST5      TBLA4 X,ACE0
TEST6      TBLA4 P,-15
TEND       DC    F'-1'      END OF TABLE MARKER
           END
```

Table for Instruction Analyzer Problem -- A5:

A macro has been provided for the generation of tables for this machine problem. The name of this macro is TBLA5.

Syntax for TBLA5:

(label)  TBLA5  'inst',length,norefs,ref1,ref2

inst - The instruction to be passed to the student.

length - The length of the instruction in bytes (2,4, or 6).

norefs - The number of core references (0,1, or 2).

ref1 - Value of first address, else 0.

ref2 - Value of second address, else 0.

The first four fullwords of the table must contain the values that registers 2 through 5 will contain when the student is called. Your table should consist of <u>five</u> entries, with no delimiter as the following example shows:

```
TABLE      CSECT
REG2       DC    F'20'
REG3       DC    F'40'
REG4       DC    F'60'
REG5       DC    F'100'
TEST1      TBLA5 'AR 2,2',2,0,0,0
TEST2      TBLA5 'CL 4,20(3,5)',4,1,160,0
TEST3      TBLA5 'LM 14,12,50(5)',4,1,150,0
TEST4      TBLA5 'TM 60(2),2',4,1,80,0
TEST5      TBLA5 'ZAP 4(3,5),15(14,2)',6,2,104,35
           END
```

Table for Roman Numeral Conversion Problem -- A6:

A macro has been provided for the generation of tables for this machine problem. The name of this macro is TBLA6.

Syntax for TBLA6:

(label)  TBLA6  number,answer

> number - The value that is to be converted to roman numeral form.

> answer - Roman numeral equivalent of this number.

Your table should consist of <u>six</u> entries. The last entry should be followed by a delimiter of X'FF', as follows:

```
TABLE     CSECT
TEST1     TBLA6 1974,MCMLXXIV
TEST2     TBLA6 153,CLIII
TEST3     TBLA6 973,CMLXXIII
TEST4     TBLA6 55,LV
TEST5     TBLA6 1776,MDCCLXXVI
TEST6     TBLA6 370,CCCLXX
          DC    X'FF'      END OF TABLE
          END
```

## 2.4   INTERNALS OF THE GRADER SYSTEM

Introduction:

     This section describes the system of macros and  subroutines
we  have  devised for grader writing, and the conventions used in
the sample graders. These conventions are of interest if you want
instructions concerning the running of sample graders, especially
JCL and parameters to apply to your new grader.

     This collection of  macros  and  subroutines  forms  a  very
powerful  system  in  which  a  new  grader may be written with a
minimum amount of effort. The layout  of  a  general  grader  is
discussed,  but  the reader is encouraged to consult the listings
of sample graders obtained when the jobs of  section  2.3.2  were
run to get a more detailed idea.

     If  this  section  appears  a  bit  sketchy, it reflects the
authors' opinion that anyone embarking on such a  project  should
already have a fair idea of what's going on. Although writing new
graders is simple, it is not trivial.

     For  your convenience we have included the source for one of
our sample graders in section 2.4.6. This grader is complete  and
fairly  sophisticated. You should read this section and the macro
descriptions before you look at this example or it probably  will
not make much sense.

### 2.4.1   How to Write a Grader

     All  graders  have  the same basic structure as indicated in
the following example. The convention <function  description>  is
used  to indicate code which is not shown, but must be present to
perform the function described.

```
GRADER     CSECT
*
*          PROLOG MACRO PERFORMS ALL INITIALIZATION
*
           PROLOG
*
*          NEXT COMES BASIC TESTING LOOP. GRADER
*          SHOULD ASSIGN STUDENT POINTS WITH THE
*          "GIVE" MACRO. ANY STUDENT
*          PROGRAM CHECK WILL AUTOMATICALLY BE HANDLED
*          BY EXITS ESTABLISHED BY PROLOG MACRO.
*
           <basic grader testing loop>
*
*          ONCE GRADER IS FINISHED, OR STUDENT
*          CAUSES PROGRAM CHECK, CONTROL IS
```

75

```
*              PASSED TO EPILOG MACRO CODE.
*
*              EPILOG
*
*              <your grader's messages and work areas>
*
*              IF THE HEXCN OR DECCN CONVERSION MACROS ARE USED,
*              THE FOLLOWING MACRO MUST BE CODED TO
*              ESTABLISH WORK AREAS.
*
*              CONST
*
               END   GRADER
```

Notes on Conventions Used in the GRADER:

1) PROLOG is used to set up the GRADER's environment, and addressability is established using base register <u>11</u>. Do <u>not</u> alter the contents of register 11. You do not need a USING statement in your program.

2) PROLOG, EPILOG, and CONST generate statement labels. To avoid multiply defined labels, do not use any of the following statement labels in your grader:

ALLDONE, BADNAME, BASEPNT, BDNM1, CLOSE, DECMASK, DECTEMP, DECTEMP2, DUMMY, ENTRY, HDR3, INTRO, MSGM, NAME, NOWOK, OLDSPIE, SAVEAREA, SCORE, TEMPLATE, TRTBL, and WORKAREA.

3) Many of the subroutine utilities are passed parameters in a parameter list pointed to by register 4. It is therefore advisable <u>not</u> to use register 4 when you are using the macro utilities.

4) If your GRADER accesses subroutines that you have written which use the STORE and RESTORE macros, you must use the following calling sequence:

```
        L     15,=V(subroutine name)
        BALR  14,15              Branch to the subroutine
```

Since this calling sequence is used by the macro utilities provided, you should not use registers 14 and 15.

5) PROLOG generates a call to PARMPROC which scans the PARM field of the EXEC card and then returns control to the GRADER. PARMPROC requires a PARM processor table (PTBL) which must be provided for each grader (see the subroutine description for PARMPROC).

6) Your GRADER can use any of the following macros in
   performing its desired tasks:

   BOUNDS, DECCN, DUMP, GIVE, HEXCN, MSG, PRNT, and
   REGDUMP

   (see macro descriptions). Note- the GIVE macro
   destroys the contents of register 0.

Setting up a GRADER for Student Runs:

   A good technique to use in your GRADER is to make the test
cases table driven. This enables the instructor to change the
problem test data easily, without incurring the cost of
re-linking the entire grader.

   To reduce the cost of running each student, graders should be
stored as pre-linked load modules (refer to section 2.3.2). You
should be aware that the macro "DUMP" used to dump a student's
program gets its starting address from V(MP1) and its stopping
address from V(DUMMY). Given this constraint and the fact that
your grader should be table driven, the pre-linked load module
should have three unresolved external references:

   1. MP1 - The student's CSECT, to be tested.
   2. DUMMY - The dummy CSECT included behind the student.
   3. TABLE - The test case driving table, whose format you
      must define.


## 2.4.2  Subroutine and Macro Utilities Overview

   This section includes a brief description of the macros and
subroutines available to provide the user with an overview of
what is available.


Subroutines:

   DCBEXIT - Changes the DCB attributes for the output file
      SYSPRINT to:  RECFM=VBA,LRECL=125,MACRF=(PM), and
      DSORG=PS.  BLKSIZE is taken from the DD-card for
      SYSPRINT. (the minimum value for BLKSIZE is 129).

   ERROR - Handles the processing of program interrupts.
      Calls RDUMP and SNAP to give the student additional
      diagnostic information.

   OUTPUT - PUTs records out onto SYSPRINT and checks for
      MAXLINES being exceeded.

PARMPROC - Obtains all keyword information from   the  PARM
   field  of  the  EXEC  card  and  puts  the  appropriate
   information into the locations specified in   the   table
   named PTBL.

RDUMP   -  Produces  a  formatted  dump  of  the   registers
   specified and then calls OUTPUT.

SNAP - Produces a formatted dump  of  the   core   locations
   specified and then calls OUTPUT.

TIMEOUT - Handles timer exits which occur when the student
   exceeds  the  maximum   execution time set by "MAXTIME".
   This  subroutine  uses  RDUMP  and  SNAP  to  dump  the
   student's  registers,  PSW, and program. The method used
   to find all of this information is fairly involved, but
   well documented in the code for TIMEOUT.


Static CSECTS:

PTBL - A keyword table used by  PARMPROC  to  process  the
   PARM field of the EXEC card.

TABLE - A testing table used by  the  sample  table-driven
   GRADERs.  Each sample GRADER has a unique TABLE format.
   A  new  grader  does  not have to have a CSECT labelled
   TABLE.


Macros:

BOUNDS - Checks validity of pointers by the student.

CONST - Generates work areas for DECCN and  HEXCN   macros.

DECCN - Converts a binary value  to  a  decimal  character
   string representation.

DUMP - Produces a call to the SNAP routine to  dump  core.

EPILOG - Generates  work  areas  and  executable  code  to
   perform  GRADER  house-keeping before returning control
   to the supervisor.

GIVE - Adds and subtracts a  specified  number  of  points
   from the student's score.

HEXCN - Converts a binary value to a hexadecimal character
   string representation.

MSG - Generates messages in a  format  acceptable  to  the
   OUTPUT routine.

PRNT - Generates a call to OUTPUT for printing messages to
   student.

PROLOG  -   Generates   code   to   perform   all   GRADER
   initilization functions.

RESTORE  -  Restores  registers  for  subroutine  return
   sequence.

STORE - Saves  registers  and  establishes  addressability
   upon entry to subroutines.


## 2.4.3  Macro Descriptions

BOUNDS Macro Description:

Purpose:

   Determines  whether an address returned in a register points
to a location within the student's program.

Syntax:

   label   BOUNDS      REG=n,OUT=lab

Operands:

   n -- register that contains the address to be checked

   lab -- label that is branched to if address is out of bounds

Uses:

   Used  to  check  pointers  returned  by  student.    Prevents
addressing interrupts

Special Features:

   If  address  is  within the student's program (i.e. OK) this
macro  does  nothing  and  processing  continues  with  the  next
instruction


CONST Macro Description:

Purpose:

   Generates  work areas and tables to be used by the HEXCN and
DECCN macros.

Syntax:

   (no label) CONST (no operand field)

Operands:   (none)

Uses:

   Used to create work areas  for the HEXCN and  DECCN  macros.
   If  neither of these macros are to be used in the CSECT, the
   CONST macro is unnecessary.

Special Features:

   - if you use the CONST macro, do not use any of the  following
     labels in your CSECT:

     WORKAREA,  TEMPLATE,  TRTBL, DECTEMP, DECTEMP2, and DECMASK.


DECCN Macro Description:

Purpose:

   Performs binary to decimal (character) conversion.

Syntax:

   label   DECCN    register,result,length,CORE

Operands:

   register - register that contains the binary number to be
              converted
   result   - address where result of conversion is to be moved
   length   - result field length in bytes (if ommitted,
              default is 15)
   CORE     - if  specified  the  four  bytes pointed to by
register  are  converted  rather  than  the contents of register.
These four bytes need not be aligned.

Uses:

   Used to convert student's score or type of program interrupt
to decimal, etc.

Special Features:

   - leading zeros are blanked out
   - with result field lengths < 15, only the right-most digits
     are moved (i.e. stored right-justified in result field)
   - maximum field length is 15 bytes
   - your CSECT must contain a macro call for CONST in order

to properly initialize the workareas for DECCN.

DUMP Macro Description:

Purpose:

To create a call with the proper parameter list for the SNAP routine which will produce a formatted dump of selected portions of core

Syntax:

label     DUMP     label1,label2

Operands:

label1- address of first location to be dumped
label2- last location to be dumped

Uses:

When student has an incorrect answer or gets an interrupt, this macro is used to dump his program

Special Features:

- if you are using labels, they must be local to  the  CSECT issuing  the  macro,  or there must be corresponding EXTRN statements for the external addresses
- the lower and upper bounds specified are rounded down  and up to a multiple of 16 bytes respectively

Examples:

```
LAB1    DUMP    PROG1,PROG2
        DUMP    PTA,PTB
```

If  at  execution time, PTA is absolute location 20 (decimal) and PTB is absolute location 30 (decimal), a dump  of  locations  16 through 32 (inclusive)  is  produced  as a result of the second macro call.


EPILOG Macro Description:

Purpose:

Generates DC's for work areas to be used by the PROLOG macro expansion  and  performs  all  GRADER  housekeeping   before returning control to the operating system.

Syntax:

     (no label) EPILOG
                    or
     (no label) EPILOG LEVELS=n

Operands:

     One of EPILOG's functions is to generate a DC labelled
     SAVEAREA to be used as a register save area stack by the
     GRADER's routines. This stack will consist of "n" entries,
     where n is the number of 18 full-word saveareas that should
     be allocated during assembly of the GRADER. The minimum
     value for "n" is 9 - since it is possible for there to be 9
     levels of subroutine calls by the grader and its
     accompanying routines (this figure is a little high, but it
     is a safe guess). If your GRADER contains recursive
     routines and more than 9 routines will be called before a
     savearea is freed, then you should specify the LEVELS option
     for the EPILOG macro.

Uses:

     - Allocates space for a SAVEAREA stack.
     - Prints the student's total score.
     - Restores the supervisor's SPIE interrupt handler.
     - Returns control to the supervisor, passing the student's
       score in the condition code.

Special Features:

     - Do not use any of the following statement labels in your
       GRADER if you are using the PROLOG and EPILOG macros:

       ALLDONE, BADJCL, BJCL1, HDR3, INTRO, JCLOK, MSGM, NOWOK,
       OLDSPIE, and SCORE.

     - later sections will contain additional information on how to
       use the PROLOG and EPILOG macros when writing a GRADER.


GIVE Macro Description:

Purpose:

     To add or subtract from student's score a specified number
     of points

Syntax:

     label    GIVE    n

Operands:

         label - label of the GIVE statement
            n - decimal number prefixed with an optional sign

Special Features:

    - It is recommended that a total  score  <  0  should  not  be
      possible.
    - The GIVE macro destroys the contents of register 0.

    Examples:

                L1    GIVE    3           - adds 3 to score
                      GIVE    +2          - adds 2 to score
                      GIVE    -5          - subtracts 5 from score

HEXCN Macro Description:

Purpose:

    Performs    internal-binary    to    hexadecimal    (character)
    conversion

Syntax:

    label    HEXCN    reg,result,length,CORE

Operands:

    reg    - register containing value to be converted
    result - area where result of conversion is to be
             converted
    length - result field length (if ommitted, default is
             8)
    CORE   - if specified the four bytes pointed to by register,
    rather than the contents of register are  converted.  These  four
    bytes need not be aligned.

Uses:

    Used for printing core, registers, addresses

Special Features:

    - with result field lengths < 8, only the right-most  digits
      are moved (i.e. stored right-justified in result field)
    - your CSECT must contain a macro call for CONST in order to
      properly initialize the workareas for HEXCN.

Examples:

                HEXCN   3,AREA

This instruction would take the contents of register 3 and convert them to hexadecimal in printable form.  If register 3 contained X°0F12361A° then AREA would contain after the conversion C°0F12361A°

        LAB1   HEXCN  0,AREA2,5

Assuming register 0 contained X°F1234567°, after the conversion AREA2 would contain C°34567°


MSG Macro Description:

Purpose:

    Generates a variable length record in an acceptable format
    for the OUTPUT
subroutine

Syntax:

    label    MSG    (lab1,°string°,lab2,°string°,...)
                       or               or
                     num1             num2

Operands:

    label  - name of message that the PRNT macro will  reference
    string - a character string enclosed in quotes
    num1   - a decimal number specifying how many bytes to
             reserve
    num2   - same as num1
    lab1   - label of the field that follows
    lab2   - same as lab1


Uses:

    Used to create all message to be printed by the grader

Special Features:

    - message is padded to an even byte length
    - the first character of the message is used as the carriage
      control character (I/O routine OUTPUT accepts only ANSI
      control characters- (+,-,0,1,ƀ)
    - note that the label of the MSG macro points to the record
      descriptor word, not the first operand field
    - if you want to omit the label on a field, just have a °,,°
      instead of a °,label,° in your operand list.
    - when you specify a number instead of a string, the

        reserved space is initialized to blanks
    - do not use quotes as characters within your MSG
    - your CSECT must contain a macro call for CONST in order to
      properly initialize the workareas for DECCN

Examples:

        FINAL    MSG    (,' YOUR SCORE IS',SCORE,8)

This instruction would create this structure:

    FINAL    DC   AL2(26,0)              record descriptor word
             DC   C' YOUR SCORE IS'
    SCORE    DC   CL8' '

You would probably use an MVC to move in score, then the message
would be ready for a PRNT instruction. Note that the first label
in the operand field was omitted by just having the comma
present. As a result, the character string ' YOUR SCORE IS' does
not have a label.

(For an explanation of record descriptor words see the IBM Data
Management Services Manual. (Refer to the sections on QSAM I/O,
which is the I/O method used by the GRADER)).


PRNT Macro Description:

Purpose:

    Used to print a prepared message (by generating a call to
    the OUTPUT subroutine)

Syntax:

    label    PRNT    lab1

Operands:

    label - label of the PRNT statement
    lab1  - label of the message to be printed

Uses:

    Used to print all of the grader's messages

Special Features:

    - the address specified by lab1 is the address of the record
      descriptor word (RDW) for the message to be printed

Examples:

```
        INTRO   PRNT    MSG1
                  •
                  •
                  •
        MSG1    MSG     (,' PRINT OUT THIS MESSAGE')
```

This would generate a call to the OUTPUT routine which would then print MSG1

PROLOG Macro Description:

Purpose:

   This macro sets up the GRADER's environment upon entry to the GRADER by the operating system.

Syntax:

   (no label) PROLOG (no operand field)

Operands:  (none)

Uses:

   When a GRADER is given control by the operating system, certain functions must be performed to properly initialize the GRADER's environment (i.e.- establish addressability, chain new save areas, open SYSPRINT, print introductory headings, etc.). PROLOG has been provided so as to facilitate the writing of your GRADER.

   See later sections for more detailed information on how to write a grader.

Special Features:

   You must always use EPILOG in conjunction with PROLOG since EPILOG generates workareas that are used by the PROLOG macro.

REGDUMP Macro Description:

Purpose:

   This macro produces a call to RDUMP which dumps a given set of registers from a series of core locations specified.

Syntax:

   label REGDUMP R1,R2,lab1

Operands:

    R1-    Starting register number.
    R2-    Stopping register number.
    lab1- Address of a register contents table.

Uses:

    This macro is used to dump the student's registers when he
either returns incorrect answers or gets an interrupt during
execution.

Special Features:

    - R1 can be > R2, in which case the dump "wraps around".
    - lab1 points to a series of full-words that contain the
      values to be dumped (i.e.- lab1 contains the value to be
      printed for R1). The remainder of the locations are to
      contain the values for R1+1 through R2 (in ascending order
      until register 15 is reached, in which case the values
      continue from register 0 through R2).

Examples:

    REGDUMP 5,7,PTR1

    where PTR1
           !
           !
           V

        _____
      ! REG 5 ! REG 6 ! REG 7 !

    This macro would dump locations PTR1 through PTR1+11
(inclusive) with the headings: REG 5, REG 6, and REG 7 above
the full-word dumps.

    EXAMPLE2 REGDUMP 13,2,PTR2
              .
              .
              .
              .
              .
    PTR2     DC       A(2,4,6,8,10,12)

    This macro call would produce the following dump by RDUMP:

    REG 13     REG 14     REG 15     REG 0     REG 1     REG 2
    00000002  00000004  00000006  00000008  0000000A  0000000C

RESTORE Macro Description:

Purpose:

This macro generates code to restore the caller's environment and then returns control to him.

Syntax:

label    RESTORE    (no operands)

Operands: (none)

Uses:

Used in subroutines to chain back through the present register save area to the caller's save area. After the old save area is re-established, the caller's registers are restored and control is given back to the caller.

For more information on RESTORE, see later sections on how to write GRADER subroutines.


STORE Macro Description:

Purpose:

This routine saves all of the caller's registers and then establishes the proper environment for its execution. This process includes establishing addressibility (using base register 11) and then setting register 13 to point to a new save area for future calls to subroutines

Syntax:

label    STORE

Uses:

Is used at the beginning of most grader routines to set up save areas, etc.

Special Features:

The STORE macro must be the first instruction of your routine since the macro generates a CSECT statement

Examples:

```
ROUTINE1    STORE
EX2         STORE
```

these statements would generate appropriate code for the initialization of the routines ROUTINE1 and EX2

## 2.4.4   Subroutine Descriptions

DCBEXIT Subroutine Description:

The assembly language problem GRADER was designed to output all diagnostic information directly after the student's Assembly listing.   Since QSAM was used for the GRADER's I/O, the attributes for SYSPRINT had to be compatible with QSAM.

The Assembler requires SYSPRINT to be a fixed block sequential access file; these attributes are incompatible with the GRADER under QSAM.  In order to circumvent this problem, the DCBEXIT routine creates an acceptable data control block (DCB) for QSAM and then re-opens SYSPRINT for the GRADER.

The file attributes supplied for the DCB are: DSORG=PS, RECFM=VBA, LRECL=125, and MACRF=(PM).

The BLKSIZE is obtained from the DD-card for SYSPRINT. Error checking is performed on the given BLKSIZE and a minimum BLKSIZE of 129 is used by default.

ERROR Subroutine Description:

This routine is entered when a program interrupt occurs. The SPIE macro in the GRADER creates a program interruption control area (PICA) which points to this routine for handling the error condition.

After taking control from the supervisor, ERROR proceeds to dump the student's PSW, registers and his MP1 CSECT at the time of the interrupt. If the cause of the interrupt was an operation exception with the offending instruction being either X'000F' or an execute instruction with an object instruction of X'000F', ERROR interprets this to be a request for a debugging dump.

In this case control is returned to the student for further testing. Otherwise control is returned to the supervisor after the program interruption element (PIE) is modified so that control will return to an entry point in the GRADER.  If an error occurs outside of the student's CSECT, the student's score is reset to zero.

OUTPUT Subroutine Description:

This routine is called with register 4 pointing to a record descriptor word (RDW) for the variable length record that is to be printed.  The format of the message must be:

```
| ROW | C | CHARACTER STRING |
```

where C is an ANSI carriage control character (0,-,1,or +).

The macro used to call OUTPUT is PRNT. In order to insure the proper formatting of your output messages, macro MSG has been supplied (-see macro descriptions).

The following parameters can be modified in the OUTPUT routine using PARMPROC:

LINESIZE- Specifies the number of lines to be printed per page (default value is 55).

MAXLINES- Specifies maximum number of lines a student can print (default value is 500).

PARMPROC Subroutine Description:

       This routine processes the PARM field on the EXEC card for the assembly language problem GRADER. By convention, upon entry to a main program CSECT by the operating system, register 1 points to the following chained data structure:

```
| REGISTER 1 | ---> | POINTER | ---> | LENGTH | the PARM list |
```

A valid PARM list consists of:

"keyword1=value1,keyword2=value2,.....keywordn=valuen"

where keyword(n) is a character string ($\leq 8$ characters) and value(n) is either a character string ($\leq 8$ characters) or a decimal integer.

       The PARM list is scanned for keywords followed by an equal sign. After finding a keyword in the PARM list, PARMPROC then searches a keyword table named PTBL and finds out where to store the value following the equal sign.

The format of PTBL is:

```
PTBL      CSECT
*
*PARM processor table for your machine problem GRADER
*
          EXTRN address1,address2,....,addressn
*
          DC      F'n'                  There are 'n' keywords in PTBL
key1      DC      CL8'keyword1'         The name of your keyword
```

```
            DC      A(address1)           Address in GRADER where default
 *                                        value is stored.
key2        DC      CL8'keyword2'
            DC      A(address2)
                .
                .
                .
keyn        DC      CL8'keywordn'
            DC      A(addressn)
            END
```

An example of a valid PTBL would be:

```
PTBL        CSECT
            EXTRN LINESIZE,MAXLINES
*Both of these external loacations are in the OUTPUT routine
            DC      F'2'     this table will have 2 keywords
ONE         DC      CL8'LINESIZE'
            DC      A(LINESIZE)
TWO         DC      CL8'MAXLINES'
            DC      A(MAXLINES)
            END
```

Your GRADER must always have a PTBL CSECT and the table must contain at least 1 entry. When a keyword is found in the PARM list, a pointer to a location in one of the GRADER's routines is obtained from PTBL. The value following the equal sign is then moved into the area specified by the table entry. If the value is a character string, the address must point to a static area of 8 bytes in length. If the value following the equal sign is a decimal value, then the number is converted to binary, and the address must specify a full-word location.

If there are no keywords in the PARM field, then PARMPROC leaves the default values and returns to the caller.


RDUMP Subroutine Description:

This routine dumps the values of a given set of registers from the core locations specified in a parameter list. Upon entry, register 4 points to a parameter list containing:

1) The starting register number
2) The ending register number
3) The address of a register contents table
   (on a full-word boundary)

REGDUMP is a supplied macro that generates a call to RDUMP (-see macro description). The following is an example showing how to use RDUMP:

```
        L       15,=A(RDUMP)    standard subroutine calling sequence
        LA      4,PARAMS        set pointer to parameter list
        BALR    14,15           branch to subroutine RDUMP
        .
        .
        .
PARAMS  DC      F'1'            starting register is REG 1
        DC      F'4'            last register is REG 4
        DC      A(REGS)         Address of register contents table
REGS    DC      A(7,9,11,13)    This is the sample table
```

After executing the above subroutine call, the following dump
will be printed:

```
 REG 1      REG 2      REG 3      REG 4
00000007   00000009   0000000B   0000000D
```

SNAP Subroutine Description:

    This routine is used to dump core in a form similar to the
system supplied "SNAP" macro, but on our OCB without special
attributes.  This subroutine is called with register 4 pointing
to a two word parameter list, the first word of which contains
the starting address to dump, and the second word containing the
stopping address.

    The "DUMP" macro should be used to generate calls to this
subroutine.


TIMEOUT Subroutine Description:

    This routine is called when the student's execution time
limit is exceeded.  An EXTRACT is performed to get the address of
the floating point register save area in the TCB.  Adding 32
(dec.) to this address gives us the TCB's anchor for the RB
chain. The first cell on this chain is the IRB which the Stage 2
Exit Effector created for the STIMER exit routine. The RBGRSAVE
field of this IRB (offset 32 dec.) contains the student's
registers that were active.

    Chaining from this RB, the previous RB is the PRB for the
Grader/student. The RBOPSW field of this PRB (offset 16 dec.)
contains the PSW we are interested in. These registers and the
PSW are formatted and printed and then the student's program is
dumped.

    Next files are closed, buffers freed and the student's **task**
is abended with a completion code of 322 (dec.). MAXTIME, which
determines the student's maximum execution time, is specified in
hundredths of seconds.

## 2.4.5   How to Write Subroutines for a Grader

Using the macro utilities, it is very   simple   to   write   an
external   subroutine   for   a   grader.   A   typical   routine would
consist of the following code:

```
*
*Generate a CSECT labelled (name) and establish addressability
*

(name)      STORE      (see macro description)

*
*Note-      The STORE macro establishes addressability using
*           Base Register 11.  Do not destroy the contents
*           of this register.
*
*           STORE also saves all registers and obtains a new
*           save area (pointed to by Register 13).
*
               .
               .
(Your subroutine goes here)
               .
               .
*
*Restore all registers and return
*

            RESTORE    (see macro description)

*
*If your routine uses the macros HEXCN or DECCN, you should
*insert the following card:
*

            CONST      (see macro description)
            END
```

**Subroutine Calling Sequence:**

You must use the following calling sequence if your   routine
uses the STORE and RESTORE macro utilities:

```
            L     15,=V(name)
            BALR  14,15
```

**Passing Parameters to Your Routine:**

The standard method for passing parameters to O.S. subroutines is by pointing register 1 to a parameter list.

This convention was not used by the GRADER's routines since O.S. system macros often destroy registers 0,1,14, and 15. The convention adopted for the GRADER's subroutines was that Register 4 will point to a parameter list for the subroutine (if one is needed).

Programming Notes:

If CONST is used, do not use any of the following statement labels in your routine to avoid multiply defined labels:

DECMASK, DECTEMP, DECTEMP2, DUMMY, SAVEAREA, TEMPLATE, TRTBL, and WORKAREA.

## 2.4.6  Example Grader Source Listing

This section contains a photo-reduced source listing of a sample grader. This grader is for the DC-Simulator problem, A4. A "PRINT NOGEN" statement has been added to this deck for readability.

A4G    GRADER FOR CONSTANT PROCESSOR -- A4 02/16/74                                           PAGE    2

```
   LOC  OBJECT CODE      ADDR1 ADDR2  STMT   SOURCE STATEMENT                                    10 JUN 74

 000000                                5 GRADER  CSECT
                                       6 *
                                       7 *INITIALIZE GRADER
                                       8 *

                                      10          PROLOG
                                      11+         ENTRY   BASEPNT,ALLDONE,SCORE,SAVEAREA,NAME,BADJCL,BADNAME
                                      12+         EXTRN   MP1,DUMMY,ERROR,SNAP,OUTPUT,TABLE,RDUMP,DCBOUT
                                      13+         EXTRN   TIMEOUT,MAXTIME
 000000                               14+BASEPNT DS      0H
 000000 90EC D00C      0000C          15+        STM     14,12,12(13) SAVE REGISTERS
 000004 41B0 F000      00000          16+        LA      11,0(0,15) CLEAR OUT TOP BYTE AND
 000000                               17+        USING   BASEPNT,11 ESTABLISH ADDRESSABILITY
 000008 4120 B734      00734          18+        LA      2,SAVEAREA GET PTR TO REGISTER SAVE AREA
 00000C 5000 2004      00004          19+        ST      13,4(,2) STORE ADDR OF PREVIOUS SAVE AREA
 000010 5020 D008      00008          20+        ST      2,8(,13) STORE ADDR OF NEW SA IN OLD SA
 000014 1802                          21+        LR      13,2 INITIALIZE PTR TO REG SAVE AREA
 000016 58F0 BEB8      00EB8          22+        L       15,=V(PARMPROC) PROCESS PARM FIELD OF EXEC CARD
 00001A 05EF                          23+        BALR    14,15
                                      24+**
                                      25+**OPEN SYSPRINT FOR MP1 GRADER- WILL USE QSAM
                                      26+**
                                      27+        CNOP    0,4 ALIGN LIST TO FULLWORD
 00001C 4510 B024      00024          28+        BAL     1,*+8 LOAD REG1 W/LIST ADDR.
 000020 8F                            29+        DC      AL1(143) OPTION BYTE
 000021 000000                        30+        DC      AL3(DCBOUT) DCB ADDRESS
 000024 0A13                          31+        SVC     19 ISSUE OPEN SVC
                                      32+**
                                      33+**INITIALIZE PROGRAM INTERRUPTION HANDLER
                                      34+**
 000026                               35+        CNOP    2,4
 000026 4110 B032      00032          36+        LA      1,*+12 LOAD BRANCH ADDRESS
 00002A 0511                          37+        BALR    1,1 BRANCH AROUND PARAMS.
 00002C 0F                            38+        DC      B'00001111' PROGRAM MASK BITS
 00002D 000000                        39+        DC      AL3(ERROR) EXIT ROUTINE ADDRESS
 000030 7F                            40+        DC      B'01111111'
 000031 FF                            41+        DC      B'11111111' INTERRUPTION MASK
 000032 0A0E                          42+        SVC     14 ISSUE SPIE SVC
                                      43+**SAVE ADDRESS OF OLD PROGRAM INTERRUPTION CONTROL AREA
 000034 5010 B5E0      005E0          44+        ST      1,OLDSPIE SAVE PICA IN OLDSPIE
                                      45+**
                                      46+**
                                      47+**    ISSUE STIMER
                                      48+**
 000038 5820 BEBC      00EBC          49+        L       2,=V(TIMEOUT)
 00003C 5810 BEC0      00EC0          50+        L       1,=V(MAXTIME)
 000040 1802                          51+        LR      0,2 LOAD PARAMETER REG 0
 000042 41E0 0010      00010          52+        LA      14,16(0,0) LOAD FLAG BYTE
 000046 89E0 0018      00018          53+        SLL     14,24(0) SHIFT TO HI-ORDER BYTE
 00004A 160E                          54+        OR      0,14 AND PACK WITH EXIT ADDR
 00004C 0A2F                          55+        SVC     47 ISSUE STIMER SVC
                                      56+**
                                      57+**PRINT HEADING FOR STUDENTS EXECUTION
                                      58+**
 00004E 58F0 BEC4      00EC4          59+        L       15,=V(OUTPUT) .   GET ADDRESS OF OUTPUT SUBROUTINE

 000052 0700                          60+        CNOP    0,4
 000054 4540 B05C      0005C          61+        BAL     4,*+8 .           REG4 POINTS TO PARAMETER LIST
 000058 000005E4                      62+        DC      A(INTRO) .        ADDR OF ROW FOR MESSAGE TO BE PRINTED
 00005C 05EF                          63+        BALR    14,15 .           CALL OUTPUT ROUTINE
 00005E 58F0 BEC8      00EC8          64+        L       15,=V(MP1)
 000062 50F0 B674      00674          65+        ST      15,WORKAREA .     PUT GIVEN VALUE INTO WORKAREA
 000066 F143 BE7D BE74 00E7D 00E74    66+        MVO     TEMPLATE(5),WORKAREA(4)
 00006C F384 BE74 BE7D 00E74 00E7D    67+        UNPK    WORKAREA(9),TEMPLATE(5)
 000072 DC07 BE75 BD92 00E75 00D92    68+        TR      WORKAREA+1(8),TRTBL-240 USE HEX TRANSLATE TABLE
 000078 D205 B646 BE77 00646 00E77    69+        MVC     ENTRY(6),WORKAREA+3
 00007E 58F0 BEC4      00EC4          70+        L       15,=V(OUTPUT) .   GET ADDRESS OF OUTPUT SUBROUTINE
 000082 0700                          71+        CNOP    0,4
 000084 4540 B08C      0008C          72+        BAL     4,*+8 .           REG4 POINTS TO PARAMETER LIST
 000088 0000062C                      73+        DC      A(HDR3) .         ADDR OF ROW FOR MESSAGE TO BE PRINTED
 00008C 05EF                          74+        BALR    14,15 .           CALL OUTPUT ROUTINE

                                      76        PRNT    M1                10 POINTS FOR ASSEMBLING
 00008E 58F0 BEC4      00EC4          77+        L       15,=V(OUTPUT) .   GET ADDRESS OF OUTPUT SUBROUTINE
 000092 0700                          78+        CNOP    0,4
 000094 4540 B09C      0009C          79+        BAL     4,*+8 .           REG4 POINTS TO PARAMETER LIST
 000098 000000AD8                     80+        DC      A(M1) .           ADDR OF ROW FOR MESSAGE TO BE PRINTED
 00009C 05EF                          81+        BALR    14,15 .           CALL OUTPUT ROUTINE
                                      82        GIVE    10
 00009E 5800 B684      00684          83+        L       0,SCORE
 0000A2 4A00 BEEC      00EEC          84+        AH      0,=H'10'
 0000A6 5000 B684      00684          85+        ST      0,SCORE
 0000AA 58A0 BECC      00ECC          86+        L       10,=V(TABLE)      REG 10 POINTS TO TEST TABLE
 000000                               87        USING   DATA,10

 0000AE                               89 LOOP    EQU     *                 BASIC TESTING LOOP

                                      91 *
                                      92 *CHECK FOR END OF TABLE
                                      93 *

 0000AE 5800 A000      00000          95        L       0,TYPE            GET TYPE OF CONSTANT
 0000B2 5900 BED0      00ED0          96        C       0,=F'-1'          IS THIS THE END OF TABLE MARKER
 0000B6 4780 B50E      0050E          97        BE      DONE              YES, BRANCH TO END OF LOOP

                                      99 *
                                     100 *PREPARE AN OPENING MESSAGE FOR THE STUDENT
                                     101 *

 0000BA D201 BB41 A032 00B41 00032   103        MVC     MT(2),CHAR        GET DATA CONVERSION TYPE
 0000C0 D227 BB52 A004 00B52 00004   104        MVC     MSTR(40),STRING   GET STRING OF DATA
                                     105        PRNT    M2                PRINT OPENING MESSAGE
 0000C6 58F0 BEC4      00EC4         106+        L       15,=V(OUTPUT) .   GET ADDRESS OF OUTPUT SUBROUTINE
 0000CA 0700                         107+        CNOP    0,4
 0000CC 4540 B0D4      000D4         108+        BAL     4,*+8 .           REG4 POINTS TO PARAMETER LIST
 0000D0 00000B22                     109+        DC      A(M2) .           ADDR OF ROW FOR MESSAGE TO BE PRINTED
 0000D4 05EF                         110+        BALR    14,15 .           CALL OUTPUT ROUTINE

                                     112 *
                                     113 *SET UP TESTING AREA FOR STUDENT
```

95

```
    LOC  OBJECT CODE    ADDR1 ADDR2 STMT   SOURCE STATEMENT                                     10 JUN 74

                                     114 *
  0000D6 900F B9F0          009F0   116        STM     0,15,GREGS       SAVE ALL OF THE GRADER'S REGISTERS
  0000DA D200 BA30 A030 00A30 00030 117        MVC     BREGS(1),IVLEN   GET LENGTH OF INPUT DATA
  0000E0 D202 BA31 BEF6 00A31 00EF6 118        MVC     BREGS+1(3),=AL3(MSTRING) GET ADDRESS OF INPUT DATA
  0000E6 D227 BEFC A004 00EFC 00004 119        MVC     MSTRING(40),STRING GET INPUT STRING FROM TABLE
  0000EC D227 BAAC A004 00AAC 00004 120        MVC     COPY(40),STRING    SAVE A COPY OF THE DATA

                                     122 *
                                     123 *FORMAT COPY OF DATA FOR MESSAGE TO STUDENT
                                     124 *
  0000F2 5810 BA30          00A30   126        L       1,BREGS          LOAD REG 1 TO BE SENT
                                     127        HEXCN   1,R11            PUT IN MESSAGE
  0000F6 5010 BE74          00E74   128+       ST      1,WORKAREA .     PUT GIVEN VALUE INTO WORKAREA
  0000FA F143 BE7D BE74 00E7D 00E74 129+       MVO     TEMPLATE(5),WORKAREA(4)
  000100 F384 BE74 BE7D 00E74 00E7D 130+       UNPK    WORKAREA(9),TEMPLATE(5)
  000106 DC07 BE75 BD92 00E75 00D92 131+       TR      WORKAREA+1(8),TRTBL-240 USE HEX TRANSLATE TABLE
  00010C D207 BE37 BE75 00E37 00E75 132+       MVC     R11(8),WORKAREA+1
  000112 D205 BE46 BE39 00E46 00E39 133        MVC     R1(6),R11+2      PUT IN MESSAGE
  000118 9812 1000          00000   134        LM      1,2,0(1)         LOAD INDIRECT WORD
                                     135        HEXCN   1,CONT1          PUT IN MESSAGE
  00011C 5010 BE74          00E74   136+       ST      1,WORKAREA .     PUT GIVEN VALUE INTO WORKAREA
  000120 F143 BE7D BE74 00E7D 00E74 137+       MVO     TEMPLATE(5),WORKAREA(4)
  000126 F384 BE74 BE7D 00E74 00E7D 138+       UNPK    WORKAREA(9),TEMPLATE(5)
  00012C DC07 BE75 BD92 00E75 00D92 139+       TR      WORKAREA+1(8),TRTBL-240 USE HEX TRANSLATE TABLE
  000132 D207 BE4E BE75 00E4E 00E75 140+       MVC     CONT1(8),WORKAREA+1
                                     141        HEXCN   2,CONT1+8        PUT IN MESSAGE
  000138 5020 BE74          00E74   142+       ST      2,WORKAREA .     PUT GIVEN VALUE INTO WORKAREA
  00013C F143 BE7D BE74 00E7D 00E74 143+       MVO     TEMPLATE(5),WORKAREA(4)
  000142 F384 BE74 BE7D 00E74 00E7D 144+       UNPK    WORKAREA(9),TEMPLATE(5)
  000148 DC07 BE75 BD92 00E75 00D92 145+       TR      WORKAREA+1(8),TRTBL-240 USE HEX TRANSLATE TABLE
  00014E D207 BE56 BE75 00E56 00E75 146+       MVC     CONT1+8(8),WORKAREA+1
                                     147        PRNT    M15              HEADER
  000154 58F0 BEC4          00EC4   148+       L       15,=V(OUTPUT) .  GET ADDRESS OF OUTPUT SUBROUTINE
  000158                             149+       CNOP    0,4
  000158 4540 B160          00160   150+       BAL     4,*+8 .          REG4 POINTS TO PARAMETER LIST
  00015C 00000DA2                   151+       DC      A(M15)           ADDR OF RDW FOR MESSAGE TO BE PRINTED
  000160 05EF                       152+       BALR    14,15 .          CALL OUTPUT ROUTINE
                                     153        PRNT    M20              'XX --> XXXXXX'
  000162 58F0 BEC4          00EC4   154+       L       15,=V(OUTPUT) .  GET ADDRESS OF OUTPUT SUBROUTINE
  000166 0700                       155+       CNOP    0,4
  000168 4540 B170          00170   156+       BAL     4,*+8 .          REG4 POINTS TO PARAMETER LIST
  00016C 00000E32                   157+       DC      A(M20) .         ADDR OF RDW FOR MESSAGE TO BE PRINTED
  000170 05EF                       158+       BALR    14,15 .          CALL OUTPUT ROUTINE

                                     160 *
                                     161 *SET UP REGISTERS AND BRANCH TO STUDENT
                                     162 *
  000172 981F BA30          00A30   164        LM      1,15,BREGS       SET UP REGISTERS FOR STUDENT
  000176 07FF                       165        BR      15               BRANCH TO STUDENT

                                     167 *
                                     168 *STUDENT RETURNS HERE


                                     169 *
  000178 05F0                       171 RETURN BALR    15,0             ESTABLISH TEMPORARY ADDRESSABILITY
  00017A                            172        USING   *,15
  00017A 900D F8F2          00A6C   173        STM     0,13,SREGS       SAVE REGISTERS RETURNED BY STUDENT

                                     175 *
                                     176 *RESTORE GRADER ENVIROMENT AND TELL STUDENT WHAT HE OR SHE RETURNED
                                     177 *
  00017E 5880 FD5A          00ED4   179        L       11,=A(BASEPNT)   RE-ESTABLISH ADDRESSABILITY
  000182                            180        DROP    15
  000182 980F B9F0          009F0   181        LM      0,15,GREGS       RESTORE ALL OF GRADER'S REGISTERS

                                     183 *
                                     184 **
                                     185 *** FOLLOWING CODE BY PGG
                                     186 **
                                     187 *
  000186 92FF BAD6          00AD6   189        MVI     BADR1SW,X'FF'    IN CASE ERROR IS FOUND
  00018A 92FF BAD7          00AD7   190        MVI     BADIWSW,X'FF'    LIKEWISE
  00018E 926F BDE1          00DE1   191        MVI     CONTA,C'?'       THIS CODE FILLS ANSWER AREAS
  000192 D20E BDE2 BDE1 00DE2 00DE1 192        MVC     CONTA+1(15),CONTA WITH QUESTION MARKS IN CASE
  000198 D207 BDCA BDE1 00DCA 00DE1 193        MVC     IWORD(8),CONTA   ONE OR MORE OF A STUDENT'S ANSWERS
  00019E D205 BDD9 BDE1 00DD9 00DE1 194        MVC     IADR(6),CONTA    ARE OUT OF BOUNDS
  0001A4 5810 BA70          00A70   196        L       1,SREGS+4        LOAD STUDENT'S REGISTER 1
                                     197        HEXCN   1,REGONE,8       PUT IN MESSAGE
  0001A8 5010 BE74          00E74   198+       ST      1,WORKAREA .     PUT GIVEN VALUE INTO WORKAREA
  0001AC F143 BE7D BE74 00E7D 00E74 199+       MVO     TEMPLATE(5),WORKAREA(4)
  0001B2 F384 BE7D BE74 00E7D 00E74 200+       UNPK    WORKAREA(9),TEMPLATE(5)
  0001B8 DC07 BE75 BD92 00E75 00D92 201+       TR      WORKAREA+1(8),TRTBL-240 USE HEX TRANSLATE TABLE
  0001BE D207 BDB3 BE75 00DB3 00E75 202+       MVC     REGONE(8),WORKAREA+1
  0001C4 D205 BDC2 BDB5 00DC2 00DB5 203        MVC     REGON(6),REGONE+2 MOVE IN ADDRESS PORTION
                                     204        BOUNDS  REG=1,OUT=PRINT  CHECK ADDRESS FOR VALIDITY
  0001CA 4110 1000          00000   205+       LA      1,0(1)           CLEAR OUT TOP BYTE
  0001CE 5800 BEC8          00EC8   206+       L       0,=V(MPL)        DOES REGISTER POINT IN
  0001D2 1901                       207+       CR      0,1              FRONT OF CSECT?
  0001D4 4720 B27A          0027A   208+       BH      PRINT            YES,BRANCH
  0001D8 5800 BED8          00ED8   209+       L       0,=V(DUMMY)      DOES REGISTER POINT
  0001DC 1901                       210+       CR      0,1              BEHIND CSECT?
  0001DE 4700 B27A          0027A   211+       BNH     PRINT            YES,BRANCH
                                     212 *                             IF ADDRESS IS NO GOOD, DON'T TRY
                                     213 *                             TO LOAD IT.
  0001E2 9200 BAD6          00AD6   215        MVI     BADR1SW,X'00'    THIS MEANS ADDRESS IS GOOD
  0001E6 D203 B9BC 1000 009BC 00000 216        MVC     TSAVE(4),0(1)
  0001EC 5810 B9BC          009BC   217        L       1,TSAVE          GET A(ANSWER)
                                     218        HEXCN   1,IWORD,8        PUT IN MESSAGE
  0001F0 5010 BE74          00E74   219+       ST      1,WORKARLA .     PUT GIVEN VALUE INTO WORKAREA
  0001F4 F143 BE7D BE74 00E7D 00E74 220+       MVO     TEMPLATE(5),WORKAREA(4)
  0001FA F384 BE7D BE74 00E7D 00E74 221+       UNPK    WORKAREA(9),TEMPLATE(5)
  000200 DC07 BE75 BD92 00E75 00D92 222+       TR      WORKAREA+1(8),TRTBL-240 USE HEX TRANSLATE TABLE
  000206 D207 BDCA BE75 00DCA 00E75 223+       MVC     IWORD(8),WORKAREA+1
```

96

A4G    GRADER FOR CONSTANT PROCESSOR -- A4 02/16/74                                    PAGE   4

```
   LOC   OBJECT CODE   ADDR1 ADDR2  STMT   SOURCE STATEMENT                                    10 JUN 74

00020C D205 BDD9 BDCC 00DD9 00DCC   224         MVC    IADR(6),IWORD+2     PUT ADDRESS PART IN MESSAGE AGAIN
                                    225         ROUNDS REG=1,OUT=PRINT   CHECK ADDRESS OF ANSWER FOR VALIDITY
000212 4110 1000       00000        226+        LA     1,0(,1) CLEAR OUT TOP BYTE
000216 5800 BEC8       00EC8        227+        L      0,=V(MP1) DOES REGISTER POINT IN
00021A 1901                         228+        CR     0,1 FRONT OF CSECT?
00021C 4720 B27A       0027A        229+        BH     PRINT YES,BRANCH
000220 5800 BED8       00ED8        230+        L      0,=V(DUMMY) DOES REGISTER POINT
000224 1901                         231+        CR     0,1 BEHIND CSECT?
000226 47D0 B27A       0027A        232+        BNH    PRINT YES,BRANCH

00022A 9200 BAD7       00AD7        234         MVI    BADIWSW,X'00'        MUST BE GOOD
00022E D203 B99C 1000 0099C 00000   235         MVC    TSAVE(4),0(1)
000234 5820 B99C       0099C        236         L      2,TSAVE
000238 D203 B99C 1004 0099C 00004   237         MVC    TSAVE(4),4(1)
00023E 5830 B99C       0099C        238         L      3,TSAVE
                                    239         HEXCN  2,CONTA,8           PUT FIRST WORD IN MESSAGE
000242 5020 BE74       00E74        240+        ST     2,WORKAREA .        PUT GIVEN VALUE INTO WORKAREA
000246 F143 BE7D BE74 00E7D 00E74   241+        MVO    TEMPLATE(5),WORKAREA(4)
00024C F384 BE7D BE74 00E7D 00E74   242+        UNPK   WORKAREA(9),TEMPLATE(5)
000252 DC07 BE75 BD92 00E75 00D92   243+        TR     WORKAREA+1(8),TRTBL-240 USE HEX TRANSLATE TABLE
000258 D207 BDE1 BE75 00DE1 00E75   244+        MVC    CONTA(8),WORKAREA+1
                                    245         HEXCN  3,CONTA+8,8         PUT SECOND WORD IN MESSAGE
00025E 5030 BE74       00E74        246+        ST     3,WORKAREA .        PUT GIVEN VALUE INTO WORKAREA
000262 F143 BE7D BE74 00E7D 00E74   247+        MVO    TEMPLATE(5),WORKAREA(4)
000268 F384 BE7D BE74 00E7D 00E74   248+        UNPK   WORKAREA(9),TEMPLATE(5)
00026E DC07 BE75 BD92 00E75 00D92   249+        TR     WORKAREA+1(8),TRTBL-240 USE HEX TRANSLATE TABLE
000274 D207 BDE9 BE75 00DE9 00E75   250+        MVC    CONTA+8(8),WORKAREA+1

                                    252 PRINT   PRNT   M17                 'YOU HAVE RETURNED'
00027A 58F0 BEC4       00EC4        253+PRINT   L      15,=V(OUTPUT) .     GET ADDRESS OF OUTPUT SUBROUTINE
00027E 0700                         254+        CNOP   0,4
000280 4540 B288       00288        255+        BAL    4,*+8 .             REG4 POINTS TO PARAMETER LIST
000284 00000DF2                     256+        DC     A(M17) .            ADDR OF ROW FOR MESSAGE TO BE PRINTED
000288 05EF                         257+        BALR   14,15 .             CALL OUTPUT ROUTINE
                                    258         PRNT   M15                 HEADER
00028A 58F0 BEC4       00EC4        259+        L      15,=V(OUTPUT) .     GET ADDRESS OF OUTPUT SUBROUTINE
00028E 0700                         260+        CNOP   0,4
000290 4540 B298       00298        261+        BAL    4,*+8 .             REG4 POINTS TO PARAMETER LIST
000294 00000DA2                     262+        DC     A(M15) .            ADDR OF ROW FOR MESSAGE TO BE PRINTED
000298 05EF                         263+        BALR   14,15 .             CALL OUTPUT ROUTINE
                                    264         PRNT   M16                 'XXX --> XXX --> XXX'
00029A 58F0 BEC4       00EC4        265+        L      15,=V(OUTPUT) .     GET ADDRESS OF OUTPUT SUBROUTINE
00029E 0700                         266+        CNOP   0,4
0002A0 4540 B2A8       002A8        267+        BAL    4,*+8 .             REG4 POINTS TO PARAMETER LIST
0002A4 00000DAE                     268+        DC     A(M16) .            ADDR OF ROW FOR MESSAGE TO BE PRINTED
0002A8 05EF                         269+        BALR   14,15 .             CALL OUTPUT ROUTINE

                                    271         PRNT   M3                  2 PTS FOR RETURNING
0002AA 58F0 BEC4       00EC4        272+        L      15,=V(OUTPUT) .     GET ADDRESS OF OUTPUT SUBROUTINE
0002AE 0700                         273+        CNOP   0,4
0002B0 4540 B2B8       002B8        274+        BAL    4,*+8 .             REG4 POINTS TO PARAMETER LIST
0002B4 00000B7A                     275+        DC     A(M3) .             ADDR OF ROW FOR MESSAGE TO BE PRINTED
0002B8 05EF                         276+        BALR   14,15 .             CALL OUTPUT ROUTINE
                                    277         GIVE   2
0002BA 5800 B684       00684        278+        L      0,SCORE
0002BE 4A00 BEEE       00EEE        279+        AH     0,=H'2'
0002C2 5000 B684       00684        280+        ST     0,SCORE
0002C6 D52F BA74 BA34 00A74 00A34   281         CLC    SREGS+3(48),BREGS+4   WERE REGS 2-13 RESTORED
0002CC 4780 B332       00332        282         BE     OK1                 YES,BRANCH
                                    283 TAMPER  PRNT   M5                  YOU DIDN'T RESTORE REGS
0002D0 58F0 BEC4       00EC4        284+TAMPER  L      15,=V(OUTPUT) .     GET ADDRESS OF OUTPUT SUBROUTINE
0002D4                              285+        CNOP   0,4
0002D4 4540 B2DC       002DC        286+        BAL    4,*+8 .             REG4 POINTS TO PARAMETER LIST
0002D8 00000BCE                     287+        DC     A(M5) .             ADDR OF ROW FOR MESSAGE TO BE PRINTED
0002DC 05EF                         288+        BALR   14,15 .             CALL OUTPUT ROUTINE
                                    289         REGDUMP 1,13,SREGS         DUMP REGS 1-13
0002DE 58F0 BEDC       00EDC        290+        L      15,=V(RDUMP) .      GET ADDR OF REG DUMPING ROUTINE
0002E2 0700                         291+        CNOP   0,4
0002E4 4540 B2F4       002F4        292+        BAL    4,*+16
0002E8 00000001                     293+        DC     F'1' .              STARTING REG NUMBER
0002EC 0000000D                     294+        DC     F'13' .             STOPPING REG NUMBER
0002F0 00000A70                     295+        DC     A(SREGS+4) .        ADDRESS WHERE REGS ARE LOCATED
0002F4 05EF                         296+        BALR   14,15
                                    297         PRNT   M6                  REGISTERS SENT WERE:
0002F6 58F0 BEC4       00EC4        298+        L      15,=V(OUTPUT) .     GET ADDRESS OF OUTPUT SUBROUTINE
0002FA 0700                         299+        CNOP   0,4
0002FC 4540 B304       00304        300+        BAL    4,*+8 .             REG4 POINTS TO PARAMETER LIST
000300 00000C12                     301+        DC     A(M6) .             ADDR OF ROW FOR MESSAGE TO BE PRINTED
000304 05EF                         302+        BALR   14,15 .             CALL OUTPUT ROUTINE
                                    303         REGDUMP 1,13,BREGS         DUMP REGS 1-13
000306 58F0 BEDC       00EDC        304+        L      15,=V(RDUMP) .      GET ADDR OF REG DUMPING ROUTINE
00030A 0700                         305+        CNOP   0,4
00030C 4540 B31C       0031C        306+        BAL    4,*+16
000310 00000001                     307+        DC     F'1' .              STARTING REG NUMBER
000314 0000000D                     308+        DC     F'13' .             STOPPING REG NUMBER
000318 00000A30                     309+        DC     A(BREGS) .          ADDRESS WHERE REGS ARE LOCATED
00031C 05EF                         310+        BALR   14,15
                                    311         PRNT   DOUBLE
00031E 58F0 BEC4       00EC4        312+        L      15,=V(OUTPUT) .     GET ADDRESS OF OUTPUT SUBROUTINE
000322 0700                         313+        CNOP   0,4
000324 4540 B32C       0032C        314+        BAL    4,*+8 .             REG4 POINTS TO PARAMETER LIST
000328 00000E5E                     315+        DC     A(DOUBLE) .         ADDR OF ROW FOR MESSAGE TO BE PRINTX
00032C 05EF                         *           ED
00032E 47F0 B34E       0034E        316+        BALR   14,15 .             CALL OUTPUT ROUTINE
                                    317         B      OK2
                                    318 OK1     PRNT   M4                  3 PTS FOR RESTORING REGISTERS
000332 58F0 BEC4       00EC4        319+OK1     L      15,=V(OUTPUT) .     GET ADDRESS OF OUTPUT SUBROUTINE
000336 0700                         320+        CNOP   0,4
000338 4540 B340       00340        321+        BAL    4,*+8 .             REG4 POINTS TO PARAMETER LIST
00033C 00000BA8                     322+        DC     A(M4) .             ADDR OF ROW FOR MESSAGE TO BE PRINTED
000340 05EF                         323+        BALR   14,15 .             CALL OUTPUT ROUTINE
                                    324         GIVE   3
000342 5800 B684       00684        325+        L      0,SCORE
000346 4A00 BEF0       00EF0        326+        AH     0,=H'3'
00034A 5000 B684       00684        327+        ST     0,SCORE
00034E                              328 OK2     EQU    *

00034E 9500 BAD6       00AD6        330         CLI    BADR1SW,X'00'       IS REGISTER ONE ALRIGHT
000352 4770 B4B2       004B2        331         BNE    OUTOFB              NO, TELL STUDENT
000356 9500 BAD7       00AD7        332         CLI    BADIWSW,X'00'       IS INDIRECT WORD OK
```

```
LOC   OBJECT CODE    ADDR1 ADDR2 STMT   SOURCE STATEMENT                                    10 JUN 74

00035A 4770 B49A          0049A 333        BNE    BADIDR               NO, TELL STUDENT

00035E 5810 B470          00A70 335        L      1,SREGS+4            GET STUDENT'S REGISTER 1
003362 1851                     336        LR     5,1                  SAVE FOR LATER LENGTH CHECK
000364 D203 B98C 1000 009BC 00000 337      MVC    TSAVE(4),0(1)
00036A 5810 B98C          0098C 338        L      1,TSAVE              WAS PROPER LENGTH RETURNED
00036E D500 A031 5000 00031 00000 339      CLC    OUTLEN(1),0(5)       NO, BRANCH
000374 4770 B3E6          003E6 340        BNE    BADLEN               2 POINTS FOR PROPER LENGTH
                                341        PRNT   M10
000378 58F0 BEC4          00EC4 342+       L      15,=V(OUTPUT) .      GET ADDRESS OF OUTPUT SUBROUTINE
00037C                          343+       CNOP   0,4
00037C 4540 B384          00384 344+       BAL    4,*+8 .              REG4 POINTS TO PARAMETER LIST
000380 00000C7E                 345+       DC     A(M10) .             ADDR OF ROW FOR MESSAGE TO BE PRINTED
000384 05EF                     346+       BALR   14,15 .              CALL OUTPUT ROUTINE
                                347        GIVE   2
000386 5800 B684          00684 348+       L      0,SCORE
00038A 4A00 BEEE          00EEE 349+       AH     0,=H'2'
00038E 5000 B684          00684 350+       ST     0,SCORE

000392 1B33                     352        SR     3,3                  CLEAR REG 3
000394 4330 A031          00031 353        IC     3,OUTLEN             GET LENGTH OF ANSWER
000398 0630                     354        BCTR   3,0                  DECREMENT FOR AN EXECUTE
00039A 4430 B42E          0042E 355        EX     3,COMP               COMPARE STUDENT'S ANSWER WITH TABLE
00039E 4770 B43A          0043A 356        BNE    WRONG                IF WRONG, BRANCH
                                357        PRNT   M12                  8 PTS FOR RIGHT ANSWER
0003A2 58F0 BEC4          00EC4 358+       L      15,=V(OUTPUT) .      GET ADDRESS OF OUTPUT SUBROUTINE
0003A6 0700                     359+       CNOP   0,4
0003A8 4540 B3B0          003B0 360+       BAL    4,*+8 .              REG4 POINTS TO PARAMETER LIST
0003AC 00000CFA                 361+       DC     A(M12) .             ADDR OF ROW FOR MESSAGE TO BE PRINTED
0003B0 05EF                     362+       BALR   14,15 .              CALL OUTPUT ROUTINE
                                363        GIVE   8
0003B2 5800 B684          00684 364+       L      0,SCORE
0003B6 4A00 BEF2          00EF2 365+       AH     0,=H'8'
0003BA 5000 B684          00684 366+       ST     0,SCORE

0003BE D527 BAAC BEFC 00AAC 00EFC 368      CLC    COPY(40),MSTRING     WAS ANY DATA MODIFIED
0003C4 4780 B4C6          004C6 369        BE     LOOPEND              NO, BRANCH TO END OF LOOP

                                371        PRNT   M13                  -5 PTS FOR ALTERING DATA
0003C8 58F0 BEC4          00EC4 372+       L      15,=V(OUTPUT) .      GET ADDRESS OF OUTPUT SUBROUTINE
0003CC                          373+       CNOP   0,4
0003CC 4540 B3D4          003D4 374+       BAL    4,*+8 .              REG4 POINTS TO PARAMETER LIST
0003D0 0000001A                 375+       DC     A(M13) .             ADDR OF ROW FOR MESSAGE TO BE PRINTED
0003D4 05EF                     376+       BALR   14,15 .              CALL OUTPUT ROUTINE
                                377        GIVE   -5
0003D6 5800 B684          00684 378+       L      0,SCORE
0003DA 4A00 BEF4          00EF4 379+       AH     0,=H'-5'
0003DE 5000 B684          00684 380+       ST     0,SCORE
0003E2 47F0 B4C6          004C6 381        B      LOOPEND

0003E6 92FF BAD5          00AD5 383 BADLEN MVI    ERRFLAG,X'FF'        SET ERROR FLAG
0003EA 1B33                     384        SR     3,3                  CLEAR A REGISTER
0003EC 4330 A031          00031 385        IC     3,OUTLEN             PICK UP CORRECT LENGTH
                                386        DECCN  3,CLEN,4             PUT CORRECT LENGTH IN MESSAGE

0003F0 4E30 BE68          00E68 387+       CVD    3,DECTEMP            CONVERT REG TO PACKED DECIMAL
0003F4 D20F BE92 BEA2 00E92 00EA2 388+     MVC    DECTEMP2(16),DECMASK .  PUT MASK INTO TEMPORARY AREA
0003FA 5010 BE70          00E70 389+       ST     1,EDCROCK PRESERVE 1
0003FE 4110 BEA1          00EA1 390+       LA     1,DECTEMP2+15        MAKE UP FOR FORCED SIGNIFICANCE
000402 DF0F BE92 BE68 00E92 00E68 391+     EDMK   DECTEMP2(16),DECTEMP .  UNPACK NUMBER & EDIT ZEROS
000408 47B0 B412          00412 392+       BNL    **+10 IF RESULT NON-NEGATIVE, SKIP SIGN
00040C 0610                     393+       BCTR   1,0 DECREMENT ADDRESS
00040E 9260 1000          00000 394+       MVI    0(1),C'-' MOVE IN MINUS SIGN
000412 5810 BE70          00E70 395+       L      1,EDCROCK RESTORE REGISTER 1
000416 D203 BCF5 BE9E 00CF5 00E9E 396+     MVC    CLEN(4),DECTEMP2+12  MOVE RESULT INTO ANSWER AREA
                                397        PRNT   M11                  INVALID LENGTH FIELD
00041C 58F0 BEC4          00EC4 398+       L      15,=V(OUTPUT) .      GET ADDRESS OF OUTPUT SUBROUTINE
000420                          399+       CNOP   0,4
000420 4540 B428          00428 400+       BAL    4,*+8 .              REG4 POINTS TO PARAMETER LIST
000424 00000CB2                 401+       DC     A(M11) .             ADDR OF ROW FOR MESSAGE TO BE PRINTED
000428 05EF                     402+       BALR   14,15 .              CALL OUTPUT ROUTINE
00042A 47F0 B4C6          004C6 403        B      LOOPEND

00042E D500 A034 1000 00034 00000 405 COMP CLC    ANSWER(0),0(1)       DO ANSWERS MATCH
000434 D200 BD92 89C0 00D92 009C0 406 CMOVE MVC   CANS(0),BOZO         MOVE CORRECT ANSWER TO MESSAGE

00043A 92FF BAD5          00AD5 408 WRONG  MVI    ERRFLAG,X'FF'        SET ERROR FLAG
00043E 9240 BD92          00D92 409        MVI    CANS,C' '            BLANK OUT THE ANSWER AREA
000442 D20E BD93 BD92 00D93 00D92 410      MVC    CANS+1(15),CANS      IN MESSAGE FOR SHORT ANSWERS

000448 4160 0005          00005 412        LA     6,5                  SET LOOP COUNTER
00044C 4110 A030          00030 413        LA     1,ANSWER-4           GET START OF SOURCE FIELD
000450 4120 B988          00988 414        LA     2,BOZO-8             AND OBJECT FIELD

000454 4110 1004          00004 416 LOOPER LA     1,4(,1)              BUMP SOURCE POINTER
000458 4120 2008          00008 417        LA     2,8(,2)              BUMP OBJECT POINTER
                                418        HEXCN  1,ZORCH,,CORE        CONVERT 4 BYTES OF SOURCE
00045C D203 BE74 1000 00E74 00000 419+     MVC    WORKAREA(4),0(1) .PUT GIVEN VALUE INTO WORKAREA
000462 F143 BE7D BE74 00E7D 00E74 420+     MVO    TEMPLATE(5),WORKAREA(4)
000468 F384 BE74 BE7D 00E74 00E7D 421+     UNPK   WORKAREA(9),TEMPLATE(5)
00046E DC07 BE75 BD92 00E75 00D92 422+     TR     WORKAREA+1(8),TRTBL-240 USE HEX TRANSLATE TABLE
000474 D207 BE9E BE75 00E9E 00E75 423+     MVC    ZORCH(8),WORKAREA+1
00047A D207 2000 B9E8 00000 009E8 424+     MVC    0(8,2),ZORCH         PUT IN OBJECT FIELD
000480 4660 B454          00454 425        BCT    6,LOOPER             PROCESS WHOLE FIELD

000484 4430 B434          00434 427        EX     3,CMOVE              MOVE ANSWER TO AREA
                                428        PRNT   M14                  INCORRECT ANSWER RETURNED
000488 58F0 BEC4          00EC4 429+       L      15,=V(OUTPUT) .      GET ADDRESS OF OUTPUT SUBROUTINE
00048C                          430+       CNOP   0,4
00048C 4540 B494          00494 431+       BAL    4,*+8 .              REG4 POINTS TO PARAMETER LIST
000490 00000D56                 432+       DC     A(M14) .             ADDR OF ROW FOR MESSAGE TO BE PRINTED
000494 05EF                     433+       BALR   14,15 .              CALL OUTPUT ROUTINE
000496 47F0 B4C6          004C6 434        B      LOOPEND

00049A 92FF BAD5          00AD5 436 BADIDR MVI    ERRFLAG,X'FF'        CAUSE DUMP
                                437        PRNT   M19
00049E 58F0 BEC4          00EC4 438+       L      15,=V(OUTPUT) .      GET ADDRESS OF OUTPUT SUBROUTINE
```

98

```
   LOC   OBJECT CODE      ADDR1 ADDR2  STMT    SOURCE STATEMENT                                              10 JUN 74

 0004A2 0700                            439+         CNOP  0,4
 0004A4 4540 B4AC          004AC        440+         BAL   4,**8 .         REG4 POINTS TO PARAMETER LIST
 0004A8 00000E0C                        441+         DC    A(M19) .        ADDR OF ROW FOR MESSAGE TO BE PRINTED
 0004AC 05EF                            442+         BALR  14,15 .         CALL OUTPUT ROUTINE
 0004AE 47F0 B4C6          004C6        443          B     LOOPEND         END OF THIS TEST


 0004B2 92FF BAD5    00AD5              445 OUTOFB   MVI   ERRFLAG,X'FF'    INDICATE ERROR TO CAUSE DUMP LATER
                                        446          PRNT  M9              "INVALID ADDRESS RETURNED"
 0004B6 58F0 BEC4          00EC4        447+         L     15,=V(OUTPUT) . GET ADDRESS OF OUTPUT SUBROUTINE
 0004BA 0700                            448+         CNOP  0,4
 0004BC 4540 B4C4          004C4        449+         BAL   4,**8 .         REG4 POINTS TO PARAMETER LIST
 0004C0 00000C52                        450+         DC    A(M9) .         ADDR OF ROW FOR MESSAGE TO BE PRINTED
 0004C4 05EF                            451+         BALR  14,15 .         CALL OUTPUT ROUTINE


 0004C6 95FF BAD5    00AD5              453 LOOPEND  CLI   ERRFLAG,X'FF'    WAS AN ERROR ENCOUNTERED
 0004CA 4770 B506          00506        454          BNE   AGAIN           NO,BRANCH

 0004CE D200 BAD5 0000 00AD5 00000      456          MVC   ERRFLAG,X'00'   CLEAR ERROR FLAG
                                        457          PRNT  M8              HERE IS A DUMP OF YOUR PROGRAM
 0004D4 58F0 BEC4          00EC4        458+         L     15,=V(OUTPUT) . GET ADDRESS OF OUTPUT SUBROUTINE
 0004D8                                 459+         CNOP  0,4
 0004D8 4540 B4E0          004E0        460+         BAL   4,**8 .         REG4 POINTS TO PARAMETER LIST
 0004DC 00000C2C                        461+         DC    A(M8) .         ADDR OF ROW FOR MESSAGE TO BE PRINTED
 0004E0 05EF                            462+         BALR  14,15 .         CALL OUTPUT ROUTINE
                                        463          PRNT  DOUBLE
 0004E2 58F0 BEC4          00EC4        464+         L     15,=V(OUTPUT) . GET ADDRESS OF OUTPUT SUBROUTINE
 0004E6 0700                            465+         CNOP  0,4
 0004E8 4540 B4F0          004F0        466+         BAL   4,**8 .         REG4 POINTS TO PARAMETER LIST
                                        467+         DC    A(DOUBLE) .     ADDR OF ROW FOR MESSAGE TO BE PRINTX
 0004EC 00000E5E                        +                  ED
 0004F0 05EF                            468+         BALR  14,15 .         CALL OUTPUT ROUTINE
                                        469          DUMP  MP1,DUMMY       DUMP THE STUDENT'S PROGRAM
 0004F2 58F0 BEE0          00EE0        470+         L     15,=V(SNAP) .   GET ADDR OF SNAP ROUTINE
 0004F6 0700                            471+         CNOP  0,4 .           ALIGN TO FULL WORD BOUNDARY
 0004F8 4540 B504          00504        472+         BAL   4,**12 .        REG 4 POINTS TO PARAMETER LIST
 0004FC 0000000000000000              473+         DC    A(MP1,DUMMY) .  A(STARTING ADDR, STOPPING ADDR)
 000504 05EF                            474+         BALR  14,15 .         BRANCH TO SNAP
                                        475 *                             THE REGISTERS HAVE ALREADY
                                        476 *                             BEEN DUMPED IF THEY WERE NOT
                                        477 *                             RESTORED. OTHERWISE THEY ARE USELESS


 000506                                 479 AGAIN    EQU   *
 000506 58A0 A02C          0002C        480          L     10,NEXT         GET ADDRESS OF NEXT ENTRY IN TABLE
 00050A 47F0 B0AE          000AE        481          B     LOOP            GO THRU LOOP AGAIN


 00050E                                 483 DONE     EQU   *               FINISHED WITH THIS TUDENT
                                        484 *
                                        485 *PERFORM GRADER HOUSE-KEEPING AND RETURN TO SUPERVISOR
                                        486 *

                                        488+         EPILOG
                                        489+         ENTRY OLDSPIE
 00050E                                 490+ALLDONE  EQU   *
 00050E D603 B688 B688 00688 00688      491+         OC    BADJCL(4),BADJCL DID STUDENT HAVE PROPER CONTROL CARDS
 000514 4780 B53A          0053A        492+         BZ    JCLOK YES, BRANCH
 000518 58F0 BEC4          00EC4        493+         L     15,=V(OUTPUT) . GET ADDRESS OF OUTPUT SUBROUTINE
 00051C                                 494+         CNOP  0,4
 00051C 4540 B524          00524        495+         BAL   4,**8 .         REG4 POINTS TO PARAMETER LIST
                                        496+         DC    A(BJCL1) .      ADDR OF ROW FOR MESSAGE TO BE PRINTEX
 000520 0000068C                        +                  D
 000524 05EF                            497+         BALR  14,15 .         CALL OUTPUT ROUTINE
 000526 47F0 B588          00588        498+         B     CLOSE FINISH GRADER PROCESSING FOR RETURN
 00052A 58F0 BEC4          00EC4        499+BADNAME  L     15,=V(OUTPUT) . GET ADDRESS OF OUTPUT SUBROUTINE
 00052E 0700                            500+         CNOP  0,4
 000530 4540 B538          00538        501+         BAL   4,**8 .         REG4 POINTS TO PARAMETER LIST
                                        502+         DC    A(BDNM1) .      ADDR OF ROW FOR MESSAGE TO BE PRINTEX
 000534 000006EC                        +                  D
 000538 05EF                            503+         BALR  14,15 .         CALL OUTPUT ROUTINE
 00053A 5840 B684          00684        504+JCLOK    L     4,SCORE GET STUDENTS TOTAL SCORE
 00053E 1244                            505+         LTR   4,4 IF TOTAL SCORE IS NEGATIVE,
 000540 4720 B546          00546        506+         BP    NOWOK SET SCORE TO 0
 000544 1844                            507+         SR    4,4
 000546                                 508+NOWOK    EQU   * CONVERT SCORE TO DECIMAL STRING
 000546 4E40 BE68          00E68        509+         CVD   4,DECTEMP .     CONVERT REG TO PACKED DECIMAL
 00054A D20F BE92 BEA2 00E92 00EA2      510+         MVC   DECTEMP2(16),DECMASK . PUT MASK INTO TEMPORARY AREA
 000550 5010 BE70          00E70        511+         ST    1,EDCROCK PRESERVE 1
 000554 4110 BEA1          00EA1        512+         LA    1,DECTEMP2+15 MAKE UP FOR FORCED SIGNIFICANCE
 000558 DF0F BE92 BE68 00E92 00E68      513+         EDMK  DECTEMP2(16),DECTEMP . UNPACK NUMBER & EDIT ZEROS
 00055E 47B0 B568          00568        514+         BNL   **10 IF RESULT NON-NEGATIVE, SKIP SIGN
 000562 0610                            515+         BCTR  1,0 DECREMENT POINTER
 000564 9260 1000    00000              516+         MVI   0(1),C'-' MOVE IN MINUS SIGN
 000568 5810 BE70          00E70        517+         L     1,EDCROCK RESTORE REGISTER 1
 00056C D202 B67D BE9F 0067D 00E9F      518+         MVC   TOTSCORE(3),DECTEMP2+13 . MOVE RESULT INTO ANSWER AREA
 000572 58D0 BEE4          00EE4        519+         L     13,=A(SAVEAREA) POINT TO REGISTER SAVE AREA
 000576 58F0 BEC4          00EC4        520+         L     15,=V(OUTPUT) . GET ADDRESS OF OUTPUT SUBROUTINE
 00057A 0700                            521+         CNOP  0,4
 00057C 4540 B584          005B4        522+         BAL   4,**8 .         REG4 POINTS TO PARAMETER LIST
                                        523+         DC    A(NSGM) .       ADDR OF ROW FOR MESSAGE TO BE PRINTED
 000580 0000064E                        +
 000584 05EF                            524+         BALR  14,15 .         CALL OUTPUT ROUTINE
 000586 0700                            525+         CNOP  0,4 ALIGN LIST TO FULLWORD
 000588 4510 B590          00590        526+CLOSE    BAL   1,**8 LOAD REG1 W/LIST ADDR
 00058C 80                             527+         DC    AL1(128) OPTION BYTE
 00058D 000000                          528+         DC    AL3(DCBOUT) DCB ADDRESS
 000590 0A14                            529+         SVC   20 ISSUE CLOSE SVC
                                        530+*
                                        531+*        STOP TIMER
                                        532+*
 000592 4110 0001          00001        533+         LA    1,1 CANCEL THIS TASK                          20272
 000596 0A2E                            534+         SVC   46 ISSUE TTIMER                               20272
 000598 5810 BEE8          00EE8        535+         L     1,=V(DCBOUT) .  GET ADDRESS OF DCB
 00059C 58F0 1014          00014        536+         L     15,20(0,1) LOAD BUFCB ADDRESS
 0005A0 9601 1017    00017              537+         OI    23(1),1 INDICATE NO BUFCB ADDR
 0005A4 1BEE                            538+         SR    14,14 CLEAR REGISTER
 0005A6 43E0 F005          00005        539+         IC    14,5(0,15) COMPUTE SIZE
 0005AA 4CE0 F006          00006        540+         MH    14,6(0,15) TO BE FREED
 0005AE 4100 E008          00008        541+         LA    0,8(0,14) ACCOUNT FOR BCB
```

# 2. ASSEMBLY LANGUAGE PROBLEMS

2-85

A4G    GRADER FOR CONSTANT PROCESSOR -- A4 02/16/74                                                       PAGE   7

```
  LOC  OBJECT CODE   ADDR1 ADDR2  STMT   SOURCE STATEMENT                                                     10 JUN 74

0005B2 9140 F004      00004       542+        TM    4(15),X'40' IS BUFCB 16 BYTES
0005B6 47E0 B58E      0058E       543+        BNO   **3 BRANCH IF BUFCB = 8 BYTES
0005BA 4100 E010      00010       544+        LA    0,16(0,14) AJUST SIZE PLUS 16
0005BE 4110 F000      00000       545+        LA    1,0(0,15) LOAD AREA ADDRESS
0005C2 0A0A                       546+        SVC   10 ISSUE FREEMAIN SVC
                                  547+**
                                  548+**RESTORE CONTROL TO OLD SPIE AND RETURN
                                  549+**
0005C4 58C0 B5E0      005E0       550+        L     12,OLDSPIE LOAD A(OLD PICA)
0005C8 181C                       551+        LR    1,(12) LOAD PARAMETER REG 1
0005CA 0A0E                       552+        SVC   14 ISSUE SPIE SVC
0005CC 58D0 D004      00004       553+        L     13,4(,13) CHAIN BACK TO SA IN SUPERVISOR
0005D0 58F0 B684      00684       554+        L     15,SCORE SET RETURN CODE TO SCORE
0005D4 58E0 D00C      0000C       555+        L     14,12(13,0) RESTORE REGISTER 14
0005D8 98DC D014      00014       556+        LM    0,12,20(13) RESTORE THE REGISTERS
0005DC 07FE                       557+        BR    14 RETURN
                                  558+        DROP  11
0005E0                            559+OLDSPIE DS    F ADDRESS OF OLD PICA
0005E4 00480000                   560+INTRO   DC    AL2(72,0) . GENERATE RECORD DESCRIPTOR WORD
                                  561+        DC    CL60'1**** ASSEMBLER PROBLEM GRADER HAS BEEN ENTERED FORX
0005E8 F15C5C5C40C1E2                 +             STUDENT '
00062C 4040404040404040          562+NAME    DC    CL8' ' .        ASSIGN STORAGE FOR THE VARIABLE
00062C 00220000                   563+HDR3    DC    AL2(34,0) . GENERATE RECORD DESCRIPTOR WORD
000630 F0D7D9D6C7D9C1D4           564+        DC    CL22'0PROGRAM ENTRY POINT: '
000646 4040404040404040          565+ENTRY   DC    CL8' ' .        ASSIGN STORAGE FOR THE VARIABLE
00064E 00340000                   566+MSGM    DC    AL2(52,0) . GENERATE RECORD DESCRIPTOR WORD
000652 605C5C5C40E3C5E2           567+        DC    CL43'-*** TESTING COMPLETE, YOUR TOTAL SCORE IS '
00067D 4040404040                 568+TOTSCORE DC   CL5' ' .        ASSIGN STORAGE FOR THE VARIABLE
000682 0000
000684 00000000                   569+SCORE   DC    F'0' RUNNING TOTAL FOR STUDENT
000688 00000000                   570+BADJCL  DC    F'0' FLAG FOR THE BATCH MONITOR
00068C 00600000                   571+BJCL1   DC    AL2(96,0) . GENERATE RECORD DESCRIPTOR WORD
                                  572+        DC    CL92'-***YOUR DECK DID NOT HAVE THE PROPER MONITOR CONTRX
000690 605C5C5CE8D6E4D9                +             OL CARDS...YOUR SCORE HAS BEEN NULLIFIED.'
0006EC 00480000                   573+BDNM1   DC    AL2(72,0) . GENERATE RECORD DESCRIPTOR WORD
                                  574+        DC    CL68'-***YOUR CSECT IS NOT LABELLED MP1 ... EXECUTION HAX
0006F0 605C5C5CE8D6E4D9                +             S BEEN TERMINATED'
                                  575+**
                                  576+**REGISTER SAVE AREA STACK TO BE USED BY MP1 GRADER'S SUBROUTINES
                                  577+**
                                  578+**--ASSUMPTION: SUBROUTINE CALLS WILL BE AT MOST 9 LEVELS DEEP
                                  579+**
000734                            580+SAVEAREA DS   (9*18)F
                                  581+**


                                  583 *
                                  584 *GRADER'S MESSAGES AND WORKAREAS
                                  585 *

00098C                            587 TSAVE   DS    F                          ALIGNED TEMPORARY SAVE AREA
0009C0                            588 BOZO    DS    10F                        INTERMEDIATE ANSWER AREA
0009E8                            589 ZORCH   DS    2F                         DITTO
0009F0                            590 GREGS   DS    16F                        GRADER'S SAVE AREA
000A30 00000EFCFFFFFFFF           591 BREGS   DC    A(MSTRING),11F'-1',A(ISTUDSAVE),A(RETURN),A(MP1)
000A6C                            592 SREGS   DS    16F                        REGS 0-15 RETURNED BY STUDENT
000AAC                            593 COPY    DS    CL40                       COPY OF DATA SENT TO STUDENT
000AD4                            594 ALEN    DS    AL1                        LENGTH FROM TABLE OF ANSWER
000AD5 00                         595 ERRFLAG DC    X'00'                      GRADER ERROR FLAG, ERROR=X'FF'
000AD6 00                         596 BADR1SW DC    X'00'                      SWITCH FOR REGISTER 1 CHECKING
000AD7 00                         597 BADIWSW DC    X'00'                      SWITCH FOR INDIRECT WORD CHECKING

                                  599 M1      MSG   (,'0YOU HAVE RECEIVED 10 POINTS FOR SUCCESSFULLY ASSEMBL?
                                                    ING YOUR PROGRAM')
000AD8 004A0000                   600+M1      DC    AL2(74,0) . GENERATE RECORD DESCRIPTOR WORD
                                  601+        DC    CL70'0YOU HAVE RECEIVED 10 POINTS FOR SUCCESSFULLY ASSEMX
000ADC F0E8D6E440C8C1E5                +             BLING YOUR PROGRAM'
                                  602 M2      MSG   (,'-***WE WILL PASS YOU A TYPE',MT,2,,' CONVERSION ON ',X
                                                    MSTR,40)
000B22 00580000                   603+M2      DC    AL2(88,0) . GENERATE RECORD DESCRIPTOR WORD
000B26 605C5C5CE6C540E6           604+        DC    CL27'-***WE WILL PASS YOU A TYPE'
000B41 4040                       605+MT      DC    CL2' ' .        ASSIGN STORAGE FOR THE VARIABLE
000B43 40C3D6D5E5C5D9E2           606+        DC    CL15' CONVERSION ON '
000B52 4040404040404040           607+MSTR    DC    CL40' ' .       ASSIGN STORAGE FOR THE VARIABLE
                                  608 M3      MSG   (,'02 POINTS FOR RETURNING CONTROL TO GRADER')
000B7A 002E0000                   609+M3      DC    AL2(46,0) . GENERATE RECORD DESCRIPTOR WORD
000B7E F0F240D7D6C9D5E3           610+        DC    CL42'02 POINTS FOR RETURNING CONTROL TO GRADER'
                                  611 M4      MSG   (,' 3 POINTS FOR RESTORING REGISTERS')
000BA8 00260000                   612+M4      DC    AL2(38,0) . GENERATE RECORD DESCRIPTOR WORD
000BAC 40F340D7D6C9D5E3           613+        DC    CL34' 3 POINTS FOR RESTORING REGISTERS'
                                  614 M5      MSG   (,'0YOU HAVE NOT RESTORED REGISTERS 2-13 ... VALUES RETUX
                                                    RNED WERE:')
000BCE 00440000                   615+M5      DC    AL2(68,0) . GENERATE RECORD DESCRIPTOR WORD
                                  616+        DC    CL64'0YOU HAVE NOT RESTORED REGISTERS 2-13 ... VALUES REX
000BD2 F0E8D6E440C8C1E5                +             TURNED WERE:'
                                  617 M6      MSG   (,'0REGISTERS SENT WERE:')
000C12 001A0000                   618+M6      DC    AL2(26,0) . GENERATE RECORD DESCRIPTOR WORD
000C16 F0D9C5C7C9E2E3C5           619+        DC    CL22'0REGISTERS SENT WERE:'
                                  620 M8      MSG   (,'-***HERE IS A DUMP OF YOUR PROGRAM')
000C2C 00260000                   621+M8      DC    AL2(38,0) . GENERATE RECORD DESCRIPTOR WORD
000C30 605C5C5CC8C5D9C5           622+        DC    CL34'-***HERE IS A DUMP OF YOUR PROGRAM'
                                  623 M9      MSG   (,'0INVALID ADDRESS RETURNED IN REGISTER 1')
000C52 002C0000                   624+M9      DC    AL2(44,0) . GENERATE RECORD DESCRIPTOR WORD
000C56 F0C9D5E5C1D3C9C4           625+        DC    CL40'0INVALID ADDRESS RETURNED IN REGISTER 1'
                                  626 M10     MSG   (,' 2 POINTS FOR SPECIFYING PROPER LENGTH OF RESULT')
000C7E 00340000                   627+M10     DC    AL2(52,0) . GENERATE RECORD DESCRIPTOR WORD
000C82 40F240D7D6C9D5E3           628+        DC    CL48' 2 POINTS FOR SPECIFYING PROPER LENGTH OF RESULT'
                                  629 M11     MSG   (,'0YOU HAVE RETURNED WRONG LENGTH FOR ANSWER, CORRECT LX
                                                    ENGTH IS: ',CLEN,4)
000CB2 00480000                   630+M11     DC    AL2(72,0) . GENERATE RECORD DESCRIPTOR WORD
                                  631+        DC    CL63'0YOU HAVE RETURNED WRONG LENGTH FOR ANSWER, CORRECTX
000CB6 F0E8D6E440C8C1E5                +             LENGTH IS: '
000CF5 4040404040                 632+CLEN    DC    CL5' ' .        ASSIGN STORAGE FOR THE VARIABLE
                                  633 M12     MSG   (,' 8 POINTS FOR CORRECT ANSWER')
000CFA 00200000                   634+M12     DC    AL2(32,0) . GENERATE RECORD DESCRIPTOR WORD
000CFE 40F840D7D6C9D5E3           635+        DC    CL28' 8 POINTS FOR CORRECT ANSWER'
                                  636 M13     MSG   (,'0-5 POINTS FOR ALTERING DATA TRANSMITTED TO YOUR PROGX
                                                    RAM')
00001A 003C0000                   637+M13     DC    AL2(60,0) . GENERATE RECORD DESCRIPTOR WORD
                                  638+        DC    CL56'0-5 POINTS FOR ALTERING DATA TRANSMITTED TO YOUR PRX
```

100

```
    LOC   OBJECT CODE      ADDR1 ADDR2  STMT   SOURCE STATEMENT                                        10 JUN 74

                                          +              OGRAM'
  000D1E  F060F54007D6C9D5              639 M14    MSG   (,'OYOU HAVE RETURNED INCORRECT ANSWER, CORRECT ANSWER IX
                                                         S: ',CANS,16)
  000D56  004C0000                      640+M14    DC    AL2(76,0) . GENERATE RECORD DESCRIPTOR WORD
                                        641+       DC    CL56'OYOU HAVE RETURNED INCORRECT ANSWER, CORRECT ANSWERX
  000D5A  FOE8D6E440C8C1E5                                IS: '
  000D92  4040404040404040              642+CANS   DC    CL16' ' .         ASSIGN STORAGE FOR THE VARIABLE
                                        643 M15    MSG   (,'O',,' REG 1')
  000DA2  000C0000                      644+M15    DC    AL2(12,0) . GENERATE RECORD DESCRIPTOR WORD
  000DA6  F0                            645+       DC    CL1'0'
  000DA7  40D9C5C740F140                646+       DC    CL7' REG 1'
                                        647 M16    MSG   (,' ',REGONE,8,,' ----> ',REGON,6,,': ',IWORD,8,,' ----->X
                                                         ',IADR,6,,': ',CONTA,16)
  000DAE  00440000                      648+M16    DC    AL2(68,0) . GENERATE RECORD DESCRIPTOR WORD
  000DB2  40                            649+       DC    CL1' '
  000DB3  4040404040404040              650+REGONE DC    CL8' ' .         ASSIGN STORAGE FOR THE VARIABLE
  000DBB  40606060606060E40             651+       DC    CL7' ----> '
  000DC2  404040404040                  652+REGON  DC    CL5' ----> '     ASSIGN STORAGE FOR THE VARIABLE
  000DC8  7A40                          653+       DC    CL2': ' .
  000DCA  4040404040404040              654+IWORD  DC    CL8' ' .         ASSIGN STORAGE FOR THE VARIABLE
  000DD2  40606060606060E40             655+       DC    CL7' ----> '
  000DD9  404040404040                  656+IADR   DC    CL6' ----> '     ASSIGN STORAGE FOR THE VARIABLE
  000DDF  7A40                          657+       DC    CL2': ' .
  000DE1  4040404040404040              658+CONTA  DC    CL17' ' .        ASSIGN STORAGE FOR THE VARIABLE
                                        659 M17    MSG   (,'-***YOU HAVE RETURNED:')
  000DF2  001A0000                      660+M17    DC    AL2(26,0) . GENERATE RECORD DESCRIPTOR WORD
  000DF6  605C5C5CE8D6E440              661+       DC    CL22'-***YOU HAVE RETURNED:'
                                        662 M19    MSG   (,'OINVALID ADDRESS IN INDIRECT WORD')
  000E0C  00260000                      663+M19    DC    AL2(38,0) . GENERATE RECORD DESCRIPTOR WORD
  000E10  FOC9D5E5C1D3C9C4              664+       DC    CL34'OINVALID ADDRESS IN INDIRECT WORD'
                                        665 M20    MSG   (,' ',R11,8,,' ----> ',R1,6,,': ',CONTI,16)
  000E32  002C0000                      666+M20    DC    AL2(44,0) . GENERATE RECORD DESCRIPTOR WORD
  000E36  40                            667+       DC    CL1' '
  000E37  4040404040404040              668+R11    DC    CL8' ' .         ASSIGN STORAGE FOR THE VARIABLE
  000E3F  40606060606060E40             669+       DC    CL7' ----> '
  000E46  404040404040                  670+R1     DC    CL6' ----> '     ASSIGN STORAGE FOR THE VARIABLE
  000E4C  7A40                          671+       DC    CL2': ' .
  000E4E  4040404040404040              672+CONTI  DC    CL16' ' .        ASSIGN STORAGE FOR THE VARIABLE
                                        673 DOUBLE MSG   (,'O')
  000E5E  00060000                      674+DOUBLE DC    AL2(6,0) . GENERATE RECORD DESCRIPTOR WORD
  000E62  F040                          675+       DC    CL2'0'

                                        677 *
                                        678 *FOR DECCN AND HEXCN
                                        679 *

                                        681        CONST
                                        682+**
                                        683+*CONSTANTS AREA USED BY SUPPLIED MACROS
                                        684+**
  000E68                                685+DECTEMP DS   D AREA USED BY DECCN
  000E70                                686+EDCROCK DS   F AREA USED BY DECCN
  000E74                                687+WORKAREA DS  OF AREA USED BY HEXCN
  000E74                                688+       DS    XL9

  000E7D  000000000F                    689+TEMPLATE DC  XL5'F' AREA USED BY HEXCN
  000E82  FOF1F2F3F4F5F6F7              690+TRTBL  DC    C'0123456789ABCDEF' TABLE FOR TRANSLATE IN HEXCN
  000E92                                691+DECTEMP2 DS  CL16 AREA USED BY DECCN
  000EA2  4020202020202020              692+DECMASK DC   X'40202020202020202020202020202120' EDIT MASK FOR DECCN
  000EB8                                693+       LTORG
  000EB8  00000000                      694        =V(PARMPROC)
  000EBC  00000000                      695        =V(TIMEOUT)
  000EC0  00000000                      696        =V(MAXTIME)
  000EC4  00000000                      697        =V(OUTPUT)
  000EC8  00000000                      698        =V(MP1)
  000ECC  00000000                      699        =V(TABLE)
  000ED0  FFFFFFFF                      700        =F'-1'
  000ED4  00000000                      701        =A(BASEPNT)
  000ED8  00000000                      702        =V(DUMMY)
  000EDC  00000000                      703        =V(RDUMP)
  000EE0  00000000                      704        =V(SNAP)
  000EE4  00000734                      705        =A(SAVEAREA)
  000EE8  00000000                      706        =V(DCBOUT)
  000EEC  000A                          707        =H'10'
  000EEE  0002                          708        =H'2'
  000EF0  0003                          709        =H'3'
  000EF2  0008                          710        =H'8'
  000EF4  FFFB                          711        =H'-5'
  000EF6  000EFC                        712        =AL3(MSTRING)

                                        714 *
                                        715 *DATA AREA FOR STUDENT
                                        716 *

  000EFC                                718        DS    OF                PUT ON A FULL WORD BOUNDARY
  000EFC                                719 MSTRING DS   CL40
  000F24                                720 STUDSAVE DS  16F               STUDENT'S SAVE AREA

                                        722 *
                                        723 *FORMAT OF TABLE ENTRY FOR GRADER
                                        724 *

  000000                                726 DATA   DSECT
  000000                                727 TYPE   DS    F                 TYPE OF CONSTANT
  000004                                728 STRING DS    CL40              CHARACTER STRING
  00002C                                729 NEXT   DS    A                 ADDRESS OF NEXT ENTRY
  000030                                730 INLEN  DS    AL1               LENGTH OF STRING
  000031                                731 OUTLEN DS    AL1               LENGTH OF ANSWER
  000032                                732 CHAR   DS    CL2               CHARACTER STRING OF TYPE
  000034                                733 ANSWER DS    CL20              VARIABLE LENGTH ANSWER
  000000                                734        END GRADER
```

## 2.5    SOLUTIONS FOR EXAMPLE PROBLEMS

## 2.5.1    Palindrome Problem -- A1

```
A1S    SAMPLE SOLUTION TO PALINDROME PROBLEM -- A1                                    PAGE    2

  LOC    OBJECT CODE    ADDR1 ADDR2    STMT    SOURCE STATEMENT                       11 JUN 74

000000                                  2 MP1      CSECT
000000                                  3          USING *,15            TELL THE ASSEMBLER MY BASE REGISTER
000000 902C D000            00000        4          STM   2,12,0(13)     SAVE REGISTERS

                                         6 *        FOLLOWING CODE REVERSES THE SECOND WORD OF THE DOUBLE-
                                         7 *        WORD STRING WE ARE CHECKING. THEN IF THE STRING WAS A PALIN-
                                         8 *        DROME THE SECOND WORD REVERSED WILL EQUAL THE FIRST WORD.

000004 1873                             10          LR    7,3            GET SECOND HALF OF STRING
000006 4190 F02F            0002F       11          LA    9,WORD-1       GET START OF STORAGE AREA
00000A 4180 0004            00004       12          LA    8,4            GET LOOP COUNT
00000E 8D60 0008            00008       13 LOOP     SLDL  6,8            PUT A HIGH ORDER BYTE IN 6
000012 4268 9000            00000       14          STC   6,0(8,9)       STORE IT IN CORE
000016 4680 F00E            0000E       15          BCT   8,LOOP         PROCESS ALL BYTES

                                        17 *        NOW THE SECOND HALF IS REVERSED

00001A 1B11                             19          SR    1,1            JUST IN CASE
00001C 5520 F030            00030       20          CL    2,WORD         IS IT A PALINDROME
000020 4770 F028            00028       21          BNE   *+8            NO, REGISTER 1 IS CORRECT

000024 4110 0001            00001       23          LA    1,1            YES, FIX REGISTER 1

000028 982C D000            00000       25          LM    2,12,0(13)     RESTORE REGISTERS
00002C 07FE                             26          BR    14             RETURN

000030                                  28 WORD     DS    F              WORK AREA
                                        29          END
```

**** ASSEMBLER PROBLEM GRADER HAS BEEN ENTERED FOR STUDENT

PROGRAM ENTRY POINT: 12F790


***YOU WILL BE SENT IN REGISTERS 2-3: ABCDBCBA


***YOU HAVE RETURNED IN REGISTER 1 : 00000001

5 POINTS FOR RETURNING CONTROL
5 POINTS FOR RESTORING REGISTERS 2-12
10 POINTS FOR CORRECT ANSWER


***YOU WILL BE SENT IN REGISTERS 2-3: ABCDABCD


***YOU HAVE RETURNED IN REGISTER 1 : 00000000

5 POINTS FOR RETURNING CONTROL
5 POINTS FOR RESTORING REGISTERS 2-12
10 POINTS FOR CORRECT ANSWER


***YOU WILL BE SENT IN REGISTERS 2-3: SUPERMAN


***YOU HAVE RETURNED IN REGISTER 1 : 00000000

5 POINTS FOR RETURNING CONTROL
5 POINTS FOR RESTORING REGISTERS 2-12
10 POINTS FOR CORRECT ANSWER


***YOU WILL BE SENT IN REGISTERS 2-3: XXZZZZXX


***YOU HAVE RETURNED IN REGISTER 1 : 00000001

5 POINTS FOR RETURNING CONTROL
5 POINTS FOR RESTORING REGISTERS 2-12
10 POINTS FOR CORRECT ANSWER


***YOU WILL BE SENT IN REGISTERS 2-3: FINISHED


***YOU HAVE RETURNED IN REGISTER 1 : 00000000

5 POINTS FOR RETURNING CONTROL
5 POINTS FOR RESTORING REGISTERS 2-12
10 POINTS FOR CORRECT ANSWER



*** TESTING COMPLETE, YOUR TOTAL SCORE IS 100

## 2.5.2 Comma Counting Problem -- A2

```
A2S    SAMPLE SOLUTION TO COMMA COUNTING PROBLEM -- A2  01/16/74 PGG                                        PAGE    3

  LOC   OBJECT CODE    ADDR1 ADDR2  STMT   SOURCE STATEMENT                                                 11 JUN 74
000000                               2 MP1    CSECT
000000                               3         USING *,15                ESTABLISH ADDRESSABILITY
000000 902C D000         00000       4         STM   2,12,0(13)          SAVE REGISTERS
000004 1B11                          5         SR    1,1                 CLEAR COUNTER
000006 4150 0008         00008       6         LA    5,8                 GET LOOP COUNT
00000A 47F0 F012         00012       7         B     *+8                 SKIP SHIFT FIRST TIME

00000E 8C20 0008         00008       9 LOOP    SRDL  2,8                 GET NEXT BYTE READY
000012 4430 F028         00028      10         EX    3,TESTCLI           COMPARE LOW ORDER BYTE TO COMMA
000016 4770 F01E         0001E      11         BNE   *+8                 NOT A COMMA, DON'T BUMP COUNTER
00001A 4110 1001         00001      12         LA    1,1(,1)             COMMA, BUMP COUNTER
00001E 4650 F00E         0000E      13         BCT   5,LOOP              PROCESS ALL BYTES

000022 982C D000         00000      15         LM    2,12,0(13)          RESTORE REGISTERS
000026 07FE                         16         BR    14                  RETURN TO GRADER

000028 9500 F02C   0002C            18 TESTCLI CLI   COMMA,X'00'         COMPARE TO COMMA
00002C 6B                           19 COMMA   DC    C','               COMMA CONSTANT
                                    20         END
```

104

**** ASSEMBLER PROBLEM GRADER HAS BEEN ENTERED FOR STUDENT

PROGRAM ENTRY POINT: 12F790

***YOU WILL BE SENT IN REGISTERS 2-3: A,B,C,D,

***YOU HAVE RETURNED IN REGISTER 1 : 00000004

5 POINTS FOR RETURNING CONTROL
5 POINTS FOR RESTORING REGISTERS 2-12
10 POINTS FOR CORRECT ANSWER

***YOU WILL BE SENT IN REGISTERS 2-3: NONEHERE

***YOU HAVE RETURNED IN REGISTER 1 : 00000000

5 POINTS FOR RETURNING CONTROL
5 POINTS FOR RESTORING REGISTERS 2-12
10 POINTS FOR CORRECT ANSWER

***YOU WILL BE SENT IN REGISTERS 2-3: - - - -,

***YOU HAVE RETURNED IN REGISTER 1 : 00000001

5 POINTS FOR RETURNING CONTROL
5 POINTS FOR RESTORING REGISTERS 2-12
10 POINTS FOR CORRECT ANSWER

***YOU WILL BE SENT IN REGISTERS 2-3: ,,HOPE,,

***YOU HAVE RETURNED IN REGISTER 1 : 00000004

5 POINTS FOR RETURNING CONTROL
5 POINTS FOR RESTORING REGISTERS 2-12
10 POINTS FOR CORRECT ANSWER

***YOU WILL BE SENT IN REGISTERS 2-3: FINISHED

***YOU HAVE RETURNED IN REGISTER 1 : 00000000

5 POINTS FOR RETURNING CONTROL
5 POINTS FOR RESTORING REGISTERS 2-12
10 POINTS FOR CORRECT ANSWER

*** TESTING COMPLETE, YOUR TOTAL SCORE IS 100

## 2.5.3   Arithmetic Operations Problem -- A3

A3S     SAMPLE SOLUTION TO ARITHMETIC OPERATIONS PROBLEM -- A3 02/16/74                        PAGE    3

```
 LOC  OBJECT CODE     ADDR1 ADDR2 STMT   SOURCE STATEMENT                                       11 JUN 74

000000                             2 MP1     CSECT

                                   4 ***************************************************************************
                                   5 *                                                                         *
                                   6 *      SOLUTION FOR MACHINE PROBLEM A3 - ARITHMETIC OPERATION ANALYZER    *
                                   7 *                                                                         *
                                   8 *                                                                         *
                                   9 *      UPON ENTRY: REGISTER 0 POINTS TO 3 CONSECUTIVE FULLWORDS WHICH     *
                                  10 *                  EACH CONTAIN A 1 BYTE LENGTH FIELD FOLLOWED BY A 3     *
                                  11 *                  BYTE ADDRESS FIELD.  THE FIRST FULLWORD DESCRIBES THE  *
                                  12 *                  FIRST OPERAND, THE SECOND FULLWORD DESCRIBES THE       *
                                  13 *                  OPERATION TO BE PERFORMED ON THE FIRST AND THIRD       *
                                  14 *                  OPERANDS.  THE THIRD FULLWORD DESCRIBES THE SECOND     *
                                  15 *                  OPERAND.  THE OPERANDS ARE IN CHARACTER FORMAT         *
                                  16 *                  WITH AN OPTIONAL SIGN IN FRONT.  THE OPERATION WILL    *
                                  17 *                  BE ONE OF THESE CHARACTER STRINGS:                     *
                                  18 *                       + - / * **                                       *
                                  19 *                                                                         *
                                  20 *      UPON RETURN: REGISTER 0 WILL POINT TO A FULLWORD WHICH CONTAINS    *
                                  21 *                  A 1 BYTE LENGTH FIELD FOLLOWED BY A 3 BYTE ADDRESS     *
                                  22 *                  FIELD THAT POINTS TO THE ANSWER OF THE ARITHMETIC      *
                                  23 *                  OPERATION.  THE ANSWER IS IN ZONED DECIMAL FORMAT.     *
                                  24 *                                                                         *
                                  25 ***************************************************************************

000002                            27 P       EQU   2
000003                            28 OPA     EQU   3
000004                            29 OPB     EQU   4
000005                            30 OPLEN   EQU   5
000006                            31 CNTR    EQU   6
000007                            32 LEN     EQU   7
000008                            33 RES     EQU   8                    (MUST PRECEDE ANS AND BE EVEN)
000009                            34 ANS     EQU   9                    (MUST FOLLOW RES AND BE ODD)
00000A                            35 ADR     EQU   10

000000                            37         USING *,15
000000 90EC D000          00000   38         STM   14,12,0(13)         SAVE GRADER'S REGISTERS
000004 50D0 F1B0          00130   39         ST    13,PTSAVE           SAVE ADDRESS OF GRADER'S SAVEAREA
000008 41D0 F174          00174   40         LA    13,SAVEAREA         LOAD ADDRESS OF OUR SAVEAREA FOR FIX
00000C 1810                       41         LR    1,0                 PUT REG 0 INTO REG 1 SO WE CAN USE IT
00000E 4121 0000          00000   42         LA    P,0(1)              LOAD POINTER TO FIRST OPERAND
000012 45E0 F0F4          000F4   43         BAL   14,FIX              FIX UP FIRST OPERAND
000016 1832                       44         LR    OPA,P               PUT RESULT OF CONV INTO OPA
000018 4121 0008          00008   45         LA    P,8(1)              LOAD PTR TO SECOND OPERAND
00001C 45E0 F0F4          000F4   46         BAL   14,FIX              FIX UP SECOND OPERAND
000020 1842                       47         LR    OPB,P               PUT RESULT OF CONVERSION IN OPB
000022 5811 0004          00004   48         L     1,4(1)              LOAD PTR TO OPERATION CODE
000026 D201 F161 1000 00161 00000 49         MVC   OP,0(1)             MOVE OPERATION INTO OP
00002C 954E F161          00161   50         CLI   OP,C'+'             IS IT AN ADDITION ?
000030 47B0 F054          00054   51         BE    ADD
000034 956D F161          00161   52         CLI   OP,C'-'             IS IT A SUBTRACTION ?
000038 47B0 F05C          0005C   53         BE    SUBTRACT
00003C 9561 F161          00161   54         CLI   OP,C'/'             IS IT A DIVISION ?
000040 47B0 F054          00054   55         BE    DIVISION
000044 955C F162          00162   56         CLI   OP+1,C'*'           IS IT AN EXPONENTIATION ?
```

```
  LOC   OBJECT CODE    ADDR1 ADDR2  STMT    SOURCE STATEMENT                                      11 JUN 74

000048 4780 F070         00070    57            RE    EXPON

00004C                            59 MULTIPLY EQU    *              NONE OF THE ABOVE, SO MUST BE A MULT
00004C 1893                       60            LR    ANS,OPA        LOAD EVEN REG WITH OPA
00004E 1C84                       61            MR    RES,OPB        MULTIPLY, RESULT IS IN ANS
000050 47F0 FOAE         000AE    62            B     CALCDONE       DONE WITH ADDITION

000054                            64 ADD      EQU    *
000054 1893                       65            LR    ANS,OPA        LOAD OPA INTO ANS
000056 1A94                       66            AR    ANS,OPB        ADD OPB TO OPA
000058 47F0 FOAE         000AE    67            B     CALCDONE

00005C                            69 SUBTRACT EQU    *
00005C 1893                       70            LR    ANS,OPA        LOAD OPA INTO ANS
00005E 1B94                       71            SR    ANS,OPB        SUBTRACT OPB
000060 47F0 FOAE         000AE    72            B     CALCDONE       DONE WITH SUBTRACTION

000064                            74 DIVISION EQU    *
000064 1883                       75            LR    RES,OPA        LOAD OPA INTO EVEN REGISTER
000066 8E80 0020         00020    76            SRDA  RES,32         FILL EVEN REGISTER WITH PROPER SIGN
00006A 1D84                       77            DR    RES,OPB        DIVIDE OPA BY OPB
00006C 47F0 FOAE         000AE    78            B     CALCDONE       DONE WITH DIVISION

000070                            80 EXPON    EQU    *
000070 1244                       81            LTR   OPB,OPB        IS EXPONENT POSITIVE ?
000072 4720 F082         00082    82            BP    POSEXP
000076 4770 F092         00092    83            BNZ   NEGEXP
00007A 4190 0001         00001    84            LA    ANS,1          EXPONENT IS 0, ANS = 1
00007E 47F0 FOAE         000AE    85            B     CALCDONE       DONE WITH EXPONENTIATION

000082                            87 POSEXP   EQU    *              EXPONENT IS POSITIVE
000082 1864                       88            LR    CNTR,OPB       SET UP LOOP COUNTER
000084 1883                       89            LR    RES,OPA        PUT OPA INTO EVEN REG

000086                            91 LOOPSTRT EQU    *
000086 1C83                       92            MR    RES,OPA        MULTIPLY OPA BY OPA
000088 1889                       93            LR    RES,ANS        PUT RESULT BACK IN EVEN REG
00008A 4660 F086         00086    94            BCT   CNTR,LOOPSTRT  LOOP THROUGH OPB TIMES
00008E 47F0 FOAE         000AE    95            B     CALCDONE       DONE WITH EXPONENTIATION

000092                            97 NEGEXP   EQU    *              EXPONENT IS NEGATIVE
                                  98 *                              MUST TEST FOR SPECIAL CASE OF -1 TO
                                  99 *                              -1 POWER
000092 5930 F188         00188   100            C     OPA,=F'-1'     WAS BASE = -1 ?
000096 4770 FOAA         000AA   101            BNE   SETZERO
00009A 5940 F188         00188   102            C     OPB,=F'-1'     WAS EXPONENT = -1 ?
00009E 4770 FOAA         000AA   103            BNE   SETZERO
0000A2 5890 F188         00188   104            L     ANS,=F'-1'     -1 TO -1 POWER = -1
0000A6 47F0 FOAE         000AE   105            B     CALCDONE
0000AA 4190 0000         00000   106 SETZERO  LA    ANS,0(0)       FOR REST OF NEGATIVE EXPONENTS, THE
                                 107 *                              RESULT WILL ALWAYS BE ZERO
```

```
 LOC  OBJECT CODE      ADDR1 ADDR2  STMT    SOURCE STATEMENT                                    11 JUN 74

0000AE                                 109 CALCDONE EQU  *                 NOW CONVERT ANSWER
0000AE 4E90 F168                00168  110          CVD  ANS,ANSWER        CONVERT ANSWER TO ZONED DECIMAL
0000B2 F373 F168 F16C 00168 0016C 111          UNPK ANSWER(8),ANSWER+4(4)  UNPACK ANSWER
0000B8 4120 F168                00168  112          LA   P,ANSWER          LOAD P WITH ADDRESS OF ANSWER
0000BC 4170 0008                00008  113          LA   LEN,8             LENGTH STARTS OUT AT 8

0000C0                                 115 LOOP     EQU  *                 LOOP TO STRIP LEADING ZEROS
0000C0 95F0 2000          00000        116          CLI  0(P),X'F0'        IS LEADING DIGIT A ZERO ?
0000C4 4780 F0D0                00000  117          BE   STRIP             YES, STRIP
0000C8 95FF 2000          00000        118          CLI  0(P),X'FF'        IS LEADING DIGIT GARBAGE ?
0000CC 4770 F0DA                0000A  119          BNE  DONE
0000D0 0670                             120 STRIP    BCTR LEN,0             YES - SUBTRACT ONE FROM LENGTH
0000D2 4122 0001                00001  121          LA   P,1(P)            ADD TO POINTER TO SKIP ZERO BYTE
0000D6 47F0 F0C0                000C0  122          B    LOOP              GO TEST NEXT DIGIT

0000DA                                 124 DONE     EQU  *                 DONE WITH STRIPPING
0000DA 4100 F170                00170  125          LA   0,ANSPOINT        ANSPOINT POINTS AT ANSWER
0000DE 58D0 F180                00180  126          L    13,PTSAVE         LOAD PTR TO SAVE AREA
0000E2 5000 0008                00008  127          ST   0,8(13)           STORE ADDRESS OF ANSWER IN SAVE AREA
0000E6 5020 F170                00170  128          ST   P,ANSPOINT        STORE POINTER TO ANSWER
0000EA 4270 F170                00170  129          STC  LEN,ANSPOINT      STORE LENGTH OF ANSWER
0000EE 98EC 0000                00000  130          LM   14,12,0(13)       RESTORE REGISTERS
0000F2 07FE                             131          BR   14                RETURN TO GRADER
```

```
                                    133 ****************************************************************
                                    134 *                                                              *
                                    135 *    THE FIX ROUTINE CONVERTS NUMBERS IN CHARACTER FORM TO BINARY *
                                    136 *                                                              *
                                    137 *        INPUT -  REG P POINTS TO A FULLWORD CONTAINING A 1 BYTE *
                                    138 *                 LENGTH FIELD FOLLOWED BY A 3 BYTE ADDRESS OF THE *
                                    139 *                 AREA TO BE CONVERTED.  THE AREA TO BE CONVERTED *
                                    140 *                 SHOULD BE A NUMBER IN CHARACTER FORM PRECEDED BY AN *
                                    141 *                 OPTIONAL SIGN.                               *
                                    142 *                                                              *
                                    143 *        OUTPUT - REG P WILL CONTAIN THE BINARY RESULT          *
                                    144 *                                                              *
                                    145 ****************************************************************
0000F4                              147 FIX      EQU   *
00000B                              148 LAST     EQU   11

0000F4 90EC D000          00000     150          STM   14,12,0(13)          SAVE REGISTERS
0000F8 05F0                         151          BALR  15,0
0000FA                              152          USING *,15
0000FA 1B77                         153          SR    LEN,LEN              CLEAR OUT LEN
0000FC 4372 0000          00000     154          IC    LEN,0(P)             LOAD LENGTH
000100 0670                         155          BCTR  LEN,0                SUBTRACT 1 FROM LEN
000102 58A2 0000          00000     156          L     ADR,0(P)             LOAD ADDRESS
000106 D207 F05F A000 00159 00000   157          MVC   WRK,0(ADR)           MOVE OPERAND INTO WORK AREA
00010C 95F0 F05F          00159     158          CLI   WRK,X'F0'            IS FIRST BYTE A DIGIT ?
000110 47B0 F02A          00124     159          BNL   PLUS                 YES, SKIP
000114 0670                         160          BCTR  LEN,0                SUBTRACT ONE FROM LEN
000116 D207 F05E F05F 00158 00159   161          MVC   SIGN(8),WRK          SHIFT WORK AREA OVER 1 BYTE TO LEFT
00011C 954E F05E          00158     162          CLI   SIGN,C'+'            IS SIGN POSITIVE ?
000120 4770 F036          00130     163          BNE   MINUS
000124                              164 PLUS     EQU   *                    SIGN IS POSITIVE
000124 41B7 F05F          00159     165          LA    LAST,WRK(LEN)        LAST POINTS TO LAST BYTE OF OPERAND
000128 94CF B000          00000     166          NI    0(LAST),X'CF'        PUT PLUS ZONE IN OPERAND
00012C 47F0 F03E          00138     167          B     CONVERT

000130                              169 MINUS    EQU   *                    SIGN IS NEGATIVE
000130 41B7 F05F          00159     170          LA    LAST,WRK(LEN)        LAST POINTS TO LAST BYTE OF OPERAND
000134 94DF B000          00000     171          NI    0(LAST),X'DF'        PUT MINUS ZONE IN OPERAND

000138                              173 CONVERT  EQU   *
000138 4470 F050          0014A     174          EX    LEN,PACK             CONVERT TO PACKED DECIMAL
00013C 4F20 F056          00150     175          CVB   P,PK                 CONVERT TO BINARY

000140                              177 EXIT     EQU   *
                                    178 *
                                    179 *    THE NEXT INSTRUCTION NEEDS TO KNOW WHAT REG P IS
                                    180 *
000140 502D 0010          00010     181          ST    P,16(13)
000144 98EC D000          00000     182          LM    14,12,0(13)          RESTORE REGISTERS
000148 07FE                         183          BR    14                   RETURN TO CALLER

                                    185 *    CONSTANTS FOR FIX GO HERE

00014A F270 F056 F05F 00150 00159   187 PACK     PACK  PK,WRK(0)
```

A3S    SAMPLE SOLUTION TO ARITHMETIC OPERATIONS PROBLEM -- A3 02/16/74                    PAGE    7

   LOC  OBJECT CODE    ADDR1 ADDR2  STMT    SOURCE STATEMENT                              11 JUN 74

000150                            188 PK        DS    D
000158                            189 SIGN      DS    CL1          SIGN CHARACTER (MUST IMMED. PRECEDE WRK)
000159                            190 WRK       DS    CL8              WORK AREA

                                  192 *         CONSTANTS FOR MP1 GO HERE

000161                            194 OP        DS    CL2          OP CODE
000168                            195 ANSWER    DS    D            ANSWER FOR GRADER
000170                            196 ANSPOINT  DS    F            POINTER TO ANSWER
000174                            197 SAVEAREA  DS    15F          SAVE AREA FOR FIX
000180                            198 PTSAVE    DS    F            SAVE AREA FOR PTR TO GRADER'S SAVE -
                                  199 *                           AREA
                                  200           END
000188 FFFFFFFF                   201                 =F'-1'

**** ASSEMBLER PROBLEM GRADER HAS BEEN ENTERED FOR STUDENT

PROGRAM ENTRY POINT: 12FD60

YOU HAVE RECEIVED 10 POINTS FOR SUCCESSFULLY ASSEMBLING YOUR PROGRAM

***WE WILL PASS YOU -> (-1        ) ** (0        ):

```
 REG  0
0012E764 ----> 12E764: 0212E770 ----> 12E770: 60F1404040404040
                       0212E778 ----> 12E778: 5C5CF04040404040
                       0112E77A ----> 12E77A: F040404040404040
```

***YOU HAVE RETURNED:

```
 REG  0
0012FED0 ----> 12FED0: 0112FECF ----> 12FECF: C10112FECF9F12FD
```

2 POINTS FOR RETURNING CONTROL TO GRADER
3 POINTS FOR RESTORING REGISTERS
2 POINTS FOR SPECIFYING PROPER LENGTH OF RESULT
8 POINTS FOR CORRECT ANSWER

***WE WILL PASS YOU -> (-8        ) * (+8        ):

```
 REG  0
0012E764 ----> 12E764: 0212E770 ----> 12E770: 60F8404040404040
                       0112E778 ----> 12E778: 5C404EF840404040
                       0212E77A ----> 12E77A: 4EF8404040404040
```

***YOU HAVE RETURNED:

```
 REG  0
0012FED0 ----> 12FED0: 0212FECE ----> 12FECE: F6D40212FECE9F12
```

2 POINTS FOR RETURNING CONTROL TO GRADER
3 POINTS FOR RESTORING REGISTERS
2 POINTS FOR SPECIFYING PROPER LENGTH OF RESULT
8 POINTS FOR CORRECT ANSWER

***WE WILL PASS YOU -> (-23       ) + (+7        ):

```
 REG  0
0012E764 ----> 12E764: 0312E770 ----> 12E770: 60F2F34040404040
                       0112E778 ----> 12E778: 4E404EF740404040
                       0212E77A ----> 12E77A: 4EF7404040404040
```

***YOU HAVE RETURNED:

```
 REG  0
0012FED0 ----> 12FED0: 0212FECE ----> 12FECE: F1D60212FECE9F12
```

2 POINTS FOR RETURNING CONTROL TO GRADER
3 POINTS FOR RESTORING REGISTERS
2 POINTS FOR SPECIFYING PROPER LENGTH OF RESULT
8 POINTS FOR CORRECT ANSWER


***WE WILL PASS YOU -> (+2        ) / (3           ):

```
 REG  0
0012E764 ----> 12E764: 0212E770 ----> 12E770: 4EF2404040404040
                       0112E778 ----> 12E778: 6140F34040404040
                       0112E77A ----> 12E77A: F340404040404040
```


***YOU HAVE RETURNED:

```
 REG  0
0012FED0 ----> 12FED0: 0112FECF ----> 12FECF: C00112FECF9F12FD
```

2 POINTS FOR RETURNING CONTROL TO GRADER
3 POINTS FOR RESTORING REGISTERS
2 POINTS FOR SPECIFYING PROPER LENGTH OF RESULT
8 POINTS FOR CORRECT ANSWER


***WE WILL PASS YOU -> (5         ) - (-6        ):

```
 REG  0
0012E764 ----> 12E764: 0112E770 ----> 12E770: F540404040404040
                       0112E778 ----> 12E778: 604060F640404040
                       0212E77A ----> 12E77A: 60F6404040404040
```


***YOU HAVE RETURNED:

```
 REG  0
0012FED0 ----> 12FED0: 0212FECE ----> 12FECE: F1C10212FECE9F12
```

2 POINTS FOR RETURNING CONTROL TO GRADER
3 POINTS FOR RESTORING REGISTERS
2 POINTS FOR SPECIFYING PROPER LENGTH OF RESULT
8 POINTS FOR CORRECT ANSWER


***WE WILL PASS YOU -> (-1        ) ** (-1        ):

```
 REG  0
0012E764 ----> 12E764: 0212E770 ----> 12E770: 60F1404040404040
                       0212E778 ----> 12E778: 5C5C60F140404040
                       0212E77A ----> 12E77A: 60F1404040404040
```

***YOU HAVE RETURNED:

 REG  0
0012FED0 ----> 12FED0: 0112FECF ----> 12FECF: D10112FECF9F12FD

2 POINTS FOR RETURNING CONTROL TO GRADER
3 POINTS FOR RESTORING REGISTERS
2 POINTS FOR SPECIFYING PROPER LENGTH OF RESULT
8 POINTS FOR CORRECT ANSWER


*** TESTING COMPLETE, YOUR TOTAL SCORE IS 100

## 2.5.4   DC-Simulator Problem -- A4

```
LOC   OBJECT CODE    ADDR1 ADDR2  STMT   SOURCE STATEMENT                                                                   11 JUN 74
000000                            2 MP1       CSECT
                                  3 *****************************************************************************************
                                  4 *                                                                                     *
                                  5 *             SAMPLE SOLUTION TO PROBLEM A4                                            *
                                  6 *                                                                                     *
                                  7 *                                                                                     *
                                  8 *DC-PROCESSOR ENTRY POINT                                                             *
                                  9 *                                                                                     *
                                 10 *UPON ENTRY:                                                                          *
                                 11 *                                                                                     *
                                 12 *REGISTER 0:                                                                          *
                                 13 *                                                                                     *
                                 14 *             CONTAINS THE TYPE OF CONVERSION TO BE PERFORMED                         *
                                 15 *             0- CHARACTER STRING CONVERSION                                          *
                                 16 *             1- HEXADECIMAL STRING CONVERSION                                        *
                                 17 *             2- PACKED DECIMAL STRING CONVERSION                                     *
                                 18 *             3- FULL-WORD STRING CONVERSION                                          *
                                 19 *                                                                                     *
                                 20 *REGISTER 1:                                                                          *
                                 21 *                                                                                     *
                                 22 *             TOP BYTE CONTAINS LENGTH OF INPUT STRING                                *
                                 23 *             LOW ORDER 3 BYTES CONTAIN ADDRESS OF INPUT STRING                       *
                                 24 *                                                                                     *
                                 25 *                                                                                     *
                                 26 *UPON RETURN:                                                                         *
                                 27 *                                                                                     *
                                 28 *             REGISTER 1 CONTAINS THE LENGTH AND ADDRESS OF THE ANSWER                *
                                 29 *                                                                                     *
                                 30 *****************************************************************************************
000000 90EC D00C      0000C      32           STM    14,12,12(13)       SAVE REGISTERS
000004 05F0                      33           BALR   15,0               ESTABLISH ADDRESSABILITY
000006                           34           USING  *,15
000006 1B33                      35           SR     3,3                CLEAR REGISTER 3
000008 433D 0018      00018      36           IC     3,12+3*4(13)       GET LENGTH OF INPUT STRING FROM
                                 37 *                                   REGISTER SAVE AREA (IN REG1)
00000C 4230 F1D6      001DC      38           STC    3,LENGTH           IN CASE C CONVERSION CALLED FOR
000010 0630                      39           BCTR   3,0                DECREMENT LENGTH BY 1 FOR AN EXECUTE
000012 4430 F038      0003E      40           EX     3,MOVE             MOVE INPUT STRING INTO ANSWER
000016 1840                      41           LR     4,0                PUT CONVERSION TYPE INTO REGISTER 4
000018 8940 0002      00002      42           SLL    4,2                MULTIPLY LENGTH BY 4
00001C 4404 F01A      00020      43           EX     0,BRANCH(4)        BRANCH TO PROPER HANDLER
000020 47F0 F02A      00030      44 BRANCH    B      CHAR               CHARACTER CONVERSION
000024 47F0 F03E      00044      45           B      HEX                HEXADECIMAL CONVERSION
000028 47F0 F080      00086      46           B      PACK               PACKED DECIMAL CONVERSION
00002C 47F0 F0EE      000F4      47           B      FULL               FULL-WORD CONVERSION
                                 48 *****************************************************************************************
                                 49 *                                                                                     *
                                 50 *             CHARACTER CONVERSION ROUTINE                                            *
                                 51 *                                                                                     *
                                 52 *****************************************************************************************
000030                           54 CHAR      EQU    *
                                 55 *****************************************************************************************
                                 56 *                                                                                     *
```

# 2. ASSEMBLY LANGUAGE PROBLEMS

2-99

A45   SAMPLE SOLUTION TO DC-SIMULATOR PROBLEM -- A4 02/15/74                                        PAGE   3

```
  LOC  OBJECT CODE    ADDR1 ADDR2 STMT  SOURCE STATEMENT                                        11 JUN 74

                                    57 *           SET UP REGISTER 1 IN THE REGISTER SAVE AREA AND RETURN     *
                                    58 *                                                                     *
                                    59 *************************************************************************
000030 4110 F1D6       001DC        61 RETURN  LA    1,LENGTH            GET A(INDIRECT WORD)
000034 5010 D018       00018        62         ST    1,12+3*4(,13)      PUT A(INDIRECT WORD) IN REGISTER 1
000038 98EC D00C       0000C        63         LM    14,12,12(13)       RESTORE REGISTERS
00003C 07FE                         64         BR    14                 RETURN TO GRADER
00003E D200 F14A 1000 00150 00000   65 MOVE    MVC   ANSWER(0),0(1)     COPY STRING INTO ANSWER
                                    66 *************************************************************************
                                    67 *                                                                     *
                                    68 *           HEXADECIMAL CONVERSION ROUTINE                             *
                                    69 *                                                                     *
                                    70 *************************************************************************
000044                              72 HEX     EQU   *
000044 4430 F07A       00080        73         EX    3,TRANS            CONVERT CHARACTERS TO NUMBERS
000048 4130 3001       00001        74         LA    3,1(,3)            SET REG 3 TO CHARACTER COUNT OF INPUT
00004C 1853                         75         LR    5,3                PUT REG 3 INTO REG 5
00004E 8850 0001       00001        76         SRL   5,1                DIVIDE BY 2
000052 4250 F1D6       001DC        77         STC   5,LENGTH           SAVE OUTPUT LENGTH
000056 4150 F14A       00150        78         LA    5,ANSWER           POINT TO ANSWER AREA
00005A 1865                         79         LR    6,5                SET REG6 TO RESULT AREA
00005C 4340 6000       00000        80 LOOP1   IC    4,0(,6)            GET A CHARACTER
000060 8940 0004       00004        81         SLL   4,4                MOVE NUMBER TO TOP 4 BITS
000064 4240 5000       00000        82         STC   4,0(,5)            SAVE SHIFTED INFORMATION
000068 D600 5000 6001 00000 00001   83         OC    0(1,5),1(6)        OR IN THE NEXT HEX DIGIT
00006E 4150 5001       00001        84         LA    5,1(,5)            INCREMENT ANSWER BY 1
000072 4160 6002       00002        85         LA    6,2(,6)            INCREMENT INPUT WORK AREA BY 2
000076 0630                         86         BCTR  3,0                DECREMENT INPUT COUNT BY 1
000078 4630 F056       0005C        87         BCT   3,LOOP1            DECREMENT COUNT AGAIN AND LOOP
00007C 47F0 F02A       00030        88         B     RETURN             BEGIN RETURNING SEQUENCE
000080 DC00 F14A F0B1 00150 000B7   89 TRANS   TR    ANSWER(0),HEXTBL-C'A' CONVERT STRING
                                    90 *************************************************************************
                                    91 *                                                                     *
                                    92 *           PACKED DECIMAL CONVERSION ROUTINE                          *
                                    93 *                                                                     *
                                    94 *************************************************************************
000086                              96 PACK    EQU   *
000086 95F0 1000       00000        97         CLI   0(1),C'0'          SEE IF FIRST CHAR IS A SIGN
00008A 47B0 F0AA       00030        98         BNL   NOSIGN             BRANCH IF NOT TO NOSIGN
00008E 4140 F14A       00150        99 SIGN    LA    4,ANSWER           GET ADDRESS OF WORK AREA
000092 4154 3000       00000       100         LA    5,0(4,3)           POINT TO LAST BYTE OF INPUT STRING
000096 954E 1000       00000       101         CLI   0(1),C'+'          IS FIRST CHAR A PLUS?
00009A 4770 F0A0       000A6       102         BNE   NOTPLUS            NO,BRANCH
00009E 94CF 5000       00000       103         NI    0(5),X'CF'         CHANGE HIGH ORDER 4 BITS TO X'C' FOR
                                   104 *                                A PLUS (+) SIGN
0000A2 47F0 F0A4       000AA       105         B     NOWPACK            BRANCH TO CONVERSION ROUTINE
0000A6 94DF 5000       00000       106 NOTPLUS NI    0(5),X'DF'         CHANGE HIGH ORDER 4 BITS TO X'D' FOR
                                   107 *                                A MINUS (-) SIGN
0000AA 4140 4001       00001       108 NOWPACK LA    4,1(,4)            INCREMENT POINTER BY 1
0000AE 0630                        109         BCTR  3,0                DECREMENT LENGTH VALUE BY 1
0000B0 4150 3001       00001       110 NOSIGN  LA    5,1(,3)            COPY LENGTH INTO REG 5
0000B4 4250 F1AE       00184       111         STC   5,COPY             USE COPY FOR TEMPORARY TEST
```

115

```
       LOC   OBJECT CODE      ADDR1 ADDR2  STMT   SOURCE STATEMENT                                              11 JUN 74

     0000B8 9101 F1AE          00184        112         TM    COPY,X'01'          IS LENGTH OF INPUT DIGITS ODD?
     0000BC 4710 F0BE                000C4   113         BO    ODD                 YES,BRANCH
     0000C0 4150 5001                00001   114 EVEN    LA    5,1(,5)             INCREMENT LENGTH BY 1
     0000C4 4150 5001                00001   115 ODD     LA    5,1(,5)             INCREMENT LENGTH BY 1
     0000C8 8850 0001                00001   116         SRL   5,1                 DIVIDE LENGTH BY 2
     0000CC 4250 F1D6                001DC   117         STC   5,LENGTH            SAVE OUTPUT LENGTH
     0000D0 0650                             118         BCTR  5,0                 DECREMENT REG 5 FOR AN EXECUTE
     0000D2 8950 0004                00004   119         SLL   5,4                 MOVE LENGTH INTO BITS 24-27
     0000D6 1635                             120         OR    3,5                 OR BOTH LENGTHS INTO REGISTER 3
     0000D8 4430 F0E2                000E8   121         EX    3,PACK2             EXECUTE A PACK INSTRUCTION
     0000DC 8850 0004                00004   122         SRL   5,4                 MOVE LENGTH BACK TO BITS 28-31
     0000E0 4450 F0E8                000EE   123         EX    5,MOVE2             MOVE RESULT INTO ANSWER
     0000E4 47F0 F02A                00030   124         B     RETURN              BRANCH TO RETURN SEQUENCE
     0000E8 F200 F1AE 4000 00184 00000 125 PACK2   PACK  COPY(0),0(0,4)
     0000EE D200 F14A F1AE 00150 00184 126 MOVE2   MVC   ANSWER(0),COPY
                                        127 ****************************************************************************
                                        128 *                                                                          *
                                        129 *           FULL WORD CONVERSION ROUTINE                                   *
                                        130 *                                                                          *
                                        131 ****************************************************************************

     0000F4                              133 FULL    EQU   *
     0000F4 4140 F14A                00150   134         LA    4,ANSWER            GET POINTER TO WORK AREA
     0000F8 95F0 1000          00000   135         CLI   0(1),C'0'           IS FIRST CHARACTER A SIGN?
     0000FC 4780 F118                0011E   136         BNL   NOSIGN2             NO,BRANCH
     000100 4154 3000                00000   137         LA    5,0(4,3)            POINT TO LAST BYTE OF INPUT STRING
     000104 954E 1000          00000   138         CLI   0(1),C'+'           IS IT A PLUS?
     000108 4770 F10E                00114   139         BNE   NOTPLUS2            NO, BRANCH
     00010C 94CF 5000          00000   140         NI    0(5),X'CF'          CHANGE HIGH ORDER 4 BITS TO X'C' FOR
                                        141 *                                     A PLUS (+) SIGN
     000110 47F0 F112                00118   142         B     NOWPACK2            BRANCH TO CONVERSION ROUTINE
     000114 940F 5000          00000   143 NOTPLUS2 NI    0(5),X'0F'          CHANGE HIGH ORDER 4 BITS TO X'D' FOR
                                        144 *                                     A MINUS(-) SIGN
     000118 4140 4001                00001   145 NOWPACK2 LA    4,1(,4)             INCREMENT POINTER BY 1
     00011C 0630                             146         BCTR  3,0                 DECREMENT LENGTH VALUE BY 1
     00011E 4160 000E                0000E   147 NOSIGN2 LA    6,14                PUT 14 INTO REG 5
     000122 1B63                             148         SR    6,3                 SUBTRACT (LENGTH - 1) FROM 14
     000124 D70E F1AE F1AE 00184 00184 149 XC    COPY(15),COPY       CLEAR OUT COPY AREA
     00012A 4166 F1AE                00184   150         LA    6,COPY(6)           POINT TO SPOT FOR A MOVE
     00012E 4430 F142                00148   151         EX    3,MOVE3             MOVE UNPACKED VALUE INTO COPY AREA
     000132 F27E F14A F1AE 00150 00184 152 PACK  ANSWER(8),COPY(15)  PERFORM A PACK
     000138 4F60 F14A                00150   153         CVB   6,ANSWER            CONVERT STRING TO A FULL-WORD
     00013C 5060 F14A                00150   154         ST    6,ANSWER            PUT ANSWER IN ANSWER
     000140 9204 F1D6          001DC   155         MVI   LENGTH,X'04'         FORCE LENGTH TO 4
     000144 47F0 F02A                00030   156         B     RETURN              PERFORM RETURN SEQUENCE
     000148 D200 6000 4000 00000 00000 157 MOVE3   MVC   0(0,6),0(4)
                                        158 ****************************************************************************
                                        159 *                                                                          *
                                        160 *           WORK AREAS AND TABLES USED BY THE DC-PROCESSOR                 *
                                        161 *                                                                          *
                                        162 ****************************************************************************

     000150                              164         DS    0D                  DOUBLE-WORD BOUNDARY
     000150                              165 ANSWER  DS    CL40
     000178 0A0B0C0D0E0F                 166 HEXTBL  DC    AL1(10,11,12,13,14,15)
```

116

```
 LOC  OBJECT CODE   ADDR1 ADDR2 STMT   SOURCE STATEMENT

00017E 0001A7                    167        ORG    HEXTBL-C'A'+C'O'
0001A7 0001020304050607          168        DC     AL1(0,1,2,3,4,5,6,7,8,9)
0001B4                           169        DS     0F                FULL-WORD BOUNDARY
0001B4                           170 COPY   DS     CL40              COPY OF INPUT STRING
0001DC                           171        DS     0F                 FORCE ALIGNMENT
0001DC                           172 LENGTH DS     XL1                ANSWER AREA
0001DD 000150                    173 ADDR   DC     AL3(ANSWER)       ADDRESS OF ANSWER TO BE RETURNED
                                 174        END
```

**** ASSEMBLER PROBLEM GRADER HAS BEEN ENTERED FOR STUDENT

PROGRAM ENTRY POINT: 12FDD0

YOU HAVE RECEIVED 10 POINTS FOR SUCCESSFULLY ASSEMBLING YOUR PROGRAM

***WE WILL PASS YOU A TYPE X CONVERSION ON A101

```
 REG 1
0412E70C ----> 12E70C: C1F1F0F140404040
```

***YOU HAVE RETURNED:

```
 REG 1
0012FFAC ----> 12FFAC: 0212FF20 ----> 12FF20: A1010001FFFFFFFF
```

2 POINTS FOR RETURNING CONTROL TO GRADER
3 POINTS FOR RESTORING REGISTERS
2 POINTS FOR SPECIFYING PROPER LENGTH OF RESULT
8 POINTS FOR CORRECT ANSWER

***WE WILL PASS YOU A TYPE F CONVERSION ON -1

```
 REG 1
0212E70C ----> 12E70C: 60F1404040404040
```

***YOU HAVE RETURNED:

```
 REG 1
0012FFAC ----> 12FFAC: 0412FF20 ----> 12FF20: FFFFFFFF0000001D
```

2 POINTS FOR RETURNING CONTROL TO GRADER
3 POINTS FOR RESTORING REGISTERS
2 POINTS FOR SPECIFYING PROPER LENGTH OF RESULT
8 POINTS FOR CORRECT ANSWER

***WE WILL PASS YOU A TYPE P CONVERSION ON -1

```
 REG 1
0212E70C ----> 12E70C: 60F1404040404040
```

***YOU HAVE RETURNED:

```
 REG 1
0012FFAC ----> 12FFAC: 0112FF20 ----> 12FF20: 1DD1FFFF0000001D
```

2 POINTS FOR RETURNING CONTROL TO GRADER
3 POINTS FOR RESTORING REGISTERS
2 POINTS FOR SPECIFYING PROPER LENGTH OF RESULT

8 POINTS FOR CORRECT ANSWER

***WE WILL PASS YOU A TYPE C CONVERSION ON WHY?

 REG 1
0412E70C ----> 12E70C: E6C8E86F40404040

***YOU HAVE RETURNED:

 REG 1
0012FFAC ----> 12FFAC: 0412FF20 ----> 12FF20: E6C8E86F0000001D

2 POINTS FOR RETURNING CONTROL TO GRADER
3 POINTS FOR RESTORING REGISTERS
2 POINTS FOR SPECIFYING PROPER LENGTH OF RESULT
8 POINTS FOR CORRECT ANSWER

***WE WILL PASS YOU A TYPE X CONVERSION ON ACE0

 REG 1
0412E70C ----> 12E70C: C1C3C5F040404040

***YOU HAVE RETURNED:

 REG 1
0012FFAC ----> 12FFAC: 0212FF20 ----> 12FF20: ACE00E0000000001D

2 POINTS FOR RETURNING CONTROL TO GRADER
3 POINTS FOR RESTORING REGISTERS
2 POINTS FOR SPECIFYING PROPER LENGTH OF RESULT
8 POINTS FOR CORRECT ANSWER

***WE WILL PASS YOU A TYPE P CONVERSION ON -15

 REG 1
0312E70C ----> 12E70C: 60F1F54040404040

***YOU HAVE RETURNED:

 REG 1
0012FFAC ----> 12FFAC: 0212FF20 ----> 12FF20: 015DD5000000001D

2 POINTS FOR RETURNING CONTROL TO GRADER
3 POINTS FOR RESTORING REGISTERS
2 POINTS FOR SPECIFYING PROPER LENGTH OF RESULT
8 POINTS FOR CORRECT ANSWER

*** TESTING COMPLETE, YOUR TOTAL SCORE IS 100

## 2.5.5   Instruction Analyzer Problem -- A5

A5    SAMPLE SOLUTION TO INSTRUCTION ANALYZER PROBLEM -- A5 07/16/74 CHC                                    PAGE   1

```
 LOC  OBJECT CODE     ADDR1 ADDR2 STMT   SOURCE STATEMENT                                              11 JUN 74

000000                              2 MP1     CSECT
000000                              3         USING     *,12                R12 IS THE BASE REGISTER
                                    4 *                                     BASE REGISTER IS CHANGED FROM R15 TO
                                    5 *                                     R12 BECAUSE R15 WILL LATER BE USED AS
                                    6 *                                     THE FIRST OPERAND REGISTER IN THE
                                    7 *                                     LOAD ADDRESS INSTRUCTION
000000 90EC D00C          0000C     8 HERE    STM       14,12,12(13)        SAVE REG IN AREA POINTED BY R13
000004 18CF                         9         LR        12,15               LOAD R12 WITH BEGINNING ADDRESS
000006 D203 C0A8 C0C0 000A8 000C0  10         MVC       LENGTH(4),=F'0'     CLEARS OUT ANSWER BLOCK
00000C D203 C0AC C0C0 000AC 000C0  11         MVC       ADDR(4),=F'0'
000012 D203 C0B0 C0C0 000B0 000C0  12         MVC       OP1(4),=F'0'
000018 D203 C0B4 C0C0 000B4 000C0  13         MVC       OP2(4),=F'0'
                                   14 *                                     CONSTRUCT A LOAD ADDRESS INSTRUCTION
                                   15 *                                     AT A LOCATION CALLED INSTR
00001E 92F0 C089        00089      16         MVI       INSTR+1,X'F0'       FORMS R1=15,X2=0
000022 D201 C0BA 1002 000BA 00002  17         MVC       INSTR+2(2),2(1)     FORMS BASE REG AND OFFSET
000028 91C0 1000        00000      18         TM        0(1),B'11000000'    TESTS OP CODE
00002C 4710 C07C        0007C      19         BO        SSTYPE              OP CODE IS X'11'
000030 4780 C050        00050      20         BZ        RRTYPE              OP CODE IS X'00'
000034 9140 1000        00000      21         TM        0(1),B'01000000'    TEST FOR X'01' OP CODE
000038 4710 C058        00058      22         BO        RXTYPE              OP CODE IS X'01'
00003C 9204 C0AB        000AB      23         MVI       LENGTH+3,X'04'      RS OR SI TYPE, LENGTH=4
000040 9201 C0AF        000AF      24         MVI       ADDR+3,X'01'        ONE REFERENCED ADDRESS
000044 4400 C0B8        00088      25         EX        0,INSTR             LOADS THE ADDRESS INTO R15
000048 50F0 C0B0        00080      26         ST        15,OP1              STORE THE ADDRESS IN OP1
00004C 47F0 C09E        0009E      27         B         DONE
000050 9202 C0AB        000AB      28 RRTYPE  MVI       LENGTH+3,X'02'      LENGTH=2 FOR RRTYPE
000054 47F0 C09E        0009E      29         B         DONE
000058 9204 C0AB        000AB      30 RXTYPE  MVI       LENGTH+3,X'04'      LENGTH=4 FOR RX TYPE
00005C 9201 C0AF        000AF      31         MVI       ADDR+3,X'01'        ONE REFERENCED ADDRESS
000060 5860 C0C4        000C4      32         L         6,=F'240'           LOAD R6 WITH X'F0' IN PREPARATION
                                   33 *                                     FOR THE OR FUNCTION IN THE EX INSTR
000064 5870 1000        00000      34         L         7,0(0,1)            LOAD R7 WITH THE INSTRUCTION
000068 5070 C0B8        00088      35         ST        7,INSTR             STORE INSTRUCTION IN TEMP LOC
00006C 9241 C0B8        00088      36         MVI       INSTR,X'41'         CHANGE OP CODE TO LOAD ADDRESS
000070 4460 C0B8        00088      37         EX        6,INSTR             LOAD ADDRESS OF OPERAND INTO R15
000074 50F0 C0B0        00080      38         ST        15,OP1              STORE ADDRESS IN OP1
000078 47F0 C09E        0009E      39         B         DONE
00007C 9206 C0AB        000AB      40 SSTYPE  MVI       LENGTH+3,X'06'      LENGTH=6 FOR SSTYPE
000080 9202 C0AF        000AF      41         MVI       ADDR+3,X'02'        TWO REFERENCED ADDRESSES
000084 4400 C0B8        00088      42         EX        0,INSTR             LOADS ADDRESS OF 1ST OPERAND INTO R15
000088 50F0 C0B0        00080      43         ST        15,OP1              STORES ADDRESS IN OP1
00008C D201 C0BA 1004 000BA 00004  44         MVC       INSTR+2(2),4(1)     FORMS THE INSTR LA 15,ADDR OF 2ND OP
000092 4400 C0B8        00088      45         EX        0,INSTR             LOADS ADDRESS OF 2ND OPERAND INTO R15
000096 50F0 C0B4        00084      46         ST        15,OP2              STORES 2ND OPERAND ADDRESS IN OP2
00009A 47F0 C09E        0009E      47         B         DONE
00009E 98EC D00C          0000C    48 DONE    LM        14,12,12(13)        RESTORE REGISTERS
                                   49         DROP      12
000000                             50         USING     HERE,15
0000A2 4110 F0A8        000A8      51         LA        1,ANSWER            R1 POINTS TO ANSWER
0000A6 07FE                        52         BR        14                  RETURN TO GRADING PROGRAM
0000A8                             53 ANSWER  DS        0F                  NAME OF ANSWER BLOCK
0000A8 00000000                    54 LENGTH  DC        F'0'
0000AC 00000000                    55 ADDR    DC        F'0'
0000B0 00000000                    56 OP1     DC        F'0'
0000B4 00000000                    57 OP2     DC        F'0'
0000B8 41F0 C000        00000      58 INSTR   LA        15,0(0,12)          INSTRUCTION FOR LOADING ADDRESSES
                                   59         END
0000C0 00000000                    60                   =F'0'
0000C4 000000F0                    61                   =F'240'
```

```
     2 POINTS FOR CORRECT LENGTH
     2 POINTS FOR CORRECT NUMBER OF ADDRESS FIELDS
     3 POINTS FOR CORRECT OPERAND 1
     3 POINTS FOR CORRECT OPERAND 2
```

***WE WILL PASS YOU:

```
 REG 1                         INSTRUCTION
 0012E602 ----> 12E602: 98EC503207000700

 REG  2      REG  3      REG  4      REG  5      REG  6      REG  7      REG  8      REG  9
 00000014    00000028    0000003C    00000064    0014CF50    000000FF    00000000    0014CE90

 REG 10      REG 11      REG 12      REG 13      REG 14      REG 15
 001300B0    0012D810    4014D04C    0012E60C    0012D998    001300F8
```

***YOU HAVE RETURNED:

```
 REG 1                         ANSWER
 001301A0 ----> 1301A0:  00000004
                         00000001
                         00000096
                         00000000
```

```
     5 POINTS FOR RETURNING CONTROL TO GRADER
     5 POINTS FOR RESTORING REGISTERS
     2 POINTS FOR CORRECT LENGTH
     2 POINTS FOR CORRECT NUMBER OF ADDRESS FIELDS
     3 POINTS FOR CORRECT OPERAND 1
     3 POINTS FOR CORRECT OPERAND 2
```

***WE WILL PASS YOU:

```
 REG 1                         INSTRUCTION
 0012E602 ----> 12E602: 9102203C07000700

 REG  2      REG  3      REG  4      REG  5      REG  6      REG  7      REG  8      REG  9
 00000014    00000028    0000003C    00000064    0014CF50    000000FF    00000000    0014CE90

 REG 10      REG 11      REG 12      REG 13      REG 14      REG 15
 001300C8    0012D810    4014D04C    0012E60C    0012D998    001300F8
```

***YOU HAVE RETURNED:

```
 REG 1                         ANSWER
 001301A0 ----> 1301A0:  00000004
                         00000001
                         00000050
                         00000000
```

```
     5 POINTS FOR RETURNING CONTROL TO GRADER
```

```
**** ASSEMBLER PROBLEM GRADER HAS BEEN ENTERED FOR STUDENT

PROGRAM ENTRY POINT: 1300F8


***WE WILL PASS YOU:

 REG 1                      INSTRUCTION
0012E602 ----> 12E602: 1A22070007000700

 REG  2     REG  3     REG  4     REG  5     REG  6     REG  7     REG  8     REG  9
00000014   00000028   0000003C   00000064   0014CF50   000000FF   00000000   0014CE90

 REG 10     REG 11     REG 12     REG 13     REG 14     REG 15
00130080   0012D810   4014D04C   0012E60C   0012D998   001300F8


***YOU HAVE RETURNED:

 REG 1                      ANSWER
001301A0 ----> 1301A0: 00000002
                       00000000
                       00000000
                       00000000

   5 POINTS FOR RETURNING CONTROL TO GRADER
   5 POINTS FOR RESTORING REGISTERS
   2 POINTS FOR CORRECT LENGTH
   2 POINTS FOR CORRECT NUMBER OF ADDRESS FIELDS
   3 POINTS FOR CORRECT OPERAND 1
   3 POINTS FOR CORRECT OPERAND 2


***WE WILL PASS YOU:

 REG 1                      INSTRUCTION
0012E602 ----> 12E602: 5543501407000700

 REG  2     REG  3     REG  4     REG  5     REG  6     REG  7     REG  8     REG  9
00000014   00000028   0000003C   00000064   0014CF50   000000FF   00000000   0014CE90

 REG 10     REG 11     REG 12     REG 13     REG 14     REG 15
00130098   0012D810   4014D04C   0012E60C   0012D998   001300F8


***YOU HAVE RETURNED:

 REG 1                         ANSWER
001301A0 ----> 1301A0: 00000004
                       00000001
                       000000A0
                       00000000

   5 POINTS FOR RETURNING CONTROL TO GRADER
   5 POINTS FOR RESTORING REGISTERS
```

```
5 POINTS FOR RESTORING REGISTERS
2 POINTS FOR CORRECT LENGTH
2 POINTS FOR CORRECT NUMBER OF ADDRESS FIELDS
3 POINTS FOR CORRECT OPERAND 1
3 POINTS FOR CORRECT OPERAND 2
```

***WE WILL PASS YOU:

```
 REG 1                         INSTRUCTION
0012E602 ----> 12E602: F82D5004200F0700
```

| REG 2 | REG 3 | REG 4 | REG 5 | REG 6 | REG 7 | REG 8 | REG 9 |
|-------|-------|-------|-------|-------|-------|-------|-------|
| 00000014 | 00000028 | 0000003C | 00000064 | 0014CF50 | 000000FF | 00000000 | 0014CE90 |

| REG 10 | REG 11 | REG 12 | REG 13 | REG 14 | REG 15 |
|--------|--------|--------|--------|--------|--------|
| 001300E0 | 0012D810 | 4014D04C | 0012E60C | 0012D998 | 001300F8 |

***YOU HAVE RETURNED:

```
 REG 1                       ANSWER
001301A0 ----> 1301A0:  00000006
                        00000002
                        00000068
                        00000023
```

```
5 POINTS FOR RETURNING CONTROL TO GRADER
5 POINTS FOR RESTORING REGISTERS
2 POINTS FOR CORRECT LENGTH
2 POINTS FOR CORRECT NUMBER OF ADDRESS FIELDS
3 POINTS FOR CORRECT OPERAND 1
3 POINTS FOR CORRECT OPERAND 2
```

*** TESTING COMPLETE, YOUR TOTAL SCORE IS 100

## 2.5.6 Roman Numeral Conversion Problem -- A6

```
LOC   OBJECT CODE     ADDR1 ADDR2  STMT   SOURCE STATEMENT

000000                               2 MP1      CSECT
                                     3 ************************************************************************
                                     4 *                                                                      *
                                     5 *      SAMPLE SOLUTION FOR ROMAN NUMERAL CONVERSION PROBLEM             *
                                     6 *                                                                      *
                                     7 *UPON ENTRY:                                                           *
                                     8 *                                                                      *
                                     9 *      REGISTER 0 CONTAINS A POINTER TO A TWO FULLWORD BLOCK:          *
                                    10 *                                                                      *
                                    11 *      THE FIRST WORD POINTS TO A CONVERSION TABLE                     *
                                    12 *                                                                      *
                                    13 *      THE SECOND WORD CONTAINS THE LENGTH (TOP BYTE) AND              *
                                    14 *      ADDRESS (LOW ORDER 3 BYTES) OF THE DECIMAL STRING TO BE         *
                                    15 *      CONVERTED                                                       *
                                    16 *                                                                      *
                                    17 *UPON RETURN:                                                          *
                                    18 *                                                                      *
                                    19 *      REGISTER 1 CONTAINS THE LENGTH AND ADDRESS OF THE ANSWER        *
                                    20 *                                                                      *
                                    21 ************************************************************************
000000 90EC D00C          0000C     23          STM    14,12,12(13)        SAVE REGISTERS
000004 05F0                         24          BALR   15,0                ESTABLISH ADDRESSABILITY
000006                              25          USING  *,15
000006 1840                         26          LR     4,0                 PUT ADDRESS OF BLOCK INTO REG 4
000008 5870 4000          00000     27          L      7,0(,4)             PUT ADDRESS OF ROMAN NUMERAL
                                    28 *                                    CONVERSION TABLE INTO REG 7
000000                              29          USING  ROMAN,7
00000C 1833                         30          SR     3,3                 CLEAR REGISTER 3
00000E 4330 4004          00004     31          IC     3,4(,4)             GET LENGTH OF INPUT STRING FROM BLOCK
000012 0630                         32          BCTR   3,0                 DECREMENT LENGTH BY 1 FOR AN EXECUTE
000014 5860 4004          00004     33          L      6,4(,4)             PUT ADDRESS OF INPUT STRING INTO REG6
000018 4430 F096          0009C     34          EX     3,MOVE              MOVE DECIMAL STRING INTO ANSWER
00001C                              35 CONVERT  EQU    *                   CONVERT INPUT STRING INTO A 32 BIT
                                    36 *                                    BINARY VALUE
00001C 4140 F0A2          000A8     37          LA     4,ANSWER            GET POINTER TO WORK AREA
000020 92FF F0C4          000CA     38          MVI    SIGN,X'FF'          SET SIGN TO PLUS BY DEFAULT
000024 4160 000E          0000E     39 NOSIGN   LA     6,14                PUT 14 INTO REG 6
000028 1863                         40          SR     6,3                 SUBTRACT (LENGTH - 1) FROM 14
00002A D70E F0B2 F0B2 000B8 000B8   41          XC     COPY(15),COPY       CLEAR OUT COPY AREA
000030 4166 F0B2          000B8     42          LA     6,COPY(6)           POINT TO SPOT FOR A MOVE
000034 4430 F09C          000A2     43          EX     3,MOVE3             MOVE UNPACKED VALUE INTO COPY AREA
000038 F27E F0A2 F0B2 000A8 000B8   44          PACK   ANSWER(8),COPY(15)  PERFORM A PACK
00003E 4F60 F0A2          000A8     45          CVB    6,ANSWER            CONVERT STRING TO A FULL-WORD
000042 4150 F0B2          000B8     46          LA     5,COPY              POINT REG 5 TO WORK AREA
000046 1833                         47          SR     3,3                 CLEAR REG 3
000048 4960 7002          00002     48 LOOP     CH     6,VALUE             IS RESIDUE VALUE SMALLER THAN
                                    49 *                                    THE TABLE VALUE ENTRY?   .
00004C 4740 F070          00076     50          BL     TOOBIG              NO, BRANCH
000050 D201 5000 7000 00000 00000   51          MVC    0(2,5),CHARS        MOVE ROMAN NUMERAL INTO AREA
000056 4860 7002          00002     52          SH     6,VALUE             DECREMENT REGISTER 6 BY ENTRY VALUE
00005A 9540 7001          00001     53          CLI    CHARS+1,C' '        IS 2ND ROMAN NUMERAL A BLANK
00005E 4780 F064          0006A     54          BE     BLANK               YES, BRANCH
000062 4150 5001          00001     55          LA     5,1(,5)             INCREMENT POINTER IN WORK AREA BY 1
000066 4130 3001          00001     56          LA     3,1(,3)             INCREMENT REG 3 FOR CHARACTER COUNT
```

A6S    SAMPLE SOLUTION TO ROMAN NUMERAL CONVERSION PROBLEM -- A6 02/16/74                    PAGE   4

```
  LOC  OBJECT CODE    ADDR1 ADDR2  STMT   SOURCE STATEMENT                                           11 JUN 74

00006A 4150 5001           00001    57 BLANK    LA    5,1(,5)       INCREMENT POINTER IN WORK AREA BY 1
00006E 4130 3001           00001    58          LA    3,1(,3)       INCREMENT REG 3 FOR CHARACTER COUNT
000072 47F0 F042           00048    59          B     LOOP          TRY LOOP AGAIN
000076 1266                         60 TOOBIG   LTR   6,6           CHECK STATUS OF REG 6
000078 4780 F07E           00084    61          BZ    DONE          BRANCH IF RESIDUE IS ZERO
00007C 4170 7004           00004    62          LA    7,4(,7)       INCREMENT POINTER IN CONVERSION TABLE
000080 47F0 F042           00048    63          B     LOOP          TRY LOOP AGAIN
000084                              64 DONE     EQU   *
000084 0650                         65          BCTR  5,0           RESET POINTER TO LAST CHARACTER
000086 D400 5000 F0C4 00000 000CA   66          NC    0(1,5),SIGN   INSERT SIGN INTO LAST DIGIT
00008C 423D 0018           00018    67          STC   3,12+3*4(13)  PUT LENGTH OF ANSWER INTO REGISTER 1
                                    68 *                            IN THE SAVE AREA POINTED TO BY REG13
000090 D202 0019 F0C1 00019 000C7   69          MVC   12+3*4+1(3,13),ADDR MOVE THE ADDRESS OF COPY IN ALSO
000096 98EC D00C           0000C    70          LM    14,12,12(13)  RESTORE ALL REGISTERS
00009A 07FE                         71          BR    14            RETURN TO THE GRADER
                                    72 ****************************************************************
                                    73 *                                                              *
                                    74 *             WORK AREAS AND CONSTANTS                          *
                                    75 *                                                              *
                                    76 ****************************************************************

00009C D200 F0A2 6000 000A8 00000   78 MOVE     MVC   ANSWER(0),0(6)
0000A2 D200 6000 4000 00000 00000   79 MOVE3    MVC   0(0,6),0(4)
0000A8                              80 ANSWER   DS    2D            SCRATCH AREA
0000B8                              81 COPY     DS    CL15          SCRATCH AREA
0000C7 0000B8                       82 ADDR     DC    AL3(COPY)     ADDRESS OF RESULT FOR GRADER
0000CA                              83 SIGN     DS    CL1           MASK FOR SIGN OF LAST ROMAN DIGIT

000000                              85 ROMAN    DSECT               CONVERSION TABLE ENTRY FORMAT
000000                              86 CHARS    DS    CL2
000002                              87 VALUE    DS    H
                                    88          END
```

```
**** ASSEMBLER PROBLEM GRADER HAS BEEN ENTERED FOR STUDENT

PROGRAM ENTRY POINT: 12FE70

YOU HAVE RECEIVED 10 POINTS FOR SUCCESSFULLY ASSEMBLING YOUR PROGRAM


***YOU WILL BE PASSED: 1974

  REG 0
0012E604 ----> 12E604: 0012E60C ----> 12E60C: CONVERSION TABLE
                       0412E640 ----> 12E640: F1F9F7F440404040
                                      CHARACTER FORM: 1974


***YOU HAVE RETURNED:

 REG 1
0812FF28 ----> 12FF28: D4C3D4D3E7E7C9E5000000F1F9F7F412FF28FFFFFFFFFFFF
        CHARACTER FORM: MCMLXXIV    1974

2 POINTS FOR RETURNING CONTROL TO GRADER
3 POINTS FOR RESTORING REGISTERS
2 POINTS FOR SPECIFYING PROPER LENGTH OF RESULT
8 POINTS FOR CORRECT ANSWER


***YOU WILL BE PASSED: 153

  REG 0
0012E604 ----> 12E604: 0012E60C ----> 12E60C: CONVERSION TABLE
                       0312E640 ----> 12E640: F1F5F34040404040
                                      CHARACTER FORM: 153


***YOU HAVE RETURNED:

 REG 1
0512FF28 ----> 12FF28: C3D3C9C9C940000000000000F1F5F312FF28FFFFFFFFFFFF
        CHARACTER FORM: CLIII        153

2 POINTS FOR RETURNING CONTROL TO GRADER
3 POINTS FOR RESTORING REGISTERS
2 POINTS FOR SPECIFYING PROPER LENGTH OF RESULT
8 POINTS FOR CORRECT ANSWER


***YOU WILL BE PASSED: 973

  REG 0
0012E604 ----> 12E604: 0012E60C ----> 12E60C: CONVERSION TABLE
                       0312E640 ----> 12E640: F9F7F34040404040
                                      CHARACTER FORM: 973
```

***YOU HAVE RETURNED:

 REG 1
0812FF28 ----> 12FF28: C3D4D3E7E7Z9C9C940000000F9F7F312FF28FFFFFFFFFFFF
        CHARACTER FORM: CMLXXIII     973

2 POINTS FOR RETURNING CONTROL TO GRADER
3 POINTS FOR RESTORING REGISTERS
2 POINTS FOR SPECIFYING PROPER LENGTH OF RESULT
8 POINTS FOR CORRECT ANSWER


***YOU WILL BE PASSED: 55

 REG 0
0012E604 ----> 12E604: 0012E60C ----> 12E60C: CONVERSION TABLE
                       0212E640 ----> 12E640: F5F5404040404040
                                  CHARACTER FORM: 55


***YOU HAVE RETURNED:

 REG 1
0212FF28 ----> 12FF28: D3E540000000000000000000000F5F512FF28FFFFFFFFFFFF
        CHARACTER FORM: LV              55

2 POINTS FOR RETURNING CONTROL TO GRADER
3 POINTS FOR RESTORING REGISTERS
2 POINTS FOR SPECIFYING PROPER LENGTH OF RESULT
8 POINTS FOR CORRECT ANSWER


***YOU WILL BE PASSED: 1776

 REG 0
0012E604 ----> 12E604: 0012E60C ----> 12E60C: CONVERSION TABLE
                       0412E640 ----> 12E640: F1F7F7F640404040
                                  CHARACTER FORM: 1776


***YOU HAVE RETURNED:

 REG 1
0912FF28 ----> 12FF28: D4C4C3C3D3E7E7E5C94000F1F7F7F612FF28FFFFFFFFFFFF
        CHARACTER FORM: MDCCLXXVI  1776

2 POINTS FOR RETURNING CONTROL TO GRADER
3 POINTS FOR RESTORING REGISTERS
2 POINTS FOR SPECIFYING PROPER LENGTH OF RESULT
8 POINTS FOR CORRECT ANSWER


***YOU WILL BE PASSED: 370

 REG 0

```
0012E604 ----> 12E604: 0012E60C ----> 12E60C: CONVERSION TABLE
                       0312E640 ----> 12E640: F3F7F04040404040
                                CHARACTER FORM: 370
```

***YOU HAVE RETURNED:

```
 REG 1
0612FF28 ----> 12FF28: C3C3C3D3E7E7400000000000000F3F7F012FF28FFFFFFFFFFFF
         CHARACTER FORM: CCCLXX       370
```

2 POINTS FOR RETURNING CONTROL TO GRADER
3 POINTS FOR RESTORING REGISTERS
2 POINTS FOR SPECIFYING PROPER LENGTH OF RESULT
8 POINTS FOR CORRECT ANSWER


*** TESTING COMPLETE, YOUR TOTAL SCORE IS 100

```
 _____
|           |
| CHAPTER 3 |
|_____|
```

## 3.1  INTRODUCTION

This chapter describes a set of exercises designed to
introduce a student to the facilities and uses of the PL/1
language. These exercises cover a broad spectrum of difficulty
and complexity. They have been selected to reinforce a student's
understanding of the fundamentals of programming in a high-level
language as well as the fundamentals of language processors
themselves.

The first four of these six exercises do not use a grading
program, rather the student codes his or her assignment as a main
procedure. To guard against an expensive student error a
governing program has been developed which "steals" control just
before a student's main procedure.

This governor establishes execution time limits for printed
output and CPU time, as well as default error handlers and a
timing facility which prints how much time a student's program
took. These limits may be controlled by execution parameters,
discussed in the third section of this chapter. In conjunction
with the batch monitor, described in chapter 7, this governor
provides a vehicle for efficiently running several students in
one job step.

The last two problems in this chapter require the student to
code their solutions as subroutines which are then called by
driving procedures. These driving procedures provide debugging
routines mainly to print formatted dumps of complex list
structures, but they also enforce execution limits accepting the
same execution parameters as the governor.

## 3.2   STUDENT WRITEUPS

### 3.2.1   Cipher Problem -- P1

**Introduction:**

Computers play a key role in the modern science of cryptography. Special purpose systems and languages have been devised soley to aid in breaking codes and ciphers. On a simpler plane programs have been devised which "scramble" files using a key not stored in the computer. This way if someone could gain access to read your files, he or she could still not readily understand them.

One of the oldest and simplest coding schemes is called the Caesar Cipher. Briefly the Caesar Cipher involves a shifting process. You take each letter of a message and substitute a letter that is a fixed number ahead in the alphabet, wrapping around. For example, the message "FEZ" shifted two positions would be "HGB". Although this might not be such a clever code to use these days as it is easy to "break", it conveys the ideas involved in coding.

**Problem Description:**

Your assignment is to write a program which could be used to encode and decode messages using the Caesar Cipher. Your program will be a PL/1 main procedure which reads its input from the file SYSIN and prints results on the file SYSPRINT.

The input to your program will be ten cards. For each card the number of places to shift will appear in columns 1-4, while the text of the message will appear in columns 5-80. Note that the amount to shift is a <u>signed</u> integer. That is it may be positive to encode or negative to decode. For each card you should print the number of places you are shifting, the input message, and the output message. This output will be used to check your program.

Your program should only shift the characters A-Z. All numbers and special characters, including blanks should <u>not</u> be changed.

**Examples:**

    input  card:    ⱶⱶ2ⱶⱶHELLO!ⱶⱶ...
    output message:    ⱶⱶJGNNQ!ⱶⱶ...

    input  card:    ⱶⱶ26ⱶGOODBYE--...
    output message:    ⱶGOODBYE--...

```
        input   card:      ███1HAL██...
        output message:       IBM██...

        input   card:      ██-2JGNNQ
        output message:       HELLO!
```

Deck Setup:

```
        /* your name - your instructor's name */
    CIPHER: PROCEDURE OPTIONS(MAIN);
    DECLARE
        (N, J) FIXED BINARY,
        INPUT CHAR(76);
            .
            .     /* DECLARATIONS, ETC. */
            .
    ON ERROR SNAP BEGIN;
        ON ERROR STOP;
        PUT DATA;
    END;
    DO J = 1 to 10;     /* READ ALL CARDS */
        GET EDIT (N, INPUT) (F(4,0), A(76));
            .
            .     /* PROCESSING */
            .
    END;
    END CIPHER;
```

Run Schedule:

   TO BE ANNOUNCED

### 3.2.2   Sorting Problem -- P2

**Introduction:**

While on the surface very mundane, sorting appears to some degree in almost every large scale non-numeric program. Assemblers and compilers sort the symbol table before it is printed to make it easier to read, while operator and keyword tables are sorted to speed access. Whenever the number of items to be sorted is very small, say less than 1,000, the algorithm used is not too critical.

Consider, however a bank which has its checking account files ordered by account number to speed processing transactions. If a listing organized by customer's last name is wanted, the entire file must be sorted. When you are dealing with very large files like Chase Manhatten's, this can be very time consuming unless a very efficient algorithm is used. For this reason several software companies offer sorting packages and the market is very competative.


**Problem Description:**

Your assignment is to write a PL/1 main procedure which sorts cards into ascending order. You are to use the basic interchange, or "bubble sort" algorithm. Simply stated the algorithm goes something like this:

   1. Declare a switch and an index. Set this switch to "on". This switch will be used to detect when the list has been sorted.

   2. Check the switch. If it is off then you have made a full pass through the list without changing it, so the list is sorted. Otherwise shut the switch off and continue with this step. Start at the top of the list of items to be sorted (N = 1).

   3. If the N+1th item is less than the Nth item, switch the two in the list and turn on the switch.

   4. Go to the next item in the list (N = N +1). If this brings you to the end of the list, ie., N is the last entry, then go back to step 2. Otherwise repeat step 3.

Although this algorithm works, it is less than optimal and may be improved considerably. For instance why do you have to wait until one whole pass is made with no changes before you can stop, and why continually scan parts of the list which are already sorted? You may feel free to jazz up this algorithm.

132

You will be given exactly ten (10) cards to sort. You should read the cards in from the file SYSIN, echo print them on the file SYSPRINT, sort the cards, print the number of passes you needed to sort them, and finally print the sorted cards. The amount of CPU time required by your program in execution will be printed at the end of your output. You are encouraged to compete with your classmates on two levels- number of passes used, and CPU time used.

Deck Setup:

      Your deck should have the following structure:

```
        /* your name - your instructor's name */
      SORT: PROCEDURE OPTIONS(MAIN);
            .
            .    /* DECLARATIONS */
            .
      ON ERROR SNAP BEGIN;
         ON ERROR STOP;
         PUT DATA;
      END;
            .
            .    /* PROCESSING */
            .
      END SORT;
```

Run Schedule:

      TO BE ANNOUNCED

### 3.2.3  Desk Directory Problem -- P3

**Introduction:**

A computer application especially common in the business sector is the so-called transaction oriented system. The input to such a system consists of requests for action to be performed upon a database. An example would be a bank's checking account inquiry system. Using a touch tone telephone a teller calls a central location and requests actions. He or she may check a customer's balance, "hold" amounts of money, terminate accounts, etc..

Since transaction systems usually interface with people who are not programmers, two very important parameters are response time and input consistency checking. Often simple checks applied to input data can detect expensive or hard to find mistakes before they are made. The response time issue is complicated by the fact that for most transaction systems the amount of data managed as well as the general workload steadily increases.

A system which initially functions well may begin to fall behind when the work load is increased. On the other hand, a very complicated system designed for a large workload may be totally uneconomical when used with a small workload. Clever design can minimize these effects by making the system "tunable".

**Problem Description:**

Your assignment is to complete a program which functions as a desk telephone directory system. This system takes the place of a rather old fashioned "flip top" telephone directory. For convenience in debugging all requests are enterred via a small desk top card reader in a fixed format. The requests to be processed are:

1. INSERT request. This request adds listings to your private directory.

   ```
   col. 1    col. 10    col. 20
   ▼         ▼          ▼
   INSERT    CHUNGA     2535716
   ```

   This request adds CHUNGA to the directory with a phone number of 253-5716.

2. DELETE request. The request deletes entries from your directory.

   ```
   col. 1    col. 10
   ▼         ▼
   DELETE    CHUNGA
   ```

This request deletes the entry CHUNGA from the directory.

3. SEARCH request. This request asks for the number associated with a name in the directory.

```
col. 1   col. 10
▼        ▼
SEARCH   CHUNGA
```

This request causes the phone number for CHUNGA to be printed.

4. PRINT request. This request prints the contents of the entire directory. This might be necessary if your system is unreliable and you need to manually look up a number while it is down!

```
col. 1
▼
PRINT
```

You will be provided with a partially completed program (described later) which you must complete in four steps:

1. DELETE handling. The program you are supplied does not process DELETE requests. Instead it prints "DELETE ACTION NOT AVAILABLE YET, REQUEST IGNORED". You must insert the appropriate code to process DELETE requests.

2. INSERT duplications. The program supplied does not check for duplications in INSERT requests. A request to add a name and number is honored, even if the name is already in the directory.

    You must fix the program so that INSERT requests for names already in the directory are not honored, but instead cause an error message to be printed. Optionally, you may want to allow requests that add an existent name, with the same number and just note that the action was not necessary.

3. Binary search and alphabetic PRINT. The provided program maintains the directory in the order entries were INSERT'ed. Thus the PRINT request prints in this order and the SEARCH request must use a linear search.

    You must change the INSERT and DELETE routines so that the directory is maintained in alphabetical order. Thus the PRINT request will print names in alphabetical order. Then you should change the SEARCH routine to use a binary search.

4. UPDATE request. You should implement a new request
   which updates existing directory entries. The format
   of this request should be the same as the INSERT
   request, for example:

```
col. 1    col. 10   col. 20
▼         ▼         ▼
UPDATE    CHUNGA    2534674
```

This requests corrects the phone number for CHUNGA.

   Your UPDATE request processing routine should
print an error message if the requested name cannot be
found.


**Notes:**

1. Please put your name and your recitation instructor's
   name on the comment card at the beginning of your
   program. This helps the operations staff.

2. Remember that PL/1 statements must begin beyond column
   1 and stop before column 73. If your statements spill
   over, the portions not between columns 2-72 are ignored
   by the compiler, even though they may print on your
   listing.

3. In the interest of debuggability (Shakespeare did it)
   the provided program contains few GO TO's. You should
   strive to keep the program as neat as possible, since
   this will have a direct bearing on your grade.


**Run Schedule:**

   TO BE ANNOUNCED

## Distributed Program:

The following program will be distributed in deck form:

```
/* DESK TOP DIRECTORY PROBLEM -- P3 DISTRIBUTION DECK */                        PAGE    2

STMT LEVEL NEST
                  /* DESK TOP DIRECTORY PROBLEM -- P3 DISTRIBUTION DECK */
  1               (SUBSCRIPTRANGE):  (STRINGRANGE):
                  TABLE:  PROCEDURE  OPTIONS(MAIN);

                  /*  'SEARCH' WILL BE AN INTERNAL FUNCTION PROCEDURE WHICH WHEN PASSED
                      A NAME WILL RETURN THE ENTRY INDEX IN THE DIRECTORY IF THE
                      NAME EXISTS THERE, OTHERWISE IT WILL RETURN A ZERO.    */

  2    1          DECLARE SEARCH ENTRY (CHAR(8)) RETURNS (FIXED(15));


                  /*****************************************************************/
                  /*****                DIRECTORY DECLARATIONS                *****/
                  /*****************************************************************/
  3    1          DECLARE
                        1 SYMBOL_TABLE(10),  /* ONLY 10 ENTRIES ALLOWED  */
                          2 SYMBOL CHARACTER(8),
                          2 VALUE FIXED DECIMAL(7);
  4    1          DECLARE
                        NUMBER_OF_SYMBOLS FIXED BINARY INITIAL (0);
                        /* NUMBER_OF_SYMBOLS KEEPS COUNT OF CURRENT NUMBER
                      OF NAMES STORED IN THE DIRECTORY */

                  /*****************************************************************/
                  /*****              OTHER NECESSARY DECLARATIONS            *****/
                  /*****************************************************************/
  5    1          DECLARE
                        ACTION CHARACTER(6),        /* EITHER 'DELETE', 'INSERT',
                                                    'PRINT', 'SEARCH', OR 'UPDATE' */
                        TSYMBOL CHARACTER(8),       /* HOLDS NAME BEING PROCESSED */
                        TVALUE FIXED DECIMAL(7),    /* HOLDS NUMBER BEING PROCESSED */
                        EOF_SW BIT(1) INITIAL('0'B),
                        I FIXED BINARY;             /* ENTRY INDEX  */

                  /*****************************************************************/
                  /*****              FUNCTION PROCEDURE SEARCH               *****/
                  /*****************************************************************/
  6    1          SEARCH:  PROCEDURE (NAME) RETURNS (FIXED(15));
  7    2            DECLARE NAME CHAR(8);
  8    2            DECLARE INDEX FIXED BIN(15);
  9    2            DO INDEX = 1 TO NUMBER_OF_SYMBOLS;
                          /* EXAMINE EVERY NAME IN DIRECTORY */
 10    2   1          IF SYMBOL_TABLE(INDEX).SYMBOL = NAME
                          /* DOES THE I-TH SYMBOL MATCH? */
 11    2   1              THEN RETURN (INDEX);
 12    2   1          END;
                      /* IF WE GET HERE, THE NAME WAS NOT IN THE DIRECTORY-RETURN 0*/
 13    2          INDEX = 0;
 14    2          RETURN (INDEX);
 15    2        END SEARCH;
```

```
/* DESK TOP DIRECTORY PROBLEM -- P3 DISTRIBUTION DECK */                                    PAGE    3

STMT LEVEL NEST

16    1           ON ERROR SNAP                      /* IF AN ERROR OCCURS, TELL WHERE */
17    1              BEGIN;
18    2                 ON ERROR STOP;               /* AVOID A LOOP */
20    2                 PUT DATA;                    /* FOR DEBUGGING */
21    2              END;

22    1           ON ENDFILE(SYSIN) EOF_SW = '1'B; /* STOP WHEN NO MORE CARDS */


                  /*************************************************************************/
                  /*****               PROCESSING STARTS HERE                        *****/
                  /*************************************************************************/

                  /*****  READ INPUT REQUEST CARD AND COPY ONTO OUTPUT              *****/
24    1           LOOP:  IF EOF_SW
25    1                     THEN STOP;               /* STOP WHEN NO MORE CARDS */

26    1                  GET EDIT(ACTION, TSYMBOL, TVALUE)
                            ( A(6), COL(10), A(8), COL(20), F(7) );
27    1                  GET SKIP;
28    1                  PUT SKIP(2) EDIT(ACTION, TSYMBOL, TVALUE)
                            ( A(6), COL(10), A(8), COL(20), F(7) );

                  /****  CHECK IF 'DELETE' ACTION *****/
29    1                  IF ACTION = 'DELETE'
30    1                  THEN DO;      /* IT IS 'DELETE', PROCESS IT */
31    1    1                PUT SKIP EDIT
                              ('DELETE ACTION NOT AVAILABLE YET, REQUEST IGNORED.')
                              (A);
32    1    1                END;
                  /*****  CHECK IF 'INSERT' ACTION *****/
33    1                  ELSE IF ACTION = 'INSERT'
34    1                  THEN DO;   /* IT IS 'INSERT', PROCESS IT */
35    1    1                IF NUMBER_OF_SYMBOLS = 10    /*TEST FOR OVERFLOW */
36    1    1                THEN PUT SKIP EDIT
                              ('DIRECTORY FULL, REQUEST IGNORED. ') (A);
37    1    1                ELSE DO;  /* INSERT NEW ENTRY AT END OF DIRECTORY */
38    1    2                   NUMBER_OF_SYMBOLS = NUMBER_OF_SYMBOLS+1;
39    1    2                   SYMBOL_TABLE(NUMBER_OF_SYMBOLS).SYMBOL = TSYMBOL;
40    1    2                   SYMBOL_TABLE(NUMBER_OF_SYMBOLS).VALUE = TVALUE;
41    1    2                   END;
42    1    1                END;

                  /*****  CHECK IF 'PRINT' ACTION *****/
43    1                  ELSE IF ACTION = 'PRINT'
                         THEN     /* IT IS 'PRINT', PROCESS IT */
44    1                  DO I = 1 TO NUMBER_OF_SYMBOLS;     /* PRINT ALL SYMBOLS */
45    1    1                PUT SKIP EDIT(SYMBOL_TABLE(I).SYMBOL,
                                          SYMBOL_TABLE(I).VALUE)
```

138

/* DESK TOP DIRECTORY PROBLEM -- P3 DISTRIBUTION DECK */                          PAGE    4

STMT LEVEL NEST
```
                                     (COL(10), A(8), COL(20), F(7) );
46    1    1                 END;

               /***** CHECK IF 'SEARCH' ACTION *****/
47    1                 ELSE IF ACTION = 'SEARCH'
48    1                 THEN DO;   /* IT IS 'SEARCH', PROCESS IT */
49    1    1                 I = SEARCH (TSYMBOL);

                             /* USE FUNCTION SEARCH TO GET THE ENTRY INDEX IN THE
                                DIRECTORY IF THE NAME WAS FOUND, OR A ZERO IF NOT */

50    1    1                 IF I = 0 THEN
51    1    1                 PUT SKIP EDIT('NAME REQUESTED NOT FOUND IN DIRECTORY. ')
                                     (A);
52    1    1                 ELSE
52    1    1                         PUT SKIP EDIT
                                         (SYMBOL_TABLE(I).VALUE)
                                         (COL(20), F(7) );
53    1    1                 GO TO LOOP;   /* GO ON TO NEXT REQUEST */
54    1    1                 END;

               /***** IF WE GET HERE, ACTION REQUESTED IS INVALID   *****/
55    1                 ELSE PUT SKIP EDIT('ACTION REQUESTED IS INVALID, IGNORED.')(A);

               /***** GO BACK AGAIN AND PROCESS NEXT INPUT DATA CARD        *****/
56    1                 GO TO LOOP;

57    1        ENC;
```

```
DELETE    CHUNGA          0
DELETE ACTION NOT AVAILABLE YET, REQUEST IGNORED.

INSERT    GREGORY    9361234

PRINT                     0
          GREGORY    9361234

INSERT    LINNELL    2536021

INSERT    DEJONG     2533213

INSERT    SMITH      8906123

IMSERT    SPELLING   2535716
ACTION REQUESTED IS INVALID, IGNORED.

SEARCH    GREGORY          0
                     9361234

INSERT    GREGORY    2611890

PRINT                     0
          GREGORY    9361234
          LINNELL    2536021
          DEJONG     2533213
          SMITH      8906123
          GREGORY    2611890

DELETE    SMITH           0
DELETE ACTION NOT AVAILABLE YET, REQUEST IGNORED.

PRINT                     0
          GREGORY    9361234
          LINNELL    2536C21
          DEJONG     2533213
          SMITH      8906123
          GREGORY    2611890

INSERT    NANGLE     2535716

INSERT    ALTMAN     6371234

INSERT    LINNELL    2536C21

PRINT                     0
          GREGORY    9361234
          LINNELL    2536C21
          DEJONG     2533213
          SMITH      8906123
          GREGORY    2611890
          NANGLE     2535716
          ALTMAN     6371234
          LINNELL    2536021

SEARCH    SPELLING         0
NAME REQUESTED NOT FOUND IN DIRECTORY.
```

```
INSERT     CALOGGER   2534643

UPDATE     CHUNGA      2611890
ACTION REQUESTED IS INVALID, IGNORED.

INSERT     DAVENPOR   2534600

INSERT     SMULLIN    2531000
DIRECTORY FULL, REQUEST IGNORED.

INSERT     BYER        2534608
DIRECTORY FULL, REQUEST IGNORED.

INSERT     WESTCOTT   2534608
DIRECTORY FULL, REQUEST IGNORED.

INSERT     MARTIN      2532411
DIRECTORY FULL, REQUEST IGNORED.

INSERT     JOHNSON    4235600
DIRECTORY FULL, REQUEST IGNORED.

INSERT     CHUCK       2582475
DIRECTORY FULL, REQUEST IGNORED.

INSERT     ALBEE       2534609
DIRECTORY FULL, REQUEST IGNORED.

INSERT     DEBBIE      2534674
DIRECTORY FULL, REQUEST IGNORED.

UPDATE     GREGORY    2611890
ACTION REQUESTED IS INVALID, IGNORED.

PRINT                         0
             GREGORY   9361234
             LINNELL   2536021
             DEJONG    2533213
             SMITH     8906123
             GREGORY   2611890
             NANGLE    2535716
             ALTMAN    6371234
             LINNELL   2536021
             CALOGGER  2534643
             DAVENPOR  2534600
```

### 3.2.4  Assembler Problem -- P4

Introduction:

     Often  in  automation and process control a machine is built
for one specific application. In  many  cases  special  op-codes
exist.  For  instance  a  machine  built to control a drill press
might have a "lower press" op-code.  In  view  of  the  special
nature  of these machines and the small number of actual programs
written for them, assemblers and other system software is  rarely
provided.

     Further,  you  find  that  such machines usually do not have
enough memory to support an assembler. A seperate machine is used
to run an assembler which produces object code  for  the  special
machine.

     Given  the  one-shot  nature  of such a project you wouldn't
want to spend a lot  of  time,  so  you  could  write a quickie
assembler  in  PL/1.  By eliminating such features as free format
input  and  linkage  facilities  an  assembler  can  be  greatly
simplified.


Problem Description:

     Your  assignment  is  to  write  a PL/1 main procedure which
assembles a simple language similar to BAL. In  the  interest  of
simplicity,  the language is very small and restricted in format.
The input to your assembler will consist of cards which you  must
read in from the file SYSIN.

     Your  assembler  must be a standard two-pass variety with no
macro  processing.  Pass  one  should  build  a  symbol  table
containing  symbol names and values (offsets).  Pass two utilizes
this symbol table to produce code. To implement a second pass you
must read the cards for a program into an array,  and  then  work
upon this array.


Input:

     To  simplify the task of decoding input, your assembler will
deal with fixed format input:

     column 1        10        16          18  19
            |         |         |          |   |
            V         V         V          V   V
            LABEL  OPCODE  REGISTER    ,   ADDRESS
                                            -or-
                                           REGISTER

(refer to the example for clarification)

LABEL - (cols 1-8) is the label field.  Labels  must  begin
    with  a  letter and may be from 1 to 8 characters long.
    This field may be blank.

OPCODE - (cols 10-15) is the mnemonic operation code.  This
    may  be  either  a  machine op-code  or  an  assembler
    instruction (pseudo-op code).

REGISTER - (cols 16-17) this field will be a 2 digit  number
    (00-15) which denotes a general purpose register.

ADDRESS - (cols 19-27) this field will  contain  a  symbolic
    reference  to a label (ie., a name), or it will contain
    a 2 digit register number.

You must recognize and process  the  following  machine  op-codes
(values are decimal):

| op-code | length in bytes | op-code value |
|---------|-----------------|---------------|
| A       | 4               | 12            |
| AR      | 2               | 13            |
| BC      | 4               | 17            |
| BCR     | 2               | 18            |
| L       | 4               | 10            |
| LR      | 2               | 11            |
| S       | 4               | 14            |
| SR      | 2               | 15            |
| ST      | 4               | 16            |

Your assembler must process the following pseudo-op codes:

| | |
|---|---|
| DC    | F'nn'  (where nn is a two digit number) |
| DROP  | register |
| DS    | F |
| END   | |
| START | |
| USING | register,label (backwards from real 360 BAL) |

Output:

    Rather  than  output  machine code, your assembler will just
have to print an assembly listing  for  the  input  program.  The
format  of  this  listing  is  similar  to  that  produced by the
standard System/360 assembler, except all numbers are in decimal

instead  of  hexadecimal.    Your output should have the following
format:

```
  _   _  _         _   _        _   _                      _
 |     | |          | |          | |                        |
 | LOC | | OP-CODE  | | REGISTER | | DISP(INDEX,BASE)       |
 |     | | VALUE    | |          | |  -or- REGISTER         |
 |_   _| |_        _| |_        _| |_                      _|
```

Where:

LOC - the decimal value of the location counter.

OP-CODE VALUE - the  decimal  number  corresponding  to  the
     mnemonic  op-code of the instruction, or in the case of
     DC instructions, the value of the constant itself, that
     is for DC F'nn' the value printed is nn.

REGISTER  -  the  value  of  the  REGISTER  field  from  the
     corresponding input statement.

DISP - a two digit decimal displacement, calculated by  your
     assembler.

INDEX - the index register, which will always be 00.

BASE -  base  register,  chosen  by  your  assembler.   This
     decision  is made in conjunction with the Base Register
     Table (described later).


Databases:

     Although you do not have to use  these  databases,  you  may
find  them  instructive  and  they  are intended to accompany the
algorithm outlined later. Many of these databases are structures,
a conglomerate of data types.  If  you  are  not  familiar  with
structures  and their use you should refer to  the PL/1 reference
manual section of that name.

   1. Input Program Array. This array is  used  to  hold  the
      cards  for  the input program so that two passes may be
      made. Associated with this array  is  the  Card  Number
      Counter  which  is  used to hold the number of cards in
      the current program. The  PL/1  declaration  for  these
      databases is:

            DECLARE
                INPUT (30) CHAR(80),   /* INPUT CARDS */
                CARD_NO FIXED BINARY(15) INITIAL(0);
                                    /* NUMBER OF CARDS */

2. Location Counter(LC). This is used to hold the next available location in the output object segment. Note that in the case of this assembler there is no object segment, but the counter is needed to print values in the output listing.

   This database is used by both pass one and two. Its PL/1 declaration is:

```
DECLARE
    LC FIXED BINARY(31) INITIAL(0);
                            /* LOCATION COUNTER */
```

3. Mnemonic Table (MT). This table is used to associate a mnemonic with its op-code or pseudo-op meaning. It contains one entry for each machine and pseudo-op code, sorted in alphabetic order. The following PL/1 declaration may be used:

```
DECLARE
    1 MNEMONIC_TABLE (15),
        2 MNEMONIC CHAR(5) INITIAL('A', 'AR',
          'BC', 'BCR', 'DC', 'DROP', 'DS',
          'END', 'L', 'LR', 'S', 'SR', 'ST',
          'START', 'USING'),
        2 MTYPE BIT(1) INITIAL( (4)(1)'1'B,
          (4)(1)'0'B, (5)(1)'1'B, (2)(1)'0'B),
        2 OPCODE FIXED BINARY(15) INITIAL(12,
          13, 17, 18, 1, 2, 3, 4, 10, 11, 14,
          15, 16, 5, 6),
        2 MLEN FIXED BINARY(15) INITIAL(4, 2, 4,
          2, 4, 0, 4, 0, 4, 2, 4, 0, 4, 0, 0);
```

Where:

MNEMONIC - the mnemonic character string for this table entry. Note that this may be either a machine or pseudo-op.

MTYPE - a switch which is set to '1'B for machine op-codes and '0'B for pseudo op-codes.

OPCODE - if this entry is for a machine op-code (MTYPE = '1'B) this is the decimal value of the op-code. Otherwise, for pseudo op-codes this is the pseudo op number. In the case of pseudo-ops this number may be used with a label array to decode pseudo-ops.

MLEN - this is the length of the instruction for machine op-codes and set to zero for pseudo-ops which generate no code.

4. **Symbol Table (ST).** This database is built by the first pass and then used by the second pass in code generation. It contains one entry for each symbol (eg., statement label) and its value. The value of a symbol is its _location_ (offset) in the output object segment.

```
       DECLARE
          1 SYMBOL_TABLE (30),
             2 SYMBOL CHAR(8),  /* SYMBOL NAME */
             2 VALUE FIXED BINARY(31),
          SYMBOL_NO FIXED BINARY(15) INITIAL(0);
```

Where:

SYMBOL - the name of a symbol, or statement label.

VALUE - the symbol's value, or location.

SYMBOL_NO - the number of symbols in the symbol table.

5. **Base Register Table (BRT).** This database is used only by pass 2. It is used to keep track of base registers and their contents. This table is added to by USING pseudo-ops and entries are deleted by DROP. The following declaration may be used:

```
       DECLARE
          1 BASE_TABLE (16),
             2 REGISTER FIXED BINARY(15),
             2 VALUE FIXED BINARY(31),
          BASE_NO FIXED BINARY(15) INITIAL(0);
```

Where:

REGISTER - base register number.

VALUE - the value this base register contains, if in use.

BASE_NO - number of currently active base registers.

This table should be maintained so that registers with the largest absolute value appear first. Sorting the table this way will help when it comes to code generation in pass two. As a byproduct, however you will have to be careful to prevent the same register from appearing twice in the table.

When you need to generate a base register-displacement pair from an absolute address, you search the BRT from the top down looking for a base

register which has a value less than   the    address   you
are   generating.    The first one you find is guaranteed
to have the smallest offset, so you   use   it.   Subtract
the   base   register value from the absolute address and
the result is the displacement.

6. Pass Switch. This is a switch   used   by   the   assembler
subroutines to detect which pass they are in. It may be
declared as:

        DECLARE
            PS BIT(1) INITIAL('0');

This   switch is off ('0') for the first pass and on for
thesecond pass.


Basic Algorithm:

        This section gives a sketch for an algorithm   which   may   be
used   with   the   preceding databases. This is not a very detailed
algorithm, but should serve to get you started:

                            Read In

1. Read the program into the input   array.   The   following
code will suffice:

        DECLARE EOF_SYSIN BIT(1) INITIAL('1'B);

        ON ENDFILE(SYSIN) EOF_SYSIN = '0'B;
        DO WHILE(EOF_SYSIN);
            CARD_NO = CARD_NO +1;
            GET LIST (INPUT(CARD_NO));
        END;
        CARD_NO = CARD_NO -1;

                            Pass One

2. Start at the first input card.

3. If a label is present for this   card,   add   it   to   the
Symbol   Table,   with   the current value of the Location
Counter.

4. Search the Mnemonic Table to get   the   length   for   the
opcode   of this card, from MLEN.   Add this value to the
Location Counter. Note that this correctly   handles   DS
and DC instructions.

5. Bump to the next input card. If this is   not   past   the
end   of the program, repeat step 3. Otherwise go to the
next step.

## Pass Two

The rest is left to you. Remember that the Base Register Table must be maintained and consulted whenever you need to generate an address from a label. The Symbol Table contains the absolute address of a symbol. To generate a base register and displacement the BRT must be searched to find the base register which yields the lowest displacement.

You might find the "GET STRING EDIT" statement and LABEL arrays most useful.

Example:

The following example should be helpful:

Input to your assembler-

```
    HARRY       START
                USING       12,HERE
    HERE        L           01,TEN
                A           01,TWO
                ST          01,TEMP1
                L           02,FOUR
                SR          01,02
                ST          01,TEMP2
                BCR         15,14
    TEN         DC          F'10'
    TWO         DC          F'02'
    TEMP1       DS          F
    FOUR        DC          F'04'
    TEMP2       DS          F
    DUMMYWRD    DS          F
                END
```

Output from your assembler-

| LOC | OP | REG1 | DISP(INDEX,BASE) -or- REG2 |
|-----|-----|------|----------------------------|
| 0   | 10 | 01   | 24(00,12)                  |
| 4   | 12 | 01   | 28(00,12)                  |
| 8   | 16 | 01   | 32(00,12)                  |
| 12  | 10 | 02   | 36(00,12)                  |
| 16  | 15 | 01   | 02                         |
| 18  | 16 | 01   | 40(00,12)                  |
| 22  | 18 | 15   | 14                         |
| 24  | 10 |      |                            |
| 28  | 02 |      |                            |
| 32  |    |      |                            |
| 36  | 04 |      |                            |
| 40  |    |      |                            |
| 44  |    |      |                            |

148

**Notes:**

1. All numbers are in decimal -- no hexadecimal at all.

2. The last statement of a program will always be an END statement.  No program will be longer than thirty (30) cards.

3. You do not have to enforce fullword alignment for DC and DS pseudo-ops.

4. Remember to reserve 4 bytes for a DS or a DC pseudo-op. Note how only the location counter is printed for a DS pseudo-op, while for DC pseudo-ops the value of the operand is printed in the operand field of the output listing.

5. The instructions that reference only registers (AR,SR,LR,BCR) do not have a displacement and index, etc. - rather, they have a second register specification.

**Deck Setup:**

The following deck structure should be used:

```
        /* your name - your instructor's name */
    ASMBLR: PROCEDURE OPTIONS(MAIN);
                .
                .    /* DECLARATIONS */
                .
    ON ERROR SNAP BEGIN;
       ON ERROR STOP;
       PUT DATA;
    END;
                .
                .    /* PROCESSING */
                .
    END ASMBLR;
```

**Run Schedule:**

TO BE ANNOUNCED

### 3.2.5   Lexical Analyzer Problem -- P5

Introduction:

The operation of a a compiler can be divided into seven
phases: lexical, syntactic, interpretation, optimization,
storage assignment, code generation, and assembly. The purpose
of the lexical phase is to build a symbol table and remove any
external format dependencies from statements.

Given almost any high-level language, statements can be
decomposed into elements of three general classes: operators,
identifiers, and literals. The set of operators consists of
keywords and all punctuation marks. Identifiers generally are
symbolic names of variables, and literals are the constants that
appear in a program.

Grouping elements of a language into general classes
simplifies the syntactic phase of the compiler. Further
simplification arises from the fact that the syntacic phase is
freed from dealing with character string representations of the
elements. Consider the following PL/1 statement:

        DO KK = J + 1 TO 10 ;

In this statement, we classify elements as follows:

| Operators | Identifiers | Literals |
|-----------|-------------|----------|
| DO | KK | 1 |
| = | J | 10 |
| + | | |
| TO | | |
| ; | | |

The lexical analyzer reads the input program, scans each
line and extracts each element. These elements are "typed" as
either operator, identifier, or literal and stored in a uniform
structure called a token. Thus each statement produces a series
of tokens. The tokens are implemented as a linked list (based
structures in PL/1), with forward chaining only. For example,
after lexical analysis the above DO statement would be converted
into this token chain:

| DO |->| KK |->| = |->| J |->| + |->| 1 |->| TO |->| 10 |->| ; |

(note: this is an idealized model of the token chain -- the
actual implementation is described later)

Problem Description:

Your assignment is to implement as a PL/1 subroutine a
general purpose lexical analyzer. Your subroutine will be called
by a grading program which will provide you with two driving

tables (described later) which completely specify the syntactical features of the language cogent to lexical analysis.

In addition to these two tables your subroutine will share another database, the symbol table, with the grader. Once your program is called it will procede to obtain card images of the source program by invoking a provided functional subroutine in the grader. As you scan each of these card images, you must allocate structures for tokens as required.

The grader provides a functional subroutine which you **must** use for allocating tokens. You share a pointer with the grader which you must use as the "anchor" to your token chain. This anchor, named START, is used by the grader's debugging routines to know the start of your token chain. Since the grader keeps track of your token allocations it will be able to tell you if your chaining is incorrect.

The two databases the grader will pass you contain the following information (complete description and declaration later):

OPTBL - This is an array of all the strings defined as operators within the language.

BRKTBL - This is an array of all those characters which are used to delimit (mark the end of) language elements. Generally, this set consists of all punctuation characters including the blank (ℓ). In some cases, elements of BRKTBL will also be in OPTBL. For example, again consider the DO statement, this time spaced differently:

DO  KK=J+1  TO 10;

In this example, the three sets of blanks serve as break characters while the characters '=','+', and ';' serve as break characters as well as operators since their appearance signifies the end of the language element immediately preceding it.

The generation of the token chain proceeds from left to right within a particular input character string. Each successive character is checked against the entries in BRKTBL for identity as a break character. If the character is not a break character, the scan proceeds to the next character in the string.

As soon as a break character is encountered, all the characters (if any) since the last break character constitute a language element. Note that the break character which delimits this element is not considered as part of the element. Having "isolated" an element you must decide what kind it is (operator, identifier, or literal) and allocate a token for it.

First you check for an operator by searching the OPTBL for the element. If the element is found in OPTBL, it is an operator and its value is the index into OPTBL.

If the element cannot be found in OPTBL, then it is either an identifier or a literal. Since we restrict identifiers to have an alphabetic or national ("a", "#", or "$") first character, it is easy to separate identifiers and literals. If the first character of the element is a number (0-9), then the element is a literal, else it is an identifier.

If you find an identifier, you must check the symbol table (IDNTAB, defined later) to see if the identifier is already known. If the identifier is not known (it doesn't exist in IDNTAB), it must be added.

Now that you know the type and value of the element you allocate a token for it (using ALOC), place it in the token, and chain the token on to the end of your token chain.

Having completely processed an element, it is time to examine the break character which delimited the element to see if it is an operator. If the break character is itself an operator (present in OPTBL), then it must be added to the token chain. If the break character is not in OPTBL, then it is ignored.

You then continue your examination of the card image at the character past the last break character. This continues until the end of the card image is reached. Then you ask the grader for another card image and this process is repeated until you run out of card images. At that point you return to the grader which will print and check your token chain.


Data Bases:

### Driving Tables

```
DECLARE 1 BRKTBL BASED (PBRKT),
        2 LEN FIXED BIN,
        2 C (J REFER (BRKTBL.LEN)) CHAR(1),
        1 OPTBL BASED (POPT),
        2 LEN FIXED BIN,
        2 C (J REFER (OPTBL.LEN)) CHAR(8),
        (PBRKT,POPT) POINTER EXTERNAL;
```

The OPTBL and BRKTBL will be supplied by the grader. They should be declared exactly as given above, and may be referenced in the same manner as any PL/I structure. Note that J is a dummy variable. You should not use this variable in your program, nor should it appear in any other declare statement.

BRKTBL.C is an array of character strings of length 1. You
may determine the length of the array at execution time by
referencing BRKTBL.LEN, which will contain the length.

OPTBL is similar to BRKTBL, except that it consists of
strings of length 8. The operator code will be its index in
OPTBL.C.

PBRKT and POPT will point to BRKTBL and OPTBL when your program
is entered, so you do not allocate these tables.

### Identifier (Symbol) Table

The identifier table consists of two parts. An array which
contains the names of identifiers, and a variable which contains
the number of entries currently in use. The following
declaration should be used:

```
DECLARE IDNTAB (50) CHAR(8) EXTERNAL,
        IDNNUM FIXED BIN(31) EXTERNAL;
```

This declaration implies a restriction of 50 as the maximum
number of identifiers and 8 as the maximum number of characters
in an identifier name. You will be called with IDNNUM equal to
zero. When you return, IDNNUM should indicate the number of
identifier table entries.

### Token Chain

In its actual implementation a token will not contain the
identifier, literal or operator it represents. Rather the token
consists of :

1) A pointer to the next token.
2) The type of token (operator, identifier, literal).
3) A pointer to a fixed binary(31) based variable which
   contains the value for the token. This value depends
   on the token type as follows:

   Operators: The value is the index of the operator in
        the operator table (OPTBL).

   Identifiers: The index of the identifier in the
        identifier table (IDNTAB).

   Literals: The actual value of the constant.

The format of each token block is given below :

```
DECLARE 1 TOKEN BASED (PT),
          2 NEXT POINTER,
          2 TYPE BIT(32) ALIGNED,
          2 VALUE FIXED BIN(31),
```

          START POINTER EXTERNAL;

TOKEN is a based structure.  Its fields are used as follows:

TOKEN.NEXT - This field is a pointer to the next token block
     in the chain.  The last token block in the chain should
     have  the  value  (returned  by  the built-in function)
     NULL.

TOKEN.TYPE - This is a bit string  of  length   32,   used   to
     indicate the type of token, as follows:

                   '100'B means OPERATOR
                   '010'B means IDENTIFIER
                   '001'B means LITERAL

TOKEN.VALUE - This is a FIXED BIN(31) number.   The  use  of
     this  variable  depends  on the token type as mentioned
     above.

START is a pointer (of external scope) which the grader will
     use to find the beginning  of  the  token  chain.   You
     should set START to the first token on the chain.

Diagramatically:

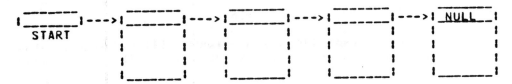

     The group of characters (--->) represents a pointer.


NULL  is a special pointer value used to signal the last block in
a chain.


Token Allocation:

     The token chain is a dynamic list with one list  member  (or
token)  for  each  element of a source program. You must allocate
tokens for  elements  as  you  analyze  a  program.   To  aid  in
debugging,  we  have  provided a functional subroutine you are to
use for token allocation.

     This routine remembers the tokens you allocate so that DEBUG
may print your token chain even if the  chaining  is  goofed  up.
Under  no circumstances should you use the normal PI/1 statements
"ALLOCATE" or "FREE". The following statements  may  be  used  to
allocate  a  token, assuming token is declared to be based on PT:

```
DECLARE ALOC ENTRY RETURNS (PTR);
   ...
PT = ALOC;
   ...
```

The ALLOC routine **must** be declared as shown for proper results.


Input:

The input to your analyzer will be a collection of 80 character cards, or "card images". To save you the tribulations of I/O the grader provides a functional subroutine (NXTCARD) which returns card images.  Each time this function is invoked it will return to you the next "card" of the program you are analyzing.

The mechanism by which NXTCARD informs you that there are no more cards available for input is very similar to the standard. When you request a card (via a function reference) and no more exist, NXTCARD raises an on-condition named EOF.  You can intercept this condition with code similar to the following:

```
DECLARE CARD CHAR(80);
DECLARE EOF_SW BIT(1) INITIAL ('1'B);
DECLARE NXTCARD ENTRY RETURNS(CHAR(80));
   ...
ON CONDITION (EOF) EOF_SW = '0'B;
   ...
CARD = NXTCARD;
DO WHILE(EOF_SW);
   ...      /* PROCESSING LOOP */
   CARD = NXTCARD;
END;
/* CONTROL REACHES HERE WHEN THERE ARE NO MORE CARDS */
   ...
   ...
```

The ON statement **must** be executed to take effect. It informs the compiler that when the condition "EOF" is signalled the variable "EOF_SW" is to be set to zero.  This technique will stop your card processing loop without a GO TO in your program.

In conformance with standard PL/1 conventions, you should ignore columns 1 and 73-80 of each card. In addition you should force a break at column 73 to insure that elements ending in column 72 are correctly recognized.

**Output:**

The output from your analyzer consists of two parts: an identifier table and a token chain. These are printed and checked by the grading program when you return control.

**Assumptions:**

Some PL/1 operators are longer than one character, but collectively act as one break character. Examples would be "**" and "||". For this problem we do not consider these operators, and the extension is left to your imagination.

**Hints:**

Certain advanced features of PL/I which you will need are not widely known. As an introduction to these features, read in the PL/I Language Reference Manual the sections on exceptional condition handling and program checkout, and list processing.

**Debugging:**

One of the nicer features of PL/1 is its error handling facilities. Correct use of these facilities drastically reduces the number of runs you need for most problems. You should look up the "ON ERROR" condition and code an error on-unit in your program.

The CHECK statement prefix may be used to trace modifications to a variable, but it is expensive in terms of CPU time. Alternatively you could place PUT LIST and PUT DATA statements at strategic points in your program to trace control flow.

You will be limited in the amount of output you may produce. Excessive output will cause your program to be terminated. It is to your advantage to obtain a lot of debugging information on your first run, perhaps being terminated for maximum output. This is far better than a non-working program with little or no information.

The grader provides a routine named DEBUG which you may use to obtain a formatted dump of your identifier table and token chain. Note that this routine does not depend upon your chaining for the token chain dump. You may call this routine at any time and it is especially meaningful to call it in your error on-unit.

If you neglect to provide an ERROR handler and an error occurs in your program the grader will call DEBUG for you. Also DEBUG will be called when your program terminates.

The following code may be used  to  print  the  value  of  a pointer:

```
DECLARE HEX ENTRY(POINTER) RETURNS(CHAR(6));

PUT SKIP LIST('START= ',HEX(START));
```

Deck Setup:

Your  program  must be a procedure labelled LEXPROC, and must not have OPTIONS(MAIN) specified.  It is important that  you  use the  declarations given in this writeup, otherwise the grader may not grade your program properly.

Your deck should have the following structure:

```
    /* your name - your instructor's name */
(SUBSCRIPTRANGE, STRINGRANGE):
LEXPROC:  PROC;
DCL  ...;              /* ALL NECESSARY DECLARATIONS */
     ...
     ...
ON ERROR SNAP BEGIN;
    ON ERROR STOP;  /* THIS STATEMENT HANDLES ERRORS */
        ...         /* OCCURRING WITHIN THIS BLOCK */
        ...
        ...         /* DEBUGGING STATEMENTS */
    CALL DEBUG;
    END;
        ...
        ...             /* BODY OF PROGRAM */
        ...
END LEXPROC;
```

Run Schedule:

TO BE ANNOUNCED

### 3.2.6   SICK Interpreter Problem -- P6

Introduction:

A compiler requires for input an algorithm encoded in a source language and produces as output a sequence of machine instructions which, when executed will realize the input algorithm. An interpreter accepts the same source language representation of an algorithm as input, but rather than output machine instructions the interpreter examines or "interprets" each source statement performing the indicated function.

An interpreter closely resembles a compiler in internal construction, with one important exception. Both start out by performing a lexical analysis of the source program to produce a list of language elements, or "tokens". Next both perform a reductions analysis upon the token list to extract the encoded algorithm.  Herein lies the crucial distinction. A compiler generates as output from the reduction step a matrix which is later used to generate code. An interpreter, however actually executes statements as the reductions step progresses.

For example, when a compiler reduces the statement  "A=B+C", a representation of the operations needed to add B to C and store the result in A are stored in the matrix.  An interpreter, on the other hand looks in the symbol table, finds the current values of B and C, adds them, and stores the result in the symbol table entry for A.

Generally speaking, an interpreter interpreting a source program takes much more CPU time than executing the machine instructions a compiler would produce for the same program.   If, however you compare the sum of time spent compiling a program and the time spent executing the compiled code to the time spent interpreting the same program you find that for small "one shot" programs the interpreter is faster. This is due to the high amount of overhead associated with a compiler.


Problem Description:

Your assignment is to write a  PL/1  subroutine  (procedure) which interprets a simple subset of PL/1 called the Simple Interpretive Computer Kludge (SICK) language. Your procedure must be named SICK and should not be a main procedure, i.e., don't use OPTIONS(MAIN).

You are to implement this problem in three steps. The first two are required to obtain complete credit and the last one is optional for extra credit.  Accordingly we provide three separate test programs which exercise increasingly advanced features of your interpreter. The features tested are:

Program 1 - All features of the language except DO-END, GOTO, IF-THEN, parenthesized expressions, and procedure invocation (internal procedures).

Program 2 - All facilities of the language except procedure invocation.

Program 3 - All facilities of the language (this part is optional).

You decide which program(s) you wish to try as described later in this writeup.

We do not provide a grading program to test your results. Rather these test programs perform calculations and print results. If your interpreter is functioning correctly the numbers printed will be correct. The output for a successful run will be posted so you can tell if yours is correct.


Required Databases:

Your interpreter must use the following standard databases:

1. Token Chain - This is a linked list of "tokens" or language elements for the SICK program you are processing. This chain is the primary input to your interpreter and is produced by a lexical analyzer we have provided.

2. Symbol Name Table (SNT) - This is a based structure containing the total number of symbols and an array of symbol names for all the symbols found by the lexical analyzer.

3. Symbol Value Stack (SVS) - This is a linked list of "cells". Each cell contains the index of a variable's name in the SNT and its value. This stack is necessary for the correct handling of internal procedures as explained later.

4. Push-Down Stack (PDS) - This is a linked list of elements which forms the heart of your interpreter. This stack is used in conjunction with a set of reductions to process the Token Chain. This process will be described fully below.

The declarations for these databases will be summarized at the end of this writeup in the section titled "Deck Setup".

Service Subroutines:

To expedite the writing and debugging of your interpreter we have provided several subroutines. These subroutines communicate by static external pointers, which you must maintain. These pointers, which are described later serve as anchors to various linked lists as well as place holders. The routines provided are:

1. LEXPROC - This is the lexical analyzer. It must be declared in your procedure with the following declaration:

   DECLARE LEXPROC ENTRY (CHAR(6));

   The argument you provide indicates which test program you wish to try. The names you may pass are 'PROGM1', 'PROGM2', and 'PROGM3'. LEXPROC communicates back to you by three static external pointers. Upon return START points to the start of a token chain for the desired program, PSNT points to the Symbol Name Table (SNT), and SVS points to the initialized Symbol Value Stack (SVS).

   If you pass LEXPROC an invalid program name (possibly the result of incorrectly declaring LEXPROC) you will be informed of your error. Be advised that if you misspell the names of any of the three pointers LEXPROC uses to communicate with you, you may experience obscure run-time errors.

   Just before LEXPROC returns to you it will print a formatted dump of the token chain, the value of START, a formatted dump of the SNT, the value of PSNT, a formatted dump of the initial SVS, and the value of SVS.

2. STMTSKP - As your interpreter processes the token chain it should keep track of the current token in a static external pointer named LOC. If you call this routine it advances LOC to the first token past the current statement. For example, if LOC points at the token for "A" in the chain:

   A = B * 3; FOO;

   And STMTSKP is called, LOC will point to the token for "FOO" upon return. If LOC points to a "PROCEDURE" or "DO" token (or a label before one), STMTSKP will skip to the statement past the end of the "PROCEDURE" or "DO" block, skipping any nested blocks as well. This routine is used to skip THEN clauses of IF statements, and internal procedures encountered in execution flow.

3. SVSDUMP - This subroutine produces a formatted dump  of
   the SVS and SNT whenever it is called.

4. PDSDUMP - This subroutine produces a formatted dump  of
   the PDS whenever it is called.

5. HEX    - This  subroutine  may  be  used  to  obtain  a
   printable  representation  of  pointers.   It  must  be
   declared as follows:

            DECLARE HEX ENTRY (POINTER) RETURNS (CHAR(6));

   It's use is fairly obvious. Suppose you wanted to  know
   where LOC was pointing:

            PUT SKIP LIST ('LOC =',HEX(LOC));

Note  that  if you misspell the name of any of these routines you
will get no output other than your  compilation,  due  to  loader
errors.

     The PDSDUMP and SVSDUMP routines should be used sparingly as
you  will  be  limited  in  the  amount of printed output you may
produce and they print copiously.


Description of Overall Algorithm:

     The general algorithm you should use is really very  simple.
A  brief  description  follows  to  get  you started in the right
direction:

1. First you call  LEXPROC  indicating  the  desired  test
   program.   This  will get you a token chain, an initial
   SVS, and a SNT.

2. Now you initialize the LOC pointer to the start of  the
   token chain (LOC = START;).

3. Take the token pointed to by LOC and put it on the  top
   of the  PDS.

4. Check to see if a reduction applies to the  PDS  stack.

5. If a reduction applies, perform the appropriate action,
   which  will  change the PDS.  Repeat step 4 to see if a
   reduction applies to this changed stack.

6. Set LOC to point to  the  next  token  (LOC  =  LOC  ->
   TOKEN.NEXT;).   If  LOC is not now NULL, repeat step 3.

     You should readily verify that the most challenging part  of
this  problem  is checking the PDS for applicable reductions. You

should strive to make this a logical step and as simple as
possible.


Comments on Based Storage:

    You should review the PL/1 manual with respect to based
storage, the ALLOCATE and FREE statements, and pointer-qualified
references. Keep in mind that only one level of pointer
qualification is allowed, that is where:

        DECLARE (P1, P2) POINTER,
        DUMMY FIXED BINARY(31) BASED(P);
        P1 -> DUMMY = P2 -> DUMMY;

is a valid collection of statements, the following is not:

        DECLARE P1 POINTER,
        P2B POINTER BASED(P3),
        DUMMY FIXED BINARY(31) BASED (PB);
        P1 -> P2 -> DUMMY = 3;

We require that all allocations be perfomed in an area declared
as follows:

        DECLARE AREAM AREA (10000) STATIC EXTERNAL;

Your allocate and free statements should use the "IN" option as
in the following example:

        DECLARE FIX FIXED BINARY(31) BASED(P);
        ALLOCATE FIX IN(AREAM);
        FREE FIX IN(AREAM);

Notes: if you free something without the "IN(AREAM)" option,
your program will be terminated with a completion code of
(system) 30A. If you attempt to free the same variable twice,
your program will go into a loop.


Lexical Analysis:

    Upon return from a LEXPROC call the pointer START will be
set to the start of a token chain with the following format:

```
 _____        _____      _____             _____
|START|-->|  NEXT  |--->|  NEXT  |-->...-->|NEXT=NULL|
         |  TYPE  |    |  TYPE  |         |  TYPE   |
         | VALUE |    | VALUE |         | VALUE  |
```

The declarations for the token cells and the static external
communicating pointers are as follows:

```
                DECLARE 1 TOKEN BASED (PT),
                        2 NEXT POINTER,
                        2 TYPE BIT(32) ALIGNED,
                        2 VALUE POINTER;
                DECLARE START POINTER EXTERNAL;
                DECLARE LOC POINTER EXTERNAL;
```

NEXT - A pointer to the next token in the chain, or the value of
       NULL for the last token in the chain.

TYPE - Specifies whether the token is an operator, identifier, or
       a literal. For our minimal interpreter there is only one
       data type, and hence one type of literal, fixed
       binary(31,0). The unused bits (rightmost 29) in TYPE are
       for expansion to more data types.

       '100'B        operator.
       '010'B        identifier.
       '001'B        fixed binary(31,0) literal.

VALUE - A pointer to a based fixed binary(31,0) variable. This
        variable contains the value of the token. This variable
        may be declared as:

            DECLARE VCELL FIXED BIN(31) BASED(VP);

        To obtain the value associated with a token, assuming PT
        pointed to the token in question, the following code
        could be used:

            VP = PT->TOKEN.VALUE;
            N = VCELL;

        The interpretation of a token's value depends on its
        type, as follows:

        operator: Number, according to the table on the
              following page.
        identifier: An index in the symbol name table (SNT),
              which is the array of identifier names set up
              by LEXPROC.
        literal: The value of the literal.

     In addition to producing a token chain LEXPROC creates a
Symbol Name Table and initial SVS for the test program. The
format for the SNT declaration, along with its communication
pointer is:

```
            DECLARE PSNT POINTER EXTERNAL,
                1 SNT BASED (PSNT),
                    2 ICOUNT FIXED BIN,
                    2 NAME (NS REFER (SNT.ICOUNT)) CHAR(8),
                NS FIXED BIN;
```

The number of symbols in the table is stored in ICOUNT.

For example, if a source program consisted of just the assignment statement:

    "A=3*B"

LEXPROC would set up the token chain and SNT as follows:

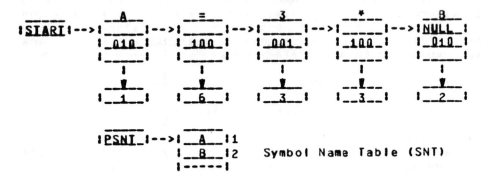

The codes for the various operators are:

| value | operator |
|-------|----------|
| 1     | **       |
| 2     | /        |
| 3     | *        |
| 4     | -        |
| 5     | +        |
| 6     | =        |
| 7     | >        |
| 8     | <        |
| 9     | IF       |
| 10    | (        |
| 11    | )        |
| 12    | ,        |
| 13    | THEN     |
| 14    | GOTO     |
| 15    | CALL     |
| 16    | RETURN   |
| 17    | DO       |
| 18    | PROCEDURE |
| 19    | END      |
| 20    | :        |
| 21    | ;        |
| 22    | PUT      |
| 23    | DECLARE  |

The Symbol Value Stack:

A product of lexical analysis, the Symbol Name Table contains one entry for each unique name in a program. The token chain contains only the SNT index for an identifier. For purposes of procedure invocation, most notably recursion a seperate database is used to hold the values of variables.

This database is a linked list called the Symbol Value Stack (SVS). The SVS contains entries for each generation of a given variable, identified by an SNT offset. To access the value of a variable, given its index in the SNT the SVS must be searched.

The SVS is modified -- that is, entries added and deleted -- only upon entry to or return from a procedure. When a procedure is enterred, SVS entries must be created for:

1. The formal argument of that procedure (appears in the "PROCEDURE" statement).

2. All variables declared with a "DECLARE" statement in the procedure, but not those declared in procedures internal to the called procedure.

3. All statement labels contained in the procedure, except those appearing inside procedures internal to the called one. Note that the label appearing on a second level PROCEDURE statement must be added to allow a call to take place.

The Symbol Value Stack is pointed to by a static external pointer called SVS. The declaration for SVS cells is as follows:

```
            DECLARE SVS POINTER EXTERNAL,
                    1 SYMVAL BASED (PS),
                      2 NEXT POINTER,
                      2 TYPE BIT(32) ALIGNED,
                      2 SYMBOL FIXED BIN(31,0),
                      2 VALUE POINTER;
```

NEXT  -   pointer to the next cell up on the chain, or NULL.
TYPE -    For this minimal interpreter, an identifier can
          only be a statement label or a fixed binary(31)
          variable.
             '010'B      statement label.
             '001'B      fixed binary(31) variable.
SYMBOL - index of the symbol in the SNT.
VALUE -   a pointer, to be interpreted according to TYPE. For
          statement labels, this points to the label's cell
          in the token chain. For variables, this pointer
          points to a fixed binary(31) based cell which
          contains the value of the variable. This cell

could be declared as follows:

                OCL ALPHA FIXED BIN(31,0) BASED(PA);

Since the SICK language allows recursion storage for variables internal to a procedure is not allocated until that procedure is entered. If the procedure calls itself recursively a new allocation of these variables is stacked. This treatment is analagous to PL/1 automatic class storage.

Consider the following example.

```
            DECLARE X;
            . . .
            CALL BAR;
            . . .
   BAR: PROCEDURE;
            DECLARE Y;
            . . .
            CALL BAR; /* RECURSIVE CALL */
            . . .
            . . .
            . . .
            END;
```

Assume we are in the main procedure. Storage for X has been allocated by LEXPROC. Now the procedure BAR is called and storage for Y must be allocated. Finally, BAR calls itself. At this point it is necessary to stack a new allocation for Y. Any reference to Y must refer to this new allocation. When BAR returns, the second allocation of Y is deleted, and references to Y again refer to the first occurrence.

This example is a little misleading in that all procedures in the SICK language must have exactly one argument. This argument is considered declared in the procedure and thus must obtain an SVS cell (of course the value cell for this SVS entry must be initialized with the value of the variable in the call statement). Procedure arguments will not be explicitly declared in a procedure.

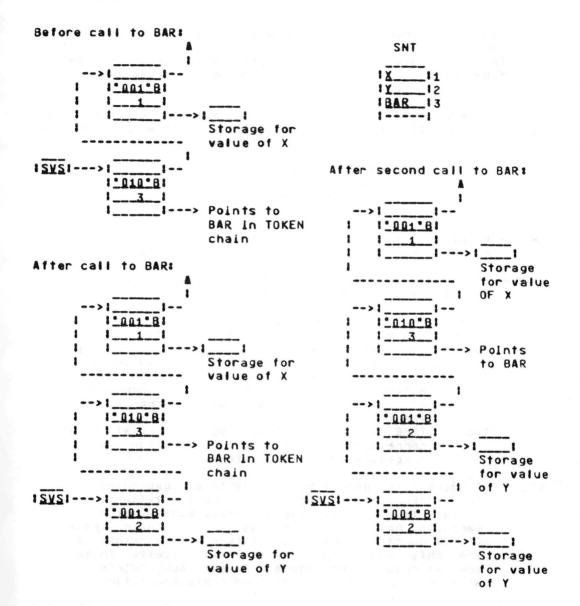

The Pushdown Stack:

    The operation of this interpreter is centered around a
single pushdown stack (PDS). This stack is a Last In First Out
(LIFO) linked list which is used to hold tokens, or uniform
symbols during the reductions process. It should be noted that
two characteristics make this separate stack (as opposed to token
chain only) necessary:

1) Reductions change the stack, elements are deleted and value cells changed.
2) The GOTO could cause you to re-process parts of the token chain. If the first time through altered tokens, the second time would not work the same.

The PDS is pointed to by a static external pointer of that name, and consists of a chain of elements, declared as follows:

```
DECLARE PDS POINTER EXTERNAL,
        1 PDCELL BASED (PP),
          2 UP POINTER,
          2 TYPE BIT (32) ALIGNED,
          2 VALUE POINTER;
```

UP    - Pointer to the previous cell on the pushdown stack, or NULL, for the oldest element in the chain.

TYPE - This field indicates the TYPE of element, similar to the TYPE field in the TOKEN cells:

'100'B  The cell corresponds to an operator.
'010'B  The cell corresponds to an identifier.
'001'B  The cell corresponds to value, fixed binary(31). A value might represent a temporary in the evaluation of an expression. Notice the difference between an occurrence of an identifier and an occurrence of a value.
'000'B  TYPE being zero indicates a special cell corresponding to the invocation of a procedure (described later).

VALUE - A pointer to another based data item, depending on the TYPE field. For operators, identifiers, and values, this cell is always a fixed binary(31) based variable. Operators are represented by their index in the operator table, identifiers by their index in the SNT, and values by the value itself. In the special case for procedure entries, VALUE points at another structure which will be explained later.

The action required to add a token to the PDS depends on the type of token. For identifiers or operators this action is a straight forward copying operation, since the PDS value pointer should point to the same fixed binary(31) cell as the token value pointer and the PDS cell type is the same as the token cell type. The following code will suffice to add an operator or identifier token to the PDS, assuming PT points to the token in question:

```
ALLOCATE PDCELL IN (AREAM);
PP->PDCELL.UP = PDS;
PDS = PP    /*NEW CELL NOW CHAINED ON PDS*/;
```

```
PP->PDCELL.TYPE = PT->TOKEN.TYPE;
PP->PDCELL.VALUE = PT->TOKEN.VALUE;
```

Notice that the value cell for the token is the _same_ _one_ used by the PDS cell, and therefore should _never_ be freed. Also the types are the same.

The action required to place a literal token on the stack is a little different. Again the type fields agree, that is to say that the type of a value PDS element is the same as the type of a literal token, but this time the value cells are _not shared_. This is because some value elements on the PDS are the intermediate results of expression evaluations. As such these are _temporary_ values which will be freed when their PDS cell is released.

Since an intermediate PDS element is indistinguishable from a literal PDS element, you must allocate a new intermediate value cell for literals to avoid freeing the literal token's value cell. To add a literal token to the PDS you must prefix the "ALLOCATE" statement in the next section of code with the following statements:

```
PDUMMY = PT->TOKEN.VALUE;
N = PDUMMY -> FIX;
```

Note that this assumes that PT points to the token for the literal.

The remaining type of element you put on the pushdown stack is a value cell for intermediate values, which may result from the evaluation of arithmetic expressions. For these you must allocate a cell for storing the value itself, and point the VALUE field of the PDS element at that cell. For this simple interpreter, there is only one data type. To put a temporary fixed binary(31) value on the PDS, you may use the following code:

```
DCL FIX FIXED BIN (31,0) BASED (PDUMMY);

ALLOCATE PDCELL IN (AREAM);
PDCELL.UP = PDS;
PDS = PP;
PDCELL.TYPE = '001'B; /* INDICATES VALUE TYPE */
ALLOCATE FIX IN (AREAM); /*GET CELL FOR VALUE*/
PDCELL.VALUE = PDUMMY;
FIX = N;    /* N IS VALUE TO BE STORED */
```

Remember that the value cells for value (type '001'B) elements _must_ be freed before you free the owning PDS elements:

```
PP = PDS;    /* THIS CODE FREES BOTTOM PDS CELL */
IF PP->PDCELL.TYPE = '001'B
```

```
        THEN DO;
            PDUMMY = PP->PDCELL.VALUE;
            FREE FIX IN(AREAM);
        END;
     PDS = PP->PDCELL.UP;
     FREE PDCELL IN (AREAM);
```

Additional data types could be added to SICK by assigning meanings to more of the bits of TYPE and declaring appropriate variables like FIX for the new data types.


Reductions:

The following reductions may be used in conjunction with the PDS and appropriate action routines to process SICK programs. The previously mentioned algorithm should be used. The column on the left is the initial pushdown stack, most recent entry at the bottom. The middle column is the form that the PDS is to be changed to after the reduction has been applied. The rightmost column describes the necessary semantic processing.

| | | |
|---|---|---|
| DO<br>; | DO | |
| DO<br>END<br>; | (nothing) | DO-END blocks don't have any action.  They are merely place keepers. |
| <ident><br>=<br><value><br>; | (nothing) | This is an assignment statement.  All of the tokens are removed from the PDS and the assignment is executed by placing the value in the appropriate SVS value cell. |
| <ident><br>: | (nothing) | Statement labels are ignored during interpretation. |
| GOTO<br><ident> | (nothing) | Change the LOC pointer.  The identifier's value is looked up in the SVS. Remember that for statement labels the SVS value pointer points to the label's token in the token chain. |
| <op1><br><ident><br>(1) | <op1><br><value> | Where: <op1>::= +|-|*|**|/|=|>|<|IF|(<br>These are all the operators which require values as operators (on the right) and not variables.  This reduction causes a variable to be replaced by its value. |

------------------------------------------------------------

(1)
This reduction does <u>not</u> apply if ident is a procedure name.
  Example:    FOO = FUNCT (A+B)

| | | |
|---|---|---|
| &lt;value&gt;<br>&lt;op2&gt;<br>&lt;value&gt; | &lt;value&gt; | Where: &lt;op2&gt;::= +¦-¦*¦**¦/¦=¦&gt;¦&lt;<br>This reduction does all arithmetic and<br>comparative operations. |
| PUT<br>&lt;ident&gt;<br>; | (nothing) | Print on the output listing as described in<br>the input-output section. |
| DECLARE<br>&lt;ident&gt; | DECLARE | During interpretation, DECLARE statements<br>are ignored. |
| DECLARE<br>; | (nothing) | See above. |
| IF<br>&lt;value&gt;<br>THEN | (nothing) | The value is either 0 or 1, being the<br>result of a comparison operator.  A single<br>SICK statement follows (it may be a DO block).<br>If the value is 1, do nothing, and the<br>then clause will be executed automatically.<br>If value is 0, then call STMTSKP to skip<br>the then clause. |
| (<br>&lt;value&gt;<br>) | &lt;value&gt; | This causes parenthesized expressions<br>to be replaced by their value. |

The next four reductions are necessary for procedure  invocation,
but their implementation is optional.

| | | |
|---|---|---|
| &lt;ident&gt;<br>&lt;value&gt; | &lt;proc&gt; | This reduction invokes a procedure.<br>Regardless of whether the invocation is<br>functional or by CALL, a procedure can<br>be recognized by an identifier followed<br>by a parenthesized expression.  The<br>resulting PDS entry &lt;proc&gt; is the special<br>type described in the section on procedure<br>invocations.  The semantic operations<br>for the procedure prologue are also<br>explained there. |
| &lt;proc&gt;<br>RETURN<br>&lt;value&gt; | &lt;value&gt; | This performs RETURN statements.  The<br>procedure epilogue is performed, as<br>explained later. |
| CALL<br>&lt;value&gt;<br>; | (nothing) | All procedures return a value, but in the<br>case of CALL, this value is not used. |
| PROCEDURE | (nothing) | Internal procedures must be skipped over<br>when they occur in the program sequence.<br>A call to STMTSKP will accomplish this.<br>LOC should be pointing at the PROCEDURE<br>token at the time of the call. |

**Example of Reductions In Action:**

    The  following  example traces the database activity for the
reduction of "A=3*B;". Assume the initial values for A and B  are
0   and 25, respectively and that the program consists of only one
statement.

Upon return from Lexproc:

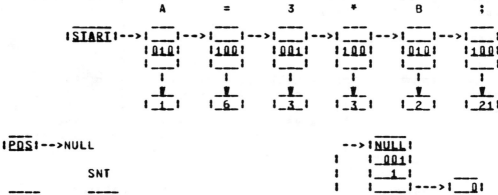

SYMBOL VALUE STACK

You should readily verify that as we add tokens onto the PDS,  no
reduction  will apply until we have "A=3*B" on the stack. At this
point the stack will look like:

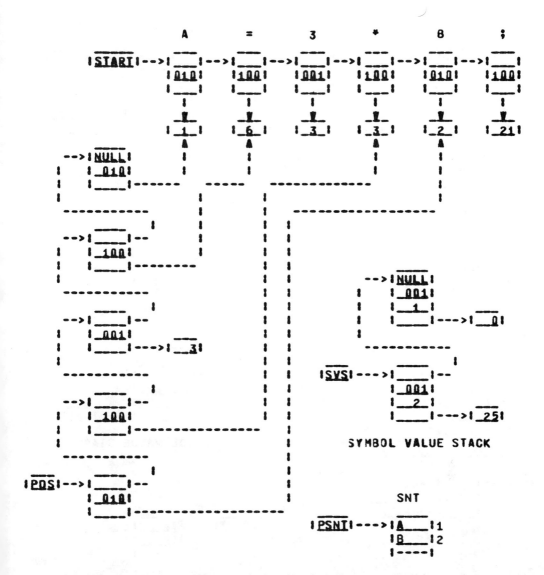

It is clear at this point that the reduction for <op1> <ident> applies. The purpose of this reduction is to replace the name of B with its value, so the expression "3*B" can be evaluated. This is how the databases will look after this reduction has been performed:

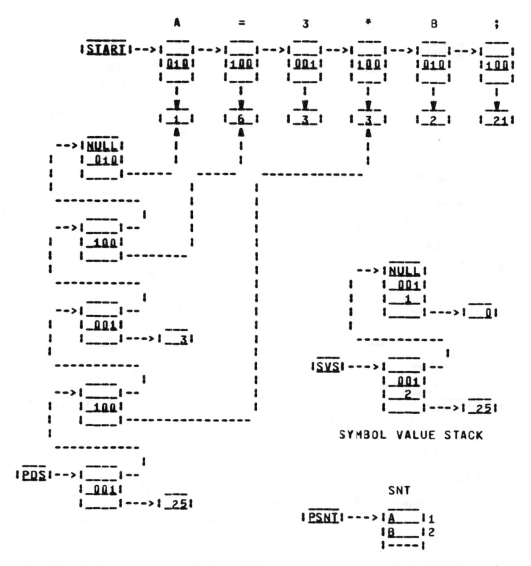

Now you can see that the reduction <value> <op2> <value> applies. The purpose of this reduction is to evaluate expressions. To this end the top two (bottom two in this backwards diagram) elements of the PDS will be purged, along with the value cell. The result of the expression will be stuck in the then top element thusly:

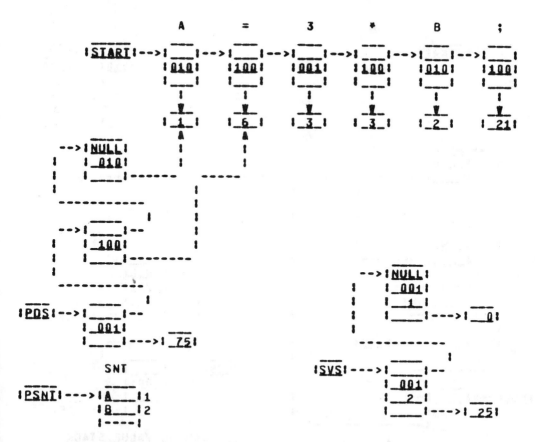

At this point no reduction matches the stack   and   the   next
token must be added!

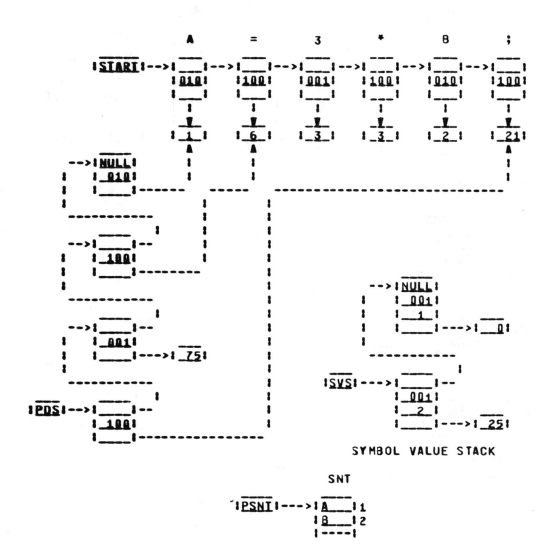

SYMBOL VALUE STACK

SNT

Now you see that the reduction for <ident> = <value> ;
applies. This is the reduction to perform assignment statements.
Note that this reduction leaves the PDS empty, as follows:

176

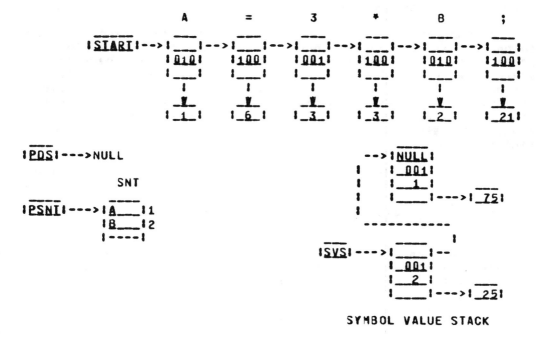

SYMBOL VALUE STACK


Input-Output Operations:

    You will not be asked to implement any input statements.  As
a  substitute  for  an  input operation, the LEXPROC routine will
provide  an  initial  SVS  which  will  simulate  input  to   the
interpreted program.

    You  will, however be responsible for implementing an output
statement so you can see if your  interpreter  works.   Given  the
following statements:

            FOOBAR = 3;
            PUT FOOBAR;

    Your interpreter should output (without the quotes):

    "FOOBAR =            3"

    This format isn't very pretty but is easy to implement.  The
following  single statement will have the desired result.  Assume
that NUM contains the  index  of  FOOBAR  in  the  SNT,  and  FIX
contains  the  value of FOOBAR, gleaned from a search of the SVS:

PUT LIST (SNT.NAME(NUM)  || '=', FIX) SKIP;

177

Invocation of Procedures:

    Perhaps the most complex function your interpreter will have
to perform is procedure invocation, that is handle internal
procedures. In the interest of simplicity we have imposed
several restrictions upon procedures and their use. In particular
all procedures have exactly one argument which is not explicity
declared (ie. does not appear in a DECLARE statement), the last
statement of each procedure is an END statement, and control is
always transferred out of a procedure with a "RETURN (<expr>);"
statement.

    A procedure may be invoked either with a functional
reference or a CALL statement as follows:

        functional reference:        A = SUBR(N);
        call reference:               CALL SUBR(N);

    In the case of invocation by call, the value returned by the
procedure is ignored (remember all procedures return a value). In
either case a procedure reference may be recognized by the
occurrence of:

        <ident>
        <value>

on the PDS. The action routine for this reduction is called the
procedure prologue. Basically the prologue saves the current
value of LOC and SVS for a return, generates SVS entries for all
declared variables and statement labels in the procedure, creates
an SVS entry for the procedure's formal argument, and transfers
control to the first statement of the procedure.

    The following detailed algorithm may be used for the
procedure prologue:

1. Save the value cell from the <value> PDS entry. Free
   the PDCELL for this entry, but not it's value cell. You
   will need a scratch pointer to hold down this cell.

2. Search the SVS to get the value pointer associated with
   the <ident> PDS cell. This pointer will point to the
   procedure label token in the token chain. Save this
   value in another scratch pointer. Free the <ident> PDS
   cell.

3. Allocate one of the special procedure invocation
   structures (PRCCELL, decsribed later). Save the current
   values of SVS and LOC in this structure. Allocate and
   chain on a PDS cell of type '000'B which points to this
   special procedure invocation structure.

4. Set LOC to the value of the second scratch pointer, the address of the procedure label token. Call STMTSKP to set LOC to the first token <u>after</u> the end of the procedure. Save this value in a third scratch pointer.

5. Set LOC back to the procedure label (scratch pointer 2). Execute this code:

```
DO JR = 1 TO 4;
LOC = LOC->TOKEN.NEXT;
END;
```

This will set LOC to the <ident> token for the formal argument of the procedure. Looking at the value cell for this token will get you the SNT index for the procedure's formal argument. Using this index allocate a variable SVS entry, using the value cell pointed to by scratch pointer 1. This initializes the formal argument of the procedure.

6. Now use the following code:

```
LOC = LOC->TOKEN.NEXT;
LOC = LOC->TOKEN.NEXT;
LOC = LOC->TOKEN.NEXT;
```

This will set LOC to the first statement of the procedure. Save this value in the second scratch pointer.

<u>Formal Aside</u>: The next part of this algorithm scans through the internal procedure, starting at the token specified by LOC and stopping when the token pointed to by scratch pointer 3 is reached. The purpose of this scan is to make SVS entries for all the declared variables and statement labels in the procedure.

7. Declare a bit switch and set it to '0'B; This switch will be used to tell if a DECLARE is being processed.

8. (Loop entry point): If the current token is a literal token, ignore it.

9. If the current token is an identifier, set the first scratch pointer to the value of LOC. This is necessary for statement labels. If the switch is set to '1'B, allocate an SVS <u>value</u> cell and set it to zero. Then allocate and chain an SVS entry with the variable type and pointing to this value cell. The symbol number for this SVS entry may be obtained from the value cell of the current token.

10. If the current token is an operator, set the switch to '0'B. Then you have to look at the operator number. If

the operator is "**;**" (20) then you must allocate an SVS
entry for a statement label, using the value cell
belonging to the token pointed to by scratch pointer
one as the symbol number, and scratch pointer one as
the value pointer.

If the operator is "DECLARE" (23), set the switch
to "1"B.

If the operator is "PROCEDURE" (18), call STMTSKP
and go to step 12.

11. Chain to the next token in the chain, ie. LOC =
LOC->TOKEN.NEXT;

12. If LOC = scratch pointer 3 then go to step 13.
Otherwise, go to step 8. (End of loop)

13. Now set LOC to the value of scratch pointer 2. This
will be the first statement of the procedure. Return to
your reduction processing loop and process the
procedure normally.

The special procedure invocation PDS cell has a VALUE of
"000"B. It is represented in the reductions by the symbol
"<proc>". For this PDS cell the value cell has the following
declaration:

```
DECLARE
     1 PRCCELL BASED(PPRC),
        2 OLDLOC POINTER,
        2 OLDSVS POINTER;
```

The OLDLOC field is used to save the value of LOC that existed at
the time the prologue was enterred. This is necessary for
returning. The OLDSVS field is used to hold the value of SVS
that existed prior to prologue execution. This is necessary for
deleting any SVS entries created by the prologue.

The procedure return reduction is triggered by the following
PDS configuration:

```
<proc>
RETURN
<value>
```

The action routine for this reduction is called the procedure
epilogue. Basically, the epilogue frees all SVS allocations made
by the prologue routine for this procedure and restores LOC to
the value it had before the prologue.

The following detailed algorithm may be used for the procedure
epilogue routine:

1. Save the VALUE pointer from the <value> PDS cell in
   scratch pointer one. Free the <value> PDS cell, but
   don't free the value cell.

2. Free the RETURN PDS cell.

3. Pick up the OLDSVS pointer from the value structure of
   the <proc> PDS cell. Save this value in scratch
   pointer 2.

4. If SVS = scratch pointer 2 then go to step 7.

5. Set PS to the value of SVS. Set SVS to SYMVAL.NEXT. If
   SYMVAL.TYPE = '001'B (variable value) then free the
   associated value cell. Free SYMVAL using PS.

6. Go to step 4 to see if you are finished with SVS
   freeing loop.

7. Set LOC to the value contained in the OLDLOC field of
   the procedure invocation value cell.

8. Free the special procedure invocation value cell and
   its owning <proc> PDS cell.

9. Allocate and chain a <value> PDS cell. Use scratch
   pointer one as its VALUE pointer.

This concludes procedure processing. Reductions procede as usual.


The SICK Language:

    The SICK language is a weak subset of PL/1 with statements
composed of three general classes of elements. These three
classes are:

LITERAL -- A constant appearing in a program. Since SICK has
    only one data type corresponding to FIXED BINARY(31),
    all literals are decimal integers.

OPERATOR -- A keyword which calls for action, as
    distinguished from literals or identifiers. An example
    would be "+".

IDENTIFIER -- A unique name which names either a value cell
    (variable) or acts as a statement label.


    It is very important that you be able to distinguish between
an identifier bound to a value (a variable) and a value. In the
example "A=B", A and B are both identifiers. However, in the
evaluation of this statement, the value bound to B will have to

be looked up and assigned to the value cell associated with A.


PROCEDURE - END - CALL - RETURN:

A procedure is a block terminated by an END statement,  just as in PL/I.  The procedure header statement can be described as

<idn> : PROCEDURE (<idn>);

A procedure is invoked either by appearing as a functional reference (such as A=SIN(B)), or in a CALL statement.  When invoked by a CALL, the returned value is ignored.  Execution of a procedure is always terminated by execution of a RETURN statement, which can be described as

RETURN (<expr>);


DECLARE:

Since there is only one data type (i.e., FIXED BIN(31))  in elementary SICK, there need be no attributes in a declaration statement.  An example is

DECLARE A B C ;

Note that the variables list is not parenthesized and the individual elements are separated by spaces, not commas.


IF . . . THEN:

The IF - THEN statement is similar to the corresponding PL/I statement except that ELSE clauses cannot be used.  The syntax is:

IF <value> <comp> <value> THEN <stmt>

where:  <comp>::= >|<|= (greater than, less than, equals)

See "assignment statements" for a description of <value>.


DO - groups:

All you need to handle here is the simple do-group:

DO; <stmt list> END;

There won't be iterative do-loops or WHILE clauses.

Assignment Statements and Expressions:

Assignment statements are of the form

<var> = <expr>;

where expr is a one-operator expression, i.e.,

<expr> ::= <value> <op> <value> | <value>

<op> ::= + | - | * | / | **

<value> ::= <var>|<function>|(<expr>)|<literal>

Unconditional Transfer:

The form is:
              GOTO <label>;

Statement Labels:

Again, the same as PL/I:

: <stmt>;

Output Statement:

PUT <ident>;

Run Schedule:

TO BE ANNOUNCED

Deck Structure:

    The following deck structure is recommended:

```
    /* your name - your instructor's name */
SICK: PROCEDURE;
DECLARE
    (LOC,
    PSNT,
    START,
    POS,
    SVS) POINTER STATIC EXTERNAL,
    1 TOKEN BASED(PT),
        2 NEXT POINTER,
        2 TYPE BIT(32) ALIGNED,
        2 VALUE POINTER,
    TVALUE FIXED BIN(31) BASED(PTV),
    1 SNT BASED(PSNT),
        2 ICOUNT FIXED BIN,
        2 NAME(NS REFER(SNT.ICOUNT)) CHAR(8),
    1 SYMVAL BASED(PS),
        2 NEXT POINTER,
        2 TYPE BIT(32) ALIGNED,
        2 SYMBOL FIXED BIN(31),
        2 VALUE POINTER,
    SVALUE FIXED BIN(31) BASED(PSV),
    1 PDCELL BASED(PP),
        2 UP POINTER,
        2 TYPE BIT(32) ALIGNED,
        2 VALUE POINTER,
    PVALUE FIXED BIN(31) BASED(PPV),
    1 PRCCELL  BASED(PPV),
        2 OLDLOC POINTER,
        2 OLDSVS POINTER,
    LEXPROC ENTRY(CHAR(6)),
    STMTSKP ENTRY,
    SVSDUMP ENTRY,
    PDSDUMP ENTRY,
    HEX ENTRY(POINTER) RETURNS(CHAR(6));
            .
            .
ON ERROR SNAP BEGIN;
    ON ERROR STOP;
    CALL SVSDUMP;
    CALL PDSDUMP;
END;
            .
            .
            .
END SICK;
```

## Example Program!

This example shows grader output and reductions in action for a PROGM1. The output from the grader stops at the statement "LEXPROC RETURNING". Subsequent output was produced by a sample solution. A line of output is produced every time a token is added to the stack or the stack is alterred by a reduction.

The number on the left of each line is the address of the next token to be added to the stack. The rest of the stack is a cannonic representation of the PDS, most recent entry to the left.

```
GRADER ENTERRED FOR STUDENT

LEXPROC CALLED
THE FOLLOWING PROGRAM WAS READ AS INPUT:

*****************************************************************************
*                   DECLARE D E F;                                         *
*                   D = 3;                                                  *
*                   E = D + 5;                                              *
*         A:        F = 9;                                                  *
*                   PUT D;                                                  *
*                   PUT E;                                                  *
*                   PUT F;                                                  *
*                   F = F * D;                                              *
*                   PUT F;                                                  *
*****************************************************************************

DEBUG CALLED, TOKEN CHAIN DUMP FOLLOWS


                                              ADDRESS
                                              -------
                                              NEXT
START->0FF538            LOC--->0FF538        TYPE      (LEFTMOST 3 BITS)
                                              VALUE
                                                V
                                              (VALUE)

DECLAR  D       E       F       ;       D       =       3       ;       E       =       D       +       5       ;
0FF538  0FF550  0FF580  0FF580  0FF5E0  0FF5F8  0FF610  0FF628  0FF640  0FF658  0FF670  0FF688  0FF6A0  0FF6B8  0FF6D0
------  ------  ------  ------  ------  ------  ------  ------  ------  ------  ------  ------  ------  ------  ------
0FF550  0FF580  0FF580  0FF5E0  0FF5F8  0FF610  0FF628  0FF640  0FF658  0FF670  0FF688  0FF6A0  0FF6B8  0FF6D0  0FF6E8
'100'B  '010'B  '010'B  '010'B  '100'B  '010'B  '100'B  '001'B  '100'B  '010'B  '100'B  '010'B  '100'B  '001'B  '100'B
0FF548  0FF560  0FF590  0FF5C0  0FF5F0  0FF608  0FF620  0FF638  0FF650  0FF668  0FF680  0FF698  0FF680  0FF6C8  0FF6E0
  V       V       V       V       V       V       V       V       V       V       V       V       V       V       V
  23      1       2       3       21      1       6       3       21      2       6       1       5       5       21

A       :       F       =       9       ;       PUT     D       ;       PUT     E       ;       PUT     F       ;
0FF6E8  0FF710  0FF728  0FF740  0FF758  0FF770  0FF788  0FF7A0  0FF7B8  0FF7D0  0FF7E8  0FF800  0FF818  0FF830  0FF848
------  ------  ------  ------  ------  ------  ------  ------  ------  ------  ------  ------  ------  ------  ------
0FF710  0FF728  0FF740  0FF758  0FF770  0FF788  0FF7A0  0FF7B8  0FF7D0  0FF7E8  0FF800  0FF818  0FF830  0FF848  0FF860
'010'B  '100'B  '010'B  '100'B  '001'B  '100'B  '100'B  '010'B  '100'B  '100'B  '010'B  '100'B  '100'B  '010'B  '100'B
0FF6F8  0FF720  0FF738  0FF750  0FF768  0FF780  0FF798  0FF7B0  0FF7C8  0FF7E0  0FF7F8  0FF810  0FF828  0FF840  0FF858
  V       V       V       V       V       V       V       V       V       V       V       V       V       V       V
  4       20      3       6       9       21      22      1       21      22      2       21      22      3       21

F       =       F       *       D       ;       PUT     F
0FF860  0FF878  0FF890  0FF8A8  0FF8C0  0FF8D8  0FF8F0  0FF908  0FF920
------  ------  ------  ------  ------  ------  ------  ------  ------
0FF878  0FF890  0FF8A8  0FF8C0  0FF8D8  0FF8F0  0FF908  0FF920  $NULL$
'010'B  '100'B  '010'B  '100'B  '010'B  '100'B  '100'B  '010'B  '100'B
0FF870  0FF888  0FF8A0  0FF8B8  0FF8D0  0FF8E8  0FF900  0FF918  0FF930
  V       V       V       V       V       V       V       V       V
  3       6       3       3       1       21      22      3       21

SVSDUMP CALLED
```

```
SVS-->OFF568          LCC--->OFF538                    NEXT
                                                       TYPE    (LEFTMOST 3 BITS)
                                                       SYMBOL
                                                       VALUE
                                                          V
                                                       (VALUE)


D           E        F        A
OFF568      OFF598   OFF5C8   OFF700
------      ------   ------   ------
OFF598      OFF5C8   OFF700   $NULL$
'001'B      '001'B   '001'B   '010'B
   1           2        3        4
OFF578      OFF5A8   OFF5D8   OFF6E8
   V           V        V
   0           0        0

SNT - SYMBOL NAME TABLE:
   1      D
   2      E
   3      F
   4      A

LEXPROC RETURNING
OFF550   DECLARE
OFF580   <IDN> DECLARE
OFF5B0   <IDN> DECLARE
OFF5E0   <IDN> DECLARE
OFF5F8   ; DECLARE
OFF610   <IDN>
OFF628   <OP2> <IDN>
OFF640   <VAL> <OP2> <IDN>
OFF658   ; <VAL> <OP2> <IDN>
OFF670   <IDN>
OFF688   <OP2> <IDN>
OFF6A0   <IDN> <OP2> <IDN>
OFF6A0   <VAL> <OP2> <IDN>
OFF6B8   <OP2> <VAL> <OP2> <IDN>
OFF6D0   <VAL> <OP2> <VAL> <OP2> <IDN>
OFF6E8   ; <VAL> <OP2> <IDN>
OFF710   <IDN>
OFF728   ; <IDN>
OFF740   <IDN>
OFF758   <OP2> <IDN>
OFF770   <VAL> <CP2> <IDN>
OFF788   ; <VAL> <OP2> <IDN>
OFF7A0   PUT
OFF7B8   <IDN> PUT
OFF7D0   ; <IDN> PUT
D        =                              3
OFF7E8   PUT
OFF800   <IDN> PUT
OFF818   ; <IDN> PUT
E        =                              8
OFF830   PUT
OFF848   <IDN> PUT
OFF860   ; <IDN> PUT
F        =                              9
OFF878   <IDN>
OFF890   <OP2> <IDN>
OFF8A6   <IDN> <OP2> <IDN>
OFF8A8   <VAL> <OP2> <IDN>
OFF8C0   <OP2> <VAL> <OP2> <IDN>
OFF8D8   <IDN> <OP2> <VAL> <OP2> <IDN>
OFF8D8   <VAL> <OP2> <VAL> <OP2> <IDN>
OFF8F0   ; <VAL> <OP2> <IDN>
OFF908   PUT
OFF920   <IDN> PUT
$NULL$   ; <IDN> PUT
F        =                             27

STUDENT PROGRAM USED     0.28 SECONDS
```

## 3.3  INSTALLING AND USING THE PROBLEMS

### 3.3.1  Introduction

In order to minimize the cost associated with a student error and provide the student with the best possible error reporting enviroment, each of the PL/1 problems has associated with it a monitoring program. Every monitoring program accepts execution parameters setting limits for CPU time and printed output. In addition, each monitor provides a default error handler to give the student information in the event the student has not provided an error handler.

The monitoring programs for the Lexical Analyzer Problem (P5) and the SICK Interpreter Problem (P6) in addition to this basic limiting support provide the student with subroutines and checking facilities to aid in debugging. As such these programs contain highly specialized sections of code. The monitoring program used for problems without grader-provided subroutines (e.g. P1-P4 and any other user-written problems) is the same physical program. In the interest of JCL simplicity it has been given the names P1-P4.

This simple monitor program allows the student to call his procedure a main one with the OPTIONS(MAIN) clause on his or her procedure declaration. However, before the student's program gets control the monitor is enterred and limits set.

All monitor programs consist of both a PL/1 component and an assembly language component. It is necessary to use assembly language subroutines to interface to the operating system's timing facilities, and to "steal" control for the simple monitor.

Through careful design all of the monitor programs accept the same execution parameters. If you write another monitor program you should strive to use the same parameters. These parameters and their meanings are described later.


System Requirements:

Since the monitor programs make use of full PL/1 (F) facilities and operating system timing facilities, they are tied down to IBM 360 or 370 systems using either OS or VS as an operating system. With much effort these monitors could be made to work under DOS.

When executing under operating systems without the programmer controlled timer feature, the monitors cannot limit a student's execution time. For this reason it is strongly suggested that your system possess this feature. Also if the monitors are run under a system without subtasking there is no way to determine a student's location when a timeout occurs, so the monitor terminates.

The storage requirements for that part of a monitor program dedicated to execution limit enforcing is quite small. Essentially the core requirement for each of the problems is determined by the complexity of the problem and the size of a student's solution. All of these problems may be run in a 128 K-byte partition, except the SICK interpreter problem (P6), which requires a region of 160 K-bytes. These figures include the overhead for the Batch Monitor which will be described later.

### 3.3.2  Installing The Monitor Programs

In order to use any of the PL/1 problems, two datasets are necessary:

1. A library (PDS) of load modules containing the monitor programs as members P1-P6. Note that P2, P3, and P4 are just aliases for the simple monitor program P1.

2. A library (PDS) containing the test data for the problems.  Members P1-P4 are the input (SYSIN) for the respective problems, P5 and P6 are dummy entries so the JCL can be generic, MAST is the control data for the Lexical Analyzer problem (P5), while PROGM1, PROGM2, and PROGM3 are test cases for the SICK Interpreter problem (P6).

These datasets are created in three steps. The distribution tape contains JCL for accomplishing this (see section 8.3).

Creating The Monitor Program Library:

Three assembly language modules are used by the monitor programs. These modules must be placed into a library for inclusion by the automatic call facility of the linkage editor. This is made necessary by the lack of a "PUNCH" analog in the PL/1 language. At the same time, however, the standard PL/1 library must be included in the automatic call library used by the linkage editor.

Due to a restriction of the linkage editor, load modules and object modules cannot be mixed in the automatic call library. You must therefore create a library containing these three load modules. The name of this library will be "PL1MP.ASM.LOAD".

The distribution tape contains the object for these three modules, complete with necessary linkage editor control statements. The following job may be run to generate the assembly language subroutine automatic call library:

```
//MAKEL     EXEC PGM=IEWL
//SYSPRINT  DD   SYSOUT=A
//SYSUT1    DD   UNIT=SYSDA,SPACE=(CYL,(2,1))
//SYSLIN    DD   UNIT=2400,DISP=(OLD,PASS),....
//SYSLMOD   DD   DSN=PL1MP.ASM.LOAD,DISP=(NEW,CATLG),
//               UNIT=2314,VOL=SER=nnnnnn,
//               SPACE=(TRK,(1,1,1))
/*
```

Notes:

1. The file referenced by SYSLIN is on the distribution tape, as is this JCL (see section 8.3).

2. nnnnnn should be replaced by the volume serial of the receiving volume. If this volume is other than a 2314, the UNIT and SPACE parameters of the SYSLMOD dd statement should be changed accordingly.

After this job has created a suitable call library, the monitor programs themselves can be linked. At the end of this next job step the previously created call library may be deleted if you do not plan to use the subroutines.

This following job reads the object modules for all the graders, complete with linkage editor control statements and produces the monitor PDS. The name of this PDS will be "PL1MP.LOAD", with the members P1-P6.

```
//MAKELO   EXEC PGM=IEWL,PARM="LET,MAP,LIST"
//SYSPRINT DD   SYSOUT=A
//SYSUT1   DD   UNIT=SYSDA,SPACE=(CYL,(2,1))
//SYSLIB   DD   DSN=SYS1.PL1LIB,DISP=SHR
//         DD   DSN=PL1MP.ASM.LOAD,DISP=SHR
//SYSLIN   DD   UNIT=2400,DISP=(OLD,PASS)..
//SYSLMOD  DD   DSN=PL1MP.LOAD,DISP=(NEW,CATLG),
//              UNIT=2314,VOL=SER=nnnnnn,
//              SPACE=(TRK,(40,5,2))
/*
```

Notes:

1. The dataset "SYS1.PL1LIB" contains the PL/1 run time library routines. This is the standard IBM name, but it may have been changed at your installation.

2. The file referenced by the SYSLIN dd statement resides on the distribution tape. It was produced by the PL/1 (F) compiler in the batching mode.

3. nnnnnn should be replaced by the volume serial of the receiving volume. If this is other than a 2314, the UNIT and SPACE parameters should be changed

appropriately.

4. The dataset "PL1MP.ASM.LOAD" may now be deleted if  you
do not wish to use these subroutines for anything else.


## Creating The Data PDS:

The purpose of this step is to create a library of test data
for the problems. The distribution tape contains this data in
IEBUPDTE (1) input format. This dataset is created with extra
(unused) space to allow for changing the test cases without
regenerating the entire PDS.

```
//MAKED    EXEC PGM=IEBUPDTE,PARM='NEW'
//SYSPRINT DD   SYSOUT=A
//SYSUT2   DD   DSN=PL1MP.DATA,DISP=(NEW,CATLG),
//              UNIT=2314,VOL=SER=nnnnnn,
//              SPACE=(TRK,(5,1,2)),
//              DCB=(RECFM=FB,LRECL=80,BLKSIZE=1600)
//SYSIN    DD   UNIT=2400,DISP=(OLD,PASS),...
/*
```

## Notes:

1. nnnnnn should be replaced by the volume serial  of  the
receiving volume.  If  this is other than a 2314, the
UNIT  and  SPACE  parameters  should  be  changed
accordingly.

2. The  dataset  referenced  by  SYSIN  resides  on  the
distribution tape.


## 3.3.3  Running The Problems

Having created the two necessary datasets, the next decision
you must make is how to run the problems. You are faced with
essentially two choices:

1. Using an in-stream or catalogued  procedure  to  reduce
the number of JCL cards involved for the student, allow
each student to be compiled and run in two seperate job
steps.  This method would use just the compiler and the
linkage loader.

2. Use the special purpose batch monitor to  run  all  the
students  as  one job step, providing extensive logging
and control card error recovery.

―――――――――――――――――――――――――――――――――――――――――――

(1) A discussion of  this  program  may  be  found  in  the  IBM
publication number GC28-6586, OS Utilities.

The first method places the lowest possible demand for core upon the system. This method has several drawbacks, however which make it unatractive if core is available. The student is required to punch up a few JCL cards, which if goofed up could cause an entire run to be lost. Each student is run as two seperate steps, and hence must undergo initiator overhead as well as any "step charges" imposed by the system. Finally, since each student's output is merged onto SYSPRINT, separating student output becomes a real nuisance.

To overcome these drawbacks we have implemented a simple batch monitor. This monitor greatly reduces the cost of running several students while making things operationally simpler as well. A run log is kept listing all students and relevant information, while student output separators are printed at the instructor's option.

The only drawbacks for the batch monitor are its increased core requirement and fixed overhead. That is there is a certain amount of overhead which is incurred only once by the batch monitor, that is not incurred by the first method. Generally speaking, running four students under the batch monitor is less expensive than stand-alone, while three student's under the batch monitor is _more_ expensive. If you want to use the batch monitor please refer to chapter 7 for details on its installation and use.

Regardless of which method you use, you should know the parameters which all of the monitor programs accept:

1. MAXTIME - Maximum amount of execution time student will be allowed, in hundredths of a second, _not counting compilation time_. This must be a non-signed integer value. A value of 100 corresponds to one second.

   If this limit is exceeded, the student is informed of his or her error and the ERROR condition is raised as if it occurred at the point of the loop.

2. STLIMIT - Maximum amount of time the student will be allowed in his or her ERROR ON-UNIT after exceeding MAXTIME. This is again expressed in hundredths of a second and must be a non-signed integer.

   If this limit is exceeded the students task is abended with a completion code of 322.

3. MAXPAGES - Maximum number of pages a student will be allowed to print, _not counting compilation_. This must be a non-signed integer. The method used to count this is an ENDPAGE ON-UNIT for SYSPRINT.

When this limit is exceeded, the student is informed and his or her job is stopped.

4. LINESIZE - Number of characters printed on each line of SYSPRINT. The default for this parameter is universally 120. This parameter must be a non-signed integer.

This parameter is used in a "LINESIZE" clause of the OPEN statement for SYSPRINT.

5. PAGESIZE - Number of lines printed on each page. The universal default is 55. This parameter must be a non-signed integer.

This parameter appears in a "PAGESIZE" clause of the OPEN statement for SYSPRINT.

6. NAME - An eight character string which is printed as the student's name on the execution output. This name may be passed by the batch monitor, which may pick it off of a student's "$JOB" card. The default for this parameter is all blank.

7. BADJCL - This is a switch used by our batch monitor to tell a monitor program that a student goofed up his or her control card(s). This is necessary since the batch monitor can correct several types of errors.

If this parameter is set to a non-zero integer value then the student is informed of a control card error on his or her execution output.

The method you use to pass these parameters depends on which method you are using to run students. With the stand-alone method these parameters are coded in the PARM field of the loader EXEC statement. When using the batch monitor these parameters are coded as part of the GP subparameter of the PARM field on the EXEC statement for the batch monitor.

JCL Using In-Stream Procedure:

```
//PL1       PROC N=
//C         EXEC PGM=IEMAA,PARM='LD,ND,NOL,NE'
//SYSPRINT DD  SYSOUT=A,DCB=(RECFM=VBA,LRECL=125,BLKSIZE=129)
//SYSUT1    DD  UNIT=SYSDA,SPACE=(CYL,(2,1))
//SYSUT2    DD  UNIT=SYSDA,SPACE=(CYL,(2,1))
//SYSUT3    DD  UNIT=SYSDA,SPACE=(CYL,(2,1))
//SYSLIN    DD  DSN=&&TEMP,DISP=(OLD,PASS)
//G         EXEC PGM=IEWLDRGO,PARM=' NOPRINT/BADJCL=0'
//SYSLOUT   DD  DUMMY
//SYSPRINT DD  SYSOUT=A,DCB=(RECFM=VBA,LRECL=125,BLKSIZE=129)
//SYSLIN    DD  DSN=PL1MP.LOAD(&N),DISP=SHR
```

```
//          DD   DSN=&&TEMP,DISP=(OLD,PASS)
//SYSIN     DD   DSN=PL1MP.DATA(&N),DISP=SHR
//MAST      DD   DSN=PL1MP.DATA(MAST),DISP=SHR
//PROGM1    DD   DSN=PL1MP.DATA(PROGM1),DISP=SHR
//PROGM2    DD   DSN=PL1MP.DATA(PROGM2),DISP=SHR
//PROGM3    DD   DSN=PL1MP.DATA(PROGM3),DISP=SHR
//          PEND
//ALLOC     EXEC PGM=IEFBR14
//DD1       DD   DSN=&&TEMP,DISP=(NEW,PASS),
//               UNIT=SYSDA,SPACE=(TRK,(10,4)),
//               DCB=(RECFM=FB,LRECL=80,BLKSIZE=1600)
//SMITH     EXEC PL1,N=Pn
//C.SYSIN   DD   *
                 .
(Smith's deck goes here)
                 .
/*
//JONES     EXEC PL1,N=Pn
//C.SYSIN   DD   *
                 .
(Jone's deck goes here)
                 .
/*
```

Notes:

1. Every occurence of n on the student's EXEC card should
   be changed to the number of the PL/1 problem, ie., for
   the Lexical Analyzer n-->5.

2. Each student is run as a seperate invocation of the
   catalogued procedure "PL1". To smooth things along you
   should provided pre-punched JCL. Then all a student
   would have to do is punch his or her name in columns
   3-10 of your pre-punched EXEC card.


JCL Using Batch Monitor:

```
//MPL1      PROC N=
//A         EXEC PGM=IEFBR14
//DD1       DD   DSN=&&TEMP,DISP=(NEW,PASS),
//               SPACE=(CYL,(2,1)),UNIT=SYSDA,
//               DCB=(RECFM=FB,LRECL=80,BLKSIZE=1600)
//DD2       DD   DSN=&&WORK,DISP=(NEW,PASS),
//               SPACE=(CYL,(2,1)),UNIT=SYSDA,
//               DCB=(RECFM=FB,LRECL=80,BLKSIZE=1600)
//DD3       DD   DSN=&&UT1,DISP=(NEW,PASS),
//               SPACE=(CYL,(2,1)),UNIT=SYSDA,
//               DCB=(RECFM=FB,LRECL=80,BLKSIZE=1600)
//M         EXEC PGM=MONITOR,
// PARM='TP=(LD,ND,NOL,NE),TN=IEMAA,SEP,LP=(NOPRINT)'
//STEPLIB   DD   DSN=MONITOR.LOAD,DISP=SHR
```

```
//SYSLOG    DD   SYSOUT=A,DCB=(RECFM=VBA,LRECL=125,BLKSIZE=129)
//SYSWORK   DD   DSN=*.A.DD2,VOL=REF=*.A.DD2,
//               DCB=*.A.DD2,DISP=(OLD,PASS)
//SYSPRINT  DD   SYSOUT=A,DCB=(RECFM=VBA,LRECL=125,BLKSIZE=129)
//SYSLIB    DD   DSN=SYS1.PL1LIB,DISP=SHR
//SYSUT1    DD   DSN=*.A.DD3,VOL=REF=*.A.DD3,
//               DISP=(OLD,PASS)
//SYSGO     DD   DSN=*.A.DD1,VOL=REF=*.A.DD1,
//               DCB=*.A.DD1,DISP=(OLD,PASS)
//SYSLOUT   DD   DUMMY
//SYSLIN    DD   DSN=PL1MP.LOAD(&N),DISP=SHR
//          DD   DSN=*.A.DD1,VOL=REF=*.A.DD1,
//               DCB=*.A.DD1,DISP=(OLD,PASS)
//MAST      DD   DSN=PL1MP.DATA(MAST),DISP=SHR
//PROGM1    DD   DSN=PL1MP.DATA(PROGM1),DISP=SHR
//PROGM2    DD   DSN=PL1MP.DATA(PROGM2),DISP=SHR
//PROGM3    DD   DSN=PL1MP.DATA(PROGM3),DISP=SHR
//          PEND
//          EXEC MPL1,N=Pn
//M.MONIN   DD   DATA,DCB=(RECFM=FB,LRECL=80,BLKSIZE=80)
$JOB name        student job 1
            .
            .
$EOJ
$JOB name        student job 2
            .
            .
$EOJ

... repeated for rest of students ...

/*
```

Notes:

1. The dataset "MONITOR.LOAD" contains the batch monitor
   and its support routines, refer to chapter 7 for more
   details.

2. If you wish to use the PL/1 include facility, the file
   used by the compiler has been changed from SYSLIB to
   TLIB.

3. The file SYSGO is the output from the compiler. The
   batch monitor has told the compiler to use this file
   instead of SYSLIN.

4. The occurence of $n$ on the EXEC statement for the
   catalogued procedure should be changed to the number of
   the problem. Thus, for the Lexical Analyzer problem,
   $n \rightarrow 5$.

5. All the students' jobs are run together after the
   M.MONIN dd statement.  The batch monitor is able to
   detect and correct most control card errors, but you
   are still advised to use pre-punched $JOB and $EOJ
   cards.

6. The field name on the $JOB card is used to label the
   students output.  This name may be from one to eight
   characters and the rest of the card is printed on the
   logging sheets.  This name is generated on a full-page
   seperator if the batch monitor option SEP is specified.

## 3.3.4  Modifying The Problem Test Data

The advantage to giving every student the same input is that
grading is made easier since the results are well known.  On the
other hand, this may get boring after awhile.  All that is
required to change the test data is to change the appropriate
member(s) in the PDS "PL1MP.DATA".  The following job may be used:

```
//CHANGED EXEC PGM=IEBUPDTE,PARM='NEW'
//SYSPRINT DD   SYSOUT=A
//SYSUT2   DD   DSN=PL1MP.DATA,DISP=OLD
//SYSIN    DD   *
./ ADD NAME=name
           .
           . new data
           .
./ ADD NAME=name
           .
           . second set, if desired
           .
./ ENDUP
/*
```

**Notes:**

1. You may only update a PDS a certain number of times.
   Every time you replace a member, its space is not
   freed, it goes into hyperspace.  After a while your
   updating jobs will abend for lack of secondary extents.

   You can avoid this by compressing the dataset with
   the IBM Utility IEBCOPY. (1)  Once you get the error,
   however your only recourse is to recreate the PDS as
   outlined in a previous section.

-------------------------------------------------------------

(1) Refer to the IBM publication number GC28-6586, OS
Utilities, for a description of this program and its use.

2. **name** is the name of the member to be replaced. The appropriate member names are P1-P6, MAST, and PROGM1-PROGM3. The individual meanings and formats of these members will be explained later.

3. Any number of members may be updated in one run. Just keep adding "./ ADD" cards followed by the data. The last input card to IEBUPDTE should be a "./ ENDUP" to signal the end of the run.

The rest of this section contains detailed information on the members involved in each problem and their formats, organized by problem.

Test Data for Cipher Problem -- P1:

The only test data needed by this problem exists as member P1 in the dataset "PL1MP.DATA". This data must be <u>exactly</u> <u>ten</u> card images of the following format:

Columns 1-4: optionally signed integer $-26 \leq n \leq 26$.  This number specifies how many places the next character string is to be shifted.

Columns 5-80: character string including any special characters or punctuation.  This string is to be "shifted" by the student. You should try to pick strings which when shifted the correct number of places (as specified by the number in cols. 1-4) make sense. This will encourage the student.

In particular you might want to start with a sensible string and have the student encode it (perhaps with a positive shift), then give the encoded string with a negative shift of the same amount.

An Example set of Test Data for P1:

```
1    5
▼    ▼
  1HAL
 -1IBM
 14 TRY THIS ON FOR SIZE
 26 THIS SHOULD NOT BE CHANGED
-26 NEITHER SHOULD THIS, SINCE BOTH ARE NO-OPS
  6 TRY SOME SPECIAL CHARACTERS:;a#%.*$<.+>)_!="?!(-/&.
  0 DON'T CHANGE THIS, EITHER
 -3 LI BRX JRW WKLV IDU, BRX'00 SUREDEOB PDNH LW.
  5 WPO, JI OCZ JOCZM CVIY...
    DID THIS CAUSE  A CONVERSION CHECK???
```

**Test Data for Sorting Problem -- P2:**

The only test data required by this problem exists as
member P2 in the dataset "PL1MP.DATA". This should consist of
exactly ten card images. Since the student is asked to sort
these cards, you should pick data which is obvious when it is
sorted correctly.

Perhaps sequence numbers near the end of each card, or some
such scheme could be used. When you arrange these cards you
should be aware that the students are competing to see if
refinements to the basic interchange algorithm can reduce the
number of passes necessary. If you place the data in exact
reverse order, everybody will have to have the same number of
passes.

**An Example Set of Test Data for P2:**

```
===================================================================04
1 ******    * ***        ******      ******     ******    * ***       **      ** 05
THEN THE NUMBERS C-9.                                                            03
** ****  **            *******   **  ****  **    **  **              ** ** 07
THEN CCME ANY SPECIAL SYMBCLS AND SCREWBALL GRAPHICS.                            02
BLANKS SHOULD BE THE LOWEST, FOLLCWED BY THE LETTERS A-Z.                        01
**    **  **          **        **   **  **    **  **                ***  08
******   **            ******   ******    ******   **               **   09
**           *** **   **   **  **        **   **   *** **     **    ** 06
                                                             ****  10
```

**Test Data for Desk Directory Problem -- P3:**

The only test data required by this problem is the member
P3. This should exist of any number of card images. These images
should be in the format discussed in the student writeup for this
problem. When you are creating test data you should be aware of
the following considerations:

1. You should provide enough test data to cause a symbol
   table overflow.

2. You should insert and delete in an order that would
   cause the table to not be in alphabetic order. This
   will give the student something to do.

3. You should include a few insert duplications, and one
   of these should be a complete duplication, that is
   inserting something with the same name and number as an
   existent item in the directory.

4. Since the only way a student's program is checked is
   with its ouput, you should include a liberal sprinkling
   of print requests at appropriate points.

5. You should include some update requests, with at  least
   one referring to a nonexistent item.

6. A liberal smattering of mispelled request  would  check
   the  student's  cleverness, as would some blank fields,
   if you are that mean.

An Example  Set of Test Data for P3:

```
    DELETE      CHUNGA
    INSERT      GREGORY     9361234
    PRINT
    INSERT      LINNELL     2536021
    INSERT      DEJONG      2533213
    INSERT      SMITH       8906123
    IMSERT      SPELLING    2535716
    SEARCH      GREGORY
    INSERT      GREGORY     2611890
    PRINT
    DELETE      SMITH
    PRINT
    INSERT      NANGLE      2535716
    INSERT      ALTMAN      6371234
    INSERT      LINNELL     2536021
    PRINT
    SEARCH      SPELLING
    INSERT      CALOGGERO   2534643
    UPDATE      CHUNGA      2611890
    INSERT      DAVENPORT   2534600
    INSERT      SMULLIN     2531000
    INSERT      BYER        2534608
    INSERT      WESTCOTT    2534608
    INSERT      MARTIN      2532411
    INSERT      JOHNSON     4235600
    INSERT      CHUCK       2582475
    INSERT      ALBEE       2534609
    INSERT      DEBBIE      2534674
    UPDATE      GREGORY     2611890
    PRINT
```

Test Data for Assembler Problem -- P4:

     The only test data required by this problem exists as member
P4.  This dataset must contain no more than 30 card images. These
card images are to be an  assembly  language  program  using  the
language specified in the student writeup for this problem.

     You  should  be  very  careful  to  insure  that the program
contains no errors or deviations from the format specified in the
writeup.  The only complicated features of this problem are  base
register  handling.  You should include a sequence of USING's and
DROP's designed to work it out. Especially try  two  active  base

registers   at   once   to   insure the one with the lowest offset is
used.

An Example Set of Data for P4:

```
CHUNGA      START
            USING 12,NOWHERE
NOWHERE     L     01,TEN
            A     01,TWO
            LR    03,01
            USING 14,THERE
            ST    01,TEMP1
THERE       L     02,FOUR
            SR    02,03
            DROP  14
            ST    02,TEMP2
            BC    15,SKIP
SKIP        DROP  12
            BCR   15,14
TEN         DC    F'10'
TWO         DC    F'02'
TEMP1       DS    F
FOUR        DC    F'04'
TEMP2       DS    F
MADNICK     DS    F
            END
```

Test Data for Lexical Analyzer Problem -- P5:

    The only test data required by this problem exists as member
MAST. In order to keep the JCL generic, however  a  dummy  member
named  P5 has been added to the dataset "PL1MP.DATA".  This input
data consists of three components, one after  the other:

1. The set of break characters to be used.  This  consists
   of  an  integer  specifying  how  many break characters
   there are, followed by the individual break  characters
   surrounded  by  quotes and seperated by blanks, thusly:

       n 'op1' 'op2' 'op3' ........

   Note that as many cards as necessary may  be  used  for
   the operators.

2. The set of operators to be used. This  data  starts  on
   the next card after the end of the break characters. It
   has the same format as the set of break characters.

3. The program to be analyzed. This should  start  on  the
   first  card  after the end of the operators and  use as
   many cards as necessary.

   After the last card of the program **two** special
cards must appear. These cards signal the end of the
program and are absolutely necessary. They should both
start in column one and read "$END".

   Remember that as we have specified the problem the student
looks at only columns 2-72. You may sequence number the program
in columns 73-80, but **do not** sequence number the break character
or operator character cards as a "GET LIST" statement is used.

   In theory, by changing the tables and program a student's
lexical analyzer could analyze FORTRAN programs, as long as
statement numbers started in column two. You might want to try
this, for dinks.

An Example Set of Data for MAST:

```
     15
     ' '  '+'  '-'  '*'  '/'
     '='  '>'  '<'  '.'  '-'
     ';'  ':'  ','  '('  ')'
     23
     '+'  '-'  '*'  '/'  '='  '>'  '<'  '.'
     '('  ')'  ';'  ':'  ','  '-'
     'PROC'  'DO'  'END'  'IF'  'THEN'  'ELSE'  'GOTO'  'PUT'  'GET'
       CROCK:    PROC;                                              000000
                 IF A < 37 THEN DO;   $IPC = BQ + 9;                000000
       GOTO XLBL; END;                                             000000
                 ELSE DO;                                           000000
                     %XID=                          3;              000000
                     PUT (A,$IPC);                                  000000
                     END;                                          000000
                 IF A=(B*D-08096)THEN GOTO X;     ELSE DO;          000000
                 PUT A;              END;                          000000
       X:        A=B *   C /2;                                     000000
                 END;                                              000000
       XLBL:                                                       00000
                 END CROCK;                                        00000
```

Test Data for SICK Interpreter Problem -- P5:

   This problem as stated, requires three sets of test data,
members PROGM1, PROGM2, and PROGM3. These members are essentially
PL/1 test programs for the interpreter. However initial values
for variables (to simulate input data) are also in these members.

   The format of these members is as follows:

1. First the sample program. This program must be a valid
   program as specified in the student's writeup. Remember
   that the three programs test increasingly advanced
   features. This program should use columns 1-80 of the

card images.  Therefore, they **may** **not** be sequenced.

2. Immediately following the last card of the program should be a card with just "$END" starting in column 1. This delimits the program and will not be passed to the student.

3. Next come cards with initial values for variables. These cards, one for each variable to be initialized, are used to initialize SVS entries created by LEXPROC. These cards consist of a variable name surrounded in quotes, followed by a comma, and then the value to be assigned the variable.

   The name must be the name of a previously declared variable from the SICK program. Further, this variable must have been declared in the **main** portion of the test program.

4. Even if no variables are to be initialized the next card should be another "$END" delimiter.

An example Set of Data for PROGM1:

```
          DECLARE D E F;
          D = 3;
          E = D + 5;
    A:    F = 9;
          PUT D;
          PUT E;
          PUT F;
          F = F * D;
          PUT F;
    $END
    $END
```

An Example Set of Data for PROGM2:

```
          DECLARE NUMBER START NUM TEMP TEST PRIME RES COUNT T S V;
          COUNT=0;
          NUMBER=START-1;
   NEXT:  COUNT=COUNT+1;
          IF COUNT=NUM THEN GOTO DONE;
          NUMBER=NUMBER+1;
          TEST=NUMBER/2;
          TEST=TEST*2;
          TEMP=NUMBER-1;
          IF TEST=TEMP THEN DO;
              PUT NUMBER;
              T=1;
   LOOP:      T=T+1;
              S=T**2;
              IF S>NUMBER THEN GOTO YES;
```

```
                        S=NUMBER/T;
                        S=S*T;
                        IF S=NUMBER THEN GOTO NO;
                        GOTO LOOP;
        YES:            RES=1;
                        GOTO D;
        NO:             RES=0;
        D:              END;
                IF TEST=NUMBER THEN GOTO NEXT;
                IF RES=0 THEN GOTO NEXT;
                PRIME=NUMBER;
                PUT PRIME;
                GOTO NEXT;
        DONE:
        $END
        'START', 5
        'NUM', 7
        $END
```

An Example Set of Data for PROGM3:

```
                DECLARE NUMBER START NUM TEMP TEST PRIME RES COUNT;
                COUNT=0;
                NUMBER=START-1;
        NEXT:   COUNT=COUNT+1;
                IF COUNT=NUM THEN GOTO DONE;
                NUMBER=NUMBER+1;
                TEST=NUMBER/2;
                TEST=TEST*2;
                TEMP=NUMBER-1;
                IF TEST=TEMP THEN DO;
                    PUT NUMBER;
                    RES=PRINE(NUMBER);
                    END;
        PRINE:  PROCEDURE (NUM);
                DECLARE TEST SQ VAL;
                TEST=1;
        LOOP:   TEST=TEST+1;
                SQ=TEST**2;
                IF SQ>NUM THEN GOTO YES;
                SQ=NUM/TEST;
                SQ=SQ*TEST;
                IF SQ=NUM THEN GOTO NO;
                GOTO LOOP;
        YES:    VAL=1;
                GOTO DONE;
        NO:     VAL=0;
        DONE:   RETURN (VAL);
                END;
                IF TEST=NUMBER THEN GOTO NEXT;
                IF RES=0 THEN GOTO NEXT;
                PRIME=NUMBER;
                PUT PRIME;
```

```
            GOTO NEXT;
DONE:
$END
'START', 5
'NUM', 7
$END
```

You may wish to create new programs for students, in
addition to these three. It may seem like all you have to do is
add an entry in the dataset PL1MP.DATA with the right name. This
is not all there is to it. In addition to the program existing
somewhere, not necessarily in the dataset "PL1MP.DATA", a new DD
statement must be added to the JCL used for running students.

This statement must have as its name the name that the
student will pass to LEXPROC. This means you should be careful
and not use any names which would conflict with existent files,
like SYSPRINT.

## 3.4   ASSEMBLY LANGUAGE SUBROUTINES USED BY MONITORS

Introduction:

Three basic assembly language packages are used by the
monitor programs. These functions are performed in assembler for
two reasons. In the case of the HEX routine an assembly language
version is much faster, which is important since the debugging
routines used by P5 and P6 make extensive use of this routine. In
the case of the remaining two packages, features of the operating
system not directly available to a PL/1 programmer are used.

This section describes the assembly language routines, there
usage, and internal details. The source for these routines exists
on the distribution tape, refer to section 8.3, if you are
interested.

### 3.4.1   HEX

The purpose of the HEX routine is to convert a PL/1 pointer
to a hexadecimal representation of the address it contains. This
function is performed in an assembly language routine in the
interest of efficiency. Recognizing that only the low order three
bytes of a pointer are significant, this routine ignores the high
order byte.

The low order three bytes of the pointer are checked for a
value of zero. If this is true the returned character string is
"$NULL$". This signifies a pointer with the value of NULL.
Otherwise these three bytes are converted to their hexadecimal
character representation and this is returned.


Declaration and Use:

The HEX routine should be declared as follows:

DECLARE HEX ENTRY(POINTER) RETURNS(CHARACTER(6));

Suppose we wanted to print the "value" of a pointer named
START. The following code would do:

PUT FILE(SYSPRINT) LIST("START= ",HEX(START));


Conversion Algorithm:

First the low order three bytes of the pointer are moved
left-justified into a four byte area. Then the one byte constant
X"0C" is moved into the last byte of the area. An unpack
instruction is used to change this "packed decimal number" into
unpacked format. This correctly pulls apart the 4 bit hex

digits, but the low order byte with the "sign" is goofed up. The result of this unpack is seven characters long, but the last byte is ignored.

Finally this character string is translated. This is necessary since the hex digits have been changed to X"F□". The translation table maps X"FA" to X"C1", etc.  Visually:

Input Pointer:        X"0010B2F8"

4 Byte Area:          X"10B2F80C"

Unpack Area:          X"F1F0FBF2FFF8C0"

After Translation:    X"F1F0C2F2C6F8"

### 3.4.2   Timing Package(SETTIME, CANTIME, USETIME)

The purpose of these routines is to provide the PL/1 programmer with a convenient interface to the STIMER timing facilities of the operating system. This package is fairly complicated internally and strongly tied to OS/MVT or VS.  Quite simply stated this package provides a mechanism for limiting the amount of time a PL/1 program will be allowed to use.

To use this package a programmer calls an initialization entry point specifying a primary and secondary time allocation, both in hundredths of a second. Once the primary time allocation has been used the secondary limit is installed and the programmer defined condition (TIMEOUT) is raised.

This condition handler should close and re-open SYSPRINT to clear any hanging I/O. If the (TIMEOUT) condition handler returns, the timing package will cause the ERROR condition to be raised at whatever point execution was suspended.  If the secondary time allotment is used up either by the (TIMEOUT) or subsequent ERROR handler, the task is abended with a completion code of 322.

Another set of entry points is provided to tell how much time has been used out of the allotments. One of these entry points cancels the timing as well. Thus if your program doesn't use its whole allotment (or at least if it doesn't use up the secondary one) you can find out how much time you did use.

This package is used by the monitors in the following manner (refer to the sample listing later for details):

1. First SETTIME is called to establish limits for the student. The values passed to SETTIME may be altered at execution time.

2. The grader establishes a (TIMEOUT) handler which closes
   SYSPRINT,  opens  it, prints an informatory message for
   the student, and then returns.

3. The grader establishes a FINISH condition handler which
   uses the USETIME entry point to determine how much time
   a student has used. This value is printed whenever  the
   FINISH condition is raised.

4. The student is called. If the student returns, the  end
   of  the  monitor is reached and the FINISH condition is
   raised. Otherwise  the  student  does  something  that
   causes the FINISH to be raised.


PL/1 Callable Entry Points:

SETTIME( FIXED BINARY(31), FIXED BINARY(31));

     The  first  argument is the primary time limit, in
hundredths of a second (ie., a value of 100 corresponds
to 1 second). The second argument is the secondary time
limit, again in hundredths of a second.

     This entry point performs initialization  for  the
timing package. It should be called as soon as possible
in  a  program  to be monitored.  Note that the program
calling this  entry  point  **must**  provide  a  condition
handler for the programmer defined condition (TIMEOUT).
This  handler,  in  turn must close and reopen the file
SYSPRINT, to avoid problems.


CANTIME(FIXED BINARY(31), FIXED BINARY(31));

     This entry point cancels the  timing  feature  and
returns  an  indication  of  how  much  of the original
interval remains. The first argument is a switch.   Its
value  is  one  if the primary allocation was used, and
zero if the  primary  allocation  has  not  been  used.
Obviously if this value is one you are operating in the
secondary limit.

     The  second  argument is the number of timer units
remaining  in  the  most  recently  set  interval  (the
secondary  interval if the first switch is on). A timer
unit is approximately equal to  26.04166  microseconds.
The code necessary to determine the amount of time used
in shown in an example monitor listing, later.

USETIME(FIXED BINARY(31), FIXED BINARY(31));

This entry point functions exactly as CANTIME, except that the remaining interval, be it primary or secondary is reestablished. The routine which gains control if this interval is exceeded abends the task with a completion code of 322. This entry point is recommended because you may have a loop in your (TIMEOUT) or ERROR handler.

Timer Internals:

When SETTIME is called it issues a STIMER macro naming EXITRTN as the exit routine and the primary time interval as the interval. Then the secondary time interval is stored in a known location for later use and the entry returns.

When CANTIME is called it issues a TTIMER macro instruction with the CANCEL option. This returns the remaining time interval and cancels the timing. Next a switch is checked to see if a previous interval has expired. This switch and the remaining interval are returned.

The entry USETIME functions exactly like CANTIME, except that before returning it uses an STIMER macro to reestablish the remaining interval specifying SABEND as the exit routine. This routine loads 322 into register one and abends.

EXITRTN is called by the operating system when the primary time limit has been exceeded. The first thing this routine does is issue an STIMER macro instruction to establish the secondary time limit with SABEND as the exit routine. Then a switch is set so the CANTIME and USETIME entry points will know that the primary allocation has been used.

The rest of this routine is very complicated. This routine is entered by the operating system stage two exit effector. For proper results this routine **must** return to the operating system or abend. Further, there is no attempt on the operating system's part to provide you information about where your program was when it ran out.

To satisfy the condition that we return to the operating system we must first find out where we were and what the registers were (method described later). Register 13 is used as the save area pointer by OS convention. For a PL/1 procedure or begin block, bit 0 of this save area (the first bit of the PL/1 reserved header word) will be on. If we are in a PL/1 procedure we perform the following:

1. Using the PSW, which points to the next instruction to be executed in the halted program, we save the next 14

bytes of the program. A switch is set in EXITRTN for later use.

2. We move into these "evacuated" 14 bytes a sequence of instructions which, when executed will cause control to flow to the label STEP2 in EXITRTN. Care is taken to check the alignment of the starting address so the code will function on a 360.

3. When STEP2 is entered it checks its switch. Noting that it was on it restores the instruction sequence previously saved.

4. Then EXITRTN returns to the operating system, only to receive control back at STEP2.

If this bit is not on, we are in either a PL/1 run-time library routine or a system I/O routine. Either way it is dangerous to suspend activity, and unlikely that these routines would loop. What we do is thread back up the save area chain until we find a save area with the magic bit on.

This save area is the lowest level procedure or begin block involved. It is used by the subroutine which was called by the procedure. We place the address of STEP2 into register 14's slot in this save area. When the subroutine is finished it will return to STEP2.

STEP2 then signals the programmer defined condition (TIMEOUT). If this condition returns then the condition ERROR is signalled. Just in case the ERROR condition returns, the next set of code is for SABEND.

Finding Registers and PSW in a STIMER Exit:

This method may be used to find the registers and PSW that were active when an STIMER exit was effected. This code functions under OS/MVT and VS releases one and two. This algorithm may work under OS/MFT with the multitasking option, but it hasn't been tried. The algorithm goes something like this:

1. Finding the TCB address. An EXTRACT macro is used with the FIELDS=(FRS) option to get the address of the floating point save area for the task. This area is a prefix to the TCB. Adding 32 (decimal) to this address gives the start (offset 0) of the TCB.

The first field in the TCB (that is, at offset 0) is the anchor pointer for the Request Block (RB) chain.

2. The first RB on this chain is the IRB created by the stage two exit effector for the STIMER exit routine.

The RBGRSAVE field of this IRB (offset 32 decimal) contains the registers of the interrupted program, stored in the order 0-15.

3. The RBLINK field of this IRB (offset 28 decimal, low order three bytes) points to the previous RB on the RB chain. This is the PRB for the student. The RBOPSW field of this PRB contains the PSW current when the timer ran out. The low order word (offset 20 decimal) of this field contains the address of the next instruction to be executed when the STIMER exit routine returns to the operating system.

## 3.4.3   STEAL Package

These routines provide the support necessary for a monitor program to "steal" control from a student's program that has been compiled with the "OPTIONS(MAIN)" clause. This process requires assembly language subroutines since the student could ostensibly name his or her procedure anything, hence a simple call statement can not be coded in the monitor.

The linkage editor is used to create a load module containing a monitor program and the STEAL package. Using linkage editor control statements STEAL is identified as the entry point for this load module. A linkage editor LI3RARY statement is used to stop resolution of the external references to IHEMAIN, IHENTRY, GOVERN, and IHESAFQ.

When the student is to be executed, his or her compiler output is appended to this load module as input to the linkage loader. The STEAL routine is enterred by the loader when loading is complete.  It saves the parameters passed, saves the address of the student's main procedure, which is contained in the CSECT IHEMAIN, and places the address of STAGE2 in this CSECT.

Then the routine IHENTRY is called. This is the initialization entry point for the PL/1 run time library. It creates the PL/1 enviroment and then branches to the address contained in IHEMAIN. This is the mechanism whereby the run time initializer knows the "name" of the main procedure.

This causes STAGE2 to be enterred, with the PL/1 enviroment created. STAGE2 creates a String Dope Vector (SDV) for the parameters saved by STEAL, and calls the PL/1 routine GOVERN. This routine is the monitor routine, an example is shown later. This monitor program processes paramters, establishes default error handlers, and execution limits.

When the monitor is ready to call the student, it calls the entry point PAYBACK. This routine retrieves the student's address which STEAL garnered from IHEMAIN, places this address in register 15, and branches to it.

When the student is finished, or when an exceptional condition causes control to return to GOVERN, it performs any post processing necessary. Now a slight crock enters into play. Since we want the IHEMAIN CSECT to point ·to the student's procedure, the GOVERN procedure **must not** use OPTIONS(MAIN). However, the procedure epilogue for a main procedure is slightly different from that of a subroutine.

If GOVERN's epilogue is allowed to gain control, it will receive a protection check (system completion code of 0C4). The entry point BAILOUT has been provided to get around this problem. This entry point causes control to be passed to the PL/1 run time library routine IHESAFQ. This routine closes all files, frees all automatic storage and returns to the operating system (loader, in our case).

PL/1 Callable Entry Points:

PAYBACK - This entry causes control to be passed to the student's main procedure. It takes any arguments the monitor wishes to pass to the student's program.

BAILOUT - This entry is called by the monitor program when it is finished processing and wishes to terminate the run.

Use of this facility is demonstrated in the next section.

## 3.5   EXAMPLE MONITOR PROGRAM

### 3.5.1   Introduction

This is the monitor program used by all the PL/1 problems which require the student to be a main procedure. It is stored as member P1 in the partitioned dataset "PL1MP.LOAD", with aliases P2, P3, and P4.

This procedure is named GOVERN, as it functions with the STEAL package. It uses the timing package, but does not make use of the HEX routine, since no pointers of debugging interest are involved. This routine is compiled and linked with the following JCL:

```
//CROCKO    EXEC PGM=IEBGENER
//SYSPRINT  DD   SYSOUT=A
//SYSIN     DD   DUMMY
//SYSUT2    DD   DSN=&&TEMP,DISP=(NEW,PASS),
//               UNIT=SYSDA,SPACE=(CYL,(1,1)),
//               DCB=(RECFM=FB,LRECL=80,BLKSIZE=1600)
//SYSUT1    DD   *
  INCLUDE SYSLIB(PAYBACK)
  LIBRARY   (IHEMAIN,IHENTRY,GOVERN,IHESAFQ)
  ENTRY STEAL
  ALIAS P2,P3,P4
/*
//COMPILE EXEC PGM=IEMAA,PARM='NE,LO,ND,OBJNM=P1'
//SYSPRINT  DD   SYSOUT=A
//SYSUT1    DD   UNIT=SYSDA,SPACE=(CYL,(2,1))
//SYSUT2    DD   UNIT=SYSDA,SPACE=(CYL,(2,1))
//SYSUT3    DD   UNIT=SYSDA,SPACE=(CYL,(2,1))
//SYSLIN    DD   DSN=&&TEMP,DISP=(MOD,PASS)
//SYSIN     DD   *

  _
  !
  ! source for GOVERN
  !_

/*
//LINK      EXEC PGM=IEWL,PARM='MAP,LIST,LET'
//SYSPRINT  DD   SYSOUT=A
//SYSUT1    DD   UNIT=SYSDA,SPACE=(CYL,(2,1))
//SYSLIB    DD   DSN=PL1MP.ASM.LOAD,DISP=SHR
//          DD   DSN=SYS1.PL1LIB,DISP=SHR
//SYSLIN    DD   DSN=&&TEMP,DISP=(OLD,DELETE)
//SYSLMOD   DD   DSN=PL1MP.LOAD,DISP=(NEW,CATLG),
//               UNIT=2314,VOL=SER=nnnnnn,
//               SPACE=(TRK,(30,5,2),RLSE)
/*
```

## 3.5.2   Example Monitor Program Listing

```
/* GOVERNING PROCEDURE ESTABLISHES LIMITS FOR STUDENTS. */        GOV 0010              PAGE    2

STMT LEVEL NEST        /*  GOVERNING PROCEDURE ESTABLISHES LIMITS FOR STUDENTS. */    GOV 0010
  1                    GOVERN: PROC(PARMS);                                           GOV 0020

                       /* THIS PROCEDURE IS USED IN CONJUNCTION WITH AN ASSEMBLY      GOV 0030
                       LANGUAGE PACKAGE (STEAL) TO ACT AS AN INVISIBLE GOVERNOR       GOV 0040
                       FOR PL/1 MAIN PROCEDURES. THIS PROCEDURE IS LINKED WITH        GOV 0050
                       THE ASSEMBLY LANGUAGE SUBROUTINES AND PLACED IN A PDS.         GOV 0060
                       THEN IT IS PREFIXED TO THE OUTPUT FROM THE COMPILER FOR        GOV 0070
                       A STUDENT'S PROGRAM AND FED INTO THE LOADER. THIS ROUTINE      GOV 0080
                       WILL RECEIVE CONTROL FIRST WITH ITS ARGUMENT AS A VARYING      GOV 0090
                       CHARACTER STRING. THIS STRING WILL CONTAIN THE PARAMETERS      GOV 0100
                       PASSED FROM THE LOADER. THESE PARAMETERS ARE USED TO CONTROL   GOV 0110
                       THE SETTING OF LIMITS AND OPTIONALLY TO LABEL A STUDENT'S      GOV 0120
                       OUTPUT     */                                                  GOV 0130

  2    1               DCL  PARMS CHAR(100) VARYING,                                  GOV 0140
                       MAXPAGES FIXED BIN INIT(15),                                   GOV 0150
                       STLIMIT FIXED BIN(31) INIT(100),                               GOV 0160
                       SETTIME ENTRY(FIXED BIN(31),FIXED BIN(31)),                    GOV 0170
                       USETIME ENTRY(FIXED BIN(31),FIXED BIN(31)),                    GOV 0180
                       BAILOUT ENTRY,                                                 GOV 0190
                       NUM_PAGES FIXED BIN INIT(0),                                   GOV 0200
                       IPARMS CHAR(101) VARYING,                                      GOV 0210
                       SWITCH FIXED BIN(31),                                          GOV 0220
                       INTERVAL_REMAINING FIXED BIN(31),                             GOV 0230
                       IHESARC ENTRY(FIXED BIN(31)),                                  GOV 0240
                       MULT FLOAT DEC(8) STATIC INT INIT(2.604166E-3),                GOV 0250
                       TIME_USED FLOAT DEC(8),                                        GOV 0260
                       INTERVAL FIXED DEC(8,2),                                       GOV 0270
                       BADJCL FIXED BINARY INIT(0),                                   GOV 0280
                       NAME CHAR(8) INIT(' '),                                        GOV 0290
                       LINESIZE FIXED BIN INIT(120),                                  GOV 0300
                       PAGESIZE FIXED BIN INIT(60),                                   GOV 0310
                       MAXTIME FIXED BIN(31) INIT(500);                               GOV 0320

                       /* PARAMETER PROCESSING BLOCK */                               GOV 0330

  3    1               BEGIN;                                                         GOV 0340
  4    2               ON ERROR PUT SKIP EDIT('*** ERROR *** THE PARAMETER STRING:',  GOV 0350
                       '''',PARMS,''' CONTAINS AN UNRECOGNIZED PARAMETER')            GOV 0360
                                                                                      GOV 0370
  6    2               (A,SKIP,A,A,A);                                                GOV 0380
  7    2               IPARMS = PARMS || ';';                                         GOV 0390
                       GET STRING(IPARMS)                                             GOV 0400
                       DATA(MAXPAGES,LINESIZE,PAGESIZE,MAXTIME,STLIMIT,NAME,BADJCL);  GOV 0410
  8    2               END;                                                           GOV 0420

                       /* OPEN SYSPRINT WITH SUPPLIED VALUES */                       GOV 0420

  9    1               OPEN FILE(SYSPRINT) STREAM OUTPUT PRINT PAGESIZE(PAGESIZE)     GOV 0430
```

```
        /*  GOVERNING PROCEDURE ESTABLISHES LIMITS FOR STUDENTS. */        GOV 0010              PAGE    3

STMT LEVEL NEST

                            LINESIZE(LINESIZE);                                        GOV 0440

                            /* SET UP CONDITION HANDLERS */                            GOV 0450

10    1        ON  FINISH BEGIN;                    /* THIS WAY TO CATCH STOP, ETC */   GOV 0460
12    2            ON ERROR GO TO EXIT;                   /* AVOID LOOPS */             GOV 0470
14    2            CALL USETIME(SWITCH, INTERVAL_REMAINING);                            GOV 0480
                                       /* GET AMOUNT OF TIME REMAINING IN MOST          GOV 0490
                                          RECENT INTERVAL, IN TIMER UNITS */            GOV 0500
15    2            TIME_USED = FLOAT(DECIMAL(INTERVAL_REMAINING,8,0),8);                GOV 0510
                                       /* GET TIME REMAINING IN FLOAT FORM */           GOV 0520
16    2            TIME_USED = TIME_USED * MULT;                                        GOV 0530
                                       /* GET TIME REMAINING IN HUNDREDTHS              GOV 0540
                                          OF SECONDS */                                 GOV 0550
17    2            INTERVAL = - FIXED(TIME_USED,8);                                     GOV 0560
                                       /* GET NEGATIVE OF INTERVAL REMAINING */         GOV 0570
18    2            INTERVAL = INTERVAL + DECIMAL(MAXTIME,8,0);                          GOV 0580
                                       /* GET AMOUNT USED FROM PRIMARY INTERVAL */GOV 0590
19    2            IF SWITCH ¬= 0                                                       GOV 0600
                   THEN                                                                 GOV 0610
                                       /* THIS MEANS SOME WAS USED FROM THE             GOV 0620
                                          SECONDARY INTERVAL'*/                         GOV 0630
20    2                INTERVAL = INTERVAL + DECIMAL(STLIMIT,8,0);                      GOV 0640
                                       /* ADD IN AMOUNT USED IN SECONDARY LIMIT */GOV 0650
21    2            PUT EDIT('STUDENT PROGRAM USED ',INTERVAL/100.0,' SECONDS')          GOV 0660
                       (SKIP(2),A,F(8,2),A);                                            GOV 0670

22    2        EXIT:                                                                    GOV 0680
23    2            CALL BAILOUT;                    /* DEFEAT EPILOGUE */               GOV 0690
              END;                                                                      GOV 0700

24    1        ON ENDPAGE(SYSPRINT)                                                     GOV 0710
25    1            BEGIN;                                                               GOV 0720
26    2            PUT PAGE;                                                            GOV 0730
27    2            NUM_PAGES = NUM_PAGES + 1;                                           GOV 0740
28    2            IF NUM_PAGES > MAXPAGES                                              GOV 0750
29    2                THEN DO;                                                         GOV 0760
30    2    1              PUT SKIP(2) EDIT                                              GOV 0770
                          ('**** MAX PAGE LIMIT EXCEEDED, EXECUTION STOPPED')(A);       GOV 0780
31    2    1              STOP;                                                         GOV 0790
32    2    1              END;                                                          GOV 0800
33    2            END;                                                                 GOV 0810

34    1        ON CONDITION(TIMEOUT)                                                    GOV 0820
35    1            BEGIN;                                                               GOV 0830
36    2            CLOSE FILE(SYSPRINT);                                                GOV 0840
37    2            OPEN FILE(SYSPRINT) STREAM OUTPUT PRINT PAGESIZE(PAGESIZE)           GOV 0850
                       LINESIZE(LINESIZE);                                              GOV 0860
38    2            PUT EDIT('**** EXECUTION TIME LIMIT EXCEEDED, ERROR SIGNALLED.')     GOV 0870
                       (SKIP(2),A);                                                     GOV 0880
```

/* GOVERNING PROCEDURE ESTABLISHES LIMITS FOR STUDENTS. */          GOV 0010                    PAGE   4

STMT LEVEL NEST

| 39 | 2 | END; | GOV 0890 |

/* TELL STUDENT HE'S COOL */          GOV 0900

| 40 | 1 | PUT EDIT('**** PROGRAM SUCCESSFULLY LOADED FOR STUDENT ',NAME) | GOV 0910 |
|    |   | (SKIP,A,A); | GOV 0920 |

/* SET TIME LIMIT */          GOV 0930

                                                                    GOV 0940
| 41 | 1 | CALL SETTIME(MAXTIME,STLIMIT); | |
/* THIS USES THE TIMING PACKAGE WHICH GOV 0950
SIGNALS CONDITION(TIMEOUT) WHEN THEGOV 0960
STUDENT RUNS OUT. WHEN THE TIMEOUT GOV 0970
HANDLER RETURNS, ERROR IS SIGNALLEDGOV 0980
FROM THE STUDENT'S PROGRAM.   */     GOV 0990

| 42 | 1 | CALL PAYBACK;        /* CALL STUDENT */ | GOV 1000 |

| 43 | 1 | SIGNAL FINISH;       /* AVOID EPILOGUE */ | GOV 1010 |

| 44 | 1 | END GOVERN; | GOV 1020 |

## 3.6  SAMPLE SOLUTIONS

## 3.6.1  Cipher Problem -- P1

/* SAMPLE SOLUTION TO CIPHER PROBLEM -- P1  BY ED DEJONG */                    PAGE     2

```
STMT LEVEL NEST
                /* SAMPLE SOLUTION TO CIPHER PROBLEM -- P1  BY ED DEJONG */
                /* INPUT: A CARD WHERE                                       */
                /*    COL.S 1-4  CONTAIN A NUMBER TELLING HOW MANY PLACES TO */
                /*             SHIFT THE INPUT STRING                        */
                /*    COL.S 5-80 CONTAIN THE INPUT STRING TO BE SHIFTED      */
                /*                                                           */
                /* OUTPUT: PRINT THE INPUT STRING SHIFTED ALPHABETICALLY     */
                /*         THE SPECIFIED NUMBER OF PLACES                    */
                /*                                                           */
                /* EXAMPLE: THE STRING 'ABYZ' SHIFTED ONE PLACE OVER IS 'BCZA'*/
                /*          (NOTE THE WRAP-AROUND)                           */
                /*                                                           */
                /* NOTE: THIS PROGRAM WILL ACCEPT NUMBERS FROM -999 TO 999   */
                /*       SPECIFYING HOW MANY PLACES TO SHIFT                 */
                /*                                                           */
  1                 SHIFT:  PROC OPTIONS(MAIN);

                /*    I IS A LOOP COUNTER                                    */
                /* NUM IS THE NUMBER OF PLACES THE INPUT STRING IS TO BE SHIFTED */
                /* STR IS THE INPUT STRING                                   */
                /* ANS IS THE ANSWER I.E., STR SHIFTED NUM PLACES            */
                /* ALPH IS A CONSTANT STRING CONTAINING THE ALPHABET         */
                /* NUMB IS NUM REDUCED MODULO 26                             */
  2     1           DCL (NUM,NUMB,I) FIXED BIN, (STR,ANS) CHAR(76),
                        ALPH CHAR(26) INIT('ABCDEFGHIJKLMNOPQRSTUVWXYZ');

                /* LOOP THROUGH TEN TIMES TO TEST PROGRAM                    */

  3     1           DO I = 1 TO 10;

                /* READ A TEST CARD                                          */

  4     1   1       GET EDIT(NUM,STR)(F(4),A(76));

                /* REDUCE NUM TO SMALLEST POSSIBLE NUMBER                    */

  5     1   1       NUMB = MOD(ABS(NUM),26)*SIGN(NUM);

                /* PERFORM THE SHIFTING                                      */

  6     1   1       ANS = TRANSLATE(STR,SUBSTR(REPEAT(ALPH,3),NUMB+27,26),ALPH);

                /* PRINT OUT THE ANSWER                                      */

  7     1   1       PUT EDIT('THE STRING: ',STR,'SHIFTED ',NUM,' PLACES IS: ',ANS)
                        (SKIP(2),X(12),A,A(76),SKIP,A,F(4),A,A(76));

  8     1   1   EXIT: END SHIFT;
```

```
                THE STRING: HAL
SHIFTED   1 PLACES IS: IBM

                THE STRING: IBM
SHIFTED  -1 PLACES IS: HAL

                THE STRING:  TRY THIS ON FOR SIZE
SHIFTED  14 PLACES IS:  HFM HVWG CB TCF GWNS

                THE STRING:  THIS SHOULD NOT BE CHANGED
SHIFTED  26 PLACES IS:  THIS SHOULD NOT BE CHANGED

                THE STRING:  NEITHER SHOULD THIS, SINCE BOTH ARE NO-OPS
SHIFTED -26 PLACES IS:  NEITHER SHOULD THIS, SINCE BOTH ARE NO-OPS

                THE STRING:  TRY SOME SPECIAL CHARACTERS:;a#%,*$<.+>)_|="? (-/&
SHIFTED   6 PLACES IS:  ZXE YUSK YVKIOGR INGXGIZKXY:;a#%,*$<.+>)_|="? (-/&

                THE STRING:  DON'T CHANGE THIS, EITHER
SHIFTED   0 PLACES IS:  DON'T CHANGE THIS, EITHER

                THE STRING:  LI BRX JRW WKLV IDU, BRX'OO SUREDEOB PDNH LW.
SHIFTED  -3 PLACES IS:  IF YOU GOT THIS FAR, YOU'LL PROBABLY MAKE IT.

                THE STRING:  WPO, JI OCZ JOCZM CVIY...
SHIFTED   5 PLACES IS:  BUT, ON THE OTHER HAND...

                THE STRING:  DID THIS CAUSE A CONVERSION CHECK???
SHIFTED   0 PLACES IS:  DID THIS CAUSE A CONVERSION CHECK???
```

## 3.6.2   Sorting Problem -- P2

```
STMT LEVEL NEST
                    /* SAMPLE SOLUTION FOR SORTING PROBLEM -- P2  BY PGG */

  1                 SORT: PROCEDURE OPTIONS(MAIN);
                                            /* THIS PROGRAM READS TEN CARDS AND
                                               PRINTS A SORTED LISTING. */
  2    1            DCL INPUT(10) CHAR(80),      /* CARDS TO SORT */
                        WORK CHAR(80),           /* USED IN INTERCHANGE */
                        PASSES FIXED BIN INITIAL(1),   /* NUMBER OF PASSES USED */
                        I FIXED BIN(15),         /* RANDOM LOOP INDEX */
                        SW BIT(1) INITIAL('1'B);  /* OFF WHEN LIST SORTED */

  3    1            PUT FILE(SYSPRINT) EDIT('INPUT CARDS:') (SKIP,A(12));
  4    1            PUT FILE(SYSPRINT) SKIP(2);

  5    1            DO I = 1 TO 10;             /* READ IN ALL THE CARDS */
  6    1   1          GET FILE(SYSIN) EDIT(INPUT(I)) (A(80));
  7    1   1          PUT FILE(SYSPRINT) EDIT(INPUT(I)) (SKIP,COL(20),A(80));
  8    1   1        END;

  9    1            DO WHILE(SW);               /* AS MANY PASSES AS NECESSARY
                                                   THIS LOOPS UNTIL NO SWITCHES ARE
                                                   MADE */
 10    1   1          SW = '0'B;               /* IF NOTHING IS CHANGED, WE ARE
                                                   FINISHED */
 11    1   1          DO I = 1 TO 9;           /* LOOK AT ALL ENTRIES */
 12    1   2            IF INPUT(I+1) < INPUT(I)
                           THEN                 /* IF ORDER INCORRECT, SWITCH */
 13    1   2               DO;
 14    1   3                  WORK = INPUT(I);
 15    1   3                  INPUT(I) = INPUT(I+1);
 16    1   3                  INPUT(I+1) = WORK;
 17    1   3                  SW = '1'B;
 18    1   3               END;
 19    1   2          END;
 20    1   1          PASSES = PASSES + 1;     /* BUMP PASS COUNTER */
 21    1   1        END;

 22    1            PUT FILE(SYSPRINT) EDIT('OUTPUT CARDS, AFTER ',PASSES,' PASSES:')
                        (SKIP(2),A,F(2,0),A);
 23    1            PUT FILE(SYSPRINT) SKIP(2);
 24    1            PUT FILE(SYSPRINT) EDIT((INPUT(I) DO I = 1 TO 10))
                        (SKIP,COL(20),A(80));
 25    1            END SORT;
```

```
                 ==================================================================04
             1     ******  * ***    ******    ******    ******   * ***     **    ** 05
                 THEN THE NUMBERS C-9.                                               03
             S     **  ****  **      ******   **  ****  **    **  **       ** **     07
                 THEN CCME ANY SPECIAL SYMBOLS AND SCREWBALL GRAPHICS.               02
                 ELANKS SHOULD BE THE LOWEST, FCLLCWED BY THE LETTERS A-Z.           01
             A     **   **  **        **       **   **   **   **            ***      08
             A:    ******  **         **       ******   ******   **         **       09
             1     **       *** **    **   **  **   **   **    ** *** **     ** ** 06
             CO                                                              ****     10

                 BLANKS SHOULD BE THE LOWEST, FOLLOWED BY THE LETTERS A-Z.           01
             A     **   **  **         **      **   **  **   **             ***      08
             A:    ******  **         ******   ******   ******   **         **       09
             1     **       *** **    **   **  **      **   ** *** **     ** ** 06
             00                                                              ****     10
```

OUTPUT CARDS, AFTER  7 PASSES:

```
                 BLANKS SHOULD BE THE LOWEST, FOLLOWED BY THE LETTERS A-Z.           01
                 THEN COME ANY SPECIAL SYMBOLS AND SCREWBALL GRAPHICS.               02
                 THEN THE NUMBERS 0-9.                                               03
                 ==================================================================04
             1     ******  * ***    ******    ******    ******   * ***     **    ** 05
             1     **       *** **    **   **  **   **   **    ** *** **     ** ** 06
             S     **  ****  **      ******   **  ****  **    **            ***      07
             A     **   **  **        **       **   **   **   **            ***      08
             A:    ******  **         ******   ******   ******   **         **       09
             00                                                              ****     10
```

## 3.6.3  Desk Directory Problem -- P3

```
STMT LEVEL NEST

                    /* SAMPLE SOLUTION FOR DESK TOP DIRECTORY PROBLEM -- P3 BY PGG */
  1                 TABLE:  PROCEDURE  OPTIONS(MAIN);

                    /*  'SEARCH' WILL BE AN INTERNAL FUNCTION PROCEDURE WHICH WHEN PASSED
                        A NAME WILL RETURN THE ENTRY INDEX IN THE DIRECTORY IF THE
                        NAME EXISTS THERE, OTHERWISE IT WILL RETURN A ZERO.    */

  2    1            DECLARE SEARCH ENTRY (CHAR(8)) RETURNS (FIXED(15));

                    /*****************************************************************/
                    /*****              DIRECTORY DECLARATIONS                  *****/
                    /*****************************************************************/
  3    1            DECLARE
                            1 SYMBOL_TABLE(10),  /* ONLY 10 ENTRIES ALLOWED */
                              2 SYMBOL CHARACTER(8),
                              2 VALUE FIXED DECIMAL(7);
  4    1            DECLARE
                            NUMBER_OF_SYMBOLS FIXED BINARY INITIAL (0);
                            /* NUMBER_OF_SYMBOLS KEEPS COUNT OF CURRENT NUMBER
                            OF NAMES STORED IN THE DIRECTORY */

                    /*****************************************************************/
                    /*****              OTHER NECESSARY DECLARATIONS            *****/
                    /*****************************************************************/
  5    1            DECLARE
                            ACTION CHARACTER(6),      /* EITHER 'DELETE', 'INSERT',
                                                         'PRINT', 'SEARCH', OR 'UPDATE' */
                            TSYMBOL CHARACTER(8),     /* HOLDS NAME BEING PROCESSED */
                            TVALUE FIXED DECIMAL(7),  /* HOLDS NUMBER BEING PROCESSED */
                            EOF_SW BIT(1) INITIAL('0'B),
                            (UL,                      /* CURRENT UPPER BOUND FOR BINARY
                                                         SEARCH */
                            LL,                       /* CURRENT LOWER BOUND */
                            J) FIXED BIN(15),         /* RANDOM LOOP INDEX */
                            I FIXED BINARY;           /* ENTRY INDEX */

                    /*****************************************************************/
                    /*****              FUNCTION PROCEDURE SEARCH               *****/
                    /*****************************************************************/
  6    1            SEARCH:  PROCEDURE (NAME) RETURNS (FIXED(15));
  7    2              DECLARE NAME CHAR(8);
  8    2              DECLARE INDEX FIXED BIN(15);

                      /* THIS ROUTINE PERFORMS A BINARY SEARCH UPON AN ORDERED
                         DIRECTORY. THIS SEARCH IS ENGINEERED SUCH THAT IF A NAME
                         IS NOT FOUND IT BELONGS IN THE ENTRY OBTAINED BY ADDING
                         ONE TO THE CURRENT LOWER BOUND. */

  9    2                LL = 0;                       /* INITIALIZE LOWER BOUND */
```

```
            /* SAMPLE SOLUTION FOR DESK TOP DIRECTORY PROBLEM -- P3 BY PGG */                    PAGE    3

STMT LEVEL NEST
  10    2                    UL = NUMBER_OF_SYMBOLS + 1;
  11    2                    DO WHILE('1'B);                /* LOOP AS NECESSARY */
  12    2     1                 IF ((UL-LL)/2) <1    /* IF THIS IS TRUE THE STEPS WILL */
                                   THEN              /* REPEAT SO WE KNOW THE NAME */
  13    2     1                       RETURN(0); /* IS NOT IN THE DIRECTORY */

  14    2     1                 INDEX = ((UL-LL)/2) + LL; /* INDEX TO CHECK */
  15    2     1                 IF SYMBOL_TABLE(INDEX).SYMBOL = NAME
                                   THEN
  16    2     1                       RETURN(INDEX); /* NAME IS FOUND */
  17    2     1                   ELSE
  17    2     1                       IF SYMBOL_TABLE(INDEX).SYMBOL < NAME
                                           THEN        /* TOO LOW, MOVE UP LOWER LIMIT */
  18    2     1                             LL = INDEX;
  19    2     1                         ELSE        /* TOO HIGH, MOVE DOWN UPPER LIMIT */
  19    2     1                             UL = INDEX;

  20    2     1                 END;                    /* END OF LOOP */
  21    2               END SEARCH;

  22    1         ON ERROR SNAP                     /* IF AN ERROR OCCURS, TELL WHERE */
  23    1           BEGIN;
  24    2             ON ERROR STOP;                /* AVOID A LOOP */
  26    2             PUT DATA;                     /* FOR DEBUGGING */
  27    2           END;

  28    1         ON ENDFILE(SYSIN) EOF_SW = '1'B; /* STOP WHEN NO MORE CARDS */


            /***********************************************************************/
            /*****               PROCESSING STARTS HERE                      *****/
            /***********************************************************************/

            /***** READ INPUT REQUEST CARD AND COPY ONTO OUTPUT              *****/
  30    1   LOOP:    IF EOF_SW
  31    1                 THEN STOP;                /* STOP WHEN NO MORE CARDS */

  32    1             GET EDIT(ACTION, TSYMBOL, TVALUE)
                         ( A(6), COL(10), A(8), COL(20), F(7) );
  33    1             GET SKIP;
  34    1             PUT SKIP(2) EDIT(ACTION, TSYMBOL, TVALUE)
                         ( A(6), COL(10), A(8), COL(20), F(7) );

            /**** CHECK IF 'DELETE' ACTION *****/
  35    1             IF ACTION = 'DELETE'
  36    1             THEN DO;     /* 'T IS 'DELETE', PROCESS IT */
  37    1     1           I = SEARCH(TSYMBOL); /* FIND NAME IN DIRECTORY */
  38    1     1           IF I = 0
                              THEN              /* NAME IS NOT IN DIRECTORY, ERROR */
```

220

/* SAMPLE SOLUTION FOR DESK TOP DIRECTORY PROBLEM -- P3 BY PGG */                          PAGE      4

```
STMT LEVEL NEST

 39    1    1                              DO;
 40    1    2                                  PUT SKIP EDIT('NAME REQUESTED CANNOT BE' ||
                                               ' FOUND IN DIRECTORY.') (A);
 41    1    2                                  GO TO LOOP;
 42    1    2                              END;

 43    1    1                          DO J = I TO NUMBER_OF_SYMBOLS - 1;
                                              /* FILL HOLE LEFT BY DELETION */
 44    1    2                              SYMBOL_TABLE(J).SYMBOL = SYMBOL_TABLE(J+1).SYMBOL;
 45    1    2                              SYMBOL_TABLE(J).VALUE = SYMBOL_TABLE(J+1).VALUE;
 46    1    2                          END;

 47    1    1                          NUMBER_OF_SYMBOLS = NUMBER_OF_SYMBOLS - 1;
                                              /* SHOW WE ARE ONE LESS */
 48    1    1                          END;
                           /***** CHECK IF 'INSERT' ACTION *****/
 49    1                   ELSE IF ACTION = 'INSERT'
 50    1                   THEN DO;   /* IT IS 'INSERT', PROCESS IT */
 51    1    1                  IF NUMBER_OF_SYMBOLS = 10   /*TEST FOR OVERFLOW */
 52    1    1                  THEN PUT SKIP EDIT
                                  ('DIRECTORY FULL, REQUEST IGNORED. ') (A);
 53    1    1                  ELSE DO;  /* INSERT NEW ENTRY AT END OF DIRECTORY */
 54    1    2                      I = SEARCH(TSYMBOL);
                                              /* CHECK TO SEE IF NAME ALREADY IN
                                                 DIRECTORY, AND IF SO IS THIS THE
                                                 SAME VALUE AS WELL */
 55    1    2                      IF I ¬= 0
                                   THEN      /* NAME DUPLICATION */
 56    1    2                          DO;
 57    1    3                              IF SYMBOL_TABLE(I).VALUE = TVALUE
                                           THEN
 58    1    3                                  PUT SKIP EDIT('REQUESTED' ||
                                               ' INSERT IS AN ' ||
                                               'EFFECTIVE NO-OP.')
                                               (A);
 59    1    3                              ELSE
 59    1    3                                  PUT SKIP EDIT('SYMBOL TO' ||
                                               ' BE INSERTED ALREADY'
                                               || ' EXISTS IN ' ||
                                               'DIRECTORY.') (A);
 60    1    3                              GO TO LOOP;
 61    1    3                          END;
                           /* IF I = 0, LL + 1 IS WHERE THE NAME SHOULD GO IN THE
                              DIRECTORY. WE MUST MOVE ENTRIES DOWN TO CREATE A SLOT
                              FOR THE NAME. */
 62    1    2                      DO I = NUMBER_OF_SYMBOLS TO LL+1 BY -1;
 63    1    3                          SYMBOL_TABLE(I+1).SYMBOL =
```

221

```
STMT LEVEL NEST

                                                SYMBOL_TABLE(I).SYMBOL;
   64    1    3                    SYMBOL_TABLE(I+1).VALUE = SYMBOL_TABLE(I).VALUE;
   65    1    3                   END;

                                 /* NOW WE INSERT THE ENTRY AND BUMP THE COUNT */

   66    1    2                     SYMBOL_TABLE(LL+1).SYMBOL = TSYMBOL;
   67    1    2                     SYMBOL_TABLE(LL+1).VALUE = TVALUE;
   68    1    2                     NUMBER_OF_SYMBOLS = NUMBER_OF_SYMBOLS + 1;

   69    1    2                  END;
   70    1    1                END;

                 /***** CHECK IF 'PRINT' ACTION *****/
   71    1            ELSE IF ACTION = 'PRINT'
                      THEN    /* IT IS 'PRINT', PROCESS IT */
   72    1            DO I = 1 TO NUMBER_OF_SYMBOLS;       /* PRINT ALL SYMBOLS */
   73    1    1           PUT SKIP EDIT(SYMBOL_TABLE(I).SYMBOL,
                                      SYMBOL_TABLE(I).VALUE)
                                     (COL(10), A(8), COL(20), F(7) );
   74    1    1           END;

                 /***** CHECK IF 'SEARCH' ACTION *****/
   75    1            ELSE IF ACTION = 'SEARCH'
   76    1            THEN DO;    /* IT IS 'SEARCH', PROCESS IT */
   77    1    1           I = SEARCH (TSYMBOL);

                          /* USE FUNCTION SEARCH TO GET THE ENTRY INDEX IN THE
                             DIRECTORY IF THE NAME WAS FOUND, OR A ZERO IF NOT */

   78    1    1           IF I = 0 THEN
   79    1    1           PUT SKIP EDIT('NAME REQUESTED NOT FOUND IN DIRECTORY. ')
                                     (A);
   80    1    1           ELSE
   80    1    1                   PUT SKIP EDIT
                                      (SYMBOL_TABLE(I).VALUE)
                                      (COL(20), F(7) );
   81    1    1           GO TO LOOP;    /* GO ON TO NEXT REQUEST */
   82    1    1           END;

                 /***** CHECK IF 'UPDATE' ACTION *****/
   83    1            ELSE IF ACTION = 'UPDATE'
   84    1            THEN DO;              /* IT IS UPDATE, PROCESS IT */
   85    1    1           I = SEARCH(TSYMBOL); /* SEE IF NAME EXISTS */
   86    1    1           IF I = 0
                          THEN            /* NAME DOES NOT EXIST, ERROR */
   87    1    1                   PUT SKIP EDIT('NAME TO BE UPDATED DOES NOT' ||
                                      ' EXIST') (A);
                                    .
   88    1    1                   ELSE          /* UPDATE VALUE */
```

222

/* SAMPLE SOLUTION FOR DESK TOP DIRECTORY PROBLEM -- P3 BY PGG */                              PAGE     6

```
STMT LEVEL NEST

  88    1    1                                  SYMBOL_TABLE(I).VALUE = TVALUE;

  89    1    1                        GO TO LOOP;
  90    1    1                        END;

                       /***** IF WE GET HERE, ACTION REQUESTED IS INVALID    *****/
  91    1                 ELSE PUT SKIP EDIT('ACTION REQUESTED IS INVALID, IGNORED.')(A);

                       /***** GO BACK AGAIN AND PROCESS NEXT INPUT DATA CARD              *****/
  92    1                 GO TO LOOP;

  93    1            END;
```

```
DELETE    CHUNGA           0
NAME REQUESTED CANNOT BE FOUND IN DIRECTORY.

INSERT    GREGORY    9361234

PRINT                      0
          GREGORY    9361234

INSERT    LINNELL    2536021

INSERT    DEJONG     2533213

INSERT    SMITH      8906123

INSERT    SPELLING   2535716
ACTION REQUESTED IS INVALID, IGNORED.

SEARCH    GREGORY          0
                     9361234

INSERT    GREGORY    2611890
SYMBOL TO BE INSERTED ALREADY EXISTS IN DIRECTORY.

PRINT                      0
          DEJONG     2533213
          GREGORY    9361234
          LINNELL    2536021
          SMITH      8906123

DELETE    SMITH            0

PRINT                      0
          DEJONG     2533213
          GREGORY    9361234
          LINNELL    2536021

INSERT    NANGLE     2535716

INSERT    ALTMAN     6371234

INSERT    LINNELL    2536021
REQUESTED INSERT IS AN EFFECTIVE NO-OP.

PRINT                      0
          ALTMAN     6371234
          DEJONG     2533213
          GREGORY    9361234
          LINNELL    2536021
          NANGLE     2535716

SEARCH    SPELLING         0
NAME REQUESTED NOT FOUND IN DIRECTORY.

INSERT    CALOGGER   2534643

UPDATE    CHUNGA     2611890
NAME TO BE UPDATED DOES NOT EXIST
```

```
INSERT    DAVENPOR   2534600

INSERT    SMULLIN    2531000

INSERT    BYER       2534608

INSERT    WESTCOTT   2534608

INSERT    MARTIN     2532411
DIRECTORY FULL, REQUEST IGNORED.

INSERT    JOHNSON    4235600
DIRECTORY FULL, REQUEST IGNORED.

INSERT    CHUCK      2582475
DIRECTORY FULL, REQUEST IGNORED.

INSERT    ALBEE      2534609
DIRECTORY FULL, REQUEST IGNORED.

INSERT    DEBBIE     2534674
DIRECTORY FULL, REQUEST IGNORED.

UPDATE    GREGORY    2611890

PRINT                        0
          ALTMAN     6371234
          BYER       2534608
          CALOGGER   2534643
          DAVENPOR   2534600
          DEJONG     2533213
          GREGORY    2611890
          LINNELL    2536021
          NANGLE     2535716
          SMULLIN    2531000
          WESTCOTT   2534608
```

## 3.6.4  Assembler Problem -- P4

```
                /* SAMPLE SOLUTION FOR ASSEMBLER PROBLEM -- P4 BY PGG */                              PAGE   2

STMT LEVEL NEST
                    /* SAMPLE SOLUTION FOR ASSEMBLER PROBLEM -- P4 BY PGG */
    1               ASMBLR: PROC OPTIONS(MAIN);

                                            /* THIS PROCEDURE ASSEMBLES A SIMPLE
                                               SUBSET OF BAL, PROVIDING AN
                                               OUTPUT LISTING ONLY */


    2     1         DECLARE
                        INPUT (30) CHAR(80),          /* HOLDS INPUT CARDS */
                        CARD_NO FIXED BIN INIT(0),    /* NUMBER OF CARDS IN PROGRAM */

                        LC   FIXED BIN(31) INIT(0),   /* OUTPUT LOCATION COUNTER */

                        1 MNEMONIC_TABLE(15),         /* TO DECODE MNEMONICS */
                            2 MNEMONIC CHAR(5) INIT('A', 'AR', 'BC', 'BCR', 'DC',
                                'DROP', 'DS', 'END', 'L', 'LR', 'S', 'SR', 'ST',
                                'START', 'USING'),
                            2 MTYPE BIT(1) INIT((4)(1)'1'B, (4)(1)'0'B, (5)(1)'1'B,
                                (2)(1)'0'B),
                            2 OPCODE FIXED BIN(15) INIT(12, 13, 17, 18, 1, 2, 3, 4, 10,
                                11, 14, 15, 16, 5, 6),
                            2 MLEN FIXED BIN(15) INIT(4, 2, 4, 2, 4, 0, 4, 0, 4, 2, 4,
                                0, 4, 0, 0),

                        1 SYMBOL_TABLE (30),
                            2 SYMBOL CHAR(8),         /* SYMBOL NAME */
                            2 VALUE FIXED BIN(31),    /* SYMBOL VALUE */
                        SYMBOL_NO FIXED BIN(15) INIT(0),

                        1 BASE_TABLE(16),
                            2 REGISTER FIXED BIN(15),
                            2 VALUE FIXED BIN(31),
                        BASE_NO FIXED BIN(15) INIT(0),

                        PS BIT(1) INIT('0'B),

                        BLAB (18) LABEL,

                        MSM BIT(1),

                        (N,I,J,L,B,D,R,V) FIXED BIN(15),

                        EOF_SYSIN BIT(1) INIT('1'B);

    3     1         ON ERROR SNAP
    4     1             BEGIN;
    5     2                 ON ERROR STOP;
    7     2                 PUT FILE(SYSPRINT) DATA;
```

/* SAMPLE SOLUTION FOR ASSEMBLER PROBLEM -- P4 BY PGG */                    PAGE     3

```
STMT LEVEL NEST

   8    2            END;

   9    1            ON ENDFILE(SYSIN) EOF_SYSIN = '0'B;

  11    1            OPEN FILE(SYSIN), FILE(SYSPRINT);

  12    1            DO WHILE(EOF_SYSIN);              /* READ WHOLE PROGRAM */
  13    1    1          CARD_NO = CARD_NO + 1;         /* BUMP COUNTER */
  14    1    1          GET FILE(SYSIN) EDIT(INPUT(CARD_NO)) (A(80));
  15    1    1       END;
  16    1            CARD_NO = CARD_NO - 1;

  17    1            PUT FILE(SYSPRINT) EDIT ('INPUT PROGRAM:') (SKIP,A);
  18    1            PUT FILE(SYSPRINT) SKIP(2);
  19    1            DO N = 1 TO CARD_NO;             /* PASS ONE THROUGH PROGRAM */
  20    1    1          PUT FILE(SYSPRINT) EDIT (INPUT(N)) (SKIP,A(80));
  21    1    1          IF SUBSTR(INPUT(N),1,1) ¬= ' '
                          THEN
  22    1    1             DO;                        /* ADD LABEL TO SYMBOL TABLE */
  23    1    2                SYMBOL_NO = SYMBOL_NO + 1;
  24    1    2                SYMBOL(SYMBOL_NO) = SUBSTR(INPUT(N),1,8);
  25    1    2                SYMBOL_TABLE.VALUE(SYMBOL_NO) = LC;
  26    1    2             END;
  27    1    1          MSW = '1'B;                   /* FIND MNEMONIC TO GET LENGTH */
  28    1    1          DO I = 1 TO 15 WHILE(MSW);    /* TRY ALL OP-CODES */
  29    1    2             IF MNEMONIC(I) = SUBSTR(INPUT(N),10,5)
                             THEN
  30    1    2                DO;                     /* WE FOUND IT */
  31    1    3                   LC = LC + MLEN(I);
  32    1    3                   MSW = '0'B;
  33    1    3                END;
  34    1    2          END;
  35    1    1       END;


                                                  /* FOR DEBUGGING */
  36    1            PUT FILE(SYSPRINT) EDIT ('SYMBOL TABLE:') (SKIP(2),A);
  37    1            PUT FILE(SYSPRINT) SKIP(2);
  38    1            PUT FILE(SYSPRINT) EDIT ((SYMBOL(I),SYMBOL_TABLE.VALUE(I)  DO I = 1
                        TO SYMBOL_NO)) (SKIP,A(8),X(2),F(6,0));


                                                  /* PASS TWO */

  39    1            PS = '1'B;                     /* INDICATE PASS TWO */
  40    1            LC = 0;

  41    1            PUT FILE(SYSPRINT) EDIT ('OUTPUT LISTING:') (SKIP(2),A);
```

```
/* SAMPLE SOLUTION FOR ASSEMBLER PROBLEM -- P4 BY PGG */                          PAGE    4

STMT LEVEL NEST

 42    1              PUT FILE(SYSPRINT) SKIP(2);

 43    1              DO N = 1 TO CARD_NO;              /* PROCESS ALL STATEMENTS */
 44    1    1           DO I = 1 TO 15;                /* GET ENTRY IN MNEMONIC TABLE */
 45    1    2             IF SUBSTR(INPUT(N),10,5) = MNEMONIC(I)
 46    1    2               THEN GO TO BLAB(OPCODE(I));
 47    1    2           END;

 48    1    1         BLAB(11): BLAB(13): BLAB(15): BLAB(18):
                                                     /* RR TYPES */
                        PUT FILE(SYSPRINT) EDIT(LC,OPCODE(I),SUBSTR(INPUT(N),16,2),',',
                          SUBSTR(INPUT(N),19,2)) (SKIP,F(6,0),COL(10),F(2,0),
                          COL(16),A(2),A(1),A(2));
 49    1    1         GO TO NEXT;                      /* PROCESS NEXT STATEMENT */

 50    1    1         BLAB(10): BLAB(12): BLAB(14): BLAB(16): BLAB(17):
                                                     /* RX TYPES */
                        MSW = '1'B;                    /* FIRST WE FIND SYMBOLS VALUE */
 51    1    1           DO J = 1 TO SYMBOL_NO WHILE(MSW);
 52    1    2             IF SYMBOL(J) = SUBSTR(INPUT(N),19,8)
                            THEN;
 53    1    2               DO;
 54    1    3                 V = SYMBOL_TABLE.VALUE(J);
 55    1    3                 MSW = '0'B;
 56    1    3               END;
 57    1    2           END;

 58    1    1         MSW = '1'B;                      /* NOW WE FIND A BASE REGISTER */
 59    1    1         DO J = 1 TO BASE_NO WHILE(MSW);
 60    1    2           IF BASE_TABLE.VALUE(J) -> V
 61    1    2             THEN;
 62    1    2               DO;
 63    1    3                 B = REGISTER(J);
 64    1    3                 D = V - BASE_TABLE.VALUE(J);
 65    1    3                 MSW = '0'B;
 66    1    3               END;
 67    1    2           END;

                                                     /* NOW WE PRINT LINE */
 68    1    1         PUT FILE(SYSPRINT) EDIT(LC,OPCODE(I),SUBSTR(INPUT(N),16,2),',',
                        D,'(00,',B,')') (SKIP,F(6,0),COL(10),F(2,0),COL(16),A(2),
                        A(1),F(2,0),A(4),F(2,0),A(1));
 69    1    1         GO TO NEXT;

 70    1    1         BLAB(1):                         /* DC PSEUDO OP */
```

228

```
          /* SAMPLE SOLUTION FOR ASSEMBLER PROBLEM -- P4 BY PGG */                    PAGE    5

STMT LEVEL NEST
                    PUT FILE(SYSPRINT) EDIT(LC,SUBSTR(INPUT(N),18,2)) (SKIP,F(6,0),
                        COL(10),A(2));
  71   1   1         GO TO NEXT;


  72   1   1         BLAB(3):                       /* DS PSEUDO OP */
                    PUT FILE(SYSPRINT) EDIT(LC) (SKIP,F(6,0));
  73   1   1         GO TO NEXT;


  74   1   1         BLAB(2):                       /* DROP PSEUDO OP */
                    GET STRING(SUBSTR(INPUT(N),16,2)) EDIT (R) (F(2,0));

  75   1   1         MSW = '1'B;                    /* FIND ENTRY */
  76   1   1         DO J = 1 TO BASE_NO WHILE(MSW);
  77   1   2             IF REGISTER(J) = R
                            THEN
  78   1   2                 DO;
  79   1   3                     DO L = J TO BASE_NO - 1;
  80   1   4                         REGISTER(L) = REGISTER(L+1);
  81   1   4                         BASE_TABLE.VALUE(L) = BASE_TABLE.VALUE(L+1)
                                                                             ;
  82   1   4                     END;
  83   1   3                     MSW = '0'B;
  84   1   3                 END;
  85   1   2         END;
  86   1   1         BASE_NO = BASE_NO -1;
  87   1   1         GO TO NEXT;


  88   1   1         BLAB(6):                       /* USING */
                    GET STRING(SUBSTR(INPUT(N),16,2)) EDIT(R) (F(2,0));

  89   1   1         MSW = '1'B;                    /* GET VALUE OF LABEL */
  90   1   1         DO J = 1 TO SYMBOL_NO WHILE(MSW);
  91   1   2             IF SYMBOL(J) = SUBSTR(INPUT(N),19,8)
                            THEN
  92   1   2                 DO;
  93   1   3                     MSW = '0'B;
  94   1   3                     V = SYMBOL_TABLE.VALUE(J);
  95   1   3                 END;
  96   1   2         END;

  97   1   1         MSW = '1'B;                    /* FIND SLOT IN BRT */
  98   1   1         DO J = 1 TO BASE_NO WHILE(MSW);
  99   1   2             IF BASE_TABLE.VALUE(J) < V
                            THEN
 100   1   2                 DO;
 101   1   3                     DO L = BASE_NO TO J BY -1;
 102   1   4                         REGISTER(L+1) = REGISTER(L);
```

```
        /* SAMPLE SOLUTION FOR ASSEMBLER PROBLEM -- P4 BY PGG */                              PAGE    6

STMT LEVEL NEST
  103    1    4                              BASE_TABLE.VALUE(L+1) =
                                                  BASE_TABLE.VALUE(L);
  104    1    4                      END;
  105    1    3                      MSW = '0'B;
  106    1    3                      J = J -1; /* SINCE WHILE IS TESTED AFTER INC */
  107    1    3                  END;
  108    1    2          END;

  109    1    1          REGISTER(J) = R;
  110    1    1          BASE_TABLE.VALUE(J) = V;

  111    1    1          BASE_NO = BASE_NO + 1;


  112    1    1      BLAB(4): BLAB(5): NEXT:        /* END OF PASS TWO LOOP */

                      LC = LC + MLEN(I);            /* BUMP LOCATION COUNTER */
  113    1    1      END;

  114    1          END ASMBLR;
```

INPUT PROGRAM:

```
CHUNGA      START
            USING   12,NOWHERE
NOWHERE     L       01,TEN
            A       01,TWO
            LR      03,01
            USING   14,THERE
            ST      01,TEMP1
THERE       L       02,FOUR
            SR      02,03
            DROP    14
            ST      02,TEMP2
            BC      15,SKIP
SKIP        DROP    12
            BCR     15,14
TEN         DC      F'10'
TWO         DC      F'02'
TEMP1       DS      F
FOUR        DC      F'04'
TEMP2       DS      F
MADNICK     DS      F
            END
```

SYMBOL TABLE:

```
CHUNGA            0
NOWHERE           0
THERE            14
SKIP             26
TEN              28
TWO              32
TEMP1            36
FOUR             40
TEMP2            44
MADNICK          48
```

OUTPUT LISTING:

```
    0    10    01,28(00,12)
    4    12    01,32(00,12)
    8    11    03,01
   10    16    01,22(00,14)
   14    10    02,26(00,14)
   18    15    02,03
   18    16    02,44(00,12)
   22    17    15,26(00,12)
   26    18    15,14
   28    10
   32    02
   36
   40    04
   44
   48
```

## 3.6.5  Lexical Analyzer Problem -- P5

```
          /* SOLUTION TO LEXICAL ANALYZER PROBLEM -- P5, BY CHAD CARPENTER */                    PAGE      2

STMT LEVEL NEST
                    /* SOLUTION TO LEXICAL ANALYZER PROBLEM -- P5, BY CHAD CARPENTER */
  1                 LEXPROC: PROC;
  2      1             DECLARE
                          1 BRKTBL BASED(PBRKT),
                            2 LEN FIXED BIN,
                            2 C(J REFER(BRKTBL.LEN)) CHAR(1),
                          1 OPTBL BASED(POPT),
                            2 LEN FIXED BIN,
                            2 C(J REFER(OPTBL.LEN)) CHAR(8),
                          (PBRKT,POPT) PTR EXT,
                          CARD CHAR(80),
                          NXTCARD ENTRY RETURNS(CHAR(80)),
                          IDNTAB(50) CHAR(8) EXT,
                          IDNNUM FIXED BIN(31) EXT,
                          1 TOKEN BASED(PT),
                            2 NEXT PTR,
                            2 TYPE BIT(32) ALIGNED,
                            2 VALUE FIXED BIN(31),
                          PT PTR,
                          START PTR EXT,
                          ALOC ENTRY RETURNS(PTR);
  3      1             DECLARE
                          CRD(80) CHAR(1) DEF CARD,
                          C1 CHAR(1),
                          STR CHAR(8),
                          MYPTR PTR,
                          CONTINUE LABEL(NEW_CARD,DOBREAK),
                          NULL BUILTIN,
                          DEBUG ENTRY,
                          (I,J,LIM1,NCHAR) FIXED BIN;
  4      1             ON CONDITION(EOF) GO TO DONE;
  6      1             START=NULL;
  7      1          NEW_CARD:
                       CARD=NXTCARD;
  8      1             I=1;
  9      1          MORE:
                       LIM1=I+1;
 10      1             IF LIM1>72 THEN GO TO NEW_CARD;
 12      1             DO I=LIM1 TO 72;
 13      1    1          C1=CRD(I);
 14      1    1          DO J=1 TO BRKTBL.LEN;
 15      1    2             IF C1=BRKTBL.C(J) THEN GO TO BREAK_CHAR;
 17      1    2          END;
 18      1    1        END;
 19      1             NCHAR=I-LIM1;   /*    I=73 IF FALLS THROUGH LOOP   */
 20      1             CONTINUE=NEW_CARD;
 21      1          ID_OR_OPER_OR_LIT:
                       PT=ALOC;
 22      1             IF START=NULL THEN START=PT;
 24      1             ELSE MYPTR->TOKEN.NEXT=PT;
 25      1             MYPTR=PT;
```

/* SOLUTION TO LEXICAL ANALYZER PROBLEM -- P5, BY CHAD CARPENTER */          PAGE    3

```
STMT LEVEL NEST
 26    1                   STR=SUBSTR(CARD,LIM1,NCHAR);
 27    1                   DO J=1 TO OPTBL.LEN;
 28    1     1                 IF STR=OPTBL.C(J) THEN DO;
 30    1     2                     TOKEN.TYPE='100'B;
 31    1     2                     TOKEN.VALUE=J;
 32    1     2                     GO TO CONTINUE;
 33    1     2                 END;
 34    1     1             END;
 35    1                   DO J=LIM1 TO I-1;
 36    1     1                 IF CRD(J)<'0' | CRD(J)>'9' THEN GO TO ID;
 38    1     1             END;
 39    1                   TOKEN.TYPE='001'B;
 40    1                   GET STRING(STR) EDIT(TOKEN.VALUE) (F(8));
 41    1                   GO TO CONTINUE;
 42    1             ID:
                          TOKEN.TYPE='010'B;
 43    1                   DO J=1 TO IDNNUM;
 44    1     1                 IF STR=IDNTAB(J) THEN DO;
 46    1     2                     TCKEN.VALUE=J;
 47    1     2                     GO TO CONTINUE;
 48    1     2                 END;
 49    1     1             END;
 50    1                   IDNNUM=J;
 51    1                   IDNTAB(J)=STR;
 52    1                   TOKEN.VALUE=J;
 53    1                   GO TO CONTINUE;
 54    1             BREAK_CHAR:
                          NCHAR=I-LIM1;    /*   BREAK CHAR IS NOT PART OF STRING    */
 55    1                   IF NCHAR>0 THEN DO;
 57    1     1                 CONTINUE=DOBREAK;
 58    1     1                 GO TO ID_OR_OPER_OR_LIT;    /*   NCHAR=0 MEANS 2 BREAKS    */
 59    1     1             END;
 60    1             DOBREAK:
 61    1                   IF C1¬=' ' THEN DO J=1 TO OPTBL.LEN;
 62    1     1                 IF C1=OPTBL.C(J) THEN DO;
 64    1     2                     PT=ALOC;
 65    1     2                     IF START=NULL THEN START=PT;
 67    1     2                     ELSE MYPTR->TOKEN.NEXT=PT;
 68    1     2                     MYPTR=PT;
 69    1     2                     TOKEN.TYPE='100'B;
 70    1     2                     TOKEN.VALUE=J;
 71    1     2                     GO TO MORE;
 72    1     2                 END;
 73    1     1             END;
 74    1                   GO TO MORE;
 75    1             DONE:
                          TOKEN.NEXT=NULL;
 76    1             END;
```

```
*** GRADER ENTERRED FOR STUDENT
20 POINTS FOR SUCCESSFUL COMPILATION

DUMP OF SUPPLIED TABLES:

                    BRKTBL           OPTBL
                    ------           -----
          1            +                +
          2            +                -
          3            -                *
          4            *                /
          5            /                =
          6            =                >
          7            >                <
          8            <                .
          9            .                (
         10            ¬                )
         11            ;                ;
         12            :                :
         13            ,                ,
         14            (                ¬
         15            )              PROC
         16                            DO
         17                           END
         18                            IF
         19                          THEN
         20                          ELSE
         21                          GOTO
         22                           PUT
         23                           GET

STUDENT PROGRAM NOW IN CONTROL

NEW INPUT LINE >>--->| CROCK:  PROC;                                    00000010|<---<<
NEW INPUT LINE >>--->|          IF A < 37 THEN DO;  $IPC = BQ + 9;      00000020|<---<<
NEW INPUT LINE >>--->| GOTO XLBL; END;                                  00000030|<---<<
NEW INPUT LINE >>--->|          ELSE DO;                                00000040|<---<<
NEW INPUT LINE >>--->|             %XID=                        3;      00000050|<---<<
NEW INPUT LINE >>--->|             PUT (A,$IPC);                        00000060|<---<<
NEW INPUT LINE >>--->|          END;                                    00000070|<---<<
NEW INPUT LINE >>--->|          IF A=(B*D-08096)THEN GOTO X;     ELSE DO; 00000080|<---<<
NEW INPUT LINE >>--->|          PUT A;         END;                     00000090|<---<<
NEW INPUT LINE >>--->| X:       A=B *  C /2;                            00000100|<---<<
NEW INPUT LINE >>--->|          END;                                    00000110|<---<<
NEW INPUT LINE >>--->| XLBL:                                            00000120|<---<<
NEW INPUT LINE >>--->|          END CROCK;                              00000130|<---<<

*** 10 POINTS FOR RETURNING CONTROL TO GRADER

*** 35 POINTS FOR CORRECT IDNTAB

                         YOUR VERSION        MINE
                         ------------        ----

           IDNNUM            10               10
              1             CROCK            CROCK
              2              A                A
```

```
3    $IPC      $IPC
4    BQ        BQ
5    XLBL      XLBL
6    %XID      %XID
7    B         B
8    D         D
9    X         X
10   C         C
```

DEBUG CALLED

DUMP OF TOKENS IN ORDER OF ALLOCATION:            ADDRESS
                                                  -------
                                                  NEXT
                     START->OFE4C8                TYPE    (LEFTMOST 3 BITS)
                                                  VALUE

| Token | Address | Next | Type | Value |
|---|---|---|---|---|
| CROCK | OFE4C8 | OFE4B0 | '010'B | 1 |
| : | OFE4E0 | OFE4F8 | '100'B | 12 |
| PROC | OFE4F8 | OFE510 | '100'B | 15 |
| ; | OFE510 | OFE528 | '100'B | 11 |
| IF | OFE528 | OFE540 | '100'B | 18 |
| A | OFE540 | OFE558 | '010'B | 2 |
| < | OFE558 | OFE570 | '100'B | 7 |
| 37 | OFE570 | OFE588 | '001'B | 37 |
| THEN | OFE588 | OFE5A0 | '100'B | 19 |
| DO | OFE5A0 | OFE5B8 | '100'B | 16 |
| ; | OFE5B8 | OFE5D0 | '100'B | 11 |
| $IPC | OFE5D0 | OFE5E8 | '010'B | 3 |
| = | OFE5E8 | OFE600 | '100'B | 5 |
| BQ | OFE600 | OFE618 | '010'B | 4 |
| + | OFE618 | OFE630 | '100'B | 1 |

| Token | Address | Next | Type | Value |
|---|---|---|---|---|
| 9 | OFE630 | OFE648 | '001'B | 9 |
| ; | OFE648 | OFE660 | '100'B | 11 |
| GOTO | OFE660 | OFE678 | '100'B | 21 |
| XLBL | OFE678 | OFE690 | '010'B | 5 |
| ; | OFE690 | OFE6A8 | '100'B | 11 |
| END | OFE6A8 | OFE6C0 | '100'B | 17 |
| ; | OFE6C0 | OFE6D8 | '100'B | 11 |
| ELSE | OFE6D8 | OFE6F0 | '100'B | 20 |
| DO | OFE6F0 | OFE708 | '100'B | 16 |
| ; | OFE708 | OFE720 | '100'B | 11 |
| %XID | OFE720 | OFE738 | '010'B | 6 |
| = | OFE738 | OFE750 | '100'B | 5 |
| 3 | OFE750 | OFE768 | '001'B | 3 |
| ; | OFE768 | OFE780 | '100'B | 11 |
| PUT | OFE780 | OFE798 | '100'B | 22 |

| Token | Address | Next | Type | Value |
|---|---|---|---|---|
| ( | OFE798 | OFE7B0 | '100'B | 9 |
| A | OFE7B0 | OFE7C8 | '010'B | 2 |
| * | OFE7C8 | OFE7E0 | '100'B | 13 |
| $IPC | OFE7E0 | OFE7F8 | '010'B | 3 |
| ) | OFE7F8 | OFE810 | '100'B | 10 |
| ; | OFE810 | OFE828 | '100'B | 11 |
| END | OFE828 | OFE840 | '100'B | 17 |
| ; | OFE840 | OFE858 | '100'B | 11 |
| IF | OFE858 | OFE870 | '100'B | 18 |
| A | OFE870 | OFE888 | '010'B | 2 |
| = | OFE888 | OFE8A0 | '100'B | 5 |
| ( | OFE8A0 | OFE8B8 | '100'B | 9 |
| B | OFE8B8 | OFE8D0 | '010'B | 7 |
| * | OFE8D0 | OFE8E8 | '100'B | 3 |
| D | OFE8E8 | OFE900 | '010'B | 8 |

| Token | Address | Next | Type | Value |
|---|---|---|---|---|
| - | OFE900 | OFE918 | '100'B | 2 |
| 8096 | OFE918 | OFE930 | '001'B | 8096 |
| ) | OFE930 | OFE948 | '100'B | 10 |
| THEN | OFE948 | OFE960 | '100'B | 19 |
| GOTO | OFE960 | OFE978 | '100'B | 21 |
| X | OFE978 | OFE990 | '010'B | 9 |
| ; | OFE990 | OFE9A8 | '100'B | 11 |
| ELSE | OFE9A8 | OFE9C0 | '100'B | 20 |
| DO | OFE9C0 | OFE9D8 | '100'B | 16 |
| ; | OFE9D8 | OFE9F0 | '100'B | 11 |
| PUT | OFE9F0 | OFEA08 | '100'B | 22 |
| A | OFEA08 | OFEA20 | '010'B | 2 |
| ; | OFEA20 | OFEA38 | '100'B | 11 |
| END | OFEA38 | OFEA50 | '100'B | 17 |
| ; | OFEA50 | OFEA68 | '100'B | 11 |

| Token | Address | Next | Type | Value |
|---|---|---|---|---|
| X | OFEA68 | OFEA80 | '010'B | 9 |
| ; | OFEA80 | OFEA98 | '100'B | 12 |
| A | OFEA98 | OFEAB0 | '010'B | 2 |
| = | OFEAB0 | OFEAC8 | '100'B | 5 |
| B | OFEAC8 | OFEAE0 | '010'B | 7 |
| * | OFEAE0 | OFEAF8 | '100'B | 3 |
| C | OFEAF8 | OFEB10 | '010'B | 10 |
| / | OFEB10 | OFEB28 | '100'B | 4 |
| 2 | OFEB28 | OFEB40 | '001'B | 2 |
| ; | OFEB40 | OFEB58 | '100'B | 11 |
| END | OFEB58 | OFEB70 | '100'B | 17 |
| ; | OFEB70 | OFEB88 | '100'B | 11 |
| XLBL | OFEB88 | OFEBA0 | '010'B | 5 |
| ; | OFEBA0 | OFEBB8 | '100'B | 12 |
| END | OFEBB8 | OFEBD0 | '100'B | 17 |

| Token | Address | Next | Type | Value |
|---|---|---|---|---|
| CROCK | OFEBD0 | OFEBE8 | '010'B | 1 |
| ; | OFEBE8 | $NULLS | '10C'B | 11 |

*** 5 PCINTS FOR START PCINTING TO FIRST TOKEN

*** 10 POINTS FOR CORRECT NUMBER OF TOKENS

*** 10 POINTS FOR CORRECT TOKEN VALUES AND TYPES

*** 10 PCINTS FCR CCRRECT CHAINING

*** SCORE FCR THIS RUN: 1CO

STLCENT PROGRAM USED    1.21 SECONDS

## 3.6.6  SICK Interpreter Problem -- P6

```
STMT LEVEL NEST
                    /* SAMPLE SICK INTERPRETER BY PGG */

   1                SICK: PROCEDURE;

                                        /* THIS PROGRAM INTERPRETS A WEAK SUBSET
                                           OF PL/1 CALLED SICK. ITS SALIENT
                                           FEATURES ARE:

                                            1) HIGH DEGREE OF MODULARITY.

                                            2) CANNONIC FORM OF REDUCTIONS USED
                                               IN TABLE DRIVEN FORM.
                                                                    */

                           /* DECLARATIONS - ALL ARE IN ONE STATEMENT FOR CONTEST */

                              /* COMMUNICATION POINTERS */

   2     1        DECLARE

                    (LOC,                  /* PLACE HOLDER IN TOKEN CHAIN */
                     PSNT,                 /* BASE FOR SYMBOL TABLE */
                     START,                /* ANCHOR FOR TOKEN CHAIN */
                     PDS,                  /* ANCHOR FOR PUSHDOWN STACK */
                     SVS)                  /* ANCHOR FOR SYMBOL VALUE STACK */
                           POINTER STATIC EXTERNAL,

                              /* SHARED ALLOCATION AREA */

                    AREAM AREA(32000) STATIC EXTERNAL,

                              /* TOKEN CHAIN CELLS */

                    1 TOKEN BASED(PT),      /* TOKEN PRODUCED BY LEXPROC */
                      2 NEXT POINTER,       /* POINTER TO NEXT TOKEN OR NULL */
                      2 TYPE BIT(32) ALIGNED,
                                            /* TYPE OF TOKEN, '100'B = OPERATOR,
                                                              '010'B = IDENTIFIER,
                                                              '001'B = LITERAL */
                      2 VALUE POINTER,      /* POINTER TO FIXED BIN(31) VALUE CELL */

                              /* TOKEN VALUE CELL */

                    TVALUE FIXED BIN(31) BASED(PTV),
                                            /* HOLDS VALUE FOR TOKEN, MEANING DEPENDS
                                               ON TYPE OF TOKEN:
                                                    FOR OPERATOR = INDEX IN OPERATOR
```

/* SAMPLE SICK INTERPRETER BY PGG */

STMT LEVEL NEST

```
                                        TABLE,
                        IDENTIFIER = INDEX IN SYMBOL NAME
                                        TABLE,
                        LITERAL = VALUE OF LITERAL. */

        /* SYMBOL NAME TABLE (SNT) */

1 SNT BASED(PSNT),          /* SYMBOL NAME TABLE PRODUCED BY LEXPROC */
  2 ICOUNT FIXED BIN, /* NUMBER OF SYMBOLS IN TABLE */
  2 NAME(NS REFER(SNT.ICOUNT)) CHAR(8),
                            /* ARRAY OF SYMBOL NAMES */

        /* SYMBOL VALUE STACK (SVS) */

1 SYMVAL BASED(PS),         /* SYMBOL VALUE CELL */
  2 NEXT POINTER,           /* POINTER TO NEXT CELL, OR NULL */
  2 TYPE BIT(32) ALIGNED,
                   /* TYPE OF SYMBOL '010'B = STATEMENT LABEL,
                                     '001'B = FIXED BIN(31)
                                              VALUE. */
  2 SYMBOL FIXED BIN(31),
                   /* INDEX OF THIS SYMBOLS NAME IN THE SNT */
  2 VALUE POINTER,    /* POINTER TO EITHER:
                         1) VALUE CELL IF TYPE = '001'B, OR
                         2) LOCATION OF IDENTIFIER IN TOKEN
                            CHAIN FOR '010'B.      */

        /* SYMBOL VALUE STACK VALUE CELL */

SVALUE FIXED BIN(31) BASED(PSV),
                   /* HOLDS VALUE FOR IDENTIFIER */

        /* PUSH DOWN STACK (PDS) */

1 PDCELL BASED(PP),         /* PDS ELEMENT */
  2 UP POINTER,             /* POINTER TO PREVIOUS ELEMENT OR NULL */
  2 TYPE BIT(32) ALIGNED,
                   /* TYPE OF CELL, '100'B = OPERATOR,
                                    '010'B = IDENTIFIER,
                                    '001'B = VALUE,
                                    '000'B = SPECIAL PROCEDURE
                                             CALL CELL */
  2 VALUE POINTER,    /* POINTER TO BASED DATA STRUCTURE */

        /* SYMBOL VALUE STACK VALUE CELL FOR STANDARD ELEMENTS */

PVALUE FIXED BIN(31) BASED(PPV),
                   /* HOLDS VALUE FOR STANDARD PDS CELLS */

        /* SYMBOL VALUE STACK VALUE CELL FOR SPECIAL ELEMENT */
```

```
/* SAMPLE SICK INTERPRETER BY PGG */                                          PAGE      4

STMT LEVEL NEST

                 1 PRCCELL BASED(PPV),     /* SPECIAL PROCEDURE CALL CELL */
                    2 OLDLOC POINTER,       /* SAVES OLD VALUE OF LCC */
                    2 SYMPNT POINTER,       /* SAVES OLD VALUE OF SVS */

                     /* EXTERNAL SUBROUTINES */

                 LEXPROC ENTRY(CHAR(6)),    /* LEXICAL ANALYZER, TAKES AS ARGUMENT TEST
                                               PROGRAM NAME FROM:
                                               PROGM1 - NO DO-END, GOTO, IF-THEN, OR
                                                        INTERNAL PROCEDURES.
                                               PROGM2 - NO INTERNAL PROCEDURES.
                                               PROGM3 - ALL FEATURES OF SICK. */
                 STMTSKP ENTRY,             /* SKIPS STATEMENTS AND BLOCKS */
                 SVSDUMP ENTRY,             /* PRINTS FORMATTED DUMP OF SVS */
                 PDSDUMP ENTRY,             /* PRINTS FORMATTED DUMP OF PDS */
                 HEX ENTRY(POINTER) RETURNS(CHAR(6)),
                                            /* FORMATS POINTERS FOR PRINTING */

                     /* INTERNAL PROCEDURES */

                 CANNONICALIZE_ ENTRY(CHAR(*)) RETURNS(BIT(1)),
                                            /* BUILDS CANNONIC REPRESENTATION OF PDS TO
                                               BE USED IN REDUCTIONS PROCESSING. VALUE
                                               RETURNED IS ZERO WHEN PDS IS EMPTY */
                 POP_PDS_ ENTRY(FIXED BIN),
                                            /* POPS N ENTRIES FROM THE PDS */
                 PUSH_PDS_ ENTRY(BIT(32) ALIGNED, POINTER),
                                            /* ALLOCATES AND CHAINS PDS CELLS */
                 PUSH_TOKEN_ ENTRY (PTR) RETURNS(BIT(1)),
                                            /* PUTS TOKEN ON PDS. THE VALUE RETURNED
                                               IS ZERO WHEN THERE ARE NO MORE TOKENS */
                 REDUCE_ ENTRY(CHAR(*)) RETURNS(BIT(1)),
                                            /* CHECKS CANNONIC REPRESENTATION OF PDS
                                               AND PERFORMS REDUCTIONS INDICATED,
                                               RETURNED VALUE IS ZERO IF NO REDUCTION
                                               APPLIED */
                 SVS_ALLOCATE_ ENTRY(FIXED BIN(31), BIT(32) ALIGNED, POINTER),
                                            /* ALLOCATES AND CHAINS SVS CELLS */
                 SVS_SEARCH_ ENTRY(FIXED BIN(31)) RETURNS(POINTER),
                                            /* SEARCHES SVS FOR IDENTIFIER, RETURNING
                                               VALUE POINTER */

                     /* TYPE VARIABLES */

                 LITERAL BIT(32) ALIGNED INIT('001'B),
                 VALUE BIT(32) ALIGNED INIT('001'B),
                 OPERATOR BIT(32) ALIGNED INIT('100'B),
```

```
/* SAMPLE SICK INTERPRETER BY PGG */                                    PAGE      5

STMT LEVEL NEST

                IDENTIFIER BIT(32) ALIGNED INIT('010'B),
                PROCEDURE BIT(32) ALIGNED INIT('000'B),

                    /* INTERNAL DECLARATIONS */

                LAST_IDN_PTR POINTER,

                                    /* NORMAL CANNONIC TABLE */
                1 OP_CANNONIC_TABLE (23) STATIC INTERNAL,
                  2 OPC_LEN FIXED BIN INIT( (10) 5,1,1,4,4,4,6,2,4,3,1,1,3,7),
                  2 OPC_CHAR CHAR(8) INIT( (8)(1)'<OP2>', (2)(1)'<OP1>', ')', ','
                      , 'THEN', 'GOTO', 'CALL', 'RETURN', 'DO', 'PROC', 'END',
                      ':', ';', 'PUT', 'DECLARE'),

                CANNONIC_STRING CHAR(64),      /* HOLDS CANNONIC FORM */

                RC(16) CHAR(20) INIT(      /* REDUCTION ARRAY */
                  '; DO',
                  '; END DO',
                  '; <VAL> <OP2> <IDN>',
                  ': <IDN>',
                  '<IDN> GOTO',
                  '<IDN> <OP1>',
                  '<IDN> <OP2>',
                  '<VAL> <OP2> <VAL>',
                  '; <IDN> PUT',
                  '<IDN> DECLARE',
                  '; DECLARE',
                  'THEN <VAL> <OP1>',
                  ') <VAL> <OP1>',
                  '<VAL> <IDN>',
                  '<VAL> RETURN <PROC>',
                  '; <VAL> CALL'),

                RL (16) FIXED BIN INIT(  /* LENGTH OF REDUCTION STRINGS */
                  4, 8, 19, 7, 10, 11, 11, 17, 11, 13, 9, 16, 13, 11, 19, 12),

                1 P_STRUCTURE,                  /* A SLICK TRICK */
                  2 PTR1 PTR,
                  2 PTR2 PTR,
                  2 PTR3 PTR,
                  2 PTR4 PTR,
                  2 PTR5 PTR,
                  2 PTR6 PTR,
                  2 PTR7 PTR,
                  2 PTR8 PTR,
                  2 PTR9 PTR,
                  2 PTR10 PTR,
```

```
          /* SAMPLE SICK INTERPRETER BY PCG */                                    PAGE     5

STMT LEVEL NEST

            P_ARRAY (10) POINTER BASED(PPTR),

            1 C_STRUCTURE,            /* YET ANOTHER CROCK */
               2 CTR1 PTR,
               2 CTR2 PTR,
               2 CTR3 PTR,
               2 CTR4 PTR,
               2 CTR5 PTR,
               2 CTR6 PTR,
               2 CTR7 PTR,
               2 CTR8 PTR,
               2 CTR9 PTR,
               2 CTR10 PTR,

            C_ARRAY(10) POINTER BASED(CPTR),

                            /* FOR DECODING TOKEN TYPES */
            1 CROCK_STRUCTURE BASED(PP),
               2 D1 POINTER,
               2 SC BIT(3),           /* LOOK AT TYPE AS THREE BIT NUMBER */

                            /* FOR PASSING TO LEXPROC */
            CURRENT_PROGRAM CHAR(6),

                            /* FOR IGNORING RETURNED BITS */
            IGNORE BIT(1),

                   /* BUILTIN FUNCTIONS */

            (NULL,
            ADDR,
            FIXED,
            BINARY,
            SUBSTR,
            INDEX) BUILTIN;

                   /* END OF DECLARATIONS */

                   /* INITIALIZATION */
3     1     PPTR = ADDR(P_STRUCTURE);
4     1     CPTR = ADDR(C_STRUCTURE);

                      /* ON ERROR UNIT FOR DEBUGGING ONLY */
5     1     ON ERROR SNAP BEGIN;
```

```
        /* SAMPLE SICK INTERPRETER BY PGG */                              PAGE    7

STMT LEVEL NEST
   7    2              ON ERROR STOP;                 /* AVOID LOOPS */
   9    2              PUT FILE(SYSPRINT) EDIT (CANNONIC_STRING, HEX(LOC))
                          (SKIP,A(64),X(6),A(6));
  10    2              CALL PDSDUMP;
  11    2              CALL SVSDUMP;
  12    2              END;

                    /* BASIC PROCESSING LOOP */

  13    1          TRICK:                           /* A STATEMENT SAVER */
                    DO CURRENT_PROGRAM = 'PROGM1', 'PROGM2', 'PROGM3';

  14    1    1        CALL LEXPROC(CURRENT_PROGRAM); /* GET PROGRAM LEXICALLY ANALYZED */

  15    1    1        LOC = START;                 /* INITIALIZATION FOR PROGRAM */
  16    1    1        PDS = NULL;

  17    1    1        DO WHILE(PUSH_TOKEN_(NULL)); /* PROCESS ALL TOKENS */

  18    1    2           IGNORE = CANNONICALIZE_(CANNONIC_STRING);
                                             /* CONVERT STACK TO CANNONIC FORM */

  19    1    2           DO WHILE(REDUCE_(CANNONIC_STRING) & IGNORE);
                                             /* LOOP PERFORMS REDUCTIONS UNTIL NO
                                                MORE APPLY */
  20    1    3              IGNORE = CANNONICALIZE_(CANNONIC_STRING);
                                             /* CONVERT STACK TO CANNONIC FORM */

  21    1    3     END TRICK;                      /* CLOSES ALL OPEN DO'S */

  24    1          CANNONICALIZE_: PROCEDURE(CSTRING) RETURNS(BIT(1));

                                             /* THIS PROCEDURE SCANS THE PDS FROM
                                                THE TOP DOWN AND CREATES A
                                                CANNONICAL REPRESENTATION OF THE
                                                STACK IN CHARACTER FORM. THIS
                                                CHARACTER FORM IS THEN USED TO
                                                EXPEDITE REDUCTIONS ANALYSIS. ALSO
                                                I BUILD AN ARRAY OF VALUE POINTERS
                                                CONTAINING THE POINTERS FROM THE
                                                CELLS. THIS EXPEDITES REDUCTIONS
                                                PROCESSING. */
  25    2              DCL  CSTRING CHAR(*),        /* STRING TO HOLD CANNONIC FORM */
```

```
        /* SAMPLE SICK INTERPRETER BY PCG */                                      PAGE     8

STMT LEVEL NEST
                         CPOS FIXED BIN INIT(1),   /* CURRENT POSITION IN CANNONIC
                                                      STRING. */
                         TBL (0:4) LABEL,          /* USED IN GO TO */
                         (N,I) FIXED BIN;          /* RANDOM LOOP INDEXES */

26    2              CSTRING = ' ';                /* BLANK OUT STRING */

27    2              IF PDS = NULL                 /* FOR EFFICIENCY'S SAKE ONLY */
28    2                 THEN RETURN('0'B);         /* SHOW NO TOKENS */

29    2              PP = ADDR(PDS);               /* FIRST TIME CROCK */

30    2              DO I = 1 TO 10 WHILE(PDCELL.UP ¬= NULL);
                                                   /* PROCESS AT MOST TEN ELEMENTS */

31    2    1             PP,C_ARRAY(I) = PP -> PDCELL.UP;
                                                   /* CHAIN TO NEXT ELEMENT */

32    2    1             PPV,P_ARRAY(I) = PDCELL.VALUE;
                                                   /* GET VALUE POINTER */

33    2    1             GO TO TBL(FIXED(BINARY(SC,15,0),15,0));
                                                   /* A COMPUTED GO TO */

34    2    1                 TBL(0):               /* SPECIAL PROCEDURE CALL CELL */
                                SUBSTR(CSTRING,CPOS,6) = '<PROC>';
                                                   /* CANNONIC FORM */
35    2    1                     CPOS = CPOS + 7;
                                                   /* LENGTH OF FORM PLUS BLANK */
36    2    1                     GO TO NEXT;       /* FINISHED WITH THIS ELEMENT */

37    2    1                 TBL(4):               /* OPERATOR */
                                SUBSTR(CSTRING,CPOS,OPC_LEN(PVALUE)) =
                                    OPC_CHAR(PVALUE);
                                                   /* CORRECT CANNONIC FORM */
38    2    1                     CPOS = CPOS + (OPC_LEN(PVALUE) +1);
39    2    1                     GO TO NEXT;       /* FINISHED */

40    2    1                 TBL(1):               /* VALUE */
                                SUBSTR(CSTRING,CPOS,5) = '<VAL>';
41    2    1                     GO TO INCREMENT;

42    2    1                 TBL(2):               /* IDENTIFIER */
                                SUBSTR(CSTRING,CPOS,5) = '<IDN>';

43    2    1                 INCREMENT:
                                CPOS = CPOS + 6;
```

/* SAMPLE SICK INTERPRETER BY PGG */

STMT LEVEL NEST

```
44   2   1              NEXT:                  /* CHECK NEXT ELEMENT OF PDS */
                  END;                         /* END OF CHAINING LOOP */

                                               /* FOLLOWING STATEMENT COULD BE USED

                  PUT FILE(SYSPRINT) EDIT (HEX(LOC), CSTRING) (SKIP,A(6),X(2),A(64));
45   2                                         /* FOR DEBUGGING PURPOSES */
                      RETURN('1'B);            /* SHOW ELEMENTS EXIST */
46   2            END CANNONICALIZE_;

47   1        POP_PDS_: PROCEDURE(NTP);

                                               /* THIS PROCEDURE POPS THE TOPMOST NTP
                                                  ELEMENTS FROM THE PDS, FREEING
                                                  ANY VALUE CELLS NECESSARY. */
48   2            DCL  NTP FIXED BIN,          /* NUMBER OF ELEMENTS TO POP */
                       N FIXED BIN;            /* RANDOM LOOP INDEX */

49   2            DO N = 1 TO NTP;

                                               /* FOLLOWING STATEMENT COULD BE USED
                  IF PDS = NULL THEN SIGNAL ERROR;
                                               /* FOR DEBUGGING PURPOSES */
50   2   1            PP = PDS;                /* GET READY FOR FREE */
51   2   1            PDS = PDCELL.UP;         /* UNCHAIN ELEMENT */
52   2   1            PPV = PDCELL.VALUE;      /* GET READY FOR FREE */
53   2   1            IF PDCELL.TYPE = LITERAL
54   2   1               THEN FREE PVALUE IN(AREAM);
                                               /* FREE VALUE CELL FOR <VAL> */
55   2   1            FREE PDCELL IN(AREAM);   /* FREE PDS ELEMENT */
56   2   1            END;                     /* END OF FREEING LOOP */
57   2            END POP_PDS_;

58   1        PUSH_PDS_: PROCEDURE(ATYPE,VPOINTER);

                                               /* THIS PROCEDURE PUSHES (ADDS)
                                                  ELEMENTS TO THE PDS. THE CALLER
                                                  MUST PROVIDE A VALUE POINTER */
59   2            DCL  ATYPE BIT(32) ALIGNED,  /* TYPE OF PDS ELEMENT */
                       VPOINTER POINTER;       /* VALUE POINTER */
60   2            ALLOCATE PDCELL IN(AREAM);   /* GET A NEW CELL */
```

/* SAMPLE SICK INTERPRETER BY PGG */                                    PAGE    10

```
STMT LEVEL NEST
   61    2              PDCELL.UP = PDS;              /* GET POINTER TO PREVIOUS ELEMENTS */
   62    2              PDS = PP;                     /* COMPLETE CHAINING */

   63    2              PDCELL.TYPE = ATYPE;          /* SET TYPE */
   64    2              PDCELL.VALUE = VPOINTER;      /* SET VALUE POINTER */
   65    2         END PUSH_PDS_;

   66    1         PUSH_TOKEN_: PROCEDURE (STOP) RETURNS(BIT(1));

                                                     /* THIS PROCEDURE ADDS TOKENS TO
                                                        THE PDS. IF LOC = STOP A VALUE
                                                        OF '0'B IS RETURNED, OTHERWISE
                                                        THE TOKEN POINTED TO BY LOC IS
                                                        ADDED AND LOC IS ADVANCED. */

   67    2              DCL  STOP POINTER;            /* POINT TO STOP AT IN CHAIN */

   68    2         CHECK:
                        IF LOC = STOP
   69    2                 THEN RETURN('0'B);         /* IF THIS IS END, SAY SO */

   70    2              PRANDO,PTV = LOC -> TOKEN.VALUE;
                                                     /* SAVE POINTER TO TOKEN VALUE CELL
                                                        FOR OPERATORS AND IDENTIFIERS */

   71    2              IF (LOC -> TOKEN.TYPE ¬= OPERATOR | TVALUE ¬= 18)
   72    2                 THEN GO TO OKTOC;          /* NOT A 'PROCEDURE' TOKEN */

   73    2              CALL STMTSKP;                 /* SKIP INTERNAL PROCEDURE */
   74    2              GO TO CHECK;                  /* CHECK AGAIN */

   75    2         OKTOC:                             /* NOT A PROCEDURE, KEEP GOING */

                        IF LOC -> TOKEN.TYPE = LITERAL
   76    2                 THEN ALLOCATE TVALUE IN(AREAM);
                                                     /* IF LITERAL, ALLOCATE VALUE CELL TO
                                                        AVOID CONFUSION ON FREE */

   77    2              TVALUE = PRANDO -> TVALUE;    /* THIS IS A NULL STATEMENT, UNLESS
                                                        TVALUE WAS ALLOCATED */

   78    2              CALL PUSH_PDS_(LOC -> TOKEN.TYPE, PTV);
                                                     /* PUSH TOKEN ONTO PDS */

   79    2              LOC = LOC -> TOKEN.NEXT;      /* CHAIN TO NEXT TOKEN */

   80    2              RETURN('1'B);                 /* SHOW MORE TOKENS TO GO */
   81    2         END PUSH_TOKEN_;
```

```
                    /* SAMPLE SICK INTERPRETER BY PGG */

STMT LEVEL NEST

 82    1            REDUCE_: PROCEDURE(CANNONIC) RETURNS(BIT(1));

                                        /* THIS PROCEDURE TAKES A CANNONIC
                                           STRING AND REDUCTION TABLE INFOR-
                                           MATION AND PROCESSES REDUCTIONS. */

 83    2            DCL  CANNONIC CHAR(*),        /* CANNONIC INPUT STRING */

                         N FIXED BIN,
                         PINT POINTER,
                         PUNT POINTER,
                         DCL_SWITCH BIT(1),

                         L(16) LABEL,             /* LABEL ARRAY FOR REDUCTIONS */
                         BL(0:4) LABEL,

                         EVALUATE_ ENTRY RETURNS(FIXED BIN(31));

                                        /* FOLLOWING LOOP CHECKS FOR A MATCH
                                           BETWEEN THE CANNONIC STRING AND A
                                           REDUCTION IN THE TABLE. */
 84    2            DO N = 1 TO 16;              /* PROCESS ALL REDUCTIONS */
 85    2   1            IF SUBSTR(CANNONIC,1,RL(N)) = SUBSTR(RC(N),1,RL(N))
                           THEN
 86    2   1                GO TO L(N);          /* REDUCTION HAS BEEN FOUND */
 87    2   1        END;                         /* END OF REDUCTIONS CHECK LOOP */

 88    2            RETURN('0'B);                 /* SHOW NO MATCH */

 89    2            L(1):                 /* '; DO' */
                    L(10):                /* '<IDN> DECLARE' */
 90    2                CALL POP_PDS_(1);        /* POP TOP ELEMENT */
                        RETURN('0'B);

 91    2            L(4):                 /* ': <IDN>' */
                    L(11):                /* '; DECLARE' */
 92    2                CALL POP_PDS_ (2);       /* POP 2 ELEMENTS */
                        RETURN('0'B);

 93    2            L(2):                 /* '; END DO' */
                    L(16):                /* '; <VAL> CALL' */
 94    2                CALL POP_PDS_(3);        /* POP 3 ELEMENTS */
                        RETURN('0'B);
```

```
/* SAMPLE SICK INTERPRETER BY PGG */                                    PAGE    12

STMT LEVEL NEST
   95    2          L(3):                    /* '; <VAL> <OP2> <IDN>' */
                        PINT = SVS_SEARCH_(PTR4 -> PVALUE);
                                             /* GET SVS VALUE POINTER */
   96    2                  PINT -> SVALUE = PTR2 -> PVALUE;
                                             /* MAKE ASSIGNMENT */
   97    2                  CALL POP_PDS_(4);      /* CLEAR STACK */
   98    2                  RETURN('0'B);

   99    2          L(5):                    /* '<IDN> GOTO' */
                        PT,LOC = SVS_SEARCH_(PTR1 -> PVALUE);
                                             /* GET ADDRESS OF BRANCH TOKEN */
  100    2                  CALL POP_PDS_(2);      /* CLEAR PDS */
  101    2                  RETURN('0'B);          /* CAUSE TOKEN TO BE STACKED */

  102    2          L(6):                    /* '<IDN> <OP1>' */
                    L(7):                    /* '<IDN> <OP2>' */
                        PSV = SVS_SEARCH_(PTR1 -> PVALUE);
                                             /* GET POINTER TO VALUE CELL */

  103    2                  IF PS -> SYMVAL.TYPE = IDENTIFIER
  104    2                     THEN RETURN('0'B);  /* THIS IS NECESSARY FOR PROCEDURES.
                                             NOTE THAT SVS_SEARCH_ LEAVES PS
                                             POINTING TO THE SVS CELL FOR FOUND
                                             IDENTIFIER. */

  105    2                  ALLOCATE PVALUE IN(AREAM);
                                             /* ALLOCATE VALUE CELL */
  106    2                  PVALUE = SVALUE;       /* REPLACE IDENT WITH VALUE */
  107    2                  PDS -> PDCELL.VALUE = PPV;
  108    2                  PDS -> PDCELL.TYPE = LITERAL;
                                             /* SWITCH PDS CELL TO VALUE TYPE */
  109    2                  RETURN('1'B);

  110    2          L(8):                    /* '<VAL> <OP2> <VAL>' */
                                             /* EXPRESSION EVALUATION */
                        PTR3 -> PVALUE = EVALUATE_;
                                             /* EVALUATE EXPRESSION */
  111    2                  GO TO L(4);            /* CLEAN UP STACK */

  112    2                  EVALUATE_: PROCEDURE RETURNS(FIXED BIN(31));
  113    3                     DECLARE OPL(8) LABEL; /* LABEL ARRAY FOR EXPRESSIONS */

  114    3                     GO TO OPL(PTR2 -> PVALUE);
                                             /* DECODE OPERATOR */

  115    3                     OPL(1):               /* '**' */
```

246

```
                        /* SAMPLE SICK INTERPRETER BY PGG */                                    PAGE    13

STMT LEVEL NEST
                                    RETURN(PTR3 -> PVALUE ** PTR1 -> PVALUE);

116    3              OPL(2):                /* '/' */
                                    RETURN(PTR3 -> PVALUE  / PTR1 -> PVALUE);

117    3              OPL(3):                /* '*' */
                                    RETURN(PTR3 -> PVALUE  * PTR1 -> PVALUE);

118    3              OPL(4):                /* '-' */
                                    RETURN(PTR3 -> PVALUE  - PTR1 -> PVALUE);

119    3              OPL(5):                /* '+' */
                                    RETURN(PTR3 -> PVALUE  + PTR1 -> PVALUE);

120    3              OPL(6):                /* '=' */
                                    RETURN(PTR3 -> PVALUE  = PTR1 -> PVALUE);

121    3              OPL(7):                /* '>' */
                                    RETURN(PTR3 -> PVALUE  > PTR1 -> PVALUE);

122    3              OPL(8):                /* '<' */
                                    RETURN(PTR3 -> PVALUE  < PTR1 -> PVALUE);

123    3              END EVALUATE_;

124    2          L(9):                     /* '; <IDN> PUT' */
                      PPV = SVS_SEARCH_(PTR2 -> PVALUE);
125    2                                    /* GET VALUE POINTER */
                      PUT FILE(SYSPRINT) SKIP LIST(SNT.NAME(PTR2 -> PVALUE)
                                               || '=', PVALUE);
126    2                                    /* PRINT IDENTIFIER AND VALUE */
                      GO TO L(2);           /* CLEAR STACK */

127    2          L(12):                    /* 'THEN <VAL> <OP1>' */
128    2              IF PTR2 -> PVALUE = 0   /* IS VALUE TRUE */
129    2                THEN CALL STMTSKP;  /* NO SKIP THEN CLAUSE */
                      GO TO L(2);           /* CLEAR STACK */

130    2          L(13):                    /* ') <VAL> <OP1>' */
                      CTR2 -> PDCELL.TYPE = OPERATOR;
131    2                                    /* STOP VALUE CELL FROM BEING FREED */
132    2              CALL POP_PDS_(3);       /* CLEAR STACK */
                      CALL PUSH_PDS_(VALUE,PTR2);
```

247

/* SAMPLE SICK INTERPRETER BY PGG */                                          PAGE    14

STMT LEVEL NEST
                                                /* PUT VALUE CELL BACK ON PDS */
133      2              RETURN('1'B);

134      2        L(14):                 /* '<VAL> <IDN>' */

                                        /* THIS REDUCTION PROCESSES PROCEDURE
                                           PROLOGUES. PINT IS USED TO HOLD
                                           THE ADDRESS OF THE VALUE CELL FROM
                                           THE TOP PDS ELEMENT. THIS VALUE IS
                                           THEN REUSED IN THE SVS ENTRY FOR
                                           THE PROCEDURE'S FORMAL PARAMETER */

                         PINT = PTR1;             /* SAVE VALUE CELL POINTER */
135      2               CTR1 -> PDCELL.TYPE = OPERATOR;
                                                /* PREVENT FREEING VALUE CELL */

                                        /* PUNT HOLDS THE LOCATION IN THE
                                           TOKEN CHAIN FOR THE PROCEDURE
                                           LABEL IN QUESTION. */

136      2               PUNT = SVS_SEARCH_(PTR2 -> PVALUE);
                                                /* GET PROCEDURE LABEL LOCATION */

                                        /* NOW A SPECIAL PROCEDURE CELL
                                           (<PROC>) IS ALLOCATED TO HOLD
                                           OUR PLACE IN THE TOKEN CHAIN AND
                                           SVS. NOTE THAT AT THIS POINT THE
                                           PDS MAY BE CLEARED. */

137      2               ALLOCATE PRCCELL IN(AREAM) SET(PTR9);
                                                /* GET A SPECIAL CELL */
138      2               PTR9 -> PRCCELL.OLDLOC = LOC;
                                                /* SAVE LOC */
139      2               PTR9 -> PRCCELL.SYMPNT = SVS;
                                                /* SAVE SVS */
140      2               CALL POP_PDS_(2);       /* THROW AWAY OLD CELLS */
141      2               CALL PUSH_PDS_(PROCEDURE,PTR9);
                                                /* PUT ON PROCEDURE CELL */

                                        /* NOW WE CREATE AN SVS ENTRY FOR THE
                                           FORMAL PARAMETER OF THE PROCEDURE,
                                           USING THE OLD PDS VALUE CELL.
                                           RECALL PUNT POINTS TO THE PROCEDURE
                                           LABEL TOKEN. WE ADVANCE TO THE
                                           FORMAL PARAMETER TOKEN. */

142      2               PUNT = PUNT -> TOKEN.NEXT; /* SEMICOLON */
143      2               PUNT = PUNT -> TOKEN.NEXT; /* PROCEDURE */

/* SAMPLE SICK INTERPRETER BY PGG */

STMT LEVEL NEST

```
144    2                    PT = PUNT -> TOKEN.NEXT; /* '(' */
145    2                    PT =    PT -> TOKEN.NEXT; /* FORMAL PARAMETER */
146    2                    PTV = PT -> TOKEN.VALUE; /* GET VALUE POINTER (TVALUE BASE) */
147    2                    CALL SVS_ALLOCATE_(TVALUE,VALUE,PINT);
                                            /* MAKE SVS CFLL FOR FORMAL PARAMETER
                                               AS SPECIAL CASE */

                                            /* NOW THE PROCEDURE MUST BE SCANNED,
                                               MINUS ANY INTERNAL PROCEDURES WHICH
                                               ARE SKIPPED BY PUSH_TOKEN_, TO
                                               CREATE SVS ENTRIES FOR IDENTIFIERS
                                               IMPLICITLY OR EXPLICITLY DECLARED.
                                                                            */
148    2                    LOC = PUNT;              /* 'PROCEDURE' TOKEN */
149    2                    CALL STMTSKP;            /* ADVANCE LOC TO TOKEN AFTER END OF
                                                        PROCEDURE */
150    2                    PINT = LOC;              /* REMEMBER FOR END OF SVS FILLING
                                                        SCAN. */

151    2                    LOC = PUNT -> TOKEN.NEXT; /* GET READY FOR SCAN */
152    2                    DCL_SWITCH = '0'B;        /* INITIALIZE FOR SCAN */

                                            /* FOLLOWING LOOP DOES SVS SCAN */

153    2                    DO WHILE(LOC ¬= PINT);    /* SCAN TO END */
154    2     1                  PTV = LOC -> TOKEN.VALUE;
155    2     1                  GO TO BL(FIXED(BINARY(LOC -> SC,15,0),15,0));
                                            /* DECODE TYPE */

156    2     1                  BL(4):                /* OPERATOR */
                                    DCL_SWITCH = '0'B;
                                            /* IN CASE */
157    2     1                       IF TVALUE = 23 /* 'DECLARE' */
158    2     1                          THEN DCL_SWITCH = '1'B;
159    2     1                          ELSE IF TVALUE = 20
160    2     1                                  THEN /* STATEMENT LABEL IS PREVIOUS */
161    2     1                                      DO;
162    2     2                                          PTV = LAST_IDN_PTR->TOKEN.VALUE;
                                                         CALL SVS_ALLOCATE_(TVALUE,
                                                            IDENTIFIER,LAST_IDN_PTR);
163    2     2                                      END;
164    2     1                                  ELSE IF TVALUE = 18
165    2     1                                          THEN CALL STMTSKP;
                                            /* SKIP INTERNAL PROCEDURES */
166    2     1                  GO TO BL(0);         /* PROCESS NEXT TOKEN */

167    2     1                  BL(2):               /* IDENTIFIER */
```

```
/* SAMPLE SICK INTERPRETER BY PGG */
```

STMT LEVEL NEST

```
                                    IF DCL_SWITCH  /* ARE WE IN DECLARE */
                                         THEN
168     2    1                            DO;  /* YES, ALLOCATE SVS CELL */
169     2    2                               ALLOCATE SVALUE;
170     2    2                               SVALUE = 0;
171     2    2                               CALL SVS_ALLOCATE_(TVALUE,VALUE,PSV);
172     2    2                            END;
173     2    1                         ELSE LAST_ION_PTR = LOC;

174     2    1            BL(0); BL(1); BL(3); /* DON'T CARES */
                                   LOC = LOC -> TOKEN.NEXT;
                                              /* ADVANCE NEXT TOKEN */
175     2    1         END;
                                              /* AT THIS POINT THE SVS IS BUILT AND
                                                 PROCESSING CONTINUES AS IF A
                                                 TRANSFER HAD TAKEN PLACE */

176     2              DO N = 1 TO 5;         /* SKIP PROCEDURE, '(', FORMAL PARM,
                                                 ')', AND ';' TOKENS */
177     2    1            PUNT = PUNT -> TOKEN.NEXT;
178     2    1         END;
179     2              LOC = PUNT;            /* LOC IS SET */
180     2              RETURN('0'B);          /* SHOW NEED TO ADD TOKENS */

181     2              L(15);                 /* '<VAL> RETURN <PROC>' */
                                              /* THIS REDUCTION PROCESSES RETURN AND
                                                 EPILOG. THE SVS MUST BE DEALLOCATED
                                                 APPROPRIATELY AND LOC RESTORED. */

                       PUNT = PTR3 -> PRCCELL.SYMPNT;
                                              /* GET OLD SVS VALUE */
182     2              DO WHILE(SVS ¬= NULL & SVS ¬= PUNT);
                                              /* WIND UP THE STACK */
183     2    1            PS = SVS;           /* CURRENT ENTRY */
184     2    1            PSV = SYMVAL.VALUE; /* IN CASE */
185     2    1            IF SYMVAL.TYPE = VALUE
186     2    1                 THEN FREE SVALUE IN(AREAM);
                                              /* FREE VALUE CELL IF IT EXISTS */
187     2    1            SVS = SYMVAL.NEXT;  /* CHAIN UP TO NEXT */
188     2    1            FREE SYMVAL IN(AREAM);
                                              /* FREE SVS CELL */
189     2    1         END;                   /* END OF SVS FREEING LOOP */

190     2              LOC = PTR3 -> PRCCELL.OLDLOC;
                                              /* RESTORE LOC */

191     2              CTR1 -> PDCELL.TYPE = OPERATOR;
```

/* SAMPLE SICK INTERPRETER BY PGG */

STMT LEVEL NEST

```
                                            /* PREVENT FREEING OF VALUE CELL */
192    2                CALL POP_PDS_(3);        /* CLEAR PDS */
193    2                CALL PUSH_PDS_(VALUE,PTR1);
                                            /* ADD BACK VALUE CELL */
194    2                RETURN('1'B);            /* KEEP GOING */
195    2            END REDUCE_;
```

```
          /* SAMPLE SICK INTERPRETER BY PGG */                              PAGE    13

STMT LEVEL NEST

196    1          SVS_ALLOCATE_: PROCEDURE(SYMBOL#,ATYPE,VPOINTER);

                                               /* THIS PROCEDURE ALLOCATES AND CHAINS
                                                  A CELL ONTO THE SVS. NOTE THAT THE
                                                  CALLER MUST ALLOCATE A VALUE CELL
                                                  FOR VARIABLES AND PASS A POINTER */

197    2          DCL  SYMBOL# FIXED BIN(31),    /* SYMBOL # FOR NEW ELEMENT */
                       ATYPE BIT(32) ALIGNED,    /* TYPE FOR NEW ELEMENT */
                       VPOINTER POINTER;         /* POINTER FOR VALUE FIELD */

198    2          ALLOCATE SYMVAL IN(AREAM);     /* ALLOCATE A SVS CELL */

199    2          SYMVAL.NEXT = SVS;             /* ADDRESS OF PREVIOUS ELEMENT */
200    2          SVS = PS;                      /* CHAIN IN NEW CELL */

201    2          SYMVAL.TYPE = ATYPE;           /* SET TYPE FOR NEW ELEMENT */
202    2          SYMVAL.SYMBOL = SYMBOL#;        /* SET SYMBOL NUMBER */
203    2          SYMVAL.VALUE = VPOINTER;       /* SET VALUE POINTER OF NEW CELL */
204    2          END SVS_ALLOCATE_;

205    1          SVS_SEARCH_: PROCEDURE(SYMBOL#) RETURNS(POINTER);

                                               /* THIS PROCEDURE SEARCHES THE SVS TO
                                                  FIND THE VALUE FOR A GIVEN SYMBOL.
                                                  THE VALUE RETURNED IS THE VALUE
                                                  POINTER FROM THE APPROPRIATE CELL
                                                  AS DETERMINED FROM A BOTTOM UP
                                                  SEARCH. */

                                               /* NOTE THAT THIS SUBROUTINE LEAVES PS
                                                  POINTING TO THE SVS CELL FOUND
                                                  BY A SEARCH. THIS IS NECESSARY FOR
                                                  THE <IDN> <OPN> REDUCTION TO SEE
                                                  IF <IDN> IS BOUND TO A PROCEDURE */

206    2          DCL  SYMBOL# FIXED BIN(31);    /* SYMBOL NUMBER TO SEARCH FOR */

207    2          PS = ADDR(SVS);                /* FIRST TIME CROCK */

208    2          DO WHILE(SYMVAL.NEXT ¬= NULL); /* CHECK ALL TOKENS IF NECESSARY */
209    2  1           PS = SYMVAL.NEXT;          /* CHAIN TO NEXT ELEMENT */
210    2  1           IF SYMVAL.SYMBOL = SYMBOL#
211    2  1               THEN RETURN(SYMVAL.VALUE);
                                               /* IF FOUND, RETURN VALUE POINTER */

212    2  1       END;
```

252

```
        /* SAMPLE SICK INTERPRETER BY PGG */                                    PAGE    19

STMT LEVEL NEST
                                        /* FOLLOWING STATEMENT FOR DEBUGGING
                    SIGNAL ERROR;       /* I CAN'T FIND IT */
213    2            END SVS_SEARCH_;

214    1            END SICK;               /* END OF PROGRAM */
```

GRADER ENTERED FOR STUDENT

LEXPADC CALLED
THE FOLLOWING PROGRAM WAS READ AS INPUT:

```
•••••••••••••••••••••••••••••••••••••••••••••••••••••••••••••••••••••••••••••
•                  DECLARE D E F;                                           •
•                  D = 3;                                                   •
•                  E = C + 5;                                               •
•          A:      F = 9;                                                   •
•                  PUT D;                                                   •
•                  PUT E;                                                   •
•                  PUT F;                                                   •
•                  F = F + D;                                               •
•                  PUT F;                                                   •
•••••••••••••••••••••••••••••••••••••••••••••••••••••••••••••••••••••••••••••
```

DEBUG CALLED, TOKEN CHAIN DUMP FOLLOWS

```
                                      ADDRESS
                                      -------
                                      NEXT
START=>0FF538        LOC--->0FF538    TYPE    (LEFTMOST 3 BITS)
                                      VALUE
                                      V
                                      (VALUE)
```

| DECLAR | C | E | F | ; | D | = | 3 | ; | E | = | D | + | 5 | ; |
|--------|-----|-----|-----|-------|------|------|------|------|------|------|------|------|------|------|
| 0FF538 | 0FF550 | 0FF580 | 0FF5B0 | 0FF5E0 | 0FF5F8 | 0FF610 | 0FF628 | 0FF640 | 0FF658 | 0FF670 | 0FF688 | 0FF6A0 | 0FF6B8 | 0FF6D0 |
| ------ | ------ | ------ | ------ | ------ | ------ | ------ | ------ | ------ | ------ | ------ | ------ | ------ | ------ | ------ |
| 0FF550 | 0FF580 | 0FF5B0 | 0FF5E0 | 0FF5F8 | 0FF610 | 0FF628 | 0FF640 | 0FF658 | 0FF670 | 0FF688 | 0FF6A0 | 0FF6B8 | 0FF6D0 | 0FF6E8 |
| '100'B | '010'B | '010'B | '010'B | '100'B | '010'B | '100'B | '001'B | '100'B | '010'B | '100'B | '010'B | '100'B | '001'B | '100'B |
| 0FF548 | 0FF560 | 0FF590 | 0FF5C0 | 0FF5F0 | 0FF608 | 0FF620 | 0FF638 | 0FF650 | 0FF668 | 0FF680 | 0FF698 | 0FF6B0 | 0FF6C8 | 0FF6E0 |
| V | V | V | V | V | V | V | V | V | V | V | V | V | V | V |
| 23 | 1 | 2 | 3 | 21 | 1 | 6 | 3 | 21 | 2 | 6 | 1 | 5 | 5 | 21 |

| A | : | D | = | 9 | ; | PUT | D | ; | PUT | E | ; | PUT | F | ; |
|--------|-----|-----|-----|-------|------|------|------|------|------|------|------|------|------|------|
| 0FF6E0 | 0FF710 | 0FF728 | 0FF740 | 0FF758 | 0FF770 | 0FF788 | 0FF7A0 | 0FF7B8 | 0FF7D0 | 0FF7E8 | 0FF800 | 0FF818 | 0FF830 | 0FF848 |
| ------ | ------ | ------ | ------ | ------ | ------ | ------ | ------ | ------ | ------ | ------ | ------ | ------ | ------ | ------ |
| 0FF710 | 0FF728 | 0FF740 | 0FF758 | 0FF770 | 0FF788 | 0FF7A0 | 0FF7B8 | 0FF7D0 | 0FF7E8 | 0FF800 | 0FF818 | 0FF830 | 0FF848 | 0FF860 |
| '010'B | '100'B | '010'B | '100'B | '001'B | '1C0'B | '100'B | '010'B | '100'B | '100'B | '010'B | '100'B | '100'B | '010'B | '100'B |
| 0FF6F8 | 0FF720 | 0FF738 | 0FF750 | 0FF768 | 0FF780 | 0FF798 | 0FF7B0 | 0FF7C8 | 0FF7E0 | 0FF7F8 | 0FF810 | 0FF828 | 0FF840 | 0FF858 |
| V | V | V | V | V | V | V | V | V | V | V | V | V | V | V |
| 4 | 20 | 3 | 6 | 9 | 21 | 22 | 1 | 21 | 22 | 2 | 21 | 22 | 3 | 21 |

| F | = | F | + | D | ; | PUT | F | ; |
|--------|-----|-----|-----|-------|------|------|------|------|
| 0FF860 | 0FF878 | 0FF890 | 0FF8A8 | 0FF8C0 | 0FF8D8 | 0FF8F0 | 0FF908 | 0FF920 |
| ------ | ------ | ------ | ------ | ------ | ------ | ------ | ------ | ------ |
| 0FF878 | 0FF890 | 0FF8A8 | 0FF8C0 | 0FF8F0 | 0FF8F0 | 0FF908 | 0FF920 | $NULL$ |
| '010'B | '100'B | '010'B | '100'B | '010'B | '1C0'B | '100'B | '010'B | '100'B |
| 0FF870 | 0FF888 | 0FF8A0 | 0FF8B8 | 0FF8D0 | 0FF8E8 | 0FF900 | 0FF918 | 0FF930 |
| V | V | V | V | V | V | V | V | V |
| 3 | 6 | 3 | 3 | 1 | 21 | 22 | 3 | 21 |

SYSDUMP CALLED

```
SVS--->OFF568          LOC--->OFF538
```

```
                                    ADDRESS
                                    -------
                                    NEXT
                                    TYPE     (LEFTMOST 3 BITS)
                                    SYMBOL
                                    VALUE
                                      V
                                    (VALUE)
```

```
D         E         F         A
OFF568    OFF598    OFF5C8    OFF700
------    ------    ------    ------
OFF598    OFF5C8    OFF700    $NULL$
'001'B    '001'B    '001'B    '010'B
  1         2         3         4
OFF578    OFF5A8    OFF5D8    OFF6E8
  V         V         V         V
  0         0         0
```

```
SNT - SYMBOL NAME TABLE:
   1     D
   2     E
   3     F
   4     A
```

```
LEXPROC RETURNING
D     =                          3
E     =                          8
F     =                          9
F     =                         27
```

```
LEXPROC CALLED
THE FOLLOWING PROGRAM WAS READ AS INPUT:
```

```
*************************************************************************
*            DECLARE NUMBER START NUM TEMP TEST PRIME RES COUNT T S V;  *
*            COUNT=0;                                                    *
*            NUMBER=START-1;                                            *
*   NEXT:    COUNT=COUNT+1;                                             *
*            IF COUNT=NUM THEN GOTO DONE;                               *
*            NUMBER=NUMBER+1;                                           *
*            TEST=NUMBER/2;                                             *
*            TEST=TEST*2;                                               *
*            TEMP=NUMBER-1;                                             *
*            IF TEST=TEMP THEN DO;                                      *
*                PUT NUMBER;                                            *
*                T=1;                                                   *
*   LOOP:        T=T+1;                                                 *
*                S=T**2;                                                *
*                IF S>NUMBER THEN GOTO YES;                             *
*                S=NUMBER/T;                                            *
*                S=S*T;                                                 *
*                IF S=NUMBER THEN GOTO NO;                              *
*                GOTO LOOP;                                             *
*   YES:     RES=1;                                                     *
*                GOTO D;                                                *
*   NO:      RES = 0;                                                   *
*   D:       END;                                                       *
*            IF TEST=NUMBER THEN GOTO NEXT;                             *
*            IF RES=0 THEN GOTO NEXT;                                   *
*            PRIME = NUMBER;                                            *
*            PUT PRIME;                                                 *
*            GOTO NEXT;                                                 *
*   DONE:                                                               *
*************************************************************************
```

DEBUG CALLFC, TOKEN CHAIN DUMP FOLLOWS

```
START->0FF538        LCC--->0FF538
```

Legend (cell format):

```
                ADDRESS
                -------
                NEXT
                TYPE    (LEFTMOST 3 BITS)
                VALUE
                  V
                (VALUE)
```

```
DECLAR  NUMBER  START   NUM     TEMP    TEST    PRIME   RES     COUNT   T       S       V       ;       COUNT   =
0FF538  0FF550  0FF580  0FF5B0  0FF5E0  0FF610  0FF640  0FF670  0FF6A0  0FF6D0  0FF700  0FF730  0FF760  0FF778  0FF790
------  ------  ------  ------  ------  ------  ------  ------  ------  ------  ------  ------  ------  ------  ------
0FF550  0FF580  0FF5B0  0FF5E0  0FF610  0FF640  0FF670  0FF6A0  0FF6D0  0FF700  0FF730  0FF760  0FF778  0FF790  0FF7A8
'100'B  '010'B  '010'B  '010'B  '010'B  '010'B  '010'B  '010'B  '010'B  '010'B  '010'B  '010'B  '100'B  '010'B  '100'B
0FF548  0FF560  0FF590  0FF5C0  0FF5F0  0FF620  0FF650  0FF680  0FF6B0  0FF6E0  0FF710  0FF740  0FF770  0FF788  0FF7A0
  V       V       V       V       V       V       V       V       V       V       V       V       V       V       V
  23      1       2       3       4       5       6       7       8       9       10      11      21      8       6
```

```
0       ;       NUMBER  =       START   -       1       ;       NEXT    :       COUNT   =       COUNT   +       1
0FF7A8  0FF7C0  0FF7D8  0FF7F0  0FF808  0FF820  0FF838  0FF850  0FF868  0FF890  0FF8A8  0FF8C0  0FF8D8  0FF8F0  0FF908
------  ------  ------  ------  ------  ------  ------  ------  ------  ------  ------  ------  ------  ------  ------
0FF7C0  0FF7D8  0FF7F0  0FF808  0FF820  0FF838  0FF850  0FF868  0FF890  0FF8A8  0FF8C0  0FF8D8  0FF8F0  0FF908  0FF920
'001'B  '100'B  '010'B  '100'B  '010'B  '100'B  '001'B  '100'B  '010'B  '100'B  '010'B  '100'B  '010'B  '100'B  '001'B
0FF7B8  0FF7D0  0FF7E8  0FF800  0FF818  0FF830  0FF848  0FF860  0FF878  0FF8A0  0FF8B8  0FF8D0  0FF8E8  0FF900  0FF918
  V       V       V       V       V       V       V       V       V       V       V       V       V       V       V
  0       21      1       6       2       4       1       21      12      20      8       6       8       5       1
```

```
;       IF      COUNT   =       NUM     THEN    GOTO    DONE    ;       NUMBER  =       NUMBER  +       1       ;
0FF920  0FF938  0FF950  0FF968  0FF980  0FF998  0FF9B0  0FF9C8  0FF9F0  0FFA08  0FFA20  0FFA38  0FFA50  0FFA68  0FFA80
------  ------  ------  ------  ------  ------  ------  ------  ------  ------  ------  ------  ------  ------  ------
0FF938  0FF950  0FF968  0FF980  0FF998  0FF9B0  0FF9C8  0FF9F0  0FFA08  0FFA20  0FFA38  0FFA50  0FFA68  0FFA80  0FFA98
'100'B  '100'B  '010'B  '100'B  '010'B  '100'B  '100'B  '010'B  '100'B  '010'B  '100'B  '010'B  '100'B  '001'B  '100'B
0FF930  0FF948  0FF960  0FF978  0FF990  0FF9A8  0FF9C0  0FF9D8  0FFA00  0FFA18  0FFA30  0FFA48  0FFA60  0FFA78  0FFA90
  V       V       V       V       V       V       V       V       V       V       V       V       V       V       V
  21      9       8       6       3       13      14      13      21      1       6       1       5       1       21
```

```
TEST    =       NUMBER  /       2       ;       TEST    =       TEST    *       2       ;       TEMP    =       NUMBER
0FFA98  0FFAB0  0FFAC8  0FFAE0  0FFAF8  0FFB10  0FFB28  0FFB40  0FFB58  0FFB70  0FFB88  0FFBA0  0FFBB8  0FFBD0  0FFBE8
------  ------  ------  ------  ------  ------  ------  ------  ------  ------  ------  ------  ------  ------  ------
0FFAB0  0FFAC8  0FFAE0  0FFAF8  0FFB10  0FFB28  0FFB40  0FFB58  0FFB70  0FFB88  0FFBA0  0FFBB8  0FFBD0  0FFBE8  0FFC00
'010'B  '100'B  '010'B  '100'B  '001'B  '100'B  '010'B  '100'B  '010'B  '100'B  '001'B  '100'B  '010'B  '100'B  '010'B
0FFAA8  0FFAC0  0FFAD8  0FFAF0  0FFB08  0FFB20  0FFB38  0FFB50  0FFB68  0FFB80  0FFB98  0FFBB0  0FFBC8  0FFBE0  0FFBF8
  V       V       V       V       V       V       V       V       V       V       V       V       V       V       V
  5       6       1       2       2       21      5       6       5       3       2       21      4       6       1
```

```
-       1       ;       IF      TEST    =       TEMP    THEN    DO      ;       PUT     NUMBER  ;       T       =
0FFC00  0FFC18  0FFC30  0FFC48  0FFC60  0FFC78  0FFC90  0FFCA8  0FFCC0  0FFCD8  0FFCF0  0FFD08  0FFD20  0FFD38  0FFD50
------  ------  ------  ------  ------  ------  ------  ------  ------  ------  ------  ------  ------  ------  ------
0FFC18  0FFC30  0FFC48  0FFC60  0FFC78  0FFC90  0FFCA8  0FFCC0  0FFCD8  0FFCF0  0FFD08  0FFD20  0FFD38  0FFD50  0FFD68
'100'B  '001'B  '100'B  '100'B  '010'B  '100'B  '010'B  '100'B  '100'B  '100'B  '100'B  '010'B  '100'B  '010'B  '100'B
0FFC10  0FFC28  0FFC40  0FFC58  0FFC70  0FFC88  0FFCA0  0FFCB8  0FFCD0  0FFCE8  0FFD00  0FFD18  0FFD30  0FFD48  0FFD60
  V       V       V       V       V       V       V       V       V       V       V       V       V       V       V
  4       1       21      9       5       6       4       13      17      21      22      1       21      9       6
```

| Symbol | Addr | Addr2 | Bits | Addr3 | Value |
|---|---|---|---|---|---|
| 1 | OFFD68 | OFFD80 | '001'B | OFFD78 | 1 |
| ; | OFFD80 | OFFD98 | '100'B | OFFD90 | 21 |
| LOOP | OFFD98 | OFFDC0 | '010'B | OFFDA8 | 14 |
| ; | OFFDC0 | OFFDD8 | '100'B | OFFDD0 | 20 |
| T | OFFDD8 | OFFDF0 | '010'B | OFFDE8 | 9 |
| = | OFFDF0 | OFFE08 | '100'B | OFFE00 | 6 |
| T | OFFE08 | OFFE20 | '010'B | OFFE18 | 9 |
| + | OFFE20 | OFFE38 | '100'B | OFFE30 | 5 |
| 1 | OFFE38 | OFFE50 | '001'B | OFFE48 | 1 |
| ; | OFFE50 | OFFE68 | '100'B | OFFE60 | 21 |
| S | OFFE68 | OFFE80 | '010'B | OFFE78 | 10 |
| = | OFFE80 | OFFE98 | '100'B | OFFE90 | 6 |
| T | OFFE98 | OFFEB0 | '010'B | OFFEA8 | 9 |
| ** | OFFEB0 | OFFEC8 | '100'B | OFFEC0 | 1 |
| 2 | OFFEC8 | OFFEE0 | '001'B | OFFED8 | 2 |

| Symbol | Addr | Addr2 | Bits | Addr3 | Value |
|---|---|---|---|---|---|
| ; | OFFEE0 | OFFEF8 | '100'B | OFFEF0 | 21 |
| IF | OFFEF8 | OFFF10 | '100'B | OFFF08 | 9 |
| S | OFFF10 | OFFF28 | '010'B | OFFF20 | 10 |
| > | OFFF28 | OFFF40 | '100'B | OFFF38 | 7 |
| NUMBER | OFFF40 | OFFF58 | '010'B | OFFF50 | 1 |
| THEN | OFFF58 | OFFF70 | '100'B | OFFF68 | 13 |
| GOTO | OFFF70 | OFFF88 | '100'B | OFFF80 | 14 |
| YES | OFFF88 | OFFFB0 | '010'B | OFFF98 | 15 |
| ; | OFFFB0 | OFFFC8 | '100'B | OFFFC0 | 21 |
| S | OFFFC8 | OFFFE0 | '010'B | OFFFD8 | 10 |
| = | OFFFE0 | OFFFF8 | '100'B | OFFFF0 | 6 |
| NUMBER | OFFFF8 | 100010 | '010'B | 100008 | 1 |
| / | 100010 | 100028 | '100'B | 100020 | 2 |
| T | 100028 | 100040 | '010'B | 100038 | 9 |
| ; | 100040 | 100058 | '100'B | 100050 | 21 |

| Symbol | Addr | Addr2 | Bits | Addr3 | Value |
|---|---|---|---|---|---|
| S | 100058 | 100070 | '010'B | 100068 | 10 |
| = | 100070 | 100088 | '100'B | 100080 | 6 |
| S | 100088 | 1000A0 | '010'B | 100098 | 10 |
| * | 1000A0 | 1000B8 | '100'B | 1000B0 | 3 |
| T | 1000B8 | 1000D0 | '010'B | 1000C8 | 9 |
| ; | 1000D0 | 1000E8 | '100'B | 1000E0 | 21 |
| IF | 1000E8 | 100100 | '100'B | 1000F8 | 9 |
| S | 100100 | 100118 | '010'B | 100110 | 10 |
| = | 100118 | 100130 | '100'B | 100128 | 6 |
| NUMBER | 100130 | 100148 | '010'B | 100140 | 1 |
| THEN | 100148 | 100160 | '100'B | 100158 | 13 |
| GOTO | 100160 | 100178 | '100'B | 100170 | 14 |
| NO | 100178 | 1001A0 | '010'B | 100188 | 16 |
| ; | 1001A0 | 1001B8 | '100'B | 1001B0 | 21 |
| GOTO | 1001B8 | 1001D0 | '100'B | 1001C8 | 14 |

| Symbol | Addr | Addr2 | Bits | Addr3 | Value |
|---|---|---|---|---|---|
| LOOP | 1001D0 | 1001E8 | '010'B | 1001E0 | 14 |
| ; | 1001E8 | 100200 | '100'B | 1001F8 | 21 |
| YES | 100200 | 100218 | '010'B | 100210 | 15 |
| ; | 100218 | 100230 | '100'B | 100228 | 20 |
| RES | 100230 | 100248 | '010'B | 100240 | 7 |
| = | 100248 | 100260 | '100'B | 100258 | 6 |
| 1 | 100260 | 100278 | '001'B | 100270 | 1 |
| ; | 100278 | 100290 | '100'B | 100288 | 21 |
| GOTO | 100290 | 1002A8 | '100'B | 1002A0 | 14 |
| D | 1002A8 | 1002D0 | '010'B | 1002B8 | 17 |
| ; | 1002D0 | 1002E8 | '100'B | 1002E0 | 21 |
| NO | 1002E8 | 100300 | '010'B | 1002F8 | 16 |
| ; | 100300 | 100318 | '100'B | 100310 | 20 |
| RES | 100318 | 100330 | '010'B | 100328 | 7 |
| ; | 100330 | 100348 | '100'B | 100340 | 6 |

| Symbol | Addr | Addr2 | Bits | Addr3 | Value |
|---|---|---|---|---|---|
| 0 | 100348 | 100360 | '100'B | 100358 | 0 |
| ; | 100360 | 100378 | '100'B | 100370 | 21 |
| D | 100378 | 100390 | '010'B | 100388 | 17 |
| ; | 100390 | 1003A8 | '100'B | 1003A0 | 20 |
| END | 1003A8 | 1003C0 | '100'B | 1003B8 | 19 |
| ; | 1003C0 | 10C3D8 | '1C0'B | 1003D0 | 21 |
| IF | 1003D8 | 1003F0 | '100'B | 1003E8 | 9 |
| TEST | 1003F0 | 100408 | '010'B | 100400 | 5 |
| = | 100408 | 100420 | '100'B | 100418 | 6 |
| NUMBER | 100420 | 100438 | '010'B | 100430 | 1 |
| THEN | 100438 | 100450 | '100'B | 100448 | 13 |
| GOTO | 100450 | 100468 | '100'B | 100460 | 14 |
| NEXT | 100468 | 100480 | '010'B | 100478 | 12 |
| ; | 100480 | 100498 | '100'B | 100490 | 21 |
| IF | 100498 | 1004B0 | '100'B | 1004A8 | 9 |

| Symbol | Addr | Addr2 | Bits | Addr3 | Value |
|---|---|---|---|---|---|
| RES | 1004B0 | 1004C8 | '010'B | 1004C0 | 7 |
| = | 1004C8 | 1004E0 | '100'B | 1004D8 | 6 |
| 0 | 1004E0 | 1004F8 | '001'B | 1004F0 | 0 |
| THEN | 1004F8 | 100510 | '100'B | 100508 | 13 |
| GOTO | 100510 | 100528 | '100'B | 100520 | 14 |
| NEXT | 100528 | 100540 | '010'B | 100538 | 12 |
| ; | 100540 | 100558 | '100'B | 100550 | 21 |
| PRIME | 100558 | 100570 | '010'B | 100568 | 6 |
| = | 100570 | 100588 | '100'B | 100580 | 6 |
| NUMBER | 100588 | 1005A0 | '010'B | 100598 | 1 |
| ; | 1005A0 | 1005B8 | '100'B | 1005B0 | 21 |
| PUT | 1005B8 | 1005D0 | '100'B | 1005C8 | 22 |
| PRIME | 1005D0 | 1005E8 | '010'B | 1005E0 | 6 |
| ; | 1005E8 | 100600 | '100'B | 1005F8 | 21 |
| GOTO | 100600 | 100618 | '100'B | 100610 | 14 |

```
NEXT       :        DONE      :
100618    100630   100648    100660
------    ------   ------    ------
100630    100648   100660    $NULL$
'010'B    '100'B   '010'B    '100'B
100628    1C0640   100658    1C0670
  v         v        v          v
 12        21       13         20
```

SVSDUMP CALLED

```
                                         ADDRESS
                                         -------
                                         NEXT
                                         TYPE    (LEFTMOST 3 BITS)
SVS--->0FF568          LOC--->0FF538     SYMBOL
                                         VALUE
                                           v
                                        (VALUE)
```

| NUMBER | START | NUM | TEMP | TEST | PRIME | RES | COUNT | T | S | V | NEXT | DONE | LOOP | YES |
|--------|-------|-----|------|------|-------|-----|-------|---|---|---|------|------|------|-----|
| OFF568 | OFF598 | OFF5C8 | OFF5F8 | OFF628 | OFF658 | OFF688 | OFF6B8 | OFF6E8 | OFF718 | OFF748 | OFF880 | OFF9E0 | OFFDB0 | OFFFA0 |
| ------ | ------ | ------ | ------ | ------ | ------ | ------ | ------ | ------ | ------ | ------ | ------ | ------ | ------ | ------ |
| OFF598 | OFF5C8 | OFF5F8 | OFF628 | OFF658 | OFF688 | OFF6B8 | OFF6E8 | OFF718 | OFF748 | OFF880 | OFF9E0 | OFFDB0 | OFFFA0 | 100190 |
| '001'B | '001'B | '001'B | '001'B | '001'B | '001'B | '001'B | '001'B | '001'B | '001'B | '001'B | '010'B | '010'B | '010'B | '010'B |
| 1 | 2 | 3 | 4 | 5 | 6 | 7 | 8 | 9 | 10 | 11 | 12 | 13 | 14 | 15 |
| OFF578 | OFF5A8 | OFF5D8 | OFF608 | OFF638 | OFF668 | OFF698 | OFF6C8 | OFF6F8 | OFF728 | OFF758 | OFF868 | 100648 | OFFD98 | 100200 |
| v | v | v | v | v | v | v | v | v | v | v | | | | |
| 0 | 5 | 7 | 0 | 0 | 0 | 0 | 0 | 0 | 0 | 0 | | | | |

```
NO        D
100190    1002C0
------    ------
1002C0    $NULL$
'010'B    '010'B
  16        17
1002E8    100378
```

```
SNT - SYMBOL NAME TABLE:
 1      NUMBER
 2      START
 3      NUM
 4      TEMP
 5      TEST
 6      PRIME
 7      RES
 8      COUNT
 9      T
10      S
11      V
12      NEXT
```

```
13      DCNE
14      LOOP
15      YES
16      NO
17      D
```

LEXPROC RETURNING
```
NUMBER  =                        5
PRIME   =                        5
NUMBER  =                        7
PRIME   =                        7
NUMBER  =                        9
```

LEXPROC CALLED
THE FOLLOWING PROGRAM WAS READ AS INPUT:

```
*******************************************************************************
*                   DECLARE NUMBER START NUM TEMP TEST PRIME RES COUNT;        *
*                   COUNT=0;                                                   *
*                   NUMBER=START-1;                                            *
*          NEXT:    COUNT=COUNT+1;                                             *
*                   IF CCUNT=NUM THEN GOTO DONE;                               *
*                   NUMBER=NUMBER+1;                                           *
*                   TEST=NUMBER/2;                                             *
*                   TEST=TEST*2$                                               *
*                   TEMP=NUMBER-1;                                             *
*                   IF TEST=TEMP THEN DO;                                      *
*                        PUT NUMBER;                                           *
*                        RES=PRINE(NUMBER);                                    *
*                        END;                                                  *
*          PRINE:   PROCECURE (NUM);                                           *
*                   DECLARE TEST SQ VAL;                                       *
*                   TEST=1;                                                    *
*          LOOP:    TEST=TEST+1;                                               *
*                   SQ=TEST**2;                                                *
*                   IF SQ>NUM THEN GOTO YES;                                   *
*                   SQ=NUM/TEST;                                               *
*                   SQ=SC*TEST;                                                *
*                   IF SQ=NUM THEN GOTO NO;                                    *
*                   GOTO LOOP;                                                 *
*          YES:     VAL=1;                                                     *
*                   GOTO DONE;                                                 *
*          NO:      VAL=C;                                                     *
*          CONE:    RETURN(VAL);                                               *
*                   END;                                                       *
*                   IF TEST=NUMBER THEN GOTO NEXT;                             *
*                   IF RES=0 THEN GOTO NEXT;                                   *
*                   PRIME=NUMBER;                                              *
*                   PUT PRIME;                                                 *
*                   GOTO NEXT;                                                 *
*          CCNE:                                                               *
*******************************************************************************
```

DEBUG CALLEC, TOKEN CHAIN DUMP FOLLOWS

```
                                          ADDRESS
                                          -------
                                          NEXT
START->OFF538          LCC--->OFF538       TYPE    (LEFTMOST 3 BITS)
                                          VALUE
                                            V
                                          (VALUE)
```

| DECLAR | NUMBER | START | NUM | TEMP | TEST | PRIME | RFS | COUNT | ; | COUNT | = | 0 | ; | NUMBER |
|---|---|---|---|---|---|---|---|---|---|---|---|---|---|---|
| OFF538 | OFF550 | OFF580 | OFF5B0 | OFF5E0 | OFF610 | OFF640 | OFF670 | OFF6A0 | OFF6D0 | OFF6E8 | OFF700 | OFF718 | OFF730 | OFF748 |
| ------ | ------ | ------ | ------ | ------ | ------ | ------ | ------ | ------ | ------ | ------ | ------ | ------ | ------ | ------ |
| OFF550 | OFF580 | OFF5B0 | OFF5E0 | OFF610 | OFF640 | OFF670 | OFF6A0 | OFF6D0 | OFF6E8 | OFF700 | OFF718 | OFF730 | OFF748 | OFF760 |
| '100'B | '010'B | '010'B | '010'B | '010'B | '010'B | '010'B | '010'B | '010'B | '100'B | '010'B | '100'B | '100'B | '100'B | '010'B |
| OFF548 | OFF560 | OFF590 | OFF5C0 | OFF5F0 | OFF620 | OFF650 | OFF680 | OFF6B0 | OFF6E0 | OFF6F8 | OFF710 | OFF728 | OFF740 | OFF758 |
| v | v | v | v | v | v | v | v | v | v | v | v | v | v | v |
| 23 | 1 | 2 | 3 | 4 | 5 | 6 | 7 | 8 | 21 | 8 | 6 | 0 | 21 | 1 |

| = | START | - | 1 | ; | NEXT | : | COUNT | = | COUNT | + | 1 | ; | IF | COUNT |
|---|---|---|---|---|---|---|---|---|---|---|---|---|---|---|
| OFF760 | OFF778 | OFF790 | OFF7A8 | OFF7C0 | OFF7D8 | OFF800 | OFF818 | OFF830 | OFF848 | OFF860 | OFF878 | OFF890 | OFF8A8 | OFF8C0 |
| ------ | ------ | ------ | ------ | ------ | ------ | ------ | ------ | ------ | ------ | ------ | ------ | ------ | ------ | ------ |
| OFF778 | OFF790 | OFF7A8 | OFF7C0 | OFF7D8 | OFF800 | OFF818 | OFF830 | OFF848 | OFF860 | OFF878 | OFF890 | OFF8A8 | OFF8C0 | OFF8D8 |
| '100'B | '010'B | '100'B | '001'B | '100'B | '010'B | '100'B | '010'B | '010'B | '010'B | '100'B | '001'B | '100'B | '100'B | '010'B |
| OFF770 | OFF788 | OFF7A0 | OFF788 | OFF7D0 | OFF7E8 | OFF810 | OFF828 | OFF840 | OFF858 | OFF870 | OFF888 | OFF8A0 | OFF888 | OFF8D0 |
| v | v | v | v | v | v | v | v | v | v | v | v | v | v | v |
| 6 | 2 | 4 | 1 | 21 | 9 | 20 | 8 | 6 | 8 | 5 | 1 | 21 | 9 | 0 |

| = | NUM | THEN | GOTO | DONE | ; | NUMBER | = | NUMBER | + | 1 | ; | TEST | = | NUMBER |
|---|---|---|---|---|---|---|---|---|---|---|---|---|---|---|
| OFF8D8 | OFF8F0 | OFF908 | OFF920 | OFF938 | OFF960 | OFF978 | OFF990 | OFF9A8 | OFF9C0 | OFF9D8 | OFF9F0 | OFFA08 | OFFA20 | OFFA38 |
| ------ | ------ | ------ | ------ | ------ | ------ | ------ | ------ | ------ | ------ | ------ | ------ | ------ | ------ | ------ |
| OFF8E8 | OFF908 | OFF920 | OFF938 | OFF960 | OFF978 | OFF990 | OFF9A8 | OFF9C0 | OFF9D8 | OFF9F0 | OFFA08 | OFFA20 | OFFA38 | OFFA50 |
| '100'B | '010'B | '100'B | '100'B | '010'B | '100'B | '010'B | '100'B | '010'B | '001'B | '100'B | '010'B | '100'B | '010'B | '010'B |
| OFF8E8 | OFF900 | OFF918 | OFF930 | OFF948 | OFF970 | OFF988 | OFF9A0 | OFF9B8 | OFF9D0 | OFF9E8 | OFFA00 | OFFA18 | OFFA30 | OFFA48 |
| v | v | v | v | v | v | v | v | v | v | v | v | v | v | v |
| 6 | 3 | 13 | 14 | 10 | 21 | 1 | 6 | 1 | 5 | 1 | 21 | 5 | 6 | 1 |

| / | 2 | ; | TEST | = | TEST | * | 2 | ; | TEMP | = | NUMBER | - | 1 | ; |
|---|---|---|---|---|---|---|---|---|---|---|---|---|---|---|
| OFFA50 | OFFA68 | OFFA80 | OFFA98 | OFFAB0 | OFFAC8 | OFFAE0 | OFFAF8 | OFFB10 | OFFB28 | OFFB40 | OFFB58 | OFFB70 | OFFB88 | OFFBA0 |
| ------ | ------ | ------ | ------ | ------ | ------ | ------ | ------ | ------ | ------ | ------ | ------ | ------ | ------ | ------ |
| OFFA68 | OFFA80 | OFFA98 | OFFAB0 | OFFAC8 | OFFAE0 | OFFAF8 | OFFB10 | OFFB28 | OFFB40 | OFFB58 | OFFB70 | OFFB88 | OFFBA0 | OFFBB8 |
| '100'B | '001'B | '100'B | '010'B | '100'B | '010'B | '100'B | '001'B | '100'B | '010'B | '100'B | '010'B | '100'B | '001'B | '100'B |
| OFFA60 | OFFA78 | OFFA90 | OFFAA8 | OFFAC0 | OFFAD8 | OFFAF0 | OFFB08 | OFFB20 | OFFB38 | OFFB50 | OFFB68 | OFFB80 | OFFB98 | OFFBB0 |
| v | v | v | v | v | v | v | v | v | v | v | v | v | v | v |
| 2 | 2 | 21 | 5 | 6 | 5 | 3 | 2 | 21 | 4 | 6 | 1 | 4 | 1 | 21 |

| IF | TEST | = | TEMP | THEN | DO | ; | PUT | NUMBER | ; | RES | = | PRINE | ( | NUMBER |
|---|---|---|---|---|---|---|---|---|---|---|---|---|---|---|
| OFFBB8 | OFFBD0 | OFFBE8 | OFFC00 | OFFC18 | OFFC30 | OFFC48 | OFFC60 | OFFC78 | OFFC90 | OFFCA8 | OFFCC0 | OFFCD8 | OFFD00 | OFFD18 |
| ------ | ------ | ------ | ------ | ------ | ------ | ------ | ------ | ------ | ------ | ------ | ------ | ------ | ------ | ------ |
| OFFBC8 | OFFBE8 | OFFC00 | OFFC18 | OFFC30 | OFFC48 | OFFC60 | OFFC78 | OFFC90 | OFFCA8 | OFFCC0 | OFFCD8 | OFFD00 | OFFD18 | OFFD30 |
| '100'B | '010'B | '100'B | '010'B | '100'B | '100'B | '100'B | '100'B | '010'B | '100'B | '010'B | '100'B | '010'B | '100'B | '010'B |
| OFFBC8 | OFFBE0 | OFFBF8 | OFFC10 | OFFC28 | OFFC40 | OFFC58 | OFFC70 | OFFC88 | OFFCA0 | OFFCB8 | OFFCD0 | OFFCE8 | OFFD10 | OFFD28 |
| v | v | v | v | v | v | v | v | v | v | v | v | v | v | v |
| 9 | 5 | 6 | 4 | 13 | 17 | 21 | 22 | 1 | 21 | 7 | 6 | 11 | 10 | 1 |

| ) | ; | END | ; | PRINE | : | PROCED | ( | NUM | ) | ; | DECLAR | TEST | SQ | VAL |
|---|---|---|---|---|---|---|---|---|---|---|---|---|---|---|
| OFFD30 | OFFD48 | OFFD60 | OFFD78 | OFFD90 | OFFDA8 | OFFDC0 | OFFDD8 | OFFDF0 | OFFE08 | OFFE20 | OFFE38 | OFFE50 | OFFE68 | OFFE80 |
| ------ | ------ | ------ | ------ | ------ | ------ | ------ | ------ | ------ | ------ | ------ | ------ | ------ | ------ | ------ |
| OFFD40 | OFFD60 | OFFD78 | OFFD90 | OFFDA8 | OFFDC0 | OFFDD8 | OFFDF0 | OFFE08 | OFFE20 | OFFE38 | OFFE50 | OFFE68 | OFFE80 | OFFE98 |
| '100'B | '100'B | '100'B | '100'B | '010'B | '100'B | '100'B | '100'B | '010'B | '100'B | '100'B | '100'B | '010'B | '010'B | '010'B |
| OFFD40 | OFFD58 | OFFD70 | OFFD88 | OFFDA0 | OFFDB8 | OFFDD0 | OFFDE8 | OFFE00 | OFFE18 | OFFE30 | OFFE48 | OFFE60 | OFFE78 | OFFE90 |
| v | v | v | v | v | v | v | v | v | v | v | v | v | v | v |
| 11 | 21 | 19 | 21 | 11 | 20 | 18 | 10 | 3 | 11 | 21 | 23 | 5 | 12 | 13 |

| Name | Addr | Link | Bits | Ptr | v |
|---|---|---|---|---|---|
| ; | OFFE98 | OFFEB0 | '100'B | OFFEA8 | 21 |
| TEST | OFFEB0 | OFFEC8 | '010'B | OFFEC0 | 5 |
| = | OFFEC8 | OFFEE0 | '100'B | OFFED8 | 6 |
| 1 | OFFEE0 | OFFEF8 | '001'B | OFFEF0 | 1 |
| ; | OFFEF8 | OFFF10 | '100'B | OFFF08 | 21 |
| LOOP | OFFF10 | OFFF28 | '010'B | OFFF20 | 14 |
| : | OFFF28 | OFFF40 | '100'B | OFFF38 | 20 |
| TEST | OFFF40 | OFFF58 | '010'B | OFFF50 | 5 |
| = | OFFF58 | OFFF70 | '100'B | OFFF68 | 6 |
| TEST | OFFF70 | OFFF88 | '010'B | OFFF80 | 5 |
| + | OFFF88 | OFFFA0 | '100'B | OFFF98 | 5 |
| 1 | OFFFA0 | OFFFB8 | '001'B | OFFFB0 | 1 |
| ; | OFFFB8 | OFFFD0 | '100'B | OFFFC8 | 21 |
| SQ | OFFFD0 | OFFFE8 | '010'B | OFFFE0 | 12 |
| = | OFFFE8 | 100000 | '100'B | OFFFF8 | 6 |

| Name | Addr | Link | Bits | Ptr | v |
|---|---|---|---|---|---|
| TEST | 100000 | 100018 | '010'B | 100010 | 5 |
| ** | 100018 | 100030 | '100'B | 100028 | 1 |
| 2 | 100030 | 100048 | '001'B | 100040 | 2 |
| ; | 100048 | 100060 | '100'B | 100058 | 21 |
| IF | 100060 | 100078 | '100'B | 100070 | 9 |
| SQ | 100078 | 1C0090 | '010'B | 100088 | 12 |
| > | 100090 | 1000A8 | '100'B | 1000A0 | 7 |
| NUM | 1000A8 | 1000C0 | '010'B | 1000B8 | 3 |
| THEN | 1000C0 | 1C00D8 | '100'B | 1000D0 | 13 |
| GOTO | 1000D8 | 1000F0 | '100'B | 1000E8 | 14 |
| YES | 1000F0 | 100108 | '010'B | 100100 | 15 |
| ; | 100108 | 100120 | '100'B | 100118 | 21 |
| SQ | 100120 | 100138 | '010'B | 100130 | 12 |
| = | 100138 | 100150 | '100'B | 100148 | 6 |
| NUM | 100150 | 100168 | '010'B | 100160 | 3 |

| Name | Addr | Link | Bits | Ptr | v |
|---|---|---|---|---|---|
| / | 100168 | 100180 | '100'B | 100178 | 2 |
| TEST | 100180 | 100198 | '010'B | 100190 | 5 |
| ; | 100198 | 1001B0 | '100'B | 1001A8 | 21 |
| SQ | 1001B0 | 1001C8 | '010'B | 1001C0 | 12 |
| = | 1001C8 | 1001E0 | '100'B | 1001D0 | 6 |
| SQ | 1001E0 | 1001F8 | '010'B | 1001F0 | 12 |
| * | 1001F8 | 100210 | '100'B | 100208 | 3 |
| TEST | 100210 | 100228 | '010'B | 100220 | 5 |
| ; | 100228 | 100240 | '100'B | 100238 | 21 |
| IF | 100240 | 100258 | '100'B | 100250 | 9 |
| SQ | 100258 | 100270 | '010'B | 100268 | 12 |
| = | 100270 | 100288 | '100'B | 100280 | 6 |
| NUM | 100288 | 1002A0 | '010'B | 100298 | 3 |
| THEN | 1002A0 | 1002B8 | '100'B | 1002B0 | 13 |
| GOTO | 1002B8 | 1002D0 | '100'B | 1002C8 | 14 |

| Name | Addr | Link | Bits | Ptr | v |
|---|---|---|---|---|---|
| NO | 1002D0 | 1002E8 | '010'B | 1002E0 | 16 |
| ; | 1002E8 | 100300 | '100'B | 1002F8 | 21 |
| GOTO | 100300 | 100318 | '100'B | 100310 | 14 |
| LOOP | 100318 | 100330 | '010'B | 100328 | 14 |
| ; | 100330 | 100348 | '100'B | 100340 | 21 |
| YES | 100348 | 100360 | '010'B | 100358 | 15 |
| : | 100360 | 100378 | '100'B | 100370 | 20 |
| VAL | 100378 | 100390 | '010'B | 100388 | 13 |
| = | 100390 | 1003A8 | '100'B | 1003A0 | 6 |
| 1 | 1003A8 | 1003C0 | '001'B | 1003B8 | 1 |
| ; | 1003C0 | 1003D8 | '100'B | 1003D0 | 21 |
| GOTO | 1003D8 | 1003F0 | '100'B | 1003E8 | 14 |
| DONE | 1003F0 | 100408 | '010'B | 100400 | 10 |
| ; | 100408 | 100420 | '100'B | 100418 | 21 |
| NO | 100420 | 100438 | '010'B | 100430 | 16 |

| Name | Addr | Link | Bits | Ptr | v |
|---|---|---|---|---|---|
| : | 100438 | 100450 | '100'B | 100448 | 20 |
| VAL | 100450 | 100468 | '010'B | 100460 | 13 |
| = | 100468 | 100480 | '100'B | 100478 | 6 |
| 0 | 100480 | 100498 | '001'B | 100490 | 0 |
| ; | 100498 | 1004B0 | '100'B | 1004A8 | 21 |
| DONE | 1004B0 | 1004C8 | '010'B | 1004C0 | 10 |
| : | 1004C8 | 1004E0 | '100'B | 1004D8 | 20 |
| RETURN | 1004E0 | 1004F8 | '100'B | 1004F0 | 16 |
| ( | 1004F8 | 100510 | '100'B | 100508 | 10 |
| VAL | 100510 | 100528 | '010'B | 100520 | 13 |
| ) | 100528 | 100540 | '100'B | 100538 | 11 |
| ; | 100540 | 100558 | '100'B | 100550 | 21 |
| END | 100558 | 100570 | '100'B | 100568 | 19 |
| ; | 100570 | 100588 | '100'B | 100580 | 21 |
| IF | 100588 | 1005A0 | '100'B | 100598 | 9 |

| Name | Addr | Link | Bits | Ptr | v |
|---|---|---|---|---|---|
| TEST | 1005A0 | 1005B8 | '010'B | 1C05B0 | 5 |
| = | 1005B8 | 1005D0 | '100'B | 1005C8 | 6 |
| NUMBER | 1005D0 | 1005E8 | '010'B | 1005E0 | 1 |
| THEN | 1005E8 | 100600 | '100'B | 1005F8 | 13 |
| GOTO | 100600 | 100618 | '100'B | 100610 | 14 |
| NEXT | 100618 | 100630 | '010'B | 100628 | 9 |
| ; | 100630 | 100648 | '100'B | 100640 | 21 |
| IF | 100648 | 100660 | '100'B | 100658 | 9 |
| RES | 1C0660 | 100678 | '010'B | 100670 | 7 |
| = | 100678 | 100690 | '100'B | 100688 | 6 |
| 0 | 100690 | 1006A8 | '001'B | 1006A0 | 0 |
| THEN | 1006A8 | 1006C0 | '100'B | 1006B8 | 13 |
| GOTO | 1006C0 | 1006D8 | '100'B | 1006D0 | 14 |
| NEXT | 1006D8 | 1006F0 | '010'B | 1006E8 | 9 |
| ; | 1006F0 | 100708 | '100'B | 100700 | 21 |

261

```
PRIME     =     NUMBER  ;     PUT    PRIME  ;     GOTO   NEXT   ;     DONE   :
1007C8 100720 100738 100750 100768 100780 100798 1007B0 1007C8 1007E0 1007F8 100810
------ ------ ------ ------ ------ ------ ------ ------ ------ ------ ------ ------

100720 100738 100750 100768 100780 100798 1007B0 1007C8 1007E0 1007F8 100810 $NULL$
'010'B '100'B '010'B '100'B '100'B '010'B '100'B '100'B '010'B '100'B '010'B '100'B
100718 100730 100748 100760 100778 100790 1007A8 1007C0 1007D8 1007F0 100808 100820
  v      v      v      v      v      v      v      v      v      v      v      v
  6      6      1     21     22      6     21     14      9     21     10     20


SVSDUMP CALLED

                                          ADDRESS
                                          -------
                                          NEXT
SVS-→->0FF568          LOC--->0FF538      TYPE    (LEFTMOST 3 BITS)
                                          SYMBOL
                                          VALUE
                                            v
                                          (VALUE)

NUMBER  START   NUM    TEMP   TEST   PRIME  RES    COUNT  NEXT   DONE   PRINE
0FF568 0FF598 0FF5C8 0FF5F8 0FF628 0FF658 0FF688 0FF6B8 0FF7F0 0FF950 0FFCF0
------ ------ ------ ------ ------ ------ ------ ------ ------ ------ ------

0FF598 0FF5C8 0FF5F8 0FF628 0FF658 0FF688 0FF6B8 0FF7F0 0FF950 0FFCF0 $NULL$
'001'B '001'B '001'B '001'B '001'B '001'B '001'B '001'B '010'B '010'B '010'B
  1      2      3      4      5      6      7      8      9     10     11
0FF578 0FF5A8 0FF5D8 0FF608 0FF638 0FF668 0FF698 0FF6C8 0FF7D8 1007F8 0FFD90
  v      v      v      v      v      v      v      v
  0      5      7      0      0      0      0      0
```

SNT - SYMBOL NAME TABLE:
```
 1    NUMBER
 2    START
 3    NUM
 4    TEMP
 5    TEST
 6    PRIME
 7    RES
 8    COUNT
 9    NEXT
10    DONE
11    PRINE
12    SQ
13    VAL
14    LCOP
15    YES
16    NO
```

LEXPROC RETURNING
```
NUMBER  =                      5
PRIME   =                      5
NUMBER  =                      7
PRIME   =                      7
NUMBER  =                      9
```

STUDENT PROGRAM USED    2.86 SECONDS

```
 _____
|           |
| CHAPTER  4 |
|_____|
```

## 4.1  User's Guide

### 4.1.1  Introduction

The System/360 Simulator (SIM360) is a collection of PL/1 and BAL (assembler language for IBM 360-370 series) modules which may be executed under any IBM 360 or 370 operating system which allows a user partition of 200 K-bytes or more. The effect of these modules in execution is to provide the user with a virtual machine; a bare 360 whose entire resources are available. (1)

As such it is powerful pedagogical aid, but even more important, a debugging tool, since it is possible for the simulator to give "snapshots" depicting the status of the virtual machine without upsetting the program undergoing simulation. Thus, it can help to isolate program faults, locate timing problems, and generally provide the programmer with a wealth of information he or she could not obtain from a real machine.

The simulator was designed primarily as a vehicle to provide students the access to a bare machine necessary to test programs related to interrupt and I/O processing. See sections 4.1.6 and 4.1.7 for a list of implemented and unimplemented instructions. Given the nitty-gritty nature of programs commonly run on the simulator, the usual source language is BAL. The following publications, therefore should be useful:

        System/360 Principles of Operation        (GA22-6821)
            or
        System/370 Principles of Operation        (GA22-7000)
        OS Assembler Language                      (GC28-6514)

----------------------------------------------------------------

(1) This simulator is the result of the Bachelor's Thesis, "SIM360: A S/360 Simulator", by Wm. Arthur McCray, MIT, MAY 1972. Many students have since been involved in refining and extending the simulator, most notably Geoffry J. Bunza. This work was sponsored (in part) by the Advanced Research Projects Agency of the Department of Defense under ARPA Order No. 2095, and was monitored by ONR under contract No. N00014-70-A-0362-0006. The work was reported in Project MAC Technical Memorandum 30, May 1972.

## 4.1.2  Program Requirements

To run a program on the virtual machine provided by the simulator, certain procedures must be followed to enter your program and start its execution. These procedures are analagous to the IPL function on a real machine. The simulator contains a rudimentary loader which takes standard format OS/360 object decks and loads them absolutely into the virtual machine's core, ignoring RLD cards.

This loader does not have the ability to resolve external references, or link multiple CSECT's, so programs must consist of just one control section. The simulator uses the name of each CSECT to label simulator output.

Once this loading process is completed, the simulator loads the double word at location zero and uses it as the initial PSW. Execution will begin at the location specified by the address portion of this PSW. As a consequence of this loading/start up procedure:

1. Your program must contain only one CSECT.

2. The first 128 (decimal) bytes of your program must be properly initialized as the System/360 low core area. This includes the initial PSW (bytes 0-7) and all new PSW's which define interrupt handling routines.

At this point an example should be instructive. Suppose you have a program which has been executing as a problem program under some operating system. Such a program could look like the following:

```
EXAMPLE   CSECT                     THIS PROGRAM CLEARS A
*                                   256 WORD BLOCK
*
          USING EXAMPLE,15          ESTABLISH ADDRESSABILITY
*
          STM   14,12,12(13)        SAVE OS REGISTERS
          LA    4,BLOCK             A(BLOCK TO ZERO)
          SR    5,5                 CLEAR REGISTER
          LA    6,256               GET LENGTH
*
LOOP      ST    5,0(,4)             CLEAR A WORD
          LA    4,4(,4)             ADVANCE POINTER
          BCT   6,LOOP              GET ALL WPORDS
*
WINDUP    LM    14,12,12(13)        GET REGISTERS
          BR    14                  RETURN
*
BLOCK     DS    256F                WORK AREA
          END
```

All that is necessary to run this program under the simulator is low core initialization, since the program is already one CSECT. Noticing that this program makes no use of the 360's interrupt handling facility, all the new PSW's may be set to wait state PSW's. Thus, if one is loaded through some error, the simulator will stop (this is a special case, a wait state PSW with no interrupts enabled). An initial PSW pointing to the start of the program is necessary and a QUIT macro must be issued to terminate simulation. The same program, prepared to run on the simulator, would look like:

```
EXAMPLE   CSECT                    SAME PROGRAM TO RUN ON
*                                  SIM360
*
          USING EXAMPLE,0          ASSEMBLE REFERENCES
*                                  ABSOLUTE
*
*               LOW CORE DEFINITIONS
IPLPSW    DC    A(0,START)         INITIAL PSW
UNUSED    DC    14F'0'             RESERVED OLD PSW'S ETC
CSWPLUS   DC    6F'0'              FILLER
NOINTRPT  DC    5XL8'00020000000000000' WAIT STATE PSW'S
*
START     LA    4,BLOCK            A(BLOCK TO ZERO)
          SR    5,5                CLEAR REGISTER
          LA    6,256              GET LENGTH
*
LOOP      ST    5,0(,4)            CLEAR A WORD
          LA    4,4(,4)            ADVANCE POINTER
          BCT   6,LOOP             GET ALL WPORDS
*
WINDUP    QUIT                     TELL SIMULATOR TO
*                                  QUIT
*
BLOCK     DS    256F               WORK AREA
          END
```

For a more complicated example showing low core initialization and simulator output see section 4.1.9.

Details to remember:

1. Low core locations 0-127 (decimal) must be properly initialized by the programmer.

2. Simulation must be terminated by means of the QUIT macro, which expands to form a special instruction with op-code X'FF'.

3. If you do not wish to use the interval timer (location 80), that is you do not wish to provide an external interrupt handler, you must mask off the timer by always keeping bit 7 in the PSW set to 0. Remember, the

timer **always** runs.

An external interrupt for the timer is generated when the timer area changes from a positive number to a negative number (zero is a positive number). Core locations 80-82 (decimal) are updated every 1/300-th of a second. Thus, if the timer area is initialized to zero, an external interrupt will occur at 3,333 microseconds.

4. You must provide the assembler with a base register and properly initialize the register before use. It should be noted that you may tell the assembler to use register 0 as a base register. This will cause the assembler to produce absolute code, obviously only good for the first 4 K-bytes of your program.

### 4.1.3   Input/Output Enviroment

The current version of the simulator (Version 1.3) implements only a byte multiplexor channel with two attached 2821 control units. Each 2821 has, in turn, one 2540 card reader-punch and two 1403 printers.  The assigned device addresses are:

| | | |
|---|---|---|
| First 2821: | X'00C' | Reader |
| | X'00D' | Punch |
| | X'00E' | First Printer |
| | X'00F' | Second Printer |
| Second 2821: | X'012' | Reader |
| | X'013' | Punch |
| | X'010' | First Printer |
| | X'011' | Second Printer |

The  functional characteristics of these devices are detailed in:

| | |
|---|---|
| System/360 Principles of Operation | (GA22-6821) |
| IBM 2821 Control Unit Component Description | (GA24-3312) |
| IBM S/360 Reference Data Card | (GX20-1703) |

Programming considerations involved in supporting these devices on the simulator are:

1. No special features are implemented.

2. Stacker select commands to the reader-punch are not simulated. Stacker select information in 2540 commands must be valid, but is ignored by the simulator.

3. For a carriage skip, commands to the printer are all interpreted as a skip to channel 1 (head of form). Carriage skip information in 1403 commands must be valid, but regardless of the channel specified, the

paper is positioned at the top of the form.

## 4.1.4   Program Tracing

When running on a real machine, the only information available to a programmer concerning the status of his or her program is either the results of I/O operations or hardware provided snapshots. Such snapshots usually require stopping the machine and displaying parameters on the front pannel. This is often not enough information to effectively debug I/O programs since stopping the machine interferes with the timing.

The simulator provides extensive tracing facilities which may be used to display detailed information concerning the status of the virtual machine and its channels, devices, etc., without upsetting the virtual machine's timing.

Proper use of these facilities will significantly reduce the number of runs required to solve a given programming problem. The trace facilities are dynamically controlled at execution time (turned on and turned off) by the use of the TRACE and TRACEOFF macro instructions, which generate op-codes X'02' and X'03', respectively. With the exception of the TRACE macro with the DUMP option specified, when these macro expansions are executed by the simulator they will enable or disable subsequent program conditions.

When the TRACE macro is coded the user may specify special supplemental information of particular interest. Whenever the specified trace condition is encountered, a message will be printed containing the default information plus this optional information. A TRACE macro with the DUMP (immediate) specification causes information to be printed immediately and does not interfere with other trace conditions. The TRACE macro takes operands of the following form:

   <opt. label> TRACE <program condition><,opt. trace info.>

The following program conditions may be "TRACE'ed": (keywords for TRACE macro shown in parentheses):

1.  Branch Tracing (BRANCH):
    Whenever a successful branch is taken, as a result of any branch instruction, a standard trace message and any optionally specified trace information will be printed. If a conditional branch instruction is executed, but no branch is taken, no trace information will be printed. Example syntax:

        LABELA  TRACE   BRANCH

2. Address Tracing (ADDRS):
Whenever the specified location is referenced as an
instruction operand, standard and any optionally
specified trace information will be printed. The
location to be used in the address trace as a trigger
follows the keyword and may either be a label name or a
decimal number. For example:

```
LABELB   TRACE   ADDRS,ENTRY
LABELC   TRACE   ADDRS,128
```

3. Execution Tracing (EXEC):
Whenever the specified location is referenced for
execution, standard and any optionally specified trace
information will be printed. The location to trigger
this trace follows the keyword "EXEC" and may be either
a label name or decimal number.  Example syntax:

```
LABELD   TRACE   EXEC,FOO
LABELE   TRACE   EXEC,400
```

4. Instruction Tracing (INSTR):
Whenever the specified op-code is executed, standard
and any optionally specified trace information will be
printed. The op-code, in hexadecimal, to be traced
follows the keyword "INSTR" as in the example (to trace
LPSW's):

```
LABELE   TRACE   INSTR,82
```

5. Interrupt Tracing (INTRPT):
Whenever the specified type of interrupt occurs, a
short form of the standard trace information as well as
any optionally specified trace information will be
printed. the interrupt type follows the keyword
"INTRPT", and must be from the following list:

```
PGM      I/O      EXT      SVC      MCK
```

For example:

```
LABELF   TRACE   INTRPT,PGM
LABELG   TRACE   INTRPT,SVC
```

6. Channel Tracing (CHANL):
Whenever the specified channel performs a significant
operation an explanatory message is printed. Note: No
optional trace information may be specified using TRACE
with the CHANL option. The channel number must be an
integer from 0 to 6, and must follow the keyword
"CHANL", as in the example:

         LABELH  TRACE  CHANL,0

7. Snapshot Dump Traces (DUMP):
   Whenever  the  TRACE  macro  with  tha  DUMP operand is
   executed,  a  short  form  of  the  standard  trace
   information  as  well as any optionally specified trace
   information will be  printed.   Please  note  that  the
   TRACE  with  DUMP operand  is  the  only  trace  macro
   expansion which causes output  immediately,  not  as  a
   consequence of some other condition(s). Example syntax:

         LABELI  TRACE  DUMP

NOTE:
     All  of  the  examples  above  specify only the program
     condition being traced. With the exception  of  channel
     tracing (CHANL), additional operands may be supplied to
     the  TRACE  macro instruction.  These optional operands
     will cause additional information to be  printed  along
     with  the  standard  trace  information, when the trace
     takes place.


Standard Trace Information (description):

     The standard trace information mentioned above contains  the
following information:

(a) The  current  value  of  the  location  counter  in
    hexadecimal.

(b) The type of trace request which caused this message  to
    be printed. Examples:

          PGM INTERRUPT        ADDRESS: 00F8
          LPSW INSTRUCTION     SNAPSHOT
          SVC INTERRUPT        I/O INTERRUPT
          EXECUTION: 00A2      EXT INTERRUPT

(c) The count of the number of instructions  the  simulator
    has executed up to the present time.

(d) The elapsed simulated time in  microseconds  since  the
    start of execution.

(e) The contents of the current PSW  in  hexadecimal  (see
    below).

(f) The  assembler  op-code  mnemonic of  the  instruction
    associated with this trace message.

(g) A hexadecimal dump of the instruction  associated  with
    this trace message.

(h) The absolute address, in hex, of operands 1 and 2, if present, as computed by the simulator.

(i) The first four bytes of operands 1 and 2, if present.


Standard Trace Output Breakdown:

Part One of Heading:

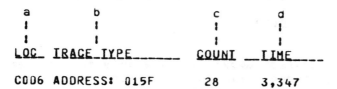

```
     a           b              c        d
     |           |              |        |
     |           |              |        |
    LOC  TRACE_TYPE_____  COUNT __TIME___

    C006 ADDRESS: 015F        28      3,347
```

Part Two of Heading:

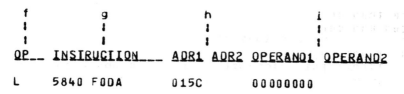

```
     f           g              h              i
     |           |              |              |
     |           |              |              |
    OP__ INSTRUCTION___  ADR1 ADR2 OPERAND1 OPERAND2

     L    5840 F0DA        015C      00000000
```

PSW Breakdown:

```
     e      Key  IC           CC    Instruction Address
     |       |    |            |         |
    PSW: 00  0 0 0000  '10'B  '00'B 0 000006
     |       |    |            |
    I/O Mask AMWP         ILC    Program Mask
```

Instruction count and simulated time are expressed in decimal. ILC and CC in the PSW are expressed in binary; all other values in hexadecimal.


Optional Trace Information,
Functional Specification and Syntax:

    Optional operands may be specified in a TRACE macro instruction which cause information in addition to that which is standard to be printed. These optional operands fall into three classes: status dumps, register dumps, and core dumps.

    Status information is that contained in the permanently assigned low core area from location 24 (decimal) to 127 (decimal). This includes the old and new PSW's for the five interrupt classes, the channel status word, and the timer. A register dump includes any or all of the sixteen general purpose registers. Registers are dumped both in hexadecimal and decimal and are individually identified. Core dumps are in hexadecimal and character format.

The TRACE macro operands which specify these dumps of optional information follow the program condition, delimited by a comma, with no intervening spaces. Each specification of status, register, or core dumps may appear either once or not at all. They may appear in any order as well.

A status dump is identified by the keyword "STATUS=", followed by a list of the status information to be dumped. Valid keywords for the status list are:

```
OLDPGM     NEWPGM     OLDI/O     NEWI/O     OLDEXT
NEWEXT     OLDSVC     NEWSVC     OLDMCK     NEWMCK
TIMER      CSW        CAW
```

If more than one keyword is specified, the list must be parenthesized and delimited by commas. Valid examples include:

```
LABELJ   TRACE   DUMP,STATUS=(OLDI/O,OLDPGM,OLDSVC)
LABELK   TRACE   INTRPT,SVC,STATUS=OLDSVC
LABELL   TRACE   BRANCH,STATUS=(OLDSVC,OLDPGM,TIMER,CSW)
```

A register dump is identified by the keyword "REGS=". One to sixteen registers may be specified in any order; parentheses must be used when more than one register is specified. Legal examples include:

```
LABELM   TRACE   ADDRS,700,REGS=(0,5,3,14,15)
LABELN   TRACE   DUMP,REGS=(0,1,2,3,4,5,6,7,8,9,10,11,12)
LABELO   TRACE   BRANCH,REGS=15
LABELP   TRACE   INSTR,50,REGS=(7)
```

A core dump is identified by the keyword "CORE=". The core option also requires a list, but the list must be parenthesized, and specifications are listed in groups of two. The first parameter is the address of the first word to be dumped; the argument immediately following this address is the count of the number of words of core to be dumped.

This starting address must be a valid, program defined address, symbol, or absolute decimal number. If this address does not specify a fullword boundary, it will be moved back to the previous fullword boundary, and the length will not be changed. You may specify a maximum of eight core dump pairs (addresses and word counts). Some examples:

```
LABELQ    TRACE    DUMP,CORE=(LABELW,7,ADDRESS,1,FOO,120)
LABELR    TRACE    INTRPT,PGM,CORE=(284,3)
```

**Note:** A maximum of 128 (decimal) words may be dumped per
address specified.

```
QUARF1    EQU      400
QUARF2    EQU      528
          TRACE    DUMP,CORE=(QUARF1,128,QUARF2,64)
* THIS EFFECTIVELY DUMPS 192 WORDS STARTING AT 400
```

Now, what may not be obvious from the preceeding discussion
is that the STATUS, REGS, and CORE specifications may all be used
in one TRACE macro instruction.  Examples follow:

```
LABELS    TRACE    DUMP,REGS=15,CORE=(ZAP,77),STATUS=(CSW,CAW)
LABELT    TRACE    CHANL,1,STATUS=CSW,REGS=(8,2,3,7)
LABELU    TRACE    ADDRS,128,CORE=(BARF,2),REGS=(0,4)
```


Turning off Tracing:

Any trace facility that you request may be removed when you
no longer need it by means of the TRACEOFF macro instruction. The
syntax of this macro is identical to that of the TRACE macro,
except that no optional operands are included.  In addition, if
you wish to turn off all traces of a given type, you may replace
the explicit specification (the address in ADDRS tracing, the
op-code in INSTR tracing, the type in INTRPT tracing, or the
channel number in CHANL tracing) with the word "ALL".  Examples:

```
TRACEOFF INSTR,ALL          TRACEOFF INTRPT,SVC
TRACEOFF BRANCH             TRACEOFF CHANL,2
TRACEOFF ADDRS,ALL
```

There is no "TRACEOFF DUMP" for the obvious reason.


### 4.1.5   Comments and Suggestions

1. The simulator takes as input object decks produced by the
   OS/360 assembler.  The following student deck setup is
   recommended:

```
Col. 1          10   16
                TITLE 'your name - instructors name'
    name        CSECT
                *
    your program
                *
                END
```

2. Your deck should have only <u>one</u> CSECT and <u>one</u> END card.

3. Do not use the EXTRN or ENTRY statements, or Q and V type address constants.

4. The first 128 (decimal) locations (16 double words) must be properly initialized.

5. Your instructor sets the maximum number of instructions you will be allowed to execute and the amount of virtual time that you are given. Be efficient in your coding and use the wait state properly. <u>NEVER</u> sit looping waiting for I/O to complete.

6. If you do not plan to use the timer, disable its interrupt by setting the external mask in the PSW (bit 7) to 0. Remember, the timer always runs and will interrupt if you give it a chance.

7. The information printed in a trace message associated with instruction execution (BRANCH, ADDRS, EXEC, or INSTR) reflects the state of the CPU at a theoretical point in time after instruction fetch and address generation, but before any data has been changed by the execution of the instruction.

8. The information printed in a trace message associated with an interrupt (INTRPT) reflects the state of the CPU after the then-current PSW has been stored and before the new PSW has been fetched.

9. The information associated with a snapshot trace (DUMP) reflects the state of the CPU after the instruction preceeding the trace macro has been processed and before the instruction following the trace request has been fetched.

## 4.1.6  Implemented Instructions

The simulator does not handle the full complement of system/360-370 instructions, however, a subset designed to be adequate for systems programming use is implemented:

1.  Add register (AR)
2.  Add (A)
3.  Add halfword (AH)
4.  And register (NR)
5.  And (N)
6.  And immediate (NI)
7.  And character (NC)
8.  Branch and link register (BALR)
9.  Branch and link (BAL)
10. Branch on condition register (BCR)
11. Branch on condition (BC)
12. Branch on count register (BCTR)
13. Branch on count (BCT)
14. Branch on index high (BXH)
15. Branch on index low or equal (BXLE)
16. Compare register (CR)
17. Compare (C)
18. Compare halfword (CH)
19. Compare logical register (CLR)
20. Compare logical (CL)
21. Compare logical characters (CLC)
22. Compare logical immediate (CLI)
23. Divide register (DR)
24. Divide (D)
25. Exclusive or register (XR)
26. Exclusive or (X)
27. Exclusive or immediate (XI)
28. Exclusive or characters (XC)
29. Execute (EX)
30. Halt I/O (HIO)
31. Insert character (IC)
32. Insert storage key (ISK)
33. Load register (LR)
34. Load (L)
35. Load address (LA)
36. Load and test register (LTR)
37. Load complement register (LCR)
38. Load halfword (LH)
39. Load multiple (LM)
40. Load negative register (LNR)
41. Load positive register (LPR)
42. Load program status word (LPSW)
43. Move immediate (MVI)
44. Move characters (MVC)
45. Move numerics (MVN)
46. Move zones (MVZ)
47. Multiply register (MR)

48. Multiply (M)
49. Multiply halfword (MH)
50. Or register (OR)
51. Or (O)
52. Or immediate (OI)
53. Or character (OC)
54. Set program mask (SPM)
55. Set storage key (SSK)
55. Set system mask (SSM)
57. Shift left double logical (SLDL)
58. Shift left single arithmetic (SLA)
59. Shift left single logical (SLL)
60. Shift right double logical (SRDL)
61. Shift right single logical (SRL)
62. Start I/O (SIO)
63. Store (ST)
64. Store character (STC)
65. Store halfword (STH)
66. Store multiple (STM)
67. Subtract register (SR)
68. Subtract (S)
69. Subtract halfword (SH)
70. Supervisor call (SVC)
71. Test and set (TS)
72. Test channel (TCH)
73. Test I/O (TIO)
74. Test under mask (TM)
75. Translate (TR)

Use of valid system/360-370 instructions that are not implemented results in a program interrupt for an operation exception. In addition to the machine instructions listed above, the TRACE, TRACEOFF, and QUIT macro instructions communicate to the assembler by use of the op-codes X'02', X'03', and X'FF', respectively. You are cautioned against using these op-codes, except through use of the provided tracing macros. will interpret them as commands.

## 4.1.7  Unimplemented Instructions

The following instructions are **not** **implemented** in the current version (1.3) of SIM360:

1.  Add logical register (ALR)
2.  Add logical (AL)
3.  Branch and store register (BASR)
4.  Branch and store (BAS)
5.  Compare decimal (CP)
6.  Compare logical characters under mask (CLM)
7.  Compare logical long (CLCL)
8.  Convert binary (CVB)
9.  Convert decimal (CVD)
10. Divide decimal (DP)
11. Edit (ED)
12. Edit and mark (EDMK)
13. Insert characters under mask (ICM)
14. Load multiple control (LMC)
15. Load real address (LRA)
16. Monitor call (MC)
17. Move long (MVCL)
17. Move with offset (MVO)
18. Multiply decimal (MP)
19. Pack (PACK)
20. Read direct (RDD)
21. Set clock (SCK)
22. Shift and round decimal (SRP)
23. Shift left double arithmetic (SLDA)
24. Shift right double arithmetic (SRDA)
25. Shift right arithmetic (SRA)
26. Start I/O fast release (SIOF)
27. Store channel ID (STIDC)
28. Store characters under mask (STCM)
29. Store clock (STCK)
30. Store CPU ID (STIDP)
31. Store control (STCTL)
32. Store multiple control (STMC)
33. Subtract decimal (SP)
34. Subtract logical register (SLR)
35. Subtract logical (SL)
36. Translate and test (TRT)
37. Unpack (UNPK)
38. Write direct (WRD)
39. Zero and add (ZAP)

In addition, none of the floating point feature instructions are implemented.

## 4.1.8  Simulator Messages

The following messages are produced by SIM360:

1. Normal simulator terminations (via QUIT macro) produce:

NORMAL SIMULATOR TERMINATION FOR PROGRAM name
                SIMULATED REAL TIME:        3,365.152
                SIMULATED CPU TIME:            47.151

Where name is the name of the CSECT that just terminated,  and
both times are given in micro-seconds.

2. What would be a "hard wait" produces:

        CPU HAS ENTERED THE WAIT STATE WITH NO INTERRUPTS
        ENABLED. SIMULATION ENDS. THE FOLLOWING SIMULATOR
        PROVIDED SNAPSHOT SHOULD HELP IN DETERMINING
        THE CAUSE OF THIS CONDITION.

In  fact  the  snapshot may not be helpful, but it is the best
that can be done. The meaning of this message is that either a
PSW was loaded which had the wait state bit on (bit  14),  and
all  interrupts  were masked off (system mask = X'00'), or one
or more interrupts were enabled in the PSW, but the interrupts
that were enabled were  not  outstanding,  ie.  nothing  would
bring the simulated CPU out of the wait state.

        As  a  possible example suppose you loaded a PSW with the
wait bit on and interrupts enabled only for channel 0 (system
mask  =  X'80'). This  is a reasonable thing to do if you are
waiting for I/O to complete on the  multiplexor  channel.  If,
however,  you  goofed up the SIO and no I/O is actually active
on the multiplexor, the simulator will correctly  notice  that
you  will  wait forever and it terminates the simulation. Note
that  if  the  timer  (external  interrupt)  is  enabled  for
interruption, this message will never result.

3. When adjacent program interrupts occur:

        A PROGRAM INTERRUPT HAS OCCURRED IN THE PROGRAM
        INTERRUPT HANDLER.
        THIS IS ALMOST CERTAINLY A FATAL ERROR.

When  two  program interrupts occur, one right after the other
with no intervening PSW swap (either from  interrupt  such  as
I/O  or  via  an  LPSW  instruction) the simulator assumes the
program is in a program  interrupt  loop  so  it  prints  this
informatory  message  and  abnormally  terminates the job. For
this abnormal termination the snapshot of the program old PSW
should be very helpful indeed.

4. For exceeding program execution limits:

    a) MAXIMUM ALLOWED INSTRUCTION COUNT EXCEEDED.

    b) MAXIMUM ALLOWED SIMULATED TIME EXCEEDED.

    c) MAXIMUM ALLOWED PAGE COUNT EXCEEDED FOR TRACE OUTPUT

When a program exceeds limits established by the instructor these self explanatory messages are produced and then the program is abnormally terminated.

5. Internal error message:

    SERIOUS SIMULATOR PROBLEM IN WAIT STATE HANDLER
    REFERENCE LABEL -GOT_IE-.
    GIVE LISTINGS TO INSTRUCTOR.

This message is caused by a severe internal error in the simulator. In order to aid in fixing any such problems all listings germane should be delivered to the person responsible for simulator maintenance.

6. Invalid trace requests produce:

    a) INVALID DATA FOUND IN TRACE COMMAND.
    PROBABLE PROGRAMMER ERROR.
    COMMAND LOCATION IS xxxxx

    b) COULD NOT FIND VALID TERMINATOR FOR TRACE.
    TAKING OPERATION INTERRUPT.

    c) FOUND VALID TERMINATOR OF TRACE COMMAND.
    COMMAND IGNORED.

    d) *****INVALID ADDRESS SPECIFICATION FOR
    SPECIFICATION NUMBER nn. IGNORED.*****

These messages are indications that you have in some way destroyed part of a trace macro expansion, or you have specified an illegal address as part of a trace macro instruction.

SIM360 EXAMPLE PROGRAM

```
LOC   OBJECT CODE     ADDR1 ADDR2  STMT   SOURCE STATEMENT
```

```
                                     2              PRINT NOGEN              FOR READABILITY
                                     3 **********************************************************************
                                     4 *
                                     5 *         EXAMPLE INTERRUPT AND I/O PROGRAM FOR THE SIM360 SIMULATOR.  *
                                     6 *
                                     7 *         THIS JOB READS AND PRINTS CARDS, PERFORMING A CALCULATION
                                     8 *         CONCURRENTLY WITH THE I/O OPERATIONS. THIS IS DESIGNED TO
                                     9 *         PROVIDE A FEEL FOR THE RELATIVE TIMINGS OF INSTRUCTIONS
                                    10 *         AND I/O OPERATIONS.
                                    11 *
                                    12 *         NOTE THAT THIS JOB WILL STOP WHEN NO MORE CARDS ARE
                                    13 *         IN THE INPUT READER. IN THIS CASE, THE JOB WILL ENTER THE
                                    14 *         WAIT STATE WITH NO INTERRUPTS PENDING (NO CARDS = NO
                                    15 *         INTERRUPTS). THE SIMULATOR RECOGNIZES THIS CONDITION AND
                                    16 *         TERMINATES SIMULATION.
                                    17 *
                                    18 **********************************************************************
000000                              20 EXAMPLE  CSECT                          THIS SIMULATOR JOB NAMED 'EXAMPLE'
00000D                              21           USING EXAMPLE,0               ESTABLISH ADDRESSABILITY

                                    23 *
                                    24 *                    SET UP LOW-CORE LOCATIONS
                                    25 *

000000 0000000000000180             27           DC    A(0,BEGIN)             IPL PSW
000008 C000000000000000             28 IPLCCW1   DC    A(0,0)                 CCW1 FOR IPL (NOT USED BY SIM360)
000010 000000C0C0C00000             29 IPLCCW2   DC    A(0,0)                 CCW2 FOR IPL (NOT USED BY SIM360)
000018 C00000000000000              30 EXTOLD    DC    A(0,0)                 OLD PSW FOR EXTERNAL INTERRUPT
000020 C000000000000000             31 SUPOLD    DC    A(0,0)                 OLD PSW FOR SUPERVISOR CALL
000028 C000000C0C000000             32 PROGOLD   DC    A(0,0)                 OLD PSW FOR PROGRAM INTERRUPT
000030 C00000000000000              33 MCKOLD    DC    A(0,0)                 OLD PSW FOR MACHINE CHECK
000038 C000000000000000             34 IOOLD     DC    A(0,0)                 OLD PSW FOR IO INTERRUPT
000040 CC000C0000000000             35 CSW       DC    A(0,0)                 CHANNEL STATUS WORD
000048 000001F8                     36 CAW       DC    A(READ1)               CHANNEL ADDRESS WORD, INITIALIZED
                                    37 *                                     TO POINT TO READER CCW
00004C C000CC000                    38 SPARE1    DC    A(0)                   UNUSED
000050 FFFFFFFF                     39 TIMER     DC    F'-1'                  TIMER AREA (WITH LARGE NUMBER)
000054 00000000                     40 SPARE2    DC    A(0)                   UNUSED
000058 C000C0000000000              41 EXTNEW    DC    A(0,0)                 EXTERNAL NEW PSW (NOT USED IN EX)
000060 000000C000000000             42 SUPNEW    DC    A(0,0)                 SVC NEW PSW (NOT USED IN EX)
000068 000000000000000              43 PROGNEW   DC    A(0,0)                 PROGRAM NEW PSW (NOT USED IN EX)
000070 CC0000C000000000             44 MCKNEW    DC    A(0,0)                 MACHINE CHECK NEW PSW (NOT USED IN
                                    45 *                                     SIM360)
000078 000000C0000001B8             46 IONEW     DC    A(0,INT)               I/O NEW PSW INITIALIZED TO POINT TO
                                    47 *                                     I/O INTERRUPT HANDLER
000080 0000000C00000000             48 SCANOUT   DC    256X'00'               DIAGNOSTIC SCAN OUT AREA, NOT USED
                                    49 *                                     BY SIM360

                                    51 *
                                    52 *                    FOLLOWING SIMULATOR TRACE REQUESTS CAUSE THE I/O OLD
                                    53 *                    PSW, THE CSW, AND REGISTER ZERO TO BE PRINTED AT EACH
                                    54 *                    I/O INTERRUPT; AND THE PROGRAM OLD PSW TO BE PRINTED
                                    55 *                    AT EVERY PROGRAM INTERRUPT.
                                    56 *
```

SIM360 EXAMPLE PROGRAM

```
LOC   OBJECT CODE    ADDR1 ADDR2  STMT   SOURCE STATEMENT

                                   58 BEGIN    TRACE  INTRPT,I/O,STATUS=(OLDI/O,CSW),REGS=(0)
                                   67          TRACE  INTRPT,PGM,STATUS=(OLDPGM)

                                   77 *
                                   78 *                START I/O ON READER
                                   79 *

000194 8C00 0274     00274         81          SSM    =X'FF'              ENABLE INTERRUPTS
000198 9C00 C00C     0C00C         82          SIO    X'00C'              START READER FOR FIRST CARD

                                   84 *
                                   85 *                FOLLOWING TRACE REQUEST SHOWS THE STATUS AFTER THE FIRST
                                   86 *                READ REQUEST, INCLUDING THE CONTENTS OF THE CAW.
                                   87 *

                                   89          TRACE  DUMP,STATUS=(CAW)

                                   99 *
                                  100 *                START COMPUTATION
                                  101 *

0001A6 5810 0260           00260  103          L      1,=F'10000'         COUNT FROM 1 TO 10,000
0001AA 1800                       104          SR     0,0                 CLEAR COUNTING REGISTER
0001AC 5A00 0264           00264  105 LOOP     A      0,=F'1'             ADD 1 TO COUNTER REGISTER
0001B0 4610 01AC           001AC  106          BCT    1,LOOP              COUNT TO PREVIOUSLY SPECIFIED NUMBER

0001B4 8200 0208     0C208        108          LPSW   WAITPSW             OUR POINT IS MADE, NOW GO INTERRUPT
                                  109 *                                   DRIVEN

                                  111 *
                                  112 *                I/O INTERRUPT HANDLER
                                  113 *

0001B8 9104 0044     0C044        115 INT      TM     CSW+4,X'04'         WAS THIS A DEVICE END INTERRUPT
0001BC 4780 01D4           001D4  116          BZ     RETURN              NO, IGNORE IT

0001C0 D501 003A 0270 0C03A 00270 118          CLC    IOOLD+2(2),=X'000C' IS IT A READER INTERRUPT
0001C6 4780 01D8           001D8  119          BE     READINT             YES, HANDLE APPROPRIATELY

0001CA D501 003A 0272 0C03A 00272 121          CLC    IOOLD+2(2),=X'00E'  IS IT A PRINTER INTERRUPT
0001D0 4780 01E6           001E6  122          BE     PRINTINT            YES, HANDLE IT

0001D4 8200 0038     0C038        124 RETURN   LPSW   IOOLD               RESTORE PREVIOUS PSW (RETURN)

                                  126 *
                                  127 *                READER INTERRUPT HANDLER, START PRINTER
                                  128 *

0001D8 D203 0048 0268 0C048 00268 130 READINT  MVC    CAW(4),=A(PRINT1)   START PRINTER AND PRINT CARD
0001DE 9C00 000E     0000E        131          SIO    X'00E'              JUST READ
0001E2 47F0 01D4           001D4  132          B      RETURN              RETURN TO POINT OF INTERRUPTION

                                  134 *
                                  135 *                PRINTER INTERRUPT HANDLER, READ CARD
                                  136 *
```

SIM360 EXAMPLE PROGRAM

| LOC | OBJECT CODE | ADDR1 | ADDR2 | STMT | SOURCE STATEMENT | | |
|-----|-------------|-------|-------|------|------------------|--|--|

```
0001E6 D203 0048 026C  00048 0026C   138 PRINTINT MVC   CAW(4),=A(READ1)    START READER TO GET NEXT CARD
0001EC 9C00 000C       0C00C          139          SIO   X'00C'
0001F0 47F0 01D4              001D4   140          B     RETURN              RETURN TO POINT OF INTERRUPTION

                                      142 *
                                      143 *                                  RANDOM STORAGE
                                      144 *

0001F4 00000000
0001F8 0200021000000050              146 READ1    CCW   X'02',BUFFER1,X'00',80
                                      147 *                                  READ 80 BYTE CARD
000200 0900021000000050              148 PRINT1   CCW   X'09',BUFFER1,X'00',80
                                      149 *                                  PRINT 80 BYTE CARD
000208 FE02000000000000              150 WAITPSW  DC    X'FE02000000000000'  I/O WAIT PSW
000210                               151 BUFFER1  DS    CL80                 BUFFER FOR 80-BYTE CARD

000260                               153          LTORG                      FORM LITERAL POOL
000260 00002710                      154                   =F'10000'
000264 00000001                      155                   =F'1'
000268 0000200                       156                   =A(PRINT1)
00026C 000001F8                      157                   =A(READ1)
000270 000C                          158                   =X'000C'
000272 000E                          159                   =X'000E'
000274 FF                            160                   =X'FF'

                                     162          END
```

```
MASSACHUSETTS INSTITUTE OF TECHNOLOGY          SYSTEM / 360 SIMULATOR                                          VERSION 1.3
EXAMPLE TRACE LISTING.   0 CONDITIONS ENABLED.                                                                      PAGE   1
                                                                          OP   INSTRUCTION      ADR1 ADR2  OPERAND1 OPERAND2
LOC  TRACE TYPE          CCUNT   TIME                                      ----  -------------   ----  ----  -------- --------
----  ---------------    -----  ----------


01A6 SNAPSHOT              2        2  PSW: FF 0 0 0000  '01'B '00'B 0 0001A6
         STATUS:
           CAW: 000001F8,        504
01AC I/O INTERRUPT        472      486  PSW: FF 0 0 000C  '10'B '10'B 0 0001AC
         STATUS:
           OLD I/O: FF 0 0 000C  '10'B '10'B 0 0001AC          CSW: 0 0 000200  0800 0000   CNT=      0
         REGISTERS:
           R 0: 000000EA,        234
0000 I/O INTERRUPT       20008   73,499  PSW: FE 0 2 000C  '10'B '00'B 0 000000
         STATUS:
           OLD I/O: FE 0 2 000C  '10'B '00'B 0 000000          CSW: 0 0 000200  0400 0000   CNT=      0
         REGISTERS:
           R 0: 00002710,      10000
0000 I/O INTERRUPT       20016   73,915  PSW: FE 0 2 000E  '10'B '00'B 0 C00000
         STATUS:
           OLD I/O: FE 0 2 000E  '10'B '00'B 0 000000          CSW: 0 0 000208  0840 0034   CNT=     52
         REGISTERS:
           R 0: 00002710,      10000
0000 I/O INTERRUPT       20019  172,216  PSW: FE 0 2 000E  '10'B '00'B 0 000000
         STATUS:
           OLD I/O: FE 0 2 000E  '10'B '00'B 0 000000          CSW: 0 0 000208  0400 0000   CNT=      0
         REGISTERS:
           R 0: 00002710,      10000
0000 I/O INTERRUPT       20029  172,711  PSW: FE 0 2 000C  '10'B '00'B 0 000000
         STATUS:
           OLD I/O: FE 0 2 000C  '10'B '00'B 0 000000          CSW: 0 0 000200  0800 0000   CNT=      0
         REGISTERS:
           R 0: 00002710,      10000
0000 I/O INTERRUPT       20032  233,500  PSW: FE 0 2 000C  '10'B '00'B 0 000000
         STATUS:
           OLD I/O: FE 0 2 000C  '10'B '00'B 0 000000          CSW: 0 0 000200  0400 0000   CNT=      0
         REGISTERS:
           R 0: 00002710,      10000
0000 I/O INTERRUPT       20040  233,915  PSW: FE 0 2 000E  '10'B '00'B 0 000000
         STATUS:
           OLD I/O: FE 0 2 000E  '10'B '00'B 0 000000          CSW: 0 0 000208  0840 0034   CNT=     52
         REGISTERS:
           R 0: 00002710,      10000
0000 I/O INTERRUPT       20043  335,216  PSW: FE 0 2 000E  '10'B '00'B 0 000000
         STATUS:
           OLD I/O: FE 0 2 000E  '10'B '00'B 0 000000          CSW: 0 0 000208  0400 0000   CNT=      0
         REGISTERS:
           R 0: 00002710,      10000
```

```
MASSACHUSETTS INSTITUTE OF TECHNOLOGY          SYSTEM / 360 SIMULATOR                                VERSION 1.3
EXAMPLE TRACE LISTING.    2 CONDITIONS ENABLED.                                                          PAGE  2

LOC  TRACE TYPE            COUNT  TIME                                        OP   INSTRUCTION        ADR1 ADR2  OPERAND1 OPERAND2
----  ----------------     -----  ----------                                 ----  --------------    ---- ----  -------- --------

0000  I/O INTERRUPT        20053    335,712  PSW: FE 0 2 000C  '10'B '00'B 0 000000
      STATUS:
         OLD I/O: FE 0 2 000C  '10'B '00'B 0 000000          CSW: 0 0 000200  0800 0000   CNT=    0
      REGISTERS:
         R 0: 00002710,        10000

0000  I/O INTERRUPT        20056    393,500  PSW: FE 0 2 000C  '10'B '00'B 0 000000
      STATUS:
         CLD I/O: FE 0 2 000C  '10'B '00'B 0 000000          CSW: 0 0 000200  0400 0000   CNT=    0
      REGISTERS:
         R 0: 00002710,        10000

0000  I/O INTERRUPT        20064    393,915  PSW: FE 0 2 000E  '10'B '00'B 0 000000
      STATUS:
         OLD I/O: FE 0 2 000E  '10'B '00'B 0 000000          CSW: 0 0 000208  0840 0034   CNT=   52
      REGISTERS:
         R 0: 00002710,        10000

0000  I/O INTERRUPT        20067    482,516  PSW: FE 0 2 000E  '10'B '00'B 0 000000
      STATUS:
         CLD I/O: FE 0 2 000E  '10'B '00'B 0 C00000          CSW: 0 0 000208  0400 0000   CNT=    0
      REGISTERS:
         R 0: 00002710,        10000


CPU HAS ENTERED THE WAIT STATE WITH NO INTERRUPTS ENABLED. SIMULATION ENDS.
THE FOLLOWING SIMULATOR-PROVIDED SNAPSHOT SHOULD HELP IN DETERMINING THE CAUSE OF THIS CONDITION.   THE PSW INTERRUPT CODE IS
1

0000  SNAPSHCT             20077    482,533  PSW: FE 0 2 0000  '10'B '00'B 0 C00000
      STATUS:
         OLD PRG: 00 0 0 0000  '00'B '00'B 0 000000
      REGISTERS:
         R 0: 00002710,        10000 R 1: 00000000,            0 R 2: FFFFFFFF,          -1 R 3: FFFFFFFF,          -1
         R 4: FFFFFFFF,           -1 R 5: FFFFFFFF,           -1 R 6: FFFFFFFF,          -1 R 7: FFFFFFFF,          -1
         R 8: FFFFFFFF,           -1 R 9: FFFFFFFF,           -1 R10: FFFFFFFF,          -1 R11: FFFFFFFF,          -1
         R12: FFFFFFFF,           -1 R13: FFFFFFFF,           -1 R14: FFFFFFFF,          -1 R15: FFFFFFFF,          -1


ABNORMAL SIMULATOR TERMINATION FOR PROGRAM EXAMPLE

         SIMULATED REAL TIME:     482,533.875

         SIMULATED CPU TIME:       20,062.187
```

```
••••••••••••••••••••••••••••••••••••••••••••••••••••••••••••••••••••••••••••••••••••••••••••••••••••••••••••••••••••••••••••
EXAMPLE                           OUTPUT TO PRINTER 00E STARTS AT HEAD OF FORM ON NEXT PAGE
••••••••••••••••••••••••••••••••••••••••••••••••••••••••••••••••••••••••••••••••••••••••••••••••••••••••••••••••••••••••••••

CARD 1 FOR LISTING
CARD 2 FOR LISTING
CARD 3 (LAST CARD) FOR LISTING
```

## 4.2   Instructor's Manual

### 4.2.1   Introduction

The purpose of this section is to support  the  installation
and use of the Simulator on two levels:

1. At  the  level  of  the  system  programmer  who  will
   implement, and may modify the programs.
2. At the level of the SIM360 user.

Discussed are the simulator's system requirements, the steps
required  to install the simulator, and the  procedures for using
it.

### 4.2.2   System Requirements

The  only  systems  supporting  the  version  of  PL/1   the
simulator is written in are the IBM 360/370 series, with an OS or
VS  operating  system.  It  would  be  possible  to recompile the
simulator to run under IBM's  DOS,  but  modifications  would  be
necessary  due  to restrictions imposed by the DOS PL/1 compiler.

The  load-module  for  the  simulator   included   on   the
distribution  tape  has  been produced by the IBM PL/1 F (version
5.4) compiler. Therefore the PL/1 (F) run time transient routines
must be available in your system before you can use this  module.

Since  the  simulator  usually  requires several input files
concurrently, it is imperative that the operating system  provide
input  spooling  capability. This implies an MFT/HASP, MVT, or VS
system (possibly DOS/POWER).

The simulator requires a region of about 200  K-bytes  under
OS/MVT.  This  requirement can be reduced by lowering the virtual
machine's core size from 32 K, or overlaying the simulator (using
the linkage editor).

Since the simulator takes as input standard OS-format object
decks, the system must possess  some  means  of  producing  these
decks.  The  most likely candidate for this job is the assembler.
Although every IBM system contains  the  IBM  F-level  assembler,
experience  has  shown  that  for  large class runs the so-called
"G-level" assembler assembler developed by  the  University  of
Waterloo  may be used in the batching mode to convert a stream of
assembly language source decks into a stream of object decks much
more  efficiently  (and  hence,  at  a  lower  cost)  than several
invocations of the F-level assembler.

To  allow  programs  under  simulation  access  to the trace
facilities of the simulator, an assembler macro library  must  be

provided. This library should also include any auxiliary macros such as machine problem testers, linkage macros, etc. which could be needed by simulated programs. The generation of this macro library is discussed in section 4.2.4. Methods for using the two assemblers to generate object deck streams are discussed in section 4.2.7.

### 4.2.3  Creating the SIM360 Load Module:

Before the simulator may be used, a load module must be created. This load module will be a member of a partitioned data set (PDS) which should be catalogued for ease of subsequent reference. We have included a load module on the distribution tape. This load module was unloaded from a 2314 using the IBM utility program IEHMOVE. If your installation has 2314 disk drives, you may simply use IEHMOVE to restore this load module (see section 8.4 for help).

If you wish to re-link the load module or load it onto non-2314 secondary storage, a new load module must be created. A load module is created by using the linkage editor to bind together several object modules. The linkage editor must be provided with object decks for each of the simulator modules. There are three ways the linkage editor can obtain these decks.

If a load module already exists on one form of storage, say a 2314, and you wish to obtain a 3330 version, you may use the 2314 version as input to the linkage editor. In the case where you have no 2314's available in your system and you do not need to change any of the simulator's modules you may obtain the object decks directly from the distribution tape (see section 8.4).

Finally, if you need to change the simulator, you may obtain the source from the distribution tape and after your changes are made, recompile (reassemble for DIVD) the source modules to obtain object decks and then proceed with the linkage editing necessary to produce a load module.

The following JCL may be used to link the object decks provided on the distribution tape. For instructions on how to use an existent load module as input to the linkage editor refer to IBM System/360 Operating System Linkage Editor and Loader, IBM publication number GC28-6538.

JCL to Link a SIM360 Load Module:

```
//STEPL    EXEC PGM=IEWL,PARM='XREF,LIST'
//SYSPRINT DD   SYSOUT=A
//SYSUT1   DD   UNIT=SYSDA,SPACE=(CYL,(5,2))
//SYSLMOD  DD   DSN=SIM360.LOAD(SIM360),UNIT=2314,
//              VOL=SER=nnnnnn,DISP=(NEW,CATLG),
//              SPACE=(TRK,(10,5,2))
//SYSLIB   DD   DSN=SYS1.PL1LIB,DISP=SHR
//SYSLIN   DD   UNIT=2400,DISP=(OLD,PASS)... (see note 1)
```

With the following assumptions:

1. This file is on the distribution tape and contains  the
   object  decks  for  the  simulator  modules (refer  to
   section 8.4).

2. The volume-serial number for the direct  access  volume
   to contain the resultant load module is nnnnnn. If this
   device  is  other than a 2314, the SPACE value and UNIT
   parameter for SYSLMOD must be changed accordingly.

3. The PL1 run-time library routines, in object form,  are
   assumed  to  reside  in  a  cataloged  dataset  named
   "SYS1.PL1LIB". This is usually the name used, but might
   be different for your installation.

4. The resultant load module is to be cataloged as  member
   "SIM360" of the partitioned datset "SIM360.LOAD".

## 4.2.4   Assembler Macro Library for SIM360

     Several  macros  are  provided  for  the  user to access the
tracing facilities of the  simulator.  In  addition,  macros  are
provided  to  act  as "testers" for student problems to be run on
the simulator.  Macros to be used in this manner (as part  of  a
machine problem) will be documented in the instructor's guide for
the  particular  problem,  but  their  source  is  included in the
simulator macro file of the distribution tape.

     This section concentrates on the steps necessary  to  create
the  assembler  macro  library.  A macro library is a partitioned
dataset which contains the individual macros as members.  One way
to generate such a  PDS  is  with  the  IBM  OS  utility  program
"IEBUPDTE"  (refer to IBM System/360 Operating System: Utilities,
IBM publication number GC28-6586).

JCL to Create New Macro Library:

```
//MCREATE EXEC PGM=IEBUPDTE,PARM='NEW'
//SYSPRINT DD  SYSOUT=A
```

```
//SYSUT2    DD   DSN=SIM360.MACLIB,DISP=(NEW,CATLG),
//               VOL=SER=nnnnnn,UNIT=2314,
//               DCB=(RECFM=FB,LRECL=80,BLKSIZE=1600),
//               SPACE=(TRK,(2,1,2))
//SYSIN     DD   <see note 3, below>
/*
```

Notes:

1. The resulting macro library is to be cataloged as the PDS "SIM360.MACLIB" on a 2314 volume nnnnnn (you provide).

2. If the receiving volume is not a 2314, the UNIT and SPACE parameters of the SYSUT2 DD statement must be modified accordingly.

3. The SYSIN DD statement defines the input to the IEBUPDTE program. This input consists of macros delimited by control statements which give the names for the macros. The distribution tape contains the macros in this form, so a file from it can be used as SYSIN (see section 8.4). If you have punched the macros and control statements onto cards, you may substitute:

```
//SYSIN     DD   *
     _
    |
    |          macros and control cards
    |_

    /*
```

Once you have created the macro library, you may wish to add your own macros. This can be accomplished with the following JCL, realizing that adding a macro with the same name as an existent one has the effect of replacing the previous one.

JCL to Add Macros to Library:

```
//MADD     EXEC PGM=IEBUPDTE,PARM='NEW'
//SYSPRINT DD   SYSOUT=A
//SYSUT2   DD   DSN=SIM360.MACLIB,DISP=OLD
//SYSIN    DD   *
./         ADD  NAME=mname

 _
|
| macro mname (from MACRO to MEND)
|_
```

```
./        ENDUP
/*
```

**Notes:**

1. **mname** is the member name the IEBUPDTE program will use to search the macro library PDS. If a member by this name is found, it will be replaced, else a new member by this name will be created. For proper results this name should be the same as the name specified on the card after the MACRO card.

2. The "ENDUP" card indicates the end of IEBUPDTE input. If more than one macro is to be added in one run, follow the first macro's MEND card with a "ADD" card for the second macro, specifying its name. Then the second macro should appear, followed by either another "ADD" card and macro or an "ENDUP" card.

3. It should be noted that every time you replace a macro in the library the space occupied by that macro "goes into hyperspace" and is unusable until the PDS is compressed. Therefore, several replacements will cause much wasted space in the library, and could eventually result in the library running out of usable space. For this reason it is suggested that the user exercise caution and add only debugged macros to the library.

4. If you wish to change the supplied macros without punching out the source and re-adding it, you may use the extended editing features of IEBUPDTE as outlined in the previously mentioned IBM Utilities publication.

### 4.2.5   JCL for Running SIM360

Assuming that the jobs to be processed are in object form and reside in the temporary dataset "&&TEMP", the JCL necessary to run the simulator is:

```
//STEPSIM  EXEC PGM=SIM360,
// PARM='optional parameters'
//STEPLIB   DD  DSNAME=SIM360.LOAD,DISP=SHR
//SIMLIN    DD  DSNAME=&&TEMP,DISP=(OLD,DELETE)
//SYSPRINT  DD  SYSOUT=A
//STRACE    DD  SYSOUT=A
//SIMPRNT   DD  SYSOUT=A
//SIMPRN2   DD  SYSOUT=A
//SIMPRN3   DD  SYSOUT=A
//SIMPRN4   DD  SYSOUT=A
//SIMPNCH   DD  SYSOUT=A
//SIMPNC2   DD  SYSOUT=A
//SIMPNC3   DD  SYSOUT=A
```

```
//SIMPNC4   DD   SYSOUT=A
//SIMIN     DD   *
 _
 I
 I         data cards for virtual reader 00C
 I_

/*
//SIMIN2    DD   *
 _
 I
 I         data cards for virtual reader 012
 I_

/*
//SIMIN3    DD   DUMMY
//SIMIN4    DD   DUMMY
/*
```

The use of the various cards, some of which are optional,  is  as
follows:

  1. //STEPSIM EXEC PGM=SIM360,

This  statement  defines  a  job  step named "STEPSIM" which will
consist  of  the  execution  of  a  program  (PDS  member)  named
"SIM360".  The  comma  after  the program name indicates that the
next card is a continuation of this statement.

  2. // PARM='optional parameters'

This statement (a continuation of the previous one)  defines  the
optional   parameters  to  be  passed  to  the  simulator.  These
parameters control output limits, virtual machine  configuration,
etc.  and  are  in  effect  for each job in the simulator's input
stream.  Refer to section 4.2.6 for a complete discussion.

  3. //STEPLIB  DD   DSNAME=      etc.

This  dataset  definition   (DD)  card  defines  the  partitioned
dataset  which  contains  the  simulator as member "SIM360". This
card may be omitted if the simulator resides in the link library.
for  additional  information  refer  to  IBM  System/360 Operating
System: Job Control Language Reference, IBM publication number
GC28-6704.

  4. //SIMLIN   DD   DSNAME=&&TEMP,DISP=(OLD,DELETE)

This statement defines the input to the simulator,  a  stream  of
object  decks.   This  dataset  will  normally  be  created  in a
previous step and then passed.  If, however, the object decks are
to be read in from cards, the  following  DD  statements  may  be
substituted:

```
//SIMLIN    DD  *
 _
I
I        object decks
I_

/*
```

5. //SYSPRINT DD   SYSOUT=A

In  the  event of a serious error, diagnostic information will be
printed on this dataset.   This  dataset  is  also  used  by  the
maintenance  and debugging features of the simulator, see section
4.2.6.

6. //STRACE    DD   SYSOUT=A

Trace information generated by the simulator is directed to  this
data  set.   Note  that  the  "MAXPGE="  parameter may be used to
prevent an erroneous program from generating too  many  pages  of
trace output.

```
 7. //SIMPRNT   DD   SYSOUT=A
 8. //SIMPRN2   DD   SYSOUT=A
 9. //SIMPRN3   DD   SYSOUT=A
10. //SIMPRN4   DD   SYSOUT=A
```

These  DD statements define the datasets which the simulator will
use for output directed to the virtual machine's  printers.   The
correspondence between virtual machine device (1403 in this case)
addresses and the DD statement names is as follows:

```
     Address    DD Statement Name
     00E        SIMPRNT
     00F        SIMPRN2
     010        SIMPRN3
     011        SIMPRN4
```

The "PRINT=" parameter controls the number of printers configured
to  the virtual machine for a given run (refer to section 4.2.6).
In order to use the 1403 at address 010, we must  have  specified
"PRINT=3"  in  the  PARM  field.  If,  however,  we don't want to
receive output from printers 00E and 00F, we  must  change  those
two DD statements as follows:

```
//SIMPRNT   DD   DUMMY
//SIMPRN2   DD   DUMMY
```

This  will  instruct  the  operating system to discard any output
directed to these two files (printers on  the  virtual  machine),
but  specification  of  either  of these two devices by a program
executing on the virtual machine will cause no error.

```
11. //SIMPNCH   DD   SYSOUT=A
12. //SIMPNC2   DD   SYSOUT=A
13. //SIMPNC3   DD   DUMMY
14. //SIMPNC4   DD   DUMMY
```

These DD statements define the datasets which the simulator will use for virtual card punches. The correspondence between virtual machine device (2540 punches in this case) addresses and DD statement names is:

| Address | DD Statement Name |
|---------|-------------------|
| 000 | SIMPNCH |
| 013 | SIMPNC2 |
| none | SIMPNC3 |
| none | SIMPNC4 |

There is a "PUNCH=" parameter which controls how many punches are configured to the virtual machine. Refer to section 4.2.6 and the previous description of the printer DD statements for help. Also note that there is currently no virtual device that uses file SIMPNC3 or SIMPNC4, but these statements should be included since an error in the "PUNCH=" parameter could cause the simulator to open one of these files.

```
15. //SIMIN    DD   *
16. //SIMIN2   DD   *
17. //SIMIN3   DD   DUMMY
18. //SIMIN4   DD   DUMMY
```

These DD statements define the input datasets which the simulator will use for the virtual card readers. The correspondence between virtual machine device (2540 readers in this case) addresses and DD statement names is:

| Address | DD Statement Name |
|---------|-------------------|
| 00C | SIMIN |
| 012 | SIMIN2 |
| none | SIMIN3 |
| none | SIMIN4 |

The "CARDS=" parameter controls the number of readers configured to the virtual machine. In its current implementation the simulator has no device which uses file SIMIN3 or SIMIN4, but these DD statements should be included as an error in the "CARDS=" parameter could cause the simulator to open one of these files. These DD statements are followed by the cards to be read into the respective virtual reader. These cards should be delimited by a card with "/*" in columns 1-2 and none of the cards to be read into the virtual reader should contain a "//" or "/*" starting in column one.

Alternatively, these DD statements could refer to a disk file. In this case the costs of reading a test deck in each time

could be avoided. These files could easily be built with the  IBM
utility program "IEBGENER".


### 4.2.6  SIM360 Parameters

The 'optional parameters' in the "PARM=" field of the EXEC
statement may specify any combination of the following
parameters, separated by commas with no imbedded blanks. The
defaults which the simulator assumes for each parameter are
underlined.


MAXTIME=n - n must be a positive decimal integer which
    represents the maximum amount of simulated real time in
    milliseconds which will be allowed to elapse for each
    program. Default is 1000, or one second.

MAXCOUNT=n - n must be a positive decimal integer which
    represents the maximum number of instructions which the
    simulator will execute for each program. Default is
    5000.

MAXPGE=n - n must be a positive decimal integer which
    represents the maximum number of pages of trace output
    which will be allowed for each program. Default is 5.

CARDS=0,1,2,3,4 - The number of virtual card readers
    configured to the simulator. A value of 1 causes 00C
    (SIMIN) to be configured by itself, a value of 2 causes
    both 00C and 012 (SIMIN2) to be configured, a value of
    3 causes 00C, 012 and file SIMIN3 to be configured -
    although no device uses this file this parameter really
    establishes the presence or absence of a file instead
    of a virtual device. A value of 4 causes file SIMIN4 to
    be added to the group of available files.

PUNCH=0,1,2,3,4 - The number of virtual card punches
    configured to the virtual machine. Corresponding DD
    statements are SIMPNCH - SIMPNC4. Only two 2540 card
    reader-punches are available in the current version of
    the simulator; the card input/output streams 3 and 4
    are available for expansion.

PRINT=0,1,2,3,4 - The number of virtual printers configured
    to the virtual machine. Corresponding DD statements are
    SIMPRNT - SIMPRN4.

PNCHDEST=PRNT,PNCH - Output directed to virtual card punches
    is by default formatted for printing (carriage control
    characters prefixed) to allow inspection.  If  PNCH  is
    coded, however, no carriage control characters will be
    prefixed to records so they may be punched. Note that

the output class of the punch files will have to be
changed to direct output to a card punch (i.e. change
SYSOUT=A to SYSOUT=B).

PGMINT=YES,NO - If 'NO', then a program interrupt which
    occurs after a program interrupt and before a PSW swap
    will cause the simulator to print a diagnostic and
    terminate the program. 'YES' causes the simulator to
    ignore this condition.

TRACE=ALL,NONE - If 'ALL', then every instruction causes the
    standard trace message to be printed. Otherwise, only
    trace conditions enabled dynamically by the program are
    printed.


The following options are for maintenance and debugging use only.
Note that they can cause many thousands of lines to be printed on
SYSPRINT.


TDUMP=0,1,2 - '1' causes the trace queue to be dumped every
    time a new trace condition is enabled. '2' causes a
    trace queue dump as for '1', and in addition on every
    occasion when a trace message is printed. '0' inhibits
    all trace queue dumps.

IQDUMP=0,1,2,3 - '1' causes the interrupt and event queue to
    be dumped each time an I/O interrupt occurs. '2'
    causes the channel specification block and the I/O
    specification block to be dumped after the initiation
    of each device operation. '3' causes both of the
    above. '0' inhibits all dumps.

PDUMP=YES,NO - The simulator's link-loader module will print
    relevant information on programs loaded and initiation
    of simulation if "YES".


        Any error in the parameter field causes the simulator to
print a terse error message and the run is terminated after the
remaining parameters have been scanned for validity. Hence all
possible errors in a parameter string will be "caught" in one
run. A correct parameter string:

// PARM='MAXTIME=10000,MAXCOUNT=4000,CARDS=2,PRINT=3,MAXPGE=11'

This string results in a virtual machine configuration of two
card readers, three printers, and one card punch which prints its
output. Each program which runs under this machine will be
allowed to execute 4,000 instructions in 10 seconds of simulated
real time, and print 11 pages of trace output.

## 4.2.7  Running a Job Stream on SIM360

The previous section describing the JCL for running SIM360 assumed that a temporary dataset named "&&TEMP" had been created containing the object decks for the program(s) to be run. SIM360 has been designed to read this file and if more than one CSECT is present each will be executed in a "batching" kind of operation. This is to cut down on the overhead of initializing SIM360 for each student in a class run.

This gives rise to three possible scenarios for using SIM360:

1. If an object deck already exists in a dataset, the SIMLIN data definition statement in the previous JCL could be changed to point to this dataset (or to DD * if you have a deck).

2. You can use the standard IBM F level assembler to assemble each deck in one job step, concatenating the output, and then execute the simulator as another step. Requiring n+1 job steps for a run of n students. If this technique was chosen you would probably provide an in-line procedure as described later.

3. You could use a batching assembler, such as the Waterloo G-level to assemble all of the students at once, producing a stream of object decks, and then execute the simulator as one step, simulating all students.

Discounting the first case as pathological, the third case is of primary interest in that it is potentially much cheaper for a run of several students at once.

The following section describes JCL for methods two and three.

JCL for Method 2:

```
//ASSEM    EXEC PGM=IEUASM,PARM='NODECK,LOAD'
//SYSPRINT DD   SYSOUT=A
//SYSLIB   DD   DSN=SIM360.MACLIB,DISP=SHR
//SYSUT1   DD   UNIT=SYSDA,SPACE=(CYL,(2,1))
//SYSUT2   DD   UNIT=SYSDA,SPACE=(CYL,(2,1))
//SYSUT3   DD   UNIT=SYSDA,SPACE=(CYL,(2,1))
//SYSLIN   DD   DSN=&&TEMP,DISP=(MOD,PASS),
//              UNIT=SYSDA,SPACE=(CYL,(1,1)),
//              DCB=(RECFM=FB,LRECL=80,BLKSIZE=1600)
//SYSIN    DD   *
```

```
|    SINGLE STUDENT SOURCE DECK
|_

/*
    .
    . as many assembly steps as students
    .
//STEPSIM EXEC PGM=SIM360,
    .
    . rest of SIM360 step JCL described previously
    .
```

JCL for Method 3:

```
//ASSEM    EXEC PGM=ASMBLRG,PARM='NODECK,LOAD,BATCH'
//SYSPRINT DD   SYSOUT=A
//SYSLIB   DD   DSN=SIM360.MACLIB,DISP=SHR
//SYSUT1   DD   UNIT=SYSDA,SPACE=(CYL,(2,1))
//SYSUT2   DD   UNIT=SYSDA,SPACE=(CYL,(2,1))
//SYSUT3   DD   UNIT=SYSDA,SPACE=(CYL,(2,1))
//SYSLIN   DD   DSN=&&TEMP,DISP=(MOD,PASS),
//              UNIT=SYSDA,SPACE=(CYL,(2,1)),
//              DCB=(RECFM=FB,LRECL=80,BLKSIZE=1600)
//SYSIN    DD   *
 _
|
|         Assembler source deck 1
|         Assembler source deck 2
|              .
|         Assembler source deck n
|_

/*
//STEPSIM EXEC PGM=SIM360,
    .
    . rest of SIM360 JCL described previously
    .
```

Macro Library:

        In  both  of  these  methods  the  dataset  referred  to  as
"SIM360.MACLIB"  should  be  a partitioned dataset containing the
TRACE, TRACEOFF, and QUIT macros, as well as any macros  required
by  a  particular  assignment  (such as BUCKET).  The creation of
this dataset has been described previously.

Student Decks:

        Each student deck must consist of only one  S/360  assembler
language  control  section.   The  simulator's loader cannot link
control sections, properly process external symbols, or  relocate

to a base address other than zero. To enable all of the simulator output to be easily collated, the name (label) on the .CSECT card is used by the simulator as an identifying tag on all output. A student deck should therefore look like;

```
          TITLE  'student name - instructor name'
name      CSECT
          .
          . student assembler program
          .
          END
```

Where name is the name that will be used to identify a student's output. For a more complete discussion of deck requirements see section 4.1.2.

## 4.3  Maintenance Manual

### 4.3.1  Overview

The Simulator is composed of four major modules coded in PL/1:

1. SIMLINK - Performs initialization including the processing of parameters, and then establishes a simple batching monitor. This monitor reads one object deck at a time from the simulator input file and loads it into a virtual core array.

2. SIMCPU - Handles the simulation of CPU functions including instruction execution, timer handling, and DMA data transfers. This module is called by SIMLINK once it has loaded a student, and returns to SIMLINK when a student has finished execution so SIMLINK can load the next student (if any).

3. TRACE - Interprets dynamic trace commands and performs the processing and formatting associated with trace output.

4. SIMIO - Performs all processing related to I/O instructions, CCW's, and coordinates the I/O subsystems.

In addition to these four major components, there is a very small (52 instruction) assembly language subroutine which simulates fullword multiplication and division. This is for efficiency's sake as PI/1 does not allow for FIXED BINARY(63) variables.

### 4.3.2  Module SIMLINK

Parameter Processing:

This module contains the initial entry point to the simulator. First the parameters passed to the simulator from the "PARM=" field on the EXEC card are processed. Processing is very straightforward and is outlined in Figure 4.3.1. Refer to section 4.2.6 for further information on parameter key-words and their effect.

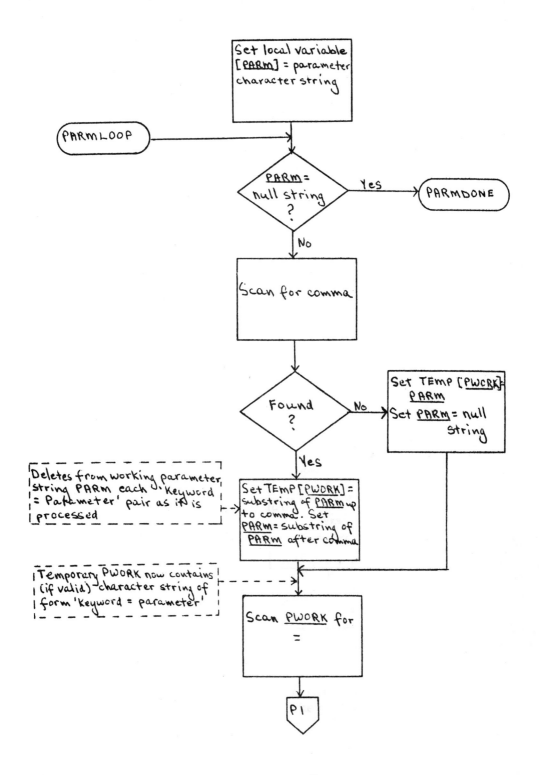

Figure 4.3.1
Parameter Processing

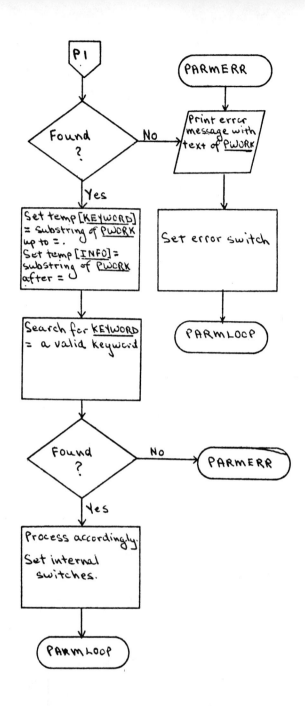

Figure 4.3.1
(continued)
Parameter Processing

| Valid Keywords | Internal Switches or Variables Affected |
|----------------|------------------------------------------|
| MAXTIME | MAXT |
| MAXCOUNT | MAXI |
| TRACE | TSWITCH |
| PGMINT | PGM_SW |
| CARDS | NOINSTR |
| PUNCH | NOPNSTR |
| PRINT | NOPRSTR |
| MAXPGE | MXPGCNT |
| PNCHDEST | PPRNTSW |
| TDUMP | TQDMPSW |
| IQDUMP | CDDMPSW, IQDMPSW |
| PDUMP | PDUMPSW |

Figure 4.3.1
(continued)
Parameter Processing

Program Loading:

     When  parameter processing is completed, the error switch is
tested and if an  error  has  occurred  the  program  terminates.
Otherwise, some initialization is performed (at the label RESTRT;
see  Figure  4.3.2),  and the output data set of the assembler is
implicitly opened and the first card read.
     Of the five valid record types produced  by  the  assembler,
only  three  are  processed by the assembler; RLD and SYM records
are ignored (without causing an error condition).  The ESD record
is used to establish the identifying name of  the  program  being
simulated.   If  the conventions for program preparation outlined
in section 4.1.2 are followed, this will be the name  (label)  on
the  CSECT  card  of the program being simulated. The END record
signals the end of the program and causes the  actual  simulation
process  to  be  initiated.   TXT  records supply the text of the
program and are loaded into the virtual core array PROG.  This is
a one dimensional array of aligned eight bit  elements  which  is
used to represent the core storage of the simulated computer.

Figure 4.3.2 shows the logical flow of the loading process.  Note
that  if  an invalid card type is detected or the student program
does not initialize the first eight bytes of core  storage  (used
as  the  initial  PSW)  the program will not be "executed".  Also
note that when the simulation of one program is finished  (return
from call to SIMCPU), SIMLINK reinitializes and continues to load
following  programs,  terminating  only  when  an  end  of  file
condition on the input stream occurs.

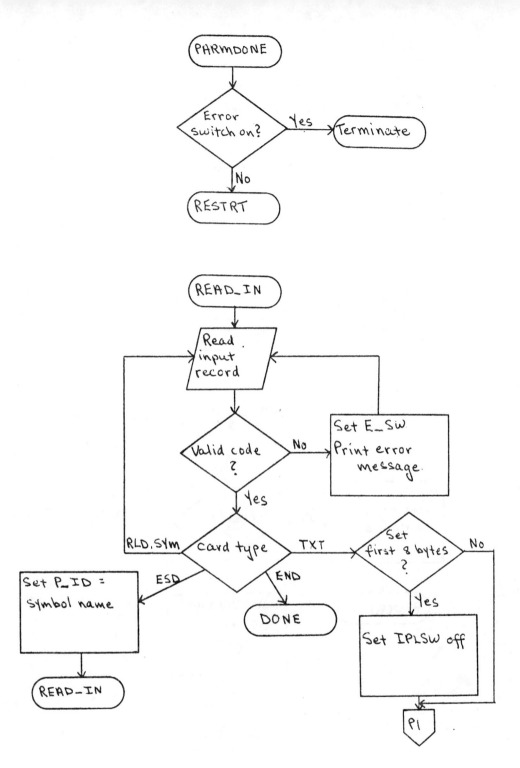

Figure 4.3.2
Program Loading

303

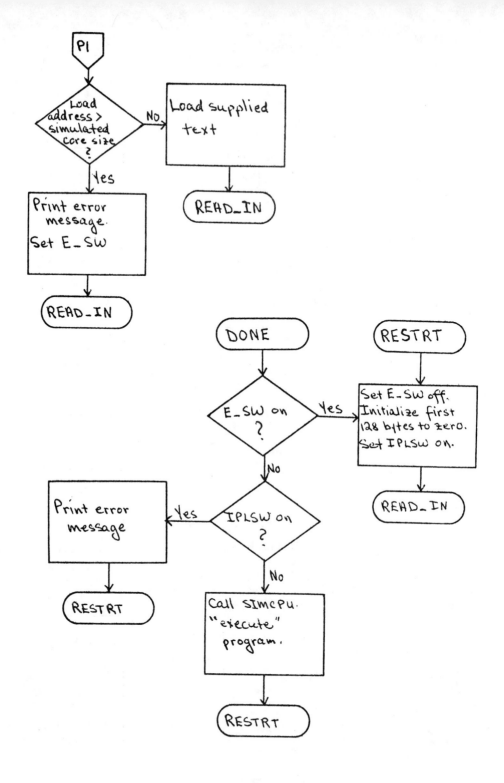

Figure 4.3.2
(continued)
Program Loading

304

### 4.3.3  Module SIMCPU

Start Up and Initialization:

On entry to this module various variables are initialized, and two calls are made to initialization entry points in the modules SIMIO and TRACE (SIMIO and SIMTRAS, respectively). The first operand address is forced to zero and the LPSW instruction is given control to load the initial PSW.

Instruction Simulation:

Instruction simulation, in itself, is quite straightforward. The interpretation and decoding of the instructions (Figure 4.3.3) is not quite so simple, and the actions taken after the completion of the simulation of each instruction are quite complex. Figure 4.3.3 shows the outline of the algorithm for instruction interpretation; reference should be made, if necessary, to IBM System/360 Principles of Operation.

Given the information in Figure 4.3.3 and the diagram showing the accessing scheme for the virtual core array (Figure 4.3.4), understanding the code which simulates the various instructions is straitforward (most instructions involve only four or five lines of PL/1 code).

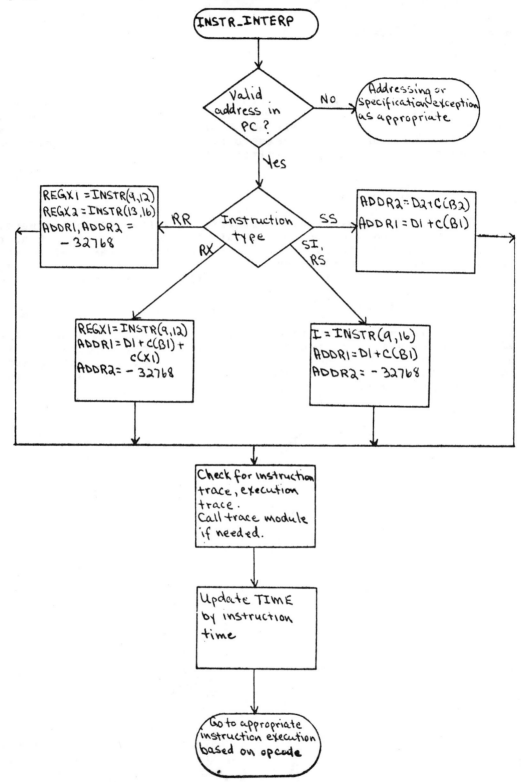

Figure 4.3.3
Instruction Interpretation

| Variable | Represents |
|----------|------------|
| ADDR1 | Address of operand one (if present- RX, SI, RS format instructions). |
| ADDR2 | Address of operand two (if present- SS format instructions only). |
| I | Value of operand two (if an immediate operand) or value of count field (if SS format instruction). |
| REGX1 | R1 specification for general purpose register operand (if RR or RX format). |
| REGX2 | R2 specification for general purpose register operand (if RR format). |

Figure 4.3.3
(continued)
Instruction Interpretation


PROG(BYTES,8 BITS)              |_|_|_|_|_|_|_|_|_|_|_|_|_|_|_|_|

BIT_HW(HALFWORD,16 BITS)        |___|___|___|___|___|___|___|___|

HW(HALFWORD,SIGN and 15 BITS)   |___|___|___|___|___|___|___|___|

BIT_FW(FULLWORD,32 BITS)        |_____|_____|_____|_____|

FW(FULLWORD,SIGN and 31 BITS)   |_____|_____|_____|_____|

BIT_DBL(DOUBLEWORD,64 BITS)     |_____|_____|


Figure 4.3.4
Accessing the Virtual Core Aray

As shown in Figure 4.3.4, the virtual core array may be accessed in six ways:

1) As a byte - 8 bit logical value.
2) As a halfword - 16 bit logical value.
3) As a halfword signed integer in the range  -32,768  to 32,767.
4) As a fullword - 32 bit logical value.
5) As a fullword signed integer in the range  -(2**31)  to (2**31)-1.
6) As a doubleword - 64 bit logical value.

The general purpose registers are also represented by an array (extent 16 -- 0:15) and are accessed in the same way as 32 bit logical, 31 bits with sign integer, and 64 bit logical values. The frequently referenced procedures AL_PROT and PROT check operand locations for boundary alignment (AL_PROT only), address tracing requests, and memory protection violation (see Figure 4.3.5).


Post-Instruction Processing:

After the execution of each instruction, and before interpreting the next instruction, the simulator must check for a variety of conditions, and perform the necessary processing associated with the conditions found.


Timer Updating and Interrupt Scheduling:

The label ND (very rarely ND2) is the point where post instruction processing begins. The instruction count is updated (and checked against the allowed maximum), and the simulated real time (R_TIME) is updated by the execution time of the instruction just completed (nominally: value of temp TIME). Then the timer counter (T_TIME) is updated and a check is made to see if 3,333 microseconds or more (virtual time) have elapsed since the timer was last decremented.

If this condition exists, then the simulated timer (fullword at location 80) is decremented by an appropriate amount, and, if the timer has gone from a positive to a negative value as a result, appropriate interrupt processing is done. If the system mask allows external interrupts (bit 7 = 1) then the interrupt is taken immediately; if external interrupts are masked off, the interrupt is scheduled to occur as soon as the external interrupt mask bit is set to allow the interrupt.

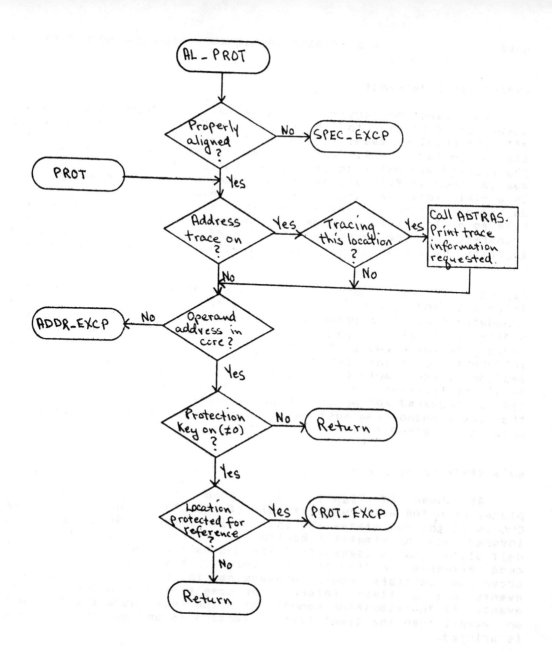

Figure 4.3.5
Alignment and Protection Checking

Search For Interrupt:

When timer processing is completed, the interrupt and event queue is searched to see if any pending (or previously masked off) interrupt or event is due to occur. An event occurs when its scheduled time (in the queue entry) is less than or equal to the elapsed virtual time in the simulation. However, an event due to occur in time may not take place, because, for example, it is a timer interrupt and the external interrupt mask bit is zero. An event which is not an interrupt might be the transfer of a byte to or from core storage by a channel in the process of data transfer, or the occurrence of a device end for an operation initiated by a channel command word with the command chaining bit on.

Figure 4.3.6 shows the outline of this process. Note that the interrupt and event queue is maintained in sorted order by scheduled time of occurrence, and that masked interrupts are simply left at the head of the queue, and thus will be examined every time the queue is searched. As shown in the figure, if an interrupt or event occurs, the post instruction processing section of the simulator is re-entered at the timer processing point (effectively the start of the section). This is because time is required for an interrupt or event to take place, and thus the elapsed time must be again updated, and a possible timer interrupt checked for.

Wait State Processing:

As shown in Figure 4.3.6, if no interrupt or event takes place, then the wait/run state bit of the CPU is checked. If the CPU is in the run state, the instruction interpretation code is invoked and the simulator continues. If the processor is in the wait state, then a somewhat clumsy and hard to follow section of code attempts to find the next point in time when an event will occur and possibly cause processing to continue. Candidate events are a timer interrupt or some type of I/O interrupt or event. If the simulator cannot determine that there exists such an event, then the simulation is terminated and an error message is printed.

Program Interrupts:

Program interrupts fall outside of the structure outlined above. Most program interrupts cannot be masked, and those which can be masked do not remain pending until enabled; they are completely ignored.

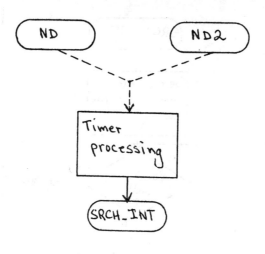

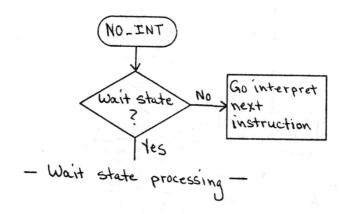

Figure 4.3.6
Interrupt and Event Processing

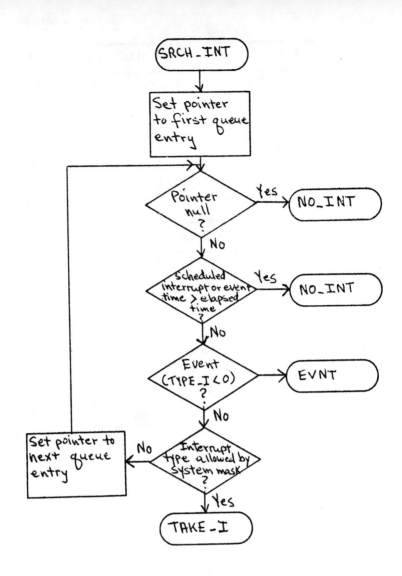

Figure 4.3.6
(continued)
Interrupt and Event Processing

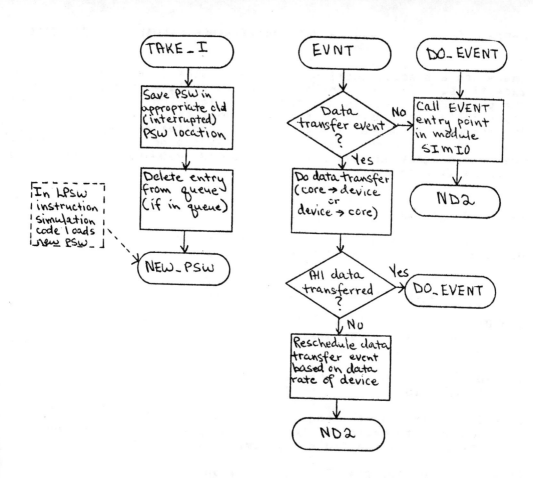

Figure 4.3.6
(continued)
Interrupt and Event Processing

Therefore a special section of code handles detected program
exceptions.   This routine sets the appropriate interrupt code in
the program old PSW (simulated core location 40), and after
appropriate processing goes to the label TAKE_1 in Figure 4.3.6.
The appropriate processing may include completing an arithmetic
operation in which overflow was detected or perhaps detecting
that the program exception which occurred was masked off, and
ignoring it altogether.


### 4.3.4  Module SIMIO

     This module has six separate entry points to perform
different functions related to I/O.  The entry points are:

SIMIO - Initialize the control blocks and data sets
     associated with I/O device simulation.

SIMIOT - Called to clean up I/O simulation on termination of
     program being simulated. Closes data sets, flushes
     buffers, etc.

HALTIO   -  Performs   processing   associated   with   HIO
     instruction.

STARTIO - Implements the SIO instruction.   Initiates
     appropriate device activity as specified by the CCW and
     the state of the I/O subsystem.

TESTIO - Simulates the TIO instruction by examining the
     state of the simulated I/O subsystem and the specified
     device, and appropriately setting the condition code
     and the status portion of the channel status word.

EVENT - Performs the processing associated with the
     occurence of an I/O event.

     Before attempting to understand the functioning of the I/O
simulation module, it is extremely important to understand in
detail the operation of the S/360 I/O subsystems. Because the
S/360 can accomodate an extremely wide range of I/O devices and
because the I/O capabilities of the 360 are very powerful, I/O
operations are quite complex. If you are not very familiar with
S/360 I/O you are encouraged to carefully study the I/O section
of Principles of Operation in conjunction with this guide and the
program listing of SIMIO.


I/O Initialization:

     As mentioned before, one of the first steps in
initialization for simulation is to call the initialization entry
point SIMIO in the I/O simulation module. Initialization is

quite straightforward.  All channels and devices are put  in  the
available  state, printer and card punch data sets are opened and
identifying headers are written, and a few entries in the  device
specification  blocks  are  initialized  to  put  the system in a
clean, ready for operation state.


I/O Termination:

The I/O termination function simply checks   to   see  if  any
data  is  contained  in the device specification blocks which has
been output by the program being simulated, but has not yet  been
written  to the appropriate print or punch data set.  If there is
any such data, it is punched or printed.


Halt I/O Instruction:

The entry point HALTIO, in simulating the  HIO  instruction,
first checks whether or not the addressed channed is operating in
burst  mode.  If the channel is so operating then the device with
which the  channel  is  communicating  is  determined,  the  data
transfer  operation is terminated, and appropriate interrupts are
scheduled.  If  the  channel  is  available,  then  the addressed
device is found and its state examined.

If  the  addressed device is working, then any data transfer
in progress (there may  be  data  transfer  in  progress  on  the
multiplexor  channel  without being in burst mode) is terminated,
and all interrupts which would normally  occur  due  to  device
operation  are  scheduled  to  occur (with appropriate changed to
reflect the HIO).  The condition code is set, and. the  simulation
of  the  HIO  is  completed.  Figure 4.3.7 shows the operation of
this routine.


Test I/O Instruction:

The entry point TESTIO first checks for the channel  working
state  (burst  operation), and, if found, sets the condition code
appropriately ('10'B) and returns.

315

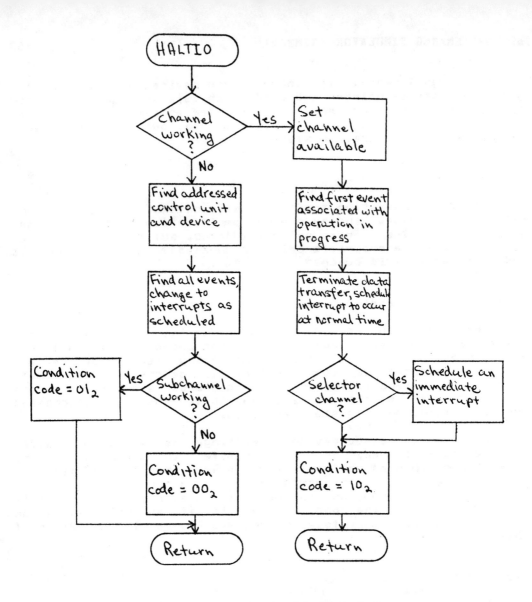

Figure 4.3.7
Simulation of Halt I/O

316

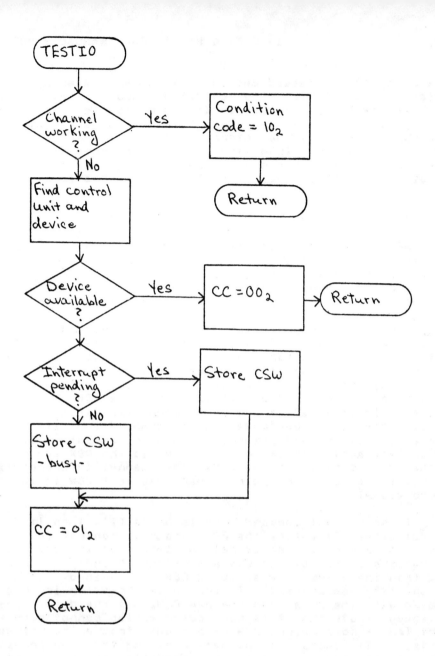

Figure 4.3.8
Simulation of Test I/O

Otherwise, the addressed device is found and examined. If the device is available, the condition code is set ("00"B) and a return to caller is executed. If the device is in the interrupt pending state, then the CSW information associated with the interrupt is stored, the interrupt is cleared, and the condition code is set to "01"B (CSW stored). If the device is working, the busy bit is set in the stored CSW, and the condition code is set to "01"B. See Figure 4.3.8 for further information.

Start I/O:

Upon entry to the STARTIO routine the channel and device are checked for availability. If one or the other is not available, action very similar to that of TESTIO for the corresponding situation is taken. If both the channel and device are available, the channel interpretation code is entered.

Channel interpretation starts by checking the channel address word (location 72 (dec)) for validity, and, if valid, setting the protection key and the CCW address. The channel command word location is checked against the key for fetch protection, and if no protection error is found, the CCW is fetched and the CCW address is updated. The CCW is first checked to see if it is a TIC (transfer in channel). If it is, then some validity checks are performed on the command and its occurrence (i.e., a TIC cannot start a command chain). If invalid, appropriate action is taken, and if valid the CCW address is set to the address given in the TIC. The channel interpretation code is reentered at the point where the next CCW is fetched (see Figure 4.3.9).

If the channel command word is not a TIC, then it is checked for validity. If valid, the PCI (program controlled interrupt) flag is examined, and if set, an interrupt is scheduled. Then the various fields of the CCW are extracted and the chain data flag from the previously executed CCW is examined. If chain data is on, the parameters of the data transfer is progress are updated with the data from the new CCW, and the data transfer is continued (note that this particular action cannot result from a start I/O -- no previous CCW -- but only from an event; see "I/O events". If there is no data chaining from the previous CCW, then a processing routine for the specific device is called to initiate the operation specified by the CCW.

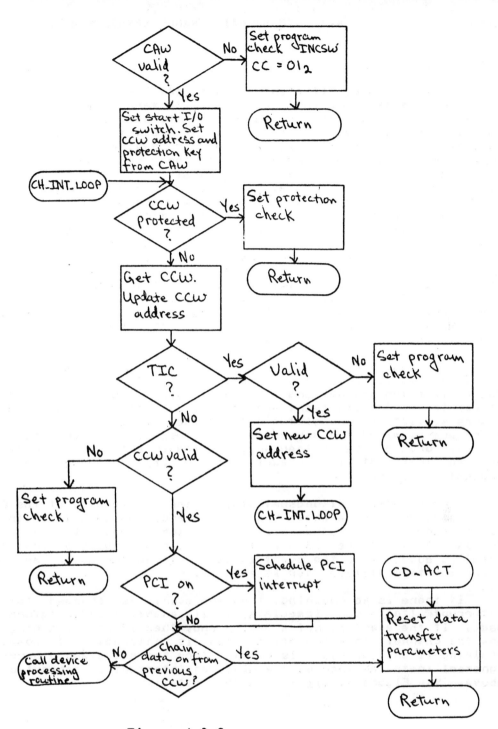

Figure 4.3.9
Channel Interpreter

319

I/O Events:

There are three different types of I/O events.  Two are data
transfer events, and their occurrence is marked by the transfer
of one or more bytes from virtual core storage to a simulated
device, or vice versa.  The remaining event type is associated
with the occurrence of a channel end or device end condition
which arises in the process of an input or output operation.
Since the termination of data transfer sometimes (on a
multiplexor channel, for example) causes a channel end condition,
a data transfer event is acted upon exactly as a normal (third
type discussed above) event when the last byte of data specified
by the operation has been transferred (see Figure 4.3.6).

All three event types are kept in the interrupt and event
queue in sorted order by time of occurrence.  They are placed in
the queue by the device processing routines and contain
information that reflects the characteristics of the device and
the operation being performed.  Figure 4.3.10 shows the PL/1
declaration of an entry in the interrupt or event queue, with
comments explaining the items.

The event processing routine (EVENT in SIMIO) handles only
normal events (data transfers are done in SIMCPU).  Upon entry to
the routine the channel and device involved in the operation
associated with the event are determined (using E_CH and E_DEV,
Figure 4.3.10) and the status bits of the CSW associated with the
event are examined for unusual status (usually an error).   If
there is unusual status then any chaining in effect is cancelled,
and an interrupt is scheduled to notify the program of the
unusual condition.

In the absence of unusual status, the status bits of the CSW
are tested for device end.  Upon device end, and data if chaining
is present, the channel interpretation loop is entered
(CH_INT_LOOP, Figure 4.3.9).  If command chaining is on from the
previous queue, then the event is deleted from the queue, and the
channel interpretation loop is entered.

If there is no chaining, then the event is changed to an
interrupt (to occur immediately, if enabled) and a return is
made.  If the event is not a device end, then if data chaining is
on, the channel interpretation loop is entered.  If command
chaining is on, the event is deleted from the queue and otherwise
ignored; in the absence of chaining, an interrupt is scheduled as
above.  See Figure 4.3.11 for further detail.

```
DECLARE
    1 INT_Q BASED(P_CI),                  /* QUEUE ENTRY */
        2 PREV_I POINTER,                 /* NULL IF FIRST ENTRY
                                             IN QUEUE */
        2 NEXT_I POINTER,                 /* NULL IF LAST ENTRY */
        2 TIME_I DEC FLOAT,               /* SCHEDULED TIME OF
                                             OCCURRENCE */
        2 P_DEV_DATA POINTER,             /* LOCATES DATA AT THE
                                             DEVICE */
        2 E_CH POINTER,                   /* IDENTIFIES ASSOCIATED
                                             CHANNEL */
        2 E_DEV POINTER,                  /* IDENTIFIES ASSOCIATED
                                             DEVICE */
        2 TIME_INTRVL DEC FLOAT,          /* FOR DATA TRANSFER EVENTS-
                                             TIME BETWEEN TRANSFERS */
        2 TYPE_I FIXED BIN(15),           /* NEGATIVE FOR EVENTS */
        2 CODE_I BIT(16) ALIGNED,         /* DEVICE ADDR. FOR PSW */
        2 CSW_I BIT(64) ALIGNED,          /* CSW ASSOCIATED WITH
                                             INTERRUPT OR EVENT */
        2 CORE_INDEX FIXED BIN(15),       /* CORE LOCATION FOR NEXT
                                             BYTE TRANSFER */
        2 DEV_INDEX FIXED BIN(15),        /* IDENTIFIES NEXT BYTE
                                             TRANSFER AT THE DEVICE */
        2 DATA_COUNT FIXED BIN(15),       /* NO. OF BYTES TO BE
                                             TRANSFERRED */
        2 INCREM FIXED BIN(15),           /* NEGATIVE FOR READ
                                             BACKWARD */
        2 CH_STAT CHAR(1),                /* A, I, or W. STATUS
                                             AFTER OCCURRENCE */
        2 DEV_STAT CHAR(1),               /* LIKEWISE FOR DEVICE */
        2 MASK_I BIT(8) ALIGNED,          /* .AND. WITH SYS. MASK TO
                                             SEE IF INTERRUPT ENABLED */
        2 IO_PROT BIT(4) ALIGNED;         /* PROTECTION KEY ASSOCIATED
                                             WITH OPERATION */
```

Figure 4.3.10
Interrupt and Event Queue Entries

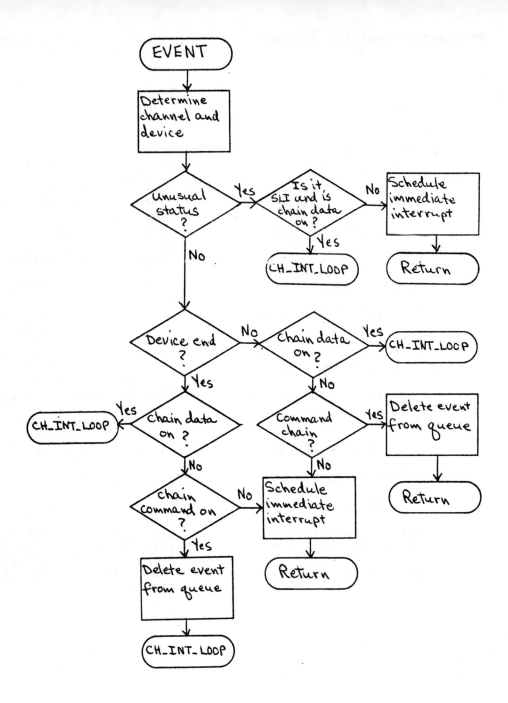

Figure 4.3.11
Event Processing

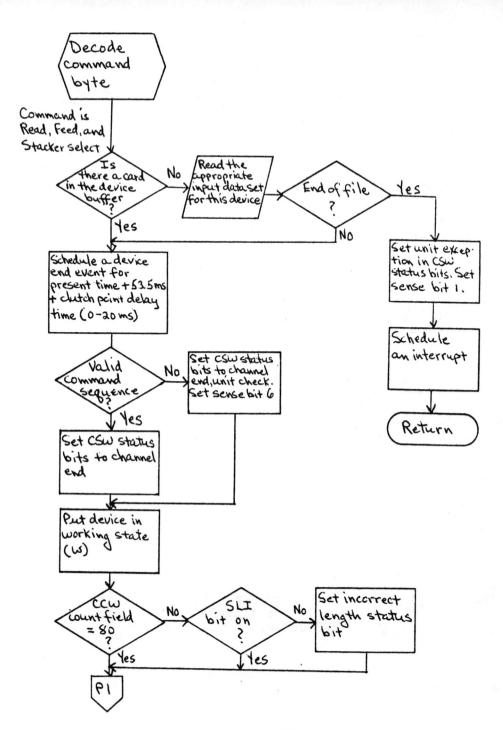

Figure 4.3.12
RFS Command to Card Reader

323

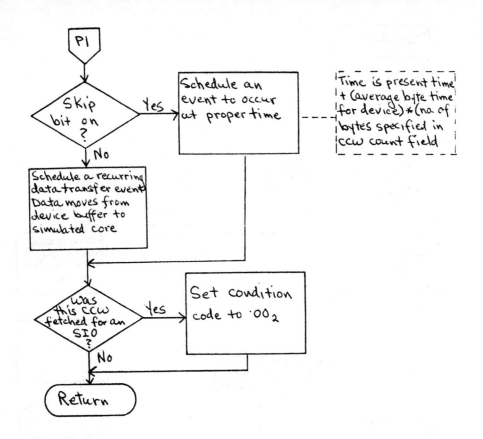

Figure 4.3.12
(continued)
RFS Command to Card Reader

Device Simulation Routines:

The details of the simulation of an I/O operation to a given device are handled by a set of routines, one for each class of devices (see Figure 4.3.9). Each individual device is defined by a device specification block (DSB) which contains all necessary information about the device and its current state; one piece of this information identifies the particular device routine which is used in simulating the device.

The device routines decode the command byte from the CCW and initiate appropriate action. Entries are placed in the interrupt and event queue as necessary. Any necessary I/O operations are performed, as in the case of a simulated card reader where an input data set of the simulator supplies the "cards" for the simulated reader. All relevant command information is checked for validity and proper sequence (there are invalid command sequences on many devices), and appropriate error action is taken if an anomaly is detected.

Since these routines vary widely in form with the device simulated, an example of such a routine is shown in some detail in Figure 4.3.12, but no attempt will be made to explain in detail the functioning of each such routine. The appropriate reference manual for a device will provide detailed information on its performance, and a complete understanding of the behavior of the device will tend to lead to an understanding of the device simulation routine.

## 4.3.5  Module TRACE

There are 9 entry points to this module, two to process dynamic trace requests by the simulated program, and 6 to do the formatting and printing associated with a trace message. The entry points are:

TRACE - Enables a trace condition in accordance with information supplied in the trace request.

NO_TRAS - Turns off any existing trace conditions of the type specified.

BTRACE - Called to do printing associated with a branch trace.

ITRACE - Called to do an instruction trace.

NTRACE - Called to do an interrupt trace.

ADTRAS - Called to do an address trace.

**ETRACE** - Called to do an execution trace.

**CTRACE** - Called to do a channel trace.

**SIMTRAS** - Initializes for simulation.

The processing done by the TRACE module is not particularly interesting or difficult to understand. With a few exceptions, it consists of getting such and such a field to print in character position n, and thus is painfully detailed but conceptually unchallenging. Discussion will therefore be brief.


Dynamic Trace Requests:

A trace request extracts information compiled into the program code by the TRACE macro instruction, checks it for validity, and makes an entry in the trace queue, a list of enabled trace conditions. Figure 4.3.13 shows the data format in the program code, and Figure 4.3.14 gives the PL/1 structure declaration of an entry in the trace queue.

The transformation from one to the other is almost one for one, and quite obvious. One item of interest is that if invalid data is found in a trace request, it is assumed that the program being simulated has erroneously modified instruction locations. In this case, an attempt is made to find the end of trace request flag, and if it can be found, the invalid trace request is ignored; otherwise, an operation exception (program interrupt for invalid op-code) is taken.

There is a separate routine to process each type of trace request, but they are very small (about five PL/1 statements) and are necessary only because a different internal indicator for each trace type is used to indicate that a trace condition is enabled.

A Traceoff command is processed at entry point NO_TRAS, and simply removes from the trace list the particular instance of the trace type specified, or, if ALL of the given type were specified, then every instance.

```
           DS    0H                ALIGN ON HALFWORD BOUNDARY
           DC    X'02'             TRACE OP-CODE
           DC    X'0n'             TRACE TYPE AS FOLLOWS:
*                                          0: BRANCH
*                                          1: INSTRUCTION
*                                          2: ADDRESS
*                                          3: INTERRUPT
*                                          4: EXECUTION
*                                          5: CHANNEL
*                                          6: UNUSED
*                                          7: UNUSED
*                                          8: DUMP
           DC    XL2'id'           INTERPRETATION DEPENDS ON TYPE,
*                                  HOLDS ADDRESS, OPCODE, INT.
*                                  TYPE, ETC.
           DC    BL2'sbsw'         BIT SWITCHES FOR STATUS DUMP
           DC    BL2'rbsw'         REGISTERS TO DUMP
*
*                FOLLOWING PAIRS ARE CORE DUMP SPECIFICATIONS:
*
           DC    AL2(address)      FIRST ADDRESS TO BE DUMPED
           DC    AL1(n,s)          n - NUMBER OF WORDS TO DUMP,
*                                  s - INDIRECT SWITCH
*
*                THERE MAY BE UP TO EIGHT PAIRS, TERMINATED
*                BY THE FOLLOWING STOPPER:
*
           DC    XL2'8000'         STOPPER
```

Figure 4.3.13
TRACE Macro Data

```
DECLARE
     1 TRACE_LIST BASED(P_C),              /* TRACE QUEUE ENTRY */
          2 PREV POINTER,                  /* NULL FOR FIRST */
          2 NEXT POINTER,                  /* NULL FOR LAST */
          2 TYPE FIXED BIN(15),            /* TYPE OF TRACE */
          2 ID BIT(16) ALIGNED,            /* DEPENDS ON TYPE */
          2 STATUS BIT(16) ALIGNED,        /* STATUS SWITCHES */
          2 REGS BIT(16) ALIGNED,          /* REGISTERS TO DUMP */
          2 DUMP_OPTIONS(8),               /* CORE PAIRS */
               3 ADDRESS FIXED BIN(15),    /* STARTING ADDRESS */
               3 DCOUNT FIXED BIN(15),     /* WORD COUNT */
```

Figure 4.3.14
Trace Queue Entries

327

Trace Output Routines:

The six entry points dealing with trace output have very similar functions. The trace list is searched for the entry associated with the trace condition. Note that because the Traceoff command only removes the entry from the trace list, the internal indicator which flags a trace condition may still be set. In this case, when the list is searched, no corresponding entry will be found, and the output routine will then reset the internal indicator and return. In the more normal case, where an entry is found in the trace list, then a call is made to an internal procedure (TDUMP) which formats and prints the trace output as specified by the information in the trace queue entry.

It should be noted that the snapshot (DUMP) type is something of an exception. Because the dynamic trace request is, in effect, the trace condition in this case, a slightly different sequence of events results. However, examination of the code will show that no difficulties are involved. Using existing code and procedures, a DUMP trace request:

1. Sets up an entry in the trace list in the normal way.

2. Calls TDUMP in the normal way to print the information requested.

3. Enters the NO_TRAS routine in an appropriate place to delete from the trace list the entry created in the first step above.

4. Returns to caller (SIMCPU).

```
 _____
|              |
| CHAPTER  5   |
|_____|
```

## 5.1  INTRODUCTION

This chapter describes four exercises designed to introduce a student to the concepts and nuances of interrupt and I/O programming on the IBM 360 or 370. These problems are graduated in complexity and difficulty, the last one requiring much time and effort.

Since these problems require a student to use privileged instructions, they obviously may not be run under a standard operating system. Running student assignments on a bare machine is inefficient and does not provide the student with any helpful debugging information. These problems may be run using a "virtual machine" provided by the IBM VM/370 operating system with great efficiency and improved debugging ease. As a third approach, we have developed a System 360 simulator (SIM360, see chapter 4) which allows these problems to be run under a standard IBM operating system, albeit at a fair cost in terms of machine resources. This simulator provides essentially a bare 360 with 32 K-bytes of memory, while itself running as a problem program of a standard operating system.

Chapter 4 provides the information necessary for installing and running this simulator, as well as a student's guide to the simulator.  In this chapter we assume that the student programs are run using the simulator. If you wish to run these problems on a virtual machine system, you are on your own.

If you use the simulator each student should have a copy of the SIM360 User's Guide, the student assignment for the given problem,  and the Principles Of Operation for either a 360 or 370 (IBM publication GA22-6821 or GA22-7000).

329

## 5.2   STUDENT ASSIGNMENTS

### 5.2.1   Instruction Simulation Problem -- OS1

Introduction:

Whereas the IBM 360/370 series is upwards compatible, i.e., any program which works on a 360 will work on a 370, there is not complete downwards compatibility.   The 370's possess several instructions not present on 360's. In general, programs which are marketed make use of only instructions present on both  machines. Using a 370-specific instruction on a 360 machine will cause a program interruption due to an operation exception. This is  very disruptive to the program trying to run.

It is possible to write a program interrupt handler to intercept operation exceptions and provide a simulator for missing instructions. Although such a project would be expensive to run in terms of CPU and interrupt overhead,  it  would  enable programs using "370-specific" instructions  to be run on a 360 without modification.


Problem Description:

Your assignment is to write a program interrupt  handler which detects an attempted execution of the 370 instruction Store Characters Under Mask (STCM), and then correctly simulates its execution.   Your interrupt handler must not alter the contents of any registers, and when simulation of the STCM is complete  it should continue executing  the  interrupted program at the next instruction.

We have provided a macro which generates a program  to  test your  interrupt handler. This program enables tracing for program interrupts, generates several operation exceptions (some  due  to STCM),  and  prints information concerning whether or not your handler appears to work correctly. The name  of  this  macro  is STCMTEST. You should code it  in your program and branch to a label placed on it, as follows:

```
         .                       INITIALIZATION
         .
         .
         B     TEST              START TESTING HANDLER
         .
TEST     STCMTEST                GENERATE TESTING PROGRAM
         END
```

STCMTEST should be coded at the end of your program,  as  it generates USING and DROP instructions.

Algorithm:

The following algorithm may be used for your program
interrupt handler:

1.  Save the general purpose registers. This is necessary
    to return to the point of interruption without changing
    the enviroment.

2.  Check the interruption code in the Program Old PSW
    (bytes 42 and 43, decimal) for operation exception
    (X'0001'). If not, load the program old PSW (byte 40,
    decimal) to return. This ignores non operation
    exception interrupts.

3.  When a program interrupt occurs, the PSW points to the
    next instruction to be executed, while the Instruction
    Length Counter contains the length of the most recently
    attempted instruction.

    Pick up the instruction address from the PSW.
    Then using the ILC, "back up" this address to the
    offending instruction. Remember that the ILC is
    expressed in 2-byte units.

4.  Check the offending instruction to see if it is a STCM
    (op-code X'BE'). If it isn't, then return. This ignores
    operation exceptions caused by non-STCM instructions.

5.  Decode the instruction to get the operand-two address
    and the masked bytes from the register, and simulate
    execution. This simulation potentially changes the
    contents of memory at the location specified by operand
    two.

6.  Return to the interrupted program and resume processing
    at the next instruction.

Description of the STCM instruction:

The STCM instruction is an RS type with an op-code of X'BE':

STCM R1,M3,D2(B2)

| BE | R1 | M3 | B2 | D2 |
|----|----|----|----|----|
| 0  | 8  | 12 | 16 20 | 31 |

The bits of the mask (M3, bits 12-15) are used to form a
variable length field. The register specified by R1 is viewed as
four contiguous bytes. From left to right these bytes are
associated with the corresponding bit in the mask. If a bit of
the mask is on, the corresponding byte is appended to the right

of a control string, which is initialized to null.

    If all the bits are zero, the control string is null, if one bit is on the string is one byte long, two bits-two bytes, and so on. After this control string is formed, it is stored in ascending locations starting at the byte addressed by the B2-D2 pair. If the control string is null, no store operation takes place, else the correct number of bytes are stored.


**Example STCM Execution:**

    Before Execution:    Reg. 1: 00000090    Reg. 2: 01020304
                         Loc. 90: 00000000 00000000

    STCM Instruction:    STCM  2,X'5',0(1)   **SELECT 1 & 3**

    After Execution:     Registers are unchanged
                         Loc. 90: 02040000 00000000


**Notes:**

    1. When you continue an interrupted program, none of the registers should be modified. The STCM macro will check this.

    2. You will not be given any invalid STCM instructions, but if you treat a non-STCM instruction as a STCM, you may experience errors.

    3. If you incorrectly decode the memory address you may receive an addressing exception.

    4. You should read the SIM360 User's Guide to learn how to use the TRACE macro instruction. The STCMTEST macro enables tracing of program interrupts, but you may want to follow control in your program, perhaps with TRACE DUMP instructions.

Deck Setup:

    Your deck should have the following structure:

```
$JOB name
            TITLE 'your name - your instructors name'
name        CSECT
            PRINT NOGEN
            .
            .                         LOW CORE DEFINITION
            .
START       EQU   *                   ANY INITIALIZATION
            .
            B     TEST                START TEST
            .
TEST        STCMTEST                  GENERATE TEST PROGRAM
            LTORG
            END
$EOJ
```

    Where  name  will be used to identify your simulator output.
You should use your last name, truncated if  necessary  to  eight
characters, or prefixed with qualifiers.


Run Schedule:

    TO BE ANNOUNCED

Example Program:

    This  program intercepts and ignores all program
interrupts. You may use it as a model for your program:

---

EXAMPLE PROGRAM FOR INTERRUPT AND I/O PROBLEM OS1                                    PAGE    1

LOC  OBJECT CODE      ADDR1 ADDR2  STMT   SOURCE STATEMENT                           31 DEC 74

```
000000                                 2 EXAMPLE CSECT
000000                                 3          USING EXAMPLE,0           ASSEMBLE ABSOLUTE ADDRESSES

                                       5 ***********************************************************************
                                       6 *                                                                     *
                                       7 *          THIS EXAMPLE DEMONSTRATES USE OF THE STCM TESTING MACRO.    *
                                       8 *          THE PROVIDED PROGRAM INTERRUPT HANDLER MERELY RETURNS       *
                                       9 *          FROM EACH INTERRUPT.                                        *
                                      10 *                                                                     *
                                      11 ***********************************************************************

                                      13 ***********************************************************************
                                      14 *                                                                     *
                                      15 *          LOW CORE INTIALIZATION                                     *
                                      16 *                                                                     *
                                      17 ***********************************************************************

000000 FE00000000000084              19 IPLPSW  DC   X'FE',AL3(0),A(START) INITIAL PSW LOADED TO START RUN
000008 0C00C0C000000000              20 IPLCCW1 DC   D'0'                   IPL CCW'S WHICH
000010 000000000000000               21 IPLCCW2 DC   D'0'                    ARE NOT USED
000018 000000000000000               22 EXTOLD  DC   D'0'                   EXTERNAL OLD PSW
000020 C00000000000000               23 SUPOLD  DC   D'0'                   SUPERVISOR OLD PSW
000028 C00000000000000               24 PGMOLD  DC   D'0'                   PROGRAM CHECK OLD PSW
000030 000000000000000               25 MCKOLD  DC   D'0'                   MACHINE CHECK OLD PSW
000038 CC00C000000000000             26 IOOLD   DC   D'0'                   INPUT/OUTPUT OLD PSW
000040 00000C0C000000000             27 CSW     DC   D'0'                   CHANNEL STATUS WORD
000048 0000C000                      28 CAW     DC   F'0'                   CHANNEL ADDRESS WORD
00004C 0000C000                      29 UNUSED1 DC   F'0'                   UNUSED WORD 1
000050 C0000C000                     30 TIMER   DC   F'0'                   TIMER AREA
000054 0000C000                      31 UNUSED2 DC   F'0'                   UNUSED WORD 2
000058 0002000000000001              32 EXTNEW  DC   X'0002',AL2(0),A(1)   EXTERNAL NEW PSW- CAUSES HALT
000060 0C0200C0u0000002              33 SUPNEW  DC   X'0002',AL2(0),A(2)   SUPERVISOR NEW PSW- CAUSES HALT
000068 00000C000000080               34 PGMNEW  DC   A(0,PGMINT)            PROGRAM CHECK NEW PSW
000070 0002000000000004              35 MCKNEW  DC   X'0002',AL2(0),A(4)   MACHINE CHECK NEW PSW- CAUSES HALT
000078 0002000000000005              36 IONEW   DC   X'0002',AL2(0),A(5)   INPUT/OUTPUT NEW PSW- CAUSES HALT

000080                               38 PGMINT  EQU  *

                                      40 ***********************************************************************
                                      41 *                                                                     *
                                      42 *          PROGRAM INTERRUPT HANDLER -- INTERRUPTS MASKED OFF          *
                                      43 *                                                                     *
                                      44 *          NOTE THAT THIS INTERRUPT HANDLER RETURNS DIRECTLY TO THE    *
                                      45 *          POINT OF INTERRUPTION WITH NO PROCESSING.                   *
                                      46 *                                                                     *
                                      47 ***********************************************************************

0C0080 8200 0028      0C028         49          LPSW PGMOLD              "RETURN" TO POINT OF INTERRUPTION
```

334

```
         EXAMPLE PROGRAM FCR INTERRUPT AND I/O PROBLEM OS1                                              PAGE    2

     LCC  CBJECT CCDE   ACCR1 ACDR2  STMT  SOURCE STATEMENT                                             31 DEC 74
                                       51 START     STCMTEST                       GENERATE TESTING PROGRAM

                                       53+************************************************************************
                                       54+*                                                                   *
                                       55+*                         STCM   TEST MACRO FOR OS1                  *
                                       56+*                                                                    *
                                       57+*            THIS MACRO GENERATES FIVE TRIALS FOR THE OS1 PROBLEM.   *
                                       58+*       TO START TESTING, BRANCH TO THE CODE GENERATED BY THIS       *
                                       59+*       MACRO. NOTE- THIS MACRO MAY BE BRANCHED TO ONLY ONCE.        *
                                       60+*                                                                    *
                                       61+************************************************************************
     000000                            63+          USING EXAMPLE,0 .           ASSEMBLE ABSOLUTE REFERENCES
     000084 980F 0350          00350   64+START     LM    0,15,SRGR0000 .       LOAD REGISTERS FOR TESTING


     000088                            67+          DS    OH
     000088 0208                       68+          DC    AL1(2,8) TRACE OP-CODE AND TYPE(KLUDGE)
     00008A C000                       69+          DC    XL2'0' ID.
     00008C CC00                       70+          DC    BL2'0000000000000000'
     00008E FFFF                       71+          DC    BL2'1111111111111111'
     000090 0324                       72+          DC    Y(SM10C000)
     000092 CC06                       73+          DC    AL1(0,6) WORD COUNT AND INDIRECT
     000094 8C00                       74+          DC    XL2'8000'


     000096                            77+          DS    OH
     00C096 0203                       78+          DC    AL1(2,3) TRACE OP-CODE AND TYPE(KLUDGE)
     000098 0002                       79+          DC    H'2' ID.
     00009A 0000                       80+          DC    BL2'0000000000000000'
     00009C CC00                       81+          DC    BL2'0000000000000000'
     00009E 8000                       82+          DC    XL2'8000'


     0000A0                            86+          DS    OH
     0C00A0 0208                       87+          DC    AL1(2,8) TRACE OP-CODE AND TYPE(KLUDGE)
     0000A2 0000                       88+          DC    XL2'0' ID.
     0000A4 C000                       89+          DC    BL2'0000000000C000000'
     0000A6 CC00                       90+          DC    BL2'0000000000000000'
     0000A8 00B0                       91+          DC    Y(STR10000)
     0000AA 0001                       92+          DC    AL1(0,1) WORD COUNT AND INDIRECT
     0000AC 8C00                       93+          DC    XL2'8000'


     0000AE 0700                       95+          CNOP  0,4 .                  FORCE ALIGNMENT FOR TRACE DUMP
     0000B0 5808 E000          00000   96+STR10000 L     0,0(8,14) .            GENERATE TRIAL 1 - ADDRESS EXCEPTION

     0000B4 9COF 0390          00390   98+          STM   0,15,STGR0000 .     SAVE STUDENT'S REGISTERS
     0000B8 D53F 0390 0350 00390 00350 99+          CLC   STGR0000(64),SRGR0000
```

335

EXAMPLE PROGRAM FOR INTERRUPT AND I/O PROBLEM OS1                                    PAGE    3

```
  LOC  OBJECT CODE    ADDR1 ADDR2  STMT  SOURCE STATEMENT                                  31 DEC 74

0000BE 4780 00D4            000D4  100+          BE    ST1ROK00 .       IF REGISTERS NOT MODIFIED

0000C2                             102+          DS    0H
0000C2 0208                        103+          DC    AL1(2,8) TRACE OP-CODE AND TYPE(KLUDGE)
0000C4 0000                        104+          DC    XL2'0' ID.
0000C6 0000                        105+          DC    BL2'0000000000000000'
0000C8 FFFF                        106+          DC    BL2'1111111111111111'
0000CA 02F4                        107+          DC    Y(SBRS0000)
0000CC 0007                        108+          DC    AL1(0,7) WORD COUNT AND INDIRECT
0000CE 8000                        109+          DC    XL2'8000'

0000D0 980F 0350            00350  111+          LM    0,15,SRGR0000 .     RESTORE REGISTERS

0000D4 0507 03E8 03D0 003E8 003D0  113+ST1ROK00 CLC   SANS0000(8),ST1A0000 CHECK ANSWER
0000DA 4780 00F4            000F4  114+          BE    ST1AOK00 .          IF OK, TELL STUDENT

0000DE                             117+          DS    0H
0000DE 0208                        118+          DC    AL1(2,8) TRACE OP-CODE AND TYPE(KLUDGE)
0000E0 C000                        119+          DC    XL2'0' ID.
0000E2 0000                        120+          DC    BL2'0000000000000000'
0000E4 0000                        121+          DC    BL2'0000000000000000'
0000E6 0310                        122+          DC    Y(SBAI0000)
0000E8 0005                        123+          DC    AL1(0,5) WORD COUNT AND INDIRECT
0000EA 03E8                        124+          DC    Y(SANS0000)
0000EC 0002                        125+          DC    AL1(0,2) WORD COUNT AND INDIRECT
0000EE 8000                        126+          DC    XL2'8000'

0000F0 47F0 0102            00102  128+          B     ST200000 .          GO TO NEXT TRIAL

0000F4                             131+          DS    0H
0000F4 0208                        132+ST1AOK00 DC     AL1(2,8) TRACE OP-CODE AND TYPE(KLUDGE)
0000F6 0000                        133+          DC    XL2'0' ID.
0000F8 C000                        134+          DC    BL2'0000000000000000'
0000FA 0000                        135+          DC    BL2'0000000000000000'
0000FC 02E4                        136+          DC    Y(SAOK0000)
0000FE 0004                        137+          DC    AL1(0,4) WORD COUNT AND INDIRECT
000100 8000                        138+          DC    XL2'8000'

000102 D707 03E8 03E8 003E8 003E8  140+ST2CC000 XC    SANS0000(8),SANS0000 CLEAR ANSWER AREA

000108                             142+          DS    0H
000108 0208                        143+          DC    AL1(2,8) TRACE OP-CODE AND TYPE(KLUDGE)
00010A C000                        144+          DC    XL2'0' ID.
00010C C000                        145+          DC    BL2'0000000000000000'
00010E CC00                        146+          DC    BL2'0000000000000000'
000110 0118                        147+          DC    Y(STR20000)
```

336

```
LOC   OBJECT CODE     ADDR1 ADDR2  STMT    SOURCE STATEMENT

000112 CC01                          148+        DC    AL1(0,1) WORD COUNT AND INDIRECT
000114 8000                          149+        DC    XL2'8C00'

000116 0700                          151+        CNOP  0,4 .                       FORCE ALIGNMENT FOR TRACE DUMP
000118 BE08F003                      152+STR2C000 DC   X'BE08F003' .               TRIAL 2 STCM 0,8,3(15)

00011C 900F 0390            00390    154+        STM   0,15,STGRCC00 .             SAVE REGISTERS FOR CHECK
000120 D53F 0390 0350 00390 00350    155+        CLC   STGR0000(64),SRGR0000 CHECK STUDENT'S REGISTERS
000126 4780 013C            0013C    156+        BE    ST2ROK00 .                  REGISTERS ARE OK

00012A                               159+        DS    0H
00012A 0208                          160+        DC    AL1(2,8) TRACE OP-CODE AND TYPE(KLUDGE)
00012C 0000                          161+        DC    XL2'0' ID.
00012E 0000                          162+        DC    BL2'0000000000000000'
000130 FFFF                          163+        DC    BL2'1111111111111111'
000132 02F4                          164+        DC    Y(SBRS0000)
000134 0007                          165+        DC    AL1(0,7) WORD COUNT AND INDIRECT
000136 8C00                          166+        DC    XL2'8000'

000138 980F 0350            00350    168+        LM    0,15,SRGR0000 .             RESTORE REGISTERS

00013C D507 03E8 03D8 003E8 003D8    170+ST2ROK00 CLC  SANSC000(8),ST2A0000 . CHECK ANSWER
000142 4780 016E            0016E    171+        BE    ST2AOK00 .                  ANSWER OK

000146                               174+        DS    0H
000146 0208                          175+        DC    AL1(2,8) TRACE OP-CODE AND TYPE(KLUDGE)
000148 C000                          176+        DC    XL2'0' ID.
00014A 0000                          177+        DC    BL2'0000000000000000'
00014C 0000                          178+        DC    BL2'0000000000000000'
00014E 0310                          179+        DC    Y(SBAI0000)
000150 0005                          180+        DC    AL1(0,5) WORD COUNT AND INDIRECT
000152 03E8                          181+        DC    Y(SANS0000)
000154 0002                          182+        DC    AL1(0,2) WORD COUNT AND INDIRECT
000156 8000                          183+        DC    XL2'8000'

000158                               186+        DS    0H
000158 0208                          187+        DC    AL1(2,8) TRACE OP-CODE AND TYPE(KLUDGE)
00015A 0000                          188+        DC    XL2'0' ID.
00015C 0000                          189+        DC    BL2'0000000000000000'
00015E C000                          190+        DC    BL2'0000000000000000'
000160 033C                          191+        DC    Y(SM200000)
000162 0005                          192+        DC    AL1(0,5) WORD COUNT AND INDIRECT
000164 03D8                          193+        DC    Y(ST2A0000)
000166 0002                          194+        DC    AL1(0,2) WORD COUNT AND INDIRECT
000168 8000                          195+        DC    XL2'8000'
```

| LOC | OBJECT CODE | ADDR1 ADDR2 | STMT | SOURCE STATEMENT | | | |
|-----|-------------|-------------|------|------------------|---|---|---|

```
00016A 47F0 0180            00180   197+    B     ST3C0000 .         GO TO NEXT TRIAL


00016E                              200+    DS    0H
00016E 0208                         201+ST2A0K00 DC   AL1(2,8) TRACE OP-CODE AND TYPE(KLUDGE)
000170 0000                         202+    DC    XL2'0' ID.
000172 0000                         203+    DC    BL2'0000000000000000'
000174 0000                         204+    DC    BL2'0000000000000000'
000176 02E4                         205+    DC    Y(SAOK0000)
000178 C004                         206+    DC    AL1(0,4) WORD COUNT AND INDIRECT
00017A 03E8                         207+    DC    Y(SANS0000)
00017C 0002                         208+    DC    AL1(0,2) WORD COUNT AND INDIRECT
00017E 8000                         209+    DC    XL2'8000'


000180 D707 03E8 03E8 003E8 003E8   212+ST3C0000 XC  SANS0000(8),SANS0000 CLEAR ANSWER AREA


000186                              214+    DS    0H
000186 0208                         215+    DC    AL1(2,8) TRACE OP-CODE AND TYPE(KLUDGE)
000188 0000                         216+    DC    XL2'0' ID.
00018A 0000                         217+    DC    BL2'000000C000000000'
00018C 0000                         218+    DC    BL2'0000000000000000'
00018E 0194                         219+    DC    Y(STR30000)
000190 0001                         220+    DC    AL1(0,1) WORD COUNT AND INDIRECT
000192 8C00                         221+    DC    XL2'8000'


000194                              223+    CNOP  0,4 .              FORCE ALIGNMENT
000194 5208F003                     224+STR30000 DC  X'5208F003' TRIAL 3 OPERATION EXCEPTION

000198 900F 0390            00390   226+    STM   0,15,STGR0000 .    SAVE REGISTERS FOR CHECK
00019C D53F 0390 0350 00390 00350   227+    CLC   STGR0000(64),SRGR0000 CHECK STUDENT'S REGISTERS
0001A2 4780 0188            00188   228+    BE    ST3ROK00 .         REGISTERS OK


0001A6                              231+    DS    0H
0001A6 0208                         232+    DC    AL1(2,8) TRACE OP-CODE AND TYPE(KLUDGE)
0001A8 0000                         233+    DC    XL2'0' ID.
0001AA 0000                         234+    DC    BL2'0000000000000000'
0001AC FFFF                         235+    DC    BL2'1111111111111111'
0001AE 02F4                         236+    DC    Y(SBRS0000)
0001B0 CC07                         237+    DC    AL1(0,7) WORD COUNT AND INDIRECT
0001B2 8000                         238+    DC    XL2'8000'


0001B4 980F 0350            00350   240+    LM    0,15,SRGR0000 .    RESTORE REGISTERS

0001B8 D507 03E8 03D0 003E8 003D0   242+ST3ROK00 CLC  SANS0000(8),ST3A0000 CHECK STUDENT'S ANSWER
0001BE 4780 01D8            001D8   243+    BE    ST3A0K00 .         ANSWER CORRECT
```

```
LOC   OBJECT CODE    ADDR1 ADDR2  STMT   SOURCE STATEMENT

0001C2                            245+        DS   0H
0001C2 0208                       246+        DC   AL1(2,8) TRACE OP-CODE AND TYPE(KLUDGE)
0001C4 CC00                       247+        DC   XL2'0' ID.
0001C6 0000                       248+        DC   BL2'0000000000000000'
0001C8 C000                       249+        DC   BL2'0C00000000000000'
0001CA 0310                       250+        DC   Y(SBAI0000)
0001CC 0005                       251+        DC   AL1(0,5) WORD COUNT AND INDIRECT
0001CE 03E8                       252+        DC   Y(SANSC000)
0001D0 CC02                       253+        DC   AL1(0,2) WORD COUNT AND INDIRECT
0001D2 8000                       254+        DC   XL2'8000'


0001D4 47F0 01E6        001E6     256+        B    ST400000 .        GO TO NEXT TRIAL


0001D8                            259+        DS   0H
0001D8 0208                       260+ST3A0K00 DC  AL1(2,8) TRACE OP-CODE AND TYPE(KLUDGE)
0001DA C000                       261+        DC   XL2'0' ID.
0001DC CC00                       262+        DC   BL2'0000000000000000'
0001DE 0000                       263+        DC   BL2'0000000000000000'
0001E0 02E4                       264+        DC   Y(SA0KC000)
0001E2 CC04                       265+        DC   AL1(0,4) WORD COUNT AND INDIRECT
0001E4 8000                       266+        DC   XL2'8000'


0001E6 D707 03E8 03E8 003E8 003E8 269+ST400000 XC SANS0000(8),SANS0C00 CLEAR ANSWER AREA


0001EC                            271+        DS   0H
0001EC 0208                       272+        DC   AL1(2,8) TRACE OP-CODE AND TYPE(KLUDGE)
0001EE 0000                       273+        DC   XL2'0' ID.
0001F0 CC00                       274+        DC   BL2'0000000000000000'
0001F2 0000                       275+        DC   BL2'0000000000000000'
0001F4 01FC                       276+        DC   Y(STR4C000)
0001F6 0001                       277+        DC   AL1(0,1) WORD COUNT AND INDIRECT
0001F8 8C00                       278+        DC   XL2'8000'


0001FA 0700                       280+        CNOP 0,4 .             FORCE ALIGNMENT
0001FC BE02F000                   281+STR40000 DC  X'BE02F000' .     TRIAL 4 STCM 0,2,0(15)

000200 900F 0390         00390    283+        STM  0,15,STGR0000 .   SAVE REGISTERS FOR CHECK
000204 D53F 0390 0350 00390 00350 284+        CLC  STGR0000(64),SRGR0000 CHECK STUDENT'S REGISTERS
00020A 4780 0220         00220    285+        BE   ST4R0K00 .        REGISTERS ARE OK


00020E                            288+        DS   0H
00020E 0208                       289+        DC   AL1(2,8) TRACE OP-CODE AND TYPE(KLUDGE)
000210 C000                       290+        DC   XL2'0' ID.
000212 0000                       291+        DC   BL2'0000000000000000'
000214 FFFF                       292+        DC   BL2'1111111111111111'
000216 02F4                       293+        DC   Y(SBRS0000)
```

339

| LOC | OBJECT CODE | ADDR1 ADDR2 | STMT | SOURCE STATEMENT | | 31 DEC 74 |
|---|---|---|---|---|---|---|

```
000218 C007                          294+        DC   AL1(0,7) WORD COUNT AND INDIRECT
00021A 8000                          295+        DC   XL2'8000'


00021C 980F 0350        00350        297+        LM   0,15,SRGR0000 .   RESTORE REGISTERS

000220 D507 03E8 03E0 003E8 003E0    299+ST4ROK00 CLC  SANS0000(8),ST4A0000 CHECK STUDENT'S ANSWER
000226 4780 0252        00252        3C0+        BE   ST4AOK00 .         ANSWER IS COOL, TELL STUDENT


00022A                               302+        DS   0H
00022A 0208                          303+        DC   AL1(2,8) TRACE OP-CODE AND TYPE(KLUDGE)
00022C C000                          304+        DC   XL2'0' ID.
00022E 0000                          305+        DC   BL2'0000000C000000000'
000230 0000                          306+        DC   BL2'0000000000000000'
000232 0310                          307+        DC   Y(SBAI0000)
000234 0005                          308+        DC   AL1(0,5) WORD COUNT AND INDIRECT
000236 03E8                          309+        DC   Y(SANS0000)
000238 0002                          310+        DC   AL1(0,2) WORD COUNT AND INDIRECT
00023A 8000                          311+        DC   XL2'8C00'


00023C                               314+        DS   0H
00023C 0208                          315+        DC   AL1(2,8) TRACE OP-CODE AND TYPE(KLUDGE)
00023E 0000                          316+        DC   XL2'0' ID.
000240 C000                          317+        DC   BL2'0000000000000000'
000242 0000                          318+        DC   BL2'0000000000000000'
000244 033C                          319+        DC   Y(SM200000)
000246 C005                          320+        DC   AL1(0,5) WORD COUNT AND INDIRECT
000248 03E0                          321+        DC   Y(ST4A0000)
00024A 0002                          322+        DC   AL1(0,2) WORD COUNT AND INDIRECT
00024C 8C00                          323+        DC   XL2'8000'


00024E 47F0 0264        00264        325+        B    ST500000 .        GO TO NEXT TRIAL


000252                               328+        DS   0H
000252 0208                          329+ST4AOK00 DC   AL1(2,8) TRACE OP-CODE AND TYPE(KLUDGE)
000254 0000                          330+        DC   XL2'0' ID.
000256 0000                          331+        DC   BL2'00000CC0000C00000'
000258 CC00                          332+        DC   BL2'00000CC000000000'
00025A 02E4                          333+        DC   Y(SAOK0000)
00025C 0004                          334+        DC   AL1(0,4) WORD COUNT AND INDIRECT
00025E 03E8                          335+        DC   Y(SANS0000)
000260 0002                          336+        DC   AL1(0,2) WORD COUNT AND INDIRECT
000262 8000                          337+        DC   XL2'8000'


000264 D707 03E8 03E8 003E8 003E8    340+ST500000 XC   SANS0000(8),SANS0000 CLEAR ANSWER AREA
```

| LCC | CBJECT CCDE | ACCR1 ACCR2 | STMT | SOURCE STATEMENT | 31 DEC 74 |
|---|---|---|---|---|---|

```
0C026A                                 342+      DS      OH
00026A 0208                            343+      DC      AL1(2,8) TRACE OP-CODE AND TYPE(KLUDGE)
00026E 0000                            344+      DC      XL2'0' ID.
00026E CC00                            345+      DC      BL2'0000000000000000'
000270 C000                            346+      DC      BL2'0000000000000000'
000272 0278                            347+      DC      Y(STR5C000)
000274 CC01                            348+      DC      AL1(0,1) WORD COUNT AND INDIRECT
000276 8C00                            349+      DC      XL2'8000'

000278                                 351+      CNOP    0,4 .                FORCE ALIGNMENT FOR DUMP
000278 BE00F000                        352+STR50000 DC   X'BE00F000' .        TRIAL 2 - STCM 0,0,0(15)

00027C 900F 0390            00390      354+      STM     0,15,STGR0000 .      SAVE REGISTERS FOR CHECK
000280 D53F 0390 0350 0C390 00350      355+      CLC     STGR0000(64),SRGR0000 CHECK STUDENT'S REGISTERS
000286 4780 029C                 0029C 356+      BE      ST5ROK00 .           REGISTERS ARE OK

00028A                                 359+      DS      OH
00028A A 0208                          360+      DC      AL1(2,8) TRACE OP-CODE AND TYPE(KLUDGE)
00028C CC00                            361+      DC      XL2'0' ID.
00028E 0000                            362+      DC      BL2'0000000000000000'
000290 FFFF                            363+      DC      BL2'1111111111111111'
000292 02F4                            364+      DC      Y(SBRS0000)
000294 0007                            365+      DC      AL1(0,7) WORD COUNT AND INDIRECT
000296 8000                            366+      DC      XL2'8000'

000298 980F 0350            00350      368+      LM      0,15,SRGR0000 .      RESTORE REGISTERS

00029C D507 03E8 03D0 003E8 003D0      370+ST5ROK00 CLC  SANS0000(8),ST5A0000 CHECK STUDENT'S ANSWER
0002A2 4780 02CE                 002CE 371+      BE      ST5A0K00 .           ANSWER IS CORRECT

0002A6                                 373+      DS      OH
0002A6 0208                            374+      DC      AL1(2,8) TRACE OP-CODE AND TYPE(KLUDGE)
0002A8 C000                            375+      DC      .XL2'0' ID.
0002AA C000                            376+      DC      BL2'0000000000000000'
0002AC C000                            377+      DC      BL2'0000000000000000'
0002AE 0310                            378+      DC      Y(SBAI0000)
0002B0 0C05                            379+      DC      AL1(0,5) WORD COUNT AND INDIRECT
0002B2 03E8                            380+      DC      Y(SANS0000)
0002B4 0002                            381+      DC      AL1(0,2) WORD COUNT AND INDIRECT
0002B6 8000                            382+      DC      XL2'8000'

0002B8                                 385+      DS      OH
0002B8 0208                            386+      DC      AL1(2,8) TRACE OP-CODE AND TYPE(KLUDGE)
0002BA C000                            387+      DC      XL2'0' ID.
0002BC 0000                            388+      DC      BL2'0000000000000000'
0002BE 0000                            389+      DC      BL2'0000000000000000'
0002C0 C33C                            390+      DC      Y(SM200000)
```

EXAMPLE PROGRAM FOR INTERRUPT AND I/O PROBLEM OS1                                    PAGE   9

```
LOC   OBJECT CODE     ADDR1 ADDR2   STMT   SOURCE STATEMENT                          31 DEC 74

0002C2 0005                         391+          DC    AL1(0,5) WORD COUNT AND INDIRECT
0002C4 03D0                         392+          DC    Y(ST5A0000)
0002C6 0002                         393+          DC    AL1(0,2) WORD COUNT AND INDIRECT
0002C8 8C00                         394+          DC    XL2'8000'


0002CA 47F0 02E0         002E0      396+          B     ST600000 .         GO TO NEXT TRIAL


0002CE                              399+          DS    0H
0002CE 0208                         400+ST5AOK00  DC    AL1(2,8) TRACE OP-CODE AND TYPE(KLUDGE)
0002D0 0000                         401+          DC    XL2'0' ID.
0002D2 0000                         402+          DC    BL2'0000000000000000'
0002D4 C000                         403+          DC    BL2'0000000000000000'
0002D6 02E4                         404+          DC    Y(SAOK0000)
0002D8 0004                         405+          DC    AL1(0,4) WORD COUNT AND INDIRECT
0002DA 03E8                         406+          DC    Y(SANS0000)
0002DC 0002                         407+          DC    AL1(0,2) WORD COUNT AND INDIRECT
0002DE 8C00                         408+          DC    XL2'8C00'


0002E0                              411+ST600000  DS    0H
0002E0 FF777777                     412+          DC    X'FF777777'

0002E4                              414+          CNOP  0,4 .               FORCE WORD ALIGNMENT FOR DUMPS
0002E4 40C1D5E2E6C5D940             415+SAOK0000  DC    C' ANSWER CORRECT '
0002F4 D9C5C7C9E2E3C5D9             416+SBRS0000  DC    C'REGISTERS HAVE BEEN CHANGED '
000310 C1D5E2E6C5D940C9             417+SBAI0000  DC    C'ANSWER INCORRECT--> '
000324 D9C5C7C9E2E3C5D9             418+SM100000  DC    C'REGISTERS FOR TESTING: '
00033C C1D5E2E6C5D940E2             419+SM200000  DC    C'ANSWER SHOULD BE:    '
000350 0102030400000001             420+SRGR0000  DC    X'01020304',F'1,2,3,4,5,6,7,0,9,10,11,12,13'
000388 FFFFFFFF000003E8             421+          DC    X'FFFFFFFF',A(SANS0000)
000390 0000000000000000             422+STGR0000  DC    16F'0'
0003D0                              423+ST1A0000  EQU   * .                 ANSWER FOR TRIAL ONE
0003D0                              424+ST3A0000  EQU   * .                 ANSWER FOR TRIAL THREE
0003D0 0000000000000000             425+ST5A0000  DC    XL8'00' .           ANSWER FOR TRIAL FIVE
0003D8 0000000100000000             426+ST2A0000  DC    X'0000000100000000' ANSWER FOR TRIAL TWO
0003E0 0300000000000000             427+ST4A0C00  DC    X'0300000000000000' ANSWER FOR TRIAL FOUR
0003E8 0C00000C000000000            428+SANS0000  DC    D'0' .              STUDENT'S ANSWER AREA

                                    430           END
```

```
MASSACHUSETTS INSTITUTE OF TECHNOLOGY          SYSTEM / 360 SIMULATOR                              VERSION 1.3
EXAMPLE TRACE LISTING.   0 CONDITIONS ENABLED.                                                        PAGE  1

LCC  TRACE TYPE          COUNT   TIME                                    OP   INSTRUCTION    ADR1 ADR2 OPERAND1 OPERAND2
---- ----------          -----   --------                               ---- -----------    ---- ---- -------- --------


0096 SNAPSHOT               1       18  PSW: FE 0 0 0000  '01'B '00'B 0 C00096
       REGISTERS:
       R  0: 01020304,    16909060 R  1: 00000001,         1 R  2: 00000002,          2 R  3: 00000003,           3
       R  4: 00000004,           4 R  5: 0C000005,         5 R  6: 0C000006,          6 R  7: 00000007,           7
       R  8: 00000000,           0 R  9: 00000009,         9 R10: 0000000A,          10 R11: 0000000B,          11
       R12: CC00000C,          12 R13: 0000000D,         13 R14: FFFFFFFF,          -1 R15: 000003E8,        1000
       CORE DUMP:
        0324,   804: D9C5C7C9 E2E3C5D9 E240C6D6 D940E3C5 E2E3C9D5 C77A4040   REGI STER S FO R TE STIN G:

00AE SNAPSHOT               1       18  PSW: FE 0 0 0000  '01'B '00'B 0 0000AE
       CORE DUMP:
        0080,   176: 5808E000                                           ????

00B4 PGM INTERRUPT          2       18  PSW: FE 0 0 0006  '10'B '00'B 0 0000B4


0102 SNAPSHOT               8       71  PSW: FE 0 0 0000  '01'B '00'B 0 000102
       CORE DUMP:
        02E4,   740: 40C1D5E2 E6C5D940 C3D6D9D9 C5C3E340                 ANS WER  CORR ECT
0116 SNAPSHOT               9       76  PSW: FE 0 0 0000  '01'B '00'B 0 000116
       CORE DUMP:
        0118,   280: BE08F003                                           ???

011C PGM INTERRUPT         10       76  PSW: FE 0 0 0001  '10'B '00'B 0 00011C


0158 SNAPSHOT              16      127  PSW: FE 0 0 0000  '01'B '01'B 0 000158
       CORE DUMP:
        0310,   784: C1D5E2E6 C5D940C9 D5C3D6D9 D9C5C3E3 60606E40        ANSW ER I NCOR RECT -->
        03E8,  1000: 00000000 00000000                                  ???? ????

016A SNAPSHOT              16      127  PSW: FE 0 0 0000  '01'B '01'B 0 00016A
       CORE DUMP:
        033C,   828: C1D5E2E6 C5D940E2 C8D6E4D3 C440C2C5 7A404040        ANSW ER S HOUL D BE :
        03D8,   984: 00000001 00000000                                  ???? ????

0194 SNAPSHOT              18      133  PSW: FE 0 0 0000  '01'B '00'B 0 000194
       CORE DUMP:
        0194,   404: 5208F003                                           ???

0198 PGM INTERRUPT         18      133  PSW: FE 0 0 0001  '10'B '00'B 0 000198

01E6 SNAPSHOT              24      185  PSW: FE 0 0 0000  '01'B '00'B 0 0001E6
       CORE DUMP:
        02E4,   740: 40C1D5E2 E6C5D940 C3D6D9D9 C5C3E340                 ANS WER  CORR ECT

01FA SNAPSHOT              25      190  PSW: FE 0 0 0000  '01'B '00'B 0 0001FA
       CORE DUMP:
        01FC,   508: BE02F000                                           ???
```

# 5.2 STUDENT ASSIGNMENT FOR INSTRUCTION SIMULATION PROBLEM

```
MASSACHUSETTS INSTITUTE OF TECHNOLOGY          SYSTEM / 360 SIMULATOR                                              VERSION 1.3
EXAMPLE TRACE LISTING.   1 CONDITIONS ENABLED.                                                                          PAGE  2

LCC  TRACE TYPE           CCUNT   TIME                                        OP    INSTRUCTION      ADR1 ADR2  OPERAND1 OPERAND2
----  ----------------    -----  ---------                                    ----  --------------   ---- ----  -------- -------


0200 PGM INTERRUPT          26       191   PSW: FE 0 0 0001   '10'B '00'B 0 C00200


023C SNAPSHOT               32       241   PSW: FE 0 0 0000   '01'B '01'B 0 00023C
        CORE DUMP:
        0310,   784: C1D5E2E6 C5D940C9 D5C3D6D9 D9C5C3E3 60606E40             ANSW ER I NCOR RECT -->
        03E8,  1000: CC0C0000 00C0C000                                       ???? ????


024E SNAPSHOT               32       241   PSW: FE 0 0 0000   '01'B '01'B 0 00024E
        CORE DUMP:
        033C,   828: C1D5E2E6 C5D940E2 C8D6E4D3 C440C2C5 7A404040            ANSW ER S HOUL D BE :
        03E0,   992: 030CC000 000CC000                                       ???? ????


0278 SNAPSHOT               34       247   PSW: FE 0 0 0C00   '01'B '00'B 0 000278
        CORE DUMP:
        0278,   632: BE00F000                                                ??0?


027C PGM INTERRUPT          34       247   PSW: FE 0 0 0C01   '10'B '00'B 0 00027C


02E0 SNAPSHOT               40       299   PSW: FE 0 0 0000   '01'B '00'B 0 0002E0
        CORE DUMP:
        02E4,   740: 40C1D5E2 E6C5D940 C3D6D9D9 C5C3E340                     ANS WER  CORR ECT
        03E8,  1000: C0000000 00000000                                       ???? ????


NORMAL SIMULATOR TERMINATION FOR PROGRAM EXAMPLE

        SIMULATED REAL TIME:       299.603

        SIMULATED CPU TIME:        299.603
```

5.2.2  Fixed-Point Overflow Fixup Problem -- OS2

Introduction:

The handling of interrupt traffic is one of the most important occupations of an operating system. For the IBM 360 or 370, interrupts are the vehicle for communication with the operating system;  be it an I/O device signalling completion of an I/O event, the timer signalling the end of an interval of time, or a problem program requesting an operating system service.

Interrupts on the 360 have been divided into five distinct classes. Processing and queueing of each class is very similar, the essential difference being the core locations of the old and new PSW's.  Of the five types of interrupts, two types are synchronous in nature and can be caused at will by a program in execution. They are program and supervisor-call interruptions. In view of the ease with which these interrupts may be generated in a controlled fashion, this problem will be primarily concerned with these two types.


Problem Description:

The purpose of this problem is to engender an understanding of interrupts and interrupt processing or programming.  You will be required to write a program interrupt handler in three distinct steps, or levels of complexity. To test your interrupt handler we have provided a macro which generates a testing program. To start testing you merely branch to a label placed on this macro.

Each of these levels will receive equal weight in grading and you must implement them in the given order.  Care should be taken to make your program as neat and well documented as possible, as this will be a factor in the grading.


Level One:

For this level you are to write a simple interrupt handler which processes just program interruptions resulting from fixed point overflow. Your handler should ignore all other types of program interrupts by returning directly to the instruction following the one which caused the interrupt.  In this case no registers or other state indicators should be modified. Note that the LPSW instruction is intended for effecting a "return" from an interrupt handler.

For a program interrupt resulting from fixed point overflow, the following processing should be performed:

1. Save all registers and state indicators (the simulator does not have floating point registers).

2. Analyze the instruction which caused the interrupt to determine which register was to contain the answer, or object of the instruction.

3. Insert the largest possible positive or negative (whichever is appropriate) value into this register.

4. Restore the other registers and state indicators.

5. Return to the instruction after the one which caused the interrupt.

**Level Two:**

For this level you are to add another type of interrupt handler to your program. This routine should perform the following functions for supervisor call interrupts:

1. Save all registers and state indicators.

2. Add one to a static "svc counter" which is intialized to zero at IPL.

3. Use TRACE to dump the contents of this counter.

4. Restore all registers and state indicators.

5. Return to the instruction after the interrupt-causing SVC.

You should then code an SVC instruction approximately halfway through your program interrupt processing routine. This will cause an SVC interrupt while you're processing a previous program interrupt.

**Level Three:**

For this final level of complexity you are to print a message whenever a fixed point overflow occurs. This message should be printed on the 1403 printer at I/O address X'00E':

"FIXED POINT OVERFLOW AT XXXXXX"

Where XXXXXX is the hexadecimal representation of the absolute address of the offending instruction.

This output should be produced between steps 3 and 4 of your level one processing. Note that you will have to add a handler for I/O interrupts to accomplish this part of the problem.

Notes:

1. Use of TIO loops is excessively expensive on the simulator and inefficient on a real machine. Therefore TIO loops will **not be allowed** and anyone using them will be docked points for the machine problem. Instead the wait state should be used.

2. If you place a zero in the timer area, you will receive an external (timer) interrupt 3333 micro-seconds after your program starts execution. You should, therefore either put a large value in the interval timer area or disable external interrupts in the PSW.

3. Several popular instructions are not currently implemented on the simulator, including ED, CVD, UNPACK and others. Consult the SIM360 User's Guide for a full list of implemented instructions.

4. After starting the I/O on printer X'00E', you should wait for a "Device End" interrupt signalling completion. Then procede to step 4 of level one processing.

CHECK Macro:

The CHECK macro generates a little test program which you **must** use to test your interrupt handler. This program enables TRACE'ing of Program Interrupts, so you can see if your handler is working. It generates several different types of program interrupts, including fixed point overflows. Before it generates an interrupt, it uses a TRACE DUMP instruction to dump the offending instruction, and upon return from your interrupt handler the answer and registers are checked.

You should code this macro at the end of your program, as it generates USING and DROP assembler instructions. Use of the CHECK macro is demonstrated later.

Deck Setup:

Your deck should have the following structure:

```
Col. 1          10      16
     $JOB name
                TITLE 'your name- your Instructor'
     name       CSECT
                PRINT NOGEN
                *
                *
     your program goes here
                *
                *
                CHECK
                END
     $EOJ
```

Where  name  will be used to identify your simulator output.
You should use your last name, truncated if  necessary  to  eight
characters, or prefixed with qualifiers.


Run Schedule:

    TO BE ANNOUNCED

## Example Interrupt Program

This   example   should   acquaint you with the
concepts of the problem and the use of CHECK. It starts
the testing   program   and   merely returns after each
interrupt.

```
EXAMPLE PROGRAM FOR INTERRUPT AND I/O PROBLEM OS2                                    PAGE   1

 LOC  OBJECT CODE    ACDR1 ADDR2  STMT   SOURCE STATEMENT                             31 DEC 74
000000                              2 EXAMPLE  CSECT
000000                              3          USING EXAMPLE,0          ASSEMBLE ABSOLUTE ADDRESSES

                                    5 *************************************************************************
                                    6 *                                                                      *
                                    7 *          THIS EXAMPLE DEMONSTRATES USE OF THE CHECK TESTING MACRO.    *
                                    8 *          THE PROVIDED PROGRAM INTERRUPT HANDLERS MERELY RETURN        *
                                    9 *          FROM EACH INTERRUPT.                                         *
                                   10 *                                                                      *
                                   11 *************************************************************************

                                   13 *************************************************************************
                                   14 *                                                                      *
                                   15 *          LOW CORE INTIALIZATION                                       *
                                   16 *                                                                      *
                                   17 *************************************************************************
000000 FE00C000000008C             19 IPLPSW   DC    X'FE',AL3(0),A(START) INITIAL PSW LOADED TO START RUN
000008 000C0000C00C00C00           20 IPLCCW1  DC    D'0'                  IPL CCW'S WHICH
000010 0000000000000000            21 IPLCCW2  DC    D'0'                     ARE NOT USED
000018 0000000000000000            22 EXTOLD   DC    D'0'                  EXTERNAL OLD PSW
000020 0000000000000000            23 SUPOLD   DC    D'0'                  SUPERVISOR OLD PSW
000028 C000000000000000            24 PGMOLD   DC    D'0'                  PROGRAM CHECK OLD PSW
000030 0C00000000000000            25 MCKOLD   DC    D'0'                  MACHINE CHECK OLD PSW
000038 0000000000000000            26 IOOLD    DC    D'0'                  INPUT/OUTPUT OLD PSW
000040 0000000000000000            27 CSW      DC    D'0'                  CHANNEL STATUS WORD
000048 C0000000                    28 CAW      DC    F'0'                  CHANNEL ADDRESS WORD
00004C 0000C000                    29 UNUSED1  DC    F'0'                  UNUSED WORD 1
000050 00000000                    30 TIMER    DC    F'0'                  TIMER AREA
000054 C000C000                    31 UNUSED2  DC    F'0'                  UNUSED WORD 2
000058 0002C0C000000001            32 EXTNEW   DC    X'0002',AL2(0),A(1)   EXTERNAL NEW PSW- CAUSES HALT
000060 0000000000000084            33 SUPNEW   DC    A(0,SVCINT)           SUPERVISOR NEW PSW
000068 C00000C000000080            34 PGMNEW   DC    A(0,PGMINT)           PROGRAM CHECK NEW PSW
000070 00020C0000000004            35 MCKNEW   DC    X'0002',AL2(0),A(4)   MACHINE CHECK NEW PSW- CAUSES HALT
000078 0000000000000088            36 IONEW    DC    A(0,IOINT)            INPUT/OUTPUT NEW PSW

000080                             38 PGMINT   EQU   *

                                   40 *************************************************************************
                                   41 *                                                                      *
                                   42 *          PROGRAM INTERRUPT HANDLER -- INTERRUPTS MASKED OFF           *
                                   43 *                                                                      *
                                   44 *          NOTE THAT THIS INTERRUPT HANDLER RETURNS DIRECTLY TO THE     *
                                   45 *          POINT OF INTERRUPTION WITH NO PROCESSING.                    *
                                   46 *                                                                      *
                                   47 *************************************************************************

000080 8200 0028       0C028       49          LPSW  PGMOLD                "RETURN" TO POINT OF INTERRUPTION
```

349

EXAMPLE PROGRAM FOR INTERRUPT AND I/O PROBLEM OS2                                          PAGE    2

LOC   OBJECT CODE    ADDR1 ADDR2  STMT   SOURCE STATEMENT                                  31 DEC 74

```
                                    51 *****************************************************************
                                    52 *                                                               *
                                    53 *          SUPERVISOR CALL INTERRUPT HANDLER -- INTERRUPTS MASKED OFF  *
                                    54 *                                                               *
                                    55 *          NOTE THAT THIS INTERRUPT HANDLER RETURNS DIRECTLY TO THE  *
                                    56 *          POINT OF INTERRUPTION WITH NO PROCESSING.             *
                                    57 *                                                               *
                                    58 *****************************************************************
000064                              60 SVCINT   EQU   *
000064 8200 0020       0C020        61          LPSW  SUPOLD                "RETURN" TO POINT OF INTERRUPTION

                                    63 *****************************************************************
                                    64 *                                                               *
                                    65 *          INPUT/OUTPUT INTERRUPT HANDLER -- INTERRUPTIONS MASKED OFF  *
                                    66 *                                                               *
                                    67 *          NOTE THAT THIS INTERRUPT HANDLER RETURNS DIRECTLY TO THE  *
                                    68 *          POINT OF INTERRUPTION WITH NO PROCESSING.             *
                                    69 *                                                               *
                                    70 *****************************************************************
000088                              72 IOINT    EQU   *
000088 8200 0038       0C038        73          LPSW  IOOLD                 "RETURN" TO POINT OF INTERRUPTION

                                    75 START    CHECK                       GENERATE TESTING PROGRAM

                                    77+****************************************************************
                                    78+*                                                               *
                                    79+*                   CHECK TEST MACRO FOR OS2                     *
                                    80+*                                                               *
                                    81+*          THIS MACRO GENERATES FIVE TRIALS FOR THE OS2 PROBLEM.  *
                                    82+*          TO START TESTING, BRANCH TO THE CODE GENERATED BY THIS  *
                                    83+*          MACRO. NOTE- THIS MACRO MAY BE BRANCHED TO ONLY ONCE.   *
                                    84+*                                                               *
                                    85+****************************************************************
000000                              87+          USING EXAMPLE,0 .          ASSEMBLE ABSOLUTE REFERENCES

00008C                              89+          CNOP  4,8 .                FORCE ALIGNMENT
00008C 8200 0090       0C090        90+START    LPSW  *+4 .                 LOAD UP THE PSW
000090 FE01C0000F                   91+CHECKPSW DC    X'FE0100000F' .       EXTERNAL DISABLED, KEY 0, PROBLEM
                                    92+*                                    STATE, ALL PROGRAM INTERRUPTS ON
000095 C00098                       93+          DC    AL3(*+3) .           ADDRESS OF CHECK PROGRAM
000098 980F 0328             00328  94+          LM    0,15,SRGR0000 .      LOAD REGISTERS FOR TESTING

00009C                              97+          DS    0H
00009C 0208                         98+          DC    AL1(2,8) TRACE OP-CODE AND TYPE(KLUDGE)
00009E 0000                         99+          DC    XL2'0' ID.
0000A0 0000                        100+          DC    BL2'CCC0000000000000'
0000A2 FFFF                        101+          DC    BL2'1111111111111111'
0000A4 02FC                        102+          DC    Y(SM100000)
0000A6 0006                        103+          DC    AL1(0,6) WORD COUNT AND INDIRECT
0000A8 8C00                        104+          DC    XL2'8C00'
```

EXAMPLE PROGRAM FOR INTERRUPT AND I/O PROBLEM OS2                                      PAGE    3

LCC   CBJECT CCDE    ADDR1 ADDR2  STMT   SOURCE STATEMENT                              31 DEC 74

```
0CC0AA                           107+        DS    OH
0000AA 0203                      108+        DC    AL1(2,3) TRACE OP-CODE AND TYPE(KLUDGE)
0CC0AC 0C02                      109+        DC    H'2' ID.
0CC0AE CC00                      110+        DC    BL2'0000000000000000'
0000B0 0000                      111+        DC    BL2'0000000000000000'
0000B2 8000                      112+        DC    XL2'8C00'


0000B4                           116+        DS    OH
0000B4 0208                      117+        DC    AL1(2,8) TRACE OP-CODE AND TYPE(KLUDGE)
0000B6 CC00                      118+        DC    XL2'0' ID.
0000 8 C000                      119+        DC    BL2'0000000000000000'
0000BA 0000                      120+        DC    BL2'000000C000C00000'
0000BC 00C4                      121+        DC    Y(STR10000)
0000BE 0001                      122+        DC    AL1(0,1) WORD COUNT AND INDIRECT
0000C0 8000                      123+        DC    XL2'8000'

0000C2 0700                      125+        CNOP  0,4 .               FORCE ALIGNMENT FOR TRACE DUMP
0C00C4 9C00 000E       0C00E     126+STR10000 SIO  X'00E' .            GENERATE TRIAL 1 - PRIVELEGED INSTR.

0000C8 900F 0368          00368  128+        STM   0,15,STGRC000 .     SAVE STUDENT'S REGISTERS
0000CC D53F 0368 0328 00368 00328 129+.      CLC   STGR0000(64),SRGR0000
0000D2 4780 00EC          000EC  130+        BE    ST1ROK00 .          IF REGISTERS NOT MODIFIED

0000D6                           132+        DS    OH
0000D6 0208                      133+        DC    AL1(2,8) TRACE OP-CODE AND TYPE(KLUDGE)
0000D8 CC00                      134+        DC    XL2'0' ID.
0000DA 0000                      135+        DC    BL2'0000000000000000'
0000DC FFFF                      136+        DC    BL2'1111111111111111'
0000DE 02CC                      137+        DC    Y(SBRS0000)
0000E0 0007                      138+        DC    AL1(0,7) WORD COUNT AND INDIRECT
0000E2 8000                      139+        DC    XL2'8000'

0000E4 980F 0328          00328  141+        LM    0,15,SRGR0000 .     RESTORE REGISTERS
0000E8 47F0 00FA          000FA  142+        B     ST200000 .          GO TO NEXT TRIAL


0000EC                           145+        DS    OH
0000EC 0208                      146+ST1ROK00 DC   AL1(2,8) TRACE OP-CODE AND TYPE(KLUDGE)
0000EE 0000                      147+        DC    XL2'0' ID.
0000F0 0000                      148+        DC    BL2'0000000000000000'
0000F2 CC00                      149+        DC    BL2'0000000000000000'
0000F4 028C                      150+        DC    Y(SAOK0000)
0000F6 0004                      151+        DC    AL1(0,4) WORD COUNT AND INDIRECT
0000F8 8C00                      152+        DC    XL2'8000'
```

351

| LOC | OBJECT CODE | ADDR1 ADDR2 | STMT | SOURCE STATEMENT | | |
|---|---|---|---|---|---|---|

```
0000FA                              156+        DS    0H
0000FA 0208                         157+ST200000 DC   AL1(2,8) TRACE OP-CODE AND TYPE(KLUDGE)
0000FC 0000                         158+        DC    XL2'0' ID.
0000FE C000                         159+        DC    BL2'0000000000000000'
000100 0000                         160+        DC    BL2'0000000000000000'
000102 0108                         161+        DC    Y(STR2C000)
000104 C001                         162+        DC    AL1(0,1) WORD COUNT AND INDIRECT
000106 8000                         163+        DC    XL2'8000'

000108                              165+        CNOP  0,4 .                  FORCE ALIGNMENT FOR TRACE DUMP
000108 10FF                         166+STR20000 LPR  15,15 .               TRIAL 2 - FIXED OVERFLOW RR

00010A 50F0 0380        003B0       168+        ST    15,SANS0000 .         SAVE ANSWER IN AREA
00010E 58F0 0364        00364       169+        L     15,SRGR0000+15*4 .    RESTORE VALUE OF 15
000112 900F 0368        00368       170+        STM   0,15,STGR0000 .       SAVE REGISTERS FOR CHECK
000116 D53F 0368 0328 00368 00328   171+        CLC   STGR0000(64),SRGR0000 CHECK STUDENT'S REGISTERS
00011C 4780 0132        00132       172+        BE    ST2ROK00 .            REGISTERS ARE OK

000120                              175+        DS    0H
000120 0208                         176+        DC    AL1(2,8) TRACE OP-CODE AND TYPE(KLUDGE)
000122 0000                         177+        DC    XL2'0' ID.
000124 C000                         178+        DC    BL2'0000000000000000'
000126 FFFF                         179+        DC    BL2'1111111111111111'
000128 02CC                         180+        DC    Y(SBRSC000)
00012A 0007                         181+        DC    AL1(0,7) WORD COUNT AND INDIRECT
00012C 8000                         182+        DC    XL2'8000'

00012E 980F 0328        00328       184+        LM    0,15,SRGR0000 .       RESTORE REGISTERS

000132 D503 03B0 03A8 003B0 003A8   186+ST2ROK00 CLC  SANS0000(4),ST2A0000 . CHECK ANSWER
000138 4780 0164        00164       187+        BE    ST2AOK00 .            ANSWER OK

00013C                              190+        DS    0H
00013C 0208                         191+        DC    AL1(2,8) TRACE OP-CODE AND TYPE(KLUDGE)
00013E 0000                         192+        DC    XL2'0' ID.
000140 0000                         193+        DC    BL2'0000000000000000'
000142 C000                         194+        DC    BL2'0000000000000000'
000144 02E8                         195+        DC    Y(SBAI0000)
000146 0005                         196+        DC    AL1(0,5) WORD COUNT AND INDIRECT
000148 03B0                         197+        DC    Y(SANS0000)
00014A 0001                         198+        DC    AL1(0,1) WORD COUNT AND INDIRECT
00014C 8000                         199+        DC    XL2'8000'

00014E                              202+        DS    0H
00014E 0208                         203+        DC    AL1(2,8) TRACE OP-CODE AND TYPE(KLUDGE)
000150 0000                         204+        DC    XL2'0' ID.
```

352

```
  LOC   OBJECT CODE      ADDR1 ADDR2   STMT    SOURCE STATEMENT                              31 DEC 74

000152 C000                            205+            DC      BL2'0CC00C0000000000'
0C0154 C000                            206+            DC      BL2'0000000000000000'
000156 C314                            207+            DC      Y(SM200000)
000158 C005                            208+            DC      AL1(0,5) WORD COUNT AND INDIRECT
00015A 03A8                            209+            DC      Y(ST2A0000)
00015C C001                            210+            DC      AL1(0,1) WORD COUNT AND INDIRECT
00015E 8000                            211+            DC      XL2'8000'


000160 47F0 0176         00176         213+            B       ST300000 .            GO TO NEXT TRIAL


000164                                 216+            DS      OH
000164 0208                            217+ST2A0K00    DC      AL1(2,8) TRACE OP-CODE AND TYPE(KLUDGE)
000166 C000                            218+            DC      XL2'0' ID.
000168 0000                            219+            DC      BL2'0000000000000000'
00016A 0000                            220+            DC      BL2'000000C0C0000000'
00016C 02BC                            221+            DC      Y(SAOK0000)
00016E 0004                            222+            DC      AL1(0,4) WORD COUNT AND INDIRECT
000170 03B0                            223+            DC      Y(SANS0000)
000172 CC01                            224+            DC      AL1(0,1) WORD COUNT AND INDIRECT
000174 8000                            225+            DC      XL2'8000'


000176                                 229+            DS      OH
000176 0208                            230+ST300000    DC      AL1(2,8) TRACE OP-CODE AND TYPE(KLUDGE)
000178 0000                            231+            DC      XL2'0' ID.
00017A 0000                            232+            DC      BL2'C0C0000000000000'
00017C C000                            233+            DC      BL2'0000000000000000'
00017E 0184                            234+            DC      Y(STR30000)
000180 0001                            235+            DC      AL1(0,1) WORD COUNT AND INDIRECT
000182 8C00                            236+            DC      XL2'8000'


000184                                 238+            CNOP    0,4 .                FORCE ALIGNMENT
000184 5A00 03A8         003A8         239+STR3C000    A       0,SMP00000 .         TRIAL 3 FIXED OVERFLOW RX

000188 5000 03B0         003B0         241+            ST      0,SANS0000 .         SAVE STUDENT'S ANSWER
00018C 5800 0328         00328         242+            L       0,SRGR0000 .         RESTORE REGISTER
000190 900F 0368         00368         243+            STM     0,15,STGR0000 .      SAVE REGISTERS FOR CHECK
000194 D53F 0368 0328 00368 00328      244+            CLC     STGR0000(64),SRGR0000 CHECK STUDENT'S REGISTERS
00019A 4780 01B0         001B0         245+            BE      ST3ROK00 .           REGISTERS OK


00019B                                 248+            DS      OH
00019E 0208                            249+            DC      AL1(2,8) TRACE OP-CODE AND TYPE(KLUDGE)
0001A0 C000                            250+            DC      XL2'0' ID.
0001A2 0000                            251+            DC      BL2'0000000000000000'
0001A4 FFFF                            252+            DC      BL2'1111111111111111'
0001A6 02CC                            253+            DC      Y(SBRS0000)
```

353

EXAMPLE PROGRAM FOR INTERRUPT AND I/O PROBLEM OS2

PAGE 6

31 DEC 74

| LOC | OBJECT CODE | ADDR1 | ADDR2 | STMT | SOURCE STATEMENT |
|---|---|---|---|---|---|
| 0001A8 | 0007 | | | 254+ | DC AL1(0,7) WORD COUNT AND INDIRECT |
| 0001AA | 8000 | | | 255+ | DC XL2'8000' |
| 0001AC | 980F 0328 | | 00328 | 257+ | LM 0,15,SRGR0000 . RESTORE REGISTERS |
| 0001B0 | D503 03B0 03A8 | 003B0 | 003A8 | 259+ST3ROK00 CLC | SANS0000(4),ST3A0000 CHECK STUDENT'S ANSWER |
| 0001B6 | 4780 01E2 | | 001E2 | 260+ | BE ST3AOK00 . ANSWER CORRECT |
| 0001BA | | | | 262+ | DS 0H |
| 0001BA | 0208 | | | 263+ | DC AL1(2,8) TRACE OP-CODE AND TYPE(KLUDGE) |
| 0001BC | 0000 | | | 264+ | DC XL2'0' ID. |
| 0001BE | 0000 | | | 265+ | DC BL2'0000000000000000' |
| 0001C0 | 0000 | | | 266+ | DC BL2'0000000000000000' |
| 0001C2 | 02E8 | | | 267+ | DC Y(SBAI0000) |
| 0001C4 | 0005 | | | 268+ | DC AL1(0,5) WORD COUNT AND INDIRECT |
| 0001C6 | 03B0 | | | 269+ | DC Y(SANS0000) |
| 0001C8 | 0002 | | | 270+ | DC AL1(0,2) WORD COUNT AND INDIRECT |
| 0001CA | 8000 | | | 271+ | DC XL2'8000' |
| 0001CC | | | | 274+ | DS 0H |
| 0001CC | 0208 | | | 275+ | DC AL1(2,8) TRACE OP-CODE AND TYPE(KLUDGE) |
| 0001CE | C000 | | | 276+ | DC XL2'0' ID. |
| 0001D0 | 0000 | | | 277+ | DC BL2'0000000000000000' |
| 0001D2 | 0000 | | | 278+ | DC BL2'000000C000000000' |
| 0001D4 | 0314 | | | 279+ | DC Y(SM200000) |
| 0001D6 | 0005 | | | 280+ | DC AL1(0,5) WORD COUNT AND INDIRECT |
| 0001D8 | 03A8 | | | 281+ | DC Y(ST3A0000) |
| 0001DA | 0001 | | | 282+ | DC ALI(0,1) WORD COUNT AND INDIRECT |
| 0001DC | 8C00 | | | 283+ | DC XL2'8000' |
| 0001DE | 47F0 01F4 | | 001F4 | 285+ | B ST400000 . GO TO NEXT TRIAL |
| 0001E2 | | | | 288+ | DS 0H |
| 0001E2 | 0208 | | | 289+ST3AOK00 DC | ALI(2,8) TRACE OP-CODE AND TYPE(KLUDGE) |
| 0001E4 | 0000 | | | 290+ | DC XL2'0' ID. |
| 0001E6 | 0000 | | | 291+ | DC BL2'0000000000000000' |
| 0001E8 | 0C00 | | | 292+ | DC BL2'0000000000000000' |
| 0001EA | 028C | | | 293+ | DC Y(SAOK0000) |
| 0001EC | 0004 | | | 294+ | DC ALI(0,4) WORD COUNT AND INDIRECT |
| 0001EE | 03B0 | | | 295+ | DC Y(SANS0000) |
| 0001F0 | 0001 | | | 296+ | DC ALI(0,1) WORD COUNT AND INDIRECT |
| 0001F2 | 8C00 | | | 297+ | DC XL2'8C00' |

LCC  CBJECT CODE    ACCR1 ADDR2  STMT   SOURCE STATEMENT

```
0001F4                                301+           DS     OH
0001F4 C208                           302+ST400000   DC     AL1(2,8) TRACE OP-CODE AND TYPE(<LUDGE)
0001F6 C000                           303+           DC     XL2'0' ID.
0001F8 CC00                           304+           DC     BL2'0000000000000000'
0001FA 0000                           305+           DC     BL2'0000000000000000'
0001FC 0204                           306+           DC     Y(STR4C000)
0001FE CC01                           307+           DC     AL1(0,1) WORD COUNT AND INDIRECT
000200 8000                           308+           DC     XL2'8000'

000202 0700                           310+           CNOP   0,4 .                FORCE ALIGNMENT
000204 CC00                           311+STR40000   DC     H'0' .               TRIAL 4 - OPERATION EXCEPTION

000206 900F 0368             00368    313+           STM    0,15,STGR0000 .     SAVE REGISTERS FOR CHECK
00020A D53F 0368 0328 00368 00328    314+           CLC    STGR0000(64),SRGR0000 CHECK STUDENT'S REGISTERS
000210 4780 022A             0022A    315+           BE     ST4AOK00 .          ANSWER IS CORRECT

000214                                318+           DS     OH
000214 0208                           319+           DC     AL1(2,8) TRACE OP-CODE AND TYPE(KLUDGE)
000216 CC00                           320+           DC     XL2'0' ID.
000218 0000                           321+           DC     BL2'0000000000000000'
00021A FFFF                           322+           DC     BL2'1111111111111111'
00021C 02CC                           323+           DC     Y(SBRS0000)
00021E 0007                           324+           DC     AL1(0,7) WORD COUNT AND INDIRECT
000220 8000                           325+           DC     XL2'8000'

000222 980F 0328             00328    327+           LM     0,15,SRGR0000 .     RESTORE REGISTERS
000226 47F0 0238             00238    328+           B      ST500000 .          GO TO NEXT TRIAL

00022A                                331+           DS     OH
00022A 0208                           332+ST4AOK00   DC     AL1(2,8) TRACE OP-CODE AND TYPE(<LUDGE)
00022C 0000                           333+           DC     XL2'0' ID.
00022E 0000                           334+           DC     BL2'0000000000000000'
000230 0000                           335+           DC     BL2'0000000000000000'
000232 02BC                           336+           DC     Y(SAOK0000)
000234 0004                           337+           DC     AL1(0,4) WORD COUNT AND INDIRECT
000236 8000                           338+           DC     XL2'8000'

000238                                342+           DS     OH
000238 0208                           343+ST500000   DC     AL1(2,8) TRACE OP-CODE AND TYPE(KLUDGE)
00023A 0000                           344+           DC     XL2'0' ID.
00023C 0000                           345+           DC     BL2'0000000000000000'
00023E 0000                           346+           DC     BL2'0000000000000000'
000240 0248                           347+           DC     Y(STR50000)
000242 0001                           348+           DC     AL1(0,1) WORD COUNT AND INDIRECT
000244 8000                           349+           DC     XL2'8C00'
```

EXAMPLE PROGRAM FOR INTERRUPT AND I/O PROBLEM OS2                                    PAGE    8

```
LOC    OBJECT CODE     ADDR1 ADDR2  STMT    SOURCE STATEMENT                                    31 DEC 74

000246 0700                         351+           CNOP  0,4 .              FORCE ALIGNMENT FOR DUMP
000248 8BB0 0001             00001   352+STR50000  SLA   11,1 .             TRIAL 5 - OVERFLOW FROM SHIFT

00024C 50B0 03B0             003B0   354+          ST    11,SANS0000 .      SAVE STUDENT'S ANSWER
000250 58B0 0354             00354   355+          L     11,SRGR0000+11*4 . RESTORE REGISTER
000254 900F 0368             00368   356+          STM   0,15,STGR0000 .    SAVE REGISTERS FOR CHECK
000258 D53F 0368 0328  00368 00328   357+          CLC   STGR0000(64),SRGR0000 CHECK STUDENT'S REGISTERS
00025E 4780 0274             00274   358+          BE    ST5ROK00 .         REGISTERS ARE OK


000262                              361+          DS    0H
000262 0208                         362+          DC    AL1(2,8) TRACE OP-CODE AND TYPE(KLUDGE)
000264 0000                         363+          DC    XL2'0' ID.
000266 0000                         364+          DC    BL2'0000000000000000'
000268 FFFF                         365+          DC    BL2'1111111111111111'
00026A 02CC                         366+          DC    Y(SBRS0000)
00026C 0007                         367+          DC    AL1(0,7) WORD COUNT AND INDIRECT
00026E 8000                         368+          DC    XL2'8000'


000270 980F 0328             00328   370+          LM    0,15,SRGR0000 .    RESTORE REGISTERS

000274 D503 03B0 03AC  003B0 003AC  372+ST5ROK00  CLC   SANS0000(4),ST5A0000 CHECK STUDENT'S ANSWER
00027A 4780 02A6             002A6   373+          BE    ST5AOK00 .         ANSWER IS CORRECT

00027E                              375+          DS    0H
00027E 0208                         376+          DC    AL1(2,8) TRACE OP-CODE AND TYPE(KLUDGE)
000280 0000                         377+          DC    XL2'0' ID.
000282 0000                         378+          DC    BL2'0000000000000000'
000284 C000                         379+          DC    BL2'0000000000000000'
000286 02E8                         380+          DC    Y(SBAI0000)
000288 0005                         381+          DC    AL1(0,5) WORD COUNT AND INDIRECT
00028A 0380                         382+          DC    Y(SANS0000)
00028C 0001                         383+          DC    AL1(0,1) WORD COUNT AND INDIRECT
00028E 8000                         384+          DC    XL2'8000'


000290                              387+          DS    0H
000290 0208                         388+          DC    AL1(2,8) TRACE OP-CODE AND TYPE(KLUDGE)
000292 0000                         389+          DC    XL2'0' ID.
000294 CC00                         390+          DC    BL2'0000000000000000'
000296 0000                         391+          DC    BL2'0000000000000000'
000298 0314                         392+          DC    Y(SM2C0000)
00029A CC05                         393+          DC    AL1(0,5) WORD COUNT AND INDIRECT
00029C 03AC                         394+          DC    Y(ST5A0000)
00029E 0001                         395+          DC    AL1(0,1) WORD COUNT AND INDIRECT
0002A0 8C00                         396+          DC    XL2'8C00'

0002A2 47F0 02B8             002B8   398+          B     ST600000 .         GO TO NEXT TRIAL
```

```
   LOC   OBJECT CODE     ACDR1 ADDR2  STMT   SOURCE STATEMENT                                          31 DEC 74

0002A6                                401+        DS    OH
0002A6 0208                           402+ST5AOK00 DC   AL1(2,8) TRACE OP-CODE AND TYPE(KLUDGE)
0002A8 CC00                           403+        DC    XL2'0' ID.
0002AA C000                           404+        DC    BL2'0000000000000000'
0002AC 0000                           405+        DC    BL2'000000C000C00000000'
0002AE 02BC                           406+        DC    Y(SAOK0000)
0002B0 0004                           407+        DC    AL1(0,4) WORD COUNT AND INDIRECT
0002B2 03B0                           408+        DC    Y(SANS0000)
0002B4 0001                           409+        DC    AL1(0,1) WORD COUNT AND INDIRECT
0002B6 8C00                           410+        DC    XL2'8000'


0002B8                                413+ST6C0000 DS   OH
0002B8 FF777777                       414+        DC    X'FF777777'

0002BC                                416+        CNOP  0,4 .                       FORCE WORD ALIGNMENT FOR DUMPS
0002BC 40C1D5E2E6C5D940               417+SAOK0000 DC   C' ANSWER CORRECT:'
0002CC D9C5C7C9E2E3C5D9               418+SBRS0000 DC   C'REGISTERS HAVE BEEN CHANGED '
0002E8 C1D5E2E6C5D940C9               419+SBA10000 DC   C'ANSWER INCORRECT--> '
0002FC D9C5C7C9E2E3C5D9               420+SM100000 DC   C'REGISTERS FOR TESTING:  '
000314 C1D5E2E6C5D940E2               421+SM200000 DC   C'ANSWER SHOULD BE:    '
000328 7000C0C0C0000001               422+SRGR0000 DC   X'70000000',F'1,2,3,4,5,6,7,8,9,10',X'8000000F'
000358 0000C00C0000000D               423+        DC    F'12,13,14',X'80000000'
000368 0000000000000000               424+STGR0000 DC   16F'0'
0003A8                                425+SMP00000 EQU  * .                         MAXIMUM POSITIVE NUMBER
0003A8                                426+ST3A0000 EQU  * .                         ANSWER FOR TRIAL THREE
0003A8 7FFFFFFF                       427+ST2A0000 DC   X'7FFFFFFF' .               ANSWER FOR TRIAL TWO
0003AC 8C00C000                       428+ST5A0000 DC   X'80000000' .              ANSWER FOR TRIAL FIVE
0003B0 0000C000                       429+SANS0000 DC   F'0' .                      STUDENT'S ANSWER AREA

                                      431         END
```

357

```
MASSACHUSETTS INSTITUTE OF TECHNOLOGY          SYSTEM / 360 SIMULATOR                                              VERSION 1.3
EXAMPLE TRACE LISTING.    0 CONDITIONS ENABLED.                                                                        PAGE  1

LOC  TRACE TYPE          COUNT  TIME                                              OP   INSTRUCTION     ADR1 ADR2 OPERAND1 OPERAND2
----  ----------------    -----  ----------                                       ----  --------------  ---- ---- -------- --------


00AA SNAPSHOT              2       21  PSW: FE 0 1 0000  '01'B '00'B F 0000AA
         REGISTERS:
         R  0: 70000000,  1879048192 R 1: 00000001,        1 R 2: 00000002,        2 R 3: 00000003,           3
         R  4: 00000004,           4 R 5: 00000005,        5 R 6: 00000006,        6 R 7: 00000007,           7
         R  8: 00000008,           8 R 9: 00000009,        9 R10: 0000000A,       10 R11: 8000000F, -2147483633
         R12: 0000000C,           12 R13: 0000000D,       13 R14: 0000000E,       14 R15: 80000000, -2147483648
         CORE DUMP:
         02FC,   764: D9C5C7C9 E2E3C5D9 E240C6D6 D940E3C5 E2E3C9D5 C77A4040   REGI STER S FO R TE STIN G:

00C2 SNAPSHOT              2       21  PSW: FE 0 1 0000  '01'B '00'B F 0000C2
         CORE DUMP:
         00C4,   196: 9C00C00E                                               ????

00C8 PGM INTERRUPT         3       21  PSW: FE 0 1 0002  '10'B '00'B F 0000C8

00FA SNAPSHOT              7       70  PSW: FE 0 1 0000  '01'B '00'B F 0000FA
         CORE DUMP:
         02BC,   700: 40C1D5E2 E6C5D940 C3D6D9D9 C5C3E37A                    ANS WER  CORR ECT:

0108 SNAPSHOT              7       70  PSW: FE 0 1 0000  '01'B '00'B F 000108
         CORE DUMP:
         0108,   264: 10FF50F0                                              ??&0

010A PGM INTERRUPT         7       70  PSW: FE 0 1 0008  '01'B '11'B F 00010A

014E SNAPSHOT             15      121  PSW: FE 0 1 0000  '01'B '10'B F 00014E
         CORE DUMP:
         02E8,   744: C1D5E2E6 C5D940C9 D5C3D6D9 D9C5C3E3 60606E40           ANSW ER I NCOR RECT -->
         03B0,   944: 80000000                                              ????

0160 SNAPSHOT             15      121  PSW: FE 0 1 0000  '01'B '10'B F 000160
         CORE DUMP:
         0314,   788: C1D5E2E6 C5D940E2 C8D6E4D3 C440C2C5 7A404040           ANSW ER S HOUL D BE :
         03A8,   936: 7FFFFFFF                                              "???

0184 SNAPSHOT             16      122  PSW: FE 0 1 0000  '01'B '10'B F 000184
         CORE DUMP:
         0184,   388: 5A0003A8                                              ???

0188 PGM INTERRUPT        16      122  PSW: FE 0 1 0008  '10'B '11'B F 000188

01CC SNAPSHOT             24      175  PSW: FE 0 1 0000  '01'B '10'B F 0001CC
         CORE DUMP:
         02E8,   744: C1D5E2E6 C5D940C9 D5C3D6D9 D9C5C3E3 60606E40           ANSW ER I NCOR RECT -->
         C3B0,   944: EFFFFFFF FFFFFFFF                                      ???? ????
01CE SNAPSHOT             24      175  PSW: FE 0 1 0000  '01'B '10'B F 0001DE
         CORE DUMP:
```

```
MASSACHUSETTS INSTITUTE OF TECHNOLOGY              SYSTEM / 360 SIMULATOR                                          VERSION 1.3
EXAMPLE TRACE LISTING.   2 CONDITIONS ENABLED.                                                                        PAGE  2

LOC  TRACE TYPE          CCUNT  TIME                                          OP   INSTRUCTION    ADR1 ADR2  OPERAND1 OPERAND2
----  --------------      -----  ---------                                    ----  --------------  ----  ----  --------  --------

        0314,   788: C1D5E2E6 C5D940E2 C8D6E4D3 C440C2C5 7A404040             ANSW ER S HOUL D BE :
        03A8,   936: 7FFFFFFF                                                 "???

0202 SNAPSHOT              25        176  PSW: FE 0 1 0000  '01'B '10'B F 000202
        CORE DUMP:
        0204,   516: 0C00900F                                                ????

0206 PGM INTERRUPT         26        176  PSW: FE 0 1 0001  '01'B '10'B F 000206

0238 SNAPSHOT              30        224  PSW: FE 0 1 0000  '01'B '00'B F 000238
        CORE DUMP:
        02BC,   700: 40C1D5E2 E6C5D940 C3D6D9D9 C5C3E37A                      ANS WER  CORR ECT:
0246 SNAPSHOT              30        224  PSW: FE 0 1 0000  '01'B '00'B F C00246
        CORE DUMP:
        0248,   584: 8BBCC001                                                ????

024C PGM INTERRUPT         31        224  PSW: FE 0 1 0008  '10'B '11'B F 00024C

0290 SNAPSHOT              39        278  PSW: FE 0 1 0000  '01'B '10'B F 000290
        CORE DUMP:
        02E8,   744: C1D5E2E6 C5D940C9 D5C3D6D9 D9C5C3E3 60606E40             ANSW ER I NCOR RECT -->
        03B0,   944: 800C001E                                                ????

02A2 SNAPSHOT              39        278  PSW: FE 0 1 0000  '01'B '10'B F 0002A2
        CORE DUMP:
        0314,   788: C1D5E2E6 C5D940E2 C8D6E4D3 C440C2C5 7A404040            ANSW ER S HOUL D BE :
        03AC,   940: 800CC000                                                ????


NORMAL SIMULATOR TERMINATION FOR PROGRAM EXAMPLE

        SIMULATED REAL TIME:      279.045

        SIMULATED CPU TIME:       279.045
```

### 5.2.3   BTB Problem -- OS3

Introduction:

     Despite the large number of instructions available on modern
computers,  additional  special  purpose  instructions  are  often
desired for specific applications. For example,  a  machine  used
for large database management might want a special instruction to
perform hash coding.

     Many computers reserve certain opcodes which actually invoke
user-written  software  routines.  These  opcodes are then called
Programmed Operators, or  User  Operators.    To  the  application
program coding one of these special instructions, it is as if the
software routine were part of the hardware.

     Whenever  an  attempt is made to execute an instruction with
an invalid opcode on an IBM 360 or 370, a program interrupt takes
place which stores the current PSW in location 40 (decimal),  and
loads  the  PSW from location 104 (decimal). The old PSW contains
an interruption code of X'0001' for operation exception.

          This loading of a new PSW effects a branch to a  routine
which  may  analyze the program interruption and take appropriate
action.  The  address  portion  of  the  old  PSW  (bytes  45-47,
decimal)  contains  the  address  of  the  next instruction to be
executed. The Instruction Length Counter of this same PSW  (first
two  bits  of  byte  44, decimal) contains the length of the last
instruction executed.

     Using this information, it is possible to "back up"  to  the
instruction  which  caused  the  interrupt. Then a routine may be
used to simulate execution of  a  new,  nonexistant  instruction.
Note  that  this  routine  must  perform any  necessary  address
calculation, condition code setting, etc.. Once this  simulation
is  completed,  control is returned to the interrupted program by
using the LPSW instruction to reload the PSW  from  location  40.
Note  that  the registers current when the LPSW is issued will be
those "passed" to the interrupted program.


Problem Description:

     Your assignment is to  write  a  program  interrupt  handler
which  simulates  execution  of  a  currently  non-existant
instruction. Your handler should ignore  any  program  interrupts
that  are  not  operation  exceptions  resulting  from this "new"
instruction.

     The instruction you are to simulate is the Bit Bucket  (BTB)
instruction,  to  be  described  later.   Your  interrupt handler
should not modify any registers except the answer register for  a
BTB instruction. Any program interrupt not caused by a BTB should

be ignored. You may wish to get fancy and allow for executed (via the EX instruction) BTB instructions, but this is not required.

BTB Instruction Specification:

This instruction is an RX instruction of the following form:

BTB R1,D2(X2,B2)

| 51 | R1 | X2 | B2 | D2 |
|---|---|---|---|---|
| 0 | 8 | 12 | 16 | 20 | 31 |

(op-code is 51 hexadecimal)

The second operand is a core location addressed by the X2-B2-D2 combination. The first operand is a general purpose register which contains the number of bytes to be examined in the second operand. If this value in register R1 is positive, then the result of the instruction is the number of bits which are on (1) in the specified string of bytes. If the value in register R1 is negative, then the result of the instruction is the number of bits in the second operand which are off (0). Either way, the result of the instruction is placed in the register R1. If the value of the R1 register is zero, the instruction should be treated as a no-op.

The following algorithm may be used to simulate the BTB instruction:

1. First you must get the address of the offending instruction and verify that it is a BTB. If so proceed, else go to step 7 (return).

2. Decode the instruction. You need to examine the instruction and pick up the R1 field. Load the value of this register into a register, we will call this LENGTH. The simplest way to do this is to store the registers in a save area, in the order 0-15 when your interrupt routine is entered. Then get the register R1 number in a register and shift it left two places (multiply by four) to get the offset in the save area. Then use this as the index in a load request from the start of the register save area.

   Next you need to get the address of the second operand. Start by clearing a register (we will call it OP2). Examine the X2 field; if it is zero, ignore it, otherwise load the value of the X2 register into OP2. Examine the B2 field if it is zero, ignore it, else add the contents of the B2 register to OP2. Then add the value of the D2 field to OP2. Now OP2 has the absolute address of the second operand.

3. Define a register ANSWER and set it to zero. This
   register will contain the output count of bits.

4. Using the Load Positive Register (LPR) instruction, get
   the absolute value of LENGTH into ALENGTH. If this is
   zero (the LPR instruction will set the condition code),
   then go to step 7. This returns to the interrupted
   program.

5. Test the sign of the value contained in LENGTH. If it
   is positive, count the one bits in the field defined
   from OP2 to OP2 + ALENGTH-1. Otherwise, count the zero
   bits. In either case place the result in ANSWER.

6. Store the value of ANSWER into the R1 register's slot
   in the register save area used by the program interrupt
   handler.

7. Restore the registers saved by the program interrupt
   handler. Then load the PSW from location 40, decimal.
   This completes a return to the interrupted program.


BTB Examples:

Assume:
        Location 100: FE045778
        Register 4:   00000100

Case 1: BTB 2,0(0,4)  --> Register 2: -3
        Answer: 11

Case 2: BTB 2,0(0,4)  --> Register 2: +4
        Answer: 17


Levels of Sophistication:

    You are to implement your solution in three distinct levels
of sophistication. Each level will count equally in the grading,
and you must code all three to get a perfect score. You will be
provided with a macro which generates a test program for your
simulator. The name of this macro is BUCKET, and its use will be
described later.


Level One:

    For this level you are to provide a program interrupt
handler which correctly simulates BTB instructions. Branching to
the generated test program will start testing of your simulator.

**Level Two:**

For this level you must add an interrupt handler for SVC interrupts. This handler should recognize only one SVC, an SVC 2 instruction. Recall that after an SVC n instruction is issued, the value of n is placed in the low order byte of the interruption code for the Supervisor Old PSW (byte 35, decimal). The purpose of this SVC will be to determine the elapsed real time, in milliseconds since IPL.

The fullword starting at location 80, decimal is the interval timer on the 360. The hardware acts so as to decrement the fullword binary integer at this location at regular intervals (once every 26.04166 microseconds). Once this value changes from positive to negative, an external interrupt is generated. If you place the largest possible positive number in this area, you will have about 15 hours before a timer interrupt.

You should initialize the timer area to the constant 0 in your program. To avoid trouble with interrupts, your program should execute with external interrupts masked off. When you receive an SVC 2 request, pick up the timer's fullword and use the "Load Positive Register" (LPR) instruction to get the number of elapsed "timer units" since IPL.

To convert this time value to milliseconds, first multiply by twenty-six (26, DEC) and then divide by nine hundred eighty (980, DEC). This will give you approximate milliseconds, in fixed point binary form.  You must convert this value to a printable decimal number eight characters long.

For instance, if the elapsed time was 100 timer units (dec) then the equivalent elapsed time in milliseconds would be 2.6. You must write a little routine to convert the fixed point binary elapsed time to decimal and then EBCDIC form. Your answer must be placed in the eight character area addressed by register 1 upon entry to your SVC handler.

**Level Three:**

This level adds I/O interrupt processing to your solution. Upon each occurrence of a fixed point overflow, the following message should be outputed on the printer at I/O address X'00E':

"A BTB INSTRUCTION OCCURRED AT LOCATION XXXXXX AT TIME YYYYYYYY MILLISECONDS."

Where XXXXXX is the (hexadecimal) location of the BTB instruction, and YYYYYYYY is the (decimal) elapsed time as returned by your SVC 2 routine.

You must provide an SVC handler for SVC 3 to perform this printer I/O. Once called this SVC should cause the line to be printed on the printer, going into the wait state until a Device End interrupt is received from device X'00E'. Then the SVC handler returns to its caller.

You should structure your program interrupt handler so that it issues an SVC 2 to fill in the time, then calculates the instruction address in printable hex form. Once the output line is completely built, then you should issue an SVC 3, from within your program interrupt handler.

Hints and Warnings:

1. You should disable external interrupts to avoid problems with the interval timer.

2. Use the TRACE macro sparingly, you will be limited to 15 pages of TRACE information.

3. You should include a "PRINT NOGEN" statement at the beginning of your program to prevent the printing of macro expansions. It saves on our printing costs.

4. You must provide an SVC handler even if you are not attempting level two, since the BUCKET test program issues an SVC 2.

Deck Setup:

The following deck structure should be used:

```
$JOB name
        TITLE 'your name - your instructors name'
name    CSECT
         PRINT NOGEN
         .
         . your program
         .
        END
$EOJ
```

Run Schedule:

TO BE ANNOUNCED

## Example Program:

This example program contains a dummy SVC handler and a program interrupt handler that merely returns. You may use it as a starting point for your program.

```
EXAMPLE PROGRAM FOR INTERRUPT AND I/O PROBLEM OS3                                    PAGE   1

LOC   OBJECT CODE     ADDR1 ADDR2  STMT   SOURCE STATEMENT                              31 DEC 74

000000                             2 EXAMPLE CSECT
000000                             3          USING EXAMPLE,0            ASSEMBLE ABSOLUTE ADDRESSES
                                   5 ***********************************************************************
                                   6 *                                                                     *
                                   7 *       THIS EXAMPLE DEMONSTRATES USE OF THE BUCKET TESTING MACRO.    *
                                   8 *       THE PROVIDED PROGRAM INTERRUPT HANDLERS MERELY RETURN         *
                                   9 *       FROM EACH INTERRUPT.                                          *
                                  10 *                                                                     *
                                  11 ***********************************************************************

                                  13 ***********************************************************************
                                  14 *                                                                     *
                                  15 *       LOW CORE INTIALIZATION                                        *
                                  16 *                                                                     *
                                  17 ***********************************************************************

000000 FE0000000000008C          19 IPLPSW   DC    X'FE',AL3(0),A(START) INITIAL PSW LOADED TO START RUN
000008 CC00C0C000000000          20 IPLCCW1  DC    D'0'                  IPL CCW'S WHICH
000010 C000CCC000000000          21 IPLCCW2  DC    D'0'                    ARE NOT USED
000018 C000CCC000000000          22 EXTOLD   DC    D'0'                  EXTERNAL OLD PSW
0C0020 C000CC000C00000           23 SUPOLD   DC    D'0'                  SUPERVISOR OLD PSW
000028 C000000000000000          24 PGMOLD   DC    D'0'                  PROGRAM CHECK OLD PSW
000030 C000000000000000          25 MCKOLD   DC    D'0'                  MACHINE CHECK OLD PSW
000038 C000000000000000          26 IOOLD    DC    D'0'                  INPUT/OUTPUT OLD PSW
000040 0C00000000000000          27 CSW      DC    D'0'                  CHANNEL STATUS WORD
000048 00000000                  28 CAW      DC    F'0'                  CHANNEL ADDRESS WORD
00004C 0000C000                  29 UNUSED1  DC    F'0'                  UNUSED WORD 1
000050 C000C000                  30 TIMER    DC    F'0'                  TIMER AREA
000054 0000C000                  31 UNUSED2  DC    F'0'                  UNUSED WORD 2
000058 0002000000000001          32 EXTNEW   DC    X'0002',AL2(0),A(1)   EXTERNAL NEW PSW- CAUSES HALT
000060 C000CCC0C0000084          33 SUPNEW   DC    A(0,SVCINT)           SUPERVISOR NEW PSW
000068 0000C00000000080          34 PGMNEW   DC    A(0,PGMINT)           PROGRAM CHECK NEW PSW
000070 0002000000000004          35 MCKNEW   DC    X'0002',AL2(0),A(4)   MACHINE CHECK NEW PSW- CAUSES HALT
000078 CC0000C000000088          36 IONEW    DC    A(0,IOINT)            INPUT/OUTPUT NEW PSW

000080                           38 PGMINT   EQU   *

                                 40 ***********************************************************************
                                 41 *                                                                     *
                                 42 *       PROGRAM INTERRUPT HANDLER -- INTERRUPTS MASKED OFF            *
                                 43 *                                                                     *
                                 44 *       NOTE THAT THIS INTERRUPT HANDLER RETURNS DIRECTLY TO THE      *
                                 45 *       POINT OF INTERRUPTION WITH NO PROCESSING.                     *
                                 46 *                                                                     *
                                 47 ***********************************************************************

00C080 8200 C028     0C028       49          LPSW  PGMOLD                "RETURN" TO POINT OF INTERRUPTION
```

EXAMPLE PROGRAM FOR INTERRUPT AND I/O PROBLEM OS3                                            PAGE    2

    LCC  CBJECT CCDE   ACCR1 ADDR2  STMT   SOURCE STATEMENT                                  31 DEC 74

```
                              51 ***************************************************************
                              52 *                                                             *
                              53 *          SUPERVISOR CALL INTERRUPT HANDLER -- INTERRUPTS MASKED OFF   *
                              54 *                                                             *
                              55 *          NOTE THAT THIS INTERRUPT HANDLER RETURNS DIRECTLY TO THE     *
                              56 *          POINT OF INTERRUPTION WITH NO PROCESSING.          *
                              57 *                                                             *
                              58 ***************************************************************
000084                        60 SVCINT  EQU   *
000084 8200 0020      0C020   61         LPSW  SUPOLD              "RETURN" TO POINT OF INTERRUPTION
                              63 ***************************************************************
                              64 *                                                             *
                              65 *          INPUT/OUTPUT INTERRUPT HANDLER -- INTERRUPTIONS MASKED OFF   *
                              66 *                                                             *
                              67 *          NOTE THAT THIS INTERRUPT HANDLER RETURNS DIRECTLY TO THE     *
                              68 *          POINT OF INTERRUPTION WITH NO PROCESSING.          *
                              69 *                                                             *
                              70 ***************************************************************
000088                        72 IOINT   EQU   *
000088 8200 0038      0C038   73         LPSW  IOOLD               "RETURN" TO POINT OF INTERRUPTION
                              75 START   BUCKET              GENERATE TESTING PROGRAM
                              77+***************************************************************
                              78+*                                                             *
                              79+*                       BUCKET TEST MACRO FOR OS3             *
                              80+*                                                             *
                              81+*          THIS MACRO GENERATES FIVE PROGRAM INTERRUPTS TO TEST   *
                              82+*          A STUDENT'S BTB INSTRUCTION SIMULATOR. SOME OF THESE     *
                              83+*          INTERRUPTS ARE NOT CAUSED BY BTB INSTRUCTIONS. AFTER     *
                              84+*          THE FIVE TRIALS, THE STUDENT'S SVC HANDLER IS TESTED     *
                              85+*          WITH AN SVC 2. TO START TESTING, BRANCH TO CODE GENERATED *
                              86+*          BY THIS MACRO. NOTE - THIS MACRO MAY BE BRANCHED TO       *
                              87+*          ONLY ONCE.                                          *
                              88+*                                                             *
                              89+***************************************************************
000000                        91+        USING EXAMPLE,0 .       ASSEMBLE ABSOLUTE REFERENCES
00008C 980F 036C      0036C   92+START   LM    0,15,SRGR0000 .   LOAD REGISTERS FOR TESTING

0CC090                        95+        DS    0H
000090 0208                   96+        DC    AL1(2,8) TRACE OP-CODE AND TYPE(KLUDGE)
000092 0000                   97+        DC    XL2'0' ID.
000094 CC00                   98+        DC    BL2'0000000000000000'
000096 FFFF                   99+        DC    BL2'1111111111111111'
000098 032C                  100+        DC    Y(SM1OC000)
00009A CC06                  101+        DC    AL1(0,6) WORD COUNT AND INDIRECT
00009C 8C00                  102+        DC    XL2'8000'
```

366

```
  LOC  OBJECT CODE    ADDR1 ADDR2    STMT   SOURCE STATEMENT                                                31 DEC 74

00009E                               105+       DS   OH
00009E 0203                          106+       DC   AL1(2,3) TRACE OP-CODE AND TYPE(KLUDGE)
0000A0 0C02                          107+       DC   H'2' ID.
0000A2 0000                          108+       DC   BL2'0000000000000000'
0000A4 0000                          109+       DC   BL2'0000000000000000'
0000A6 8C00                          110+       DC   XL2'8C00'


0000A8                               113+       DS   OH
0000A8 0203                          114+       DC   AL1(2,3) TRACE OP-CODE AND TYPE(KLUDGE)
0000AA C003                          115+       DC   H'3' ID.
0000AC 0000                          116+       DC   BL2'0000000000000000'
0000AE 0000                          117+       DC   BL2'00C0000000000000'
0000B0 8C00                          118+       DC   XL2'8C00'


0000B2                               122+       DS   OH
0000B2 0208                          123+       DC   AL1(2,8) TRACE OP-CODE AND TYPE(KLUDGE)
0000B4 C000                          124+       DC   XL2'0' ID.
0000B6 0000                          125+       DC   BL2'0000000000000000'
0000B8 0000                          126+       DC   BL2'0000000C000C00000'
0000BA C0C0                          127+       DC   Y(STR1C000)
0000BC 0001                          128+       DC   AL1(0,1) WORD COUNT AND INDIRECT
0000BE 8000                          129+       DC   XL2'8C00'

0000C0                               131+       CNOP 0,4 .                    FORCE ALIGNMENT FOR TRACE DUMP
0000C0 5800 C000              C0000  132+STR1C000 L  0,0(0,12) .              GENERATE TRIAL 1 - ADDRESSING EXCEP

0000C4 900F 03AC              003AC  134+       STM  0,15,STGRC000 .          SAVE STUDENT'S REGISTERS
0000C8 D53F 03AC 036C   003AC 0036C  135+       CLC  STGR0000(64),SRGR0000
0000CE 4780 00E8              C00E8  136+       BE   ST1ROK00 .               IF REGISTERS NOT MODIFIED

0000D2                               138+       DS   OH
0000D2 C208                          139+       DC   AL1(2,8) TRACE OP-CODE AND TYPE(KLUDGE)
0000D4 C000                          140+       DC   XL2'0' ID.
0000D6 0000                          141+       DC   BL2'00C000000C0000000'
0000D8 FFFF                          142+       DC   BL2'1111111111111111'
0000DA 02FC                          143+       DC   Y(SBRS0000)
0000DC 0007                          144+       DC   AL1(0,7) WORD COUNT AND INDIRECT
0000DE 8000                          145+       DC   XL2'8000'

0000E0 980F 036C              0036C  147+       LM   0,15,SRGR0000 .          RESTORE REGISTERS
0000E4 47F0 00F6              C00F6  148+       B    ST200000 .               GO TO NEXT TRIAL


0000E8                               151+       DS   OH
```

```
LCC  CBJECT CCDE     ACDR1 ADDR2  STMT   SOURCE STATEMENT                                           31 DEC 74

0C00E8 0208                       152+ST1ROK00 DC   AL1(2,8) TRACE OP-CODE AND TYPE(KLUDGE)
0000EA 0000                       153+        DC    XL2'0' ID.
0000EC 0000                       154+        DC    BL2'0CC0000000000000'
0000EE CCC0                       155+        DC    BL2'0000000000000000'
0000F0 02EC                       156+        DC    Y(SAOK0000)
0000F2 0004                       157+        DC    AL1(0,4) WORD COUNT AND INDIRECT
0000F4 8C00                       158+        DC    XL2'8000'


0000F6                            162+        DS    OH
0000F6 0208                       163+ST200000 DC   AL1(2,8) TRACE OP-CODE AND TYPE(KLUDGE)
0000F8 CC00                       164+        DC    XL2'0' ID.
0000FA 0000                       165+        DC    BL2'0000000000000000'
0000FC 0000                       166+        DC    BL2'0000000000000000'
0000FE 0104                       167+        DC    Y(STR20000)
000100 0001                       168+        DC    AL1(0,1) WORD COUNT AND INDIRECT
000102 8C00                       169+        DC    XL2'8C00'

000104                            171+        CNOP  0,4 .                FORCE ALIGNMENT FOR TRACE DUMP
000104 51700000                   172+STR20000 DC   X'51700000' .        GENERATE TRIAL 2 - BTB 7,0(0,0)

000108 5070 03F8       003F8      174+        ST    7,SANSC000           SAVE ANSWER IN AREA
00010C 5870 0388       00388      175+        L     7,SRGR0000+7*4 .     RESTORE VALUE OF 7
000110 900F 03AC       003AC      176+        STM   0,15,STGR0000 .      SAVE REGISTERS FOR CHECK
000114 D53F 03AC 036C  003AC 0036C 177+       CLC   STGR0000(64),SRGR0000 CHECK STUDENT'S REGISTERS
00011A 4780 0130       00130      178+        BE    ST2ROK00 .           REGISTERS ARE OK


00011E                            181+        DS    OH
00011E 0208                       182+        DC    AL1(2,8) TRACE OP-CODE AND TYPE(KLUDGE)
000120 CC00                       183+        DC    XL2'0' ID.
000122 0000                       184+        DC    BL2'0000000000000000'
000124 FFFF                       185+        DC    BL2'1111111111111111'
000126 02FC                       186+        DC    Y(SBRS0000)
000128 0007                       187+        DC    AL1(0,7) WORD COUNT AND INDIRECT
00012A 8000                       188+        DC    XL2'8C00'

00012C 980F 036C       0036C      190+        LM    0,15,SRGR0000 .      RESTORE REGISTERS

000130 D503 03EC 03F8 003F8 003EC 192+ST2ROK00 CLC  SANS0000(4),ST2A0000 . CHECK ANSWER
000136 4780 0162       00162      193+        BE    ST2AOK00 .           ANSWER OK


00013A                            196+        DS    OH
00013A 0208                       197+        DC    AL1(2,8) TRACE OP-CODE AND TYPE(KLUDGE)
00013C 0000                       198+        DC    XL2'0' ID.
00013E 0C00                       199+        DC    BL2'0000000000000000'
000140 0000                       200+        DC    BL2'0000000000000000'
```

| LOC | OBJECT CODE | ADDR1 ADDR2 | STMT | SOURCE STATEMENT | 31 DEC 74 |
|---|---|---|---|---|---|
| 000142 | 0318 | | 201+ | DC | Y(SBAI0000) |
| 000144 | 0005 | | 202+ | DC | AL1(0,5) WORD COUNT AND INDIRECT |
| 000146 | 03F8 | | 203+ | DC | Y(SANS0000) |
| 000148 | 0001 | | 204+ | DC | AL1(0,1) WORD COUNT AND INDIRECT |
| 00014A | 8000 | | 205+ | DC | XL2'8000' |
| 00014C | | | 208+ | DS | OH |
| 00014C | 0208 | | 209+ | DC | AL1(2,8) TRACE OP-CODE AND TYPE(KLUDGE) |
| 00014E | CC00 | | 210+ | DC | XL2'0' ID. |
| 000150 | 0000 | | 211+ | DC | BL2'0000000000000000' |
| 000152 | 0000 | | 212+ | DC | BL2'0000000000000000' |
| 000154 | 0344 | | 213+ | DC | Y(SM200000) |
| 000156 | 0005 | | 214+ | DC | AL1(0,5) WORD COUNT AND INDIRECT |
| 000158 | 03EC | | 215+ | DC | Y(ST2A0000) |
| 00015A | 0001 | | 216+ | DC | AL1(0,1) WORD COUNT AND INDIRECT |
| 00015C | 8C00 | | 217+ | DC | XL2'8000' |
| 00015E | 47F0 0174 | 00174 | 219+ | B | ST300000 .         GO TO NEXT TRIAL |
| 000162 | | | 222+ | DS | OH |
| 000162 | 0208 | | 223+ST2A0K00 DC | AL1(2,8) TRACE OP-CODE AND TYPE(KLUDGE) |
| 000164 | 0000 | | 224+ | DC | XL2'0' ID. |
| 000166 | C000 | | 225+ | DC | BL2'0000000000000000' |
| 000168 | 0C00 | | 226+ | DC | BL2'0000000000000000' |
| 00016A | 02EC | | 227+ | DC | Y(SA0K0000) |
| 00016C | 0004 | | 228+ | DC | AL1(0,4) WORD COUNT AND INDIRECT |
| 00016E | 03F8 | | 229+ | DC | Y(SANS0000) |
| 000170 | 0001 | | 230+ | DC | AL1(0,1) WORD COUNT AND INDIRECT |
| 000172 | 8C00 | | 231+ | DC | XL2'8C00' |
| 000174 | | | 235+ | DS | OH |
| 000174 | 0208 | | 236+ST300000 DC | AL1(2,8) TRACE OP-CODE AND TYPE(KLUDGE) |
| 000176 | CC00 | | 237+ | DC | XL2'0' ID. |
| 000178 | C000 | | 238+ | DC | BL2'0000000000000000' |
| 00017A | 0000 | | 239+ | DC | BL2'000000C000000000' |
| 00017C | 0184 | | 240+ | DC | Y(STR30000) |
| 00017E | CC01 | | 241+ | DC | AL1(0,1) WORD COUNT AND INDIRECT |
| 000180 | 8000 | | 242+ | DC | XL2'8000' |
| 000182 | 0700 | | 244+ | CNOP | 0,4 .                FORCE ALIGNMENT |
| 000184 | 51E3FC00 | | 245+STR30000 DC | X'51E3F000' .        GENERATE TRIAL 3 - BTB 14,0(3,15) |
| 000188 | 50E0 03F8 | 003F8 | 247+ | ST | 14,SANS0000 .        SAVE STUDENT'S ANSWER |
| 00018C | 58E0 03A4 | 003A4 | 248+ | L | 14,SRGR0000+14*4 .   RESTORE VALUE OF 14 |

369

EXAMPLE PROGRAM FOR INTERRUPT AND I/O PROBLEM OS3                                    PAGE    6

```
LCC   OBJECT CODE      ADDR1 ADDR2  STMT    SOURCE STATEMENT                                    31 DEC 74

000190 900F 03AC             003AC  249+           STM   0,15,STGR0000 .     SAVE REGISTERS FOR CHECK
000194 D53F 03AC 036C 003AC 0036C  250+           CLC   STGR0000(64),SRGR0000 CHECK STUDENT'S REGISTERS
00019A 4780 01B0             001B0  251+           BE    ST3ROK00 .          REGISTERS OK


00019E                              254+           DS    OH
00019E 0208                         255+           DC    AL1(2,8) TRACE OP-CODE AND TYPE(KLUDGE)
0001A0 0000                         256+           DC    XL2'0' ID.
0001A2 CC00                         257+           DC    BL2'0000000000000000'
0001A4 FFFF                         258+           DC    BL2'1111111111111111'
0001A6 02FC                         259+           DC    Y(SBRSC000)
0001A8 C007                         260+           DC    AL1(0,7) WORD COUNT AND INDIRECT
0001AA 8000                         261+           DC    XL2'8000'


0001AC 980F 036C             0036C  263+           LM    0,15,SRGR0000 .     RESTORE REGISTERS

0001B0 D503 03F8 03F0 003F8 003F0  265+ST3ROK00 CLC   SANS0000(4),ST3A0000 CHECK STUDENT'S ANSWER
0001B6 4780 01E2             001E2  266+           BE    ST3AOK00 .          ANSWER CORRECT


0001BA                              268+           DS    OH
0001BA 0208                         269+           DC    AL1(2,8) TRACE OP-CODE AND TYPE(KLUDGE)
0001BC CC00                         270+           DC    XL2'0' ID.
0001BE 0000                         271+           DC    BL2'0000000000000000'
0001C0 0000                         272+           DC    BL2'0000000000000000'
0001C2 0318                         273+           DC    Y(SBAI0000)
0001C4 0005                         274+           DC    AL1(0,5) WORD COUNT AND INDIRECT
0001C6 03F8                         275+           DC    Y(SANS0000)
0001C8 0002                         276+           DC    AL1(0,2) WORD COUNT AND INDIRECT
0001CA 8000                         277+           DC    XL2'8000'


0001CC                              280+           DS    OH
0001CC 0208                         281+           DC    AL1(2,8) TRACE OP-CODE AND TYPE(KLUDGE)
0001CE 0000                         282+           DC    XL2'0' ID.
0001D0 0000                         283+           DC    BL2'0000000000000000'
0001D2 CC00                         284+           DC    BL2'0000000000000000'
0001D4 0344                         285+           DC    Y(SM200000)
0001D6 0005                         286+           DC    AL1(0,5) WORD COUNT AND INDIRECT
0001D8 03F0                         287+           DC    Y(ST3A0000)
0001DA 0001                         288+           DC    AL1(0,1) WORD COUNT AND INDIRECT
0001DC 8000                         289+           DC    XL2'8000'


0001DE 47F0 01F4             001F4  291+           B     ST400000 .          GO TO NEXT TRIAL


0001E2                              294+           DS    OH
0001E2 0208                         295+ST3AOK00 DC   AL1(2,8) TRACE OP-CODE AND TYPE(KLUDGE)
0001E4 CC00                         296+           DC    XL2'0' ID.
```

EXAMPLE PROGRAM FOR INTERRUPT AND I/O PROBLEM OS3

```
LOC   OBJECT CODE    ADDR1 ADDR2  STMT   SOURCE STATEMENT

0001E6 0000                       297+        DC     BL2'0000000000000000'
0001E8 0000                       298+        DC     BL2'0000000000000000'
0001EA 02EC                       299+        DC     Y(SAOK0000)
0001EC C004                       300+        DC     AL1(0,4) WORD COUNT AND INDIRECT
0001EE 03F8                       301+        DC     Y(SANS0000)
0001F0 0001                       302+        DC     AL1(0,1) WORD COUNT AND INDIRECT
0001F2 8000                       303+        DC     XL2'8000'


0001F4                            307+        DS     OH
0001F4 0208                       308+ST400000 DC    AL1(2,8) TRACE OP-CODE AND TYPE(KLUDGE)
0001F6 0000                       309+        DC     XL2'0' ID.
0001F8 0000                       310+        DC     BL2'0000000000000000'
0001FA 0000                       311+        DC     BL2'0000000000000000'
0001FC 02D4                       312+        DC     Y(STR40000)
0001FE 0001                       313+        DC     AL1(0,1) WORD COUNT AND INDIRECT
000200 8000                       314+        DC     XL2'8C00'

000202 0700                       316+        CNOP   0,4 .             FORCE ALIGNMENT
000204 0000                       317+STR4C000 DC    H'0' .            TRIAL 4 - OPERATION EXCEPTION

000206 900F 03AC          003AC   319+        STM    0,15,STGR0000 .   SAVE REGISTERS FOR CHECK
00020A D53F 03AC 036C 003AC 0036C 320+        CLC    STGR0000(64),SRGR0000 CHECK STUDENT'S REGISTERS
000210 4780 022A          0022A   321+        BE     ST4AOK00 .        ANSWER IS CORRECT


000214                            324+        DS     OH
000214 0208                       325+        DC     AL1(2,8) TRACE OP-CODE AND TYPE(KLUDGE)
000216 0000                       326+        DC     XL2'0' ID.
000218 0000                       327+        DC     BL2'0000000000000000'
00021A FFFF                       328+        DC     BL2'1111111111111111'
00021C 02FC                       329+        DC     Y(SBRS0000)
00021E 0007                       330+        DC     AL1(0,7) WORD COUNT AND INDIRECT
000220 8C00                       331+        DC     XL2'8C00'


000222 980F 036C          0036C   333+        LM     0,15,SRGR0000 .   RESTORE REGISTERS
000226 47F0 0238          00238   334+        B      ST5CC000 .        GO TO NEXT TRIAL


00022A                            337+        DS     OH
00022A 0208                       338+ST4AOK00 DC    AL1(2,8) TRACE OP-CODE AND TYPE(KLUDGE)
00022C CC00                       339+        DC     XL2'0' ID.
00022E CC00                       340+        DC     BL2'0000000000000000'
000230 0000                       341+        DC     BL2'0000000000000000'
000232 02FC                       342+        DC     Y(SAOK0000)
000234 CC04                       343+        DC     AL1(0,4) WORD COUNT AND INDIRECT
000236 8C00                       344+        DC     XL2'8000'
```

371

```
     LOC  OBJECT CODE      ACDR1 ADDR2  STMT   SOURCE STATEMENT                                      31 DEC 74

   000238                                348+          DS    OH
   000238 0208                           349+ST50C000  DC    AL1(2,8) TRACE OP-CODE AND TYPE(KLUDGE)
   00023A C000                           350+          DC    XL2'0' ID.
   00023C 0000                           351+          DC    BL2'0000000000000000'
   00023E C000                           352+          DC    BL2'0000000000000000'
   000240 0248                           353+          DC    Y(STR50000)
   000242 C001                           354+          DC    AL1(0,1) WORD COUNT AND INDIRECT
   000244 8000                           355+          DC    XL2'8000'

   000246 0700                           357+          CNOP  0,4 .                           FORCE ALIGNMENT FOR DUMP
   000248 5120F003                       358+STR50000  DC    X'5120F003' .                   GENERATE TRIAL 5 - BTB 2,3(0,15)

   00024C 5020 03F8              003F8    360+          ST    2,SANSC000 .                   SAVE STUDENT'S ANSWER
   000250 5820 0374              00374    361+          L     2,SRGR0000+2*4 .               RESTORE VALUE OF 2
   000254 900F 03AC              003AC    362+          STM   0,15,STGR0000 .                SAVE REGISTERS FOR CHECK
   000258 D53F 03AC 036C  003AC 0036C     363+          CLC   STGR0000(64),SRGRC000 CHECK STUDENT'S REGISTERS
   00025E 4780 0274              00274    364+          BE    ST5ROK00 .                     REGISTERS ARE OK

   000262                                367+          DS    OH
   000262 0208                           368+          DC    AL1(2,8) TRACE OP-CODE AND TYPE(KLUDGE)
   000264 C000                           369+          DC    XL2'0' ID.
   000266 0000                           370+          DC    BL2'0000000000000000'
   000268 FFFF                           371+          DC    BL2'1111111111111111'
   00026A 02FC                           372+          DC    Y(SBRS0000)
   00026C 0007                           373+          DC    AL1(0,7) WORD COUNT AND INDIRECT
   00026E 8000                           374+          DC    XL2'8000'

   000270 980F 036C              0036C    376+          LM    0,15,SRGR0000 .                RESTORE REGISTERS

   000274 D503 03F8 03F4  003F8 003F4     378+ST5ROK00 CLC   SANS0000(4),ST5A0000 CHECK STUDENT'S ANSWER
   00027A 4780 02A6              002A6    379+          BE    ST5A0K00 .                      ANSWER IS CORRECT

   00027E                                381+          DS    OH
   00027E 0208                           382+          DC    AL1(2,8) TRACE OP-CODE AND TYPE(KLUDGE)
   000280 0000                           383+          DC    XL2'0' ID.
   000282 0000                           384+          DC    BL2'0000000000000000'
   000284 C000                           385+          DC    BL2'0000000000000000'
   000286 0318                           386+          DC    Y(SBAI0000)
   000288 0005                           387+          DC    AL1(0,5) WORD COUNT AND INDIRECT
   00028A 03F8                           388+          DC    Y(SANSC000)
   00028C 0001                           389+          DC    AL1(0,1) WORD COUNT AND INDIRECT
   00028B 8000                           390+          DC    XL2'8000'

   000290                                393+          DS    OH
   000290 0208                           394+          DC    AL1(2,8) TRACE OP-CODE AND TYPE(KLUDGE)
   000292 0000                           395+          DC    XL2'0' ID.
   000294 C000                           396+          DC    BL2'0000000000000000'
```

372

EXAMPLE PROGRAM FOR INTERRUPT AND I/O PROBLEM OS3

```
LOC    OBJECT CODE    ADDR1 ADDR2   STMT   SOURCE STATEMENT

000296 0000                          397+        DC    BL2'0000000000000000'
000298 0344                          398+        DC    Y(SM200000)
00029A 0005                          399+        DC    AL1(0,5) WORD COUNT AND INDIRECT
00029C 03F4                          400+        DC    Y(ST5A0000)
00029E 0001                          401+        DC    AL1(0,1) WORD COUNT AND INDIRECT
0002A0 8000                          402+        DC    XL2'8000'

0002A2 47F0 0288         0288        404+        B     ST600000 .        GO TO NEXT TRIAL


0002A6                               407+        DS    0H
0002A6 0208                          408+ST5A0K00 DC   AL1(2,8) TRACE OP-CODE AND TYPE(KLUDGE)
0002A8 C000                          409+        DC    XL2'0' ID.
0002AA 0000                          410+        DC    BL2'0000000000000000'
0002AC C000                          411+        DC    BL2'0000000000000000'
0002AE 02EC                          412+        DC    Y(SA0K0000)
0002B0 0004                          413+        DC    AL1(0,4) WORD COUNT AND INDIRECT
0002B2 03F8                          414+        DC    Y(SANS0000)
0002B4 CC01                          415+        DC    AL1(0,1) WORD COUNT AND INDIRECT
0002B6 8000                          416+        DC    XL2'8000'


0002B8 0A02                          419+ST600000 SVC  2 .               ISSUE SVC TO TEST STUDENT

0002BA 900F 03AC         003AC       421+        STM   0,15,STGR0000 .   SAVE STUDENT'S REGISTERS
0002BE D53F 036C 03AC 0036C 003AC    422+        CLC   SRGR0000(64),STGR0000 WERE REGISTERS MODIFIED
0002C4 4780 02D6         002D6       423+        BE    ST6R0K00 .        NO, COOL


0002C8                               425+        DS    0H
0002C8 0208                          426+        DC    AL1(2,8) TRACE OP-CODE AND TYPE(KLUDGE)
0002CA 0000                          427+        DC    XL2'0' ID.
0002CC C000                          428+        DC    BL2'0000000000000000'
0002CE FFFF                          429+        DC    BL2'1111111111111111'
0002D0 02FC                          430+        DC    Y(SBRS0000)
0002D2 CC07                          431+        DC    AL1(0,7) WORD COUNT AND INDIRECT
0002D4 8000                          432+        DC    XL2'8000'


0002D6                               436+        DS    0H
0002D6 0208                          437+ST6R0K00 DC   AL1(2,8) TRACE OP-CODE AND TYPE(KLUDGE)
0002D8 0000                          438+        DC    XL2'0' ID.
0002DA 0000                          439+        DC    BL2'00C0000000000000'
0002DC CC00                          440+        DC    BL2'0000000000000000'
0002DE 0358                          441+        DC    Y(SM300000)
0002E0 0005                          442+        DC    AL1(0,5) WORD COUNT AND INDIRECT
0002E2 03FC                          443+        DC    Y(TAREA000)
0002E4 CC02                          444+        DC    AL1(0,2) WORD COUNT AND INDIRECT
0002E6 8000                          445+        DC    XL2'8C00'
```

| LOC | OBJECT CODE | ACDR1 ADDR2 | STMT | SOURCE STATEMENT | | 31 DEC 74 |
|---|---|---|---|---|---|---|
| 0002E8 | | | 447+ | DS | OH | |
| 0002E8 | FF777777 | | 448+ | DC | X'FF777777' | |
| 0002EC | | | 450+ | CNOP | 0,4 .                      FORCE WORD ALIGNMENT FOR DUMPS | |
| 0002EC | 40C1E5E2E6C5D940 | | 451+SAOKC000 DC | | C' ANSWER CORRECT:' | |
| 0002FC | D9C5C7C9E2E3C5D9 | | 452+SBRSO000 DC | | C'REGISTERS HAVE BEEN CHANGED ' | |
| 000318 | C1D5E2E6C5D940C9 | | 453+SBAI0000 DC | | C'ANSWER INCORRECT--> ' | |
| 00032C | C9C5C7C9E2E3C5D9 | | 454+SM1C0000 DC | | C'REGISTERS FOR TESTING:  ' | |
| 000344 | C1D5E2E6C5D940E2 | | 455+SM200000 DC | | C'ANSWER SHOULD BE:   ' | |
| 000358 | E3C9D4C540E5C1D3 | | 456+SM300000 DC | | C'TIME VALUE RETURNED:' | |
| 00036C | 00000000000003FC | | 457+SRGRC000 DC | | F'0',A(TAREA000),F'-3,3,4,5,6,0,8,9,10,11',X'FFFFFFFF' | |
| 0003A0 | 0000000000000002 | | 458+ | DC | F'13,2',A(FIELD000) | |
| 0003AC | CC00C0C000000000 | | 459+STGR0000 DC | | 16F'0' | |
| 0003EC | 00000C000 | | 460+ST2A0000 DC | | F'0' .            ANSWER FOR TRIAL TWO | |
| 0003F0 | 00000009 | | 461+ST3A0000 DC | | F'9' .            ANSWER FOR TRIAL THREE | |
| 0003F4 | C000C00A | | 462+ST5A0000 DC | | F'10' .           ANSWER FOR TRIAL FIVE | |
| 0003F8 | 0000C000 | | 463+SANS0000 DC | | F'0' .            STUDENT'S ANSWER AREA | |
| 0003FC | 0000000000000000 | | 464+TAREA000 DC | | 8X'00' .          STUDENT'S SVC 2 ANSWER AREA | |
| 000404 | C7C7D9C5C7D6D9E8 | | 465+FIELD000 DC | | X'C7C7D9C5C7D6D9E8' TEST AREA | |
| | | | 467 | END | | |

374

```
MASSACHUSETTS INSTITUTE OF TECHNOLOGY           SYSTEM / 360 SIMULATOR                               VERSION 1.3
EXAMPLE TRACE LISTING.   0 CONDITIONS ENABLED.                                                             PAGE  1

LOC  TRACE TYPE          COUNT  TIME                                  OP   INSTRUCTION       ADR1 ADR2  OPERAND1 OPERAND2
----  ----------------   -----  ----------                           ----  --------------   ---- ----  -------- -------


009E SNAPSHOT              1          18  PSW: FE 0 0 0000  '01'B '00'B 0 00009E
       REGISTERS:
          R 0: 00000000,        0 R 1: 000003FC,       1020 R 2: FFFFFFFD,          -3 R 3: 00000003,              3
          R 4: 00000004,        4 R 5: 00000005,          5 R 6: 00000006,           6 R 7: 00000000,              0
          R 8: 00000008,        8 R 9: 00000009,          9 R10: 0000000A,          10 R11: 0000000B,             11
          R12: FFFFFFFF,       -1 R13: 0000000D,         13 R14: 00000002,           2 R15: 00000404,           1028
       CORE DUMP:
         032C,   812: D9C5C7C9 E2E3C5D9 E240C6D6 D940E3C5 E2E3C9D5 C77A4040   REGI STER S FO R TE STIN G:

00C0 SNAPSHOT              1          18  PSW: FE 0 0 0000  '01'B '00'B 0 0000C0
       CORE DUMP:
         00C0,   192: 5800C000                                                ????

00C4 PGM INTERRUPT         1          18  PSW: FE 0 0 0006  '10'B '00'B 0 0000C4

00F6 SNAPSHOT              5          66  PSW: FE 0 0 0000  '01'B '00'B 0 0000F6
       CORE DUMP:
         02EC,   748: 40C1D5E2 E6C5D940 C3D6D9D9 C5C3E37A                      ANS WER  CORR ECT:

0104 SNAPSHOT              5          66  PSW: FE 0 0 0000  '01'B '00'B 0 000104
       CORE DUMP:
         0104,   260: 51700000                                                ????

0108 PGM INTERRUPT         5          66  PSW: FE 0 0 0001  '10'B '00'B 0 000108

0174 SNAPSHOT             13         118  PSW: FE 0 0 0000  '01'B '00'B 0 000174
       CORE DUMP:
         02EC,   748: 40C1D5E2 E6C5D940 C3D6D9D9 C5C3E37A                      ANS WER  CORR ECT:
         03F8,  1016: 00000000                                                ????

0182 SNAPSHOT             13         118  PSW: FE 0 0 0000  '01'B '00'B 0 000182
       CORE DUMP:
         0184,   388: 51E3F000                                                ?TO?

0188 PGM INTERRUPT        14         119  PSW: FE 0 0 0001  '10'B '00'B 0 000188

01CC SNAPSHOT             22         171  PSW: FE 0 0 0000  '01'B '01'B 0 0001CC
       CORE DUMP:
         0318,   792: C1D5E2E6 C5D940C9 D5C3D6D9 D9C5C3E3 60606E40            ANSW ER I NCOR RECT -->
         03F8,  1016: 00000002 00000C00                                       ???? ????

01DE SNAPSHOT             22         171  PSW: FF 0 0 0000  '01'B '01'B 0 C001DE
       CORE DUMP:
         0344,   836: C1D5E2E6 C5D940E2 C8D6E4D3 C440C2C5 7A404040            ANSW ER S HOUL D BE :
         03F0,  100R: 00000009                                                ????

0202 SNAPSHOT             23         172  PSW: FE 0 0 0000  '01'H '01'B 0 000202
       CORE DUMP:
```

375

```
MASSACHUSETTS INSTITUTE OF TECHNOLOGY          SYSTEM / 360 SIMULATOR                                    VERSION 1.3
EXAMPLE TRACE LISTING.   3 CONDITIONS ENABLED.                                                             PAGE  2

LCC  TRACE TYPE           CCUNT   TIME                                      OP   INSTRUCTION     ADR1 ADR2  OPERAND1 OPERAND2
---- ---------------      -----   ----                                     ---- -------------   ---- ----  -------- --------


      0204,    516: 0000900F                                               ????

0206 PGM INTERRUPT         24        172  PSW: FE 0 0 0001  '01'B '01'B 0 000206

0238 SNAPSHOT              28        220  PSW: FE 0 0 0C00  '01'B '00'B 0 000238
     CORE DUMP:
       02EC,   748: 40C1D5E2 E6C5D940 C3D6D9D9 C5C3E37A                     ANS WER  CORR ECT:

0246 SNAPSHOT              28        220  PSW: FE 0 0 0000  '01'B '00'B 0 000246
     CORE DUMP:
       0248,   584: 5120F003                                               ????

024C PGM INTERRUPT         29        220  PSW: FE 0 0 0001  '10'B '00'B 0 00024C

0290 SNAPSHOT              37        272  PSW: FE 0 0 0000  '01'B '10'B 0 000290
     CORE DUMP:
       0318,   792: C1D5E2E6 C5D940C9 D5C3D6D9 D9C5C3F3 60606E40            ANSW ER I NCOR RECT -->
       03F8,  1016: FFFFFFFD                                               ????

02A2 SNAPSHOT              37        272  PSW: FE 0 0 0000  '01'B '10'B 0 0002A2
     CORE DUMP:
       0344,   836: C1D5E2E6 C5D940E2 C8D6E4D3 C440C2C5 7A404040           ANSW ER S HOUL D BE :
       03F4,  1012: 0000000A                                               ????

02BA SVC INTERRUPT         39        272  PSW: FE 0 0 0002  '01'B '10'B 0 0002BA

02E8 SNAPSHOT              43        324  PSW: FE 0 0 0000  '01'B '00'B 0 0002E8
     CORE DUMP:
       0358,   856: E3C9D4C5 40E5C1D3 E4C540D9 C5E3E4D9 D5C5C47A            TIME  VAL UE R ETUR NED:
       03FC,  1020: 00000000 00000000                                      ???? ????


NORMAL SIMULATOR TERMINATION FOR PROGRAM EXAMPLE

          SIMULATED REAL TIME:       324.485

          SIMULATED CPU TIME:        324.485
```

## 5.2.4  Airline Reservations Problem -- OS4

Introduction:

A  common application for computer systems is the real-time,
transaction-oriented system.  Such  a  system  allows  people  at
several  different  locations to interrogate and update a central
database instantaneously. Typically users access  such  a  system
through  a  terminal.  These terminals are connected to a central
computer by telephone lines.

From his or her terminal a user enters  requests  which  act
upon  the  central  database. A prime example of such a system is
the  airlines  reservations  system.  From  widely  scattered
terminals,  reservations  may  be made and deleted. A reservation
made in Boston is known in Chicago the minute it has  been  made.
This  is absolutely necessary to allow ticket sales to be made in
several cities at once. Usually these systems  are  divided  into
two  components-  a  terminal I/O handling part heavily operating
system dependent and  probably  written  in  assembler,  and   an
inquiry  processing  part  written in a high level language like
PL/1.

Since terminal input is essentially  random,  most  terminal
handling  packages  queue  terminal  I/O  to  a buffering medium,
possibly a disk.  During  periods  of  light  load  the  inquiry
program(s)  accept  input  as it is typed, but when the load gets
heavy a backlog develops in the buffering medium. In  a  buffered
system  like  this  the  inquiry program never waits for input as
long as there is a buffered backlog. This  provides  the  fastest
possible response under load.

In  a  typical  airline  reservations  system  there  may be
several  thousand  terminals.  The  IBM  360-370  I/O  device
addressing  scheme  does not allow direct addressing of this many
devices. As a solution  terminals  are  attached  to  controllers
which  act as "concentrators". Many terminals are connected to a
single controller which is then attached as <u>one</u> I/O device.   The
controller numbers each terminal attached to it. When you issue a
read  request to a controller it gives you the line inputted by a
terminal, <u>prefixed</u> with the  terminal's  number.  On  output  you
prefix a message with its terminal number.

For  example,  a  user  on terminal number eight may request
information on Pacific Airlines flight 707 by typing:

        PA707

The input controller would prefix the user's terminal  number  to
the  input  request, and the actual message passed from the input
controller to the CPU would be:

        08PA707

Similarly, suppose the inquiry program now wishes to tell the
user on terminal eight that Pacific Flight 707 is non-existant.
Perhaps the message should be:

        PACIFIC FLIGHT 707 NON-EXISTANT

The inquiry program would have to send the following message to
the output controller to accomplish this:

        08PACIFIC FLIGHT 707 NON-EXISTANT

        For this problem we will consider a controller to have
twenty terminals numbered 0-19.   In order to simplify the
assignment (and take advantage of our 360 simulator facilities),
we will assume that the input controller uses the same I/O
commands as a 2540 card reader and the output controller uses the
same I/O commands as a 1403 printer. Thus, to read a line from a
terminal, an SIO is issued to the input controller at I/O address
X'00C'. The resultant eighty character message will have a
terminal number in EBCDIC as the first two characters.

        To output messages to a terminal, an SIO is issued to the
output controller at I/O address x'00E'. Lines output in this
fashion must be prefixed with the two character number of the
terminal to receive the message.

        A deck of cards containing requests is used as input to your
program. A copy of this input will be posted so you will know
what it is. Your output will appear as printed, so again you may
check your results. This method of terminal simulation has
inherent some peculiarities. It is possible for you to write on
a terminal at the same time you are reading from it, you will
never have to wait for a person to type a request, and your run
will be terminated by an end of file condition from the reader
(unit exception in the CSW).


Problem Description:

        You will be provided with a working, but crude airline
reservations system. You are asked to embellish this program in
four distinct levels or steps. The provided system is logically
divided into a terminal handling component and an inquiry
processing component. The inquiry processing program communicates
to the terminal handler by using the supervisor call mechanism in
the following fashion:

SVC 1 - the SVC routine should return with register one
        pointing to an eighty character (including terminal
        prefix) input request. No other registers should be
        alterred.

If this request cannot be satisfied (no more requests in reader) the run should be terminated.

SVC 2 - this requests that a message be printed on a given terminal. Register one points to the message, while register zero contains the length of the message in lines.

Each line is 132 characters long, including a terminal number prefix. The only possible messages are a one line 132 character message or a two line 264 character message.

As soon as the inquiry processing program is activated it starts requesting input. It functions in a very straightforward fashion, always alternating between input requests and answers in the form of output requests.

The terminal handling (SVC handler) is also very simple. It is this part of the program you will be asked to improve. When the inquiry program issues an input request (SVC 1), the handler issues an SIO for the reader. Only when this I/O operation is complete does the SVC routine return to the inquiry program (via an LPSW instruction).

When the inquiry program issues an output request (SVC 2) the handler issues an SIO for the printer. Once this I/O is complete the handler returns and the cycle is repeated.

Embellishment One:

It should be clear that in the distributed system most of the time spent (real time) is waiting for terminal I/O. Notice the large difference between simulated real time and simulated CPU time. In particular no attempt is made to overlap the printing of a response with either the reading of the next request or the processing of a subsequent request.

This is to say that our system does not make any use of buffering. The purpose of this modification is to add buffering to the distributed system. In order to increase the efficiency of terminal I/O we are introducing the concept of read-ahead and write-behind. This is an interrupt-driven scheme with the following algorithm:

1. As soon as the first input request is received an interrupt driven input loop is started. Each input request is enterred into a buffer. As soon as one buffer is full, the card reader is started up again to fill another. This proceeds until either all the input buffers are full, or there are no more cards.

379

2. It should be noted that although interrupt-driven in
   nature this process needs to be synchronized with the
   inquiry processing program. The first request starts
   this loop, but if the buffers become full the loop must
   be stopped until a read request by the inquiry program
   frees up another buffer. Also, once end of file has
   been received from the reader a mechanism is necessary
   whereby the already buffered requests are processed.

3. Thus, when an SVC 1 is received a check is made to see
   if a request is already in a buffer. If one is, it is
   copied into an intermediate area. This is necessary
   since the buffer is about to be reused. If all the
   input buffers were full, then the reader processing
   loop must be started again now that an input buffer is
   free. Otherwise control is returned to the inquiry
   program with register one pointing to the intermediate
   area.

4. If no request is in the input buffers, you must know
   why. If EOF on the reader is the reason, the simulation
   is terminated. Otherwise the SVC handler must go into
   the wait state until an I/O interrupt signals that a
   read has been completed.

5. The output side is similar in its operation. If enough
   buffer space is available for a message, the message is
   placed in the buffer directly. If no printer I/O is
   active the output loop is started. Then the SVC handler
   returns to the inquiry program.

6. If enough buffer space is not available, the SVC
   handler must wait until completion of a previous output
   I/O operation frees more space. Note that this should
   not interfere with the reader's interrupt loop.

7. As soon as one print request is complete, the I/O
   interrupt handler must see if more output is already
   buffered. If so, it is initiated on the printer and the
   interrupted program is restarted.

       If the I/O old PSW has the wait state bit on, then
   a check is made to see if the SVC handler is waiting
   for printer buffer space. If so, the wait is cleared
   and SVC processing continues. Similar considerations
   apply to I/O interrupts for the reader.

To make the problem more interesting we make several
restrictions on this embellishment. First, the input buffer is
constrained to four cards (320 bytes) and the output buffer is
limited to three lines (396 bytes). Second, all two-line messages
should be printed using command chained CCW's. Third, the buffers
should each be managed on a FIFO basis.

To determine if your program works correctly, you should dump the contents of the input and output buffers before processing each SVC 1 request. The major indication of success will be the amount of simulated real time your solution requires to process all the requests.

**Embellishment Two:**

In a real system with buffering it is not at all unusual to find several messages queued and waiting for service. Some messages might require immediate attention. Suppose for instance a flight is cancelled an hour before it was scheduled to depart. Some of the stacked up messages may be reservations for that flight, in which case they should be turned down.

The purpose of this modification is to implement a three-level priority system. A user indicates the priority of a request by the first character he or she types. Remember that this becomes the third character after the terminal prefix is added. The following levels are defined:

Normal - as before, e.g., "04UN881...".

Important - serviced before normal requests. This level of urgency is indicated by an asterisk ("*") as the first message character; e.g., "04*UN881...".

Urgent - serviced before normal and important requests. This level is identified by an exclamation point ("!"); e.g., "04!UN881...".

Both input and output queues must be serviced by priority. Within priority levels, however, messages and requests should be processed on a FIFO basis.

**Embellishment Three:**

Even with terminal buffering our system will be I/O bound. In an effort to improve response, we will add another controller and set of buffers, dividing the present twenty terminals up accordingly.

Terminals numbered 0-9 will be connected to the present controller (reader X'00C' and printer X'00E'), while terminals numbered 10-19 will be connected to the new controller (reader X'012' and printer X'00F'). You must add four input buffers (320 bytes) and three output buffers (396 bytes) to be used by the second controller. The following points must be considered:

1. Both readers and printers should be kept as busy as possible.

2. Buffers are assigned to a particular controller (reader-printer pair) and may not be used by the other controller.

3. If the output buffer of one printer becomes full, the SVC 1 routine should only feed the inquiry routine requests from the other printer's reader. This will provide optimum throughput.

4. Priority processing should be enforced collectively for the two input buffers. That is an urgent request in any buffer takes precedence, followed by an important request in any buffer, followed by normal requests in either buffer. The important exception to this rule is when one printer is full, all of its reader requests are ignored.

5. Priority processing of output buffers is on an individual basis, for obvious reasons.


Embellishment Four:

     In keeping with the national trend, your company has noticed that good help is getting harder and harder to find. An airline ticketing operation involves two people.  One person checks baggage and issues tickets at the information desk, while another person collects tickets at the boarding gate. Due to increased costs of labor the airlines have started hiring personnel that cannot tell time.

     To make sure that the ticket collector starts passengers boarding at the right time, you are to implement a facility whereby a supervisor enters the exact time of boarding, to the nearest 1/10th of a second. When the time arrives, you send an urgent message "FIRE" to the correct terminal (the one that requested the notice). This alerts the dozing attendant who starts boarding passengers.

     Notice that this message is handled entirely by the terminal handling routines.  The activating request should not be passed to the inquiry program. This request has the following format:

     04+hh:mm:ss.d

Where 04 is the terminal number, hh is the hour, mm is the minute, ss is the second, and d is the tenths of a second that the "FIRE" message should be sent. You are to assume that the system is always IPL'ed at 10:00, and crashes before 11:00. Only one boarding message request may be outstanding for each terminal.

The plus indicates that this message should never get to the inquiry processing program.  The 360 timer feature with external interrupt should be used to implement this feature.   Make sure that the "FIRE" message has urgent priority.


Deck Setup:

You should use the following deck structure:

```
Col. 1        10        16
     $JOB name
               TITLE 'your name- your instructor'
     name      CSECT
               PRINT NOGEN
                 .
                 . distribution deck with your modifications.
                 .
               END
     $EOJ
```

Where **name** is used to identify your output. It should be your last name, truncated or prefixed with qualifiers to eight characters.


Point Assignment for Grading:

The  base  value  of  this  problem  is  ten  (10)  points. Modifications three  and  four  will  receive  extra  credit,  as follows:

| 1 | 2 | 3 | 4 | CREDIT |
|---|---|---|---|--------|
| MODIFICATIONS | | | | CREDIT |
| X |   |   |   | 8  |
| X | X |   |   | 10 |
| X | X | X |   | 16 |
| X | X |   | X | 14 |
| X | X | X | X | 20 |


Run Schedule:

TO BE ANNOUNCED

Distributed Program:

The following program will be distributed in deck form:

| LOC | OBJECT CODE | ADDR1 ADDR2 | STMT | SOURCE STATEMENT | | 31 DEC 74 |
|-----|-------------|-------------|------|------------------|---|---|

```
000000                              2 EXAMPLE CSECT
000000                              3         USING EXAMPLE,0          ASSEMBLE ABSOLUTE ADDRESSES
                                    4         PRINT NOGEN              DON'T PRINT MACRO EXPANSIONS

                                    6 *************************************************************
                                    7 *                                                           *
                                    8 *      THIS EXAMPLE DEMONSTRATES USE OF THE INQUIRY TESTING MACRO.  *
                                    9 *      IN THE INTEREST OF SIMPLICITY THIS TEST PROGRAM ONLY  *
                                   10 *      SERVICES ONE TERMINAL CONTROLLER (READER-PRINTER PAIR) *
                                   11 *      AND ATTEMPTS NO I/O OVERLAP.                          *
                                   12 *                                                           *
                                   13 *************************************************************

                                   15 *************************************************************
                                   16 *                                                           *
                                   17 *            LOW CORE INTIALIZATION                         *
                                   18 *                                                           *
                                   19 *************************************************************

000000 FE00000000000130           21 IPLPSW  DC   X'FE',AL3(0),A(START) INITIAL PSW LOADED TO START RUN
000008 CC00000000000000           22 IPLCCW1 DC   D'0'                IPL CCW'S WHICH
000010 0000000000000000           23 IPLCCW2 DC   D'0'                ARE NOT USED
000018 0000000000000000           24 EXTOLD  DC   D'0'                EXTERNAL OLD PSW
000020 CC00000000000000           25 SUPOLD  DC   D'0'                SUPERVISOR OLD PSW
000028 CC00000000000000           26 PGMOLD  DC   D'0'                PROGRAM CHECK OLD PSW
000030 0000000000000000           27 MCKOLD  DC   D'0'                MACHINE CHECK OLD PSW
000038 0C00000000000000           28 IOOLD   DC   D'0'                INPUT/OUTPUT OLD PSW
000040 0000C00C00000000           29 CSW     DC   D'0'                CHANNEL STATUS WORD
000048 0000C000                   30 CAW     DC   A(0)                CHANNEL ADDRESS WORD
00004C 0000C000                   31 UNUSED1 DC   F'0'                UNUSED WORD 1
000050 C0000000                   32 TIMER   DC   F'0'                TIMER AREA
000054 C000C000                   33 UNUSED2 DC   F'0'                UNUSED WORD 2
000058 0002000000000001           34 EXTNEW  DC   X'0002',AL2(0),A(1) EXTERNAL NEW PSW- CAUSES HALT
000060 CC000CC000000013E          35 SUPNEW  DC   A(0,SVCINT)         SUPERVISOR NEW PSW
000068 0002000000000002           36 PGMNEW  DC   X'0002',AL2(0),A(2) PROGRAM CHECK NEW PSW - CAUSES HALT
000070 0002000000000004           37 MCKNEW  DC   X'0002',AL2(0),A(4) MACHINE CHECK NEW PSW- CAUSES HALT
000078 C0000CC0000001C4           38 IONEW   DC   A(0,IOINT)          INPUT/OUTPUT NEW PSW

                                   40 *************************************************************
                                   41 *                                                           *
                                   42 *            CONSTANTS AND EQUATES                          *
                                   43 *                                                           *
                                   44 *************************************************************

000080 CC00000000000000           46 SUPSAVE DC   16F'0'              SVC SAVE AREA
0000C0 FE02CCC0CC0001B6           47 IOWAIT  DC   X'FE020000',A(IOCOMP) PSW LOADED TO WAIT FOR I/O
0000C8 CC00C00020000084           48 CCWCHAIN CCW X'00',*-*,X'20',132 WRITE CCW 1
000000 0000C00020000084           49 CCW2    CCW  X'00',*-*,X'20',132 WRITE CCW 2
00CC0B C2C0C0E020C00050           50 CCWREAD CCW  X'02',BUFFER,X'20',80 READ ONE CARD INTO BUFFER
0000E0 4040404040404040           51 BUFFER  DC   80C' '              HOLDS INPUT REQJESTS

000000                            53 R0      EQU  0                   REGISTER EQUATES
00CCC1                            54 R1      EQU  1
```

| LCC | CBJECT CODE | ADDR1 | ADDR2 | STMT | SOURCE STATEMENT | |
|---|---|---|---|---|---|---|

```
0CCCC2                            55  R2       EQU   2
000003                            56  R3       EQU   3
000004                            57  R4       EQU   4
0CC005                            58  R5       FQU   5
000006                            59  R6       EQU   6
000007                            60  R7       EQU   7
000008                            61  R8       EQU   8
000C09                            62  R9       EQU   9
00000A                            63  RA       EQU   10
00000B                            64  RB       EQU   11
00000C                            65  RC       EQU   12
00000D                            66  RD       EQU   13
00000E                            67  RE       EQU   14
00000F                            68  RF       FQU   15

00000C                            70  READER   EQU   X'00C'     ADDRESS OF READER FOR INPUT REQUESTS
00000E                            71  PRINTER  EQU   X'00E'     ADDRESS OF PRINTER FOR OUTPUT MSGS
000011                            72  PCODE1   EQU   X'11'      PRINTER CCW-CODE - PRINT-SKIP 2
000009                            73  PCODE2   EQU   X'09'      PRINTER CCW-CODE   PRINT-SKIP 1
000084                            74  WLEN     EQU   132        LENGTH OF OUTPUT REQUESTS
000001                            75  RREQ     EQU   1          SVC NUMBER FOR INPUT REQUEST
000002                            76  WREQ     EQU   2          SVC NUMBER FOR OUTPUT REQUEST
000020                            77  SLI      EQU   X'20'      SLI BIT IN CCW
000040                            78  CCHAIN   EQU   X'40'      COMMAND CHAINING BIT IN CCW
000001                            79  UNITEX   EQU   X'01'      UNIT EXCEPTION IN CSW
000004                            80  DEVEND   EQU   X'04'      DEVICE-END IN CSW
000008                            81  CHANEND  EQU   X'08'      CHANNEL-END IN CSW
0000FD                            82  WAITOFF  EQU   X'FD'      USED TO AND OFF WAIT BIT IN PSW

                                  84  START    TRACE INTRPT,SVC,REGS=(0,1) SHOW SVC CALLING SEQUENCE
00013A 47F0 01F6        001F6     93           B     BEGIN                   BEGIN TESTING

                                  95  ********************************************************************
                                  96  *                                                                  *
                                  97  *                 SUPERVISOR CALL INTERRUPT HANDLER                 *
                                  98  *                                                                  *
                                  99  *         THIS INTERRUPT HANDLER PROCESSES INPUT/OUTPUT REQUESTS    *
                                 100  *         FROM THE INQUIRY PROCESSING PROGRAM GENERATED BY THE       *
                                 101  *         INQUIRY MACRO. THIS HANDLER IS PARTICULARLY SIMPLE, IN     *
                                 102  *         THAT IT ATTEMPTS NO I/O OVERLAP.                           *
                                 103  *                                                                  *
                                 104  *         FOR INPUT REQUESTS (SVC 1) REGISTER ONE IS SET TO POINT AT *
                                 105  *         AN EIGHTY CHARACTER INPUT REQUEST FOUND IN THE CARD READER *
                                 106  *         AT ADDRESS X'00C'. IF THE CARD READER GIVES A UNIT-EXCEPTION *
                                 107  *         THEN IT IS OUT OF CARDS, SO THE SIMULATION IS TERMINATED   *
                                 108  *         WITH A QUIT MACRO.                                        *
                                 109  *                                                                  *
                                 110  *         FOR OUTPUT REQUESTS (SVC 2), REGISTER ZERO CONTAINS EITHER *
                                 111  *         A ONE OR A TWO, REPRESENTING THE NUMBER OF 132 CHARACTER   *
                                 112  *         LINES POINTED TO BY REGISTER 1. A COMMAND CHAINED CCW      *
                                 113  *         PAIR IS USED TO HANDLE THE TWO-LINE CASE.                  *
                                 114  *                                                                  *
                                 115  ********************************************************************
```

EXAMPLE PROGRAM FOR INTERRUPT AND I/O PROBLEM OS4                                      PAGE    3

| LOC | OBJECT CODE | ADDR1 ADDR2 | STMT | SOURCE STATEMENT | | | |
|---|---|---|---|---|---|---|---|
| | | | | | | | 31 DEC 74 |
| 00013E | 900F 0080 | 00080 | 117 | SVCINT | STM | R0,RF,SUPSAVE | SAVE REGISTERS |
| 000142 | 9501 0023 | 0C023 | 118 | | CLI | SUPOLD+3,RREQ | IS THIS A READ REQUEST |
| 000146 | 4780 0156 | 00156 | 119 | | BE | READ | YES, PROCESS IT |
| 00014A | 9502 0023 | 0C023 | 120 | | CLI | SUPOLD+3,WREQ | IS THIS A WRITE REQUEST |
| 00014E | 4780 017A | 0017A | 121 | | BE | WRITE | YES, DO-IT |
| 000152 | 8200 0070 | 00070 | 123 | ERROR | LPSW | MCKNEW | TERMINATE SIMULATION |
| | | | 125 | ************************************************************* | | | |
| | | | 126 | * | | | * |
| | | | 127 | * | READ ROUTINE (NO I/O OVERLAPPING) | | * |
| | | | 128 | * | | | * |
| | | | 129 | ************************************************************* | | | |
| 000156 | | | 131 | READ | EQU | * | |
| 000156 | 4120 00E0 | 000E0 | 132 | | LA | R2,BUFFER | GET A(INPUT REQUEST) |
| 00015A | 5020 0084 | 00084 | 133 | | ST | R2,SUPSAVE+4 | FIX UP REGISTER 1 IN SAVE AREA |
| 00015E | 4120 00D8 | 000D8 | 134 | | LA | R2,CCWREAD | GET A(CCW FOR READING) |
| 000162 | 5020 0048 | 00048 | 135 | | ST | R2,CAW | SET CHANNEL ADDRESS WORD |
| 000166 | 9C00 000C | 0C00C | 136 | | SIO | READER | START UP READER |
| 00016A | 4780 01B2 | 001B2 | 137 | | BZ | WAIT | SIO SUCCESSFUL |
| 00016E | 9101 0044 | 00044 | 139 | | TM | CSW+4,UNITEX | UNIT EXCEPTION IN CSW |
| 000172 | 47E0 01E4 | 001E4 | 140 | | BNO | IOERROR | NO, SOME OTHER ERROR |
| | | | 141 | | QUIT | | YES, NO MORE REQUESTS IN READER |
| | | | 145 | ************************************************************* | | | |
| | | | 146 | * | | | * |
| | | | 147 | * | WRITE ROUTINE (NO I/O OVERLAPPING) | | * |
| | | | 148 | * | | | * |
| | | | 149 | ************************************************************* | | | |
| 00017A | | | 151 | WRITE | EQU | * | |
| 00017A | 5010 00C8 | 000C8 | 152 | | ST | R1,CCWCHAIN | PUT A(LINE 1) IN CCW |
| 00017E | 9211 00C8 | 000C8 | 153 | | MVI | CCWCHAIN,PCODE1 | OP-CODE FOR ONE-LINE IN CASE |
| 000182 | 9220 00CC | 000CC | 154 | | MVI | CCWCHAIN+4,SLI | IN CASE ONLY ONE CCW NEEDED |
| 000186 | 0600 | | 155 | | BCTR | R0,R0 | SUBTRACT ONE FROM LINE COUNT |
| 000188 | 1200 | | 156 | | LTR | R0,R0 | IS IT NOW ZERO |
| 00018A | 4780 01A2 | 001A2 | 157 | | BZ | PSTART | YES, WE ARE ALL SET - ONLY ONE LINE |
| 00018E | 4110 1084 | 00084 | 159 | | LA | R1,WLEN(,R1) | BUMP TO SECOND LINE |
| 000192 | 5010 00D0 | 000D0 | 160 | | ST | R1,CCW2 | PLACE IT IN THE CCW |
| 000196 | 9211 00D0 | 0C0D0 | 161 | | MVI | CCW2,PCODE1 | MOVE IN OP-CODE FOR SECOND LINE |
| 00019A | 9260 00CC | 0C0CC | 162 | | MVI | CCWCHAIN+4,CCHAIN+SLI | SET CHAINING IN FIRST CCW |
| 00019E | 9209 00C8 | 000C8 | 163 | | MVI | CCWCHAIN,PCODE2 | SET SKIP ONE LINE IN FIRST CCW |
| 0001A2 | 4120 00C8 | 000C8 | 165 | PSTART | LA | R2,CCWCHAIN | GET A(CCW CHAIN FOR WRITE) |
| 0001A6 | 5020 0048 | 00048 | 166 | | ST | R2,CAW | SET CHANNEL ADDRESS WORD |
| 0001AA | 9C00 000E | 0C00E | 167 | | SIO | PRINTER | START I/O ON PRINTER |
| 0001AE | 4770 01E4 | 001E4 | 168 | | BNZ | IOERROR | IF UNSUCCESSFUL, ERROR |
| 0001B2 | 8200 00C0 | 0C0C0 | 170 | WAIT | LPSW | IOWAIT | WAIT FOR PREVIOUS I/O TO COMPLETE |
| 0001B6 | D707 0040 0040 | 0C040 00040 | 172 | IOCOMP | XC | CSW(8),CSW | CLEAR CSW - CONTROL RETURNS HERE |
| | | | 173 | * | | | WHEN I/O IS COMPLETE |

```
  LOC   OBJECT CODE   ACDR1 ADDR2   STMT   SOURCE STATEMENT                                        31 DEC 74

0001BC 980F 0080            00080   174         LM     R0,RF,SUPSAVE         RESTORE REGISTERS
0001C0 8200 0020      00020         175         LPSW   SUPOLD                "RETURN" TO INQUIRY PROGRAM


                                    177  ************************************************************************
                                    178  *                                                                      *
                                    179  *                  INPUT / OUTPUT INTERRUPT HANDLER                     *
                                    180  *                                                                      *
                                    181  *        THIS INTERRUPT HANDLER WAITS FOR DEVICE END, RE-DRIVING        *
                                    182  *        THE WAIT FOR CHANNEL END. ONCE DEVICE-END IS FOUND, THE        *
                                    183  *        WAIT BIT OF THE PSW IS ANDED OFF AND THE IOOLD PSW IS          *
                                    184  *        RELOADED. ANY ERROR CONDITIONS IN THE CSW CAUSE A TRACE TO     *
                                    185  *        TAKE PLACE AND THEN THE SIMULATION IS TERMINATED.              *
                                    186  *                                                                      *
                                    187  ************************************************************************

0001C4 91FF 0045      00045         189  IOINT   TM     CSW+5,X'FF'           TEST ERROR BYTE
0001C8 4770 01E4            001E4   190          BNZ    IOERROR               ANY BITS ON ARE ERROR
0001CC 91F3 0044      00044         191          TM     CSW+4,255-DEVEND-CHANEND ANY ERROR BITS IN BYTE 1
0001D0 4770 01E4            001E4   192          BNZ    IOERROR               YES, BAD NEWS
0001D4 9104 0044      00044         193          TM     CSW+4,DEVEND          IS THERE A DEVICE-END PRESENT
0001D8 47E0 01E0            001E0   194          BNO    *+8                   NO, RE-DRIVE WAIT
0001DC 94FD 0039      00039         195          NI     IOOLD+1,WAITOFF       TURN OFF WAIT BIT IN PSW
0001E0 8200 0038      00038         196          LPSW   IOOLD                 RETURN TO INTERRUPTED PROGRAM

                                    198  IOERROR TRACE DUMP,STATUS=(OLDI/O,CSW,CAW),CORE=(CCWCHAIN,6)
0001F2 8200 0070      00070         209          LPSW   MCKNEW                ABNORMALLY TERMINATE SIMULATION


                                    211  ************************************************************************
                                    212  *                                                                      *
                                    213  *        INQUIRY MACRO    (PROCESSING PROGRAM)                          *
                                    214  *                                                                      *
                                    215  ************************************************************************

                                    217          PRINT GEN
                                    218  BEGIN    INQUIRY                      GENERATE TESTING PROGRAM

                                    220 +************************************************************************
                                    221 +*                                                                      *
                                    222 +*                  INQUIRY PROCESSING PROGRAM FOR OS4                   *
                                    223 +*                                                                      *
                                    224 +*        THIS PROGRAM ISSUES AN SVC 1 TO OBTAIN A REQUEST FROM          *
                                    225 +*        A TERMINAL. THIS REQUEST IS THEN PROCESSED AND AN SVC 2        *
                                    226 +*        IS ISSUED TO PRINT THE OUTPUT FOR THE REQUEST. THIS LOOP       *
                                    227 +*        IS REPEATED UNTIL THERE ARE NO MORE REQUESTS AND THE           *
                                    228 +*        SVC 1 HANDLER DOES NOT RETURN. THAT IS TO SAY THAT THIS        *
                                    229 +*        PROGRAM DOES NOT ISSUE A QUIT MACRO.                           *
                                    230 +*                                                                      *
                                    231 +************************************************************************

000000                              233 +         USING EXAMPLE,0 .           ASSEMBLE ABSOLUTE REFERENCES
0001F6                              234 +BEGIN    DS     0H .                  START OF PROGRAM
0001F6 0A01                         235 +INQREAD  SVC    1 * .                 GET TERMINAL REQUEST FROM STUDENT
0001F8 9240 02A8      002A8         236 +         MVI    INQBUFF1,C' ' .       CLEAR ANSWER AREA FOR THIS REQUEST
```

```
        EXAMPLE PROGRAM FOR INTERRUPT AND I/O PROBLEM OS4                                          PAGE  5

    LOC  OBJECT CODE    ADDR1 ADDR2  STMT   SOURCE STATEMENT                                     31 DEC 74

  0001FC D282 02A9 02A8 002A9 002A8  237+      MVC   INQBUFF1+1(131),INQBUFF1
  000202 D283 032C 02A8 0032C 002A8  238+      MVC   INQBUFF2(132),INQBUFF1
  000208 D207 02A8 1000 002A8 00000  239+      MVC   INQBUFF1(8),0(1) .  TRANSFER FIRST 8 BYTES OF INPUT
                                     240+*                                REQUEST TO OUTPUT AREA
  00020E 4120 02AA       002AA       241+      LA    2,INQBUFF1+2 .      POINT TO THIRD CHARACTER IN INPUT
  000212 91C0 2000  00000            242+      TM    0(2),X'C0' .        IS IT ALPHANUMERIC
  000216 4710 021E       0021E       243+      BO    INQNOPR2 .          YES, NO PRIORITY CHARACTER
  00021A 4120 2001       00001       244+      LA    2,1(0,2) .          BUMP PAST PRIORITY CHARACTER

  00021E 4130 000A       0000A       246+INQNOPR2 LA 3,INQTABZ .         GET NUMBER OF ENTRIES IN MESSAGE TBL
  000222 4140 043F       0043F       247+      LA    4,INQTABLE .        GET  START OF MESSAGE TABLE FOR SCAN

  000226 D504 4000 2000 00000 00000  249+INQLOOP CLC 0(5,4),0(2) .       COMPARE FLIGHT NUMBERS
  00022C 4780 0258             00258  250+      BE    INQFOUND .          IF MATCH WE HAVE OUTPUT MESSAGE
  000230 4140 401D       0001D       251+      LA    4,L'INQTABLE(0,4) . BUMP TO START OF NEXT ENTRY IN TBL
  000234 4630 0226             00226  252+      BCT   3,INQLOOP .         CHECK ALL ENTRIES, IF NECESSARY

                                     254+**************************************************************
                                     255+*                                                            *
                                     256+**        IF CONTROL GETS HERE IT MEANS AN INVALID MESSAGE HAS BEEN  *
                                     257+**        RECEIVED. THE STUDENT PROBABLY IGNORED A MONKEY REQUEST.   *
                                     258+**        THE OUTPUT MESSAGE IS AN ERROR MESSAGE IN THIS CASE.       *
                                     259+*                                                            *
                                     260+**************************************************************
  000238 D204 03B4 2000 003B4 00000  262+      MVC   INQNONEX+4(5),0(2) .MOVE FLIGHT NUMBER TO ERROR MESSAGE
  00023E D239 02AB 03B0 002AB 003B0  263+      MVC   INQBUFF1+3(58),INQNONEX PUT ERROR MESSAGE IN OUTPUT AREA
  000244 91C0 02AA       002AA       264+      TM    INQBUFF1+2,X'C0' .  IS THIS A PRIORITY MESSAGE
  000248 47E0 0250             00250  265+      BNO   INQNOPR1 .          YES, LEAVE IT ALONE
  00024C 9240 02AA       002AA       266+      MVI   INQBUFF1+2,C' ' .   NO, BLANK PRIORITY FIELD
  000250 4100 0001       00001       267+INQNOPR1 LA 0,1 .               SET LENGTH OF MESSAGE, IN LINES
  000254 47F0 029E             0029E  268+      B     INQOUTPT .          GO PRINT ERROR MESSAGE (VIA SVC 2)

  000258 D204 03F6 2000 003F6 00000  270+INQFOUND MVC INQPATN1+12(5),0(2) MOVE FLIGHT NUMBER TO MESSAGE
  00025E D206 03EA 4016 003EA 00016  271+      MVC   INQPATN1(7),22(4) . MOVE AIRLINE NAME TO MESSAGE
  000264 D225 02AB 03EA 002AB 003EA  272+      MVC   INQBUFF1+3(38),INQPATN1 MOVE MESSAGE TO OUTPUT BUFFER
  00026A 91C0 02AA       002AA       273+      TM    INQBUFF1+2,X'C0' .  IS THIS A PRIORITY MESSAGE
  00026E 47E0 0276             00276  274+      BNO   INQNOPRY .          YES, DON'T MESS
  000272 9240 02AA       002AA       275+      MVI   INQBUFF1+2,C' ' .   NO, BLANK OUT PRIORITY FIELD
  000276 D206 02BE 4006 002BE 00006  276+INQNOPRY MVC INQBUFF1+22(7),6(4) PLACE TIME IN MESSAGE
  00027C D201 02CD 400E 002CD 0000E  277+      MVC   INQBUFF1+37(2),14(4) PLACE GATE NUMBER IN MESSAGE

  000282 D22E 032C 0410 0032C 00410  279+      MVC   INQBUFF2(47),INQPATN2 START PREPARING SECOND LINE OF MSG
  000288 D201 032C 02A8 0032C 002A8  280+      MVC   INQBUFF2(2),INQBUFF1 PUT TERMINAL NUMBER IN SECOND LINE
  00028E D201 0341 4011 00341 00011  281+      MVC   INQBUFF2+21(2),17(4) MOVE IN NUMBER OF FIRST CLASS PASS
  000294 D201 0351 4014 00351 00014  282+      MVC   INQBUFF2+37(2),20(4) THEN NUMBER OF COACH PASSENGERS
  00029A 4100 0002       00002       283+      LA    0,2 .               LENGTH OF MESSAGE, IN LINES
  00029E 4110 02A8       002A8       284+INQOUTPT LA 1,INQBUFF1 .        SET ADDRESS OF OUTPUT MESSAGE
  0002A2 0A02                        285+      SVC   2 .                 CAUSE MESSAGE TO BE PRINTED
  0002A4 47F0 01F6             001F6  286+      B     INQREAD .           GO GET NEXT REQUEST


  0002A8                             288+INQBUFF1 DS CL132 .             BUFFER FOR LINE 1 OF OUTPUT MESSAGE
  00032C                             289+INQBUFF2 DS CL132 .             BUFFER FOR LINE 2 OF OUTPUT MESSAGE
                                     290+INQNONEX DC CL58'FLT   : NONEXISTENT FLIGHT NUMBER.  PLEASE TRY X
```

```
 LOC   OBJECT CODE    ADDR1 ADDR2  STMT   SOURCE STATEMENT                                              31 DEC 74
0003B0 C6D3E34040404040                *               AGAIN. ' .              ERROR MESSAGE
0003EA 404040404040404040         291+INQPATN1 DC      CL38'          FLT        :        , GATE  . '
000410 4040404040404040          292+INQPATN2 DC       CL47'         UNRESERVED:        FIRST CLASS,     COACH. '
00043F E4D5F6F6F640F47A          293+INQTABLE DC       C'UN666 4:45 PM 21 10 20UNITED '
00045C C5C1F6F9F640F27A          294+        DC        C'EA696 2:30 PM  6 20 80EASTERN'
000479 D7C1F7F0F740F87A          295+        DC        C'PA707 8:00 AM 13  5 15PAN AM '
000496 E3E6F7F2F740F97A          296+        DC        C'TW727 9:00 AM 15  0 0TWA     '
0004B3 E4D5F7F4F740F17A          297+        DC        C'UN747 1:00 PM 12 50 90UNITED '
0004D0 C5C1F8F0F240F37A          298+        DC        C'EA802 3:00 PM 21  2  3EASTERN'
0004ED D7C1F8F7F640F37A          299+        DC        C'PA876 3:00 PM 12 12 25PAN AM '
00050A E3E6F8F8F140F97A          300+        DC        C'TW881 9:00 AM 13 15  1TWA     '
000527 E4D5F9F6F940F77A          301+        DC        C'UN969 7:00 AM 15  3  0UNITED '
000544 C5C1F9F9F940F27A          302+        DC        C'EA999 2:30 AM 21 20 80EASTERN'
00000A                           303+INQTABZ EQU       (*-INQTABLE)/L'INQTABLE
000562                           304+        DS        0H .            ALIGN ANY FOLLOWING INSTRUCTIONS
                                 306         END
```

389

MASSACHUSETTS INSTITUTE OF TECHNOLOGY          SYSTEM / 360 SIMULATOR                          VERSION 1.3
EXAMPLE TRACE LISTING.    0 CONDITIONS ENABLED.                                                      PAGE   1

LOC  TRACE TYPE          COUNT  TIME                           OP   INSTRUCTION     ADR1 ADR2  OPERAND1 OPERAND2
----  ----------------   -----  ----------                     ----  --------------  ---- ----  -------- --------

01F8 SVC INTERRUPT          2          0  PSW: FE 0 0 0001  '01'B '00'B 0 0001F8
              REGISTERS:
              R 0: FFFFFFFF,        -1 R 1: FFFFFFFF,         -1

02A4 SVC INTERRUPT         84     73,727  PSW: FE 0 0 0002  '01'B '11'B 0 0002A4
              REGISTERS:
              R 0: 00000002,         2 R 1: 000002A8,        680

01F8 SVC INTERRUPT        125    265,829  PSW: FE 0 0 0001  '01'B '11'B 0 0001F8
              REGISTERS:
              R 0: 00000002,         2 R 1: 000002A8,        680

02A4 SVC INTERRUPT        187    333,707  PSW: FE 0 0 0002  '01'B '11'B 0 0002A4
              REGISTERS:
              R 0: 00000002,         2 R 1: 000002A8,        680

01F8 SVC INTERRUPT        228    520,748  PSW: FE 0 0 0001  '01'B '11'B 0 0001F8
              REGISTERS:
              R 0: 00000002,         2 R 1: 000002A8,        680

02A4 SVC INTERRUPT        282    593,699  PSW: FE 0 0 0002  '01'B '01'B 0 0002A4
              REGISTERS:
              R 0: 00000002,         2 R 1: 000002A8,        680

01F8 SVC INTERRUPT        323    791,414  PSW: FE 0 0 0001  '01'B '01'B 0 0001F8
              REGISTERS:
              R 0: 00000002,         2 R 1: 000002A8,        680

02A4 SVC INTERRUPT        389    853,711  PSW: FE 0 0 0002  '01'B '01'B 0 0002A4
              REGISTERS:
              R 0: 00000002,         2 R 1: 000002A8,        680

01F8 SVC INTERRUPT        430  1,046,462  PSW: FE 0 0 0001  '01'B '01'B 0 0001F8
              REGISTERS:
              R 0: 00000002,         2 R 1: 000002A8,        680

02A4 SVC INTERRUPT        516  1,113,668  PSW: FE 0 0 0002  '01'B '01'B 0 0002A4
              REGISTERS:
              R 0: 00000001,         1 R 1: 000002A8,        680

01F8 SVC INTERRUPT        552  1,221,432  PSW: FE 0 0 0001  '01'B '01'B 0 0001F8
              REGISTERS:
              R 0: 00000001,         1 R 1: 000002A8,        680

02A4 SVC INTERRUPT        630  1,293,692  PSW: FE 0 0 0002  '01'B '01'B 0 0002A4
              REGISTERS:
              R 0: 00000002,         2 R 1: 000002A8,        680

01F8 SVC INTERRUPT        671  1,487,532  PSW: FE 0 0 0001  '01'B '01'B 0 0001F8
              REGISTERS:
              R 0: 00000002,         2 R 1: 000002A8,        680

```
MASSACHUSETTS INSTITUTE OF TECHNOLOGY           SYSTEM / 360 SIMULATOR
EXAMPLE TRACE LISTING.    1 CONDITIONS ENABLED.                                    VERSION 1.3
                                                                                       PAGE  3
LOC  TRACE TYPE           COUNT   TIME                      OP   INSTRUCTION    ADR1 ADR2  OPERAND1 OPERAND2
---- ---------------      -----   ----------                ----  -------------  ---- ----  -------- --------

02A4 SVC INTERRUPT          741  1,553,688  PSW: FE 0 0 0002  '01'B '01'B 0 0002A4
        REGISTERS:
        R 0: 00000002,           2 R 1: 000002A8,      680

01F8 SVC INTERRUPT          782  1,758,216  PSW: FE 0 0 0001  '01'B '01'B 0 0001F8
        REGISTERS:
        R 0: 00000002,           2 R 1: 000002A8,      680

02A4 SVC INTERRUPT          856  1,813,690  PSW: FE 0 0 0002  '01'B '11'B 0 0002A4
        REGISTERS:
        R 0: 00000002,           2 R 1: 000002A8,      680

01F8 SVC INTERRUPT          897  2,013,224  PSW: FE 0 0 0001  '01'B '11'B 0 0001F8
        REGISTERS:
        R 0: 00000002,           2 R 1: 000002A8,      680

02A4 SVC INTERRUPT          983  2,073,668  PSW: FE 0 0 0002  '01'B '01'B 0 0002A4
        REGISTERS:
        R 0: 00000001,           1 R 1: 000002A8,      680

01F8 SVC INTERRUPT         1019  2,168,032  PSW: FE 0 0 0001  '01'B '01'B 0 0001F8
        REGISTERS:
        R 0: 00000001,           1 R 1: 000002A8,      680

NORMAL SIMULATOR TERMINATION FOR PROGRAM EXAMPLE

        SIMULATED REAL TIME:  2,168,068.000

        SIMULATED CPU TIME:       3,184.000
```

```
************************************************************************************************
EXAMPLE                    OUTPUT TO PRINTER 00E STARTS AT HEAD OF FORM ON NEXT PAGE
************************************************************************************************

00 TWA    FLT TW881: 9:00 AM , GATE 13.
00     UNRESERVED:  15 FIRST CLASS,  1 COACH.

01 PAN AM  FLT PA707: 8:00 AM , GATE 13.
01     UNRESERVED:   5 FIRST CLASS, 15 COACH.

02*UNITED  FLT UN666: 4:45 PM , GATE 21.
02     UNRESERVED:  10 FIRST CLASS, 20 COACH.

03*TWA     FLT TW727: 9:00 AM , GATE 15.
03     UNRESERVED:   0 FIRST CLASS,  0 COACH.

09+FLT 10:00:  NONEXISTENT FLIGHT NUMBER.  PLEASE TRY AGAIN.

04 PAN AM  FLT PA876: 3:00 PM , GATE 12.
04     UNRESERVED:  12 FIRST CLASS, 25 COACH.

05 UNITED  FLT UN747: 1:00 PM , GATE 12.
05     UNRESERVED:  50 FIRST CLASS, 90 COACH.

06 EASTERN FLT EA802: 3:00 PM , GATE 21.
06     UNRESERVED:   2 FIRST CLASS,  3 COACH.

07 FLT PA300:  NONEXISTENT FLIGHT NUMBER.  PLEASE TRY AGAIN.
```

## 5.3   INSTALLING AND USING THE PROBLEMS

### 5.3.1   Installing The Problems

This section describes the procedures necessary to install and use the I/O and interrupt problems. All of the macros necessary for these problems are included in the macro library for the simulator. To use these problems it is necessary to have the System/360 simulator (SIM360) installed along with its macro library. The procedures necessary to accomplish this are completely described in chapter 4.

The simulator by itself is very awkward for running large student runs. Several output files must be split apart and collated for each student. To overcome this problem a special batching monitor has been implemented. This monitor invokes the simulator for each student, collating all output on one file and providing output separators.

If you want to use this special monitor in conjunction with the simulator, your installation must possess a copy of the proprietary IBM Optimizing PL/1 Compiler (release 2.0, or greater), and its run time support routines. In addition, you must be running under either an OS/MVT or VS/1-2 operating system. Detailed instructions on the installation and use of this special monitor may be found in chapter 7.

### 5.3.2   Running The Problems

**Without Special Monitor:**

If you plan to run the simulator without the monitor, your system must be either OS/MFT, OS/MVT,VS1, or VS2. At least 220 K-bytes of memory must be available in a user region. If your system does not support output spooling of print streams, the output will be very difficult to interpret.

The best way to run students on the simulator, lacking the facilities for the special monitor, is to use a cataloged or in-stream JCL procedure. Each student would then be required to use three JCL cards, which you could pre-punch to reduce the possibility of error.

The following procedure could be used for this purpose:

```
//STUDENT PROC TPARM="LOAD,NODECK"
//C         EXEC PGM=IEUASM,PARM=&TPARM
//SYSPRINT DD   SYSOUT=A
//SYSLIB    DD   DSN=SIM360.MACLIB,DISP=SHR
//          DD   DSN=SYS1.MACLIB,DISP=SHR
//SYSUT1    DD   UNIT=SYSDA,SPACE=(CYL,(2,1))
```

```
//SYSUT2    DD   UNIT=SYSDA,SPACE=(CYL,(2,1))
//SYSUT3    DD   UNIT=SYSDA,SPACE=(CYL,(2,1))
//SYSGO     DD   DDNAME=SYSLIN
//SYSLIN    DD   DSN=&&TEMP,DISP=(MOD,PASS)
//          PEND
//SIM360    PROC GPARM='CARDS=0,PRINT=0'
//G         EXEC  PGM=SIM360,PARM=&GPARM
//STEPLIB   DD   DSN=SIM360.LOAD,DISP=SHR
//SIMLIN    DD   DSN=&&TEMP,DISP=(OLD,DELETE)
//SYSPRINT  DD   SYSOUT=A
//STRACE    DD   SYSOUT=A
//SIMPRNT   DD   SYSOUT=A
//SIMPRN2   DD   SYSOUT=A
//SIMPRN3   DD   SYSOUT=A
//SIMPRN4   DD   SYSOUT=A
//SIMPNCH   DD   SYSOUT=A
//SIMPNC2   DD   SYSOUT=A
//SIMPNC3   DD   SYSOUT=A
//SIMPNC4   DD   SYSOUT=A
//SIMIN3    DD   DUMMY
//SIMIN4    DD   DUMMY
//          PEND
```

Each student is run as a separate step. The output for all the students is run together into SYSPRINT and SYSLIN. Then a final step is run which reads the SIMLIN file and simulates all the student programs. An example run might look like:

```
//ALLOC    EXEC PGM=IEFBR14
//DD1      DD   DSN=&&TEMP,DISP=(NEW,PASS),
//              SPACE=(CYL,(2,1)),UNIT=SYSDA,
//              DCB=(RECFM=FB,LRECL=80,BLKSIZE=1600)
//name1    EXEC STUDENT
//C.SYSIN  DD   *
  _
 |
 | student deck
 |_

/*
//name2    EXEC STUDENT
//C.SYSIN  DD   *
  _
 |
 | student deck
 |_

/*
     .
     . repeated for each student
     .
/*
//RUN      EXEC SIM360,GPARM= (see note 5, below)
```

```
//G.SIMIN   DD  *
00TW881
01PA707
02*UN666
03*TW727
09+10:00:00.7
04!PA876
05!UN747
07!PA300
/*
//G.SIMIN2 DD  *
12UN969
11UN747
10*EA696
19+10:00:00.7
13*EA802
14!EA999
15!TW881
16TW727
17!PA400
/*
//
```

**Notes:**

1. The program IEUASM is the IBM F-level assembler.

2. The partitioned dataset "SIM360.MACLIB" contains the macros for these problems and the simulator in general.

3. The partitioned dataset "SIM360.LOAD" contains the System/360 simulator load module as member SIM360.

4. __name__ is the student's name. This should be the last name truncated, or prefixed to eight characters.

5. The parameters specified as the GPARM field of the RUN step are determined by the problem being run. This is described in the next section.

6. All the student assignments show $JOB and $EOJ control cards. These are for use by the special batch monitor and should be removed when running without the monitor.

**With Special Monitor:**

If your system has a user partition of 256 K-bytes, the IBM Optimizing PL/1 compiler, and uses either OS/MVT or VS 1-2 you may use the special batch monitor for the simulator. This monitor vastly improves the operational aspects of using the simulator for class runs.

The students use simple job control cards in a very forgiving enviroment. This batch monitor reads its input stream, prints an output separator and invokes the simulator for each student. All of a student's output is neatly collated behind a separator.

Execution time and page limits are enforced to guard against expensive errors. The disadvantages of this approach are the increased I/O necessary to "SPOOL" the separate output files and the overhead of re-initializing the simulator for each student. The advantages of this scheme are its operational convenience, and it does beat any step charges, running as only one job step.

Again, to reduce possibility of a JCL error a cataloged or in-stream procedure is provided. This procedure, named SIM360 is described completely in chapter 4. This procedure is used in the following fashion:

```
//          EXEC SIM360,GPARM= (see note 1, below)
//G.BATCHIN DD *
$JOB name1

 _
|
| student deck
|_

$EOJ
$JOB name2

 _
|
| student deck
|_

    .
    . repeated for each student
    .
/*
```

Notes:

1. The parameters specified in the GPARM field for this procedure are passed to the simulator. Their value depends on the problem being run as the next section dictates.

2. The name field will be used to generate a full page, block-lettered paging separator for student output. It may be a maximum of nine characters and must start at least one space after the "B" of the $JOB card.

### 5.3.3  Simulator Parameters for Each Problem

This section describes the simulator parameters which should be used with each of the interrupt and I/O problems. These parameters have proven adequate for most cases, but particularly in the Airline Reservations Problem (OS4) a student may need more real time and simulated instructions to finish the problem.

Instruction Simulation Problem -- OS1:

    GPARM='MAXTIME=1000,MAXPGE=8,PUNCH=0,PRINT=0,CARDS=0'

Fixed-Point Overflow Fixup Problem -- OS2:

    GPARM='MAXTIME=5000,MAXPGE=10,PUNCH=0,CARDS=0,PRINT=1'

BTB Problem -- OS3:

    GPARM='MAXTIME=5000,PUNCH=0,CARDS=0,PRINT=1'

Airline Reservations Problem -- OS4:

    GPARM='MAXTIME=10000,MAXCOUNT=9000,CARDS=2,PRINT=2,PUNCH=0'

## 5.4  SAMPLE SOLUTIONS

## 5.4.1  Instruction Simulation Problem -- OS1

```
EXAMPLE SOLUTION FOR INTERRUPT AND I/O PROBLEM OS1 --PGG  11/11/74                        PAGE   2

  LOC  OBJECT CODE      ADDR1 ADDR2  STMT   SOURCE STATEMENT                                31 DEC 74

000000                               2 SOLUTION CSECT
000000                               3          USING SOLUTION,0      GENERATE ABSOLUTE ADDRESSES
000000                               4          PRINT NOGEN

                                     6 ****************************************************************************
                                     7 *                                                                        *
                                     8 *          EXAMPLE SOLUTION FOR INTERRUPT AND I/O PROBLEM OS1, USING      *
                                     9 *          ALGORITHM OUTLINED IN STUDENT ASSIGNMENT.                     *
                                    10 *                                                                        *
                                    11 ****************************************************************************

                                    13 ****************************************************************************
                                    14 *                                                                        *
                                    15 *          LOW CORE INTIALIZATION                                         *
                                    16 *                                                                        *
                                    17 ****************************************************************************

000000 FE00000000000154             19 IPLPSW   DC    X'FE',AL3(0),A(START) INITIAL PSW LOADED TO START RUN
000008 0000000000000000             20 IPLCCW1  DC    D'0'                   IPL CCW'S WHICH
000010 0000000000000000             21 IPLCCW2  DC    D'0'                     ARE NOT USED
000018 C000000000000000             22 EXTOLD   DC    D'0'                   EXTERNAL OLD PSW
000020 0000000000000000             23 SUPOLD   DC    D'0'                   SUPERVISOR OLD PSW
000028 0000000000000000             24 PGMOLD   DC    D'0'                   PROGRAM CHECK OLD PSW
000030 0000000000000000             25 MCKOLD   DC    D'0'                   MACHINE CHECK OLD PSW
000038 0000000000000000             26 IOOLD    DC    D'0'                   INPUT/OUTPUT OLD PSW
000040 0000000000000000             27 CSW      DC    D'0'                   CHANNEL STATUS WORD
000048 00000000                     28 CAW      DC    F'0'                   CHANNEL ADDRESS WORD
00004C 00000000                     29 UNUSED1  DC    F'0'                   UNUSED WORD 1
000050 00000000                     30 TIMER    DC    F'0'                   TIMER AREA
000054 00000000                     31 UNUSED2  DC    F'0'                   UNUSED WORD 2
000058 0002000000000001             32 EXTNEW   DC    X'0002',AL2(0),A(1) EXTERNAL NEW PSW- CAUSES HALT
000060 0002000000000002             33 SUPNEW   DC    X'0002',AL2(0),A(2) SUPERVISOR NEW PSW- CAUSES HALT
000068 00000000000000C4             34 PGMNEW   DC    A(0,PGMINT)            PROGRAM CHECK NEW PSW
000070 0002000000000004             35 MCKNEW   DC    X'0002',AL2(0),A(4) MACHINE CHECK NEW PSW- CAUSES HALT
000078 0002000000000005             36 IONEW    DC    X'0002',AL2(0),A(5) INPUT/OUTPUT NEW PSW- CAUSES HALT

                                    39 ****************************************************************************
                                    40 *                                                                        *
                                    41 *          PROGRAM CONSTANTS AND EQUATES.                                 *
                                    42 *                                                                        *
                                    43 ****************************************************************************

000080 0000000000000000             45 REGSAVE  DC    16F'0'                 REGISTER SAVE AREA
0000C0 0000FFFF                     46 HIGHCLR  DC    X'0000FFFF'            FOR CLEARING BYTES 0 AND 1

000000                              48 R0       EQU   0
000001                              49 R1       EQU   1
000002                              50 R2       EQU   2
000003                              51 R3       EQU   3
000004                              52 R4       EQU   4
000005                              53 R5       EQU   5
000006                              54 R6       EQU   6
000007                              55 R7       EQU   7
000008                              56 R8       EQU   8
```

```
  LOC  OBJECT CODE    ADDR1 ADDR2  STMT   SOURCE STATEMENT                                              31 DEC 74

000009                             57 R9        EQU   9
00000A                             58 RA        EQU   10
00000B                             59 RB        EQU   11
00000C                             60 RC        EQU   12
00000D                             61 RD        EQU   13
00000E                             62 RE        EQU   14
00000F                             63 RF        EQU   15

000001                             65 OPEX      EQU   1                INT CODE FOR OPERATION EXCEPTION
0000BE                             66 STCM      EQU   X'BE'            OP-CODE FOR STCM INSTRUCTION

                                   68 ***********************************************************************
                                   69 *                                                                     *
                                   70 *          PROGRAM INTERRUPT HANDLER -- INTERRUPTS MASKED OFF          *
                                   71 *                                                                     *
                                   72 *          THIS INTERRUPT HANDLER SIMULATES EXECUTION OF THE STORE     *
                                   73 *          CHARACTER(S) UNDER MASK (STCM) INSTRUCTION. THIS INSTRUCTION*
                                   74 *          IS DESCRIBED IN THE STUDENT ASSIGNMENT FOR INTERRUPT        *
                                   75 *          AND I/O PROBLEM OS1.                                        *
                                   76 *                                                                     *
                                   77 ***********************************************************************

0000C4                             79 PGMINT    EQU   *
0000C4 900F 0080          00080    80           STM   R0,RF,REGSAVE    SAVE REGISTERS
0000C8 9501 002B    0C028 0002B    81           CLI   PGMOLD+3,OPEX    IS THIS OPERATION EXCEPTION
0000CC 4770 014C          0014C    82           BNE   PGMRET           NO, IGNORE IT (RETURN)

                                   84 ***********************************************************************
                                   85 *                                                                     *
                                   86 *          FIRST THE ADDRESS OF THE OFFENDING INSTRUCTION IS CALCULATED*
                                   87 *          THEN THIS INSTRUCTION IS CHECKED TO INSURE A STCM (X'BE').  *
                                   88 *          IF NOT, CONTROL IS RETURNED.                                *
                                   89 *                                                                     *
                                   90 ***********************************************************************

0000D0 5820 002C          0002C    92           L     R2,PGMOLD+4      GET A(NEXT INST TO BE EXECUTED)
0000D4 4120 2000          00000    93           LA    R2,0(,R2)        CLEAR HIGH-ORDER BYTE
0000D8 1B33                         94           SR    R3,R3            CLEAR A REGISTER
0000DA 4330 002C          0002C    95           IC    R3,PGMOLD+4      PICK UP ILC, CC, AND PROG MASK
0000DE 8830 0006          00006    96           SRL   R3,6             DROP CC & PRG MASK
0000E2 8930 0001          00001    97           SLL   R3,1             GET INST LENGTH IN BYTES
0000E6 1B23                         98           SR    R2,R3            GET A(OFFENDING INSTRUCTION)

0000E8 958E 2000    00000          100          CLI   0(R2),STCM       IS THIS A STCM INSTRUCTION
0000EC 4770 014C          0014C    101          BNE   PGMRET           NO, SKIP IT

                                   103 **********************************************************************
                                   104 *                                                                    *
                                   105 *         NOW R2 POINTS TO THE OFFENDING INSTRUCTION. WE DECODE THE    *
                                   106 *         MASK AND R1 FIELDS. THE END RESULT WILL BE THE MASK LEFT-    *
                                   107 *         JUSTIFIED IN A REGISTER, AND THE CONTENTS OF THE R1 REGISTER *
                                   108 *         IN AN ODD REGISTER.                                          *
                                   109 *                                                                    *
                                   110 *         IF THE MASK FIELD IS ZERO, THE INSTRUCTION IS TREATED LIKE   *
                                   111 *         A NO-OP.                                                     *
```

# 5. INTERRUPT AND I/O PROBLEMS     5-71

| LOC | OBJECT CODE | ADDR1 ADDR2 | STMT | SOURCE STATEMENT | |
|---|---|---|---|---|---|
| | | | 112 | * | |
| | | | 113 | ************************************* | |
| 0000F0 | 1844 | | 115 | SR R4,R4 | CLEAR SOME |
| 0000F2 | 1855 | | 116 | SR R5,R5 | REGISTERS |
| 0000F4 | 4340 2001 | 00001 | 117 | IC R4,1(,R2) | GET R1 AND M3 FIELD |
| 0000F8 | 8C40 0004 | 00004 | 118 | SRDL R4,4 | R1 FIELD IN R4, MASK IN R5- LEFT J |
| 0000FC | 8940 0002 | 00002 | 119 | SLL R4,2 | MULTIPLY BY 4 TO GET OFFSET |
| 000100 | 5894 0080 | 00080 | 120 | L R9,REGSAVE(R4) | GET CONTENTS OF R1 REGISTER IN R9 |
| 000104 | 1255 | | 121 | LTR R5,R5 | IS MASK ZERO |
| 000106 | 4780 014C | 0014C | 122 | BZ PGMRET | YES, NO-OP |
| | | | 124 | ************************************* | |
| | | | 125 | * | |
| | | | 126 | *    NOW R2 POINTS TO THE INSTRUCTION, R5 HAS THE MASK LEFT- | |
| | | | 127 | *    JUSTIFIED, AND R9 CONTAINS THE CONTENTS OF THE R1 REGISTER. | |
| | | | 128 | *    NEXT THE BASE-DISPLACEMENT PAIR MUST BE EVALUATED TO | |
| | | | 129 | *    GET THE ANSWER AREA ADDRESS. | |
| | | | 130 | * | |
| | | | 131 | ************************************* | |
| 00010A | 4860 2002 | 00002 | 133 | LH R6,2(,R2) | GET B2 AND D2 FIELDS |
| 00010E | 5460 00C0 | 000C0 | 134 | N R6,HIGHCLR | CLEAR HIGH-ORDER TWO BYTES |
| 000112 | 8C60 000C | 0000C | 135 | SRDL R6,12 | B2 IN R6, RIGHT JUSTIFIED |
| 000116 | 8960 0002 | 00002 | 136 | SLL R6,2 | MULTIPLY BY FOUR TO GET OFFSET |
| 00011A | 8870 0014 | 00014 | 137 | SRL R7,20 | D2 IN R7, RIGHT-JUSTIFIED |
| 00011E | 1888 | | 138 | SR R8,R8 | IN CASE B2 IS ZERO |
| 000120 | 1266 | | 139 | LTR R6,R6 | IS B2 ZERO |
| 000122 | 4780 012A | 0012A | 140 | BZ *+8 | YES, BASE IS ABSOLUTE 0 |
| 000126 | 5886 0080 | 00080 | 141 | L R8,REGSAVE(R6) | GET CONTENTS OF B2 REGISTER |
| 00012A | 4178 7000 | 00000 | 142 | LA R7,0(R8,R7) | CALCULATE ANSWER AREA ADDRESS IN R7 |
| | | | 144 | ************************************* | |
| | | | 145 | * | |
| | | | 146 | *    NOW REGISTER 7 POINTS TO THE START OF THE ANSWER AREA, | |
| | | | 147 | *    REGISTER 5 HAS THE MASK LEFT-JUSTIFIED, AND REGISTER 9 | |
| | | | 148 | *    CONTAINS THE CONTENTS OF THE R1 REGISTER. | |
| | | | 149 | * | |
| | | | 150 | *    A SIMPLE LOOP IS USED TO PROCESS THE STCM. ONE BY ONE, FROM | |
| | | | 151 | *    HIGH-ORDER TO LOW-ORDER, THE MASK BITS ARE EXAMINED. | |
| | | | 152 | *    IF ONE IS FOUND TO BE ON, THE APPROPRIATE BYTE OF THE R1 | |
| | | | 153 | *    REGISTER IS STORED AND THE ANSWER AREA POINTER IS | |
| | | | 154 | *    INCREMENTED. THIS LOOP IS EXECUTED FOUR TIMES. | |
| | | | 155 | * | |
| | | | 156 | ************************************* | |
| 00012E | 41A0 0004 | 00004 | 158 | LA RA,4 | NUMBER OF TIMES TO LOOP |
| 000132 | 8080 0008 | 00008 | 159 LOOP | SLDL R8,8 | R8 GETS NEXT BYTE FROM R1 REGISTER |
| 000136 | 1255 | | 160 | LTR R5,R5 | TEST HIGH ORDER BIT OF MASK |
| 000138 | 4780 0144 | 00144 | 161 | BNM SKIP | POSITIVE MEANS BIT OFF--> NO STORE |
| 00013C | 4280 7000 | 00000 | 162 | STC R8,0(,R7) | STORE BYTE IN ANSWER AREA |
| 000140 | 4170 7001 | 00001 | 163 | LA R7,1(,R7) | BUMP ANSWER AREA POINTER |
| 000144 | 8950 0001 | 00001 | 165 SKIP | SLL R5,1 | MOVE MASK TO NEXT BIT |
| 000148 | 46A0 0132 | 00132 | 166 | BCT RA,LOOP | PROCESS ALL BITS OF MASK |

LOC   OBJECT CODE    ADDR1 ADDR2  STMT   SOURCE STATEMENT                                          31 DEC 74

```
                                  167  ************************************************************************
                                  168  *                                                                      *
                                  169  *         NOW CONTROL IS RETURNED TO THE INSTRUCTION AFTER THE          *
                                  170  *         OFFENDING ONE. NOTE THAT THE REGISTERS MUST BE RESTORED AS    *
                                  171  *         WELL AS THE PSW.                                             *
                                  172  *                                                                      *
                                  173  ************************************************************************

00014C 980F 0080          00080   175 PGMRET    LM    R0,RF,REGSAVE        RESTORE REGISTERS
000150 8200 0028    00028         176           LPSW  PGMOLD               "RETURN" TO POINT OF INTERRUPTION
                                  177 START     STCMTEST             GENERATE TESTING PROGRAM
                                  556           END
```

```
MASSACHUSETTS INSTITUTE OF TECHNOLOGY          SYSTEM / 360 SIMULATOR                              VERSION 1.3
SOLUTIONTRACE LISTING.    O CONDITIONS ENABLED.                                                        PAGE  1

LOC  TRACE TYPE           COUNT   TIME                                   OP   INSTRUCTION    ADR1 ADR2 OPERAND1 OPERAND2
----  ----------------    -----  ----------                             ----  ------------   ---- ---- -------- --------


0166 SNAPSHOT               1         18  PSW: FE 0 0 0000  '01'B '00'B 0 000166
         REGISTERS:
         R 0: 01020304,   16909060 R 1: 00000001,      1 R 2: 00000002,         2 R 3: 00000003,          3
         R 4: 00000004,          4 R 5: 00000005,      5 R 6: 00000006,         6 R 7: 00000007,          7
         R 8: 00000000,          0 R 9: 00000009,      9 R10: 0000000A,        10 R11: 0000000B,         11
         R12: 0000000C,         12 R13: 0000000D,     13 R14: FFFFFFFF,        -1 R15: 000004B8,       1208
         CORE DUMP:
            03F4,  1012: D9C5C7C9 E2E3C5D9 E240C6D6 D940E3C5 E2E3C9D5 C77A4040   REGI STER S FO R TE STIN G:

017E SNAPSHOT               1         18  PSW: FE 0 0 0000  '01'B '00'B 0 00017E
         CORE DUMP:
            0180,   384: 5B08E000                                                ????

0184 PGM INTERRUPT          2         18  PSW: FE 0 0 0006  '10'B '00'B 0 000184


01D2 SNAPSHOT              12        122  PSW: FE 0 0 0000  '01'B '00'B 0 0001D2
         CORE DUMP:
            03B4,   948: 40C1D5E2 E6C5D940 C3D6D9D9 C5C3E340                      ANS WER  CORR ECT

01E6 SNAPSHOT              13        127  PSW: FE 0 0 0000  '01'B '00'B 0 0001E6
         CORE DUMP:
            01E8,   488: BE08F003                                                ????

01EC PGM INTERRUPT         14        127  PSW: FE 0 0 0001  '10'B '00'B 0 0001EC


0250 SNAPSHOT              74        272  PSW: FE 0 0 0000  '01'B '00'B 0 000250
         CORE DUMP:
            03B4,   948: 40C1D5E2 E6C5D940 C3D6D9D9 C5C3E340                      ANS WER  CORR ECT
            04B8,  1208: 00000001 00000000                                       ???? ????

0264 SNAPSHOT              75        278  PSW: FE 0 0 0000  '01'B '00'B 0 000264
         CORE DUMP:
            0264,   612: 5208F003                                                ????

0268 PGM INTERRUPT         75        278  PSW: FE 0 0 0001  '10'B '00'B 0 000268


02B6 SNAPSHOT              94        387  PSW: FE 0 0 0000  '01'B '00'B 0 0002B6
         CORE DUMP:
            03B4,   948: 40C1D5E2 E6C5D940 C3D6D9D9 C5C3E340                      ANS WER  CORR ECT

02CA SNAPSHOT              95        392  PSW: FE 0 0 0000  '01'B '00'B 0 0002CA
         CORE DUMP:
            02CC,   716: BE02F000                                                ????

02D0 PGM INTERRUPT         96        393  PSW: FE 0 0 0001  '10'B '00'B 0 0002D0

0334 SNAPSHOT             155        533  PSW: FE 0 0 0000  '01'B '00'B 0 000334
```

MASSACHUSETTS INSTITUTE OF TECHNOLOGY          SYSTEM / 360 SIMULATOR                                                    VERSION 1.3
SOLUTIONTRACE LISTING.   2 CONDITIONS ENABLED.                                                                                  PAGE  2

LOC  TRACE TYPE          COUNT  TIME                                             OP   INSTRUCTION      ADR1 ADR2  OPERAND1 OPERAND2
----  ----------------    -----  ----------                                      ----  --------------   ---- ----  -------- --------

        CORE DUMP:
        0384,   948: 40C1D5E2 E6C5D940 C3D6D9D9 C5C3E340                        ANS WER  CORR ECT
        0488,  1208: 03000000 00000000                                         ????  ????

0348 SNAPSHOT            157        543  PSW: FE 0 0 0000  '01'B '00'B 0 000348
        CORE DUMP:
        0348,   840: BE00F000                                                  ??0?

034C PGM INTERRUPT       157        543  PSW: FE 0 0 0001  '10'B '00'B 0 00034C


0380 SNAPSHOT            184        659  PSW: FE 0 0 0000  '01'B '00'B 0 000380
        CORE DUMP:
        0384,   948: 40C1D5E2 E6C5D940 C3D6D9D9 C5C3E340                        ANS WER  CORR ECT
        0488,  1208: 00000000 00000000                                         ????  ????


NORMAL SIMULATOR TERMINATION FOR PROGRAM SOLUTION

        SIMULATED REAL TIME:        659.358

        SIMULATED CPU TIME:         659.358

## 5.4.2   Fixed-Point Overflow Fixup Problem -- OS2

```
  LOC  OBJECT CODE      ADDR1 ADDR2 STMT   SOURCE STATEMENT

000000                              2 SOLUTION CSECT
                                    3        PRINT NOGEN              SUPPRESS MACRO EXPANSION PRINTING
000000                              4        USING SOLUTION,0         ASSEMBLE ABSOLUTE ADDRESSES

                                    6 ************************************************************************
                                    7 *        EXAMPLE SOLUTION FOR INTERRUPT AND I/O PROBLEM OS2,          *
                                    8 *        USING ALGORITHM OUTLINED IN STUDENT ASSIGNMENT.              *
                                    9 *                                                                     *
                                   10 *        THIS PROGRAM DETECTS FIXED-POINT OVERFLOW AND "FIXES"        *
                                   11 *        THE AFFECTED REGISTER WITH THE MAXIMUM NEGATIVE OR           *
                                   12 *        MAXIMUM POSITIVE VALUE, AS APPROPRIATE.                      *
                                   13 *                                                                     *
                                   14 *                                                                     *
                                   15 ************************************************************************

                                   17 ************************************************************************
                                   18 *                                                                     *
                                   19 *            LOW CORE INTIALIZATION                                    *
                                   20 *                                                                     *
                                   21 ************************************************************************

000000 FE00000000003D4             23 IPLPSW   DC   X'FE',AL3(0),A(START) INITIAL PSW LOADED TO START RUN
000008 0000000000000000            24 IPLCCW1  DC   D'0'                IPL CCW'S WHICH
000010 0000000000000000            25 IPLCCW2  DC   D'0'                  ARE NOT USED
000018 0000000000000000            26 EXTOLD   DC   D'0'                EXTERNAL OLD PSW
000020 0000000000000000            27 SUPOLD   DC   D'0'                SUPERVISOR OLD PSW
000028 0000000000000000            28 PGMOLD   DC   D'0'                PROGRAM CHECK OLD PSW
000030 0000000000000000            29 MCKOLD   DC   D'0'                MACHINE CHECK OLD PSW
000038 0000000000000000            30 IOOLD    DC   D'0'                INPUT/OUTPUT OLD PSW
000040 0000000000000000            31 CSW      DC   D'0'                CHANNEL STATUS WORD
000048 00000080                    32 CAW      DC   A(CCWCHAIN)         CHANNEL ADDR WORD --> CCW CHAIN
00004C 00000000                    33 UNUSED1  DC   F'0'                UNUSED WORD 1
000050 00000000                    34 TIMER    DC   F'0'                TIMER AREA
000054 00000000                    35 UNUSED2  DC   F'0'                UNUSED WORD 2
000058 0002000000000001            36 EXTNEW   DC   X'0002',AL2(0),A(1) EXTERNAL NEW PSW- CAUSES HALT
000060 0000000000000388            37 SUPNEW   DC   A(0,SVCINT)         SUPERVISOR NEW PSW
000068 000000000000029A            38 PGMNEW   DC   A(0,PGMINT)         PROGRAM CHECK NEW PSW
000070 0002000000000004            39 MCKNEW   DC   X'0002',AL2(0),A(4) MACHINE CHECK NEW PSW- CAUSES HALT
000078 00000000000003AE            40 IONEW    DC   A(0,IOINT)          INPUT/OUTPUT NEW PSW

                                   42 ************************************************************************
                                   43 *                                                                     *
                                   44 *            PROGRAM CONSTANTS AND EQUATES                             *
                                   45 *                                                                     *
                                   46 ************************************************************************

000080 110001686000001E            48 CCWCHAIN CCW  X'11',BUFFER,X'60',30 PRINT OUT LINE AND CHAIN ON
000088 0300000020000001            49          CCW  X'03',*-*,X'20',1  NO-OP CAUSES SIMULTANEOUS CHANNEL
                                   50 *                                END AND DEVICE END INTERRUPTS
000090 FE0200000000037A            51 IOWAIT   DC   X'FE020000',A(IOCOMP) PSW FOR WAITING ON I/O
000098 0000000000000000            52 SVCSAVE  DC   16F'0'             SAVE AREA FOR SVC CALLS
0000D8 0000000000000000            53 PGMSAVE  DC   16F'0'             SAVE AREA FOR PROGRAM INTERRUPTS
000118 0000000000000000            54 IOSAVE   DC   16F'0'             SAVE AREA FOR I/O INTERRUPTS
000158 00000000                    55 SVCCOUNT DC   F'0'               NUMBER OF SVC'S EXECUTED SINCE IPL
00015C 7FFFFFFF                    56 MAXPOS   DC   X'7FFFFFFF'         MAXIMUM POSITIVE VALUE
```

403

```
LOC   OBJECT CODE    ADDR1 ADDR2  STMT   SOURCE STATEMENT                                    31 DEC 74

000160 80000000                    57 MAXNEG  DC    X'80000000'        MAXIMUM NEGATIVE NUMBER
000164 FFFFFFFF                     58 ALLFS   DC    X'FFFFFFFF'        ALL X'FF'S
000168 C6C9E7C5C440D7D6             59 BUFFER  DC    C'FIXED POINT OVERFLOW AT '
000180 E7E7E7E7E7E7                 60 ADDR    DC    C'XXXXXX'          FILLED IN WITH INTERRUPT ADDRESS
000186 0000                         61 WORK    DC    H'0'               WORK AREA
000188 0010                         62 MAXTV   DC    H'16'              MAXIMUM TRANSFER TABLE OFFSET

                                    64 ****************************************************************
                                    65 *                                                              *
                                    66 *         FOLLOWING TABLE USED TO DECIDE WHAT CLASS OF INSTRUCTION *
                                    67 *         CAUSED OVERFLOW. THIS AIDS IN PROCESSING INTERRUPTS. THIS *
                                    68 *         TABLE IS USED TO TRANSLATE THE OP-CODE OF THE OFFENDING *
                                    69 *         INSTRUCTION. THE RESULTANT CODES ARE:                  *
                                    70 *                                                              *
                                    71 *         00   SHOULD NOT CAUSE OVERFLOW, ERROR                 *
                                    72 *         04   R1 REGISTER SHOULD ALWAYS BE MAX POSITIVE NUMBER *
                                    73 *         08   MINUS VALUE IN R1 MEANS POSITIVE OVERFLOW, POSITIVE *
                                    74 *              VALUE IN R1 INDICATES MINUS OVERFLOW.             *
                                    75 *         12   BIT 31 OF R1 SPECIFIES ACTION: 1-MAX NEG, 0-MAX POS *
                                    76 *         16   SIMILAR TO ABOVE, EXCEPT BIT 31 OF R1+1 REGISTER USED *
                                    77 *                                                              *
                                    78 ****************************************************************

00018A 0000000000000000             80 TABLE   DC    256X'00'           TRANSLATE TABLE, FILLED IN WITH ORGS
00028A 00019A                        81         ORG   TABLE+X'10'
00019A 0400000400000000000808        82         DC    X'0400000400000000000808'
0001A6 0001D4                        83         ORG   TABLE+X'4A'
0001D4 0808                          84         DC    X'0808'
0001D6 0001E4                        85         ORG   TABLE+X'5A'
0001E4 0808                          86         DC    X'0808'
0001E6 000215                        87         ORG   TABLE+X'8B'
000215 0C00000010                    88         DC    X'0C00000010'
00021A 00028A                        89         ORG

                                    91 ****************************************************************
                                    92 *                                                              *
                                    93 *         THIS TRANSLATE TABLE IS USED IN THE CONVERSION OF BINARY *
                                    94 *         ADDRESSES TO PRINTABLE EBCDIC FORM (HEX DIGITS). AFTER *
                                    95 *         THE ADDRESS HAS BEEN "STRETCHED OUT" AND THE HOLES FILLED *
                                    96 *         WITH F'S, THIS TABLE TRANSLATES FA TO C1 FOR CORRECT *
                                    97 *         PRINTING. NOTE THAT THIS TABLE IS ONLY 16 BYTES LONG, *
                                    98 *         SINCE FILLING IN HOLES INSURES A MINIMUM BYTE VALUE *
                                    99 *         OF 240. THIS TABLE IS THEN PASSED TO THE TRANSLATE *
                                   100 *         INSTRUCTION AS STARTING AT SHORTTAB-240.              *
                                   101 *                                                              *
                                   102 ****************************************************************

00028A F0F1F2F3F4F5F6F7            104 SHORTTAB DC   C'0123456789ABCDEF' FIXES-UP HEX DIGITS OVER 9

000000                             106 R0      EQU   0
000001                             107 R1      EQU   1
000002                             108 R2      EQU   2
000003                             109 R3      EQU   3
000004                             110 R4      EQU   4
000005                             111 R5      EQU   5
```

404

```
LOC    OBJECT CODE    ADDR1 ADDR2   STMT    SOURCE STATEMENT

000006                               112 R6       EQU    6
000007                               113 R7       EQU    7
000008                               114 R8       EQU    8
000009                               115 R9       EQU    9
00000A                               116 RA       EQU    10
00000B                               117 RB       EQU    11
00000C                               118 RC       EQU    12
00000D                               119 RD       EQU    13
00000E                               120 RE       EQU    14
00000F                               121 RF       EQU    15

000008                               123 OVERFLOW EQU    X'08'          INTERRUPT CODE FOR FIXED-POINT OVFLW
0000FD                               124 WAITOFF  EQU    X'FD'          MASK TO AND-OFF WAIT BIT IN PSW
00000E                               125 PRINTER  EQU    X'00E'         ADDRESS OF 1403 TO PRINT MESSAGES ON

                                     127 *****************************************************************
                                     128 *                                                               *
                                     129 *      PROGRAM INTERRUPT HANDLER -- INTERRUPTS MASKED OFF        *
                                     130 *                                                               *
                                     131 *      THIS INTERRUPT HANDLER FIXES UP FIXED POINT OVERFLOWS.    *
                                     132 *      IT ISSUES AN SVC TO ADD TO THE SVC COUNTER AND PRINTS     *
                                     133 *      A MESSAGE ON THE PRINTER AT ADDRESS X'00E'.               *
                                     134 *                                                               *
                                     135 *****************************************************************

00029A                               137 PGMINT   EQU    *

00029A 900F 00D8            000D8    139          STM    R0,RF,PGMSAVE   SAVE REGISTERS
00029E 9508 002B      0002B 140          CLI    PGMOLD+3,OVERFLOW  WAS THIS OVERFLOW
0002A2 4770 0380            00380    141          BNE    PGMRET          NO, SKIP IT

                                     143 *****************************************************************
                                     144 *                                                               *
                                     145 *      ADDRESS OF OFFENDING INSTRUCTION IS FOUND BY "BACKING UP" *
                                     146 *      THE ADDRESS CONTAINED IN THE PROGRAM OLD PSW. THIS ADDRESS*
                                     147 *      IS THAT OF THE NEXT INSTRUCTION TO BE EXECUTED, BUT THE ILC*
                                     148 *      FIELD CONTAINS THE LENGTH OF THE OFFENDING INSTRUCTION,   *
                                     149 *      IN TWO-BYTE UNITS. THIS ADDRESS IS SAVED IN REGISTER 1 FOR*
                                     150 *      LATER USE.                                                *
                                     151 *                                                               *
                                     152 *****************************************************************

0002A6 5810 002C            0002C    154          L      R1,PGMOLD+4     GET A(NEXT INSTRUCTION)
0002AA 4110 1000            00000    155          LA     R1,0(,R1)       CLEAR HIGH-ORDER BYTE
0002AE 1B22                           156          SR     R2,R2           CLEAR A REGISTER
0002B0 4320 002C            0002C    157          IC     R2,PGMOLD+4     GET ILC, CC, AND PROG MASK
0002B4 8820 0006            00006    158          SRL    R2,6            DROP CC & PROG MASK
0002B8 8920 0001            00001    159          SLL    R2,1            GET INSTRUCTION LENGTH IN BYTES
0002BC 1B12                           160          SR     R1,R2           BACK UP TO OFFENDING INSTRUCTION
0002BE 18C1                           161          LR     RC,R1           SAVE R1 FOR LATER USE
```

```
    LOC  OBJECT CODE    ADDR1 ADDR2  STMT   SOURCE STATEMENT                                              31 DEC 74

                                     163 ****************************************************************************
                                     164 *                                                                          *
                                     165 *        NOW WE CONVERT THE ADDRESS IN REGISTER 1 TO PRINTABLE             *
                                     166 *        HEXADECIMAL (EBCDIC HEX DIGITS). THIS INVOLVES "STRETCHING        *
                                     167 *        OUT" THE HEX ADDRESS, FILLING THE HOLES WITH F'S, AND            *
                                     168 *        THEN TRANSLATING DIGITS OVER 9. FOR EXAMPLE:                     *
                                     169 *                                                                          *
                                     170 *        REGISTER 1:    X'0000001C'                                        *
                                     171 *        STRETCHED OUT: X'F0F0F0F0F1FC'                                    *
                                     172 *        FINAL FORM:    X'F0F0F0F0F1C3'                                    *
                                     173 *        PRINTS AS:     C'00001C'                                          *
                                     174 *                                                                          *
                                     175 *        NOTE THAT THE LEADING TWO BYTES ARE IGNORED. THE RESULT          *
                                     176 *        OF THIS CONVERSION IS PLACED IN ADDR. THEN THE CCW CHAIN         *
                                     177 *        SO NAMED IS STARTED ON THE 1403 PRINTER SPECIFIED BY             *
                                     178 *        PRINTER (X'00E'). A PSW IS LOADED WITH THE WAIT BIT ON           *
                                     179 *        TO AWAIT THE COMPLETION OF THIS I/O. THIS COMPLETES              *
                                     180 *        LEVEL THREE PROCESSING.                                          *
                                     181 *                                                                          *
                                     182 ****************************************************************************

   0002C0 4190 0006          00006   184        LA    R9,6                 NUMBER OF BYTES TO PROCESS
   0002C4 4180 017F          0017F   185        LA    R8,ADDR-1            A(STARTING BYTE-1)

   0002C8 41A9 8000          00000   187 LOOP   LA    RA,0(R9,R8)          GET A(CURRENT BYTE) IN ANSWER AREA
   0002CC 4210 A000          00000   188        STC   R1,0(,RA)            STORE CURRENT NIBBLE
   0002D0 96F0 A000    00000         189        OI    0(RA),X'F0'          FILL IN HOLE
   0002D4 8810 0004          00004   190        SRL   R1,4                 GET READY FOR NEXT NIBBLE
   0002D8 4690 02C8          002C8   191        BCT   R9,LOOP              PROCESS ALL BYTES
   0002DC DC05 0180 019A  00180 0019A 192       TR    ADDR(6),SHORTTAB-240 FIX-UP DIGITS OVER 9
   0002E2 9C00 000E    0000E         193        SIO   PRINTER              START UP THE PRINTER
   0002E6 4770 03C4          003C4   194        BNZ   ERROR                IF NOT SUCCESSFUL, CRY
   0002EA 181C                       195        LR    R1,RC                RESTORE INSTRUCTION ADDRESS

                                     197 ****************************************************************************
                                     198 *                                                                          *
                                     199 *        NOW WE PICK UP THE R1 REGISTER SPECIFIED IN THE OFFENDING         *
                                     200 *        INSTRUCTION. THIS VALUE IS MULTIPLIED BY 4 TO YIELD AN           *
                                     201 *        OFFSET INTO THE PROGRAM SAVE AREA FOR THE REGISTER'S             *
                                     202 *        ACTUAL VALUE. THIS OFFSET IS SAVED IN REGISTER 2. THEN           *
                                     203 *        THE TRANSLATE TABLE IS USED TO DECODE THE TYPE OF                *
                                     204 *        INSTRUCTION WHICH CAUSED THE OVERFLOW. THIS VALUE IS A           *
                                     205 *        MULTIPLE OF 4 WHICH IS USED IN A TRANSFER TABLE.                 *
                                     206 *                                                                          *
                                     207 ****************************************************************************

   0002EC 1822                       209        SR    R2,R2                CLEAR REGISTER
   0002EE 4320 1001          00001   210        IC    R2,1(,R1)            GET R1 AND GOOP
   0002F2 8820 0004          00004   211        SRL   R2,4                 DROP JUNK
   0002F6 8920 0002          00002   212        SLL   R2,2                 MULTIPLY BY FOUR
   0002FA D200 0186 1000  00186 00000 213       MVC   WORK(1),0(R1)        COPY OP-CODE TO WORK AREA
   000300 DC00 0186 018A  00186 0018A 214       TR    WORK(1),TABLE        GET OVERFLOW TYPE CODE
   000306 1B33                       215        SR    R3,R3                CLEAR A REGISTER
   000308 4330 0186          00186   216        IC    R3,WORK              PUT IN A REGISTER
```

EXAMPLE SOLUTION FOR INTERRUPT AND I/O PROBLEM 052 -- PGG 12/03/74

PAGE   6

    LOC   OBJECT CODE     ADDR1 ADDR2 STMT   SOURCE STATEMENT

```
                                     218 ****************************************************************
                                     219 *                                                              *
                                     220 *       THIS SVC IS FOR THE SECOND LEVEL OF THIS PROBLEM.      *
                                     221 *                                                              *
                                     222 ****************************************************************
    00030C 0A00                      224        SVC    0

                                     226 ****************************************************************
                                     227 *                                                              *
                                     228 *       TRANSFER VECTOR FOR DECODING OP-CODE TYPE.             *
                                     229 *                                                              *
                                     230 ****************************************************************
    00030E 4930 0188         00188   232        CH     R3,MAXTV          IS THIS A VALID CODE
    000312 47D3 0316         00316   233        BNH    *+4(R3)           YES, GO TO APPROPRIATE ROUTINE
    000316 47F0 03C4         003C4   234        B      ERROR             (R3 = 0 => ERROR)
    00031A 47F0 0338         00338   235        B      MAXONLY           (R3 = 4 => ALWAYS POSITIVE OVERFLOW)
    00031E 47F0 032A         0032A   236        B      ARITH             (R3 = 8 => ADD OR SUBTRACT)
    000322 47F0 0344         00344   237        B      SSHIFT            (R3 = 12 => OVERFLOW FROM SLA)
    000326 47F0 0358         00358   238        B      DSHIFT            (R3 = 16 => OVERFLOW CAUSED BY SLDA)

                                     240 ****************************************************************
                                     241 *                                                              *
                                     242 *       PROCESSING ROUTINES FOR EACH TYPE.                     *
                                     243 *                                                              *
                                     244 ****************************************************************
    00032A                           246 ARITH  EQU    *                 (S,SR,SH, A, AR, & AH)
    00032A 5840 0160         00160   247        L      R4,MAXNEG         ASSUME MAXIMUM NEGATIVE VALUE
    00032E 5852 00D8         000D8   248        L      R5,PGMSAVE(R2)    GET VALUE OF R1 REGISTER
    000332 1255                      249        LTR    R5,R5             TEST ITS SIGN
    000334 4720 033C         0033C   250        BP     SET               IF POSITIVE, MAX NEGATIVE IS CORRECT

    000338                           252 MAXONLY EQU   *                 (LPR & LCR WITH MAX NEGATIVE NUMBER)
    000338 5840 015C         0015C   253        L      R4,MAXPOS         MAXIMUM POSITIVE VALUE

    00033C 5042 00D8         000D8   255 SET    ST     R4,PGMSAVE(R2)    SET REGISTER VALUE
    000340 47F0 0376         00376   256        B      MWAIT             WAIT FOR MESSAGE TO BE PRINTED

    000344                           258 SSHIFT EQU    *                 (SLA)
    000344 5840 0160         00160   259        L      R4,MAXNEG         ASSUME MAXIMUM NEGATIVE NUMBER
    000348 4152 00D8         000D8   260        LA     R5,PGMSAVE(R2)    A(REGISTER R1'S VALUE)
    00034C 9180 5000   00000        261        TM     0(R5),X'80'       CHECK SIGN BIT
    000350 4710 033C         0033C   262        BO     SET               IF 1, NEGATIVE VALUE IS CORRECT
    000354 47F0 0338         00338   263        B      MAXONLY           OTHERWISE, MAXIMUM POSITIVE VALUE

    000358                           265 DSHIFT EQU    *                 (SLDA)
    000358 5880 0160         00160   266        L      R8,MAXNEG         MAXIMUM NEGATIVE VALUE
    00035C 1899                      267        SR     R9,R9             IN EVEN-ODD PAIR R8-R9
    00035E 4152 00D8         000D8   268        LA     R5,PGMSAVE(R2)    A(REGISTER R1'S VALUE)
    000362 9180 5000   00000        269        TM     0(R5),X'80'       CHECK SIGN BIT FOR DOUBLEWORD
    000366 4710 0372         00372   270        BO     DSET              IF ON, NEGATIVE VALUE IN ORDER

    00036A 5880 015C         0015C   272        L      R8,MAXPOS         MAXIMUM POSITIVE VALUE
```

| LOC | OBJECT CODE | ADDR1 | ADDR2 | STMT | SOURCE STATEMENT | |
|---|---|---|---|---|---|---|
| | | | | | | 31 DEC 74 |
| 00036E | 5890 0164 | | 00164 | 273 | L     R9,ALLFS | IN EVEN-ODD PAIR R8-R9 |
| 000372 | 9089 5000 | | 00000 | 275 DSET | STM   R8,R9,0(R5) | SET THE EVEN-ODD PAIR R1-R1+1 |

```
277 ************************************************************
278 *                                                          *
279 *       NOW WE WAIT FOR PREVIOUS I/O TO COMPLETE. THE I/O INTERRUPT *
280 *       HANDLER ANDS OFF THE WAIT BIT AND RETURNS. THIS CAUSES *
281 *       CONTROL TO FLOW TO IOCOMP WHEN I/O IS COMPLETE.     *
282 *                                                          *
283 ************************************************************
```

| 000376 | 8200 0090 | | 00090 | 285 MWAIT | LPSW  IOWAIT | WAIT FOR I/O TO COMPLETE |
| 00037A | D707 0040 0040 | 00040 | 00040 | 287 IOCOMP | XC    CSW(8),CSW | CLEAR CHANNEL STATUS WORD |
| 000380 | 980F 0008 | | 00008 | 289 PGMRET | LM    R0,RF,PGMSAVE | RESTORE REGISTERS |
| 000384 | 8200 0028 | | 00028 | 290 | LPSW  PGMOLD | "RETURN" TO POINT OF INTERRUPTION |

```
292 ************************************************************
293 *                                                          *
294 *       SUPERVISOR CALL INTERRUPT HANDLER -- INTERRUPTS MASKED OFF *
295 *                                                          *
296 *       THIS INTERRUPT HANDLER ADDS ONE TO A STATIC "SVC COUNTER" *
297 *       WHICH IS INITIALIZED TO ZERO AT IPL TIME. THEN THE VALUE *
298 *       OF THIS CELL IS DUMPED USING A TRACE INSTRUCTION.   *
299 *                                                          *
300 ************************************************************
```

| 000388 | | | | 302 SVCINT | EQU   * | |
| 000388 | 900F 0098 | | 00098 | 303 | STM   R0,RF,SVCSAVE | SAVE REGISTERS |
| 00038C | 4110 0001 | | 00001 | 304 | LA    R1,1 | GET INCREMENT IN REGISTER 1 |
| 000390 | 5A10 0158 | | 00158 | 305 | A     R1,SVCCOUNT | ADD ONE TO COUNTER |
| 000394 | 5010 0158 | | 00158 | 306 | ST    R1,SVCCOUNT | PUT VALUE BACK |
| | | | | 307 | TRACE DUMP,CORE=(SVCCOUNT,1) | DUMP CONTENTS OF COUNTER |
| 0003A6 | 980F 0098 | | 00098 | 318 | LM    R0,RF,SVCSAVE | RESTORE REGISTERS |
| 0003AA | 8200 0020 | | 00020 | 319 | LPSW  SUPOLD | "RETURN" TO POINT OF INTERRUPTION |

```
321 ************************************************************
322 *                                                          *
323 *       INPUT/OUTPUT INTERRUPT HANDLER -- INTERRUPTIONS MASKED OFF *
324 *                                                          *
325 *       THIS INTERRUPT HANDLER ASSUMES THAT A CCW CHAIN HAS BEEN *
326 *       STARTED ON THE PRINTER WHICH HAS A NO-OP CHAINED ON THE END *
327 *       TO CAUSE SIMULTANEOUS CHANNEL END/DEVICE END. THIS HANDLER *
328 *       ANDS-OFF THE WAIT BIT IN THE I/O OLD PSW AND RELOADS IT. *
329 *                                                          *
330 *                                                          *
331 ************************************************************
```

| 0003AE | | | | 333 IOINT | EQU   * | |
| 0003AE | 900F 0118 | | 00118 | 334 | STM   R0,RF,IOSAVE | SAVE REGISTERS |
| 0003B2 | 910C 0044 | 0C044 | | 335 | TM    CSW+4,X'0C' | CHANNEL END/DEVICE END |
| 0003B6 | 4710 03C8 | | 003C8 | 336 | BO    IORET | YES, COOL |

PAGE  8

31 DEC 74

| LOC | OBJECT CODE | ADDR1 | ADDR2 | STMT | SOURCE STATEMENT | |
|-----|-------------|-------|-------|------|------------------|---|
| | | | | 338 | TRACE | DUMP,STATUS=(OLDI/O,CSW,CAW) |
| 0003C4 | 8200 0070 | 00070 | | 348 ERROR | LPSW | MCKNEW | ERROR CONDITION, STOP |
| 0003C8 | 94FD 0039 | 00039 | | 350 IORET | NI | IOOLD+1,WAITOFF | TURN OFF WAIT BIT IN OLD PSW |
| 0003CC | 980F 0118 | | 00118 | 351 | LM | R0,RF,IOSAVE | RESTORE REGISTERS |
| 0003D0 | 8200 0038 | 00038 | | 352 | LPSW | IOOLD | "RETURN" TO POINT OF INTERRUPTION |
| | | | | 354 START | CHECK | | GENERATE TESTING PROGRAM |
| | | | | 710 | END | | |

```
MASSACHUSETTS INSTITUTE OF TECHNOLOGY        SYSTEM / 360 SIMULATOR                              VERSION 1.3
SOLUTIONTRACE LISTING.   0 CONDITIONS ENABLED.                                                        PAGE  1

LOC  TRACE TYPE          COUNT   TIME                               OP  INSTRUCTION     ADR1 ADR2  OPERAND1 OPERAND2
----  ----------------    -----  ----------                         ----  --------------- ---- ----  -------- --------


03F2 SNAPSHOT              2        21  PSW: FE 0 1 0000   '01'B '00'B F 0003F2
        REGISTERS:
          R  0: 70000000,  1879048192 R 1: 00000001,         1 R 2: 00000002,         2 R 3: 00000003,         3
          R  4: 00000004,             4 R 5: 00000005,        5 R 6: 00000006,         6 R 7: 00000007,         7
          R  8: 00000008,             8 R 9: 00000009,        9 R10: 0000000A,        10 R11: 8000000F, -2147483633
          R12: 0000000C,             12 R13: 0000000D,       13 R14: 0000000E,        14 R15: 80000000, -2147483648
        CORE DUMP:
          0644,  1604: D9C5C7C9 E2E3C5D9 E240C6D6 D940E3C5 E2E3C9D5 C77A4040   REGI STER S FO R TE STIN G:

040A SNAPSHOT              2        21  PSW: FE 0 1 0000   '01'B '00'B F 00040A
        CORE DUMP:
          040C,  1036: 9C00000E                                     ????

0410 PGM INTERRUPT         3        21  PSW: FE 0 1 0002   '10'B '00'B F 000410


0442 SNAPSHOT             11       121  PSW: FE 0 1 0000   '01'B '00'B F 000442
        CORE DUMP:
          0604,  1540: 40C1D5E2 E6C5D940 C3D6D9D9 C5C3E37A              ANS WER  CORR ECT:

0450 SNAPSHOT             11       121  PSW: FE 0 1 0000   '01'B '00'B F 000450
        CORE DUMP:
          0450,  1104: 10FF50F0                                     ??60

0452 PGM INTERRUPT        11       121  PSW: FE 0 1 0008   '01'B '11'B F 000452


03A6 SNAPSHOT             71       238  PSW: 00 0 0 0000   '01'B '10'B 0 0003A6
        CORE DUMP:
          0158,   344: 00000001                                    ????

04BE SNAPSHOT             96     93,511  PSW: FE 0 1 0000   '01'B '00'B F 0004BE
        CORE DUMP:
          0604,  1540: 40C1D5E2 E6C5D940 C3D6D9D9 C5C3E37A              ANS WER  CORR ECT:
          06F8,  1784: 7FFFFFFF                                    "???

04CC SNAPSHOT             96     93,511  PSW: FE 0 1 0000   '01'B '00'B F 0004CC
        CORE DUMP:
          04CC,  1228: 5A0006F0                                    ??0

04D0 PGM INTERRUPT        96     93,511  PSW: FE 0 1 0008   '10'B '11'B F 0004D0


03A6 SNAPSHOT            156     93,627  PSW: 00 0 0 0000   '01'B '10'B 0 0003A6
        CORE DUMP:
          0158,   344: 00000002                                    ????

053C SNAPSHOT            185    201,789  PSW: FE 0 1 0000   '01'B '00'B F 00053C
        CORE DUMP:
          0604,  1540: 40C1D5E2 E6C5D940 C3D6D9D9 C5C3E37A              ANS WER  CORR ECT:
          06F8,  1784: 7FFFFFFF                                    "???
```

```
MASSACHUSETTS INSTITUTE OF TECHNOLOGY              SYSTEM / 360 SIMULATOR                              VERSION 1.3
SOLUTIONTRACE LISTING.   2 CONDITIONS ENABLED.                                                            PAGE  2

LOC  TRACE TYPE           COUNT  TIME                                    OP   INSTRUCTION    ADR1 ADR2  OPERAND1 OPERAND2
----  ----------------     -----  ---------                             ----  ------------   ---- ----  -------- --------

054A SNAPSHOT               185    201,789  PSW: FE 0 1 0000  '01'B '00'B F 00054A
        CORE DUMP:
          054C,  1356: 0000900F                                         ????

054E PGM INTERRUPT          186    201,790  PSW: FE 0 1 0001  '01'B '00'B F 00054E


0580 SNAPSHOT               194    201,888  PSW: FE 0 1 0000  '01'B '00'B F 000580
        CORE DUMP:
          0604,  1540: 40C1D5E2 E6C5D940 C3D6D9D9 C5C3E37A              ANS WER  CORR ECT:

058E SNAPSHOT               194    201,888  PSW: FE 0 1 0000  '01'B '00'B F 00058E
        CORE DUMP:
          0590,  1424: 88800001                                         ????

0594 PGM INTERRUPT          195    201,888  PSW: FE 0 1 0008  '10'B '11'B F 000594


03A6 SNAPSHOT               255    202,005  PSW: 00 0 0 0000  '01'H '10'B 0 0003A6
        CORE DUMP:
          0158,   344: 00000003                                         ????

0600 SNAPSHOT               283    308,646  PSW: 0 1 0 0000  '01'B '00'B F 000600
        CORE DUMP:
          0604,  1540: 40C1D5E2 E6C5D940 C3D6D9D9 C5C3E37A              ANS WER  CORR ECT:
          06F8,  1784: 80000000                                         ????


NORMAL SIMULATOR TERMINATION FOR PROGRAM SOLUTION

        SIMULATED REAL TIME:    308,646.000

        SIMULATED CPU TIME:     1,067.812
```

```
*********************************************************************************************************************
SOLUTION                         OUTPUT TO PRINTER OOE STARTS AT HEAD OF FORM ON NEXT PAGE
*********************************************************************************************************************
```

FIXED POINT OVERFLOW AT 000450

FIXED POINT OVERFLOW AT 0004CC

FIXED POINT OVERFLOW AT 000590

```
 LOC  OBJECT CODE     ADDR1 ADDR2 STMT   SOURCE STATEMENT                                          31 DEC 74

000000                              2 SOLUTION CSECT
                                    3          PRINT NOGEN                SUPPRESS MACRO EXPANSION PRINTING
000000                              4          USING SOLUTION,0           ASSEMBLE ABSOLUTE ADDRESSES

                                    6 *****************************************************************************
                                    7 *          EXAMPLE SOLUTION FOR INTERRUPT AND I/O PROBLEM OS3,           *
                                    8 *          USING ALGORITHM OUTLINED IN STUDENT ASSIGNMENT.              *
                                    9 *                                                                        *
                                   10 *          THIS PROGRAM SIMULATES THE MYTHICAL BTB INSTRUCTION, AS       *
                                   11 *          DESCRIBED IN THE STUDENT ASSIGNMENT FOR PROBLEM OS3.          *
                                   12 *                                                                        *
                                   13 *                                                                        *
                                   14 *****************************************************************************

                                   16 *****************************************************************************
                                   17 *                                                                        *
                                   18 *          LOW CORE INTIALIZATION                                         *
                                   19 *                                                                        *
                                   20 *****************************************************************************
000000 FE00000000000816            22 IPLPSW   DC    X'FE',AL3(0),A(START) INITIAL PSW LOADED TO START RUN
000008 0000000000000000            23 IPLCCW1  DC    D'0'                   IPL CCW'S WHICH
000010 0000000000000000            24 IPLCCW2  DC    D'0'                     ARE NOT USED
000018 0000000000000000            25 EXTOLD   DC    D'0'                   EXTERNAL OLD PSW
000020 0000000000000000            26 SUPOLD   DC    D'0'                   SUPERVISOR OLD PSW
000028 0000000000000000            27 PGMOLD   DC    D'0'                   PROGRAM CHECK OLD PSW
000030 0000000000000000            28 MCKOLD   DC    D'0'                   MACHINE CHECK OLD PSW
000038 0000000000000000            29 IOOLD    DC    D'0'                   INPUT/OUTPUT OLD PSW
000040 0000000000000000            30 CSW      DC    D'0'                   CHANNEL STATUS WORD
000048 00000080                    31 CAW      DC    A(CCWCHAIN)            CHANNEL ADDR WORD --> CCW CHAIN
00004C 00000000                    32 UNUSED1  DC    F'0'                   UNUSED WORD 1
000050 00000000                    33 TIMER    DC    F'0'                   TIMER AREA
000054 00000000                    34 UNUSED2  DC    F'0'                   UNUSED WORD 2
000058 0002000000000001            35 EXTNEW   DC    X'0002',AL2(0),A(1)    EXTERNAL NEW PSW- CAUSES HALT
000060 0000000000000792            36 SUPNEW   DC    A(0,SVCINT)            SUPERVISOR NEW PSW
000068 00000000000006C0            37 PGMNEW   DC    A(0,PGMINT)            PROGRAM CHECK NEW PSW
000070 0002000000000004            38 MCKNEW   DC    X'0002',AL2(0),A(4)    MACHINE CHECK NEW PSW- CAUSES HALT
000078 00000000000007F0            39 IONEW    DC    A(0,IOINT)             INPUT/OUTPUT NEW PSW

                                   41 *****************************************************************************
                                   42 *                                                                        *
                                   43 *          PROGRAM CONSTANTS AND EQUATES                                  *
                                   44 *                                                                        *
                                   45 *****************************************************************************
000080 1100015860000048            47 CCWCHAIN CCW   X'11',BUFFER,X'60',75  PRINT OUT LINE AND CHAIN ON
000088 0300000020000001            48          CCW   X'03',*-*,X'20',1      NO-OP CAUSES SIMULTANEOUS CHANNEL
                                   49 *                                      END AND DEVICE END INTERRUPTS
000090 FE02000000007B2             50 IOWAIT   DC    X'FE020000',A(IOCOMP)  PSW FOR WAITING ON I/O
000098 0000000000000000            51 SVCSAVE  DC    16F'0'                 SAVE AREA FOR SVC CALLS
0000D8 0000000000000000            52 PGMSAVE  DC    16F'0'                 SAVE AREA FOR PROGRAM INTERRUPTS
000118 0000000000000000            53 IOSAVE   DC    16F'0'                 SAVE AREA FOR I/O INTERRUPTS
000158 C140C2E3C240C9D5            54 BUFFER   DC    C'A BTB INSTRUCTION OCCURRED AT LOCATION '
00017F E7E7E7E7E7E740C1            55 ADDR     DC    C'XXXXXX AT TIME '     FILLED IN WITH INTERRUPT ADDRESS
00018E E8E8E8E8E8E8E8E8            56 TIME     DC    C'YYYYYYYYY MILLISECONDS'
```

# 5. INTERRUPT AND I/O PROBLEMS 5-85

LOC    OBJECT CODE     ADDR1 ADDR2  STMT   SOURCE STATEMENT                                        31 DEC 74

```
0001A3 00
0001A4 0000001A                      57 TWENTY6  DC  F'26'          USED TO CONVERT FROM TIMER
0001A8 000003E6                      58 THOUSAND DC  F'998'             UNITS TO MILLISECONDS
0001AC 0000000A                      59 TEN      DC  F'10'          USED TO CONVERT FROM BINARY TO DEC
0001B0 0000000000000000             60 WORK     DC  256X'00'        WORK AREA

                                     62 **********************************************************************
                                     63 *                                                                    *
                                     64 *        FOLLOWING TABLE USED TO CONVERT FROM AN ARBITRARY            *
                                     65 *        BYTE TO THE NUMBER OF ONES IN THE BYTE. EACH ENTRY OF        *
                                     66 *        THIS TABLE IS TWO BYTES LONG. THUS, TO GET THE LENGTH OF     *
                                     67 *        A GIVEN BYTE, THE HALFWORD AT OTABLE + (BYTE VALUE) * 2      *
                                     68 *        IS ACCESSED.                                                 *
                                     69 *                                                                    *
                                     70 **********************************************************************

0002B0 0000000100010002             72 OTABLE  DC  AL2(0,1,1,2,1,2,2,3,1,2,2,3,2,3,3,4)   (00-0F)
0002D0 0001000200020003             73         DC  AL2(1,2,2,3,2,3,3,4,2,3,3,4,3,4,4,5)   (10-1F)
0002F0 0001000200020003             74         DC  AL2(1,2,2,3,2,3,3,4,2,3,3,4,3,4,4,5)   (20-2F)
000310 0002000300030004             75         DC  AL2(2,3,3,4,3,4,4,5,3,4,4,5,4,5,5,6)   (30-3F)
000330 0001000200020003             76         DC  AL2(1,2,2,3,2,3,3,4,2,3,3,4,3,4,4,5)   (40-4F)
000350 0002000300030004             77         DC  AL2(2,3,3,4,3,4,4,5,3,4,4,5,4,5,5,6)   (50-5F)
000370 0002000300030004             78         DC  AL2(2,3,3,4,3,4,4,5,3,4,4,5,4,5,5,6)   (60-6F)
000390 0003000400040005             79         DC  AL2(3,4,4,5,4,5,5,6,4,5,5,6,5,6,6,7)   (70-7F)
0003B0 0001000200020003             80         DC  AL2(1,2,2,3,2,3,3,4,2,3,3,4,3,4,4,5)   (80-8F)
0003D0 0002000300030004             81         DC  AL2(2,3,3,4,3,4,4,5,3,4,4,5,4,5,5,6)   (90-9F)
0003F0 0002000300030004             82         DC  AL2(2,3,3,4,3,4,4,5,3,4,4,5,4,5,5,6)   (A0-AF)
000410 0003000400040005             83         DC  AL2(3,4,4,5,4,5,5,6,4,5,5,6,5,6,6,7)   (B0-BF)
000430 0002000300030004             84         DC  AL2(2,3,3,4,3,4,4,5,3,4,4,5,4,5,5,6)   (C0-CF)
000450 0003000400040005             85         DC  AL2(3,4,4,5,4,5,5,6,4,5,5,6,5,6,6,7)   (D0-DF)
000470 0003000400040005             86         DC  AL2(3,4,4,5,4,5,5,6,4,5,5,6,5,6,6,7)   (E0-EF)
000490 0004000500050006             87         DC  AL2(4,5,5,6,5,6,6,7,5,6,6,7,6,7,7,8)   (F0-FF)

                                     89 **********************************************************************
                                     90 *                                                                    *
                                     91 *        THIS TABLE IS SIMILAR TO THE PREVIOUS ONE, EXCEPT IT         *
                                     92 *        CONVERTS FROM A BYTE TO ITS NUMBER OF ZERO BITS.             *
                                     93 *                                                                    *
                                     94 **********************************************************************

0004B0 0008000700070006             96 ZTABLE  DC  AL2(8,7,7,6,7,6,6,5,7,6,6,5,6,5,5,4)   (00-0F)
0004D0 0007000600060005             97         DC  AL2(7,6,6,5,6,5,5,4,6,5,5,4,5,4,4,3)   (10-1F)
0004F0 0007000600060005             98         DC  AL2(7,6,6,5,6,5,5,4,6,5,5,4,5,4,4,3)   (20-2F)
000510 0006000500050004             99         DC  AL2(6,5,5,4,5,4,4,3,5,4,4,3,4,3,3,2)   (30-3F)
000530 0007000600060005            100         DC  AL2(7,6,6,5,6,5,5,4,6,5,5,4,5,4,4,3)   (40-4F)
000550 0006000500050004            101         DC  AL2(6,5,5,4,5,4,4,3,5,4,4,3,4,3,3,2)   (50-5F)
000570 0006000500050004            102         DC  AL2(6,5,5,4,5,4,4,3,5,4,4,3,4,3,3,2)   (60-6F)
000590 0005000400040003            103         DC  AL2(5,4,4,3,4,3,3,2,4,3,3,2,3,2,2,1)   (70-7F)
0005B0 0007000600060005            104         DC  AL2(7,6,6,5,6,5,5,4,6,5,5,4,5,4,4,3)   (80-8F)
0005D0 0006000500050004            105         DC  AL2(6,5,5,4,5,4,4,3,5,4,4,3,4,3,3,2)   (90-9F)
0005F0 0006000500050004            106         DC  AL2(6,5,5,4,5,4,4,3,5,4,4,3,4,3,3,2)   (A0-AF)
000610 0005000400040003            107         DC  AL2(5,4,4,3,4,3,3,2,4,3,3,2,3,2,2,1)   (B0-BF)
000630 0006000500050004            108         DC  AL2(6,5,5,4,5,4,4,3,5,4,4,3,4,3,3,2)   (C0-CF)
000650 0005000400040003            109         DC  AL2(5,4,4,3,4,3,3,2,4,3,3,2,3,2,2,1)   (D0-DF)
000670 0005000400040003            110         DC  AL2(5,4,4,3,4,3,3,2,4,3,3,2,3,2,2,1)   (E0-EF)
```

```
   LOC  OBJECT CODE      ADDR1 ADDR2  STMT   SOURCE STATEMENT                                          31 DEC 74

   000690 0004000300030002              111           DC    AL2(4,3,3,2,3,2,2,1,3,2,2,1,2,1,1,0)   (F0-FF)

                                        113  ***********************************************************************
                                        114  *                                                                     *
                                        115  *              THIS TRANSLATE TABLE IS USED IN THE CONVERSION OF BINARY *
                                        116  *              ADDRESSES TO PRINTABLE EBCDIC FORM (HEX DIGITS). AFTER   *
                                        117  *              THE ADDRESS HAS BEEN "STRETCHED OUT" AND THE HOLES FILLED *
                                        118  *              WITH F'S, THIS TABLE TRANSLATES FA TO C1 FOR CORRECT    *
                                        119  *              PRINTING. NOTE THAT THIS TABLE IS ONLY 16 BYTES LONG,   *
                                        120  *              SINCE FILLING IN HOLES INSURES A MINIMUM BYTE VALUE     *
                                        121  *              OF 240. THIS TABLE IS THEN PASSED TO THE TRANSLATE      *
                                        122  *              INSTRUCTION AS STARTING AT SHORTTAB-240.               *
                                        123  *                                                                     *
                                        124  ***********************************************************************

   000680 F0F1F2F3F4F5F6F7              126  SHORTTAB DC    C'0123456789ABCDEF' FIXES-UP HEX DIGITS OVER 9

   000000                               128  R0       EQU   0
   000001                               129  R1       EQU   1
   000002                               130  R2       EQU   2
   000003                               131  R3       EQU   3
   000004                               132  R4       EQU   4
   000005                               133  R5       EQU   5
   000006                               134  R6       EQU   6
   000007                               135  R7       EQU   7
   000008                               136  R8       EQU   8
   000009                               137  R9       EQU   9
   00000A                               138  RA       EQU   10
   00000B                               139  RB       EQU   11
   00000C                               140  RC       EQU   12
   00000D                               141  RD       EQU   13
   00000E                               142  RE       EQU   14
   00000F                               143  RF       EQU   15

   000051                               145  BTB      EQU   X'51'             OP-CODE FOR BTB INSTRUCTION
   000001                               146  OPEX     EQU   X'01'             PROGRAM INTERRUPTION CODE FOR OP
                                        147  *                                  EXCEPTION
   000002                               148  TIMESVC  EQU   2                 SVC NUMBER FOR TIME REQUEST
   000003                               149  IOSVC    EQU   3                 SVC NUMBER FOR I/O SVC
   000008                               150  TAREALEN EQU   8                 LENGTH OF TIMER ANSWER AREA
   0000FD                               151  WAITOFF  EQU   X'FD'             MASK TO AND-OFF WAIT BIT IN PSW
   00000E                               152  PRINTER  EQU   X'00E'            ADDRESS OF 1403 TO PRINT MESSAGES ON

                                        154  ***********************************************************************
                                        155  *                                                                     *
                                        156  *              PROGRAM INTERRUPT HANDLER -- INTERRUPTS MASKED OFF      *
                                        157  *                                                                     *
                                        158  *              THIS INTERRUPT HANDLER SNARES THE OPERATION EXCEPTIONS  *
                                        159  *              CAUSED BY THE NON-EXISTANT BTB INSTRUCTION. THEN THIS   *
                                        160  *              INSTRUCTION IS SIMULATED. AN SVC 2 CALL IS USED TO GET  *
                                        161  *              THE CURRENT TIME IN MILLISECONDS, AND THEN AN SVC 3     *
                                        162  *              CALL IS USED TO PRINT A MESSAGE ON THE PRINTER.         *
                                        163  *                                                                     *
                                        164  ***********************************************************************
```

```
   LOC   OBJECT CODE    ADDR1 ADDR2  STMT    SOURCE STATEMENT
```

```
   0006C0                                 166 PGMINT   EQU   *

   0006C0 900F 00D8            000D8       168          STM   R0,RF,PGMSAVE       SAVE REGISTERS
   0006C4 950L 002B     0C02B              169          CLI   PGMOLD+3,OPEX       WAS THIS OVERFLOW
   0006C8 4770 078A            0078A       170          BNE   PGMRET              NO, SKIP IT

                                          172 ********************************************************************
                                          173 *                                                                  *
                                          174 *      AN SVC 2 CALL IS MADE TO GET THE CURRENT TIME IN THE        *
                                          175 *      MESSAGE TO BE PRINTED.                                      *
                                          176 *                                                                  *
                                          177 *      ADDRESS OF OFFENDING INSTRUCTION IS FOUND BY "BACKING UP"   *
                                          178 *      THE ADDRESS CONTAINED IN THE PROGRAM OLD PSW. THIS ADDRESS  *
                                          179 *      IS THAT OF THE NEXT INSTRUCTION TO BE EXECUTED, BUT THE ILC *
                                          180 *      FIELD CONTAINS THE LENGTH OF THE OFFENDING INSTRUCTION,     *
                                          181 *      IN TWO-BYTE UNITS. THIS ADDRESS IS SAVED IN REGISTER 1 FOR  *
                                          182 *      LATER USE.                                                  *
                                          183 *                                                                  *
                                          184 ********************************************************************

   0006CC 4110 018E            0018E       186          LA    R1,TIME             A(ANSWER AREA) FOR SVC
   0006D0 0A02                             187          SVC   TIMESVC             GET TIME IN AREA

   0006D2 5810 002C            0002C       189          L     R1,PGMOLD+4         GET A(NEXT INSTRUCTION)
   0006D6 4110 1000            00000       190          LA    R1,0(,R1)           CLEAR HIGH-ORDER BYTE
   0006DA 1822                             191          SR    R2,R2               CLEAR A REGISTER
   0006DC 4320 002C            0002C       192          IC    R2,PGMOLD+4         GET ILC, CC, AND PROG MASK
   0006E0 8820 0006            00006       193          SRL   R2,6                DROP CC & PROG MASK
   0006E4 8920 0001            00001       194          SLL   R2,1                GET INSTRUCTION LENGTH IN BYTES
   0006E8 1B12                             195          SR    R1,R2               BACK UP TO OFFENDING INSTRUCTION
   0006EA 9551 1000            00000       196          CLI   0(R1),BTB           WAS THIS OP-EX CAUSED BY BTB
   0006EE 4770 078A            0078A       197          BNE   PGMRET              NO, IGNORE IT
   0006F2 18C1                             198          LR    RC,R1               SAVE R1 FOR LATER USE

                                          200 ********************************************************************
                                          201 *                                                                  *
                                          202 *      NOW WE CONVERT THE ADDRESS IN REGISTER 1 TO PRINTABLE       *
                                          203 *      HEXADECIMAL (EBCDIC HEX DIGITS). THIS INVOLVES "STRETCHING  *
                                          204 *      OUT" THE HEX ADDRESS, FILLING THE HOLES WITH F'S, AND       *
                                          205 *      THEN TRANSLATING DIGITS OVER 9. FOR EXAMPLE:                *
                                          206 *                                                                  *
                                          207 *      REGISTER 1:    X'0000001C'                                  *
                                          208 *      STRETCHED OUT: X'F0F0F0F0F1FC'                              *
                                          209 *      FINAL FORM:    X'F0F0F0F0F1C3'                              *
                                          210 *      PRINTS AS:     C'00001C'                                    *
                                          211 *                                                                  *
                                          212 *      NOTE THAT THE LEADING TWO BYTES ARE IGNORED. THE RESULT     *
                                          213 *      OF THIS CONVERSION IS PLACED IN ADDR. THEN AN SVC 3 CALL    *
                                          214 *      IS ISSUED TO PRINT THE NOW COMPLETE MESSAGE. THIS SVC       *
                                          215 *      RETURNS WHEN THE I/O HAS BEEN COMPLETED.                    *
                                          216 *                                                                  *
                                          217 ********************************************************************

   0006F4 4190 0006            00006       219          LA    R9,6                NUMBER OF BYTES TO PROCESS
   0006F8 4180 017E            0017E       220          LA    R8,ADDR-1           A(STARTING BYTE-1)
```

| LOC | OBJECT CODE | ADDR1 | ADDR2 | STMT | SOURCE STATEMENT | | 31 DEC 74 |
|---|---|---|---|---|---|---|---|
| 0006FC | 41A9 8000 | | 00000 | 222 LOOP | LA | RA,0(R9,R8) | GET A(CURRENT.BYTE) IN ANSWER AREA |
| 000700 | 4210 A000 | | 00000 | 223 | STC | R1,0(,RA) | STORE CURRENT NIBBLE |
| 000704 | 96F0 A000 | 00000 | | 224 | OI | 0(RA),X'F0' | FILL IN HOLE |
| 000708 | 8810 0004 | | 00004 | 225 | SRL | R1,4 | GET READY FOR NEXT NIBBLE |
| 00070C | 4690 06FC | | 006FC | 226 | BCT | R9,LOOP | PROCESS ALL BYTES |
| 000710 | DC05 017F 05C0 | 0017F | 005C0 | 227 | TR | ADDR(6),SHORTTAB-240 | FIX-UP DIGITS OVER 9 |
| 000716 | 0A03 | | | 229 | SVC | IOSVC | PRINT MESSAGE |
| 000718 | 181C | | | 230 | LR | R1,RC | RESTORE INSTRUCTION ADDRESS |
| | | | | 232 | ************************************************************************ | | |
| | | | | 233 | * | | * |
| | | | | 234 | * | NOW WE PICK UP THE R1 REGISTER SPECIFIED IN THE OFFENDING | | * |
| | | | | 235 | * | INSTRUCTION. THIS VALUE IS MULTIPLIED BY 4 TO YIELD AN | | * |
| | | | | 236 | * | OFFSET INTO THE PROGRAM SAVE AREA FOR THE REGISTER'S | | * |
| | | | | 237 | * | ACTUAL VALUE. THIS OFFSET IS SAVED IN REGISTER 2. THEN | | * |
| | | | | 238 | * | THE CONTENTS OF THIS REGISTER ARE LOADED INTO REGISTER 4. | | * |
| | | | | 239 | * | THE ADDRESS OF OPERAND TWO IN THE BTB INSTRUCTION IS | | * |
| | | | | 240 | * | CALCULATED AND STORED IN REGISTER-5. | | * |
| | | | | 241 | * | | * |
| | | | | 242 | ************************************************************************ | | |
| 00071A | 1822 | | | 244 | SR | R2,R2 | CLEAR REGISTERS |
| 00071C | 1833 | | | 245 | SR | R3,R3 | FOR NEXT MOVE |
| 00071E | 4320 1001 | | 00001 | 246 | IC | R2,1(,R1) | GET R1 AND GOOP |
| 000722 | 8C20 0004 | | 00004 | 247 | SRDL | R2,4 | MOVE X2 INTO R3 |
| 000726 | 8920 0002 | | 00002 | 248 | SLL | R2,2 | MULTIPLY R1 VALUE BY FOUR |
| 00072A | 8830 001A | | 0001A | 249 | SRL | R3,26 | X2 * 4 IN R3 |
| 00072E | 4850 1002 | | 00002 | 250 | LH | R5,2(,R1) | GET B2-D2 |
| 000732 | 8950 0010 | | 00010 | 251 | SLL | R5,16 | LEFT-JUSTIFY |
| 000736 | 1844 | | | 252 | SR | R4,R4 | CLEAR REGISTER |
| 000738 | 8D40 0004 | | 00004 | 253 | SLDL | R4,4 | GET B2 IN R4,RIGHT-JUSTIFIED |
| 00073C | 8940 0002 | | 00002 | 254 | SLL | R4,2 | B2 * 4 IN REGISTER 4 |
| 000740 | 8850 0014 | | 00014 | 255 | SRL | R5,20 | D2 IN R5 |
| 000744 | 1244 | | | 256 | LTR | R4,R4 | IS B2 = 0 |
| 000746 | 4780 074E | | 0074E | 257 | BZ | *+8 | YES, ABSOLUTE ZERO |
| 00074A | 5A54 0008 | | 00008 | 258 | A | R5,PGMSAVE(R4) | NO, ADD IN C(B2) |
| 00074E | 1233 | | | 259 | LTR | R3,R3 | IS X2 = 0 |
| 000750 | 4780 0758 | | 00758 | 260 | BZ | *+8 | YES, ABSOLUTE ZERO |
| 000754 | 5A53 0008 | | 00008 | 261 | A | R5,PGMSAVE(R3) | NO, ADD IN C(X2) |
| 000758 | 5842 0008 | | 00008 | 262 | L | R4,PGMSAVE(R2) | GET VALUE OF R1 REGISTER |
| | | | | 264 | ************************************************************************ | | |
| | | | | 265 | * | | * |
| | | | | 266 | * | NOW R2 = R1 FIELD * 4, R4 = CONTENTS OF R1 REGISTER, AND | | * |
| | | | | 267 | * | R5 IS THE ADDRESS OF THE SECOND OPERAND FOR THE BTB. | | * |
| | | | | 268 | * | | * |
| | | | | 269 | ************************************************************************ | | |
| 00075C | 1034 | | | 271 | LPR | R3,R4 | GET LENGTH OF BTB OPERAND 2 |
| 00075E | 4780 078A | | 0078A | 272 | BZ | PGMRET | ZERO-LENGTH FIELD IS NO-OP |
| 000762 | 41A0 02B0 | | 002B0 | 273 | LA | RA,OTABLE | ONE'S TABLE BY DEFAULT |
| 000766 | 1244 | | | 274 | LTR | R4,R4 | WAS LENGTH NEGATIVE |
| 000768 | 4720 0770 | | 00770 | 275 | BP | *+8 | NO, ONE'S TABLE IS CORRECT |
| 00076C | 41A0 04B0 | | 004B0 | 276 | LA | RA,ZTABLE | IF COUNT NEGATIVE, COUNT ZEROES |

```
                              278 ***********************************************************************
                              279 *                                                                     *
                              280 *        R3 = LENGTH OF FIELD, RA = ADDRESS OF CORRECT CONVERSION      *
                              281 *        TABLE AND R5 = ADDRESS OF OPERAND 2.                          *
                              282 *                                                                     *
                              283 ***********************************************************************
000770 1899                   285            SR    R9,R9              INITIALIZE COUNT TO ZERO
000772 0650                   286            BCTR  R5,0               SUBTRACT ONE FROM OP 2 ADDRESS

000774 1877                   288 GLOOP      SR    R7,R7              CLEAR REGISTER
000776 4373 5000       00000  289            IC    R7,0(R3,R5)        GET CURRENT BYTE
00077A 8970 0001       00001  290            SLL   R7,1               MULTIPLY BY TWO
00077E 4A97 A000       00000  291            AH    R9,0(R7,RA)        ADD CORRECT AMOUNT TO COUNT
000782 4630 0774       00774  292            BCT   R3,GLOOP           PROCESS ALL BYTES OF OPERAND TWO

                              294 ***********************************************************************
                              295 *                                                                     *
                              296 *        NOW R9 COTAINS ANSWER. RECALLING THAT R2 = R1 FIELD * 4,      *
                              297 *        WE STORE THIS ANSWER IN THE R1 REGISTER'S SLOT IN THE         *
                              298 *        SAVE AREA AND THEN RETURN.                                    *
                              299 *                                                                     *
                              300 ***********************************************************************
000786 5092 00D8       000D8  302            ST    R9,PGMSAVE(R2)     SET R1 REGISTER IN SAVE AREA

00078A 980F 00D8       000D8  304 PGMRET     LM    R0,RF,PGMSAVE      RESTORE REGISTERS
00078E 8200 0028       00028  305            LPSW  PGMOLD             "RETURN" TO POINT OF INTERRUPTION

                              307 ***********************************************************************
                              308 *                                                                     *
                              309 *        SUPERVISOR CALL INTERRUPT HANDLER -- INTERRUPTS MASKED OFF    *
                              310 *                                                                     *
                              311 *        THIS SVC HANDLER RECOGNIZES TWO SVC'S - 2 AND 3. SVC 3        *
                              312 *        CAUSES THE LINE STARTING AT "BUFFER" TO BE PRINTED ON         *
                              313 *        THE PRINTER DEFINED BY "PRINTER", WHILE SVC 2 CAUSES THE      *
                              314 *        ELASPED TIEM IN MILLISECONDS TO BE STORED IN PRINTABLE        *
                              315 *        FORM AT THE ADDRESS SPECIFIED BY REGISTER 1.                  *
                              316 *                                                                     *
                              317 ***********************************************************************
000792                        319 SVCINT     EQU   *
000792 900F 0098       00098  320            STM   R0,RF,SVCSAVE      SAVE REGISTERS
000796 9502 0023       00023  321            CLI   SUPOLD+3,TIMESVC   IS THIS A TIME REQUEST
00079A 4780 07BC       007BC  322            BE    GETTIME            YES, PROCESS IT
00079E 9503 0023       00023  323            CLI   SUPOLD+3,IOSVC     IS THIS AN I/O REQUEST
0007A2 4770 07E8       007E8  324            BNE   SVCRET             NO, IGNORE IT

                              326 ***********************************************************************
                              327 *                                                                     *
                              328 *        SVC 3 => PRINT MESSAGE ON PRINTER.                            *
                              329 *                                                                     *
                              330 ***********************************************************************
0007A6 9C00 000E       0000E  332            SIO   PRINTER            START UP THE PRINTER
```

| LOC | OBJECT CODE | ADDR1 | ADDR2 | STMT | SOURCE STATEMENT | | | 31 DEC 74 |
|-----|-------------|-------|-------|------|------------------|---|---|-----------|
| 0007AA | 4770 0806 | | 00806 | 333 | | BNZ | ERROR | IF NOT SUCCESSFUL, CRY |
| | | | | 335 | ************************************************************************ | | | |
| | | | | 336 | * | | | |
| | | | | 337 | *      NOW WE WAIT FOR PREVIOUS I/O TO COMPLETE. THE I/O INTERRUPT  * | | | |
| | | | | 338 | *      HANDLER ANDS OFF THE WAIT BIT AND RETURNS. THIS CAUSES        * | | | |
| | | | | 339 | *      CONTROL TO FLOW TO IOCOMP WHEN I/O IS COMPLETE.              * | | | |
| | | | | 340 | * | | | |
| | | | | 341 | ************************************************************************ | | | |
| 0007AE | 8200 0090 | 00090 | | 343 MWAIT | | LPSW | IOWAIT | WAIT FOR I/O TO COMPLETE |
| 0007B2 | D707 0040 0040 | 00040 | 00040 | 345 IOCOMP | | XC | CSW(8),CSW | CLEAR CHANNEL STATUS WORD |
| 0007B8 | 47F0 07E8 | | 007E8 | 346 | | B | SVCRET | RETURN TO REQUESTING PROGRAM |
| | | | | 348 | ************************************************************************ | | | |
| | | | | 349 | * | | | |
| | | | | 350 | *      SVC 2 => TIMER REQUEST, R1 -> ANSWER AREA.                   * | | | |
| | | | | 351 | * | | | |
| | | | | 352 | ************************************************************************ | | | |
| 0007BC | 5830 0050 | | 00050 | 354 GETTIME | | L | R3,TIMER | GET TIMER VALUE |
| 0007C0 | 1033 | | | 355 | | LPR | R3,R3 | GET ELAPSED TIME, IN TIMER UNITS |
| 0007C2 | 1822 | | | 356 | | SR | R2,R2 | CLEAR HIGH-ORDER REGISTER |
| 0007C4 | 5C20 01A4 | | 001A4 | 357 | | M | R2,TWENTY6 | MULTIPLY BY 26 AND THEN DIVIDE |
| 0007C8 | 5D20 01A8 | | 001A8 | 358 | | D | R2,THOUSAND | BY A THOUSAND TO GET TIME IN MS |
| | | | | 360 | ************************************************************************ | | | |
| | | | | 361 | * | | | |
| | | | | 362 | *      NOW THE APPROXIMATE ELAPSED TIME IS IN R3. THIS IS CONVERTED * | | | |
| | | | | 363 | *      TO PRINTABLE DECIMAL FORM IN THE ANSWER AREA.               * | | | |
| | | | | 364 | * | | | |
| | | | | 365 | ************************************************************************ | | | |
| 0007CC | 4140 0008 | | 00008 | 367 | | LA | R4,TAREALEN | LENGTH OF ANSWER AREA |
| 0007D0 | 0610 | | | 368 | | BCTR | R1,0 | DECREMENT ADDRESS OF AREA BY 1 |
| 0007D2 | 4164 1000 | | 00000 | 370 SLOOP | | LA | R6,0(R4,R1) | A(CURRENT DIGIT IN ANSWER AREA) |
| 0007D6 | 1822 | | | 371 | | SR | R2,R2 | CLEAR HIGH-ORDER REGISTER |
| 0007D8 | 5D20 01AC | | 001AC | 372 | | D | R2,TEN | GET CURRENT RADIX |
| 0007DC | 4220 6000 | | 00000 | 373 | | STC | R2,0(,R6) | STORE REMAINDER IN FIELD |
| 0007E0 | 96F0 6000 | 0C000 | | 374 | | OI | 0(R6),X'F0' | STICK IN ZONE |
| 0007E4 | 4640 07D2 | | 007D2 | 375 | | BCT | R4,SLOOP | FILL ANSWER AREA |
| 0007E8 | 980F 0098 | | 00098 | 377 SVCRET | | LM | R0,9F,SVCSAVE | RESTORE REGISTERS |
| 0007EC | 8200 0020 | 00020 | | 378 | | LPSW | SUPOLD | "RETURN" TO POINT OF INTERRUPTION |

```
 LOC   OBJECT CODE   ADDR1 ADDR2  STMT    SOURCE STATEMENT                                      31 DEC 74

                                   380  ****************************************************************************
                                   381  *                                                                          *
                                   382  *          INPUT/OUTPUT INTERRUPT HANDLER -- INTERRUPTIONS MASKED OFF        *
                                   383  *                                                                          *
                                   384  *          THIS INTERRUPT HANDLER ASSUMES THAT A CCW CHAIN HAS BEEN          *
                                   385  *          STARTED ON THE PRINTER WHICH HAS A NO-OP CHAINED ON THE END       *
                                   386  *          TO CAUSE SIMULTANEOUS CHANNEL END/DEVICE END. THIS HANDLER        *
                                   387  *          ANDS-OFF THE WAIT BIT IN THE I/O OLD PSW AND RELOADS IT.          *
                                   388  *                                                                          *
                                   389  *                                                                          *
                                   390  ****************************************************************************

0007F0                             392 IOINT    EQU   *
0007F0 900F 0118            00118  393          STM   R0,RF,IOSAVE        SAVE REGISTERS
0007F4 910C 0044      00044        394          TM    CSW+4,X'0C'         CHANNEL END/DEVICE END
0007F8 4710 080A            080A   395          BO    IORET               YES, COOL

                                   397          TRACE DUMP,STATUS=(OLDI/O,CSW,CAW)

000806 8200 0070      00070        407 ERROR    LPSW  MCKNEW              ERROR CONDITION, STOP

00080A 94FD 0039      00039        409 IORET    NI    IOOLD+1,WAITOFF     TURN OFF WAIT BIT IN OLD PSW
00080E 980F 0118            00118  410          LM    R0,RF,IOSAVE        RESTORE REGISTERS
000812 8200 0038      00038        411          LPSW  IOOLD               "RETURN" TO POINT OF INTERRUPTION

                                   413 START    BUCKET                    GENERATE TESTING PROGRAM
                                   805          END
```

```
MASSACHUSETTS INSTITUTE OF TECHNOLOGY          SYSTEM / 360 SIMULATOR                                    VERSION 1.3
SOLUTIONTRACE LISTING.   0 CONDITIONS ENABLED.                                                               PAGE  1

LOC  TRACE TYPE        COUNT   TIME                                      OP   INSTRUCTION    ADR1 ADR2 OPERAND1 OPERAND2
----  ----------------  -----   ---------                               ----  --------------- ---- ---- -------- --------


0828 SNAPSHOT             1       18  PSW: FE 0 0 0000  '01'B '00'B 0 000828
       REGISTERS:
        R  0: 00000000,        0 R 1: 00000BRR,      2952 R 2: FFFFFFFD,       -3 R 3: 00000003,         3
        R  4: 00000004,        4 R 5: 00000005,         5 R 6: 00000006,        6 R 7: 00000000,         0
        R  8: 00000008,        8 R 9: 00000009,         9 R10: 0000000A,       10 R11: 0000000B,        11
        R12: FFFFFFFF,        -1 R13: 0000000D,        13 R14: 00000002,        2 R15: 00000890,      2960
       CORE DUMP:
        0AB8,  2744: D9C5C7C9 E2E3C5D9 E240C6D6 D940E3C5 E2E3C9D5 C77A4040  REGI STER S FO R TE STIN G:

084A SNAPSHOT             1       18  PSW: FE 0 0 0000  '01'B '00'B 0 00084A
       CORE DUMP:
        084C,  2124: 5800C000                                            ????

0850 PGM INTERRUPT        2       18  PSW: FE 0 0 0006  '10'B '00'B 0 000850


0882 SNAPSHOT            10      118  PSW: FE 0 0 0000  '01'B '00'B 0 000882
       CORE DUMP:
        0A78,  2680: 40C1D5E2 E6C5D940 C3D6D9D9 C5C3E37A                 ANS WER  CORR ECT:

0890 SNAPSHOT            10      118  PSW: FE 0 0 0000  '01'B '00'B 0 000890
       CORE DUMP:
        0890,  2192: 51700000                                            ????

0894 PGM INTERRUPT       10      118  PSW: FE 0 0 0001  '10'B '00'B 0 000894


06D2 SVC INTERRUPT       15      150  PSW: 00 0 0 0002  '01'B '00'B 0 0006D2


0718 SVC INTERRUPT      119      377  PSW: 00 0 0 0003  '01'B '01'B 0 000718


0900 SNAPSHOT           166   94,001  PSW: FE 0 0 0000  '01'B '00'B 0 000900
       CORE DUMP:
        0A78,  2680: 40C1D5E2 E6C5D940 C3D6D9D9 C5C3E37A                 ANS WER  CORR ECT:
        0B84,  2948: 00000000                                            ????

090E SNAPSHOT           166   94,001  PSW: FE 0 0 0000  '01'B '00'B 0 00090E
       CORE DUMP:
        0910,  2320: 51E3F000                                            ?TO?

0914 PGM INTERRUPT      167   94,001  PSW: FE 0 0 0001  '10'B '00'B 0 000914


06D2 SVC INTERRUPT      172   94,034  PSW: 00 0 0 0002  '01'B '00'B 0 0006D2


0718 SVC INTERRUPT      276   94,256  PSW: 00 0 0 0003  '01'B '01'B 0 000718
```

●●●●●●●●●●●●●●●●●●●●●●●●●●●●●●●●●●●●●●●●●●●●●●●●●●●●●●●●●●●●●●●●●●●●●●●●●●●●●●●●●●●●●●●●●●●●●●●●●●●●●●●●●●●●●●●●●●●●●●●●●●●●●●●●●●●●●●●●●●●
SOLUTION                              OUTPUT TO PRINTER 00E STARTS AT HEAD OF FORM ON NEXT PAGE
●●●●●●●●●●●●●●●●●●●●●●●●●●●●●●●●●●●●●●●●●●●●●●●●●●●●●●●●●●●●●●●●●●●●●●●●●●●●●●●●●●●●●●●●●●●●●●●●●●●●●●●●●●●●●●●●●●●●●●●●●●●●●●●●●●●●●●●●●●●

A BTB INSTRUCTION OCCURRED AT LOCATION 0008A0 AT TIME 00000000 MILLISECONDS

A BTB INSTRUCTION OCCURRED AT LOCATION 000910 AT TIME 00000186 MILLISECONDS

A BTB INSTRUCTION OCCURRED AT LOCATION 0009D4 AT TIME 00000373 MILLISECONDS

MASSACHUSETTS INSTITUTE OF TECHNOLOGY              SYSTEM / 360 SIMULATOR                                          VERSION 1.3
SOLUTIONTRACE LISTING.   3 CONDITIONS ENABLED.                                                                        PAGE  2

```
LOC  TRACE TYPE          COUNT   TIME                                    OP   INSTRUCTION      ADR1 ADR2  OPERAND1 OPERAND2
----  ----------------    -----  ---------                               ----  --------------   ---- ----  -------- --------

0980 SNAPSHOT              341    187,573  PSW: FE 0 0 0000  '01'B '00'B 0 000980
       CORE DUMP:
         0A78,  2680: 40C1D5E2 E6C5D940 C3D6D9D9 C5C3E37A                       ANS WER  CORR ECT:
         0B84,  2948: 00000009                                                  ????

098E SNAPSHOT              341    187,573  PSW: FE 0 0 0000  '01'B '00'B 0 00098E
       CORE DUMP:
         0990,  2448: 0000900F                                                  ????

0992 PGM INTERRUPT        342    187,573  PSW: FE 0 0 0001  '01'B '00'B 0 000992


06D2 SVC INTERRUPT        347    187,606  PSW: 00 0 0 0002  '01'B '00'B 0 0006D2


09C4 SNAPSHOT             421    187,865  PSW: FE 0 0 0000  '01'B '00'B 0 0009C4
       CORE DUMP:
         0A78,  2680: 40C1D5E2 E6C5D940 C3D6D9D9 C5C3E37A                       ANS WER  CORR ECT:

09D2 SNAPSHOT             421    187,865  PSW: FE 0 0 0000  '01'B '00'B 0 0009D2
       CORE DUMP:
         09D4,  2516: 5120F003                                                  ????

09D8 PGM INTERRUPT        422    187,866  PSW: FE 0 0 0001  '10'B '00'B 0 0009D8


06D2 SVC INTERRUPT        427    187,898  PSW: 00 0 0 0002  '01'B '00'B 0 0006D2


0718 SVC INTERRUPT        531    188,121  PSW: 00 0 0 0003  '01'B '01'B 0 000718


0A44 SNAPSHOT             601    296,805  PSW: FE 0 0 0000  '01'B '00'B 0 000A44
       CORE DUMP:
         0A78,  2680: 40C1D5E2 E6C5D940 C3D6D9D9 C5C3E37A                       ANS WER  CORR ECT:
         0B84,  2948: 0000000A                                                  ????

0A46 SVC INTERRUPT        602    296,805  PSW: FE 0 0 0002  '01'B '00'B 0 000A46


0A74 SNAPSHOT             665    297,037  PSW: FE 0 0 0000  '01'B '00'B 0 000A74
       CORE DUMP:
         0AE4,  2788: E3C9D4C5 40E5C1D3 E4C540D9 C5E3E4D9 D5C5C47A             TIME  VAL UE R ETUR NED:
         0B88,  2952: F0F0F0F0 F0F5F9F3                                         0000 0593


NORMAL SIMULATOR TERMINATION FOR PROGRAM SOLUTION

        SIMULATED REAL TIME:    297,037.000

        SIMULATED CPU TIME:      2,121.812
```

## 5.4.4 Airline Reservations Problem -- OS4

```
AIRLINE RESERVATION SAMPLE SOLUTION OBVIOUSLY NOT BY PGG                                    PAGE    2

  LOC  OBJECT CODE      ADDR1 ADDR2  STMT    SOURCE STATEMENT                                31 DEC 74

000000                                  2 SAMPLE   CSECT
                                        3          PRINT NOGEN
000000 FE000000000000A0                 4 IPL      DC    X'FE000000',A(BEGIN)
000008 0002000000000000                 5 TEMP     DC    10X'0002000000000000'
000058 0000000000000972                 6          DC    A(O,EXTINT)
000060 0000000000000430                 7 SVC      DC    A(0,SVCINT)
000068 0000000000000980                 8          DC    A(O,PGMINT)
000070 000000000000098E                 9          DC    A(O,MCKINT)
000078 00000000000006FC                10 IO       DC    A(O,IOINT)
000080                                  11 UNUSED   DS    8F
0000A0 1BDD                             12 BEGIN    SR    INFULL,INFULL
0000A2 1BEE                             13          SR    OUTFULL,OUTFULL
0000A4 50DD 0088             00088      14          ST    INFULL,X'88'       SAVE INFULL IN CASE OF INTERRUPT.
0000A8 50E0 008C             0008C      15          ST    OUTFULL,X'8C'      STORE OUTFULL IN CASE OF INTERRUPT.
                                        16          TRACE INTRPT,SVC,REGS=(0,1)
                                        25          TRACE INTRPT,I/O,CORE=(56,5)
                                        36          INQUIRY                  INFORMATION PROCESSING MACRO
000020                                 124 OLDSVC   EQU   X'20'
000048                                 125 CAW      EQU   X'48'
000040                                 126 CSW      EQU   X'40'
000038                                 127 OLDIO    EQU   X'38'
000018                                 128 OLDEXT   EQU   X'18'
000030                                 129 OLDMCK   EQU   X'30'
000028                                 130 OLDPGM   EQU   X'28'
00000D                                 131 INFULL   EQU   13
00000E                                 132 OUTFULL  EQU   14
000430 50F0 0054             00054     133 SVCINT   ST    15,X'54'
000434 05F0                            134          BALR  15,0
000436                                 135          USING *,15,11
000436 900E F5C2             009F8     136          STM   0,14,SAVEAREA
00043A 05B0                            137          BALR  11,0
00043C 5AB0 F992             00DC8     138          A     11,=F'4090'
000440 92FF F984       00DBA           139          MVI   SVCFLAG,X'FF'      WE'RE IN SVC PROGRAM
000444 D203 F5FE 0054  00A34 00054     140          MVC   SAVEAREA+15*4(4),X'54'
00044A 58DD 0088             00088     141          L     INFULL,X'88'       GET INFULL
00044E 58E0 008C             0008C     142          L     OUTFULL,X'8C'      GET OUTFULL
000452 8000 F985       00DBB           143          SSM   ENABLE
000456 9501 0023             00023     144          CLI   OLDSVC+3,X'01'     INTERRUPT CODE OF OLDSVC PSW
00045A 4780 F034             0046A     145          BE    READ               CONTAINS BIT POSITIONS 8-15 OF
00045E 9502 0023             00023     146          CLI   OLDSVC+3,X'02'       SUPERVISOR CALL
000462 4780 F1A4             005DA     147          BE    WRITE
000466 47F0 F52E             00964     148          B     ERROR
                                       149 ********************************************************
                                       150 *
                                       151 *
                                       152 *        READ   ROUTINE
                                       153 *
                                       154 ********************************************************
000474 8000 F980       00DB6           155 READ     TRACE DUMP,REGS=(13,14)
000478 5900 F996             00DCC     164          SSM   DISABLE
00047C 4770 F09A             004D0     165          C     INFULL,=F'0'       INPUT BUFFER EMPTY?
000480 95FF F97B       00DB1           166          BNE   NEMPTY
000484 4780 F086             004BC*    167          CLI   RFLAG,X'FF'        ALREADY READING?
000488 95FF F97D       00DB3           168          BE    WAY1               YES.
                                       169          CLI   EOFLAG,X'FF'       ARE WE OUT OF CARDS?
```

AIRLINE RESERVATION SAMPLE SOLUTION OBVIOUSLY NOT BY PGG                                                          PAGE    3

| LOC | OBJECT CODE | ADDR1 | ADDR2 | STMT | SOURCE STATEMENT | | | 31 DEC 74 |
|-----|-------------|-------|-------|------|------|------|------|------|
| 00048C | 4780 F19C | | 005D2 | 170 | | BE | OUTOF | |
| 000490 | 8000 F985 | 00DB8 | | 171 | | SSM | ENABLE | |
| 000494 | 4150 F582 | | 009B8 | 172 | | LA | 5,CCWR | LOAD ADDRESS OF FIRST READ CCW |
| 000498 | 5050 0048 | | 00048 | 173 | | ST | 5,CAW | SET IT UP AS TE CAW FOR SIO INST. |
| 00049C | 9D00 000C | 0000C | | 174 | | TIO | X'00C' | |
| 0004A0 | 4770 F086 | | 0048C | 175 | | BNZ | WAY1 | MEANS BUSY (I/O PENDING) |
| 0004A4 | 8000 F980 | 00DB6 | | 176 | | SSM | DISABLE | DON'T LET ANY I/O INTRPTS COME IN |
| 0004A8 | 9C00 000C | 0000C | | 177 | | SIO | X'00C' | |
| 0004AC | 4780 F086 | | 0048C | 178 | | BZ | WAY1 | TURN ON WAIT1 SWITCH |
| 0004B0 | 9101 0044 | | 00044 | 179 | | TM | CSW+4,X'01' | IS UNIT CHECK ON? |
| 0004B4 | 4710 F198 | | 005CE | 180 | | BO | CONTIN | |
| 0004B8 | 47F0 F52E | | 00964 | 181 | | B | ERROR | |
| 0004BC | 92FF F978 | 00DB1 | | 182 | WAY1 | MVI | RFLAG,X'FF' | |
| 0004C0 | 92FF F97A | 00DB0 | | 183 | | MVI | WAIT1,X'FF' | |
| 0004C4 | 8200 F56A | | 009A0 | 184 | | LPSW | WAITIO | |
| 0004C8 | 95F0 F97E | 00DB4 | | 185 | RINT | CLI | RDRW,X'F0' | WAS IT A READER INTERRUPT LIKE WE |
| | | | | 186 | * | | | WANT? |
| 0004CC | 4770 F086 | | 0048C | 187 | | BNE | WAY1 | PRINTER INTERRUPT-WE WANTED READER |
| 0004D0 | 8000 F980 | 00DB6 | | 188 | NEMPTY | SSM | DISABLE | MASK I/O INT. FOR SHORT TIME NOW |
| 0004D4 | 1855 | | | 189 | | SR | 5,5 | |
| 0004D6 | 186D | | | 190 | | LR | 6,INFULL | GET NO. OF CARDS IN INBUFF |
| 0004D8 | 4170 F644 | | 00A7A | 191 | LOOP1 | LA | 7,INBUFF+2 | GET THE PRIORITY BYTE |
| 0004DC | 1A75 | | | 192 | | AR | 7,5 | ADD OFFSET |
| 0004DE | 955A 7000 | 00000 | | 193 | | CLI | 0(7),X'5A' | IS IT " " PRIORITY |
| 0004E2 | 4780 F0D6 | | 0050C | 194 | | BE | FOUND | YES |
| 0004E6 | 5A50 F99A | 00DD0 | | 195 | | A | 5,=F'80' | INCREMENT TO CHECK NEXT CARD |
| 0004EA | 4660 F0A2 | | 004D8 | 196 | | BCT | 6,LOOP1 | CHECK ALL CARDS IN INBUFF |
| 0004EE | 1855 | | | 197 | | SR | 5,5 | REINITIALIZE OFFSET |
| 0004F0 | 186D | | | 198 | | LR | 6,INFULL | RESET COUNTER |
| 0004F2 | 4170 F644 | | 00A7A | 199 | LOOP2 | LA | 7,INBUFF+2 | GET PRIORITY BYTE |
| 0004F6 | 1A75 | | | 200 | | AR | 7,5 | ADD OFFSET |
| 0004F8 | 955C 7000 | 00000 | | 201 | | CLI | 0(7),X'5C' | IS IT '*'PRIORITY? |
| 0004FC | 4780 F0D6 | | 0050C | 202 | | BE | FOUND | YES |
| 000500 | 5A50 F99A | 00DD0 | | 203 | | A | 5,=F'80' | INCREMENT OFFSET |
| 000504 | 4660 F08C | | 004F2 | 204 | | BCT | 6,LOOP2 | |
| 000508 | 47F0 F136 | | 0056C | 205 | | B | REG | BRANCH IF NO PRIORITY WAS FOUND |
| | | | | 206 | FOUND | TRACE | DUMP,REGS=(5) | |
| 000516 | 5950 F996 | 00DCC | | 215 | | C | 5,=F'0' | WAS FIRST MESSAGE HIGHEST PRIORITY? |
| 00051A | 4780 F136 | | 0055C | 216 | | BE | REG | YES |
| 00051E | 5050 F972 | 00DA8 | | 217 | | ST | 5,PROFF | SAVE OFFSRT OF HIGHEST PRIORITY |
| 000522 | 4150 F642 | | 00A78 | 218 | | LA | 5,INBUFF | GET ADDR. OF INBUFF |
| 000526 | 5A50 F972 | 00DA8 | | 219 | | A | 5,PROFF | ADD OFFSET |
| 00052A | D24F F782 5000 | 00B88 | 00000 | 220 | | MVC | BUFFER(80),0(5) | PASS BACK CORRECT MESSAGE. |
| 000530 | 5850 F972 | 00DA8 | | 221 | | L | 5,PROFF | RESTORE REG FOR LATER |
| 000534 | 5BD0 F99E | 00DD4 | | 222 | | S | INFULL,=F'1' | |
| 000538 | 95FF F97B | 00DB1 | | 223 | | CLI | RFLAG,X'FF' | IS READING GOING ON NOW? |
| 00053C | 4770 F112 | | 00548 | 224 | | BNE | RUFFLE | NO--O.K. TO SHUFFLE NOW |
| 000540 | 92FF F9A2 | 00DB8 | | 225 | | MVI | PING,X'FF' | SET FLAG TO SHUFFLE LATER |
| 000544 | 47F0 F156 | | 0058C | 226 | | B | ADDR | |
| 000548 | 5950 F9A2 | 00DD8 | | 227 | RUFFLE | C | 5,=F'240' | WAS HIGHEST PRIORITY FOURTH CARD? |
| 00054C | 4780 F156 | | 0058C | 228 | | BE | ADDR | NO NEED TO SHUFFLE |
| 000550 | 5950 F99A | 00DD0 | | 229 | | C | 5,=F'80' | WAS SECOND MESS. HIGHEST PRIORITY? |
| 000554 | 4780 F12C | | 00562 | 230 | | BE | MOVEUP | YES |
| 000558 | D24F F6E2 F732 | 00818 00868 | | 231 | | MVC | INBUFF+160(80),INBUFF+240 | NO, MUST BE THIRD MESSAGE |
| 00055E | 47F0 F156 | | 0058C | 232 | | B | ADDR | |

AIRLINE RESERVATION SAMPLE SOLUTION OBVIOUSLY NOT BY PSG                    PAGE    4

```
LOC   OBJECT CODE    ADDR1 ADDR2  STMT    SOURCE STATEMENT                                          31 DEC 74

000562 D29F F692 F6E2 00AC8 00B18  233 MOVEUP   MVC   INBUFF+80(160),INBUFF+160 SECOND MESSAGE WAS MOVED OUT
000568 47F0 F156        0058C      234          B     ADDR
00056C D24F F792 F642 00B88 00A78  235 REG      MVC   BUFFER(80),INBUFF       MOVE TOP OF INBUFF TO REAL BUFFER
                                   236 *                                      FOR PROCESSING BY THE MACRO
000572 5BD0 F99E        00DD4      237          S     INFULL,=F'1'
000576 95FF F97B        00DB1      238          CLI   RFLAG,X'FF'             IS READER READING IN CARDS NOW?
00057A 4770 F150        00586      239          BNE   SHUFF                   NO, SO IT'S OK TO SHUFFLE INBUFF.
00057E 92FF F981        00DB7      240          MVI   RING,X'FF'              SET A FLAG TO INDICATE THAT WE
                                   241 *                                      WANT TO SHUFFLE INBUFF BUT WE
                                   242 *                                      CAN'T NOW SINCE READING INTO IT
000582 47F0 F156        0058C      243          B     ADDR                    SKIP AROUND THE SHUFFLING
000586 D2EF F642 F692 00A78 00AC8  244 SHUFF    MVC   INBUFF(240),INBUFF+80   DO THE SHUFFLING--I.E. MOVE
                                   245 *                                      EACH LINE IN INBUFF UP ONE NOTCH
                                   246 *                                      TO TAKE CARE OF THE FIFO ALGORITHM.
00058C 4110 F782        00B88      247 ADDR     LA    1,BUFFER                SET REG1 POINTING AT MESS FOR MACRO
000590 5010 F5C6        009FC      248          ST    1,SAVEAREA+4
000594 9500 F986        00DBC      249          CLI   FULLAG,X'00'
000598 4780 F176        005AC      250          BE    RELOAD
00059C 4130 F59A        00990      251          LA    3,CCWR+24
0005A0 5030 0048        00048      252          ST    3,CAW
0005A4 9200 F986        00DBC      253          MVI   FULLAG,X'00'
0005A8 9C00 000C        0000C      254          SIO   X'00C'
0005AC 50D0 0088        00088      255 RELOAD   ST    INFULL,X'88'
0005B0 50E0 008C        0008C      256          ST    OUTFULL,X'8C'           STORE OUTFULL IN CASE OF INTERRUPT.
0005B4 9200 F984        00DBA      257          MVI   SVCFLAG,X'00'
0005B8 980F F5C2        009F8      258          LM    0,15,SAVEAREA
                                   259          TRACE DUMP,CORE=(BUFFER,2)
0005CA 8200 0020        00020      270          LPSW  OLDSVC                  I/O INT WILL BE ENABLED IMPLICITLY
0005CE 92FF F97D        00DB3      271 CONTIN   MVI   EOFLAG,X'FF'
0005D2 8200 F57A        009B0      272 OUTOF    LPSW  EOWAIT                  PUT INTO WAIT STATE TO FINISH PRINT
0005D6 47F0 F19C        005D2      273 AGAIN    B     OUTOF
                                   274 WRITE    TRACE DUMP,REGS=(13,14)
0005F2 5800 F5C2        009F8      283          TRACE DUMP,CORE=(INQBUFF1,10)
0005F6 58C0 F5C6        009FC      294          L     0,SAVEAREA              GET LENGTH OF MESSAGE
0005FA 80E0 F980        00DB6      295          L     12,SAVEAREA+4           STORE ADDRESS OF MESSAGE
0005FE 185E                        296 REFIT    SSM   DISABLE
000600 5860 F9A6        00DDC      297          LR    5,OUTFULL
000604 1865                        298          L     6,=F'3'
000606 1906                        299          SR    6,5                     ROOM LEFT IN BUFFER
000608 47D0 F1EE        00624      300          CR    0,6                     WILL MESSAGE FIT?
00060C 92FF F97F        00DB5      301          BNH   FIT                     IT WILL FIT
000610 8200 F572        009A8      302 NOFIT    MVI   WAIT2,X'FF'             NO.
000614 8000 F980        00DB6      303          LPSW  WRWAIT                  WAIT
000618 950F F97E        00DB4      304 WINT     SSM   DISABLE
00061C 4770 F106        0060C      305          CLI   RORM,X'0F'              PRINTER INTERRUPT?
000620 47F0 F1C4        005FA      306          BNE   NOFIT                   NO
000624 189E                        307          B     REFIT                   CHECK TO SEE IF IT WILL FIT NOW
000626 187E                        308 FIT      LR    9,OUTFULL
000628 8970 0002        00002      309          LR    7,OUTFULL
00062C 5007 F966        009DC      310          SLL   7,2                     MULTIPLY BY 4 TO STORE INDICATOR
000630 5C80 F9AA        00DE0      311          ST    0,POUT+4(7)             STORE IND THAT TELLS LENGTH OF MESS
000634 41A0 F7D2        00C08      312          M     8,=F'132'               GET POSITION OF NEXT
000638 1A9A                        313          LA    10,OUTBUFF              GET ADDRESS OF OUTBUFF
00063A 5090 F95E        00D94      314          AR    9,10                    GET ADDRESS OFF OF OUTBUFF
                                   315          ST    9,OFFSET                REMEMBER IT.
```

```
         AIRLINE RESERVATION SAMPLE SOLUTION OBVIOUSLY NOT BY PGG                                    PAGE   5

LOC   OBJECT CODE     ADDR1 ADDR2  STMT   SOURCE STATEMENT                                           31 DEC 74

00063E D283 9000 C000 00000 00000  316          MVC    0(132,9),0(12)        STORE MESSAGE IN PROPER PLACE IN
                                   317  *                                    OUTBUFF
000644 5AE0 F99E            00DD4  318          A      OUTFULL,=F'1'          INCR. COUNTER.
000648 5900 F99E            00DD4  319          C      0,=F'1'
00064C 4780 F22C            00662  320          BE     TINUE                  ONE-LINE MESSAGE.
000650 58A0 F95E            00DD4  321          L      10,OFFSET              OFFSET IS POINTER TO OLD PLACE
000654 5AA0 F9AA            00DE0  322          A      10,=F'132'             GET PROPER OFFSET OFF OUTBUFF
000658 D283 A000 C084 00000 00084  323          MVC    0(132,10),132(12)       DO A MOVE FOR A TWO LINE MESSAGE
00065E 5AE0 F99E            00DD4  324          A      OUTFULL,=F'1'          INCR. COUNTER AGAIN.
                                   325  TINUE   TRACE  DUMP,CORE=(OUTBUFF,10)
                                   336          TRACE  DUMP,CORE=(OUTBUFF+132,10)
                                   347          TRACE  DUMP,CORE=(OUTBUFF+264,10)
00068C 95FF F97C      00DB2        358          CLI    WFLAG,X'FF'            IS IT PRINTING ALREADY NOW?
000690 4780 F2B2            006E8  359          BE     GOBACK                 YES.
000694 8000 F985      00DBB        360          SSM    ENABLE
000698 4110 F7D2            00C08  361          LA     1,OUTBUFF
00069C 5800 F966            00D9C  362          L      0,OUT1
0006A0 5900 F99E            00DD4  363          C      0,=F'1'                ONE LINE MESSAGE?
0006A4 4780 F284            006BA  364          BE     ONELINE                YES
0006A8 9823 F5B2            009E8  365          LM     2,3,CCW1               GET 1ST CCW
0006AC 1621                        366          OR     2,1                    PUT IN ADDRESS
0006AE 4110 1084            00084  367          LA     1,132(0,1)             INCR. BUFFER POINTER
0006B2 4160 F5A2            009D8  368          LA     6,CCWW
0006B6 47F0 F288            006BE  369          B      WNEXT
0006BA 4160 F5AA            009E0  370  ONELINE LA     6,CCWW+8               MAKE IT 2ND CCW.
0006BE 9845 F58A            009F0  371  WNEXT   LM     4,5,CCW2               GET 2ND CCW
0006C2 1641                        372          OR     4,1                    PUT IN ADDRESS.
0006C4 9240 F7D4      00C0A        373          MVI    OUTBUFF+2,X'40'        PUT BLANK IN PRIORITY SPACE
0006C8 9025 F5A2            009D8  374          STM    2,5,CCWW               STORE CCW CHAIN
0006CC 5060 0048            00048  375          ST     6,CAW                  SER UP CAW FOR SIO INSTR
0006D0 8000 F980      00DB6        376          SSM    DISABLE
0006D4 9D00 000E      0000E        377          TIO    X'00E'                 PRINTER BUSY?
0006D8 4770 F2B2            006E8  378          BNZ    GOBACK                 YES.
0006DC 92FF F97C      00DB2        379          MVI    WFLAG,X'FF'            SET FLAG THAT ABOUT TO PRINT
0006E0 9200 F983      00DB9        380          MVI    CASE,X'00'             SET FLAG FOR NORMAL HANDLING
0006E4 9C00 000E      0000E        381          SIO    X'00E'                 START PRINTING
0006E8 50D0 0088            00088  382  GOBACK  ST     INFULL,X'88'
0006EC 50E0 008C            0008C  383          ST     OUTFULL,X'8C'          STORE OUTFULL IN CASE OF INTERRUPT.
0006F0 9200 F984      00DBA        384          MVI    SVCFLAG,X'00'
0006F4 980F F5C2            009F8  385          LM     0,15,SAVEAREA
0006F8 8200 0020            00020  386          LPSW   OLDSVC                 RETURN
                                   387  *
                                   388  **********************************************************************
                                   389  *
                                   390  *     PROCESSING WILL COME HERE AFTER ANY I/O INTERRRUPT
                                   391  *
                                   392  *
                                   393  **********************************************************************
0006FC 50F0 0080            00080  394  IOINT   ST     15,X'80'
000700 05F0                        395          BALR   15,0
000702                             396          USING  *,15
000702 900E F336            00A38  397          STM    0,14,IOSAVE
000706 D203 F372 0080 00A74 00080  398          MVC    IOSAVE+15*4(4),X'80'
00070C 95FF F6B8      00DBA        399          CLI    SVCFLAG,X'FF'          DID WE COME FROM SVC ROUTINE
000710 4780 F01E            00720  400          BE     SVCLOAD                YES
```

426

AIRLINE RESERVATION SAMPLE SOLUTION OBVIOUSLY NOT BY PGG

```
   LOC   OBJECT CODE    ADDR1 ADDR2  STMT    SOURCE STATEMENT
```

```
000714 4170 0088              00088  401          LA    7,X'88'          NO, USE LOW CORE
000718 4180 008C              0008C  402          LA    8,X'8C'
00071C 47F0 F026              00728  403          B     NOW
000720 4170 F36A              00A6C  404 SVCLOAD  LA    7,IOSAVE+13*4    USE SAVEAREA.
000724 4180 F36E              00A70  405          LA    8,IOSAVE+14*4
000728 5807 0000              00000  406 NOW      L     INFULL,0(7)
00072C 58E8 0000              00000  407          L     OUTFULL,0(8)
000730 9104 0044        00044        408          TM    CSW+4,X'04'
000734 4710 F03E              00740  409          BO    CHECK
000738 980F F336              00A38  410          LM    0,15,IOSAVE
00073C 8200 0038        0C038        411          LPSW  OLDIO
000740 950E 003B        0003B        412 CHECK    CLI   OLDIO+3,X'0E'    PRINTER DEVICCE END?
000744 4780 F122              00824  413          BE    IOWRITE
000748 92F0 F6B2        00DB4        414 IOREAD   MVI   RDRW,X'FO'       SET FLAG-READER INTERRUPT
00074C 9200 F6AF        00DB1        415          MVI   RFLAG,X'00'      RESET FLAG IND THAT NOR READING
                                     416 *                              ANYMORE SINCE JUST GET DEVICE END.
000750 5AD0 F6D2              00DD4  417          A     INFULL,=F'1'     INCREMENT FLAG TO SHOW HOW MANY
                                     418 *                              MANY LINES IN INPUT BUFFER
                                     419          TRACE DUMP,REGS=(13,14)
00075E 95FF F6B6        00DB8  428          CLI   PING,X'FF'       WAS PRIORITY SHUFFLING DELAYED?
000762 4770 F090              00792  429          BNE   IT               NO CHECK REGJLAR SHUFFLING
000766 9200 F6B6        00DB8  430          MVI   PING,X'00'       YES, TURN OFF FLAG.
00076A 5850 F6A6              00DA8  431          L     5,PROFF          GET OFFSET OF CARD THAT WAS REMOVED
00076E 5950 F6D6              00DD8  432          C     5,=F'240'        WAS IT LAST CARD?
000772 4780 F0A2              007A4  433          BE    OK2              YES, DON'T SHUFFLE
000776 5950 F6CE              00DD0  434          C     5,=F'80'         WAS IT SECOND CARD?
00077A 4780 F086              00788  435          BE    ANN              YES
00077E D24F F416 F466 00B18 00B68  436          MVC   INBUFF+160(80),INBUFF+240  NO, THIRD CARD-SHUFFLE ACCORD.
000784 47F0 F0A2              007A4  437          B     OK2
000788 D29F F3C6 F416 00AC8 00B18  438 ANN      MVC   INBUFF+80(160),INBUFF+160  SHUFFLE FOR EMPT80 IND SLOT
00078E 47F0 F0A2              007A4  439          B     OK2
000792 95FF F685        00DB7  440 IT       CLI   RING,X'FF'       WAS REGULAR SHUFFLING DELAYED?
000796 4770 F0A2              007A4  441          BNE   OK2              NO, WE ALREADY DID IT
00079A 9200 F685        00DB7  442          MVI   RING,X'00'       RESET FLAG TO 0
00079E D2EF F376 F3C6 00A78 00AC8  443          MVC   INBUFF(240),INBUFF+80    MOVE UP ALL LINES FOR FIFO
0007A4 59D0 F6E2              00DE4  444 OK2      C     INFULL,=F'4'     IS INPUT BUFFER FULL?
0007A8 4770 F0BA              007BC  445          BNE   NOTFULL
0007AC 92FF F6BA        00DBC  446          MVI   FULLAG,X'FF'
0007B0 50D7 0000              00000  447          ST    INFULL,0(7)
0007B4 980F F336              00A38  448          LM    0,15,IOSAVE
0007B8 8200 0038        00038  449          LPSW  OLDIO
0007BC 182D              450 NOTFULL  LR    2,INFULL
0007BE 8920 0003              00003  451          SLL   2,3              MULTIPLY BY 8 TO READ APPROPRIATE
                                     452 *                              CCW.
0007C2 4130 F2B6              009B8  453          LA    3,CCWR
0007C6 1A32              454          AR    3,2
                                     455 *                              REG3 NOW CONTAINS ADDRESS OF CCW TO
                                                                        BE STORED IN CAW FOR AN SIO
0007C8 5030 0048        00048  456          ST    3,CAW
0007CC 95FF F6B1        00DB3  457          CLI   EOFLAG,X'FF'
0007D0 4770 F0E2              007E4  458          BNE   MORE
0007D4 50D7 0000              00000  459          ST    INFULL,0(7)
0007D8 50E8 0000              00000  460          ST    OUTFULL,0(8)
0007DC 980F F336              00A38  461          LM    0,15,IOSAVE
0007E0 8200 0038        00038  462          LPSW  OLDIO
0007E4 95FF F6AE        00DB0  463 MORE     CLI   WAIT1,X'FF'      WAS CPU IN WAIT STATE?
```

AIRLINE RESERVATION SAMPLE SOLUTION ORVIOUSLY NOT BY PGG                                    PAGE    7

```
   LOC   OBJECT CODE    ADDR1 ADDR2  STMT    SOURCE STATEMENT                                   31 DEC 74

0007E8 4770 F0F2              007F4   464          BNE     UPSTART              NO.
0007EC 9200 F6AE        00DB0         465          MVI     WAIT1,X'00'          YES IT WAS WAITING
0007F0 9200 0039        0C039         466          MVI     OLDIO+1,X'00'        TURN OFF SWITCH
0007F4 9C00 000C        0000C         467  UPSTART SIO     X'00C'
0007F8 4780 F106              00808   468          BZ      OK
0007FC 9101 0044        00044         469          TM      CSW+4,X'01'          IS IT UNIT CHECK NOW?
000800 4710 F10E              00810   470          BO      ERETURN
000804 47F0 F262              00964   471          B       ERROR
000808 92FF F6AF        00DB1         472  OK      MVI     RFLAG,X'FF'          SIO WORKED MEANS WE ARE READING NOW
00080C 47F0 F112              00814   473          B       RETURN
000810 92FF F6B1        00DB3         474  ERETURN MVI     EOFLAG,X'FF'         SET EOF FLAG
000814 50D7 0000        00000         475  RETURN  ST      INFULL,0(7)
000818 50E8 0000        00000         476          ST      OUTFULL,0(8)
00081C 980F F336              00A38   477          LM      0,15,IOSAVE
000820 8200 0038        00038         478          LPSW    OLDIO
000824 920F F6B2        00DB4         479  IOWRITE MVI     RORW,X'0F'           PRINTERRUPT.
000828 9200 F6B0        00DB2         480          MVI     WFLAG,X'00'          DONE PRINTING.
00082C 9500 F6B7        00DB9         481          CLI     CASE,X'00'           WAS IT NORAL PRINTING FROM TOP?
000830 4780 F146              00848   482          BE      NORMAL               YES
000834 D283 F58A F60E  00C8C 00D10    483          MVC     OUTBUFF+132(132),OUTBUFF+264 NO,IT PRINTED FROM SECOND
00083A 5BE0 F6D2              00DD4   484          S       OUTFULL,=F'1'
00083E D203 F69E F6A2  00DA0 00DA4    485          MVC     OUT2(4),OUT3
000844 47F0 F194              00896   486          B       WRITEON
000852 D283 F506 F58A  00C08 00C8C    487  NORMAL  TRACE   DUMP,REGS=(13,14)
000852 D283 F506 F58A  00C08 00C8C    496          MVC     OUTBUFF(132),OUTBUFF+132    MOVE UP ONE LINE
000858 58B0 F69A              00D9C   497          L       11,OUT1              GET INDICATOR
00085C 5980 F6E6              00DE8   498          C       11,=F'2'             2 LINE MESSAGE PRINTED?
000860 4780 F184              00886   499          BE      DOUBLE               YES
000864 D283 F58A F60E  00C8C 00D10    500          MVC     OUTBUFF+132(132),OUTBUFF+264    MOVE UP NEXT LINE
                                      501          TRACE   DUMP,CORE=(OUTBUFF,10)
000878 5BE0 F6D2              00DD4   512          S       OUTFULL,=F'1'        DECREMENT COUNTER
00087C D207 F69A F69E  00D9C 00DA0    513          MVC     OUT1(8),OUT2         MOVE UP BOTH INDICATORS.
000882 47F0 F194              00896   514          B       WRITEON              CONTINUE
000886 D283 F506 F60E  00C08 00D10    515  DOUBLE  MVC     OUTBUFF(132),OUTBUFF+264    MOVE UP LINE
00088C D203 F69A F6A2  00D9C 00DA4    516          MVC     OUT1(4),OUT3         MOVE UP INDICATOR
000892 5BE0 F6E6              00DE8   517          S       OUTFULL,=F'2'        DECREMENT COUNTER
000896 59E0 F6CA              00DCC   518  WRITEON C       OUTFULL,=F'0'        BUFFER EMPTY?
00089A 4780 F242              00944   519          BE      TURN
00089E 18CE                           520          LR      12,OUTFULL
0008A0 1BAA                           521          SR      10,10
0008A2 41B0 F508              00C0A   522  LOOP3   LA      11,OUTBUFF+2         GET PRIORITY BYTE
0008A6 1ABA                           523          AR      11,10                OFFSET
0008A8 955A B000        00000         524          CLI     0(11),X'5A'          IS IT ' ' PRIORITY?
0008AC 4780 F1D8              008DA   525          BE      FIND                 YES
0008B0 5AA0 F6DE              00DE0   526          A       10,=F'132'           INCREMENT OFFSET
0008B4 46C0 F1A0              008A2   527          BCT     12,LOOP3
0008B8 1BAA                           528          SR      10,10
0008BA 18CE                           529          LR      12,OUTFULL
0008BC 41B0 F508              00C0A   530  LOOP4   LA      11,OUTBUFF+2         GET PRIORITY BYTE
0008C0 1ABA                           531          AR      11,10                OF CURRENT MESSAGE
0008C2 955C B000        00000         532          CLI     0(11),X'5C'          IS IT '*' PRIORITY?
0008C6 4780 F1D8              008DA   533          BE      FIND
0008CA 5AA0 F6DE              00DE0   534          A       10,=F'132'           INCREMENT OFFSET
0008CE 46C0 F1BA              008BC   535          BCT     12,LOOP4
0008D2 9200 F6B7        00DB9         536          MVI     CASE,X'00'           NO PRIORITY WAS FOUND, SET FLAG
```

428

| LOC | OBJECT CODE | ADDR1 ADDR2 | STMT | SOURCE STATEMENT | | | 31 DEC 74 |
|---|---|---|---|---|---|---|---|
| 0008D6 | 47F0 F202 | 00904 | 537 | | B | SETUP | |
| 0008DA | 50A0 F6AA | 00DAC | 538 FIND | ST | 10,OUTOFF | |
| | | | 539 | TRACE | DUMP,REGS=(10) | |
| 0008E8 | 59A0 F6CA | 00DCC | 548 | C | 10,=F'0' | IS IT REGULAR CASE? |
| 0008EC | 4780 F1FE | 00900 | 549 | BE | REGWEST | YES |
| 0008F0 | 92FF F6B7 | 00DB9 | 550 | MVI | CASE,X'FF' | NO, IT'S SPECIAL, SECOND WAS HIGHER |
| | | | 551 * | | | PRIORITY, IT MUST BE A ONE LINE |
| 0008F4 | 4110 F58A | 00C8C | 552 | LA | 1,OUTRUFF+132 | PRINT SECOND LINE--HIGHER PRIORITY |
| 0008F8 | 9240 F58C | 00C8E | 553 | MVI | OUTBUFF+134,X'40' | GET RID OF PRIORITY BYTE |
| 0008FC | 47F0 F224 | 00926 | 554 | B | ONLY | |
| 000900 | 9240 F508 | 00C0A | 555 REGWEST | MVI | OUTBUFF+2,X'40' | GET RID OF PRIORITY IN FIRST LINE |
| 000904 | 5890 F69A | 00D9C | 556 SETUP | L | 9,OUT1 | GET LENGTH INDICATOR |
| 000908 | 4110 F506 | 00C08 | 557 | LA | 1,OUTBUFF | GET ADDR. OF OUTBUFF |
| 00090C | 5990 F6D2 | 00DD4 | 558 | C | 9,=F'1' | LENGTH = 1? |
| 000910 | 4780 F224 | 00926 | 559 | BE | ONLY | YES |
| 000914 | 9823 F2E6 | 009E8 | 560 | LM | 2,3,CCW1 | GET 1ST CCW |
| 000918 | 1621 | | 561 | OR | 2,1 | PUT ADDR IN CCW |
| 00091A | 4110 1084 | 00084 | 562 | LA | 1,132(0,1) | |
| 00091E | 4160 F2D6 | 009D8 | 563 | LA | 6,CCWW | |
| 000922 | 47F0 F228 | 0092A | 564 | B | WCONT | |
| 000926 | 4160 F2DE | 009E0 | 565 ONLY | LA | 6,CCWW+8 | USE 2ND CCW |
| 00092A | 9845 F2EE | 009F0 | 566 WCONT | LM | 4,5,CCW2 | GET 2ND CCW |
| 00092E | 1641 | | 567 | OR | 4,1 | PUT IN ADDRESS |
| 000930 | 9025 F2D6 | 009D8 | 568 | STM | 2,5,CCWW | STORE CCW'S |
| 000934 | 5060 0048 | 00048 | 569 | ST | 6,CAW | |
| 000938 | 92FF F6B0 | 00DB2 | 570 | MVI | WFLAG,X'FF' | SET FLAG THAT ABOUT TO PRINT |
| 00093C | 9C00 000E | 0000E | 571 | SIO | X'00E' | START PRINTING |
| 000940 | 4770 F262 | 00964 | 572 | BNZ | ERROR | DIDN'T WORK |
| 000944 | 95FF F6B3 | 00DB5 | 573 TURN | CLI | WAIT2,X'FF' | IS WAIT2 SWITCH ON? |
| 000948 | 4770 F252 | 00954 | 574 | BNE | WRETURN | NO |
| 00094C | 9200 F6B3 | 00DB5 | 575 | MVI | WAIT2,X'00' | YES, TURN IT OFFF |
| 000950 | 9200 0039 | 0C039 | 576 | MVI | OLDIO+1,X'00' | TURN OFF WAIT SIT IN OLDIOPSW |
| 000954 | 50E8 0000 | 00000 | 577 WRETURN | ST | OUTFULL,0(8) | |
| 000958 | 50D7 0000 | 00000 | 578 | ST | INFULL,0(7) | |
| 00095C | 980F F336 | 00A38 | 579 | LM | 0,15,IOSAVE | |
| 000960 | 8200 0038 | 00038 | 580 | LPSW | OLDIO | RETURN |
| | | | 581 ERROR | TRACE | DUMP,REGS=(0,1,2,3,4,5,6,7,8,9,10,11,12,13,14,15) | |
| 00096E | 47F0 F6BC | 00DBE | 590 | B | QUIT | |
| | | | 591 EXTINT | TRACE | DUMP,STATUS=(OLDEXT) | |
| 00097C | 8200 0018 | 00018 | 600 | LPSW | OLDEXT | |
| | | | 601 PGMINT | TRACE | DUMP,STATUS=(OLDPGM) | |
| 00098A | 8200 0028 | 00028 | 610 | LPSW | OLDPGM | |
| | | | 611 MCKINT | TRACE | DUMP,STATUS=(OLDMCK) | |
| 000998 | 8200 0030 | 00030 | 620 | LPSW | OLDMCK | |
| 0009A0 | | | 621 ALIGN | DS | 0D | |
| 0009A0 | FE02000000004C8 | | 622 WAITIO | DC | XL5'FE02000000',AL3(RINT) | |
| 0009A8 | FE02000000000614 | | 623 WRWAIT | DC | XL5'FE02000000',AL3(WINT) | |
| 0009B0 | FE02000000005D6 | | 624 EOWAIT | DC | XL5'FE02000000',AL3(AGAIN) | |
| 0009B8 | 02000A7800000050 | | 625 CCWR | CCW | X'02',INBUFF+000,X'00',80 | |
| 0009C0 | 02000AC800000050 | | 626 | CCW | X'02',INBUFF+080,X'00',80 | |
| 0009C8 | 02000B1800000050 | | 627 | CCW | X'02',INBUFF+160,X'00',80 | |
| 0009D0 | 02000B6800000050 | | 628 | CCW | X'02',INBUFF+240,X'00',80 | |
| 0009D8 | | | 629 CCWW | DS | 2D | |
| 0009E8 | 0900000040000084 | | 630 CCW1 | DC | X'0900000040000084' | |
| 0009F0 | 1900000000000084 | | 631 CCW2 | DC | X'1900000000000084' | |

| LOC | OBJECT CODE | ADDR1 ADDR2 | STMT | SOURCE STATEMENT | |
|---|---|---|---|---|---|
| 0009F8 | | | 632 | SAVEAREA DS | 16F |
| 000A38 | | | 633 | IOSAVE DS | 16F |
| 000A78 | | | 634 | INBUFF DS | 4CL80 |
| 000BB8 | | | 635 | BUFFER DS | CL80 |
| 000C08 | | | 636 | OUTBUFF DS | 3CL132 |
| 000C94 | | | 637 | OFFSET DS | F |
| 000C98 | | | 638 | POUT DS | F |
| 000C9C | | | 639 | OUT1 DS | F |
| 000CA0 | | | 640 | OUT2 DS | F |
| 000CA4 | | | 641 | OUT3 DS | F |
| 000CA8 | | | 642 | PROFF DS | F |
| 000CAC | | | 643 | OUTOFF DS | F |
| 000CB0 | 00 | | 644 | WAIT1 DC | X'00' |
| 000CB1 | 00 | | 645 | RFLAG DC | X'00' |
| 000CB2 | 00 | | 646 | WFLAG DC | X'00' |
| 000CB3 | 00 | | 647 | EOFLAG DC | X'00' |
| 000CB4 | 00 | | 648 | RORW DC | X'00' |
| 000CB5 | 00 | | 649 | WAIT2 DC | X'00' |
| 000CB6 | 00 | | 650 | DISABLE DC | X'00' |
| 000CB7 | 00 | | 651 | RING DC | X'00' |
| 000CB8 | 00 | | 652 | PING DC | X'00' |
| 000CB9 | 00 | | 653 | CASE DC | X'00' |
| 000CBA | 00 | | 654 | SVCFLAG DC | X'00' |
| 000CBB | FE | | 655 | ENABLE DC | X'FE' |
| 000CBC | 00 | | 656 | FULLAG DC | X'00' |
| | | | 657 | QUIT QUIT | |
| | | | 660 | END | |
| 000CC8 | 00000FFA | | 661 | | =F'4090' |
| 000CCC | 00000000 | | 662 | | =F'0' |
| 000CD0 | 00000050 | | 663 | | =F'80' |
| 000CD4 | 00000001 | | 664 | | =F'1' |
| 000CD8 | 000000F0 | | 665 | | =F'240' |
| 000CDC | 00000003 | | 666 | | =F'3' |
| 000CE0 | 00000084 | | 667 | | =F'132' |
| 000CE4 | 00000004 | | 668 | | =F'4' |
| 000CE8 | 00000002 | | 669 | | =F'2' |

```
MASSACHUSETTS INSTITUTE OF TECHNOLOGY        SYSTEM / 360 SIMULATOR                                      VERSION 1.3
SAMPLE  TRACE LISTING.   0 CONDITIONS ENABLED.                                                             PAGE  1

LOC  TRACE TYPE            COUNT  TIME                                        OP   INSTRUCTION    ADR1 ADR2  OPERAND1 OPERAND2
----  ----------------     -----  ----------                                 ----  --------------  ----  ----  --------  --------


00C6 SVC INTERRUPT           5        2  PSW: FE 0 0 0001  '01'B '00'B 0 0000C6
     REGISTERS:
       R 0: FFFFFFFF,        -1 R 1: FFFFFFFF,         -1

0474 SNAPSHOT               17       47  PSW: FE 0 0 0000  '01'B '00'B 0 000474
     REGISTERS:
       R13: 00000000,        0 R14: 00000000,          0

04C8 I/O INTERRUPT         35      541  PSW: FE 0 2 000C  '10'B '00'B 0 0004C8
     CORE DUMP:
       0038,    56: FE02000C 800004C8 000009C0 080C0000 000009B8      ???? ???H ???? ???? ????

04C8 I/O INTERRUPT         49   73,499  PSW: FE 0 2 000C  '10'B '00'B 0 0004C8
     CORE DUMP:
       0038,    56: FE02000C 800004C8 000009C0 040000000 000009B8     ???? ???H ???? ???? ????

075E SNAPSHOT              66   73,543  PSW: 00 0 0 0000  '01'B '10'B 0 00075E
     REGISTERS:
       R13: 00000001,        1 R14: 00000000,          0

05CA SNAPSHOT             125   73,651  PSW: 00 0 0 0000  '01'B '00'B 0 0005CA
     CORE DUMP:
       0BB8,  3000: F0F0E3E6 F8F8F140                                 00TW 881

0172 SVC INTERRUPT        180   73,854  PSW: FE 0 0 0002  '01'B '11'B 0 000172
     REGISTERS:
       R 0: 00000002,        2 R 1: 00000176,        374

05E4 SNAPSHOT             194   73,901  PSW: FE 0 0 0000  '01'B '00'B 0 0005E4
     REGISTERS:
       R13: 00000000,        0 R14: 00000000,          0

05F2 SNAPSHOT             194   73,901  PSW: FE 0 0 0000  '01'B '00'B 0 0005F2
     CORE DUMP:
       0174,   372: 00C4F0F0 40E3E6C1 40404040 40C6D3E3 40E3E6F8 F8F17A40   ?D00 TWA    FLT  TW8 81:
       018C,   396: F97AF0F0 40C1D440 6B40C7C1 E3C540F1                     9:00 AM , GA TE 1

0670 SNAPSHOT             218   74,020  PSW: 00 0 0 0000  '01'B '10'B 0 000670
     CORE DUMP:
       0C08,  3080: F0F040E3 E6C14040 404040C6 D3E340E3 E6F8F8F1 7A40F97A   00 T WA    F LT T W881 : 9:
       0C20,  3104: F0F040C1 D4406B40 C7C1E3C5 40F1F34B                     00 A M , GATE 13.

067E SNAPSHOT             218   74,020  PSW: 00 0 0 0000  '01'B '10'B 0 00067E
     CORE DUMP:
       0C8C,  3212: F0F04040 40404040 E4D5D9C5 E2C5D9E5 C5C47A40 40F1F540   00     UNRE SERV ED:   15
       0CA4,  3236: C6C9D9E2 E340C3D3 C1E2E26B 4040F140                     FIRS T CL ASS,   1

068C SNAPSHOT             218   74,020  PSW: 00 0 0 0000  '01'B '10'B 0 00068C
     CORE DUMP:
       0D10,  3344: FFFFFFFF FFFFFFFF FFFFFFFF FFFFFFFF FFFFFFFF FFFFFFFF   ???? ???? ???? ???? ???? ????
       0D28,  3368: FFFFFFFF FFFFFFFF FFFFFFFF FFFFFFFF                     ???? ???? ???? ????
```

```
MASSACHUSETTS INSTITUTE OF TECHNOLOGY        SYSTEM / 360 SIMULATOR                              VERSION 1.3
SAMPLE  TRACE LISTING.   2 CONDITIONS ENABLED.                                                       PAGE  2

LOC  TRACE TYPE           COUNT  TIME                                OP   INSTRUCTION   ADR1 ADR2  OPERAND1 OPERAND2
---- ---------------      -----  ----------                          ---- -----------   ---- ----  -------- --------

06CC I/O INTERRUPT         234    74,044  PSW: FE 0 0 000C  '10'B '01'B 0 0006CC
     CORE DUMP:
        0038,      56: FE00000C 900006CC 000009C8 38000000 000009C0          ???? ???? ???H ???? ????

00C6 SVC INTERRUPT         262    74,135  PSW: FE 0 0 0001  '01'B '11'B 0 0000C6
     REGISTERS:
        R 0: 00000002,         2 R 1: 00000176,         374

0474 SNAPSHOT              274    74,182  PSW: FE 0 0 0000  '01'B '00'B 0 000474
     REGISTERS:
        R13: 00000000,         0 R14: 00000002,           2

04C8 I/O INTERRUPT        282   133,500  PSW: FE 0 2 000C  '10'B '00'B 0 0004C8
     CORE DUMP:
        0038,      56: FE02000C 800004C8 000009C8 04000000 000009D8          ???? ???H ???H ???? ???Q

075E SNAPSHOT             299   133,543  PSW: 00 0 0 0000  '01'B '10'B 0 00075E
     REGISTERS:
        R13: 00000001,         1 R14: 00000002,           2

05CA SNAPSHOT             360   133,733  PSW: 00 0 0 0000  '01'B '00'B 0 0005CA
     CORE DUMP:
        0BB8,    3000: F0F1D7C1 F7F0F740                                     01PA 707

0172 SVC INTERRUPT        395   133,914  PSW: FE 0 0 0002  '01'B '11'B 0 000172
     REGISTERS:
        R 0: 00000002,         2 R 1: 00000176,         374

05E4 SNAPSHOT             409   133,962  PSW: FE 0 0 0000  '01'B '00'B 0 0005E4
     REGISTERS:
        R13: 00000000,         0 R14: 00000002,           2

05F2 SNAPSHOT             409   133,962  PSW: FE 0 0 0000  '01'B '00'B 0 0005F2
     CORE DUMP:
        0174,     372: 00C4F0F1 40D7C1D5 40C1D440 40CAD3E3 40D7C1F7 F0F77A40  7D01  PAN  AM   FLT  PA7 07:
        018C,     396: F87AF0F0 40C1D440 6B40C7C1 E3C540F1                     8:00  AM  , GA TE 1

0614 I/O INTERRUPT        419   134,121  PSW: FE 0 2 000C  '10'B '00'B 0 000614
     CORE DUMP:
        0038,      56: FE02000C 80000614 000009C8 08000000 000009C0          ???? ???? ???H ???? ????

0614 I/O INTERRUPT        433   174,087  PSW: FE 0 2 000E  '10'B '00'B 0 000614
     CORE DUMP:
        0038,      56: FE02000E 80000614 000009E8 08000000 000009C0          ???? ???? ???Y ???? ????

0614 I/O INTERRUPT        447   193,500  PSW: FE 0 2 000C  '10'B '00'B 0 000614
     CORE DUMP:
        0038,      56: FE02000C 80000614 000009C8 04000000 000009C0          ???? ???? ???H ???? ????

075E SNAPSHOT             464   193,543  PSW: 00 0 0 0000  '01'B '10'B 0 00075E
     REGISTERS:
        R13: 00000001,         1 R14: 00000002,           2
```

```
LOC  TRACE TYPE          COUNT   TIME                                          OP   INSTRUCTION    ADR1 ADR2  OPERAND1 OPERAND2
----  --------------      -----   ----------                                   ----  --------------  ---- ----  -------- --------

0614 I/O INTERRUPT         489    194,120  PSW: FE 0 2 000C  '10'B '00'B 0 000614
     CORE DUMP:
        0038,       56: FE02000C 80000614 000009C8 08000000 000009C0            ???? ???? ???H ???? ????

0614 I/O INTERRUPT         503    253,500  PSW: FE 0 2 000C  '10'B '00'B 0 000614
     CORE DUMP:
        0038,       56: FE02000C 80000614 000009C8 04000000 000009C0            ???? ???? ???H ???? ????

075E SNAPSHOT              520    253,543  PSW: 00 0 0 0000  '01'B '10'B 0 00075E
     REGISTERS:
        R13: 00000002,         2 R14: 00000002,          2

0614 I/O INTERRUPT         543    254,038  PSW: FE 0 2 000C  '10'B '00'B 0 000614
     CORE DUMP:
        0038,       56: FE02000C 80000614 000009D0 08000000 000009C8            ???? ???? ???? ???? ???H

0614 I/O INTERRUPT         557    272,139  PSW: FE 0 2 000E  '10'B '00'B 0 000614
     CORE DUMP:
        0038,       56: FE02000E 80000614 000009E8 04000000 000009C8            ???? ???? ???Y ???? ???H

0852 SNAPSHOT              575    272,184  PSW: 00 0 0 0000  '01'B '00'B 0 000852
     REGISTERS:
        R13: 00000002,         2 R14: 00000002,          2

0670 SNAPSHOT              618    272,425  PSW: 00 0 0 0000  '01'B '10'B 0 000670
     CORE DUMP:
        0C08,     3080: F0F140D7 C1D540C1 D44040C6 D3E340D7 C1F7F0F7 7A40F87A   01 P AN A M  F LT P A707 : B:
        0C20,     3104: F0F040C1 D4406840 C7C1E3C5 40F1F34B                     00 A M ,  GATE  13.

067E SNAPSHOT              618    272,425  PSW: 00 0 0 0000  '01'B '10'B 0 00067E
     CORE DUMP:
        0C8C,     3212: F0F14040 40404040 E4D5D9C5 E2C5D9E5 C5C47A40 4040F540   01        UNRE SERV ED:    5
        0CA4,     3236: C6C9D9E2 E340C3D3 C1E2E26B 40F1F540                     FIRS T CL ASS,  15

068C SNAPSHOT              618    272,425  PSW: 00 0 0 0000  '01'B '10'B 0 00068C
     CORE DUMP:
        0D10,     3344: FFFFFFFF FFFFFFFF FFFFFFFF FFFFFFFF FFFFFFFF FFFFFFFF   ???? ???? ???? ???? ???? ????
        0D28,     3368: FFFFFFFF FFFFFFFF FFFFFFFF FFFFFFFF                     ???? ???? ???? ????

00C6 SVC INTERRUPT         648    272,480  PSW: FE 0 0 0001  '01'B '11'B 0 0000C6
     REGISTERS:
        R 0: 00000002,         2 R 1: 00000176,        374

0474 SNAPSHOT              660    272,526  PSW: FE 0 0 0000  '01'B '00'B 0 000474
     REGISTERS:
        R13: 00000002,         2 R14: 00000002,          2

0516 SNAPSHOT              684    272,542  PSW: 00 0 0 0000  '01'B '00'B 0 000516
     REGISTERS:
        R 5: 00000000,         0

05CA SNAPSHOT              700    272,602  PSW: 00 0 0 0000  '01'B '00'B 0 0005CA
     CORE DUMP:
```

```
LOC  TRACE TYPE          COUNT  TIME                                   OP   INSTRUCTION      ADR1 ADR2 OPERAND1 OPERAND2
----  ----------------    -----  ----                                  ----  --------------   ---- ----  -------- --------

       0BB8,  3000: F0F25CE4 D5F6F6F6                                  02*U N666

0172 SVC INTERRUPT         727    272,775  PSW: FE 0 0 0002  '01'B '01'B 0 000172
        REGISTERS:
        R 0: 00000002,          2 R 1: 00000176,         374

05E4 SNAPSHOT              741    272,823  PSW: FE 0 0 0000  '01'B '00'B 0 0005E4
        REGISTERS:
        R13: 00000001,          1 R14: 00000002,           2

05F2 SNAPSHOT              741    272,823  PSW: FE 0 0 0000  '01'B '00'B 0 0005F2
        CORE DUMP:
        0174,   372: 00C4F0F2 5CE4D5C9 E3C5C44D 40C6D3E3 40E4D5F6 F6F67A40    7DD2 *UNI TED   FLT  UN6 66:
        018C,   396: F47AF4F5 40D7D440 6B40C7C1 E3C540F2                      4:45  PM  , GA TE 2

0614 I/O INTERRUPT         751    313,500  PSW: FE 0 2 000C  '10'B '00'B 0 000614
        CORE DUMP:
        0038,    56: FE02000C 80000614 000009D0 04000000 000009D8            ???? ???? ???? ???? ???Q

075E SNAPSHOT              768    313,543  PSW: 00 0 0 0000  '01'B '10'B 0 00075E
        REGISTERS:
        R13: 00000002,          2 R14: 00000002,           2

0614 I/O INTERRUPT         793    314,120  PSW: FE 0 2 000C  '10'B '00'B 0 000614
        CORE DUMP:
        0038,    56: FE02000C 80000614 000009D0 08000000 000009C8            ???? ???? ???? ???? ???H

0614 I/O INTERRUPT         807    366,676  PSW: FE 0 2 000E  '10'B '00'B 0 000614
        CORE DUMP:
        0038,    56: FE02000E 80000614 000009E8 08000000 000009C8            ???? ???? ???Y ???? ???H

0614 I/O INTERRUPT         821    373,500  PSW: FE 0 2 000C  '10'B '00'B 0 000614
        CORE DUMP:
        0038,    56: FE02000C 80000614 000009D0 04000000 000009C8            ???? ???? ???? ???? ???H

075E SNAPSHOT              838    373,543  PSW: 00 0 0 0000  '01'B '10'B 0 00075E
        REGISTERS:
        R13: 00000003,          3 R14: 00000002,           2

0614 I/O INTERRUPT         861    374,038  PSW: FE 0 2 000C  '10'B '00'B 0 000614
        CORE DUMP:
        0038,    56: FE02000C 80000614 000009D8 08000000 00000900            ???? ???? ???Q ???? ????

0614 I/O INTERRUPT         875    433,500  PSW: FE 0 2 000C  '10'B '00'B 0 000614
        CORE DUMP:
        0038,    56: FE02000C 80000614 000009D8 04000000 00000900            ???? ???? ???Q ???? ????

075E SNAPSHOT              892    433,543  PSW: 00 0 0 0000  '01'B '10'B 0 00075E
        REGISTERS:
        R13: 00000004,          4 R14: 00000002,           2

0614 I/O INTERRUPT         902    468,918  PSW: FE 0 2 000E  '10'B '00'B 0 000614
        CORE DUMP:
```

```
MASSACHUSETTS INSTITUTE OF TECHNOLOGY        SYSTEM / 360 SIMULATOR                                    VERSION 1.3
SAMPLE TRACE LISTING.  2 CONDITIONS ENABLED.                                                                PAGE 5

LOC  TRACE TYPE           COUNT  TIME                                        OP  INSTRUCTION    ADR1 ADR2 OPERAND1 OPERAND2
---- ----------------     -----  ----                                        --- -------------- ---- ---- -------- --------

        0038,     56: FE02000E 80000614 000009E8 04000000 00000900           ???? ???? ???Y ???? ????

0852 SNAPSHOT             920    468,962  PSW: 00 0 0 0000  '01'B '00'B 0 000852
     REGISTERS:
     R13: 00000004,          4 R14: 00000002,          2

0670 SNAPSHOT             963    469,204  PSW: 00 0 0 0000  '01'B '10'B 0 000670
     CORE DUMP:
     0C08,  40A0: F0F25CF4 D5C9E3C5 C44040C6 D3E340E4 D5F6F6F6 7A40F47A   020U NITE D  F LT U N666 : 4:
     0C20,  40A4: 14F540D7 D4406B40 C7C1E3C5 40F2F14B                     45 P M ,  GATE  21.

067E SNAPSHOT             963    469,204  PSW: 00 0 0 0000  '01'B '10'B 0 00067E
     CORE DUMP:
     0CAC,  3212: F0F24040 40404040 E4D5D9C5 E2C5D9E5 C5C47A40 40F1F040   02      UNRE SERV ED:   10
     0CA4,  3236: C6C9D9E2 E340C3D3 C1E2E26A 40F2F040                     FIRS T CL ASS,  20

068C SNAPSHOT             963    469,204  PSW: 00 0 0 0000  '01'B '10'B 0 00068C
     CORE DUMP:
     0D10,  3344: FFFFFFFF FFFFFFFF FFFFFFFF FFFFFFFF FFFFFFFF FFFFFFFF   ???? ???? ???? ???? ???? ????
     0D28,  3368: FFFFFFFF FFFFFFFF FFFFFFFF FFFFFFFF                     ???? ???? ???? ????

00C6 SVC INTERRUPT        993    469,258  PSW: FE 0 0 0001  '01'B '01'B 0 0000C6
     REGISTERS:
     R 0: 00000002,          2 R 1: 00000176,        374

0474 SNAPSHOT            1005    469,305  PSW: FE 0 0 0000  '01'B '00'B 0 000474
     REGISTERS:
     R13: 00000004,          4 R14: 00000002,          2

0516 SNAPSHOT            1027    469,320  PSW: 00 0 0 0000  '01'B '00'B 0 000516
     REGISTERS:
     R 5: 000000A0,        160

05CA SNAPSHOT            1055    469,417  PSW: 00 0 0 0000  '01'B '00'B 0 0005CA
     CORE DUMP:
     0BB8,  3000: F0F45AD7 C1F8F7F6                                      04 P A876

0172 SVC INTERRUPT       1106    469,623  PSW: FE 0 0 0002  '01'B '01'B 0 000172
     REGISTERS:
     R 0: 00000002,          2 R 1: 00000176,        374

05E4 SNAPSHOT            1120    469,672  PSW: FE 0 0 0000  '01'B '00'B 0 0005E4
     REGISTERS:
     R13: 00000003,          3 R14: 00000002,          2

05F2 SNAPSHOT            1120    469,672  PSW: FE 0 0 0000  '01'B '00'B 0 0005F2
     CORE DUMP:
     0174,  372: 00C4F0F4 5AD7C1D5 40C1D440 40C6D3E3 40D7C1F8 F7F67A40   7D04 PAN AM  FLT  PA8 76:
     018C,  396: F37AF0F0 40D7D440 6840C7C1 E3C540F1                     3:00 PM  , GA TE 1

0614 I/O INTERRUPT       1130    469,879  PSW: FE 0 2 000C  '10'B '00'B 0 000614
     CORE DUMP:
     0038,     56: FE02000C 80000614 000009D8 08000000 00000900           ???? ???? ???Q ???? ????
```

```
MASSACHUSETTS INSTITUTE OF TECHNOLOGY          SYSTEM / 360 SIMULATOR                                    VERSION 1.3
SAMPLE TRACE LISTING.  2 CONDITIONS ENABLED.                                                             PAGE  6

LOC  TRACE TYPE           COUNT  TIME                                            OP  INSTRUCTION    ADR1 ADR2 OPERAND1 OPERAND2
----  ----------------    -----  ----------                                      ----  -----------  ---- ---- -------- --------


0614 I/O INTERRUPT        1144    533,500  PSW: FE 0 2 000C   '10'B '00'B 0 000614
     CORE DUMP:
       0038,   56: FE02000C 80000614 000009D8 04000000 000009D0              ???? ???? ???Q ???? ????

075E SNAPSHOT             1161    533,543  PSW: 00 0 0 0000   '01'B '10'B 0 00075E
     REGISTERS:
       R13: 00000004,          4 R14: 00000002,          2

0614 I/O INTERRUPT        1171    571,832  PSW: FE 0 2 000E   '10'B '00'B 0 000614
     CORE DUMP:
       0038,   56: FE02000E 80000614 000009E8 08000000 000009D0              ???? ???? ???Y ???? ????

0614 I/O INTERRUPT        1185    675,131  PSW: FE 0 2 000E   '10'B '00'B 0 000614
     CORE DUMP:
       0038,   56: FE02000E 80000614 000009E8 04000000 000009D0              ???? ???? ???Y ???? ????

0852 SNAPSHOT             1203    675,175  PSW: 00 0 0 0000   '01'B '00'B 0 000852
     REGISTERS:
       R13: 00000004,          4 R14: 00000002,          2

0670 SNAPSHOT             1246    675,417  PSW: 00 0 0 0000   '01'B '10'B 0 000670
     CORE DUMP:
       0C08, 3080: F0F45AD7 C1D540C1 D44040C6 D3E340D7 C1F8F7F6 7A40F37A     04 P AN A M  F LT P A876 : 3:
       0C20, 3104: F0F040D7 D4406B40 C7C1E3C5 40F1F24B                       00 P M , GATE 12.

067E SNAPSHOT             1246    675,417  PSW: 00 0 0 0000   '01'B '10'B 0 00067E
     CORE DUMP:
       0C8C, 3212: F0F44040 40404040 E4D5D9C5 E2C5D9E5 C5C47A40 40F1F240     04        UNRE SERV ED:   12
       0CA4, 3236: C6C9D9E2 E340C3D3 C1E2E26B 40F2F540                       FIRS T CL ASS, 25

068C SNAPSHOT             1246    675,417  PSW: 00 0 0 0000   '01'B '10'B 0 00068C
     CORE DUMP:
       0D10, 3344: FFFFFFFF FFFFFFFF FFFFFFFF FFFFFFFF FFFFFFFF FFFFFFFF     ???? ???? ???? ???? ???? ????
       0D28, 3368: FFFFFFFF FFFFFFFF FFFFFFFF FFFFFFFF                       ???? ???? ???? ????

00C6 SVC INTERRUPT        1276    675,471  PSW: FE 0 0 0001   '01'B '01'B 0 0000C6
     REGISTERS:
       R 0: 00000002,          2 R 1: 00000176,        374

0474 SNAPSHOT             1288    675,518  PSW: FE 0 0 0000   '01'B '00'B 0 000474
     REGISTERS:
       R13: 00000004,          4 R14: 00000002,          2

0516 SNAPSHOT             1310    675,533  PSW: 00 0 0 0000   '01'B '00'B 0 000516
     REGISTERS:
       R 5: 000000A0,        160

05CA SNAPSHOT             1338    675,630  PSW: 00 0 0 0000   '01'B '00'B 0 0005CA
     CORE DUMP:
       0BBA, 3000: F0F55AE4 D5F7F4F7                                        05 U N747

0172 SVC INTERRUPT        1381    675,827  PSW: FE 0 0 0002   '01'B '01'B 0 000172
     REGISTERS:
```

```
MASSACHUSETTS INSTITUTE OF TECHNOLOGY          SYSTEM / 360 SIMULATOR                                              VERSION 1.3
SAMPLE  TRACE LISTING.   2 CONDITIONS ENABLED.                                                                          PAGE  7

LOC  TRACE TYPE          COUNT   TIME                                            OP   INSTRUCTION     ADR1 ADR2  OPERAND1 OPERAND2
---- ----------------    -----   ---------                                       ---- -------------   ---- ----  -------- -------


      R  0: 00000002,          2 R  1: 00000176,          374

05E4 SNAPSHOT            1395    675,877  PSW: FE 0 0 0000   '01'B '00'B 0 0005E4
     REGISTERS:
      R13: 00000003,          3 R14: 00000002,            2

05F2 SNAPSHOT            1395    675,877  PSW: FE 0 0 0000   '01'B '00'B 0 0005F2
     CORE DUMP:
      0174,   372: 00C4F0F5 5AE4D5C9 E3C5C440 40C6D3E3 40E4D5F7 F4F77A40      ?DQ5  UNI TED    FLT  UN7 47:
      018C,   396: F17AF0F0 40D7D440 6840C7C1 E3C54OF1                        1:00  PM , GA TE 1

0614 I/O INTERRUPT       1405    676,092  PSW: FE 0 2 000C   '10'B '00'B 0 000614
     CORE DUMP:
      0038,    56: FE02000C 80000614 000009D8 08000000 000009D0               ???? ???? ???Q ???? ????

0614 I/O INTERRUPT       1419    733,500  PSW: FE 0 2 000C   '10'B '00'B 0 000614
     CORE DUMP:
      0038,    56: FE02000C 80000614 000009D8 04000000 000009D0               ???? ???? ???Q ???? ????

075E SNAPSHOT            1436    733,543  PSW: 00 0 0 0000   '01'B '10'B 0 00075E
     REGISTERS:
      R13: 00000004,          4 R14: 00000002,            2

0614 I/O INTERRUPT       1446    764,458  PSW: FE 0 2 000E   '10'B '00'B 0 000614
     CORE DUMP:
      0038,    56: FE02000E 80000614 000009E8 08000000 000009D0               ???? ???? ???Y ???? ????

0614 I/O INTERRUPT       1460    871,983  PSW: FE 0 2 000E   '10'B '00'B 0 000614
     CORE DUMP:
      0038,    56: FE02000E 80000614 000009E8 04000000 000009D0               ???? ???? ???Y ???? ????

0852 SNAPSHOT            1478    872,027  PSW: 00 0 0 0000   '01'B '00'B 0 000852
     REGISTERS:
      R13: 00000004,          4 R14: 00000002,            2

0670 SNAPSHOT            1521    872,269  PSW: 00 0 0 0000   '01'B '10'B 0 000670
     CORE DUMP:
      0C08,  3080: F0F55AE4 D5C9E3C5 C44040C6 D3E340E4 D5F7F4F7 7A40F17A      05 U NITE D  F LT U N747 : 1:
      0C20,  3104: F0F040D7 D4406840 C7C1E3C5 40F1F24B                        00 P M , GATE 12.

067E SNAPSHOT            1521    872,269  PSW: 00 0 0 0000   '01'B '10'B 0 00067E
     CORE DUMP:
      0C8C,  3212: F0F54040 40404040 E4D5D9C5 E2C5D9E5 C5C47A40 40F5F040      05       UNRE SERV ED:   50
      0CA4,  3236: C6C9D9E2 E340C3D3 C1E2E26B 40F9F040                        FIRS T CL ASS,  90

068C SNAPSHOT            1521    872,269  PSW: 00 0 0 0000   '01'B '10'B 0 00068C
     CORE DUMP:
      0D10,  3344: FFFFFFFF FFFFFFFF FFFFFFFF FFFFFFFF FFFFFFFF FFFFFFFF      ???? ???? ???? ???? ???? ????
      0D28,  3368: FFFFFFFF FFFFFFFF FFFFFFFF FFFFFFFF                        ???? ???? ???? ????

00C6 SVC INTERRUPT       1551    872,323  PSW: FE 0 0 0001   '01'B '01'B 0 0000C6
     REGISTERS:
      R  0: 00000002,          2 R  1: 00000176,          374
```

```
MASSACHUSETTS INSTITUTE OF TECHNOLOGY          SYSTEM / 360 SIMULATOR                                      VERSION 1.3
SAMPLE  TRACE LISTING.   3 CONDITIONS ENABLED.                                                                PAGE  8

LOC  TRACE TYPE          COUNT   TIME                                          OP   INSTRUCTION    ADR1 ADR2  OPERAND1 OPERAND2
----  ----------------    -----  ----------                                    ----  --------------  ---- ----   -------- --------


0474 SNAPSHOT            1563    872,370  PSW: FE 0 0 0000  '01'B '00'B 0 000474
        REGISTERS:
        R13: 00000004,          4 R14: 00000002,          2

0516 SNAPSHOT            1591    872,389  PSW: 00 0 0 0000  '01'B '00'B 0 000516
        REGISTERS:
        R 5: 000000F0,        240

05CA SNAPSHOT            1615    872,455  PSW: 00 0 0 0000  '01'B '01'B 0 0005CA
        CORE DUMP:
        0BB8,  3000: F0F75AD7 C1F3F0F0                                         07 P A300

0172 SVC INTERRUPT       1674    872,634  PSW: FE 0 0 0002  '01'B '01'B 0 000172
        REGISTERS:
        R 0: 00000001,          1 R 1: 00000176,         374

05E4 SNAPSHOT            1688    872,682  PSW: FE 0 0 0000  '01'B '00'B 0 0005E4
        REGISTERS:
        R13: 00000003,          3 R14: 00000002,          2

05F2 SNAPSHOT            1688    872,682  PSW: FE 0 0 0000  '01'B '00'B 0 0005F2
        CORE DUMP:
        0174,   372: 00C4F0F7 5AC6D3E3 40D7C1F3 F0F07A40 40D5D6D5 C5E7C9E2      ?D07  FLT  PA3 00:    NON EXIS
        018C,   396: E3C5D5E3 40C6D3C9 C7C8E340 D5E4D4C2                        TENT  FLI GHT  NUMB

0670 SNAPSHOT            1708    872,751  PSW: 00 0 0 0000  '01'B '00'B 0 000670
        CORE DUMP:
        0C08,  3080: F0F540E4 D5C9E3C5 C44040C6 D3E340E4 D5F7F4F7 7A40F17A      05 U NITE D  F LT U N747 : 1:
        0C20,  3104: F0F040D7 D4406B40 C7C1E3C5 40F1F24B                        00 P M ,  GATE  12.

067E SNAPSHOT            1708    872,751  PSW: 00 0 0 0000  '01'B '00'B 0 00067E
        CORE DUMP:
        0C8C,  3212: F0F54040 40404040 E4D5D9C5 E2C5D9E5 C5C47A40 40F5F040      05        UNRE SERV ED:    50
        0CA4,  3236: C6C9D9E2 E340C3D3 C1E2E268 40F9F040                        FIRS T CL ASS,   90

068C SNAPSHOT            1708    872,751  PSW: 00 0 0 0000  '01'B '00'B 0 00068C
        CORE DUMP:
        0D10,  3344: F0F75AC6 D3E340D7 C1F3F0F0 7A40405 D6D5C5E7 C9E2E3C5      07 F LT P A300 :  N ONEX ISTE
        0D28,  3368: D5E340C6 D3C9C7C8 E340D5E4 D4C2C5D9                        NT F LIGH T NU MBER

00C6 SVC INTERRUPT       1717    872,778  PSW: FE 0 0 0001  '01'B '01'B 0 0000C6
        REGISTERS:
        R 0: 00000001,          1 R 1: 00000176,         374

0474 SNAPSHOT            1729    872,824  PSW: FE 0 0 0000  '01'B '00'B 0 000474
        REGISTERS:
        R13: 00000003,          3 R14: 00000003,          3

0516 SNAPSHOT            1759    872,845  PSW: 00 0 0 0000  '01'B '00'B 0 000516
        REGISTERS:
        R 5: 00000000,          0

05CA SNAPSHOT            1774    872,986  PSW: 00 0 0 0000  '01'B '00'B 0 0005CA
```

```
MASSACHUSETTS INSTITUTE OF TECHNOLOGY        SYSTEM / 360 SIMULATOR                              VERSION 1.3
SAMPLE  TRACE LISTING.  3 CONDITIONS ENABLED.                                                         PAGE  9

LOC  TRACE TYPE        COUNT  TIME                           OP    INSTRUCTION      ADR1 ADR2  OPERAND1 OPERAND2
---- ---------------   -----  ---------                      ----  ---------------  ---- ----  -------- --------

         CORE DUMP:
           0BB8,  3000: F0F35CE3 E6F7F2F7                    03*T W727

0172 SVC INTERRUPT      1813     873,165  PSW: FE 0 0 0002  '01'B '01'B 0 000172
         REGISTERS:
           R 0: 00000002,         2 R 1: 00000176,          374

05E4 SNAPSHOT           1827     873,211  PSW: FE 0 0 0000  '01'B '00'B 0 0005E4
         REGISTERS:
           R13: 00000002,         2 R14: 00000003,          3

05F2 SNAPSHOT           1827     873,211  PSW: FE 0 0 0000  '01'B '00'B 0 0005F2
         CORE DUMP:
           0174,   372: 00C4F0F3 5CE3E6C1 40404043 40C6D3E3 40E3E6F7 F2F77A40   ?D03 *TWA      FLT  TW7 27:
           018C,   396: F97AF0F0 40C1D440 6840C7C1 E3C540F1                     9:00  AM  , GA TE 1

0614 I/O INTERRUPT      1837     969,762  PSW: FE 0 2 000E  '10'B '00'B 0 000614
         CORE DUMP:
           0038,    56: FE02000E 80000614 000009E8 08000000 000009D0            ???? ???? ???Y ???? ????

0614 I/O INTERRUPT      1851   1,078,491  PSW: FE 0 2 000E  '10'B '00'B 0 000614
         CORE DUMP:
           0038,    56: FE02000E 80000614 000009E8 04000000 000009D0            ???? ???? ???Y ???? ????

0852 SNAPSHOT           1869   1,078,523  PSW: 00 0 0 0000  '01'B '00'B 0 000852
         REGISTERS:
           R13: 00000002,         2 R14: 00000003,          3

08E8 SNAPSHOT           1885   1,078,616  PSW: 00 0 0 0000  '01'B '00'B 0 0008E8
         REGISTERS:
           R10: 00000000,         0

0670 SNAPSHOT           1934   1,078,750  PSW: 00 0 0 0000  '01'B '10'B 0 000670
         CORE DUMP:
           0C08,  3080: F0F740C6 D3E340D7 C1F3F0F0 7A404005 D6D5C5E7 C9E2E3C5   07 F LT P A300 :  N ONEX ISTE
           0C20,  3104: D5E340C6 D3C9C7C8 E340D5E4 D4C2C5D9                     NT F LIGH T NU MBER

067E SNAPSHOT           1934   1,078,750  PSW: 00 0 0 0000  '01'B '10'B 0 00067E
         CORE DUMP:
           0C8C,  3212: F0F35CE3 E6C14040 404040C6 D3E340E3 E6F7F2F7 7A40F97A   03*T WA      FLT T W727 : 9:
           0CA4,  3236: F0F040C1 D4406840 C7C1E3C5 40F1F54B                     00 A M ,  GATE 15.

068C SNAPSHOT           1934   1,078,750  PSW: 00 0 0 0000  '01'B '10'B 0 00068C
         CORE DUMP:
           0D10,  3344: F0F34040 40404040 E4D5D9C5 E2C5D9E5 C5C47A40 4040F040   03        UNRE SERV ED:    0
           0D28,  3368: C6C9D9E2 E340C3D3 C1E2E26B 4040F040                     FIRS T CL ASS,  0

00C6 SVC INTERRUPT      1943   1,078,770  PSW: FE 0 0 0001  '01'B '01'B 0 0000C6
         REGISTERS:
           R 0: 00000002,         2 R 1: 00000176,          374

0474 SNAPSHOT           1955   1,078,806  PSW: FE 0 0 0000  '01'B '00'B 0 000474
         REGISTERS:
```

```
MASSACHUSETTS INSTITUTE OF TECHNOLOGY        SYSTEM / 360 SIMULATOR                                    VERSION 1.3
SAMPLE  TRACE LISTING.   3 CONDITIONS ENABLED.                                                              PAGE 10

LOC  TRACE TYPE           COUNT   TIME                                    OP   INSTRUCTION    ADR1 ADR2  OPERAND1 OPERAND2
----  ----------------    -----  ----------                              ----  ------------- ---- ----  -------- -------

           R13: 00000002,       2 R14: 00000003,          3

05CA SNAPSHOT             2001  1,078,935  PSW: 00 0 0 0000  '01'B '00'B 0 0005CA
            CORE DUMP:
             0BB8,  3000: F0F94EF1 F07AF0F0                                09+1 0:00

0172 SVC INTERRUPT        2060  1,079,077  PSW: FE 0 0 0002  '01'B '01'B 0 000172
            REGISTERS:
             R 0: 00000001,       1 R 1: 00000176,        374

05E4 SNAPSHOT             2074  1,079,113  PSW: FE 0 0 0000  '01'B '00'B 0 0005E4
            REGISTERS:
             R13: 00000001,       1 R14: 00000003,          3

05F2 SNAPSHOT             2074  1,079,113  PSW: FE 0 0 0000  '01'B '00'B 0 0005F2
            CORE DUMP:
             0174,   372: 00C4F0F9 4EC6D3E3 40F1F07A F0F07A40 40D5D6D5 C5E7C9E2  ?009 +FLT  10: 00:   NON EXIS
             018C,   396: E3C5D5E3 40C6D3C9 C7C8E340 D5E4D4C2                    TENT  FLI GHT  NUMB

0614 I/O INTERRUPT        2084  1,079,294  PSW: FE 0 2 000E  '10'B '00'B 0 000614
            CORE DUMP:
             0038,    56: FE02000E 80000614 000009E8 08000000 000009E0         ???? ???? ???Y ???? ????

0614 I/O INTERRUPT        2098  1,187,654  PSW: FE 0 2 000E  '10'B '00'B 0 000614
            CORE DUMP:
             0038,    56: FE02000E 80000614 000009E8 04000000 000009E0         ???? ???? ???Y ???? ????

0852 SNAPSHOT             2116  1,187,686  PSW: 00 0 0 0000  '01'B '00'B 0 000852
            REGISTERS:
             R13: 00000001,       1 R14: 00000003,          3

0878 SNAPSHOT             2121  1,187,776  PSW: 00 0 0 0000  '01'B '01'B 0 000878
            CORE DUMP:
             0C08,  3080: F0F35CE3 E6C14040 404040C6 D3E340E3 E6F7F2F7 7A40F97A  03*T WA    F LT T W727 : 9:
             0C20,  3104: F0F040C1 D4406840 C7C1E3C5 40F1F54B                    00 A M ,  GATE 15.

08E8 SNAPSHOT             2147  1,187,781  PSW: 00 0 0 0000  '01'B '00'B 0 0008E8
            REGISTERS:
             R10: 00000000,       0

0670 SNAPSHOT             2196  1,187,873  PSW: 00 0 0 0000  '01'B '00'B 0 000670
            CORE DUMP:
             0C08,  3080: F0F340E3 E6C14040 404040C6 D3E340E3 E6F7F2F7 7A40F97A  03 T WA    F LT T W727 : 9:
             0C20,  3104: F0F040C1 D4406840 C7C1E3C5 40F1F54B                    00 A M ,  GATE 15.

067E SNAPSHOT             2196  1,187,873  PSW: 00 0 0 0000  '01'B '00'B 0 00067E
            CORE DUMP:
             0C8C,  3212: F0F34040 40404040 E4D5D9C5 E2C5D9E5 C5C47A40 4040F040  03        UNRE SERV ED:    0
             0CA4,  3236: C6C9D9E2 E340C3D3 C1E2E26B 4040F040                    FIRS T CL ASS,   0

068C SNAPSHOT             2196  1,187,873  PSW: 00 0 0 0000  '01'B '00'B 0 00068C
            CORE DUMP:
             0D10,  3344: F0F94EC6 D3E340F1 F07AF0F0 7A4040D5 D6D5C5E7 C9E2E3C5  09+F LT 1 0:00 :  N ONEX ISTE
```

440

```
MASSACHUSETTS INSTITUTE OF TECHNOLOGY          SYSTEM / 360 SIMULATOR                               VERSION 1.3
SAMPLE  TRACE LISTING.  3 CONDITIONS ENABLED.                                                         PAGE 11

LOC  TRACE TYPE           COUNT  TIME                                    OP   INSTRUCTION    ADR1 ADR2  OPERAND1 OPERAND2
----  ---------------      -----  ----------                             ----  --------------  ----  ----  --------  -------

      0D28,  3368: D5E340C6 D3C9C7C8 E340D5E4 D4C2C5D9                    NT F LIGH T NU MBER

00C6 SVC INTERRUPT          2205  1,187,893  PSW: FE 0 0 0001  '01'B '01'B 0 0000C6
       REGISTERS:
       R 0: 00000001,            1 R 1: 00000176,         374

0474 SNAPSHOT               2217  1,187,929  PSW: FE 0 0 0000  '01'B '00'B 0 000474
       REGISTERS:
       R13: 00000001,            1 R14: 00000003,           3

05CA SNAPSHOT               2251  1,188,058  PSW: 00 0 0 0000  '01'B '00'B 0 0005CA
       CORE DUMP:
       0B88,  3000: F0F6C5C1 F8F0F240                                    06EA 802

0172 SVC INTERRUPT          2298  1,188,222  PSW: FE 0 0 0002  '01'B '11'B 0 000172
       REGISTERS:
       R 0: 00000002,            2 R 1: 00000176,         374

05E4 SNAPSHOT               2312  1,188,258  PSW: FE 0 0 0000  '01'B '00'B 0 0005E4
       REGISTERS:
       R13: 00000000,            0 R14: 00000003,           3

05F2 SNAPSHOT               2312  1,188,258  PSW: FE 0 0 0000  '01'B '00'B 0 0005F2
       CORE DUMP:
       0174,   372: 00C4F0F6 40C5C1E2 E3C5D9D5 40C6D3E3 40C5C1F8 F0F27A40  ?D06  EAS TERN  FLT   EA8 02:
       018C,   396: F37AF0F0 40D7D440 6B40C7C1 E3C540F2                    3:00  PM , GA TE 2

0614 I/O INTERRUPT          2322  1,286,757  PSW: FE 0 2 000E  '10'B '00'B 0 000614
       CORE DUMP:
       0038,    56: FE02000E 80000614 000009E8 08000000 000009D8           ???? ???? ???Y ???? ???Q

0614 I/O INTERRUPT          2336  1,398,480  PSW: FE 0 2 000E  '10'B '00'B 0 000614
       CORE DUMP:
       0038,    56: FE02000E 80000614 000009E8 04000000 000009D8           ???? ???? ???Y ???? ???Q

0852 SNAPSHOT               2354  1,398,512  PSW: 00 0 0 0000  '01'B '00'B 0 000852
       REGISTERS:
       R13: 00000000,            0 R14: 00000003,           3

0670 SNAPSHOT               2427  1,398,739  PSW: 00 0 0 0000  '01'B '10'B 0 000670
       CORE DUMP:
       0C08,  3080: F0F94EC6 D3E340F1 F07AF0F0 7A404005 D6D5C5E7 C9E2E3C5  09+F LT 1 0:00 :  N ONEX ISTE
       0C20,  3104: D5E340C6 D3C9C7C8 E340D5E4 D4C2C5D9                    NT F LIGH T NU MBER

067E SNAPSHOT               2427  1,398,739  PSW: 00 0 0 0000  '01'B '10'B 0 00067E
       CORE DUMP:
       0C8C,  3212: F0F640C5 C1E2E3C5 D9D540C5 D3E340C5 C1F8F0F2 7A40F37A  06 E ASTE RN F LT E A802 : 3:
       0CA4,  3236: F0F040D7 D44068 40 C7C1E3C5 40F2F14B                    00 P M , GATE 21.

068C SNAPSHOT               2427  1,398,739  PSW: 00 0 0 0000  '01'B '10'B 0 00068C
       CORE DUMP:
       0D10,  3344: F0F64040 40404040 E4D5D9C5 E2C5D9E5 C5C47A40 4040F240  06       UNRE SERV ED:    2
       0D28,  3368: C6C9D9E2 E340C3D3 C1E2E26B 4040F340                    FIRS T CL ASS,    3
```

441

```
MASSACHUSETTS INSTITUTE OF TECHNOLOGY        SYSTEM / 360 SIMULATOR                                    VERSION 1.3
SAMPLE TRACE LISTING.  2 CONDITIONS ENABLED.                                                              PAGE 12

                                                                        OP   INSTRUCTION    ADR1 ADR2 OPERAND1 OPERAND2
LOC  TRACE TYPE          COUNT  TIME                                     ---- ------------   ---- ---- -------- --------
----  ----------------   -----  ----------

00C6 SVC INTERRUPT        2436  1,398,759  PSW: FE 0 0 0001  '01'B '11'B 0 0000C6
     REGISTERS:
       R 0: 00000002,             2 R 1: 00000176,          374

0474 SNAPSHOT             2448  1,398,795  PSW: FE 0 0 0000  '01'B '00'B 0 000474
     REGISTERS:
       R13: 00000000,             0 R14: 00000003,            3

05D6 I/O INTERRUPT        2467  1,399,283  PSW: FE 0 2 000E  '10'B '00'B 0 0005D6
     CORE DUMP:
       0038,    56: FE02000E 800005D6 000009E8 08000000 000009B8          ???? ???0 ???Y ???? ????

05D6 I/O INTERRUPT        2481  1,497,932  PSW: FE 0 2 000E  '10'B '00'B 0 0005D6
     CORE DUMP:
       0038,    56: FE02000E 800005D6 000009E8 04000000 000009B8          ???? ???0 ???Y ???? ????

0852 SNAPSHOT             2499  1,497,964  PSW: 00 0 0 0000  '01'B '00'B 0 000852
     REGISTERS:
       R13: 00000000,             0 R14: 00000003,            3

0878 SNAPSHOT             2504  1,498,054  PSW: 00 0 0 0000  '01'B '01'B 0 000878
     CORE DUMP:
       0C08,  3080: F0F640C5 C1E2E3C5 D9D540C6 D3E340C5 C1F8F0F2 7A40F37A   06 E ASTE RN F LT E A802 : 3:
       0C20,  3104: F0F040D7 D4406840 C7C1E3C5 40F2F14B                     00 P M , GATE 21.

05D6 I/O INTERRUPT        2561  1,593,313  PSW: FE 0 2 000E  '10'B '00'B 0 0005D6
     CORE DUMP:
       0038,    56: FE02000E 800005D6 000009E8 08000000 000009D8          ???? ???0 ???Y ???? ???Q

05D6 I/O INTERRUPT        2575  1,697,592  PSW: FE 0 2 000E  '10'B '00'B 0 0005D6
     CORE DUMP:
       0038,    56: FE02000E 800005D6 000009E8 04000000 000009D8          ???? ???0 ???Y ???? ???Q

0852 SNAPSHOT             2593  1,697,624  PSW: 00 0 0 0000  '01'B '00'B 0 000852
     REGISTERS:
       R13: 00000000,             0 R14: 00000002,            2


CPU HAS ENTERED THE WAIT STATE WITH NO INTERRUPTS ENABLED. SIMULATION ENDS.
THE FOLLOWING SIMULATOR-PROVIDED SNAPSHOT SHOULD HELP IN DETERMINING THE CAUSE OF THIS CONDITION.  THE PSW INTERRUPT CODE IS
1

05D6 SNAPSHOT             2608  1,697,737  PSW: FE 0 2 0000  '10'B '00'B 0 0005D6
     STATUS:
       OLD PRG: 00 0 2 0000  '00'B '00'B 0 000000
     REGISTERS:
       R 0: 00000002,             2 R 1: 00000176,          374 R 2: 00000178,          376 R 3: 00000005,            5
       R 4: 0000039E,           926 R 5: 000009B8,         2488 R 6: FFFFFFFF,           -1 R 7: FFFFFFFF,           -1
       R 8: FFFFFFFF,            -1 R 9: FFFFFFFF,           -1 R10: FFFFFFFF,           -1 R11: 40001436, 1073746998
       R12: FFFFFFFF,            -1 R13: 00000000,            0 R14: 00000000,            0 R15: 40000436, 1073742902
```

442

ABNORMAL SIMULATOR TERMINATION FOR PROGRAM SAMPLE

         SIMULATED REAL TIME:   1,697,737.000

         SIMULATED CPU TIME:        8,498.000


```
*******************************************************************************************************************************
SAMPLE                               OUTPUT TO PRINTER OOE STARTS AT HEAD OF FORM ON NEXT PAGE
*******************************************************************************************************************************

00 TWA     FLT TW881: 9:00 AM , GATE 13.
00     UNRESERVED:  15 FIRST CLASS,  1 COACH.

01 PAN AM  FLT PA707: 8:00 AM , GATE 13.
01     UNRESERVED:   5 FIRST CLASS, 15 COACH.

02 UNITED  FLT UN666: 4:45 PM , GATE 21.
02     UNRESERVED:  10 FIRST CLASS, 20 COACH.

04 PAN AM  FLT PA876: 3:00 PM , GATE 12.
04     UNRESERVED:  12 FIRST CLASS, 25 COACH.

05 UNITED  FLT UN747: 1:00 PM , GATE 12.
05     UNRESERVED:  50 FIRST CLASS, 90 COACH.

07 FLT PA300:  NONEXISTENT FLIGHT NUMBER.  PLEASE TRY AGAIN.

03 TWA     FLT TW727: 9:00 AM , GATE 15.
03     UNRESERVED:   0 FIRST CLASS,  0 COACH.

09+FLT 10:00:  NONEXISTENT FLIGHT NUMBER.  PLEASE TRY AGAIN.

06 EASTERN FLT EA802: 3:00 PM , GATE 21.
06     UNRESERVED:   2 FIRST CLASS,  3 COACH.
```

```
I----------------I
I                I
I CHAPTER  6  I
I----------------I
```

## 6.1  STUDENT'S GUIDE

### 6.1.1  Introduction

In this chapter a sample operating system is presented as an aid to the understanding of operating systems in general. (1) This operating system is simple, making it easy for students to learn. This is in contrast to other operating systems, e.g., OS/360, MULTICS, etc., whose main purpose is not pedagogical. It is also a small operating system, as operating systems go; in its present form, it occupies less than 2500 cards of assembly language statements.

This operating system does not include language processors or utility programs, but instead implements a basic system nucleus which provides such features as multiprocessing, dynamic memory allocation, device management, etc., to which any top level supervisor and associated programs could be easily fitted. The basic features provided are the ones most important in learning fundamentals of operating systems.

This implementation does include a simple top level supervisor to provide processing of the job streams. Thus the operating system is complete, in that it could be used for some real-world application, such as controlling a large number of real-time devices, with additional background computing.

Lastly, this operating system is explicitly designed in a modular and structured manner. In particular, the relevant sections for processor management, memory management, and device management can be easily identified. Although the specific implementation is for the IBM System/360, the algorithms and techniques are applicable to most contemporary computer systems.

----------------------------------------------------------------

(1) This example operating system is based upon the Master's Thesis, "Design and Implementation of an Example Operating System", by John D. DeTreville, MIT, June 1972. Others, notably Richard Swift and Paul Fredette, assisted in debugging it. This work was supported (in part) by Project MAC, an MIT research program sponsored by the Advanced Research Projects Agency, Department of Defense, under Office of Naval Research Contract Number Nonr-4102(01).

## 6.1.2  Overview of the System

The sample operating system is a multiprogramming system
designed for the IBM System/360. Any types of I/O devices can be
supported, but currently system support is provided only for card
readers and line printers. User programs can provide their own
routines for non-standard devices, however. There is no file
system provided.

Memory allocation for the user programs is in the form of
dynamic partition allocation. The user must specify the amount of
storage required for his job in terms of 2K-byte increments from
2K-bytes upwards. The system currently requires about 6K-bytes
for its own routines; the rest of memory is available for user
programs and system tables.

The system is capable of supporting multiple job streams
coming from different input devices (here, readers), with the
output being directed to different output devices (here,
printers). Each job stream consists of a number of jobs, stacked
in order as illustrated in Figure 6.1.1.

A job consists of a $JOB card, followed by a single object
deck, followed by optional data. The format of the $JOB card is:

        $JOB,core,name=devtype,name=devtype,...

as in:

        $JOB,8K,FILEA=IN,FILEB=OUT

The core field gives the amount of core required for the
job; in this example it is 8K. The "name=devtype" field can be
repeated any number of times, including zero. The "name" gives
the name by which the user program can reference this device.
These names are up to the user; thus, flexible, device
independent referencing of devices is provided. The "devtype"
tells the type of device to be assigned. There are currently
three possibilities for this field.

The type "IN" specifies the system input unit, i.e., the
card reader for this job stream. The type "OUT" specifies the
system output unit, the line printer. The type "EXCP" indicates
a non-standard device, for which the user will supply his own
handler routine. Currently, the $JOB card can contain at most one
reference to IN, one reference to OUT, and one reference to EXCP.

445

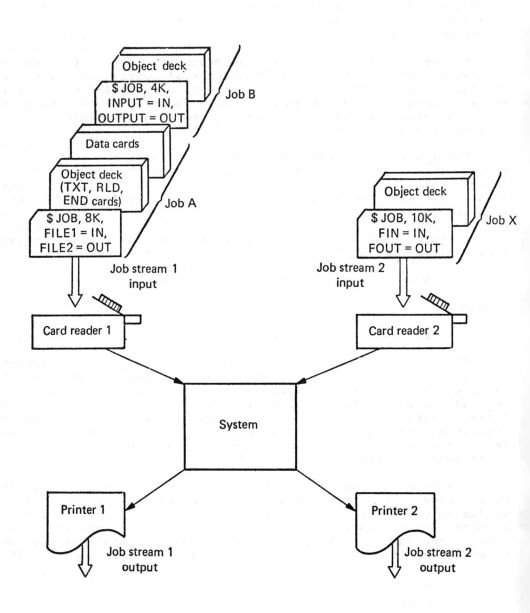

Figure 6.1.1
Overview of Multiple Job Stream
Multiprogramming System

The object deck, which immediately follows the $JOB card, has the same format as the standard OS/360 object deck. External references are not allowed, however. (i.e., subroutine linkage facilities are not provided). Following the object deck is the card input data to the user program, if there is a reference to "IN" on the $JOB card.

The user's program may specify parallel processing to take place within it (i.e., create multiple processes), and there are features to control this, along with flexible facilities for communication between different parallel execution paths of the program. The system automatically schedules the various jobs in the system, and their processes, in such a way as to tend to maximize the use of the CPU and the data channels. The sophistication of the scheduling is, of course, limited by the brevity of the implementation. The system can easily be extended to provide more advanced features and facilities.

The program listing and output for a simple job run under the sample operating system is reproduced as figure 6.1.2. This program causes one line to be printed on the system printer and then terminates. The output was produced by running the sample operating system under the System 360 simulator (SIM360), described in chapter 4.

### 6.1.3  Design and Use

The detailed design and structure of the sample system and its user interface is presented in chapter seven of Operating Systems (1) by Madnick and Donovan. This presentation includes a complete assembly listing of the system. It is strongly recommended that this reference be reviewed before attempting to modify the sample operating system.

--------------------------------------------------------------------

(1) Mc Graw - Hill, 1974.

EXAMPLE JOB FOR THE SAMPLE OPERATING SYSTEM                                          PAGE    2

```
 LOC  OBJECT CODE     ADDR1 ADDR2  STMT    SOURCE STATEMENT                            20 MAY 74

                                    2              PUNCH  '$JOB,2K,READER=IN,PRINTER=OUT'
000000                              3 USER        CSECT
000000 05F0                         4              BALR   15,0              ESTABLISH ADDRESSABILITY
000002                              5              USING  *,15              TELL ASSEMBLER

000002 4120 F00E          00010     7              LA     2,MSGONE          SEND MESSAGE TO PRINTER
000006 0AE2                         8              SVC    C'S'              ...

000008 4120 F0A6          000A8    10              LA     2,MSGTWO          WAIT FOR REPLY INDICATING
00000C 0AD9                        11              SVC    C'R'                 THAT PRINTING IS COMPLETED

00000E 0AC8                        13              SVC    C'H'              HALT JOB

000010 D7D9C9D5E3C5D940            15 MSGONE      DC     CL8'PRINTER'       NAME OF PROCESS
000018 00000008                    16              DC     F'8'              LENGTH OF MESSAGE
00001C D7D9C9D500000024            17              DC     C'PRIN',A(PRINT1) TEXT OF MESSAGE
000024 E4E2C5D940D7D9D6            18 PRINT1      DC     CL132'USER PROGRAM ENTRY SUCCESSFUL.'
                                   19 *                                    TEXT TO BE PRINTED

0000A8                             21 MSGTWO      DS     CL8               NAME OF PROCESS RETURNED HERE
0000B0 00000004                    22              DC     F'4'              LENGTH OF RETURN AREA
0000B4                             23              DS     CL4               STATUS RETURNED FROM 'PRINTER'
                                   24              END
```

```
MASSACHUSETTS INSTITUTE OF TECHNOLOGY          SYSTEM / 360 SIMULATOR                         VERSION 1.3
PROGRAM TRACE LISTING.    0 CONDITIONS ENABLED.                                                  PAGE   1

LOC  TRACE TYPE          COUNT   TIME                             OP   INSTRUCTION    ADR1 ADR2  OPERAND1 OPERAND2
----  ---------------    -----   ---------                        ----  --------------  ---- ----  -------- --------
```

CPU HAS ENTERED THE WAIT STATE WITH NO INTERRUPTS ENABLED. SIMULATION ENDS.
THE FOLLOWING SIMULATOR-PROVIDED SNAPSHOT SHOULD HELP IN DETERMINING THE CAUSE OF THIS CONDITION.  THE PSW INTERRUPT CODE IS        21
5

```
056A SNAPSHOT          46210  1,056,207  PSW: FE 0 2 0000   '10'B '00'B 0 00056A
        STATUS:
          OLD PRG: 00 0 0 0000   '00'B '00'B 0 000000
        REGISTERS:
          R 0: FFFFFFFF,            -1 R 1: 40000570,  1073743216 R 2: 00000EC0,          3776 R 3: FFFFFFFF,          -1
          R 4: 00000EC4,          3780 R 5: 00000000,           0 R 6: 00002218,          8728 R 7: 0000000C,          12
          R 8: FFFFFFFF,            -1 R 9: 400002B8,  1073742520 R10: 00001648,          5704 R11: 00001648,        5704
          R12: 00000000,             0 R13: 00F00000,    15728640 R14: 0000021C,           540 R15: 00001AB8,        6840
```

ABNORMAL SIMULATOR TERMINATION FOR PROGRAM PROGRAM

        SIMULATED REAL TIME:  1,056,207.000

        SIMULATED CPU TIME:     139,912.000

```
****************************************************************************************************************
PROGRAM                          OUTPUT TO PRINTER 00E STARTS AT HEAD OF FORM ON NEXT PAGE
****************************************************************************************************************
```

$JOB,2K,READER=IN,PRINTER=OUT
USER PROGRAM ENTRY SUCCESSFUL.
PROGRAM HALT

## 6.1.4  Sample Assignments

Since the sample operating system was designed to be a pedagogical tool, simplicity was an important constraint. However, every attempt was made to insure that general approaches were taken to allow for future expansion of the system.

From the many such possible extensions we have chosen a few suitable for assignment to students. These assignments require a detailed understanding of the sample system's internals. Depending on the time alotted for completion it may be wise to encourage groups of students to work together on the more difficult assignments.

1.  Stopped Processes:  Currently, after using the "stop process" primitive (routine XZ), the stopped process cannot be restarted by the "start process" primitive (routine XY). This is because the stopped process might be in the middle of the "leave smc section" primitive (routine XCOM) waiting on a semaphore that no other process will ever access. An assignment to test for such a condition in the "start process" routine would test the reader's basic understanding of the system and its databases.

2.  User semaphores:  Currently, the semaphore operations "P" and "V" are not allowed by user processes. This is because certain system information, for example, a pointer to the PCB of the first process waiting on the semaphore, is stored in the semaphore itself. Therefore, if the semaphore were stored in the user's partition, this pointer's integrity could not be guaranteed. Thus, the system currently allows only system routines to call the "P" and "V" routines, and these calling routines pass only system semaphores, stored outside of any user's partition and accessible only by system routines, as arguments.

The reader should provide a facility usable by the user's programs for semaphore-type synchronization. Basically, it would need an entry point for creating semaphores in a system area, at the user's request, and passing back a name for the created semaphore to be used in future pseudo-P and pseudo-V requests. The basic thing the reader should get from this, apart from gaining a familiarity with P and V, would be an awareness of the problems of memory allocation.

Full records will have to be kept of what name is associated with what semaphore, and also of what semaphores were allocated by the user's processes, so that these can be freed at the end of the job. This bookkeeping serves to get the reader into the details very quickly.

3.  Automatic Storage:  Presently, the automatic storage facility (SVC C'E') only allows one work area to be allocated per process. Extend this facility to allow multiple uses of SVC C'E' in a

449

process.

4.   Messages:   A  pointer to the sender's PCB is stored in each
message on the message chain for the receiver's PCB.  What  error
can  occur if a sender's process is destroyed before the receiver
has "read" the message? How can this problem be avoided?

5.   Accounting Information:   The  system  as  now  implemented
performs  no  accounting. This assignment is to modify the system
to  expect  another  field  on  the  $JOB  card,  of  the  form
USER=username,  where  username  is the name of the user to which
this work is to be charged. At the end of the job, an  accounting
tallsheet is printed containing the username, the resources used,
and  the  total  cost.  As an adjunct to this problem, the reader
should develop a pricing scheme implementing the  goals  for  the
installation.

6.   Deadlock Recovery:   Currently, if the processes running in
the  system  all  start  to  request  memory  to  the  extent  of
surpassing  the  ability  of the memory management to provide it,
and there is no  process  freeing  memory,  a  deadlock  will  be
reached.  All  processes  in  the system might well be waiting on
other processes either  waiting  for  other  processes  to  free
memory,  or waiting for processes that are themselves waiting for
memory.

     This can seriously degrade system performance,  if  it  does
not stop the system cold. The operating system should detect that
all  processes  in  the system are currently blocked, and that no
one is runnable or will ever be runnable (because  there  are  no
input/output  operations  currently  being performed). This test,
which  could  be  performed  by  the  traffic  controller  as  an
extention  to  a  similar  test that it currently performs, would
cause it to throw a  selected  job  off  the  system.  Here,  the
detection  of a deadlock situation is easy, but the modifications
to the system will cause problems.

     Currently, the method to throw a job off the system  has  as
part  of  it  sending  a  message  which  requires  memory  to be
allocated. The amount required here is just  a  few  words,  but
would  be very likely to be impossible to satisfy if we were ever
to  find  ourselves  in  this  situation.  A  pedagogically  more
important  problem  is that we would have the traffic controller,
the most basic part of the system,  very  far  removed  from  the
problem.  This  is  a  definite  problem  from  the viewpoint of
modularity, and its resolution is not obvious.

7.  Deadlock Avoidance:  Another problem with  memory  allocation
deadlocks  would be to detect partial deadlocks. It might be that
with five job streams in the system, four of them are involved in
a deadlock while the  fifth  has  a  long  compute-bound  program
running,  which  has  no  current  use for programs that use the
memory allocation.

When it completes its compute-bound section, it might free enough memory to allow the others to run, but it more likely will get caught in the same deadlock. An important, but intellectually difficult assignment, would be to extend the traffic controller to detect this type of deadlock coming on, and deal with it as in the previous problem.

8.  Device Assignment:   Currently, each job can request one reader and one printer, where the device to be assigned is determined before the request is made. This is certainly not the most efficient manner to proceeding, especially if there are more printers than readers, but is simple and completely avoids the problem of device deadlocks. A real improvement in system performance might be gained if, say, a reader used by a job were to be released whenever there were no more cards to be read for that job, thus allowing a then-created supervisor process to begin to process the next job.

9.  Secondary Storage Support:  One assignment would be to add routines to the system to handle other types of devices, such as disks. The modifications would come in the Job Stream Processor and in the device management routines.

10.  File System Design:  Once there is disk management, there is the possibility of adding a file system. Specifics of this might vary, but it might be noticed that from the user's viewpoint, the fields on the $JOB card make easy provision for this.

11.  Spooling and Job Scheduling:  With disk management and a simple file system, we can perform input and output spooling. And, with spooling, addition of various job scheduling algorithms becomes practical.

## 6.2  Instructor's Guide

### 6.2.1  Introduction

This sample operating system is complete in that it works and may actually be used. It serves as a useful vehicle for teaching operating system design in that it is small enough for a student to understand with a modest outlay of time, and its modularity lends readily to student assignments for extension and enhancement.

In order to test these assignments a method must be available for actually running the system. You are faced with essentially three options:

1. Use a bare 360 or 370 machine, on a stand-alone basis. Although this is the most realistic approach and the experience may be helpful to students, it is very costly in terms of resources and may prove to be totally impractical.

2. Use a virtual machine, provided by CP-67 or VM-370. This approach offers the highest economy in terms of resources while retaining many advantages of "hands-on" usage. Due to the special nature of the machine/operating system involved, however this approach may not be available to you.

3. Use the System/360 Simulator (SIM360) described in chapter 4 of this book. This is a simulator which operates as a problem program under a standard IBM batch system to provide a simulated bare machine. Although this approach does not allow for interactive use of the system (i.e. the simulator does not support an operator's console), it does allow the system to be run on a standard machine without disrupting activities.

In view of the similarities between methods two and three, this discussion will deal with two general classes: simulator versus stand-alone (virtual machine) enviroment. In deference to the people without virtual machine facilities, the distribution tape contains a version of the system compatible with the simulator. To get started you may print the listing of the system from the distribution tape, and then use the object as input to the simulator. See section 8.5 for help.

### 6.2.2  Simulator Enviroment:

The simulator essentially provides 360 model 65 processor with 32 K-bytes of memory, one multiplexor channel, four

printers, two card readers, and two card punches. A detailed
description of device addresses and types may be found in chapter
4. The important difference between the simulator-provided
machine and a real one is that the simulator provides a simple
loader, and thus accepts as input standard System/360 object
decks.

The simulator also includes a powerful tracing facility to
allow detailed examination of program flow. To use this facility
specail tracing macro instructions must be assembled in to the
system. This may be accomplished either by changing the
generating macro with the IBM utility IEBUPDTE, or through use of
the assembler ORG psuedo-op instruction coded after the POSGEN
macro for system generation (to be explained).

The ORG method basically goes back and changes previously
assembled code. Note that in the case of the svc trace listing
the TRACE macro instructions were placed in the diagnostic scan
out area to preserve program offsets.

The following assembler code was used to generate the
version of the sample operating system which produced the svc
trace printed in chapter seven of Operating Systems:

```
            POSGEN      CORE=32,READRS=(012,00C),PRINTRS=(010,00E)
            EJECT
PROGRAM     CSECT                   RESTORE CSECT
            ORG         PROGRAM+5 GO BACK TO IPL PSW ADDRESS
            DC          AL3(128)  A(DIAGNOSTIC SCAN OUT AREA)
            ORG         PROGRAM+128
            TRACE       INTRPT,SVC
            LPSW        NEWPSW     CONTINUE WITH IPL PROCESSING
            DS          0D         FORCE ALIGNMENT
NEWPSW      DC          A(0,IPLRTN)
            ORG         PROGRAM+X'123C'
            QUIT                   STOP SIMULATION
            ORG                    RESTORE LOCATION COUNTER
            END
```

## 6.2.3  Simulator Procedures

First you must generate an object deck for the sample
operating system, complete with any changes you wish. Then you
generate any test job streams, remembering that they must be
assembled and prefixed with "$JOB" cards. Then the simulator is
executed, with the file SIMLIN pointing to the object deck for
the system, and SIMIN and/or SIMIN2 containing the test job
streams. When you are using the simulator you should be aware of
the large amount of simulated instructions and real time
necessary to get anything done, and set SIM360 limits
appropriately. If you are using a two job stream system, be sure

453

to specify "CARDS=2,PRINT=2" in the SIM360 parameters.

     For  a  more  complete  discussion  of  the  parameters  and
operating procedures of SIM360, refer to chapter 4.


### 6.2.4   Simulator JCL

     This section contains sample JCL for running one job  stream
on  the  example  operating system under SIM360. This JCL assumes
that you have generated the simulator as directed in  chapter  4.


```
//SIMEXOS EXEC PGM=SIM360,
// PARM='MAXTIME=1000,MAXCOUNT=100000,CARDS=2,PUNCH=0,PRINT=2'
//STEPLIB  DD  DSN=SIM360.LOAD,DISP=SHR
//SIMLIN   DD  DSN=EXOS.OBJECT,DISP=SHR
//SYSPRINT DD  SYSOUT=A
//STRACE   DD  SYSOUT=A
//SIMPRNT  DD  SYSOUT=A
//SIMPRN2  DD  DUMMY,DCB=(RECFM=FBA,LRECL=133,BLKSIZE=133)
//SIMIN    DD  DSN=EXOS.JOBS,DISP=SHR
//SIMIN2   DD  DUMMY,DCB=(RECFM=FB,LRECL=80,BLKSIZE=80)
/*
```

Notes:

   1. SIM360.LOAD must be a PDS containing the  simulator  as
      member   "SIM360".   Instructions  for  creating  this
      dataset are in chapter 4.

   2. The dataset "EXOS.OBJECT" must contain an  object  deck
      for  the  example  system. This may be the one from the
      distribution tape, or you may create a new  version  as
      described later.

   3. The files that are DUMMY'ed are for compatibility.  The
      distributed version of the system is set up for two job
      streams,  so  the  devices  must be there, even if they
      aren't used.

   4. The dataset "EXOS.JOBS" contains jobs  for  the  sample
      operating  system  to run. Remember that a job consists
      of a $JOB card, followed by an object deck, followed by
      any optional data. Any number of jobs may be present in
      an input stream.  The best way to generate  these  jobs
      is  to  use the PUNCH assembler instruction to generate
      job cards as the previous example shows.

   5. When the system has processed all jobs, the  simulation
      will  terminate  by  going into the wait state with no
      interrupts enabled (actually  waiting  for  device  end
      interrupt  from reader). This is normal termination _for_

this system.

## 6.2.5  Stand-Alone Enviroment

The main difficulty associated with using a stand-alone machine is the IPL procedure. This is the procedure whereby the sample operating system is loaded into the machine and execution begun. A special bootstrap loader must be used to load the assembler produced object deck for the system into the machine.

Generating an IPL°able bootstrap loader is essentially a two step process. First the actual IPL program is coded in assembler and assembled. This produces a standard system/360 format object deck. This deck may not be directly loaded by the CPU, however. Another program is used to convert the object deck for the IPL program into an IPL°able form.

We have included on the distribution tape the assembler source for a bootstrap loader, the PL/1 source for a routine to transform object decks into IPL format, and the actual four card IPL deck.

On a 360 an I/O interrupt is generated every time a previously powered down device is turned on. You should exercise caution to insure that you do not generate interrupts in this fashion for devices which the sample operating system does not use. This implies that you must generate a version of the system which "knows" about any devices you wish to use.

An option available on a real machine which is absent in the simulator is console support. Through a system generation option described later you may specify that the system have console support. A clever console support routine could be implemented to ease the process of debugging any modifications to the system. For instance, you could write a routine to selectively halt processes and display/modify storage locations.

## 6.2.6  Stand-Alone Procedures

The following procedures are required to run the sample operating system on a stand-alone basis:

1. Generate the desired configuration of the system and produce an object deck.

2. Generate an IPL deck, as outlined in section 6.2.7.

3. Place the system object deck after the IPL deck in the IPL specified card reader, and press the Load button on the CPU panel. For virtual machine systems, the XFER command may be used to place the IPL deck and the

system object deck into a reader, and then the IPL command is used to start the reader.

4. When the END card of the object deck is read, the system will enter the wait state. To begin processing user job streams, press the STOP button followed by the PSW Restart button on the CPU panel. The system will begin to read jobs from the devices specified for the various job streams. If you are using a virtual machine system, the BEGIN command may be used to simulate the effect of PSW restart. To set up the job streams, the XFER command can be used to fill readers, while the START command will start the processing for that job stream.

If the console handler has been generated for the system, it is operated as follows:

1. To input a command, first press the request button on the operator's console. This will unlock the keyboard and allow input. The equivalent for virtual machine users is two attention requests in a row.

2. Type in the desired command from the set of operator commands that have been implemented. If an error is typed, end the line with a cancel and start again. If correct, end the line with EOB.

Currently only one command is implemented, but extension is straitforward. The implemented command is "DISPLAY CORE xxxxxx", which displays 32 bytes of core starting at <u>hexadecimal</u> address xxxxxx.

## 6.2.7   IPL Program Generation

IPL deck generation is inherently a two step operation. First an IPL program is assembled. The output of this step is a standard System/360 object deck. This deck must be converted to a new format, by a provided PL/1 program (refer to figure 6.2.1).

```
       BOOTSTRAP IPL LOADER FOR 2480                                            PAGE   1

   LOC  OBJECT CODE    ADDR1 ADDR2  STMT    SOURCE STATEMENT                    20 MAY 74

 000000                               2              CSECT                SOURCE CODE OF IPL DECK
 000000                               3              USING  *,0           ADDRESSIBILITY
                                      4       *      CARD 1 CONTAINS ONLY THE NEXT 24 BYTES
 000000  0000000000000070             5   IPLPSW    DC     X'00000000',A(START)
 000008  020000184C000050             6   CCW1      CCW    X'02',CCW3,X'40',80
 000010  020000604000050             7   CCW2      CCW    X'02',NEWPROG-8,X'40',80
                                      8       *      CARD 2 STARTS HERE
 000018  020000A800000050             9   CCW3      CCW    X'02',NEWPROG+64,X'00',80
 000020  0002000000000000            10   DEAD      DC     X'0002000000000000'  FINAL WAIT PSW
 000000                              11   CSW       EQU    64
 000028  000048                      12             ORG    *+X'20'
 000048  000000E0                    13   CAW       DC     A(READCCW)
 00004C                              14             DS     F
 000050  FFFFFFFF                    15   TIMER     DC     F'-1'
 000054  000068                      16             ORG    *+X'14'
                                     17       *      CARD 3 STARTS HERE
 000068  0000000000000088            18   NEWPROG   DC     F'0',A(L2)          FOR ADDR INTERRUPT CAUSED BY
 000070  05F0                        19   START     BALR   15,0                   ZEROING CORE
 000072                              20             USING  *,15               BASE REGISTER 15
 000072  4110 F076          000E8    21             LA     1,BUFFER
 000076  9200 F076          000E8    22             MVI    BUFFER,X'00'
 00007A  D2FF 1001 1000 00001 00000  23   L1        MVC    1(256,1),0(1)      ZERO CORE UNTIL YOU CAUSE
 000080  4111 0100          00100    24             LA     1,256(1)              ADDRESSING INTERRUPT
 000084  47F0 F008          0007A    25             B      L1
 000088  980E 0400          00400    26   L2        LM     0,14,X'400'        CLEAR REGISTERS
 00008C  4820 0002          00002    27             LH     2,2                GET IPL UNIT ADDRESS IN REG 2
 000090  9C00 2000          00000    28   LL1       SIO    0(2)               READ IN THE OBJECT DECK
 000094  9D00 2000          0C000    29   L3        TIO    0(2)               IF AVAILABLE, SEE WHAT KIND
 000098  4780 F03A          000AC    30             BE     L4                    OF CARD WAS READ
 00009C  9102 0044          00044    31             TM     CSW+4,X'02'        IF EXCEPTION, SET FLAG
 0000A0  47E0 F022          00094    32             BNO    L3                    AND STOP
 0000A4  92FF 0027          00027    33             MVI    DEAD+7,X'FF'       SET ERROR CODE IN PSW
                                     34       *      CARD 4 STARTS HERE
 0000A8  8200 0020          0C020    35   L6        LPSW   DEAD               LOAD PSW TO WAIT FOR OPERATOR
 0000AC  95E7 F078          0C0EA    36   L4        CLI    BUFFER+2,C'X'      IS IT A TXT CARD?
 0000B0  4780 F04E          000C0    37             BE     L5
 0000B4  95D5 F078          0C0EA    38             CLI    BUFFER+2,C'N'      IS IT AN END CARD?
 0000B8  4780 F036          000A8    39             BE     L6
 0000BC  47F0 F01E          00090    40             B      LL1                IGNORE ALL OTHERS
 0000C0  9500 F081          000F3    41   L5        CLI    BUFFER+11,X'00'    IF ZERO COUNT, IGNORE
 0000C4  4780 F01E          00090    42             BE     LL1                   THIS CARD
 0000C8  4350 F081          000F3    43             IC     5,BUFFER+11        OTHERWISE, GET COUNT FOR
 0000CC  0650                        44             BCTR   5,0                   MOVING TEXT INTO CORE AT THE
 0000CE  5890 F07A          000EC    45             L      9,BUFFER+4            CORRECT LOCATION
 0000D2  4450 F068          000DA    46             EX     5,MOVE             MOVE TEXT
 0000D6  47F0 F01E          00090    47             B      LL1                GET ANOTHER CARD
 0000DA  D200 9000 F086 0C000 000F8  48   MOVE      MVC    0(0,9),BUFFER+16
 0000E0  020000E800000050            49   READCCW   CCW    X'02',BUFFER,X'00',80
 0000E8                              50   BUFFER    DS     CL80               CARD BUFFER
                                     51             END
```

```
         /* IPL DECK GENERATOR MAY 1974 */                                    PAGE    2


STMT LEVEL NEST
                     /* IPL DECK GENERATOR MAY 1974 */

   1                 IPL: PROC OPTIONS(MAIN);

                     /* THIS PROGRAM PROCESSES THE OBJECT DECK OF AN ASSEMBLY
                        LANGUAGE IPL PROGRAM AND PREPARES IT FOR USE BY A BARE MACHINE.
                        IN SIMPLE TERMS, THIS PROGRAM STRIPS AWAY THE "TXT" CHARACTERS
                        AND ADDS SEQUENCE NUMBERS IN COLUMNS 73-80.
                        NOTE: THE FIRST 24 BYTES ARE SPECIAL.  THEY ARE PUT ON THEIR
                        OWN CARD (THESE BYTES REPRESENT THE IPL PSW AND IPL CCW'S.  */

   2    1      DCL      IN FILE EXTERNAL INPUT RECORD,
                        OUT FILE OUTPUT EXTERNAL RECORD;

   3    1      DCL      (I,J,K,COUNT) FIXED BIN INIT(1);

   4    1      DCL      A CHAR(500) INIT(' ');

   5    1      DCL      SWITCH BIT(1) INIT('1'B);

   6    1      DCL      1 TXT_CARD UNALIGNED BASED(BUFFER_PTR),
                          2 FILLER1 CHAR(1),    /* X'02' */
                          2 TYPE CHAR(3),       /* TYPE OF CARD, TXT, ESD, RLD, END */
                          2 FILLER2 CHAR(2),    /* USELESS */
                          2 ADDRESS FIXED BIN(15),
                                                /* RELATIVE ADDRESS OF THIS DATA */
                          2 FILLER25 CHAR(2),   /* MORE JUNK */
                          2 LENGTH FIXED BIN(15),
                                                /* LENGTH OF DATA AREA IN BYTES */
                          2 FILLER3 CHAR(4),    /* MORE JUNK */
                          2 DATA CHAR(56),      /* DATA FROM TEXT CARD */
                          2 SEQUENCE CHAR(8),   /* SEQUENCING INFORMATION */

                     BUFFER_PTR POINTER;

   7    1      DCL    1 OUT_CARD UNALIGNED,
                        2 OUTPUT CHAR(72),
                        2 NAME CHAR(4) INIT('IPL '),
                        2 SEQ PIC'9999';

                     /* READ IN ALL THE TXT CARDS INTO THE ARRAY "A" */

   8    1      DO WHILE(SWITCH);
   9    1  1      READ FILE(IN) SET(BUFFER_PTR); /* READ A CARD */
  10    1  1      IF TYPE = 'TXT'            /* IS THIS A TXT CARD */
  11    1  1         THEN DO;
  12    1  2            SUBSTR(A,ADDRESS,LENGTH) = DATA;
                                             /* COPY IN DATA */
  13    1  2            I = ADDRESS + LENGTH;
                                             /* BUMP PLACE HOLDER */
  14    1  2         END;
```

458

```
                /* IPL DECK GENERATOR MAY 1974 */                                    PAGE      3

STMT LEVEL NEST

  15    1    1          ELSE IF TYPE = 'END'           /* IS THIS THE LAST CARD */
  16    1    1              THEN SWITCH='0'B;          /* YES, STOP PROCESSING */
  17    1    1          END;                           /* END OF READING LOOP */
                        /* SET UP FIRST CARD AS A SPECIAL CASE */

  18    1           OUTPUT = ' ';                      /* CLEAR AREA */
  19    1           SUBSTR(OUTPUT,1,24) = SUBSTR(A,1,24);
                                                       /* FIRST CARD CASE */
  20    1           J = -47;

  21    1           DO WHILE(J < I);
  22    1    1          SEQ = COUNT;                   /* SET SEQUENCE NUMBER */
  23    1    1          WRITE FILE(OUT) FROM(OUT_CARD);
  24    1    1          COUNT = COUNT + 1;
  25    1    1          J = J +72;
  26    1    1          OUTPUT = SUBSTR(A,J,72);       /* GET NEXT CARD WORTH */
  27    1    1          END;
  28    1           END IPL;
```

459

## 6.3  Maintenance Guide

### 6.3.1  Introduction

This section is intended as a reference and guide to those persons responsible for implementing and maintaining the sample operating system. The system is distributed on a standard distribution tape, described in chapter 8.

The first step towards generating a version of the system is to create a generating macro library. The distribution tape contains the generating macros in a form suitable for input to the IBM utility program IEBUPDTE. The following job may be run to generate a macro library:

```
//MACLIB   EXEC PGM=IEBUPDTE,PARM='NEW'
//SYSPRINT DD   SYSOUT=A
//SYSUT2   DD   DSN=EXOS.MACLIB,DISP=(NEW,CATLG),
//              UNIT=2314,VOL=SER=nnnnnn,
//              DCB=(RECFM=FB,LRECL=80,BLKSIZE=1111),
//              SPACE=(TRK,(35,5),RLSE)
//SYSIN    DD   UNIT=2400,DCB=(RECFM=FB,LRECL=80,BLKSIZE=3200),
//              LABEL=(36,NL)  (see note 3)
/*
```

Notes:

1. nnnnnn should be replaced with the volume serial of the receiving volume. If this volume is other than a 2314, the SPACE and UNIT parameters should be changed accordingly.

2. 1111 should be the same as your installation's blocksize for the dataset "SYS1.MACLIB". This is important!

3. This is a file on the distribution tape, see section 8.5.

Once this macro library has been created, you are free to generate the system as you please.

### 6.3.2  System Generation

The system is coded as one giant macro and two auxiliary macros. To tailor a version of the system to your local needs/configuration, an assembly job of the following form is run:

```
//ASSEM    EXEC PGM=IEUASM,PARM=LOAD,NODECK°
//SYSPRINT DD  SYSOUT=A
//SYSLIB   DD  DSN=EXOS.MACLIB,DISP=SHR
//         DD  DSN=SYS1.MACLIB,DISP=SHR
//SYSUT1   DD  UNIT=SYSDA,SPACE=(CYL,(2,1))
//SYSUT2   DD  UNIT=SYSDA,SPACE=(CYL,(2,1))
//SYSUT3   DD  UNIT=SYSDA,SPACE=(CYL,(2,1))
//SYSGO    DD  whatever you want
//SYSIN    DD  *
         TITLE 'anything that turns you on'
         POSGEN parameters (see below)
         END
/*
```

The POSGEN macro takes several keyword parameters, as follows:

CORE=n, where n is the number of thousand of bytes of core storage to which the system has access. This includes the core necessary to hold the entire system, system and user PCBs and automatic storage, and any free storage desired. Default is 32K (the maximum allowed for the simulator). The amount specified must not exceed the address space of the installation using the system.

READRS=(r1,r2,...,rN), where ri is the channel-device number in hexadecimal (three digits) for the ith card reader of the system. The number of readers specified by this argument list determines the number of job streams that the system will support.

PRINTRS=(p1,p2,...,pN), where pi is the channel-device number in three hexadecimal digits of the ith line printer of the system. The number of printers must match the number of readers, and the devices are paired for the separate job streams in the order specified.

EXCPDEV=(e1,e2,...,eN), where ei is the channel-device number in three hexadecimal digits of the ith exceptional (i.e., non-standard) device on the system. These devices will not be used to process job streams but may be accessed via the EXCP handler by user or system processes.

RDRFPR,PRTFPR,EXCPFPR=(fpr1,fpr2,...,fprN), where each entry corresponds to a device and indicates whether Fast Processing is required. If the field indicates YES, the FAST_PROCESSING_REQUIRED bit in the UCB for that device will be set; default is no fast processing.

CONSOLE=num, where num is the channel-device number in three hexadecimal digits of the operator's console. This

option causes the console handler process to be
generated in the system. The UCB for the console has
Fast Processing Required in effect.


### 6.3.3  Maintenance

The generating macros for the example operating system are
sequenced with an increment of ten, so you may use a standard
on-line editor or the IBM utility program IEBUPDTE to change this
source without getting your hands dirty.

For permanent system changes, the IEBUPDTE route is
suggested as this gives you a permanent copy (the update deck) of
changes made. For temporary changes the editor approach, or if
nothing better the cards and keypunch approach is called for.


### 6.3.4  Operational Problems

The system has been designed to run on any IBM 360/370 model
without major revisions. Any peculiarities due to the
installation to be used should be considered before trying to run
it. For example, the I/O routines provided all assume no
difficulty with channels being busy since a multiplexor channel
is assumed with devices dedicated to a given job stream.

If the channel used is a selector instead of multiplexor
channel, a busy channel could cause problems. One solution is to
associate a channel semaphore as a lock so that more than one I/O
request will not be attempted on a busy channel. Such problems
are, however, very installation-dependent and so there is no
attempt to compensate for them in the system as presented.

```
 _____
|           |
| CHAPTER 7 |
|_____|
```

## 7.1  INTRODUCTION

The processing of large volumes of relatively small student
programs can be handled in a much less general environment than
that provided by IBM's standard Operating System/360.  It is
possible to produce a more specialized environment that
eliminates much unnecessary overhead and, at the same time,
simplifies and streamlines the handling of the student programs.

## 7.2  BATCH MONITOR CONCEPT

### 7.2.1  Purpose

The basic idea of the batch monitor is to eliminate
repetitious overhead normally incurred by each student, by
incurring it once for all students run in a batch.  The monitor
adds its own overhead to the execution of each student, as
discussed below, but job step initiation overhead is only
incurred once.  Assuming the overhead added by the monitor is
lower than step initiation overhead, this approach lowers the
marginal cost of running a student program.

### 7.2.2  Processing of Student Programs

A typical programming exercise consists of the functional
description of a program which the student is to write.  The
student prepares an input deck containing his or her program.
This program is then tested and the results examined to determine
a grade.

Partially to protect the student from the system and
partially to protect the system from the student, a student's
prepared program (deck) is generally entered into the computer
system by a course employee, who has knowledge of Job Control
Language and such things.  As far as the student is concerned, he
or she prepares a program, leaves the deck somewhere, and comes
back later for the results.  While keeping the student somewhat
in the dark about the details of actual job submission
procedures, it does free the course to address itself to only the
pure, system independent aspects of programming.

Once a student's program is prepared, it must be tested. This
testing process usually involves the following four steps, which
must be performed for each program:

1. Input the student's program. This entails reading in the deck which the student has prepared.

2. Translate the student's program into machine language (via a compiler or assembler).

3. If no errors were detected during translation, bind the program with any external subroutines it may require and initiate its execution.

4. Print the output from translation and (if any) execution.

### 7.2.3  Standard OS/360 Processing

In IBM terminology, a job step is, "...that unit of work associated with one processing program." The language translators written by IBM accept as input a source program and output machine language when they are invoked. No further processing is performed. The loader accepts this machine language, loads it into memory, and executes it.

Since each job step may specify only one major program to be executed, two job steps are required to test a student's program. One to translate the program and another to load and execute it. Thus, if the straightforward and obvious method were used for testing n students, 2*n job steps would be required.

### 7.2.4  Batch Monitor Processing

The batch monitor is executed by one job step, which contains all the file definitions (JCL) for the translator and loader. For input, the monitor takes a stream or "batch" of student program decks, separated by special delimiter cards. After its execution is initiated, the monitor performs the following processing:

1. Interpretation of parameters entered from the JCL. These parameters control the optional features of the monitor, such as logging of students and their results, and convey required information like the names of the translator and loader programs.

2. Location of the translator and loader programs in the file system. This involves use of the BLDL macro.

3. Spooling of a student's deck. If the input file is empty, proceed to step eight, else copy cards from the monitor input file to a disk scratch file, until a terminator is reached, or there are no more cards. At this point the scratch file contains one complete student program.

4. Invocation of the translator. The specified translator
   is invoked, passing it the program collected in the
   scratch file. Output from the translator is saved in
   another scratch file.

5. Return code checking. Examine the translator return
   code to see if errors were encountered. If so, repeat
   step three to process the next student.

6. Student execution. The program specified as the loader
   is invoked to bind the student's program with any
   needed external subroutines, load it into core, and
   execute it.

7. Loader termination handling. When the loader
   terminates, the student's program has finished
   executing. Note that this may be an abnormal
   termination. When the current student is finished,
   step three is repeated to process the next student.

8. Monitor termination handling. When all students have
   been processed, the monitor must terminate its
   execution. This releases any resources allocated to the
   monitor's job step.

In addition to this bare minimum processing, the monitor may
perform several amenities which expedite the student running
process. These include: keeping a log of student names, along
with their translator and loader return codes; printing paging
separators identifying student output; and rewarding of students.
These facilities are described in more detail in the next
section.

## 7.3   OPERATION AND USE OF BATCH MONITOR

This section describes the operation and use of the batch monitor. This program may be used for virtually any two step computing task. It is driven from a large set of execution time parameters to allow greater flexibility.

### 7.3.1   Operating Sequence

Basically, the batch monitor reads an input stream of student decks, performing the same processing for each deck. Decks are preceded by a "$JOB" card specifying the student's name, and terminated by a "$EOJ" card. The processing performed for each deck is fairly simple, as follows:

1. Each student's deck is spooled onto a dataset defined by SYSWORK. This spooling process strips off the two control cards.

2. If the separator option is specified, a program named by a parameter is linked to, to print student separators. This routine's input specifications appear in Section 7.5.1.

3. A parameter-defined translater program is invoked for the student. The alternate ddname list option is used by this call, therefore the translator must be IBM compatible. (See, for example, either page 47 of "Assembler(F) Programmer's Guide," IBM publication number GC26-3756, or page 62 of "PL/I(F) Programmer's Guide," IBM publication number GC28-6594.) The ddname SYSIN is changed to SYSWORK, the ddname SYSLIB is changed to TLIB, and the ddname SYSLIN is changed to SYSGO. These changes avoid confusion with loader and run-time datasets, which would result from all of the JCL for two steps appearing at once.

4. The translator's return code is compared to a parameter to see if the student will be allowed to run. If not, the loader phase is skipped.

5. If the student's translater return code was acceptable, the loader is invoked to run the student. Parameters may be specified for the loader and the student, and the loader program's name is a parameter.

6. If the rewarding option has been specified, the loader completion code is examined. Except for the case of loader errors, this is a return code from the student's program. If this value is equal to a supplied parameter, a program is linked to. This allows grading programs to indicate a student's score, for possible

rewarding. The input description for this routine is
given in Section 7.5.2.

7. If the logging option is specified, the student's name
   from his or her "SJOB" card is saved, along with
   translator and loader return codes. This information is
   formatted on the file SYSLOG.

8. This concludes processing of the current student. Step
   one is repeated for the next student, until the input
   stream is empty.

This monitor is very tolerant of student control card
errors, including omission. All but the most pathological cases
are correctly handled. The loader program is attached, so a
student abend will not affect the monitor, unless the STEP option
was coded. The monitor is reentrant, so it may be installed in
the Link Pack Area to prevent student damage.


## 7.3.2 Options

The monitor accepts many options. Some of these options may
contain subfields, for instance to pass the translator two
parameters "LOAD" and "NODECK", you would code
"TP=(LOAD,NODECK)". The parentheses are necessary for correct
monitor parameter parsing, but are not passed to the translator.
Whenever a program name is called for, its length must be less
than or equal to eight characters. The monitor options, with
their abbreviations, and default values, are:

SEP, SEPERATOR- If specified, the paging separator option is
   turned on. This causes a special module to be LINK'ed
   to print output separators for a student. The default
   for this option is on.

NOSEP, NOSEPERATOR- If specified, turns off the student
   output separator feature.

SN, SNAME- Specifies the name of a load module in the
   current STEPLIB or LINKLIB, which will be invoked to
   print separators, if the SEP option is in effect. The
   default for this parameter is SEPRTN.

LOG- If specified, causes the student log to be maintained.
   This requires the monitor file SYSLOG. The default for
   this option is on.

NOLOG- If specified, turns off the logging option.

LC, LINECNT- An unsigned integer specifying the number of
   lines to be printed per page of the SYSLOG dataset. The
   default is 55.

REW- If specified, indicates the student rewarding option is
in effect. The default for this option is off. This
option uses the following two parameters.

RS, REWARDSCORE- An unsigned integer specifying the loader
return code which will cause the rewarding module to be
invoked. The default is 100.

RN, RNAME- Name of module invoked to perform student
rewarding when the student's loader return code matches
the rewarding score. Same restrictions as SNAME. The
default is REWARD.

NOREW- If specified, turns off the student rewarding
feature.

TN, TNAME- Specifies name of translator program. This name
should exist either in the JOBLIB or STEPLIB; or in
LINKLIB. The default is ASMBLRF.

TP, TPARMS- A parenthesized list of options to be passed to
the translator. The default for this parameter is
(LOAD,NODECK).

MR, MAXRET- An unsigned integer specifying the maximum
allowed translator return code. Students with a value
higher than this will not be loaded. The default is 4.

LN, LNAME- Name of loader program. Same restrictions as
TNAME. The default is IEWLDRGO.

LP, LPARMS- A parenthesized list of options to be passed to
the loader program. The default is (NOPRINT).

GP, GPARMS- Parenthesized parameter string passed to the
grader, subject to the ZS parameter below. The default
is (), ie. null.

ZS, ZSCORE- A character string which will be appended to the
specified GP string whenever the current student had a
control card error. This allows the monitor to
communicate to grading programs. This parameter should
be parenthesized and its default is (BADJCL=1).


These parameters may be specified in any order in the PARM
field of the EXEC statement for the monitor's job step. The
batch monitor requires the following files, with qualifications
mentioned:

MONIN- Always required; contains the student decks with
their monitor control cards. This file should have the
DCB attributes RECFM=FB, LRECL=80, and BLKSIZE= some

multiple of 80.

SYSWORK- Always required; used to spool the  student  decks.
Should  have  DCB  attributes similar to MONIN, but not
necessarily the same block size.

SYSLOG- Required if the LOG option is in effect.  This  file
should  have  the  DCB attributes RECFM=VBA, LRECL=125,
and BLKSIZE= n*125+4 (ie. 129, 2004, etc.).

SYSPRINT- Required if the SEP or REW options are in  effect.
Also used by translator and student. DCB attributes may
be  any commonly used translator compatible attributes.

SYSGO- Required by translator to output machine  code.  Same
DCB restrictions as MONIN.

TLIB- Required if students are to use macros (assembler)  or
include  files (PL/1).  Should  point  to  a PDS with
correct attributes for translator.

SYSLIN- Provides input file for loader program. Usually this
defines a set of concatenated  file definitions,  with
SYSGO's  dataset  appearing  somewhere (refer  to  the
example, below).

SYSLIB- Used to specify a dynamic linking  library  for  the
loader.  If  PL/1  is  used  this should point to the
dataset "SYS1.PL1LIB."

Any other files  required  by  the  translator,  loader,  or
student  should  be  freely  declared,  as  long  as  they do not
conflict with the required file names. Note that  SYSIN  is  free
for student use.

The monitor is divided into three assembly language routines
totalling  2200  lines  of  code.   It requires from 8K to 20K of
storage, depending on the  options  specified  and  buffer  sizes
(file block sizes).   This  should be taken into account before
assigning a region size. Any parameter  errors  will  cause  the
monitor to terminate, with an explanator message.


7.3.3  Example

The  following  example  illustrates  the  monitor  used  to
process PL/1 assignments. A prelinked load module is used to hold
the governing procedure which watches  the  student's  execution.
Therefore,  the student is second in the concatenating order. The
allocation step cuts down overhead in the monitor step.

JCL for Running the Monitor with PL/1

```
//A          EXEC PGM=IEFBR14
//DD1        DD   DSN=&&GO,DISP=(NEW,PASS),UNIT=SYSDA,
//                SPACE=(TRK,(10,4)),
//                DCB=(RECFM=FB,LRECL=80,BLKSIZE=1600)
//DD2        DD   DSN=&&WK,DISP=(NEW,PASS),UNIT=SYSDA,
//                SPACE=(TRK,(10,4)),
//                DCB=(RECFM=FB,LRECL=80,BLKSIZE=2000)
//DD3        DD   DSN=&&T1,DISP=(NEW,PASS),UNIT=SYSDA,
//                SPACE=(TRK,(10,4)),
//                DCB=(RECFM=FB,LRECL=80,BLKSIZE=1600)
//M          EXEC PGM=MONITOR,
// PARM=('TP=(LO,NO,NOL,NE),TN=IEMAA,SEP',
//     'LP=(NOPRINT,EP=STEAL)')
//STEPLIB    DD   DSN=U.M20153.11272.MONITOR.LOAD,DISP=SHR
//           DD   DSN=U.M20153.11272.COPY.MITPL1,DISP=SHR
//SYSLOG     DD   SYSOUT=A,DCB=(RECFM=VBA,LRECL=125,BLKSIZE=2004)
//SYSWORK    DD   DSN=*.A.DD2,VOL=REF=*.A.DD2,
//                DCB=*.A.DD2,DISP=(OLD,PASS)
//SYSPRINT   DD   SYSOUT=A,DCB=(RECFM=VBA,LRECL=125,BLKSIZE=2004)
//SYSLIB     DD   DSN=SYS1.PL1LIB,DISP=SHR
//SYSUT1     DD   DSN=*.A.DD3,VOL=REF=*.A.DD3,
//                DISP=(OLD,PASS)
//SYSGO      DD   DSN=*.A.DD1,VOL=REF=*.A.DD1,
//                DCB=*.A.DD1,DISP=(OLD,PASS)
//SYSLOUT    DD   DUMMY
//SYSLIN     DD   DSN=U.M20153.11272.PL1MP.LOAD(P1),DISP=SHR
//           DD   DSN=*.A.DD1,VOL=REF=*.A.DD1,
//                DCB=*.A.DD1,DISP=(OLD,PASS)
//SYSIN      DD   DSN=U.M20153.11272.PL1MP.DATA(P1),DISP=SHR
//MONIN  DD   DATA,DCB=(RECFM=FB,LRECL=80,BLKSIZE=2000)
$JOB name of student one, in free form

 _
I
I deck for student one
I_

$EOJ
$JOB name of student two

 _
I
I deck for student two
I_

$EOJ

     repeated for other students

/*
```

## 7.4   GOVERNING PROGRAM

### 7.4.1   Purpose

In order to provide a means to test the correctness of the
student programs and to monitor student resource usage, special
procedures have been developed. The basic idea is that unknown
(invisible in all respects) to the student, a special governing
program receives control before the student's program. This
program establishes a CPU timer with the Operating System. If
the student exceeds this limit, the governing procedure regains
control and prints diagnostic information. In addition, this
procedure may be used to provide test cases to the student
program and assign a grade to the student.

### 7.4.2   Loop Prevention Procedure

IBM operating systems enforce execution limits at the job
step level. That is, a programmer may specify limits on
execution time and printed output for a job step. When one of
these limits is exceeded, the job step is terminated abruptly.
When the batch monitor is used, many students are to be run under
one job step. If each student were to be allowed ten seconds of
CPU time, then the batch monitor's job step must be given a time
limit in seconds equal to ten times the number of students.

Now suppose the first student, out of a batch of twenty,
codes a program which loops indefinitely. This student is going
to use the job step's entire time limit. Furthermore, since the
operating system terminates such a step abruptly, there is no way
to tell the student where he or she was within the program, or
the values of any variables. Since the program ostensibly looked
correct in the first place, the student will probably not be
certain of the error. In order to locate the problem, the
student may have to submit the program over and over again with
minor changes.

The simplistic approach would be to have the monitor act
like the initiator in monitoring the CPU usage of the loader when
it is invoked for a student. The IBM operating system makes this
approach very complex, and not fool-proof. Also this approach
will probably not help the student much.

An alternate approach is to execute the students program
concurrently with a loop preventing governor. This governor
would trap any potential loops and perform the correct diagnostic
action. This would be a simple program dump with PSW and
registers, for assembly language problems. For problems using a
higher-level language such as PL/I, this processing is more
complicated.

A set of subroutines and procedures has been implemented to effect the correct governing behavior, or at least make it easy to add to existing programs. The essential precept of this governing approach is that the student's program be executed as a subroutine of a procedure which establishes handlers for looping conditions.

### 7.4.3 Assembly Language Governing Procedure

An assembly language student assignment should be handled in the following fashion:

1.  All students code their programs with the same given CSECT label.

2.  A governing procedure is coded which is placed in the loader input stream physically before the student's program. Additionally, a special CSECT is placed after the student's program in the loader input stream.

3.  This governing procedure uses the STIMER macro with the TASK option to set up a CPU timer.

4.  The student's program is called, with any suitable parameters. When the student returns, the timer is cancelled.

5.  The exit routine specified in the STIMER macro should first close all open files, then obtain the student's registers and PSW, following the procedure outlined later. Then the student's program should be dumped from its start (remember, we know its CSECT name), to its end, which is found from the special CSECT we stuck after the student. Following the dump, the student's program is terminated.

### 7.4.4 PL/I Governing Procedure

For student assignments written in PL/I, a more elaborate governing package has been developed. A major benefit of this package is that is provides a convenient interface to the STIMER timing facilities of the operating system. A detailed description of the interfaces to and internals of the governing routines can be found in Section 3.4. An example monitor program illustrating the use of the governing procedure can be found in Section 3.5.

## 7.5  SEPARATOR AND REWARDING ROUTINES

### 7.5.1  Separator Routine Input Specifications

The separator routine is invoked to print output separators on the file SYSPRINT, if the SEP option is in effect. This routine is invoked dynamically by the monitor, via the LOAD macro. The name used is obtained from the SN parameter. Then the routine is BALR'ed to for each student.

Upon entry to this routine, register 15 contains a base address, register 14 contains a return address, and register one points to a five word parameter list, as follows:

1. Pointer to DCB for SYSPRINT. This DCB is opened, with any DCB attributes compatible with the translator being used. If the user leaves the DCB information off of the SYSPRINT DD card, the default attributes of RECFM=VBA, LRECL=125, BLKSIZE=129 are supplied.

2. Contains the address of a character string student identifier, obtained from the student's $JOB card.

3. Length of the student identifier from above.

4. Pointer to 80 character control card one, which was supplied by student.

5. Pointer to 80 character control card two.

The supplied default separator routine prints the student's control cards at the top of an even page, then the student identifier in block letters.

### 7.5.2  Rewarding Routine Input Specifications

If the rewarding option is in effect, this routine is LINK'ed to when a student's leader return code matches a supplied rewarding score. The name used in the LINK request is supplied as parameter RN.

Upon entry to this routine, register 15 contains a base address, register 14 contains a return address, and register one points to a one word parameter list. This word contains the address of an open DCB for the file SYSPRINT. The DCB attributes of this file may be any translator compatible combinations.

The supplied default rewarding module skips to the top of a page, prints a congratulatory message, opens the file REWARDIN, and copies it onto the SYSPRINT file. It assumes that the dataset specified by REWARDIN has the DCB attributes RECFM=FBA,

LRECL=121, and BLKSIZE= some multiple of 121. It correctly handles any popular SYSPRINT DCB attribute combination.

## 7.6  EVALUATION OF BATCH MONITOR APPROACH

### 7.6.1  Design Goals

#### 7.6.1.1  Compatibility

A difficulty with previous monitor designs had been that programs which ran under them required extensive modifications, that is the monitor provided an environment dissimilar to the standard IBM environment. Thus, programs could not be tested without the monitor, and programs used under the monitor contained non-standard coding constructs which made them hard to understand. Therefore, a design objective for this batch monitor program was that it provide an environment identical to the standard environment as far as student programs are concerned.

#### 7.6.1.2  Flexibility

It is necessary to be flexible in the action that should be taken when a student exceeds execution limits. This action, in general depends on the language which the student is using.  For assembler language, a dump of the student's program, registers, and PSW will suffice; while for PL/I, an ERROR condition sould be raised, enabling the student to perform higher level debugging. This is one of the reasons why the batch monitor leaves the issue of governing to its subordinate programs.

### 7.6.2  Operational Costs

When the batch monitor is used, it incurs a certain cost in initializing itself to accept student input. This cost is a function of monitor options and includes any job step charge. After the cost of this initialization is paid, each student saves two job step charges, plus much of the overhead of job step initiation. However, each student is penalized with an overhead cost, previously nonexistent. This is the cost of spooling the student's deck onto an intermediate scratch file before translation.

Without the monitor, each student's deck is read only once. With the monitor, each student's deck is read once and written once to get it on the scratch file, and then it is read again. This introduces an overhead factor proportional to the size of a student's deck. For suitably large decks this overhead factor outweighs the two step charges and initiation overhead savings.

This gives rise to a "break even" student deck size, above which the monitor is not cheaper. It may still be worthwhile to operate in this region if some monitor features are being used to

expedite operational efficiency of the running process.  A
quantitative determination of this breakeven point is necessarily
tied to the type of machine and billing structure being used.

## 7.6.2.1  Determining Fixed Overhead

The fixed and deck-size dependent factors of batch monitor
overhead may be quantitatively determined by two relatively
simple experiments.  To determine the fixed overhead, the
translator and loader names are set to IEFBR14, a system provided
utility which merely returns once it is invoked.  Then the
monitor is executed with all appropriate options and an empty
input stream. The monitor must undergo all fixed overhead items,
including job step initiation, monitor initialization, monitor
termination, and job step termination.

## 7.6.2.2  Determining Spool Overhead

After the fixed overhead has been determined, the spooling
overhead may be found by another experiment. The translator name
is set to a special test program, which merely reads its input
using QSAM I/O (same as translators). The monitor is then
executed three times, with 50, 100, and 200 card student decks in
the input stream. The costs for these three runs are compared,
and their difference is a direct measurement of the deck-size
dependant overhead. Three points are taken to determine if this
charge is linear, as predicted. If the charge turns out to be
nonlinear, the billing structure in use is suspect.

## 7.6.2.3  Experimental Results

These experiments may be performed at any installation using
its accounting procedures and rates to determine the break even
point, or estimate the gains derivable from use of the batch
monitor.

These experiments were performed on the MIT Information
Processing Center's Model 168 running OS/MVT. The tables below
summarize the results obtained using MIT's pricing structure
($12.00 per CPU minute, $1.20 per thousand I/O operations, $.10
per job step, and exponential memory costs). CPU times are in
seconds:

```
            w/o Log and Separators  |  w Log and Separators
CPU     .06      $0.01              |  .12       $0.02
I/O     59       $0.07              |  61        $0.07
MEMORY  16K      $0.04             |  24K       $0.05
subtotal         $0.11             |            $0.12
step charge      $0.10             |            $0.10
total            $0.21             |            $0.22
```

### Fixed Overhead for Batch Monitor

| | w/o Log and Separators per hundred cards | | w Log and Separators per hundred cards | |
|---|---|---|---|---|
| CPU | .04 | $0.01 | .04 | $0.01 |
| I/O | 6 | $0.01 | 6 | $0.01 |
| MEMORY | - | $0.01 | - | $0.01 |
| total | | $0.03 | | $0.03 |

### Spooling Overhead for Batch Monitor

As predicted, the spooling charge (deck-size dependent overhead) was linear, and did not depend on monitor options in effect. Also, the amenity options (log and separators) added only $0.01 to the fixed overhead cost.

Using these figures, a simple example can be worked. Suppose you are given six decks which average 300 cards, the spooling overhead should be $.09/deck. The fixed overhead, assuming log and separators, is 22/6 = $.04/deck. Thus the total monitor overhead is $.13/deck. Since the NET step charges are $.10, you would expect a savings of $.07/deck.

## 8.1  INTRODUCTION

The aim of this book is to provide an exportable set of
pedagogical aides for programming courses based on the IBM 360 or
370. To this end the source, listings, examples, etc. from the
previous chapters are available for a nominal charge.

The distribution medium chosen is a nine track, 800 BPI,
non-labelled 2400 foot computer tape. The charge includes postage
and cost of the tape. Inquiries may be directed to the authors.

### 8.1.1  Recovering Information From Distribution Tape

The tape is organized into 56 distinct files to facilitate
retrieval of selected components. The first file contains
in-stream procedures and jobs which may be used to restore the
tape contents and later run some of the programs. In general, it
should not be necessary to create any JCL other than installation
dependent JOB or SETUP type cards. The first step should be to
punch this file. The following job may be run:

```
//FILE1     EXEC PGM=IEBGENER
//SYSPRINT  DD   SYSOUT=A
//SYSIN     DD   DUMMY
//SYSUT1    DD   UNIT=2400,VOL=SER=PADIST,LABEL=(1,NL),
//               DISP=(OLD,PASS),DCB=(RECFM=FB,LRECL=80,
//               BLKSIZE=1600,DEN=2)
//SYSUT2    DD   SYSOUT=B,DCB=(RECFM=F,BLKSIZE=80)
//
```

The output of this job will be approximately 1500 cards. The
individual jobs and procedures of this file are in chapter order.

### 8.2  File Descriptions

Each file has one of five possible DCB formats. For
expository purposes these formats are numbered from zero to four

as follows:

  #         DCB Attributes (assuming DEN=2 for 800 BPI)

  0  RECFM=FB,LRECL=80,BLKSIZE=800
  1  RECFM=FBA,LRECL=121,BLKSIZE=1210
  2  RECFM=FBA,LRECL=133,BLKSIZE=1330
  3  RECFM=FB,LRECL=80,BLKSIZE=3200
  4  RECFM=FB,LRECL=80,BLKSIZE=1600

The following table briefly describes each of the tape files, giving the DCB attributes in terms of the previous numbering scheme. Descriptions of the jobs present in file one are in later sections of this chapter.

#--(DCB)          Description

1--(4).Retrieval and miscellaneous JCL.

2--(1).Listings of assembly language grader subroutines, example graders, and link maps.

3--(1).Assembly listings and execution output for assembly language sample solutions.

4--(3).Assembly language grader macros, in form suitable for input to IEBUPDTE (containing ./ ADD cards).

5--(4).Source for assembly language grader subroutines, one CSECT after the next.

6--(4).Object for assembly language grader subroutines, all run together.

7--(4).Source for sample assembly language graders, including PUNCH cards to produce linkage editor control statements.

8--(4).Object for sample assembly language graders, including linkage editor control statements.

9--(3).IEBUPDTE input stream to produce sample grader driving tables.

10-(4).Assembly language source for sample driving tables, including PUNCH statements to generate IEBUPDTE ./ ADD cards.

11-(3).Solutions to sample assembly language problems, including IEBUPDTE control statements to create PDS with solutions as members.

#--(DCB)              DESCRIPTION


12-(0).Unloaded PDS containing assembly language grader load
        modules as members.  Unloaded by IEHMOVE from a  2314
        with full-track blocking.

13-(1).Listings for PL/1 language  graders  including  their
        assembly language subroutines and link maps.

14-(1).Compilation listings and output for example solutions
        to PL/1 language problems.

15-(4).Source for assembly language subroutines used by PL/1
        graders.

16-(4).Object for assembly language subroutines used by PL/1
        graders,  including linkage editor control statements
        to produce a load module PDS with the subroutines  as
        members.

17-(0).Unloaded  PDS  whose  members  are  load  modules  of
        assembly  language  subroutines used by PL/1 graders.
        Produced by IEHMOVE from a 2314.

18-(4).PL/1  source  for  PL/1  language  graders,  many
        subroutines  separated  by  "*PROCESS  cards, some of
        which use the OBJNM option.

19-(4).Object for PL/1 modules of  PL/1  graders,  including
        linkage  editor  control statements to produce grader
        load module PDS.

20-(3).IEBUPDTE input to produce a  PDS  containing  driving
        tables for the PL/1 language graders.

21-(4).Source  for  PL/1  examples  and  sample  solutions,
        including IEBUPDTE  control  statements to create PDS
        with solutions as members.

22-(0).Unloaded PDS containing  PL/1  grader  load  modules.
        Produced by IEHMOVE from 2314.

23-(1).Listings of all routines and link map for  System/360
        simulator (SIM360).

24-(2).Assembly  listing  and  output  for  sample  SIM360
        program.

25-(4).Source  for  assembly  language  subroutine  used  by
        SIM360.

26-(4).Source for PL/1  (F)  modules  of  SIM360,  including
        "*PROCESS" cards.

#--(DCB)              DESCRIPTION


27-(4).Object for SIM360, including both PL/1 and  assembler
       modules.

28-(3).IEBUPDTE input stream to produce  macro  library  for
       SIM360.  This library includes testing macros for the
       interrupt and I/O machine problems.

29-(4).Assembly language source for SIM360 example  program.

30-(0).Unloaded PDS containing load  module  for  SIM360.
       Produced by IEHMOVE from 2314.

31-(2).Assembly listings and output of sample solutions  and
       examples for interrupt and I/O problems.

32-(4).Assembly language source of  examples  and  solutions
       for  interrupt  and  I/O  problems,  with  IEBUPDTE
       statements to produce a PDS.

33-(4).Null file, contains one card. For  future  expansion.

34-(4).Null file, contains one card. For  future  expansion.

35-(1).Assembly listing of Sample Operating  System  (SIM360
       compatible version).

36-(2).Assembly listing and  output  from  example  job  run
       under Sample Operating System.

37-(1).Listings  of  programs  and  output  for  IPL  deck
       generation process.

38-(3).IEBUPDTE  input  stream  to  create  macro  library
       containing  macros  used to generate Sample Operating
       System.

39-(4).Object  for  SIM360-compatible  version  of  Sample
       Operating System.

40-(4).Assembly language source for example Sample Operating
       System job, including PUNCH statement to produce $JOB
       card.

41-(4).Object  for  Sample  Operating  System  example  job,
       including "$JOB" card and data.

42-(4).Assembly  language  source  for  2540  IPL  program
       (bootstrap loader).

43-(4).PL/1 source for program to convert  assembler  output
       (object decks) to bootstrap format.

# 8. DISTRIBUTION TAPE

# 8. DISTRIBUTION TAPE

# 8. DISTRIBUTION TAPE

# 8. DISTRIBUTION TAPE

# 8. DISTRIBUTION TAPE

#-- (DCB)    DESCRIPTION

44-(4).2540 bootstrap IPL deck.

45-(1).Assembly listings and link map for simple batch monitor.

46-(1).Listings (assembly and PL/1 Optimizer) and link map for SIM360 batch monitor.

47-(4).Assembly language source for simple batch monitor.

48-(4).Source for PL/1 modules of SIM360 batch monitor.

49-(4).Source for assembly language modules of SIM360 batch monitor.

50-(4).Object for simple batch monitor.

51-(4).Object for SIM360 batch monitor.

52-(0).Unloaded PDS containing both SIM360 and simple batch monitor load modules as members. Produced by IEHMOVE from 2314.

53-(0).Unloaded PDS containing load modules of Fast PL/1 (F) compiler. Produced by IEHMOVE from 2314.

54-(3).IEBUPDTE input stream for MIT modifications to produce fast PL/1 (F) compiler. These updates apply to the source for version 5.4 of the IBM PL/1 (F) compiler.

55-(4).Jobs to create fast PL/1 (F) compiler. Punch these if you wish to restore and use the fast compiler.

56-(0).Unloaded PDS containing load modules of Fast PL/1 (F) compiler. Produced by IEHMOVE from 3330.

```
//************************************************************************  PAD00010
//*                                                                        PAD00020
//* THIS TAPE IS 9 TRACK, 800 BPI NON-LABELLED.                            PAD00030
//*                                                                        PAD00040
//* IT IS THE PRIMARY DISTRIBUTION TAPE FOR THE PEDAGOGICAL AIDES          PAD00050
//* PROJECT. IT CONTAINS 56 FILES.                                         PAD00060
//*                                                                        PAD00070
//* THIS FIRST FILE CONTAINS ALL THE JOBS NECESSARY TO GENERATE            PAD00080
//* AND USE THE PROGRAMS DESCRIBED IN THE PAD BOOK.                        PAD00090
//*                                                                        PAD00100
//* THE DCB INFORMATION FOR THIS FILE IS:                                  PAD00110
//*                                                                        PAD00120
//*      DCB= (RECFM=FB,LRECL=80;BLKSIZE=1600,DEN=2)                       PAD00130
//*                                                                        PAD00140
//*                PAUL G. GREGORY III                                     PAD00150
//*                                                                        PAD00160
//************************************************************************  PAD00170
//******************** JOB 01 ********************                          PAD00180
//PRINT    EXEC PGM=IEBGENER                                               PAD00190
//*                                                                        PAD00200
//************************************************************************  PAD00210
//*                                                                        PAD00220
//* THIS JOB PRINTS THE ASSEMBLY LANGUAGE PROBLEMS GRADER LISTINGS         PAD00230
//*   FROM THE DISTRIBUTION TAPE.                                          PAD00240
//*                                                                        PAD00250
//************************************************************************  PAD00260
//*                                                                        PAD00270
//SYSPRINT DD   SYSOUT=A                                                   PAD00280
//SYSUT2   DD   SYSOUT=A,DCB=(RECFM=FBA,LRECL=121,BLKSIZE=1210)            PAD00290
//SYSUT1   DD   UNIT=2400,DISP=(OLD,PASS),VOL=SER=PADIST,                  PAD00300
//             LABEL=(2,NL),DCB=(RECFM=FBA,LRECL=121,BLKSIZE=1210)         PAD00310
//SYSIN    DD   DUMMY                                                      PAD00320
//*                                                                        PAD00330
//******** END OF JOB, REPLACE WITH NULL (//) IF APPROPRIATE              PAD00340
//******************** JOB 02 ********************                          PAD00350
//PRINT    EXEC PGM=IEBGENER                                               PAD00360
//*                                                                        PAD00370
//************************************************************************  PAD00380
//*                                                                        PAD00390
//* THIS JOB PRINTS THE SAMPLE SOLUTION LISTINGS                           PAD00400
//*   FROM THE DISTRIBUTION TAPE.                                          PAD00410
//*                                                                        PAD00420
//************************************************************************  PAD00430
//*                                                                        PAD00440
//SYSPRINT DD   SYSOUT=A                                                   PAD00450
//SYSUT2   DD   SYSOUT=A,DCB=(RECFM=FBA,LRECL=121,BLKSIZE=1210)            PAD00460
//SYSUT1   DD   UNIT=2400,DISP=(OLD,PASS),VOL=SER=PADIST,                  PAD00470
//             LABEL=(3,NL),DCB=(RECFM=FBA,LRECL=121,BLKSIZE=1210)         PAD00480
//SYSIN    DD   DUMMY                                                      PAD00490
//*                                                                        PAD00500
//******** END OF JOB, REPLACE WITH NULL (//) IF APPROPRIATE              PAD00510
//******************** JOB 03 ********************                          PAD00520
//DOITA    PROC NAME='',UNIT=SYSDA,VOl=''                                  PAD00530
//*                                                                        PAD00540
//************************************************************************  PAD00550
```

```
                                                                      PAD00560
//*                                                                   PAD00570
//* THIS JOB PRODUCES AN ASSEMBLY LANGUAGE GRADER                     PAD00580
//* LOAD MODULE PDS ON THE DISK &VOL, OF TYPE &UNIT.                  PAD00590
//* THE NAME OF THE PDS WILL BE &NAME.ASSEMMP.LOAD                    PAD00600
//*                                                                   PAD00610
//********************************************************************PAD00620
//*                                                                   PAD00630
//COPYOBJ EXEC PGM=IEBGENER                                           PAD00640
//*                                                                   PAD00650
//********************************************************************PAD00660
//*                                                                   PAD00670
//* THIS STEP COPIES THE OBJECT FOR THE SERVICE ROUTINES              PAD00680
//* ONTO A DISK FILE FOR SUBSEQUENT INCLUSION IN THE LINKAGE          PAD00690
//* EDITING STEP.                                                     PAD00700
//*                                                                   PAD00710
//********************************************************************PAD00720
//*                                                                   PAD00730
//SYSPRINT DD    SYSOUT=A                                             PAD00740
//SYSIN    DD    DUMMY                                                PAD00750
//SYSUT2   DD    DSN=&&OBJ,DISP=(NEW,PASS),UNIT=SYSDA,                PAD00760
//               DCB=(RECFM=FB,LRECL=80,BLKSIZE=1600),                PAD00770
//               SPACE=(TRK,(10,10))                                  PAD00780
//SYSUT1   DD    UNIT=2400,VOL=SER=PADIST,DISP=(OLD,PASS),            PAD00790
//               LABEL=(6,NL),DCB=(RECFM=FB,LRECL=80,BLKSIZE=1600)    PAD00800
//*                                                                   PAD00810
//LINK     EXEC PGM=IEWL,PARM='MAP,LIST,LET'                          PAD00820
//*                                                                   PAD00830
//********************************************************************PAD00840
//*                                                                   PAD00850
//* THIS STEP PRODUCES THE ACTUAL LOAD MODULE PDS                     PAD00860
//*                                                                   PAD00870
//********************************************************************PAD00880
//*                                                                   PAD00890
//SYSPRINT DD    SYSOUT=A                                             PAD00900
//SYSUT1   DD    UNIT=SYSDA,SPACE=(CYL,(2,1))                         PAD00910
//SYSLIN   DD    UNIT=2400,VOL=SER=PADIST,DISP=(OLD,PASS),            PAD00920
//               LABEL=(8,NL),DCB=(RECFM=FB,LRECL=80,BLKSIZE=1600)    PAD00930
//OBJECT   DD    DSN=*.COPYOBJ.SYSUT2,DISP=(OLD,DELETE)               PAD00940
//SYSLMOD  DD    DSN=&NAME..ASSEMMP.LOAD,DISP=(NEW,CATLG),            PAD00950
//               UNIT=(&UNIT),VOL=SER=(&VOL),                         PAD00960
//               SPACE=(TRK,(20,15,1),RLSE)                           PAD00970
//*                                                                   PAD00980
//         PEND                                                       PAD00990
//*                                                                   PAD01000
//         EXEC DOITA                                                 PAD01010
//******** END OF JOB, REPLACE WITH NULL (//) IF APPROPRIATE          PAD01020
//******************** JOB 04 *******************                     PAD01030
//*                                                                   PAD01040
//DOIT2A   PROC NAME='',VOL='',UNIT=SYSDA                             PAD01050
//*                                                                   PAD01060
//********************************************************************PAD01070
//*                                                                   PAD01080
//* THIS JOB CREATES THE ASSEMBLY LANGUAGE PROBLEMS                   PAD01090
//* DATA PDS. THE SYMBOLIC PARAMETER NAME SETS NAME PREFIX,           PAD01100
//* RESULTING NAME WILL BE NAME.ASSEMMP.DATA, VOL GIVES
```

```
//* A VOLUME SERIAL FOR THE DATA PDS, AND UNIT ALLOWS THE USER        PAD01110
//* TO GIVE A SPECIFIC UNIT TYPE.                                     PAD01120
//*                                                                   PAD01130
//*******************************************************************  PAD01140
//*                                                                   PAD01150
//DATA     EXEC PGM=IEBUPDTE,PARM='NEW'                               PAD01160
//SYSPRINT DD  SYSOUT=A                                               PAD01170
//SYSUT2   DD  DSN=&NAME..ASSEMMP.DATA,DISP=(NEW,CATLG),              PAD01180
//             UNIT=(&UNIT),VOL=SER=(&VOL),DCB=(RECFM=FB,LRECL=80,    PAD01190
//             BLKSIZE=1600),SPACE=(TRK,(2,1,2))                      PAD01200
//SYSIN    DD  UNIT=2400,VOL=SER=PADIST,DISP=(OLD,PASS),              PAD01210
//             LABEL=(9,NL),DCB=(RECFM=FB,LRECL=80,BLKSIZE=3200)      PAD01220
//        PEND                                                        PAD01230
//        EXEC DOIT2A                                                 PAD01240
//*                                                                   PAD01250
//******** END OF JOB, REPLACE WITH NULL (//) IF APPROPRIATE         PAD01260
//********************** JOB 05 *********************                 PAD01270
//*                                                                   PAD01280
//PUNCH    EXEC PGM=IEBGENER                                          PAD01290
//*                                                                   PAD01300
//*******************************************************************  PAD01310
//*                                                                   PAD01320
//* THIS JOB PUNCHES THE ASSEMBLY LANGUAGE PROBLEMS SAMPLE SOLUTIONS  PAD01330
//*  FROM THE DISTRIBUTION TAPE.                                      PAD01340
//*                                                                   PAD01350
//*******************************************************************  PAD01360
//*                                                                   PAD01370
//SYSPRINT DD  SYSOUT=A                                               PAD01380
//SYSUT2   DD  SYSOUT=B,DCB=(RECFM=F,BLKSIZE=80)                      PAD01390
//SYSUT1   DD  UNIT=2400,DISP=(OLD,PASS),VOL=SER=PADIST,              PAD01400
//             LABEL=(11,NL),DCB=(RECFM=FB,LRECL=80,BLKSIZE=3200)     PAD01410
//SYSIN    DD  DUMMY                                                  PAD01420
//*                                                                   PAD01430
//******** END OF JOB, REPLACE WITH NULL (//) IF APPROPRIATE         PAD01440
//********************** JOB 06 *********************                 PAD01450
//*                                                                   PAD01460
//*******************************************************************  PAD01470
//*                                                                   PAD01480
//* THIS JOB RUNS A BATCH OF STUDENT ASSEMBLY                         PAD01490
//* LANGUAGE PROBLEMS, USING THE BATCH MONITOR.                       PAD01500
//*                                                                   PAD01510
//* NAME IS USED AS A PREFIX TO THE STANDARD NAMES, AND SHOULD        PAD01520
//* BE SET TO THE SAME VALUE USED TO CREATE THE GRADER LOAD           PAD01530
//* MODULE AND DATA PDS'S, AS WELL AS THE MONITOR LOAD MODULE PDS.    PAD01540
//*                                                                   PAD01550
//* N SHOULD BE SET TO THE PROBLEM NUMBER (A1-A6).                    PAD01560
//*                                                                   PAD01570
//* INBLOCK- THE BLOCKSIZE USED FOR THE                               PAD01580
//* INPUT DATASET. THIS SHOULD BE A MULTIPLE OF 80.                   PAD01590
//*                                                                   PAD01600
//* OUTBLOCK- THE BLOCKSIZE USED FOR OUTPUT DATASETS, SHOULD          PAD01610
//* BE A MULTIPLE OF 121.                                             PAD0162C
//*                                                                   PAD01630
//* THESE SHOULD BE SET TO THE LARGEST VALUE YOUR INSTALLATION        PAD0164C
//* CAN SUPPORT, FOR EFFICIENCY'S SAKE.                               PAD0165C
```

```
//*                                                              PADO1660(
//* NOTE: THIS MEANS INBLOCK=2000, OUTBLOCK=1815                 PADO1670(
//* FOR YOU AL.                                                  PADO1680(
//*                                                              PADO1690(
//****************************************************************PADO1700(
//*                                                              PADO1710(
//MONITOR PROC NAME='',N=A1,OUTBLOCK=129                         PADO1720(
//*                                                              PADO1730(
//RUN     EXEC PGM=MONITOR,                                      PADO1740(
// PARM='LP=(NOPRINT,EP=GRADER),TN=IFUASM,SEP,ZS=(BADJCL=1)'     PADO1750(
//STEPLIB  DD  DSN=&NAME..MONITOR.LOAD,DISP=SHR                  PADO1760(
//SYSLOG   DD  SYSOUT=A                                          PADO1770(
//*TLIB    DD  DSN=SYS1.MACLIB,DISP=SHR                          PADO1780(
//SYSWORK  DD  DSN=*.ALLOC.DD2,VOL=REF=*.ALLOC.DD2,              PADO1790(
//             DISP=(OLD,PASS)                                   PADO1800(
//SYSPRINT DD  SYSOUT=A,DCB=(RECFM=FBA,LRECL=121,BLKSIZE=&OUTBLOCK) PADO1810(
//SYSUT1   DD  DSN=*.ALLOC.DD3,VOL=REF=*.ALLOC.DD3,              PADO1820(
//             DISP=(OLD,PASS)                                   PADO1830(
//SYSUT2   DD  DSN=*.ALLOC.DD4,VOL=REF=*.ALLOC.DD4,              PADO1840(
//             DISP=(OLD,PASS)                                   PADO1850(
//SYSUT3   DD  DSN=*.ALLOC.DD5,VOL=REF=*.ALLOC.DD5,              PADO1860(
//             DISP=(OLD,PASS)                                   PADO1870(
//SYSGO    DD  DSN=*.ALLOC.DD1,VOL=REF=*.ALLOC.DD1,              PADO1880(
//             DISP=(OLD,PASS)                                   PADO1890(
//SYSLOUT  DD  DUMMY,DCB=BLKSIZE=121                             PADO1900(
//SYSLIN   DD  DSN=&NAME..ASSEMMP.LOAD(&N),DISP=SHR              PADO1910(
//         DD  DSN=&NAME..ASSEMMP.DATA(&N),DISP=SHR              PADO1920(
//         DD  DSN=*.ALLOC.DD1,VOL=REF=*.ALLOC.DD1,              PADO1930(
//             DISP=(OLD,PASS)                                   PADO1940(
//         DD  DSN=&NAME..ASSEMMP.DATA(DUMMY),DISP=SHR           PADO1950(
//*                                                              PADO1960(
//         PEND                                                  PADO1970(
//*                                                              PADO1980(
//*                                                              PADO1990(
//ALLOC   EXEC PGM=IEFBR14                                       PADO2000(
//*                                                              PADO2010(
//****************************************************************PADO2020(
//*                                                              PADO2030(
//* THIS STEP ALLOCATES AND FORMATS FILES                        PADO2040(
//*                                                              PADO2050(
//****************************************************************PADO2060(
//*                                                              PADO2070(
//DD1      DD  DSN=&&TEMP,DISP=(NEW,PASS),SPACE=(CYL,            PADO2080(
//             (2,1)),DCB=(RECFM=FB,LRECL=80,BLKSIZE=1600),      PADO2090(
//             UNIT=SYSDA                                        PADO2100(
//DD2      DD  DSN=&&WORK,DISP=(NEW,PASS),SPACE=(CYL,            PADO2110(
//             (2,1)),DCB=(RECFM=FB,LRECL=80,BLKSIZE=1600),      PADO2120(
//             UNIT=SYSDA                                        PADO2130(
//DD3      DD  DSN=&&UT1,DISP=(NEW,PASS),SPACE=(CYL,             PADO2140(
//             (1,1)),UNIT=SYSDA                                 PADO2150(
//DD4      DD  DSN=&&UT2,DISP=(NEW,PASS),SPACE=(CYL,             PADO2160(
//             (1,1)),UNIT=SYSDA                                 PADO2170(
//DD5      DD  DSN=&&UT3,DISP=(NEW,PASS),SPACE=(CYL,             PADO2180(
//             (1,1)),UNIT=SYSDA                                 PADO2190(
//*                                                              PADO2200(
```

```
//          EXEC MONITOR                                                        PAD02210
//RUN.MONIN DD DATA,DCB=(RECFM=FB,LRECL=80,BLKSIZE=80) <- &INBLOCK              PAD02220
* STUDENT JOBS GO HERE, WITH $JOB AND $EOJ CARDS                                PAD02230
//****** REPLACE THIS CARD WITH A FILE TERMINATOR /*  ******                    PAD02240
//******** END OF JOB, REPLACE WITH NULL (//) IF APPROPRIATE                    PAD02250
//******************** JOB 07 *******************                               PAD02260
//*                                                                             PAD02270
//******************************************************************** ****** PAD02280
//*                                                                             PAD02290
//* THIS JOB RUNS STUDENT ASSEMBLY LANGUAGE PROBLEMS                            PAD02300
//* WITHOUT THE BATCH MONITOR. EACH STUDENT IS RUN AS TWO                       PAD02310
//* STEPS, ASSEMBLY AND THEN LOAD. THE FOLLOWING                                PAD02320
//* SYMBOLIC VARIABLES ARE USED IN THE PROCEDURE:                               PAD02330
//*                                                                             PAD02340
//* NAME- A PREFIX TO THE GRADER LOAD MODULE AND DATA PDS'S.                     PAD02350
//* THIS SHOULD BE THE SAME VALUE SPECIFIED WHEN THESE DATASETS                 PAD02360
//* WHERE CREATED.                                                              PAD02370
//*                                                                             PAD02380
//* N- THE PROBLEM NUMBER BEING RUN, (A1-A6).                                   PAD02390
//*                                                                             PAD02400
//* INBLOCK- THE BLOCKSIZE USED FOR THE                                         PAD02410
//* INPUT DATASET. THIS SHOULD BE A MULTIPLE OF 80.                             PAD02420
//*                                                                             PAD02430
//* OUTBLOCK- THE BLOCKSIZE USED FOR OUTPUT DATASETS, SHOULD                    PAD02440
//* BE A MULTIPLE OF 121.                                                       PAD02450
//*                                                                             PAD02460
//* THESE SHOULD BE SET TO THE LARGEST VALUE YOUR INSTALLATION                  PAD02470
//* CAN SUPPORT, FOR EFFICIENCY'S SAKE.                                         PAD02480
//*                                                                             PAD02490
//* NOTE: THIS MEANS INBLOCK=2000, OUTBLOCK=1815                                PAD02500
//* FOR YOU AL.                                                                 PAD02510
//*                                                                             PAD02520
//******************************************************************** ****** PAD02530
//*                                                                             PAD02540
//MP1       PROC NAME=' ',N=A1,OUTBLOCK=129                                     PAD02550
//C         EXEC PGM=IEUASM,PARM=(LOAD,NODECK)                                  PAD02560
//SYSPRINT DD  SYSOUT=A,DCB=(RECFM=FBM,LRECL=121,BLKSIZE=&OUTBLOCK)             PAD02570
//SYSUT1    DD  DSN=&&UT1,DISP=(OLD,PASS)                                       PAD02580
//SYSUT2    DD  DSN=&&UT2,DISP=(OLD,PASS)                                       PAD02590
//SYSUT3    DD  DSN=&&UT3,DISP=(OLD,PASS)                                       PAD02600
//SYSLIN    DD  DDNAME=SYSGO                                                    PAD02610
//SYSGO     DD  DSN=&&TEMP,DISP=(OLD,PASS)                                      PAD02620
//G         EXEC PGM=IEWLDRGO,COND=(4,LE,C),                                    PAD02630
//               PARM='NOPRINT,EP=GRADER',                                      PAD02640
//               TIME=(0,1)                                                     PAD02650
//SYSLOUT   DD  DUMMY,DCB=BLKSIZE=121                                           PAD02660
//SYSLIN    DD  DSN=&NAME..ASSEMMP.LOAD(&N),DISP=SHR                            PAD02670
//          DD  DSN=&NAME..ASSEMMP.DATA(&N),DISP=SHR                            PAD02680
//          DD  DSN=&&TEMP,DISP=(OLD,PASS)                                      PAD02690
//          DD  DSN=&NAME..ASSEMMP.DATA(DUMMY),DISP=SHR                         PAD02700
//SYSPRINT DD  SYSOUT=A,DCB=(RECFM=FBA,LRECL=121,BLKSIZE=&OUTBLOCK)             PAD02710
//          PEND                                                                PAD02720
//*                                                                             PAD02730
//ALLOC     EXEC PGM=IEFBR14                                                    PAD02740
//*                                                                             PAD02750
```

```
//*************************************************************** PAD0276C
//*                                                             PAD02770
//* THIS STEP ALLOCATES AND FORMATS WORK DATASETS              PAD0278C
//*                                                             PAD02790
//*************************************************************** PAD02800
//*                                                             PAD02810
//DD1      DD   DSN=&&TEMP,DISP=(NEW,PASS),                     PAD02820
//              UNIT=SYSDA,SPACE=(TRK,(2,1)),                   PAD02830
//              DCB=(RECFM=FB,LRECL=80,BLKSIZE=1600)            PAD02840
//DD2      DD   DSN=&&UT1,DISP=(NEW,PASS),                      PAD02850
//              UNIT=SYSDA,SPACE=(TRK,(10,5)),                  PAD02860
//              DCB=(RECFM=FB,LRECL=80,BLKSIZE=1600)            PAD02870
//DD3      DD   DSN=&&UT2,DISP=(NEW,PASS),                      PAD02880
//              UNIT=SYSDA,SPACE=(TRK,(10,5)),                  PAD02890
//              DCB=(RECFM=FB,LRECL=80,BLKSIZE=1600)            PAD02900
//DD4      DD   DSN=&&UT3,DISP=(NEW,PASS),                      PAD02910
//              UNIT=SYSDA,SPACE=(TRK,(10,5)),                  PAD02920
//              DCB=(RECFM=FB,LRECL=80,BLKSIZE=1600)            PAD02930
//SMITH    EXEC MP1                                             PAD02940
//C.SYSIN DD   *,DCB=(RECFM=FB,LRECL=80,BLKSIZE=80) <- &INBLOCK PAD02950
* SMITH'S DECK GOES HERE, WITHOUT $JCB AND $EOJ CARDS          PAD02960
//* REPLACE THIS CARD WITH A FILE TERMINATOR /*               PAD02970
//JONES    EXEC MP1                                             PAD02980
//C.SYSIN DD   *,DCB=(RECFM=FB,LRECL=80,BLKSIZE=80) <- &INBLOCK PAD02990
* JONES' DECK GOES HERE. SUBSEQUENT DECKS AS OBVIOUS           PAD03000
//* SHOULD BE REPLACED BY TERMINATOR /*                        PAD03010
//******* END OF JOB, REPLACE WITH NULL (//) IF APPROPRIATE    PAD03020
//********************* JOB 08 *********************            PAD03030
//*                                                             PAD03040
//PRINT    EXEC PGM=IEBGENER                                    PAD03050
//*                                                             PAD03060
//*************************************************************** PAD03070
//*                                                             PAD03080
//* THIS JOB PRINTS THE PL/1 PROBLEM GRADER LISTINGS           PAD03090
//*   FROM THE DISTRIBUTION TAPE.                              PAD03100
//*                                                             PAD03110
//*************************************************************** PAD03120
//*                                                             PAD03130
//SYSPRINT DD   SYSOUT=A                                        PAD03140
//SYSUT2   DD   SYSOUT=A,DCB=(RECFM=FBA,LRECL=121,BLKSIZE=1210) PAD03150
//SYSUT1   DD   UNIT=2400,DISP=(OLD,PASS),VOL=SER=PADIST,       PAD03160
//              LABEL=(13,NL),DCB=(RECFM=FBA,LRECL=121,BLKSIZE=1210) PAD03170
//SYSIN    DD   DUMMY                                           PAD03180
//*                                                             PAD03190
//******* END OF JOB, REPLACE WITH NULL (//) IF APPROPRIATE    PAD03200
//********************* JOB 09 *********************            PAD03210
//*                                                             PAD03220
//PRINT    EXEC PGM=IEBGENER                                    PAD03230
//*                                                             PAD03240
//*************************************************************** PAD03250
//*                                                             PAD03260
//* THIS JOB PRINTS THE SAMPLE SOLUTIONS TO PL/1 PROBLEMS      PAD03270
//*   FROM THE DISTRIBUTION TAPE.                              PAD03280
//*                                                             PAD03290
//*************************************************************** PAD03300
```

```
//*                                                                    PAD03310
//SYSPRINT DD    SYSOUT=A                                              PAD03320
//SYSUT2   DD    SYSOUT=A,DCB=(RECFM=FBA,LRECL=121,BLKSIZE=1210)       PAD03330
//SYSUT1   DD    UNIT=2400,DISP=(OLD,PASS),VOL=SER=PADIST,             PAD03340
//               LABEL=(14,NL),DCB=(RECFM=FBA,LRECL=121,BLKSIZE=1210)  PAD03350
//SYSIN    DD    DUMMY                                                 PAD03360
//*                                                                    PAD03370
//******** END OF JOB, REPLACE WITH NULL (//) IF APPROPRIATE          PAD03380
//********************* JOB 10 *******************                      PAD03390
//*                                                                    PAD03400
//*************************************************************************  PAD03410
//*                                                                    PAD03420
//* THIS JOB CREATES A PDS WHOSE MEMBERS ARE LOAD MODULES              PAD03430
//* OF THE PL/1 GRADER ASSEMBLY LANGUAGE SUBROUTINES                   PAD03440
//*                                                                    PAD03450
//*************************************************************************  PAD03460
//*                                                                    PAD03470
//DOITB    PROC NAME='',UNIT=SYSDA,VOL=''                              PAD03480
//*                                                                    PAD03490
//*************************************************************************  PAD03500
//*                                                                    PAD03510
//* NAME IS A NAME PREFIX, VOL IS A VOLUME SERIAL,                     PAD03520
//* UNIT IS A UNIT SPECIFICATION, USED IF VOL IS SPECIFIED.           PAD03530
//*                                                                    PAD03540
//*************************************************************************  PAD03550
//*                                                                    PAD03560
//MAKE1    EXEC PGM=IEWL,PARM='MAP,LIST,LET'                           PAD03570
//SYSPRINT DD    SYSOUT=A                                              PAD03580
//SYSUT1   DD    UNIT=SYSDA,SPACE=(CYL,(2,1))                          PAD03590
//SYSLIN   DD    UNIT=2400,VOL=SER=PADIST,DISP=(OLD,PASS),             PAD03600
//               LABEL=(16,NL),DCB=(RECFM=FB,LRECL=80,BLKSIZE=1600)    PAD03610
//SYSLMOD  DD    DSN=&NAME..PL1MP.ASM.LOAD,DISP=(NEW,CATLG),           PAD03620
//               UNIT=(&UNIT),VOL=SER=(&VOL),                          PAD03630
//               SPACE=(TRK,(1,1,1))                                   PAD03640
//*                                                                    PAD03650
//         PEND                                                        PAD03660
//         EXEC DOITB                                                  PAD03670
//*                                                                    PAD03680
//******** END OF JOB, REPLACE WITH NULL (//) IF APPROPRIATE          PAD03690
//********************* JOB 11 *******************                      PAD03700
//*                                                                    PAD03710
//*************************************************************************  PAD03720
//*                                                                    PAD03730
//* THIS JOB CREATES THE PL/1 LANGUAGE PROBLEMS                        PAD03740
//* GRADER LOAD MODULE PDS.                                            PAD03750
//*                                                                    PAD03760
//* THE SYMBOLIC PARAMETER NAME IS PREFIXED TO THE                     PAD03770
//* STANDARD NAMES, VOL ALLOWS A SPECIFIC VOLUME REQUEST,             PAD03780
//* AND UNIT IS SPECIFIED IN CONJUNCTION WITH VOL.                     PAD03790
//*                                                                    PAD03800
//*************************************************************************  PAD03810
//*                                                                    PAD03820
//DOIT2B   PROC NAME='',VOL='',UNIT=SYSDA                              PAD03830
//*                                                                    PAD03840
//MAKELO   EXEC PGM=IEWL,PARM='LET,MAP,LIST'                           PAD03850
```

```
//SYSPRINT DD    SYSOUT=A                                             PAD03860
//SYSUT1   DD    UNIT=SYSDA,SPACE=(CYL,(2,1))                         PAD03870
//SYSLIB   DD    DSN=SYS1.PL1LIB,DISP=SHR                             PAD03880
//         DD    DSN=&NAME..PL1MP.ASM.LOAD,DISP=SHR                   PAD03890
//SYSLIN   DD    UNIT=2400,DISP=(OLD,PASS),VOL=SER=PADIST,            PAD03900
//               LABEL=(19,NL),DCB=(RECFM=FB,LRECL=80,BLKSIZE=1600)   PAD03910
//SYSLMOD  DD    DSN=&NAME..PL1MP.LOAD,DISP=(NEW,CATLG),              PAD03920
//               UNIT=(&UNIT),VOL=SER=(&VOL),                         PAD03930
//               SPACE=(TRK,(20,5,2),RLSE)                            PAD03940
//*                                                                   PAD03950
//         PEND                                                       PAD03960
//*                                                                   PAD03970
//         EXEC DOIT2B                                                PAD03980
//*                                                                   PAD03990
//******** END OF JOB, REPLACE WITH NULL (//) IF APPROPRIATE          PAD04000
//******************** JOB 12 ********************                     PAD04010
//*                                                                   PAD04020
//****************************************************************************  PAD04030
//*                                                                   PAD04040
//* THIS JOB CREATES THE PL/1 LANGUAGE  GRADER                        PAD04050
//* DATA PDS.                                                         PAD04060
//*                                                                   PAD04070
//* THE SYMBOLIC PARAMETER NAME IS USED AS A NAMING                   PAD04080
//* PREFIX, VOL ALLOWS A SPECIFIC VOLUME                              PAD04090
//* REQUEST, AND UNIT IS USED IN CONJUNCTION WITH VOL                 PAD04100
//*                                                                   PAD04110
//****************************************************************************  PAD04120
//*                                                                   PAD04130
//DOIT3B   PROC NAME='',VOL='',UNIT=SYSDA                             PAD04140
//*                                                                   PAD04150
//MAKED    EXEC PGM=IEBUPDTE,PARM='NEW'                               PAD04160
//SYSPRINT DD    SYSOUT=A                                             PAD04170
//SYSUT2   DD    DSN=&NAME..PL1MP.DATA,DISP=(NEW,CATLG),              PAD04180
//               UNIT=(&UNIT),VOL=SER=(&VOL),                         PAD04190
//               SPACE=(TRK,(3,1,2)),                                 PAD04200
//               DCB=(RECFM=FB,LRECL=80,BLKSIZE=1600)                 PAD04210
//SYSIN    DD    UNIT=2400,DISP=(OLD,PASS),VOL=SER=PADIST,            PAD04220
//               LABEL=(20,NL),DCB=(RECFM=FB,LRECL=80,BLKSIZE=3200)   PAD04230
//*                                                                   PAD04240
//         PEND                                                       PAD04250
//*                                                                   PAD04260
//         EXEC DOIT3B                                                PAD04270
//*                                                                   PAD04280
//******** END OF JOB, REPLACE WITH NULL (//) IF APPROPRIATE          PAD04290
//******************** JOB 13 ********************                     PAD04300
//*                                                                   PAD04310
//****************************************************************************  PAD04320
//*                                                                   PAD04330
//PUNCH    EXEC PGM=IEBGENER                                          PAD04340
//*                                                                   PAD04350
//****************************************************************************  PAD04360
//*                                                                   PAD04370
//* THIS JOB PUNCHES THE PL/1 PROBLEM SAMPLE SOLUTIONS                PAD04380
//*  FROM THE DISTRIBUTION TAPE.                                      PAD04390
//*                                                                   PAD04400
```

```
//********************************************************************  PAD04410
//*                                                                     PAD04420
//SYSPRINT DD   SYSOUT=A                                                PAD04430
//SYSUT2   DD   SYSOUT=B,DCB=(RECFM=F,BLKSIZE=80)                       PAD04440
//SYSUT1   DD   UNIT=2400,DISP=(OLD,PASS),VOL=SER=PADIST,               PAD04450
//              LABEL=(21,NL),DCB=(RECFM=FB,LRECL=80,BLKSIZE=1600)      PAD04460
//SYSIN    DD   DUMMY                                                   PAD04470
//*                                                                     PAD04480
//******* END OF JOB, REPLACE WITH NULL (//) IF APPROPRIATE            PAD04490
//********************** JOB 14 *******************                     PAD04500
//*                                                                     PAD04510
//********************************************************************  PAD04520
//*                                                                     PAD04530
//* THIS JOB RUNS STUDENT PL/1 LANGUAGE PROBLEMS,                       PAD04540
//* USING THE BATCH MONITOR.                                            PAD04550
//*                                                                     PAD04560
//* THE SYMBOLIC PARAMETER NAME IS A LABEL PREFIX                       PAD04570
//* WHICH SHOULD BE THE SAME AS THE ONE USED TO                         PAD04580
//* CREATE THE MONITOR AND PL/1 DATASETS.                               PAD04590
//*                                                                     PAD04600
//* THE PARAMETER N IDENTIFIES THE PROBLEM BEING                        PAD04610
//* RUN (P1-P6).                                                        PAD04620
//*                                                                     PAD04630
//* EP IS SET ACCORDING TO THE PROBLEM BEING RUN, AS FOLLOWS:           PAD04640
//*     P1-P3 EP=STEAL            FOR STAND-ALONE GOVERNOR              PAD04650
//*     P4-P6 EP=IHENTRY          FOR STANDARD PL/1 EXECUTION           PAD04660
//*                                                                     PAD04670
//* INBLOCK- THE BLOCKSIZE USED FOR THE                                 PAD04680
//* INPUT DATASET. THIS SHOULD BE A MULTIPLE OF 80.                     PAD04690
//*                                                                     PAD04700
//* OUTBLOCK- THE BLOCKSIZE USED FOR OUTPUT DATASETS, SHOULD            PAD04710
//* BE A MULTIPLE OF 125 PLUS 4, (I.E. 129, or 2004).                   PAD04720
//*                                                                     PAD04730
//* THESE SHOULD BE SET TO THE LARGEST VALUE YOUR INSTALLATION          PAD04740
//* CAN SUPPORT, FOR EFFICIENCY'S SAKE.                                 PAD04750
//*                                                                     PAD04760
//* NOTE: THIS MEANS INBLOCK=2000, OUTBLOCK=2004                        PAD04770
//* FOR YOU AL.                                                         PAD04780
//*                                                                     PAD04790
//********************************************************************  PAD04800
//*                                                                     PAD04810
//MPL1     PROC N=P1,NAME='',OUTBLOCK=129,EP=STEAL                      PAD04820
//*                                                                     PAD04830
//M        EXEC PGM=MONITOR,                                            PAD04840
// PARM='TP=(LD,ND,NOL,NE),TN=IEMAA,SEP,LP=(NOPRINT,EP=&EP)'            PAD04850
//STEPLIB  DD   DSN=&NAME..MONITOR.LOAD,DISP=SHR                        PAD04860
//SYSLOG   DD   SYSOUT=A,DCB=(RECFM=VBA,LRECL=125,BLKSIZE=&OUTBLOCK)    PAD04870
//SYSWORK  DD   DSN=*.A.DD2,VOL=REF=*.A.DD2,                            PAD04880
//              DCB=*.A.DD2,DISP=(OLD,PASS)                             PAD04890
//SYSPRINT DD   SYSOUT=A,DCB=(RECFM=VBA,LRECL=125,BLKSIZE=&OUTBLOCK)    PAD04900
//SYSLIB   DD   DSN=SYS1.PL1LIB,DISP=SHR                                PAD04910
//SYSUT1   DD   DSN=*.A.DD3,VOL=REF=*.A.DD3,                            PAD04920
//              DISP=(OLD,PASS)                                         PAD04930
//SYSGO    DD   DSN=*.A.DD1,VOL=REF=*.A.DD1,                            PAD04940
//              DCB=*.A.DD1,DISP=(OLD,PASS)                             PAD04950
```

```
//SYSLOUT    DD   DUMMY                                                        PAD04960
//SYSLIN     DD   DSN=&NAME..PL1MP.LOAD(&N),DISP=SHR                           PAD04970
//           DD   DSN=*.A.DD1,VOL=REF=*.A.DD1,                                 PAD04980
//                DCB=*.A.DD1,DISP=(OLD,PASS)                                  PAD04990
//SYSIN      DD   DSN=&NAME..PL1MP.DATA(&N),DISP=SHR                           PAD05000
//MAST       DD   DSN=&NAME..PL1MP.DATA(MAST),DISP=SHR                         PAD05010
//PROGM1     DD   DSN=&NAME..PL1MP.DATA(PROGM1),DISP=SHR                       PAD05020
//PROGM2     DD   DSN=&NAME..PL1MP.DATA(PROGM2),DISP=SHR                       PAD05030
//PROGM3     DD   DSN=&NAME..PL1MP.DATA(PROGM3),DISP=SHR                       PAD05040
//           PEND                                                             PAD05050
//*                                                                           PAD05060
//           EXEC MPL1                                                        PAD05070
//*                                                                           PAD05080
//M.MONIN    DD   DATA,DCB=(RECFM=FB,LRECL=80,BLKSIZE=80) <- &INBLOCK         PAD05090
* STUDENT JOBS GO HERE, WITH $JOB AND $EOJ CARDS.                             PAD05100
//********** REPLACE WITH FILE TERMINATOR  /*                                 PAD05110
//******** END OF JOB, REPLACE WITH NULL (//) IF APPROPRIATE                  PAD05120
//******************** JOB 15 ********************                            PAD05130
//*                                                                           PAD05140
//*********************************************************************       PAD05150
//*                                                                           PAD05160
//* THIS JOB RUNS STUDENT PL/1 LANGUAGE PROBLEMS,                             PAD05170
//* WITHOUT USING THE MONITOR.                                                PAD05180
//*                                                                           PAD05190
//* THE SYMBOLIC PARAMETER NAME IS A LABEL PREFIX                             PAD05200
//* WHICH SHOULD BE THE SAME AS THE ONE USED TO                               PAD05210
//* CREATE THE PL/1 DATASETS.                                                 PAD05220
//*                                                                           PAD05230
//* THE PARAMETER N IS USED TO SELECT THE PROBLEM                             PAD05240
//* BEING RUN (P1-P6).                                                        PAD05250
//*                                                                           PAD05260
//* EP IS SET ACCORDING TO THE PROBLEM BEING RUN, AS FOLLOWS:                 PAD05270
//*     P1-P3 EP=STEAL            FOR STAND-ALONE GOVERNOR                    PAD05280
//*     P4-P6 EP=IHENTRY          FOR STANDARD PL/1 EXECUTION                 PAD05290
//*                                                                           PAD05300
//* INBLOCK- THE BLOCKSIZE USED FOR THE                                       PAD05310
//* INPUT DATASET. THIS SHOULD BE A MULTIPLE OF 80.                           PAD05320
//*                                                                           PAD05330
//* OUTBLOCK- THE BLOCKSIZE USED FOR OUTPUT DATASETS, SHOULD                  PAD05340
//* BE A MULTIPLE OF 125 PLUS 4, (I.E. 129 OR 2004).                          PAD05350
//*                                                                           PAD05360
//* THESE SHOULD BE SET TO THE LARGEST VALUE YOUR INSTALLATION                PAD05370
//* CAN SUPPORT, FOR EFFICIENCY'S SAKE.                                       PAD05380
//*                                                                           PAD05390
//* NOTE: THIS MEANS INBLOCK=2000, OUTBLOCK=2004                              PAD05400
//* FOR YOU AL.                                                               PAD05410
//*                                                                           PAD05420
//*********************************************************************       PAD05430
//*                                                                           PAD05440
//PL1        PROC N=P1,NAME='',OUTBLOCK=129,EP=STEAL                          PAD05450
//*                                                                           PAD05460
//C          EXEC PGM=IEMAA,PARM='LD,ND,NOL,NE'                               PAD05470
//SYSPRINT   DD   SYSOUT=A,DCB=(RECFM=VBA,LRECL=125,BLKSIZE=&OUTBLOCK)        PAD05480
//SYSUT1     DD   DSN=&&UT1,DISP=(OLD,PASS)                                   PAD05490
//SYSUT2     DD   DSN=&&UT2,DISP=(OLD,PASS)                                   PAD05500
```

```
//SYSUT3    DD   DSN=&&UT3,DISP=(OLD,PASS)                              PAD05510
//SYSLIN    DD   DSN=&&TEMP,DISP=(OLD,PASS)                             PAD05520
//G         EXEC PGM=IEWLDRGO,PARM='NOPRINT,EP=&EP./EADJCL=0'           PAD05530
//SYSLOUT   DD   DUMMY                                                  PAD05540
//SYSPRINT  DD   SYSOUT=A,DCB=(RECFM=VBA,LRECL=125,BLKSIZE=&OUTBLOCK)   PAD05550
//SYSLIN    DD   DSN=&NAME..PL1MP.LOAD(&N),DISP=SHR                     PAD05560
//          DD   DSN=&&TEMP,DISP=(OLD,PASS)                             PAD05570
//SYSIN     DD   DSN=&NAME..PL1MP.DATA(&N),DISP=SHR                     PAD05580
//MAST      DD   DSN=&NAME..PL1MP.DATA(MAST),DISP=SHR                   PAD05590
//PROGM1    DD   DSN=&NAME..PL1MP.DATA(PROGM1),DISP=SHR                 PAD05600
//PROGM2    DD   DSN=&NAME..PL1MP.DATA(PROGM2),DISP=SHR                 PAD05610
//PROGM3    DD   DSN=&NAME..PL1MP.DATA(PROGM3),DISP=SHR                 PAD05620
//          PEND                                                       PAD05630
//*                                                                    PAD05640
//ALLOC     EXEC PGM=IEFBR14                                           PAD05650
//DD1       DD   DSN=&&TEMP,DISP=(NEW,PASS),                           PAD05660
//               UNIT=SYSDA,SPACE=(TRK,(10,4)),                        PAD05670
//               DCB=(RECFM=FB,LRECL=80,BLKSIZE=1600)                  PAD05680
//DD2       DD   DSN=&&UT1,DISP=(NEW,PASS),UNIT=SYSDA,                 PAD05690
//               DCB=(RECFM=FB,LRECL=80,BLKSIZE=1600)                  PAD05700
//DD3       DD   DSN=&&UT2,DISP=(NEW,PASS),UNIT=SYSDA,                 PAD05710
//               DCB=(RECFM=FB,LRECL=80,BLKSIZE=1600)                  PAD05720
//DD4       DD   DSN=&&UT3,DISP=(NEW,PASS),UNIT=SYSDA,                 PAD05730
//               DCB=(RECFM=FB,LRECL=80,BLKSIZE=1600)                  PAD05740
//*                                                                    PAD05750
//SMITH     EXEC PL1                                                   PAD05760
//C.SYSIN   DD   *,DCB=(RECFM=FB,LRECL=80,BLKSIZE=80) <-INBLOCK        PAD05770
* DECK FOR STUDENT SMITH GOES HERE, WITHOUT $JOB and $EOJ CARDS        PAD05780
//*********** FILE TERMINATOR GOES HERE /*                             PAD05790
//JONES     EXEC PL1                                                   PAD05800
//C.SYSIN   DD   *,DCB=(RECFM=FB,LRECL=80,BLKSIZE=80) <-INBLOCK        PAD05810
* DECK FOR STUDENT JONES GOES HERE, THIS IS REPEATED FOR ALL STUDENTS  PAD05820
//*********** FILE TERMINATOR GOES HERE  /*                            PAD05830
//******** END OF JOB, REPLACE WITH NULL (//) IF APPROPRIATE           PAD05840
//******************* JOB 16 *******************                       PAD05850
//*                                                                    PAD05860
//PRINT     EXEC PGM=IEBGENER                                          PAD05870
//*                                                                    PAD05880
//********************************************************************  PAD05890
//*                                                                    PAD05900
//* THIS JOB PRINTS THE SYSTEM/360 SIMULATOR (SIM360) LISTINGS         PAD05910
//*   FROM THE DISTRIBUTION TAPE.                                      PAD05920
//*                                                                    PAD05930
//********************************************************************  PAD05940
//*                                                                    PAD05950
//SYSPRINT  DD   SYSOUT=A                                              PAD05960
//SYSUT2    DD   SYSOUT=A,DCB=(RECFM=FBA,LRECL=121,BLKSIZE=1210)       PAD05970
//SYSUT1    DD   UNIT=2400,DISP=(OLD,PASS),VOL=SER=PADIST,             PAD05980
//               LABEL=(23,NL),DCB=(RECFM=FBA,LRECL=121,BLKSIZE=1210)  PAD05990
//SYSIN     DD   DUMMY                                                 PAD06000
//*                                                                    PAD06010
//******** END OF JOB, REPLACE WITH NULL (//) IF APPROPRIATE           PAD06020
//******************* JOB 17 *******************                       PAD06030
//*                                                                    PAD06040
//PRINT     EXEC PGM=IEBGENER                                          PAD06050
```

```
//*                                                                     PAD06060
//**********************************************************************  PAD06070
//*                                                                     PAD06080
//* THIS JOB PRINTS THE SIM360 EXAMPLE PROGRAM LISTINGS                 PAD06090
//*   FROM THE DISTRIBUTION TAPE.                                       PAD06100
//*                                                                     PAD06110
//**********************************************************************  PAD06120
//*                                                                     PAD06130
//SYSPRINT DD   SYSOUT=A                                                PAD06140
//SYSUT2   DD   SYSOUT=A,DCB=(RECFM=FBA,LRECL=133,BLKSIZE=1330)         PAD06150
//SYSUT1   DD   UNIT=2400,DISP=(OLD,PASS),VOL=SER=PADIST,               PAD06160
//              LABEL=(24,NL),DCB=(RECFM=FBA,LRECL=133,BLKSIZE=1330)    PAD06170
//SYSIN    DD   DUMMY                                                   PAD06180
//*                                                                     PAD06190
//******** END OF JOB, REPLACE WITH NULL (//) IF APPROPRIATE           PAD06200
//********************* JOB 18 ********************                      PAD06210
//*                                                                     PAD06220
//**********************************************************************  PAD06230
//*                                                                     PAD06240
//* THIS JOB LINKS THE SIMULATOR TO PRODUCE A LOAD                      PAD06250
//* MODULE.                                                             PAD06260
//*                                                                     PAD06270
//* THE SYMBOLIC PARAMETER NAME IS USED AS A LABEL                      PAD06280
//* PREFIX WHEN NAMING DATASETS.                                        PAD06290
//*                                                                     PAD06300
//* THE PARAMETER VOL IS USED TO GIVE A SPECIFIC                        PAD06310
//* VOLUME REQUEST, UNIT IS USED IN CONJUNCTION                         PAD06320
//* WITH VOL.                                                           PAD06330
//*                                                                     PAD06340
//**********************************************************************  PAD06350
//*                                                                     PAD06360
//DOITC    PROC NAME='',UNIT=SYSDA,VOL=''                               PAD06370
//*                                                                     PAD06380
//STEPL    EXEC PGM=IEWL,PARM='MAP,LIST'                                PAD06390
//SYSPRINT DD   SYSOUT=A                                                PAD06400
//SYSUT1   DD   UNIT=SYSDA,SPACE=(CYL,(2,1))                            PAD06410
//SYSLMOD  DD   DSN=&NAME..SIM360.LOAD(SIM360),UNIT=(&UNIT),            PAD06420
//              VOL=SER=(&VOL),DISP=(NEW,CATLG),                        PAD06430
//              SPACE=(TRK,(10,5,2),RISE)                               PAD06440
//SYSLIB   DD   DSN=SYS1.PL1LIB,DISP=SHR                                PAD06450
//SYSLIN   DD   UNIT=2400,VOL=SER=PADIST,DISP=(OLD,PASS),               PAD06460
//              LABEL=(27,NL),DCB=(RECFM=FB,LRECL=80,BLKSIZE=1600)      PAD06470
//*                                                                     PAD06480
//        PEND                                                          PAD06490
//*                                                                     PAD06500
//        EXEC DOITC                                                    PAD06510
//*                                                                     PAD06520
//******** END OF JOB, REPLACE WITH NULL (//) IF APPROPRIATE           PAD06530
//********************* JOB 19 ********************                      PAD06540
//*                                                                     PAD06550
//**********************************************************************  PAD06560
//*                                                                     PAD06570
//* THIS JOB CREATES A SIM360 MACRO LIBRARY, INCLUDING                  PAD06580
//* THE TRACE AND OTHER SIMULATOR-SPECIFIC MACROS                       PAD06590
//* AS WELL AS THE MACROS USED BY INTERRUPT AND                         PAD06600
```

```
//* I/O PROBLEMS.                                                         PAD06610
//*                                                                       PAD06620
//* THE SYMBOLIC PARAMETER NAME IS USED AS A LABEL                        PAD06630
//* PREFIX. THE SYMBOL VOL ALLOWS A SPECIFIC VOLUME                       PAD06640
//* REQUEST AND UNIT IS USED IN CONJUNCTION WITH VOL.                     PAD06650
//*                                                                       PAD06660
//* NOTE: VERY IMPORTANT: THE BLOCKSIZE USED FOR THE                      PAD06670
//* MACRO LIBRARY SHOULD BE THE SAME, OR LARGER THAN THAT                 PAD06680
//* USED FOR SYS1.MACLIB IN YOUR INSTALLATION. THIS PARAMETER             PAD06690
//* IS BLKSIZE.                                                           PAD06700
//*                                                                       PAD06710
//***********************************************************************  PAD06720
//*                                                                       PAD06730
//DOIT2C   PROC NAME='',UNIT=SYSDA,VOL='',BLKSIZE=3200                    PAD06740
//*                                                                       PAD06750
//MCREATE EXEC PGM=IEBUPDTE,PARM='NEW'                                    PAD06760
//SYSPRINT DD   SYSOUT=A                                                  PAD06770
//SYSUT2   DD   DSN=&NAME..SIM360.MACLIB,DISP=(NEW,CATLG),                PAD06780
//              VOL=SER=(&VOL),UNIT=(&UNIT),                              PAD06790
//              DCB=(RECFM=FB,LRECL=80,BLKSIZE=&BLKSIZE),                 PAD06800
//              SPACE=(TRK,(2,1,2))                                       PAD06810
//SYSIN    DD   UNIT=2400,VOL=SER=PADIST,DISP=(OLD,PASS),                 PAD06820
//              LABEL=(28,NL),DCB=(RECFM=FB,LRECL=80,BLKSIZE=3200)        PAD06830
//*                                                                       PAD06840
//         PEND                                                           PAD06850
//*                                                                       PAD06860
//         EXEC DOIT2C                                                    PAD06870
//*                                                                       PAD06880
//******** END OF JOB, REPLACE WITH NULL (//) IF APPROPRIATE             PAD06890
//********************* JOB 20 *********************                       PAD06900
//*                                                                       PAD06910
//***********************************************************************  PAD06920
//*                                                                       PAD06930
//* THIS JOB RUNS STUDENT PROGRAMS ON THE SYSTEM/360                      PAD06940
//* SIMULATOR (SIM360), USING THE MONITOR.                               PAD06950
//*                                                                       PAD06960
//* THE SYMBOLIC PARAMETER NAME IS USED AS A                             PAD06970
//* LABEL PREFIX AND SHOULD BE THE SAME AS                               PAD06980
//* SPECIFIED WHEN THE MONITOR AND SIM360                                PAD06990
//* DATASETS WHERE CREATED.                                              PAD07000
//*                                                                       PAD07010
//* THE INPUT FILE SPECIFICATIONS (DD *) DO NOT CONTAIN                   PAD07020
//* ANY DCB SPECIFICATIONS, THUS THE I/O IS NOT BLOCKED.                 PAD07030
//* FOR EFFICIENCY, YOU SHOULD BLOCK THESE FILES AS                      PAD07040
//* LARGE AS YOUR INSTALLATION PERMITS SUCH AS:                          PAD07050
//*                                                                       PAD07060
//* DD *,DCB=(RECFM=FB,LRECL=80,BLKSIZE=2000)                            PAD07070
//*                                                                       PAD07080
//***********************************************************************  PAD07090
//*                                                                       PAD07100
//SIM360   PROC TPARM='LOAD,NODECK',NAME='',                             PAD07110
//    GPARM='CARDS=2,PRINT=2,MAXTIME=9999,MAXPGE=15,MAXCOUNT=5000'       PAD07120
//*                                                                       PAD07130
//G        EXEC PGM=S360MON,PARM='ISA(4K)/&TPARM./&GPARM.'               PAD07140
//STEPLIB  DD   DSN=&NAME..MONITOR.LOAD,DISP=SHR                         PAD07150
```

```
//          DD   DSN=&NAME..SIM360.LOAD,DISP=SHR                      PAD07160
//SYSLOG   DD   SYSOUT=A                                             PAD07170
//SYSPRINT DD   SYSOUT=A                                             PAD07180
//SYSLIB   DD   DSN=&NAME..SIM360.MACLIB,DISP=SHR                    PAD07190
//SYSGO    DD   UNIT=SYSDA,SPACE=(CYL,(1,2))                         PAD07200
//SYSUT1   DD   UNIT=SYSDA,SPACE=(CYL,(1,2))                         PAD07210
//SYSUT2   DD   UNIT=SYSDA,SPACE=(CYL,(1,2))                         PAD07220
//SYSUT3   DD   UNIT=SYSDA,SPACE=(CYL,(1,2))                         PAD07230
//SIMLIN   DD   UNIT=SYSDA,SPACE=(CYL,(1,2)),                        PAD07240
//               DCB=(LRECL=80,BLKSIZE=1600,RECFM=FB)                PAD07250
//SYSIN    DD   UNIT=SYSDA,SPACE=(CYL,(1,2)),                        PAD07260
//               DCB=(LRECL=80,BLKSIZE=2000,RECFM=FB)                PAD07270
//SIMPRNT  DD   UNIT=SYSDA,SPACE=(CYL,(1,2)),                        PAD07280
//               DCB=(LRECL=125,BLKSIZE=2004,RECFM=VBA)              PAD07290
//SIMPRN2  DD   UNIT=SYSDA,SPACE=(CYL,(1,2)),                        PAD07300
//               DCB=(LRECL=125,BLKSIZE=2004,RECFM=VEA)              PAD07310
//STRACE   DD   UNIT=SYSDA,SPACE=(CYL,(1,2)),                        PAD07320
//               DCB=(LRECL=125,BLKSIZE=2004,RECFM=VBA)              PAD07330
//*                                                                  PAD07340
//          PEND                                                     PAD07350
//*                                                                  PAD07360
//RUN      EXEC SIM360                                               PAD07370
//*                                                                  PAD07380
//G.SIMIN  DD   *                                                    PAD07390
00TW881                                                              PAD07400
01PA707                                                              PAD07410
02*UN666                                                             PAD07420
03*TW727                                                             PAD07430
09+10:00:00.7                                                        PAD07440
04!PA876                                                             PAD07450
05!UN747                                                             PAD07460
06EA802                                                              PAD07470
07!PA300                                                             PAD07480
//********** SHOULD BE REPLACED BY A FILE TERMINATOR  /*             PAD07490
//G.SIMIN2 DD   *                                                    PAD07500
12UN969                                                              PAD07510
11UN747                                                              PAD07520
10*EA696                                                             PAD07530
19+10:00:00.7                                                        PAD07540
13*EA802                                                             PAD07550
14!EA999                                                             PAD07560
15!TW881                                                             PAD07570
16TW727                                                              PAD07580
17!PA400                                                             PAD07590
//********** SHOULD BE REPLACED BY A FILE TERMINATOR  /*             PAD07600
//*                                                                  PAD07610
//G.BATCHIN DD DATA                                                  PAD07620
* STUDENT DECKS GO HERE, WITH $JOB AND $EOJ CARDS.                   PAD07630
//********** SHOULD BE REPLACED BY A FILE TERMINATOR  /*             PAD07640
//********* END OF JOB, REPLACE WITH NULL (//) IF APPROPRIATE        PAD07650
//******************** JOB 21 *******************                    PAD07660
//*                                                                  PAD07670
//***************************************************************************  PAD07680
//*                                                                  PAD07690
//*   THIS JOB RUNS STUDENT PROGRAMS ON THE SYSTEM/360               PAD07700
```

```
//* SIMULATOR (SIM360), WITHOUT THE MONITOR.                            PAD07710
//*                                                                     PAD07720
//* THE SYMBOLIC PARAMETER NAME IS USED AS A LABEL                      PAD07730
//* PREFIX. THE VALUE USED SHOULD BE THE SAME SPECIFIED                 PAD07740
//* WHEN THE SIM360 AND MONITOR DATASETS WERE CREATED.                  PAD07750
//*                                                                     PAD07760
//* THE PARAMETER  GPARM IS USED TO PASS PARAMETERS                     PAD07770
//* TO THE SIMULATOR.                                                   PAD07780
//*                                                                     PAD07790
//* THE INPUT DATA FILES USED IN THIS JOB (DD *),                       PAD07800
//* ARE SHOWN WITHOUT DCB INFORMATION, I.E.                            PAD07810
//*  UNBLOCKED. FOR MAXIMUM EFFICIENCY YOU SHOULD                       PAD07820
//* BLOCK THESE FILES AS HIGH AS YOUR INSTALLATION                      PAD07830
//* PERMITS, SUCH AS:                                                   PAD07840
//*                                                                     PAD07850
//* DD *,DCB=(RECFM=FB,LRECL=80,BLKSIZE=2000)                           PAD07860
//*                                                                     PAD07870
//*********************************************************************  PAD07880
//*                                                                     PAD07890
//SIM360  PROC NAME='',                                                 PAD07900
//  GPARM='CARDS=2,PRINT=2,MAXTIME=9999,MAXPGE=15,MAXCOUNT=5000'        PAD07910
//*                                                                     PAD07920
//C       EXEC PGM=IEUASM,PARM='NODECK,LOAD'                            PAD07930
//SYSPRINT DD  SYSOUT=A                                                 PAD07940
//SYSLIB   DD  DSN=&NAME..SIM360.MACLIB,DISP=SHR                        PAD07950
//SYSUT1   DD  UNIT=SYSDA,SPACE=(CYL,(2,1))                             PAD07960
//SYSUT2   DD  UNIT=SYSDA,SPACE=(CYL,(2,1))                             PAD07970
//SYSUT3   DD  UNIT=SYSDA,SPACE=(CYL,(2,1))                             PAD07980
//SYSLIN   DD  DSN=&&TEMP,DISP=(NEW,PASS),                              PAD07990
//             UNIT=SYSDA,SPACE=(CYL,(1,1)),                            PAD08000
//             DCB=(RECFM=FB,LRECL=80,BLKSIZE=1600)                     PAD08010
//*                                                                     PAD08020
//G       EXEC PGM=SIM360,PARM=&GPARM                                   PAD08030
//STEPLIB  DD  DSN=&NAME..SIM360.LOAD,DISP=SHR                          PAD08040
//SIMLIN   DD  DSNAME=&&TEMP,DISP=(OID,DELETE)                          PAD08050
//SYSPRINT DD  SYSOUT=A                                                 PAD08060
//STRACE   DD  SYSOUT=A                                                 PAD08070
//SIMPRNT  DD  SYSOUT=A                                                 PAD08080
//SIMPRN2  DD  SYSOUT=A                                                 PAD08090
//SIMPRN3  DD  SYSOUT=A                                                 PAD08100
//SIMPRN4  DD  SYSOUT=A                                                 PAD08110
//SIMPNCH  DD  SYSOUT=A                                                 PAD08120
//SIMPNC2  DD  SYSOUT=A                                                 PAD08130
//SIMPNC3  DD  SYSOUT=A                                                 PAD08140
//SIMPNC4  DD  SYSOUT=A                                                 PAD08150
//SIMIN3   DD  DUMMY                                                    PAD08160
//SIMIN4   DD  DUMMY                                                    PAD08170
//SIMPRNT  DD  DUMMY                                                    PAD08180
//SIMPRN2  DD  DUMMY                                                    PAD08190
//*                                                                     PAD08200
//       PEND                                                           PAD08210
//*                                                                     PAD08220
//STUDENT EXEC SIM360                                                   PAD08230
//*                                                                     PAD08240
//C.SYSIN  DD  *                                                        PAD08250
```

```
* STUDENT JOB, WITHOUT $JOB AND $EOJ  CARDS                              PADO8260
//********* SHOULD BE REPLACED BY A FILE TERMINATOR  /*                  PADO8270
//G.SIMIN  DD  *                                                         PADO8280
00TW881                                                                  PADO8290
01PA707                                                                  PADO8300
02*UN666                                                                 PADO8310
03*TW727                                                                 PADO8320
09+10:00:00.7                                                            PADO8330
04!PA876                                                                 PADO8340
05!UN747                                                                 PADO8350
06EA802                                                                  PADO8360
07!PA300                                                                 PADO8370
//********* SHOULD BE REPLACED BY A FILE TERMINATOR  /*                  PADO8380
//G.SIMIN2 DD  *                                                         PADO8390
12UN969                                                                  PADO8400
11UN747                                                                  PADO8410
10*EA696                                                                 PADO8420
19+1C:00:00.7                                                            PADO8430
13*EA802                                                                 PADO8440
14!EA999                                                                 PADO8450
15!TW881                                                                 PADO8460
16TW727                                                                  PADO8470
17!PA400                                                                 PADO8480
//********* SHOULD BE REPLACED BY A FILE TERMINATOR  /*                  PADO8490
//******** END OF JOB, REPLACE WITH NULL (//) IF APPROPRIATE            PADO8500
//******************* JOB 22 *******************                         EADO8510
//*                                                                      PADO8520
//PRINT    EXEC PGM=IEBGENER                                             PADO8530
//*                                                                      PADO8540
//********************************************************************    PADO8550
//*                                                                      PADO8560
//* THIS JOB PRINTS THE SAMPLES AND SOLUTIONS TO THE                     PADO8570
//* INTERRUPT AND I/O PROBLEMS FROM THE DISTRIBUTION TAPE.               PADO8580
//*                                                                      PADO8590
//********************************************************************    PADO8600
//*                                                                      PADO8610
//SYSPRINT DD  SYSOUT=A                                                  PADO8620
//SYSUT2   DD  SYSOUT=A,DCB=(RECFM=FBA,LRECL=133,BLKSIZE=1330)           PADO8630
//SYSUT1   DD  UNIT=2400,DISP=(OLD,PASS),VOL=SER=PADIST,                 PADO8640
//             LABEL=(31,NL),DCB=(RECFM=FBA,LRECL=133,BLKSIZE=1330)      PADO8650
//SYSIN    DD  DUMMY                                                     PADO8660
//*                                                                      PADO8670
//******** END OF JOB, REPLACE WITH NULL (//) IF APPROPRIATE            PADO8680
//******************* JOB 23 *******************                         PADO8690
//*                                                                      PADO8700
//PUNCH    EXEC PGM=IEBGENER                                             PADO8710
//*                                                                      PADO8720
//********************************************************************    PADO8730
//*                                                                      PADO8740
//* THIS JOB PUNCHES THE SAMPLES AND SOLUTIONS FOR THE INTERRUPT         PADO8750
//* AND I/O PROBLEMS FROM THE DISTRIBUTION TAPE.                         PADO8760
//*                                                                      PADO8770
//********************************************************************    PADO8780
//*                                                                      PADO8790
//SYSPRINT DD  SYSOUT=A                                                  PADO8800
```

```
//SYSUT2    DD    SYSOUT=B,DCB=(RECFM=F,BLKSIZE=80)                              PAD08810
//SYSUT1    DD    UNIT=2400,DISP=(OLD,PASS),VOL=SER=PADIST,                      PAD08820
//                LABEL=(32,NL),DCB=(RECFM=FB,LRECL=80,BLKSIZE=1600)             PAD08830
//SYSIN     DD    DUMMY                                                          PAD08840
//*                                                                             PAD08850
//******** END OF JOB, REPLACE WITH NULL (//) IF APPROPRIATE                    PAD08860
//******************* JOB 24 *******************                                 PAD08870
//*                                                                             PAD08880
//EXOSL     EXEC  PGM=IEBGENER      .                                           PAD08890
//*                                                                             PAD08900
//*********************************************************************          PAD08910
//*                                                                  *          PAD08920
//*        THIS JOB PRINTS THE EXAMPLE OPERATING SYSTEM LISTINGS.    *          PAD08930
//*                                                                  *          PAD08940
//*********************************************************************          PAD08950
//*                                                                             PAD08960
//SYSPRINT  DD    SYSOUT=A                                                       PAD08970
//SYSIN     DD    DUMMY                                                          PAD08980
//SYSUT2    DD    SYSOUT=A,DCB=(RECFM=FBA,LRECL=121,BLKSIZE=1210)                PAD08990
//SYSUT1    DD    UNIT=2400,VOL=SER=PADIST,DISP=(OLD,PASS),                      PAD09000
//                LABEL=(35,NL),DCB=(RECFM=FBA,LRECL=121,BLKSIZE=1210)           PAD09010
//*                                                                             PAD09020
//******** END OF JOB, REPLACE WITH NULL (//) IF APPROPRIATE                    PAD09030
//******************* JOB 25 *******************                                 PAD09040
//*                                                                             PAD09050
//EXOSS     EXEC  PGM=IEBGENER                                                   PAD09060
//*                                                                             PAD09070
//*********************************************************************          PAD09080
//*                                                                  *          PAD09090
//*        THIS JOB PRINTS THE OUTPUT FROM A SAMPLE JOB.             *          PAD09100
//*                                                                  *          PAD09110
//*********************************************************************          PAD09120
//*                                                                             PAD09130
//SYSPRINT  DD    SYSOUT=A                                                       PAD09140
//SYSIN     DD    DUMMY                                                          PAD09150
//SYSUT2    DD    SYSOUT=A,DCB=(RECFM=FBA,LRECL=133,BLKSIZE=1330)                PAD09160
//SYSUT1    DD    UNIT=2400,VOL=SER=PADIST,DISP=(OLD,PASS),LABEL=(36,NL),        PAD09170
//                DCB=(RECFM=FBA,LRECL=133,BLKSIZE=1330)                         PAD09180
.//*                                                                            PAD09190
//******** END OF JOB, REPLACE WITH NULL (//) IF APPROPRIATE                    PAD09200
//******************* JOB 26 *******************                                 PAD09210
//*                                                                             PAD09220
//EXOSI     EXEC  PGM=IEBGENER                                                   PAD09230
//*                                                                             PAD09240
//*********************************************************************          PAD09250
//*                                                                  *          PAD09260
//*        THIS JOB PRINTS THE OUTPUT FOR AN IPL DECK GENERATION.    *          PAD09270
//*                                                                  *          PAD09280
//*********************************************************************          PAD09290
//*                                                                             PAD09300
//SYSPRINT  DD    SYSOUT=A                                                       PAD09310
//SYSIN     DD    DUMMY                                                          PAD09320
//SYSUT2    DD    SYSOUT=A,DCB=(RECFM=FEA,LRECL=121,BLKSIZE=1210)                PAD09330
//SYSUT1    DD    UNIT=2400,VOL=SER=PADIST,DISP=(OLD,PASS),LABEL=(37,NL),        PAD09340
//                DCB=(RECFM=FBA,LRECL=121,BLKSIZE=1210)                         PAD09350
```

```
//*                                                                PAD09360
//********* END OF JOB, REPLACE WITH NULL (//) IF APPROPRIATE      PAD09370
//********************** JOB 27 ********************               PAD09380
//*                                                                PAD09390
//*                                                                PAD09400
//*************************************************************************  PAD09410
//*                                                                PAD09420
//* THIS JOB CREATES A MACRO LIBRARY WHICH MAY BE USED             PAD09430
//* TO ASSEMBLE A VERSION OF THE EXAMPLE OPERATING SYSTEM.         PAD09440
//*                                                                PAD09450
//* THE SYMBOLIC PARAMETER NAME IS USED AS A LABEL PREFIX.         PAD09460
//*                                                                PAD09470
//* THE PARAMETER VOL ALLOWS A SPECIFIC VOLUME REQUEST,            PAD09480
//* AND UNIT IS USED IN CONJUNCTION WITH VOL.                      PAD09490
//*                                                                PAD09500
//* THE PARAMETER BLKSIZE IS USED TO SPECIFY THE BLKSIZE           PAD09510
//* WHICH WILL BE USED FOR THE MACRO LIBRARY. THIS VALUE           PAD09520
//* SHOULD BE AT LEAST AS LARGE AS THAT USED BY THE                PAD09530
//* SYSTEM DATASET "SYS1.MACLIB" AT YOUR INSTALLATION.             PAD09540
//*                                                                PAD09550
//*************************************************************************  PAD09560
//*                                                                PAD09570
//DOITC    PROC NAME='',VOL='',UNIT=SYSDA,BLKSIZE=3200             PAD09580
//*                                                                PAD09590
//EXOSML   EXEC PGM=IEBUPDTE,PARM='NEW'                            PAD09600
//*                                                                PAD09610
//SYSPRINT DD   SYSOUT=A                                           PAD09620
//SYSUT2   DD   DSN=&NAME..EXOS.MACLIB,DISP=(NEW,CATLG),           PAD09630
//              UNIT=(&UNIT),VOL=SER=(&VOL),                       PAD09640
//              SPACE=(TRK,(45,4,2),RISE),                         PAD09650
//              DCB=(RECFM=FB,LRECL=80,BLKSIZE=&BLKSIZE)           PAD09660
//SYSIN    DD   UNIT=24C0,VOL=SER=PADIST,DISP=(OLD,PASS),LABEL=(38,NL),  PAD09670
//              DCB=(RECFM=FB,LRECL=80,BLKSIZE=3200)               PAD09680
//*                                                                PAD09690
//******** END OF JOB, REPLACE WITH NULL (//) IF APPROPRIATE       PAD09700
//********************** JOB 28 ********************               PAD09710
//*                                                                PAD09720
//*************************************************************************  PAD09730
//*                                                                PAD09740
//* THIS JOB LOADS THE OBJECT FOR A VERSION OF THE EXAMPLE         PAD09750
//* OPERATING SYSTEM COMPATIBLE WITH THE                           PAD09760
//* SYSTEM/360 SIMULATOR (SIM360). THIS VERSION IS                 PAD09770
//* DOCUMENTED IN CHAPTER 6.                                       PAD09780
//*                                                                PAD09790
//* THE SYMBOLIC PARAMETER NAME IS USED AS A LABEL PREFIX          PAD09800
//* FOR THE OBJECT DATASET. THE PARAMETER VOL ALLOWS               PAD09810
//* A SPECIFIC VOLUME REQUEST, AND UNIT IS USED IN CONJUNCTION     PAD09820
//* WITH VOL.                                                      PAD09830
//*                                                                PAD09840
//*************************************************************************  PAD09850
//*                                                                PAD09860
//DOIT2C   PROC NAME='',VOL='',UNIT=SYSDA                          PAD09870
//*                                                                PAD09880
//STUFF    EXEC PGM=IEBGENER                                       PAD09890
//SYSPRINT DD   SYSOUT=A                                           PAD09900
```

```
//SYSIN    DD   DUMMY                                                  PAD09910
//SYSUT1   DD   UNIT=2400,VOL=SER=PADIST,DISP=(OLD,PASS),              PAD09920
//              LABEL=(39,NL),DCB=(RECFM=FB,LRECL=80,BLKSIZE=1600)     PAD09930
//SYSUT2   DD   DSN=&NAME..EXOS.OBJ,DISP=(NEW,CATLG),                  PAD09940
//              DCB=(RECFM=FB,LRECL=80,BLKSIZE=1600),UNIT=(&UNIT),     PAD09950
//              VOL=SER=(&VOL),SPACE=(TRK,(35,10),RISE)                PAD09960
//*                                                                    PAD09970
//        PEND                                                         PAD09980
//        EXEC DOIT2C                                                  PAD09990
//*                                                                    PAD10000
//******** END OF JOB, REPLACE WITH NULL (//) IF APPROPRIATE          PAD10010
//********************* JOB 29 ********************                     PAD10020
//*                                                                    PAD10030
//PUNCH    EXEC PGM=IEBGENER                                           PAD10040
//*                                                                    PAD10050
//**********************************************************************PAD10060
//*                                                                    PAD10070
//* THIS JOB PUNCHES THE SOURCE FOR A SAMPLE EXOS JOB                  PAD10080
//*  FROM THE DISTRIBUTION TAPE.                                       PAD10090
//*                                                                    PAD10100
//**********************************************************************PAD10110
//*                                                                    PAD10120
//SYSPRINT DD   SYSOUT=A                                               PAD10130
//SYSUT2   DD   SYSOUT=B,DCB=(RECFM=F,BLKSIZE=80)                      PAD10140
//SYSUT1   DD   UNIT=2400,DISP=(OLD,PASS),VOL=SER=PADIST,             PAD10150
//              LABEL=(40,NL),DCB=(RECFM=FB,LRECL=80,BLKSIZE=1600)     PAD10160
//SYSIN    DD   DUMMY                                                  PAD10170
//*                                                                    PAD10180
//******** END OF JOB, REPLACE WITH NULL (//) IF APPROPRIATE          PAD10190
//********************* JOB 30 ********************                     PAD10200
//*                                                                    PAD10210
//**********************************************************************PAD10220
//*                                                                  * PAD10230
//*       THIS JOB PUNCHES A 4 CARD IPL DECK TO BOOTSTRAP LOAD THE   * PAD10240
//*       EXAMPLE OPERATING SYSTEM.                                  * PAD10250
//*                                                                  * PAD10260
//**********************************************************************PAD10270
//*                                                                    PAD10280
//EXOSID   EXEC PGM=IEBGENER                                           PAD10290
//SYSPRINT DD   SYSOUT=A                                               PAD10300
//SYSIN    DD   DUMMY                                                  PAD10310
//SYSUT1   DD   UNIT=2400,VOL=SER=PADIST,DISP=(OLD,PASS),LABEL=(44,NL),PAD10320
//              DCB=(RECFM=FB,LRECL=80,BLKSIZE=1600)                   PAD10330
//SYSUT2   DD   SYSOUT=B,DCB=(RECFM=F,BLKSIZE=80)                      PAD10340
//*                                                                    PAD10350
//******** END OF JOB, REPLACE WITH NULL (//) IF APPROPRIATE          PAD10360
//********************* JOB 31 ********************                     PAD10370
//*                                                                    PAD10380
//PRINT    EXEC PGM=IEBGENER                                           PAD10390
//*                                                                    PAD10400
//**********************************************************************PAD10410
//*                                                                    PAD10420
//* THIS JOB PRINTS THE SIMPLE BATCH MONITOR LISTINGS                  PAD10430
//*  FROM THE DISTRIBUTION TAPE.                                       PAD10440
//*                                                                    PAD10450
```

```
//****************************************************************   PAD10460
//*                                                                 PAD10470
//SYSPRINT DD  SYSOUT=A                                             PAD10480
//SYSUT2    DD  SYSOUT=A,DCB=(RECFM=FBA,LRECL=121,BLKSIZE=1210)     PAD10490
//SYSUT1    DD  UNIT=2400,DISP=(OLD,PASS),VOL=SER=PADIST,           PAD10500
//               LABEL=(45,NL),DCB=(RECFM=FBA,LRECL=121,BLKSIZE=1210) PAD10510
//SYSIN     DD  DUMMY                                               PAD10520
//*                                                                 PAD10530
//******** END OF JOB, REPLACE WITH NULL (//) IF APPROPRIATE        PAD10540
//********************** JOB 32 ***********************              PAD10550
//*                                                                 PAD10560
//PRINT   EXEC PGM=IEBGENER                                         PAD10570
//*                                                                 PAD10580
//****************************************************************   PAD10590
//*                                                                 PAD10600
//* THIS JOB PRINTS THE SIM360 BATCH MONITOR LISTINGS              PAD10610
//*  FROM THE DISTRIBUTION TAPE.                                    PAD10620
//*                                                                 PAD10630
//****************************************************************   PAD10640
//*                                                                 PAD10650
//SYSPRINT DD  SYSOUT=A                                             PAD10660
//SYSUT2    DD  SYSOUT=A,DCB=(RECFM=FBA,LRECL=121,BLKSIZE=1210)     PAD10670
//SYSUT1    DD  UNIT=2400,DISP=(OLD,PASS),VOL=SER=PADIST,           PAD10680
//               LABEL=(46,NL),DCB=(RECFM=FBA,LRECL=121,BLKSIZE=1210) PAD10690
//SYSIN     DD  DUMMY                                               PAD10700
//*                                                                 PAD10710
//******** END OF JOB, REPLACE WITH NULL (//) IF APPROPRIATE        PAD10720
//********************** JOB 33 ***********************              PAD10730
//*                                                                 PAD10740
//****************************************************************   PAD10750
//*                                                                 PAD10760
//* THIS JOB LINKS THE SIMPLE BATCH MONITOR, USED TO EASE          PAD10770
//* RUNNING A LARGE NUMBER OF STUDENT ASSEMBLY LANGUAGE            PAD10780
//* OR PL/1 PROBLEMS.                                               PAD10790
//*                                                                 PAD10800
//* THE SYMBOLIC PARAMETER NAME IS USED TO PREFIX DATASET          PAD10810
//* NAMES USED BY THE MONITOR. THE PARAMETER VOL ALLOWS            PAD10820
//* A SPECIFIC VOLUME REQUEST, UNIT IS USED IN CONJUNCTION         PAD10830
//* WITH VOL, AND NOSIM360 IS SET TO THE VALUE 'RLSE' IF YOU       PAD10840
// DO NOT PLAN TO GENERATE THE SYSTEM/360 SIMULATOR (SIM360)       PAD10850
//* BATCH MONITOR.                                                  PAD10860
//*                                                                 PAD10870
//****************************************************************   PAD10880
//*                                                                 PAD10890
//DOITD   PROC NAME='',UNIT=SYSDA,VOL='',NOSIM360=''                PAD10900
//*                                                                 PAD10910
//LINK    EXEC PGM=IEWL,PARM='LIST,MAP,RENT'                        PAD10920
//SYSPRINT DD  SYSOUT=A                                             PAD10930
//SYSUT1    DD  UNIT=SYSDA,SPACE=(CYL,(2,1))                        PAD10940
//SYSLIN    DD  UNIT=2400,VOL=SER=PADIST,DISP=(OLD,PASS),           PAD10950
//               LABEL=(50,NL),DCB=(RECFM=FB,LRECL=80,BLKSIZE=1600) PAD10960
//SYSLMOD   DD  DSN=&NAME..MONITOR.LOAD,DISP=(NEW,CATLG),           PAD10970
//               UNIT=(&UNIT),VOL=SER=(&VOL),                       PAD10980
//               SPACE=(TRK,(15,5,2),&NOSIM360)                     PAD10990
//*                                                                 PAD11000
```

```
//       EXEC DOITD                                                      PAD11010
//*                                                                      PAD11020
//******** END OF JOB, REPLACE WITH NULL (//) IF APPROPRIATE            PAD11030
//******************** JOB 34 *******************                        PAD11040
//*                                                                      PAD11050
//*********************************************************************  PAD11060
//*                                                                      PAD11070
//* THIS JOB LINKS THE SYSTEM/360 (SIM360) SIMULATOR'S BATCH           PAD11080
//* MONITOR. THIS MONITOR IS WRITTEN IN OPTIMIZER PL/1                 PAD11090
//* WITH ASSEMBLY LANGUAGE SUBROUTINES. IF YOU DO NOT                  PAD11100
//* HAVE THE OPTIMIZER TRANSIENT LIBRARY, IT WILL NOT WORK.           PAD11110
//* IF YOU DO NOT HAVE THE OPTIMIZER LINK LIBRARY,                     PAD11120
//* THIS LINK WILL NOT WORK, BUT THE UNLOADED LOAD MODULE             PAD11130
//* FILE ON THIS TAPE MAY BE USED.                                     PAD11140
//*                                                                      PAD11150
//* THE SYMBOLIC PARAMETER NAME IS USED AS A LABEL PREFIX.            PAD11160
//* THIS JOB SHOULD NORMALLY BE RUN AFTER THE JOB WHICH CREATES       PAD11170
//* THE SIMPLE BATCH MONITOR. THIS JOB EXPECTS A CATALOGED            PAD11180
//* LOAD MODULE PDS WITH THE NAME '&NAME.MONITOR.LOAD'. THIS          PAD11190
//* DATASET MUST FURTHER HAVE ENOUGH SPACE TO ACCOMODATE              PAD11200
//* THIS MODULE (ABOUT 5 3330 TRACKS).                                PAD11210
//*                                                                      PAD11220
//*********************************************************************  PAD11230
//*                                                                      PAD11240
//DOIT2D  PROC NAME=''                                                   PAD11250
//*                                                                      PAD11260
//LNKS360 EXEC PGM=IEWL,PARM='LIST,MAP'                                  PAD11270
//SYSPRINT DD  SYSOUT=A                                                  PAD11280
//SYSLIB   DD  DSN=SYS1.PLIBASE,DISP=SHR    PL/1 (OPTIMIZER) LINK LIB    PAD11290
//SYSUT1   DD  UNIT=SYSDA,SPACE=(CYL,(2,1))                              PAD11300
//SYSLIN   DD  UNIT=2400,VOL=SER=PADIST,DISP=(OLD,PASS),                 PAD11310
//             LABEL=(51,NL),DCB=(RECFM=FB,LRECL=80,BLKSIZE=1600)        PAD11320
//SYSLMOD  DD  DSN=&NAME..MONITOR.LOAD,DISP=OLD                          PAD11330
//*                                                                      PAD11340
//       PEND                                                            PAD11350
//*                                                                      PAD11360
//       EXEC DOIT2D                                                     PAD11370
//*                                                                      PAD11380
//******** END OF JOB, REPLACE WITH NULL (//) IF APPROPRIATE            PAD11390
//******************** JOB 35 *******************                        PAD11400
//*                                                                      PAD11410
//*********************************************************************  PAD11420
//*                                                                  *   PAD11430
//*       THIS JOB PUNCHES THE JOBS NEEDED TO INTSALL THE MIT FAST   *   PAD11440
//*       PL/1 (F) COMPILER.                                         *   PAD11450
//*                                                                  *   PAD11460
//*********************************************************************  PAD11470
//*                                                                      PAD11480
//MITPL1  EXEC PGM=IEBGENER                                              PAD11490
//*                                                                      PAD11500
//SYSPRINT DD  SYSOUT=A                                                  PAD11510
//SYSIN    DD  DUMMY                                                     PAD11520
//SYSUT2   DD  SYSOUT=B,DCB=(RECFM=F,BLKSIZE=80)                         PAD11530
//SYSUT1   DD  UNIT=2400,VOL=SER=PADIST,DISP=(OLD,PASS),                 PAD11540
//             LABEL=(55,NL),DCB=(RECFM=FB,LRECL=80,BLKSIZE=1600)        PAD11550
```

```
//*                                                                PAD11560
//********** END OF JOB, REPLACE WITH NULL (//) IF APPROPRIATE     PAD11570
//*                                                                PAD11580
//*                                                                PAD11590
//*                                                                PAD11600
//*                                                                PAD11610
//*                                                                PAD11620
//*              ****************                                   PAD11630
//*              * END OF JOBS *                                   PAD11640
//*              ****************                                   PAD11650
```

## A.  MODIFIED IBM PL/I(F) COMPILER

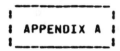

### A.1  INTRODUCTION

The standard IBM PL/I (F-level) compiler is rather expensive
to use, especially for small programs.  For a machine problem
assignment in PL/I, the major cost of running a small student job
is the compilation since execution time is typically negligible.
Close examination of the compiler's costs discloses that it is
fairly efficient in its use of CPU time, but not in its usage of
disk I/O.  With a typically small student program (fewer than 200
cards) and a well chosen region size (128K-bytes), most of the
disk I/O performed by the compiler is the result of program
fetches.  That is, the I/O is requesting program segments instead
of data.  The compiler has been restructured to reduce this
overhead and make it more efficient for small programs; the code
produced is unchanged.

### A.2  STRUCTURE OF PL-I(F) COMPILER

### A.2.1  Original Structure

The PL/I(F) compiler was originally designed to run in a 44K
partition, that being the largest user partition on a 64K machine
running OS/360.  To meet this requirement, the compiler was
designed to use 16K for its code, regardless of the actual amount
of memory available.  To accomplish this goal, it was broken down
into about 125 small overlay phases.  These phases are loaded as
needed, under the control of special subroutines in the compiler
root phase.  This loading is accomplished by either a LINK, or
LOAD and DELETE combination of operating system macros.

### A.2.2  Modified Structure

The modifications made center around changing the overlay
structure, making for fewer phases (segments) of greater length.
To allow relatively easy changing of this structure, a
combination of the linkage editor overlay supervisor and the
LOAD, DELETE, and LINK facilities of OS are used.  The linkage
editor is used in conjunction with overlay control statements to
produce a compiler load module.  Any rarely used phases such as
those required only for special features or handling disastrous
errors, are excluded from this linkage edit.

When the phase control routines in the compiler root want a certain phase, a table of address constants is checked. If the appropriate address constant is zero, indicating the phase was not linked in, the old method of obtaining the phase is used. If the constant is not zero, a standard OS CALL is used to access the phase through the overlay supervisor. This approach allows the best of both worlds.

### A.2.3   TRACEFLOW Feature

The overlay structure may easily be modified to suit different objectives, while rarely used phases do not add to the overhead of segment swapping. To aid in the determination of optimal overlay strategy, a special option, "TRACEFLOW," has been added. This option expects a file TRACE, with attributes similar to SYSPRINT. A formatted, annotated dump of control flow indicating when phases and segments were actually loaded is produced on this file. This option produces much output, hence it should be used with care.

### A.2.4   Other Changes

In addition to the structural changes, the initialization process of the compiler has been drastically streamlined. In the case of batch compilations, very little initialization is necessary after the first deck. Several new features have been added to make the compiler more convenient. This includes accurate spill file metering and size estimation. A complete description of these enhancements and their use is explained later.

### A.2.5   Status of Modifications

The PL-I(F) compiler modifications are contained in about 4000 cards worth of annotated input to IEBUPDTE, the IBM text maintenance utility. These changes apply directly to the IBM source for the following compiler modules: IEMAA, IEMAB, IEMAC, IEMAK, IEMAL, IEMAN, IEMBW, IEMFV, IEMJZ, IEMLV, IEMQU, IEMQX, and IEMXA. The bulk of the modifications apply to IEMAA and IEMAB.

The modified compiler, of course, requires a larger partition that the unmodified version. The minimum partition size is 112K. It successfully compiles small (about 150 statement) programs in 128K without opening the spill file. A good estimate is to start with 60K more than normally used. For medium size PL-I source decks, a 160K partition should be adequate.

It should be stressed that absolutely no modifications have been made to those parts of the compiler that participate in code generation or parsing. Thus, the modified compiler produces exactly the same code as the unmodified compiler. Extreme caution should be exercised when changing the compiler overlay structure, since some routines make assumptions about the availability of a module and bypass the phase acquistion routines of the root. This usually produces very subtle bugs. The way to find these is to use TRACEFLOW and compare loading activity to the old overlay structure published in the IBM compiler PLM (Appendix A, Page 383, of "IBM System/360 Operating System--PL-I(F) Compiler Program Logic Manual," IBM publication number GY28-6800).

## A.3  OPERATION AND USE OF MODIFIED PL-I(F) COMPILER

The modified PL-I(F) compiler is operationally identical to the unmodified compiler, with a few exceptions. It is recommended that a PDS be created which contains the modified compiler's load modules. Then take whatever JCL you use for the standard compiler and add a STEPLIB or JOBLIB DD statement referring to the modified compiler's PDS.

The modified compiler accepts four new options, controlling two new features. These options are:

TF, TRACEFLOW--If specified, the user must provide a file definition for the TRACE print file. The DCB attributes for this file should be RECFM=VBA, LRECL=125, and BLKSIZE= n*125+4, like 129 or 2004. If this option is specified, a formatted, annotated dump of compiler control flow is printed. The default for this option is off.

NOTF, NOTRACEFLOW--This option turns off the tracing option.

OFF, OFFSET--This option causes a statement offset map to be produced, regardless of other compiler options.

NOOFF, NOOFFSET--This option suppresses the printing of a statement offset map.

If a T is coded in the column identified for control characters (usually column one), the title line is reset and an eject to a fresh page is inserted. This may be used to provide neater listings.

In addition, changes have been made to the handling of "*PROCESS" cards. If you specify "*PROCESS('');", the system default options will be used for the compilation. If you specify "*PROCESS;", the same options supplied to the compiler upon invocation will be used.

When several subroutines are compiled at once, the "*PROCESS;" card should be used to batch the compilations, as this will result in substantial savings.

## A.4  PERFORMANCE OF MODIFIED PL-I(F) COMPILER

According to results indicated in a report by Granger and Donovan, using the M.I.T. charging algorithm, the modified compiler is ten to fifteen percent cheaper to run than the unmodified version. The gains are greatest for small decks and batched compilations. The modifications act to cut CPU time, disk I/O, and core residence time. The CPU reduction is from reduced operating system entry/exit sequences and I/O processing.

Since these modifications drastically reduce the fixed overhead for a PL-I compilation, the savings are most dramatic where small (fewer than 100 card) decks are concerned, running as high as 60 percent. Granger and Donovan compared this modified compiler to the unmodified F-level and the IBM optimizer with OPT(0) and OPT(2) specified. Their results were obtained on a IBM Model 165, running MVT 21.7. The only parameters reported were CPU time (in minutes). The prices used were $7.00 per CPU minute, $1.00 per thousand I/O operatins, and, since all core requirements were less than 400K, $0.50 per kilobyte-hour for core residence. The results which they obtained for a typical 150-card program are summarized in the table below. In fairness, it should be noted that although more expensive in the compilation phase, the optimizing compiler produces code which is cheaper to execute. However, for most student runs execution time is negligible compared to compilation time.

| CATEGORY | MOD-F | IBM-F | OPT(0) | OPT(2) |
|----------|-------|-------|--------|--------|
| CPU | .074 | .082 | .162 | .192 |
| DISK I/O | 413 | 828 | 516 | 719 |
| MEMORY | .283 | .498 | .423 | .556 |
| COST | $1.25 | $1.80 | $2.18 | $2.77 |

Similar comparisons have been made between the modified and unmodified compilers, using various size student decks. One of these decks contained 76 cards and performed very little I/O, but manipulated linked lists; the other was 348 cards and performed much more I/O and list processing. The tests were performed on an IBM Model 168 running OS MVT release 21.8, using the same accounting procedures as used by Granger and Donovan. The pricing structure was different, however. The rates were $12.00 per CPU minutes, $1.20 per thousand disk I/O operations, and $0.65 per K-byte hour for memory. The results obtained were:

|          | Small Deck |       | Larger Deck |       |
| CATEGORY | MOD-F | IBM-F | MOD-F | IBM-F |
|----------|-------|-------|-------|-------|
| CPU      | .014  | .021  | .028  | .036  |
| DISK I/O | 380   | 887   | 367   | 906   |
| MEMORY   | .205  | .461  | .214  | .481  |
| COST     | $0.88 | $1.87 | $1.08 | $2.21 |